INDUSTRIEKULTUR

• The MIT Press
Cambridge, Massachusetts
London, England

INDUSTRIEKULTUR

Peter Behrens and
the AEG, 1907–1914

by
• Tilmann Buddensieg

in collaboration with Henning Rogge

with contributions by

Gabriele Heidecker

Karin Wilhelm

Sabine Bohle

and

Fritz Neumeyer

translated by Iain Boyd Whyte

Library of Congress Cataloging in Publication Data

Buddensieg, Tilmann.
    Industriekultur : Peter Behrens and the AEG, 1907–1914.

    Includes bibliography and index.

    1. Behrens, Peter, 1868–1940—Addresses, essays, lectures. 2. Allgemeine Elektricitäts-Gesellschaft—Addresses, essays, lectures.
3. Decorative arts—Germany—Addresses, essays, lectures. 4. Architecture, Modern—20th century—Germany—Addresses, essays, lectures.
I. Rogge, Henning. II. title.
N6888.B433A4 1948   709′.2′4   83–5375

ISBN 0-262-02195-1

Contents

Translator's Introduction

In the first essay in this volume, Tilmann Buddensieg quotes Nietzsche's call for "a remodeling of the world in order to make it bearable to live in." This contrast between art and reality is of crucial importance to the understanding of Peter Behrens's work for the AEG. As a convinced Nietzschean, Behrens saw the artist as the rarely gifted being who could create an alternative to the delusions and mendacity of everyday life.[1] Nietzsche insisted: "There is only *one* world, and this is false, cruel, contradictory, seductive, without meaning. A world thus constituted is the real world. We have a need of lies in order to conquer this reality, this 'truth.' "[2] More directly: "We possess art lest we perish of the truth."[3]

Viewed metaphysically, art became a means to overcome and improve reality, a vehicle for the Nietzschean will to power. A contemporary of Behrens, the poet Gustav Landauer, said exactly this in 1903 when he wrote: "For me it is not enough simply to comprehend things for the sake of living: I want to perceive in order to form. Nietzsche called it will to power, to power over the world. But to me that is too ambiguously stated; I call it forming (Gestaltung), art."[4] That Behrens also identified the Nietzschean will to power with the act of artistic creation can be inferred from a letter he wrote to the philosopher's sister, Elisabeth Förster-Nietzsche, in December 1902. In this letter, Behrens thanked her for sending him a set of the works of her "immortal brother." She had also invited Behrens to visit her in Weimar, and the letter continued: "I regard myself as privileged to be able to pour out to you all my veneration and deepest admiration for the wise genius. . . . I only hope that I possess the power which I shall need to translate my feelings into tangible works."[5]

This Nietzschean equation of power and art worked reciprocally. If at the metaphysical level art was a means to achieving power over mundane reality, then at the material level power was viewed as the foundation of art. Clearly, this was no new phenomenon; throughout history the arts had been put to use by whichever element in the society was dominant at a particular time. In Wilhelmine Germany, however, the combination of Nietzschean aesthetics and burgeoning economic, military, and industrial influence focused particular attention on the power of art and the aesthetic qualities of power as expressions of the particularly Prussian values of organization and order.

In 1902 the city of Hamburg commissioned Behrens to design the entrance hall to the German pavilion at the First International Exhibition of Decorative Arts, in Turin. A critique of this vestibule by Behrens's friend and collaborator Georg Fuchs gives a fascinating insight into the contemporary debate on the nature and purpose of art in the new German state. Having condemned the irrelevance of nineteenth-century art and design, Fuchs hailed Behrens as the leader of a new artistic movement seeking to ennoble the realities of modern life through art. The fusion of art and political power found perfect expression, said Fuchs, in the vestibule at Turin. As a suitable inscription above the entrance he suggested "Come in stranger, the German state presides here; marvel at what it can do!"[6] The vestibule, said Fuchs, was the first point of intersection between "external and internal power,"[7] between the power of the state and the power of the creative spirit. As if to confirm the debt that his analysis owed to Nietzsche, Fuchs quoted Zarathustra: "This is what I call beauty, when power becomes benevolent and descends to the visible plane."[8]

It is unlikely that Behrens would have agreed with Fuchs's suggestion that the Behrens style represented a national style, the style of the Wilhelmine state. Only a year previously, Wilhelm II had officially opened the Siegesallee, a double row of pseudo-Classical monuments running through the Tiergarten in Berlin, and had observed in his speech that "despite all our modern feelings and knowledge we are proud when a particularly fine achievement is praised with the words: 'That is nearly as good as the art of 1900 years ago.' "[9] Clearly, Behrens's progressive art had little to do with such archconservatism or with the works of the Kaiser's favorite painters, Anton von Werner and Max Koner. What Behrens would, however, have approved of in Fuchs's critique was the Nietzschean equation of power in the abstract sense of art. By happy coincidence, Behrens exhibited a decorated book cover for *Also sprach Zarathustra* at the same exhibition in Turin. The massive cover carried a crystalline motif, the recurring symbol of purity and transcendence.

Fuchs entitled his article "The Vestibule to the House of Power and Beauty," and added "it is now up to us and our successors to build the house."[10] Behrens was given the chance to do this and more in 1907 by the directors of the Allgemeine Elektricitäts-Gesellschaft (AEG), when they appointed him artistic director to the company—a post he held until 1914.

Originally established by Emil Rathenau in 1883 as the Deutsche Edison Gesellschaft, the company changed its name in 1887 to Allgemeine Elektricitäts-Gesellschaft and expanded at an unprecedented rate over the following quarter-century. By the time Behrens took up his appointment in 1907, the AEG had a capital value exceeding 100 million marks and employed some 70,000 people. Its sales catalogs listed hundreds of different products, ranging from light switches to giant turbines, and these were manufactured in factories located on several sites in and around Berlin.

On an incrementally expanding basis, Behrens was commissioned to redesign the company's buildings, products, and publicity material, from the celebrated turbine hall right down to tiny publicity seals. While it is clear that Behrens's AEG style was in complete contrast to the "Zarathustrastil" of the Turin vestibule,[11] both can be related to the Nietzschean urge to refute nihilism and chaos by constructing an alternative, higher reality. The earlier, Jugendstil-influenced solution might be seen to represent Nietzsche's Dionysian aspect, the doctrine of chance and meaninglessness which emancipates man and leads to ecstatic joy. The AEG factories, in contrast, stand for the Apollonian element in Nietzsche's writings, representing the heroic, solemn, and serious longing to transcend human limitations through art. In this particular instance, human frailty had expressed itself in the confusion and inhumanity of industrial production. Behrens's AEG factories represent the first and perhaps the most successful attempt to ennoble the industrial process via the means at an artist's disposal, such as scale, sequence, proportion, rhythm, light, shade, and the play of materials.

By employing Behrens's talented hand to create a corporate image, the AEG brought the visual arts into the front line in the battle for productivity and turnover. The light and airy factories were designed not only to increase production directly but also to minimize discontent among the company's employees. Similarly, the construction of workers' housing, albeit on a very small scale, was also seen as a means of ensuring a loyal, productive workforce. With well-designed products being manufactured at maximum output in modern factories by contented employees, the company was in a strong position not only to challenge its domestic rivals but also to assert itself on the world markets. In bringing together design expertise and technical know-how into a potent force with which to conquer the home and foreign markets, the AEG put into practice one of the founding tenets of the Deutscher Werkbund: "Art is not only an aesthetic but also a moral force; the two together ultimately lead to the most important power of all: economic power."[12]

Behrens officially took up his post with the AEG on 1 October 1907, and the first meeting of the Werkbund was held four days later in Munich, with Behrens as a founding member. In many ways, the design policy pursued by the AEG under Behrens's guidance was a practical demonstration of the Werkbund program as it was developed between 1907 and 1914.[13] It is impossible to miss the nationalistic zeal with which both the AEG and the Werkbund set about reforming the quality of German design. Art and industry were to be put to the service of the national economy and to the glory of the new German state. It is significant that Behrens's first building for the AEG, the pavilion at the 1908 Deutsche Schiffbau-Ausstellung (German Shipbuilding Exhibition), was opened by Kaiser Wilhelm II. Nor can the Kaiser himself have missed the similarity between this shrine to technology and Charlemagne's Palatine Chapel at Aachen. Yet the very existence of new industries and of a new class of industrial entrepreneurs posed a threat to the established order. Indeed, a dominant feature in the political history of Wilhelmine Germany has been described as "the defense of inherited ruling positions by preindustrial elites against the onslaught of new forces."[14] To a certain degree, this problem was alleviated by what German historians have called the "feudalization of the bourgeoisie."[15]

This conflict between the material values of a modern industrialized society and the preindustrial modes of thought and action favored by the court and the aristocracy also had an aesthetic dimension, and led, among other things, to the establishment of the Berlin Secession in 1898.[16] The debate was also conducted within the AEG between Behrens and Walther Rathenau, the son of the founder. Yet for all his antipathy to Behrens's architecture and his reservations about reformist tendencies in general, Rathenau, as a businessman, must have recognized the value of Behrens's talent to the AEG, for in Rathenau's own definition "to be a genius means to look ten years ahead and to sense what no one else knows or foresees at the time."[17] The quality of Behrens's foresight can be judged by the caliber of the assistants who worked with him on the AEG projects, among them Walter Gropius, Adolf Meyer, Ludwig Mies van der Rohe, and Le Corbusier.

The wheel has now turned full circle. No longer does the AEG support the German economy; rather, the West German state supports the AEG with loans and guarantees intended to save the company from bankruptcy. To cut its losses or rationalize its assets, the AEG is planning to close down some or all of the Behrens-designed factories on the Brunnenstrasse site in Berlin.[18] Although this certainly is not the place for an enquiry into the reasons for the company's ills, one is tempted to speculate on the fortunes of the AEG if men as farsighted as Emil Rathenau and Peter Behrens had determined company policy after 1945.

In translating the essays in this volume I have tried to reproduce as closely as possible the various styles of the individual contributors. Where feasible, I have used the past tense, even for buildings and objects that still exist. I should like to thank Dr. Ursula Marsch-Ziegler for her untiring help in clarifying some of the more obscure passages in the original German text, and The MIT Press for its invaluable editorial contribution.

Iain Boyd Whyte
Berlin and Burnsall, 1982

Notes

1. For a detailed account of Nietzsche's influence on Behrens and on the design of the architect's own house at Darmstadt, see Tillmann Buddensieg, "Das Wohnhaus als Kultbau," in *Peter Behrens und Nürnberg*, exhibition catalog (Nuremberg, 1980), pp. 48–64.

2. Friedrich Nietzsche, *Der Wille zur Macht*, p. 853.

3. Ibid., p. 822.

4. Gustav Landauer, letter to Julius Bab, 16 June 1903, in Bruno Hillebrand (ed.), *Nietzsche und die deutsche Literatur*, volume 1 (Tübingen, 1978), p. 147.

5. Peter Behrens, letter to Elisabeth Förster-Nietzsche, 6 December 1902, in Buddensieg (above, note 1), p. 40.

6. Georg Fuchs, "Die Vorhalle zum Hause der Macht und Schönheit," *Deutsche Kunst und Dekoration* 11, no. 1 (October 1902), p. 6.

7. Ibid., p. 8.

8. Friedrich Nietzsche, *Also sprach Zarathustra*, quoted: ibid., p. 9.

9. Kaiser Wilhelm II, speech of 18 December 1901, in Johannes Penzler (ed.), *Die Reden Kaiser Wilhelms II*, volume 3 (Leipzig, 1907), p. 60. Although Behrens was emphatically opposed to the Kaiser's views on art, he was not against Wilhelmine nationalism, and he was one of the signatories to the celebrated "Aufruf an die Kulturwelt" published on 4 October 1914 in support of the German war aims and the invasion of Belgium.

10. Fuchs (note 6), p. 9.

11. The term was coined by Friedrich Ahlers-Hesterman in *Stilwende* (Berlin, 1941) (p. 87) to describe the music room in Behrens's house in Darmstadt.

12. Kurt Schumacher, speech at the founding meeting of the Deutscher Werkbund, Munich, 5–6 October 1907, in Julius Posener, *Anfänge des Funktionalismus: von Arts and Crafts zum Deutschen Werkbund* (Berlin, 1964), p. 22.

13. On the Deutscher Werkbund, see Joan Campbell, *The German Werkbund: the Politics of Reform in the Applied Arts* (Princeton, 1978).

14. Hans-Ulrich Wehler, *Das deutsche Kaiserreich 1871–1914* (Göttingen, 1973), p. 14.

15. See Richard J. Evans (ed.), *Society and Politics in Wilhelmine Germany* (London, 1980), p. 20.

16. On the Berlin Secession, see Peter Paret, *The Berlin Secession: Modernism and Its Enemies in Imperial Germany* (Cambridge, Massachusetts, 1980).

17. Gabriele Reuter, "In memoriam Walther Rathenau," *Die neue Rundschau* 33 (1922), pp. 832–833; reprinted in Ernst Schulin (ed.), *Gespräche mit Rathenau* (Munich, 1980), p. 313.

18. See Tilmann Buddensieg, "Zeitlos alt oder veraltet: die Berliner AEG-Bauten an der Brunnenstrasse," *Frankfurter Allgemeine Zeitung*, 26 August 1982.

A Survey of the Work of Peter Behrens

Peter Behrens was born in Hamburg on 14 April 1868. After attending the Realgymnasium in Altona, he began his painting studies in 1886 at the Kunstakademie in Karlsruhe. From there he moved to Düsseldorf, where he studied with Ferdinand Bütt. In December 1889, Behrens married Lilli Krämer, and in the following year the couple moved to Munich, where he continued his studies with Kotschenreiter. He became a founding member of the Munich Secession in 1893 and, shortly afterwards, a founding member of the more progressive Freie Vereinigung Münchener Künstler—together with Otto Eckmann, Max Slevogt, Wilhelm Trübner, and Lovis Corinth. He also made contacts with literary Munich and joined the circle associated with the magazine *Pan*, which included Otto Julius Bierbaum, Julius Meier-Graefe, Otto Julius Bierbaum, Franz Blei, Richard Dehmel, and Otto Eckmann.

Although Behrens exhibited regularly in the 1890s, his paintings and woodcuts from the period explain his decision at the end of the decade to abandon painting in favor of the applied arts. His first graphic works and designs for glass, porcelain, jewelry, and furniture appeared in 1898 and 1899, and his monogram for the Insel Verlag (1899) is still in use today in a modified form. In 1899 he exhibited his craft designs at the Keller and Reiner Gallery in Berlin, at the Glaspalast in Munich, and at the Kunstverein in Darmstadt. The success of these exhibitions led to his appointment, also in 1899, to the Künstler-Kolonie in Darmstadt by Ernst Ludwig, Grand Duke of Hesse.

Together with Josef Maria Olbrich, Behrens was a dominant artistic influence in the Darmstadt colony, where he became particularly involved in plans for a new theater. In July 1900 work was begun on his own house, for which he had designed everything from the structure down to the furniture, carpets, and glasses. During the Darmstadt period Behrens was strongly influenced by the writings of Friedrich Nietzsche, and this influence can be seen in his own house and in the Hamburg Vestibule at the 1902 Turin International Exhibition, dubbed the Tomb of the Unknown Superman. (At Turin he also exhibited a much more restrained design for the study of the Darmstadt publisher Alexander Koch.)

In January 1903, Behrens was appointed director of the Kunstgewerbe-schule in Düsseldorf. He tried unsuccessfully to persuade the architects Hendrik Berlage and Josef Hoffmann and the young painter Vasili Kandinsky to take up teaching posts at Düsseldorf. His interest in the work of Berlage and Hoffmann, representing the latest developments in Holland and Vienna respectively, and his own designs of this time mark his development away from the lingering Jugendstil of his Darmstadt period and toward more abstract geometrical forms based on cubes, cylinders, and framed rectangular planes. These elements all appear in his reading room for the library at Düsseldorf (1904), the cover design for a catalog for the 1904 St. Louis World's Fair, the dining room furniture exhibited at Dresden in 1904, the Haus Schede at Wetter an der Ruhr (1904–05), the restaurant at Düsseldorf (1904), and particularly the exhibition pavilion at Oldenburg (1905).

The cubistic building elements Behrens used in the design of the Obenauer house near Saarbrücken (1905–06) invite comparison with contemporary experiments in painting and sculpture, and particularly with Hoffmann's reliefs of 1902. This approach to three-dimensional design was further developed in the project for the Tietz store in Düsseldorf (1905–06), the Klein carpet shop in Hagen (1906–07), and the Catholic Gesellenhaus in Neuss (1908–1910).

Behrens gained a number of commissions through the intercession of the banker and patron Karl Ernst Osthaus. These included the Tonhaus at the Cologne Exhibition of 1906, the crematorium in Hagen (1906–07), and an unexecuted project for a Protestant church, also in Hagen. In the last two schemes, the Dutch and Viennese stimuli toward geometric abstraction were joined by strong references to the Florentine proto-Renaissance.

A notable feature in Behrens's pre-Berlin work was the development of a pioneering style of exhibition design. Typical examples were the Kunst-halle at the 1905 Oldenburg exhibition and the pavilion for the Anker Linoleum Company at the 1906 Deutsche Kunstgewerbeausstellung at Dresden. Behrens was assisted on these projects by the young Adolf Meyer, who was later to collaborate with another Behrens pupil, Walter Gropius, on the celebrated Fagus factory.

In 1907, Behrens was called to Berlin as artistic adviser to the AEG, and from this time on his work shows the marked influence of Prussian Classicism. It appears, for example, in the Villa Cuno (1909), one of the large houses Behrens built around Hagen. Gropius worked with Behrens on this project, and its lasting influence can be seen in Gropius's design for the Otte house in Zehlendorf (1921). A more Schinkelesque version of Classicism emerged in 1910–1912, the period of the Villa Wiegand in Dahlem, the alterations to the Mertens house in Potsdam, and the Kröller-Müller house in The Hague. The example of Schinkel's planning, as adapted by Behrens, was to exercise a lasting influence on one of the assistants on the Kröller-Müller project, Ludwig Mies van der Rohe.

The turn of the year 1910–11 marked the most fruitful and creative period in Behrens's life. In addition to several major schemes for the AEG, he found time to work on an almost unbelievable number of complicated projects, including the German embassy at St. Petersburg, the administration building of the Mannesmannröhren-Werke in Düsseldorf, and the Continentale-Gummi-Werke in Hanover. Perhaps the most striking was the embassy, with its vigorous references to Schinkel in the magnificent vestibule with walls clad in honey-colored marble and black porphyry columns. Mies worked here as project architect, and throughout his life he looked back proudly on the embassy building as his Gesellenstück—the piece of work that qualifies an apprentice as a journeyman.

The latent Classicism of these works became even more manifest in the schemes Behrens designed immediately before the outbreak of World War I, notably the Festhalle at the 1914 Werkbund Exhibition at Cologne, the grandiose design for a hotel in San Remo (whose construction was to have begun in July 1914), and the office building for Frank and Lehmann (which still stands in Cologne). With these designs, Behrens distanced himself from the functional, cubic, geometric style that he had used so effectively for the gasworks at Frankfurt (1911), the AEG factories, and the railway shed at the 1910 Brussels World Exhibition.

After the war, Behrens completely reassessed his architectural language and abandoned the stereometric rationality and the Classicist traits of his prewar work. The I.G.-Farben building at Höchst (1920–1924) was the most impressive product of Behrens's Expressionist phase. In its use of color, its clock tower, its belfry, and its cathedral-like memorial hall, the I.G.-Farben complex was entirely in harmony with the self-conscious medievalism that dominated radical architectural theory in Germany in the immediate postwar years and was advocated by such leading figures as Hans Poelzig, Bruno Taut, and Walter Gropius. The contemporary desire to reform architectural design and education on the model of the lodges of the medieval masons led in 1919 to Gropius's program for the Weimar Bauhaus, and in 1922 to Behrens's Dombauhütte at the Kunstgewerbeschau at Munich. Further examples of a lingering antigeometric tendency are New Ways (the house in Northampton, England, which Behrens designed in 1925), the much admired pavilion at the International Exhibition of Industrial Art held in Paris in 1925, and the bizarre design for the pavilion of the Deutsche Spiegelglasfabrikanten at the Cologne exhibition of the same year.

In 1922, Behrens was appointed director of the architecture school at the Vienna Academy. A move away from mystic asymmetry back to the cubic forms of Neue Sachlichkeit was announced in the apartment blocks that were built in Vienna between 1925 and 1929 and confirmed in his house at the Weissenhofsiedlung in Stuttgart (1927). In his major projects from the late 1920s—the competition scheme for the Centrosojuz building in Moscow (1928) and the successful project for the rebuilding of Alexanderplatz in Berlin (1928)—Behrens reverted to the regular articulation, banded fenestration, and stereometric forms of his AEG factories.

Further buildings in the International Style followed, including the Villa Levin at Berlin-Schlachtensee (1929), an apartment house at Berlin-Westend (1930), and the Villa Gans at Kronberg, near Frankfurt (1931). In 1936, Behrens was appointed director of the architecture department at the Preussische Akademie der Künste, and in the same year he designed a factory for the Austrian state tobacco administration in Linz, still in the International Style. His 1939 design for an AEG administration building on Albert Speer's North-South Axis in Berlin employed the compositional techniques of his earlier AEG buildings, but to less distinguished effect. Behrens died in Berlin in 1940.

INDUSTRIEKULTUR

Introduction

Tilmann Buddensieg

Industrial society has been condemned with equal vigor by both right-wing and left-wing critics. It has been dismissed by Alfred Rosenberg as "the lowest form of life that has ever existed"[1] and by Leo Kofler as "civilization perverted into an inhuman process."[2] Faced with verdicts like these, one is tempted to accept the view that modern industrial society is incapable of generating any spiritual or intellectual impulses beyond a simple faith in performance and the ability to organize labor.

The young Karl Marx suggested that the reactionary and the utopian are one and the same.[3] Rather than focus on the reactions of the extreme left or right, it may be more fruitful to take a more moderate stance. From such a position, the historian's interest can profitably be directed at those industrial institutions that not only possessed the obvious attributes of organization, economic power, and technical perfection but also generated "spiritual impulses," social models, and cultural ideas. One such institution was the Allgemeine Elektricitäts-Gesellschaft (AEG) under the guidance of Emil and Walther Rathenau. Between 1907 and 1914, this firm's physical reorganization, the design of its products and trademark, and the provision of housing for its employees were entrusted to the architect Peter Behrens.

Describing Behrens's work for the AEG, Franz Blei (a friend of both Walther Rathenau and Behrens) spoke of Rathenau's "passionate conviction that spiritual content and form could be given to the inert and chaotic body of trade and industry."[4] Behrens's "reorganization of everything visible"[5] also had a social and didactic dimension. It was seen as a means of alleviating the devastation that industrialization had wrought on such basic areas as labor, production, housing, and human relations. This reflected the then-novel idea that society could be improved and made more civilized by a socially oriented art, whose power would be based on the techniques of mass production and on the widespread dissemination of industrial products. Only a great industrial enterprise with a wide range of products and designs was seen to possess this potential for reform.[6] The vision of an industrial and social culture that would embrace all social classes was thus created, and this is the true subject of the present volume.

One reason for the oblivion into which the AEG-Behrens experiment has sunk is the superficiality of judgments such as those quoted above. Another is the widespread tendency to view concrete and practical attempts at reform through the rose-tinted lenses of preindustrial or postindustrial utopias and to judge them, accordingly, as failures. But the AEG experiment was an expression of a specifically bourgeois culture, and acknowledged Max Weber's plea for the unreserved acceptance of the demands of industrial capitalism. Such practical experiments have not been highly valued by those social theorists who prefer mere speculation. The authors of this book do not need Nietzsche's "cold, gray eyes" in order to see that much of this AEG model was specific to the Wilhelmine period and is now obsolete. Equally clear are the unrealized hopes, the pedagogic enthusiasm, the obsessive desire to conquer the world's markets, and the belief in a higher mission of the Zeitgeist. However, a fair assessment cannot be made until the experiment in general, and Behrens's contribution in particular, have been fully documented.

It might be argued that the relevance and validity of the AEG-Behrens experiment disappeared with the historical context in which it came into being. We would suggest, however, that Behrens's ideas and designs created standards that survived long after their initial realization. Every subsequent design in the same area—for a button console, a kettle, an advertising brochure, a factory, or a company housing estate—is unavoidably a statement of agreement or disagreement with Behrens's prototype. For proof of Behrens's lasting influence it is sufficient to look at the young men standing at the windows of his studio in the memorable photograph shown in appendix B.

In our attempt to reconstruct this important experiment, we turned to those manifestos, documents, and commentaries in which Behrens's industrial and domestic architecture, his graphics, and his product designs were described. His work for the AEG deserves to be recalled for its "graceful beauty" as well as for its social and historical significance. This task of reconstruction depended not only on the interpretative ability of the authors, but also on the collection, identification, and preservation of objects that once were produced in large numbers but now are nearly extinct. The museums, with the exception of the Science Museum in London, do not collect these relics. Indeed, more is known about the creations of the ceramic industry in Periclean Athens than about the design of electrical appliances in Wilhelmine Berlin. It was this contrast between the number and diversity of the appliances produced and their rarity today that convinced us that it would be desirable to reconstruct the original range of products as completely as possible. The exhibition held at the Internationale Design Zentrum in Berlin at the suggestion of François Burkhardt, and the accompanying catalog, assembled the surviving fragments of Behrens's work for the AEG. The quality of this work was confirmed by the comparison drawn in the exhibition between the AEG products and those of rival firms.

Although no book on twentieth-century art is complete without the AEG turbine factory and a Behrens-designed arc lamp, the subject to which this book is dedicated does not belong, by its very nature, to the art historians. Behrens's work for the AEG took him into the diverse realms of the civil, the production, and the electrical engineer, the advertising manager, and the businessman. In order to reconstruct Behrens's major contribution to twentieth-century architecture and design, one must risk a hazardous tightrope walk over pitfalls and difficulties that have nothing to do with art history, even in its most liberal definition. The competence with which my fellow authors have written on specific aspects of the general theme underlines my complete lack of technical expertise. However, it would scarcely be possible to research all aspects of the topic fully, even with the help of more experts. To combat our uneasiness, we offer the documentation and the annotated catalog.

This book came into being through the help of many individuals and institutions. It is not the work of one author, and it demands a long list of grateful acknowledgments. Particular thanks are due to Petra Behrens, the daughter of Peter and Lilli Behrens, for her generous help throughout my research. AEG-Telefunken gave us free access to the factories on the Brunnenstrasse and the library on the Hohenzollerndamm. A thousand glass negatives documenting the AEG's building activity and products up to 1914 were found in an attic at Brunnenstrasse. Similarly, a hundred or so booklets, which make up a fairly complete set of Behrens's advertising brochures, were preserved in the cellar of the Hohenzollerndamm library. Mr. Toepfer, the librarian, was able to rescue these remnants shortly before the remainder of the archival material was removed from the head office on the Karl-Friedrich-Ufer in 1945. I do not regard this material as definitely lost. AEG-Telefunken's unrestricted permission to publish these documents provided the basis for the present book.

The astonished skepticism with which the management of the AEG viewed our claims to competence in this area ultimately proved to be a great stimulus. For promoting our work in this way, we would like in particular to thank Messrs. von der Osten-Sacken, Bender, Fuchs, and Hahn.

The Fritz Thyssen Foundation (in the person of Ernst Coenen), the Friedrich Meinecke Institute of the Freie Universität Berlin, and Berlin's Senator for Art and Education variously supported the project with direct aid, with practical assistance, and by granting a sabbatical leave for two semesters. In addition, generous hospitality and incomparable working conditions were afforded by King's College, Cambridge.

Only at the Freie Universität Berlin after 1968 could an essentially sane art historian have hit upon the idea of recasting his former research on the royal gold of the Holy Roman Empire in the bourgeois brass and proletarian iron of mass production in Wilhelmine Germany. However, the "mania for gadgets" of which Rathenau speaks had already been imparted to me by my teachers Hermann Schnitzler and Erich Meyer and my friend Hans Swarzenski. The book developed out of a seminar held in the Department of Art History at the Freie Universität Berlin in the winter of 1972–73; the book's constributors also came from this seminar (except for Fritz Neumeyer, from the Technische Universität Berlin).

Credit for the homogeneity of this account of the AEG-Behrens project is due to Henning Rogge, who in over three years of joint work helped to piece the text together out of a series of disorganized lecture notes, seminar papers, and occasional contributions to Festschriften. In addition to making contributions to the text, Gabriele Heidecker and Karin Wilhelm played a major part in the creation of the book, and Sabine Bohle and Fritz Neumeyer willingly offered the relevant sections of their own dissertations. By setting a date for the exhibition, François Burkhardt also set one for the book. Heinz Peters, our German publisher, supervised its realization with an enthusiasm that enabled him to visualize the end product before even a single line had been written. He also dealt nobly with the difficulties of working with several authors at once. My secretary in Berlin, Veronika von Below, ensured that my research was given strict priority, and, together with Renate Klotz, my Bonn secretary, typed the many versions of the manuscript.

For their help, information, and references, we authors thank Ernst Busche, Berlin; Thomas Deecke, Berlin; Hans Fürstenberg, Geneva; Princess Margaret of Hesse and Rhein, Wolfsgarten; Hans-Jürgen Imiela, Mainz; Ulrich Kerkhoff, Bonn; Christiane and Jürgen Klebs, Berlin; Jürgen Krause, Berlin; Marie-Agnes von Puttkamer, Bonn; Gert Schiff, New York; Carl Schmitt,

Plettenberg; Ernst Schulin, Freiburg; Messrs. Bondzio, Drinkel, and Goltz, Kraftwerk Union, Berlin; Messrs. Neumann, Obst, and Schädel, AEG-Telefunken, Brunnenstrasse, Berlin; Mr. Salbach, Berlin, who after 1925 was responsible for the outstanding exhibitions mounted by the AEG; Mr. Monkowius, BEWAG, Berlin; Mr. Matschke, HEW Museum, Hamburg; Bodo Herzog, Gutehoffnungshütte Archive, Oberhausen; Klaus Popitz, Kunstbibliothek, Stiftung Preussischer Kulturbesitz, Berlin; Wilhelm Weber, Pfalzgalerie, Kaiserslautern; J. H. Müller and A. C. Funk, Karl Ernst Osthaus Museum, Hagen; Messrs. Berninger and Heitmeier, Deutsches Museum, Munich; the Periodicals Department of the Deutsche Staatsbibliothek, East Berlin; the Institut für Zeitungsforschung, Dortmund; the Klingspor Museum, Offenbach; and the Kaiser Wilhelm Museum, Krefeld.

I dedicate my share in this book to my wife, Daphne Buddensieg.

Notes

1. Alfred Rosenberg, "Krisis und Neugeburt Europas" (lecture, Milan, 1932), in *Blut und Ehre, Reden und Aufsätze 1919–1933*, seventeenth edition (Munich, 1938), p. 297 [see also *Blut und Ehre*, twelfth edition (Munich, 1942), II, p. 142]. Here Rosenberg, citing Nietzsche, calls the industrial age "the coarsest form of life one could imagine."

2. Leo Kofler, *Der asketische Eros. Industriekultur und Ideologie* (Vienna, Frankfurt, and Zurich, 1967), p. 284.

3. Karl Marx, "*Das Elend der Philosophie*," in *Die Frühschriften*, ed. Siegfried Landshut (Stuttgart, 1955), p. 491.

4. Franz Blei, *Männer und Masken* (Berlin, 1930), p. 260.

5. Fritz Meyer-Schönbrunn, *Peter Behrens* (Hagen and Dortmund, 1913), p. 3.

6. Joseph August Lux, *Das neue Kunstgewerbe in Deutschland* (Leipzig, 1908), p. 250.

ESSAYS

Industriekultur: Peter Behrens and the AEG, 1907–1914

Tilmann Buddensieg

Our compulsion to formulate concepts, categories, aims, and laws should not be understood as something that enables us to define the real world, but rather as a compulsion to create a world in which our existence becomes possible.
Friedrich Nietzsche[1]

In order to make a lucid, logical, and clearly articulated entity out of an arc lamp, . . . a complete transformation of our aesthetic notions was necessary.
Paul Westheim[2]

Peter Behrens and Paul Jordan: The 1907 Program and Its Consequences

On 28 July 1907 the *Berliner Tageblatt* announced on its arts page that the director of the Kunstgewerbeschule in Düsseldorf, Professor Peter Behrens, who was well known for his outstanding work in the applied arts, had agreed to take up an appointment in Berlin as artistic adviser to the Allgemeine Elektricitäts-Gesellschaft. This was followed on 29 August by a specially commissioned account entitled "Kunst in der Techik," in which Behrens described his plans and the AEG's willingness to adopt them.

Even before Behrens's appointment, some of the AEG's new products had been admired for the technical qualities of their designs; their external form, however, had been left entirely to the taste of the individual Werkmeister. This random method was now to be replaced by a new manner of design that, "following the tendency of the age," would allow for "the most intimate union possible between art and industry," and would renounce "the imitation of handcraftsmanship, of other materials, and of historical styles." The aim was to arrive at "those forms that derive directly from and which correspond to the machine and machine production." This could be achieved, said Behrens, by "concentrating on the exact implementation of the techniques of mechanical production." He then suggested that in the design of arc lamps, electric fans, switchgear, heaters, circuit breakers, contacts, and the like it would be valid, by using standard types, to "strive after a graceful beauty [anmutige Schönheit] . . . clearly constructed and appropriate to the materials used." The graceful beauty appropriate to typical products of industrial mass production should be achieved, he said, without recourse to historicism or to the stylistic individualism that had been demanded of the artist by Jugendstil. Such a manner of design would resolve the conflict between the technical character of electrical appliances and the "artistic layout of a room" in favor of an "all-embracing artistic order." Consistent with the "logical application of these intentions," the AEG would also "attach great importance to the artistic and typographic design of all its publications" and to the design of its future exhibitions. Behrens concluded the article with a look into a future in which applied art would inevitably be industrially produced. Thus, "the practical realization of these ideas" would also make possible "the conversion of artistic and creative work into material assets," and the applied arts would gain an economic and social function.

In contrast to the fine arts, which exist "independent of public life," Behrens saw the applied arts as a public utility for the use of society at large.[3] This "intimate union" between the techniques and forms of mass production and "artistic and creative work" would go beyond the interest of a few, would prepare the way for "a general improvement in public taste," and would enable art to penetrate into "the most distant strata of the population." To the concepts of public taste and art, Behrens added propriety (Anstand). His work for the AEG would help, he felt, to spread this concept throughout all sections of society. By propriety he first meant fitness or aptness of design and construction. At the same time, however, the word also had a more elevated sense and referred to the educational and instructive powers of beautiful, gracefully formed objects.

From these principles it can be seen that, from the outset, Behrens and the AEG saw their collaboration not simply as the work of a new department of product design but as something of more fundamental importance. The considerable interest Behrens's appointment excited in the press attested to the great hopes that were pinned on the collaboration between "one of our leading artists and one of the world's largest companies."[4] These hopes were to find a national forum in the Deutscher Werkbund, which was founded soon after with basic aims the same as those Behrens had outlined.

Behrens's work for the AEG began with the relatively unimportant task of redesigning the company journal. He then turned his attention to the arc lamp, and from that he went on to establish an all-embracing AEG style that extended to the design of factories, transport depots, and model housing estates for the firm's employees. In response to Behrens's work, the AEG's board of directors cautiously extended his contract step by step into what was probably the widest-ranging commission of modern times.

Although the projects Behrens had completed by 1907 were well known and had been documented in the professional literature, they were not very numerous. The list included his own house in the artists' colony at Darmstadt (1900), successful but temporary pavilions at exhibitions held at Turin (1902), St. Louis (1904), Cologne (1906), and Dresden (1906), and half a dozen smaller commissions in Saarbrücken, Wetter an der Ruhr, and Hagen. The formal consistency, intellectual rigor, and universal applicability of these works, coupled with Behrens's outstanding ability as product designer, graphic artist, and architect, must have commended him to the directors of the AEG.

Because of wartime losses, the exact circumstances and considerations that led to Behrens's appointment can no longer be reconstructed from the archives. Behrens himself said that Paul Jordan, the director responsible for the AEG's factories, had initiated the appointment,[5] and this has been confirmed by other sources. Jordan was one of the oldest and closest colleagues of Emil Rathenau, the founder of the AEG. The sure judgment the firm displayed from the outset in employing outstanding architects, designers, and even sculptors can be attributed to Jordan. With men like Emil and Walther Rathenau, Carl Fürstenberg, and Felix Deutsch connected with the AEG, expert knowledge and judgment in artistic matters was ensured.

The engagement of Behrens must be seen in the context of the AEG's history. Franz Schwechten (1841–1921), the designer of the Anhalter Bahnhof (1875), was one of Berlin's leading architects. For the AEG he built the factory on the Ackerstrasse (completed by 1889) and the monumental portal on the Brunnenstrasse (1896). Schwechten was also responsible for the buildings of the Berliner Elektrizitätswerke on the Voltastrasse (1899) and, indirectly, for other AEG factories built in his style by assistants before the arrival of Behrens.[6]

As a result of his pioneering Wertheim store (1896), Alfred Messel emerged in the late 1890s as Berlin's most prominent architect. After holding an unsuccessful competition, the AEG commissioned him to design a new administration building for the Friedrich-Karl-Ufer. In 1906, however, the prospect of further collaboration between Messel and the AEG was ruled out by his involvement with a major building project on the "Museumsinsel" in Berlin, which fully occupied him until his death in 1909.

The daring appointment of Otto Eckmann to design the AEG's catalogs and other printed material for the 1900 World Exhibition in Paris was also a brief episode, for Eckmann died in 1902. Nevertheless, his appointment confirmed the AEG's intention to entrust the design of its publicity material to outstanding artists using modern techniques, rather than follow the academic taste of the Wilhelmine court or that of the company's principal customer, the general public. Among companies of a comparable size, only the AEG had such an adventurous attitude toward design. However, neither the printed materials nor the products designed between the death of Otto Eckmann in 1902 and the arrival of Behrens in 1906 show any trace of an original hand.

An important part in the AEG's search for a unifying force was played by the Dritte Deutsche Kunstgewerbeausstellung (Third German Exhibition of Applied Arts) held in Dresden in 1906.[7] For this exhibition, Behrens produced a highly formalized design for a new type of display pavilion (illustration 2) for the Anker Linoleum Company. Behrens developed this design from a more modest one he had produced for an earlier exhibition in Oldenburg.[8] The Anker Company also commissioned Behrens to design most of its patterns, its trademark, and its advertisement on the back cover of the exhibition catalog. The formal, unified image set Anker apart from the other exhibitors and must have offered a useful starting point for those people in the AEG who were responsible for the reorganization of that firm's design policy.

At the time of the Dresden exhibition, the AEG was, without doubt, already considering its contributions to the Elektrotechnik in der Kleinindustrie exhibition planned for the summer of 1907 and the Berliner Schiffbau-Ausstellung to be held in the summer of 1908. Behrens's pavilion at the latter was his first major project for the AEG, and a comparison with the Anker pavilion reveals that the decision to appoint Behrens had its roots at Dresden. Both of these pavilions were free-standing buildings in the classical manner, physically and stylistically removed from the other, rather conventional exhibition halls.

PAVILLON DER DELMENHORSTER LINOLEUM-FABRIK

Paul Jordan seems to have been convinced by the conclusions drawn by Ernst Schur in his critique of Behrens's contribution to the Dresden exhibition: "Behrens enjoys an indisputably high standing in Germany at the present time; he stimulates industry by working with it."[9]

The press was unanimous in its approval of Behrens's explanatory manifesto, of his first, modest efforts, and of his increasingly comprehensive work for the AEG. From the wide range of contemporary comments, here are the views of some of the more influential critics: At the beginning of 1908, Joseph August Lux wrote that the "enfeebled product design" of firms like the AEG should be replaced by "typical and consistent forms derived from the practical demands made by the products themselves." This, he said, was the "true task of the century."[10] Karl Ernst Osthaus, a banker's son and a patron of the arts, celebrated the union of industry and art that economic necessity had brought about. He called it "a triumph that exceeds even the most daring hopes of recent years," and added that "art has once again gained public acceptance in Germany."[11] Two years later, a visit to the turbine factory confirmed Osthaus's enthusiastic assessment: "That which the Deutscher Werkbund has recently been striving for with great energy and gradually increasing success has been accomplished by the AEG with one bold decision: The AEG has given back to the world its right to art in the industrial process."[12] Karl Scheffler, who from the outset had vigorously supported Behrens's work for the AEG in his influential journal *Kunst und Künstler*, described the "new style" Behrens had created for the AEG as the "style of the approaching epoch of world trade."[13]

2
Peter Behrens, pavilion for Anker Linoleum Company, Dritte Deutsche Kunstgewerbe-Ausstellung, Dresden, 1906.

3
Peter Behrens, catalog for Anker Linoleum Company, 1905. Courtesy of F. Stoedtner.

Comments like these emphasized the change in the "spirit of commercial enterprise," which Scheffler said had now been made aware of "its aesthetic responsibilities."[14] Although this emphasis was quite alien to Behrens, it certainly reflected contemporary feeling. His work, however, was not merely a response to the specific problems of the period; it also pointed the way forward. The progressive, specifically twentieth-century qualities are not difficult to identify.

Behrens transformed the concept of art. In describing the "Industriekunst" of the future, he pronounced the end of industrially produced "art" in the sense of the mechanical copying of traditional ornament, materials, and craftsmanship. Instead of forcing new, mechanical appliances to conform to the formal and decorative norms of their hand-built precursors, Behrens sought to give them a form appropriate to their nature and to the means of their production. With Behrens's AEG program clearly in mind, Joseph August Lux summarized these ideas in *Die neue Zeit*, the weekly magazine of the German Social Democratic Party:

Works of art cannot be manufactured and duplicated *en masse*. The task of industry is not to produce art, . . . but rather to promote good taste. The appointment of outstanding artists to leading positions in industrial companies is of great importance to the general improvement of public taste. Practical considerations demand that the artist who works for industry should produce unadorned, correct designs that achieve their effect simply through good proportions and an enhanced sense of function. The artists themselves would be the last to claim that these designs and their industrial production were a contribution to the arts. They should merely satisfy the demands of cultivated taste. For this reason, it is essential today to employ artists, and, what is more, the best artists. It is agreed, however, that the true roots of art are not to be found here.[15]

This thoughtful description of the novel tasks confronting the "artistic advisers" to industry and the new responsibilities that had been thrust on industry by economic necessity was written by Lux in 1909. At this early date he defined an explosive contradiction: Only the very best artists could design industrial products in such a way that they would have nothing to do with art. Using nothing but "unadorned, correct designs," the artists could find an effective role as purveyors of good taste. At the same time they could escape from the traditional isolation of the artist, as their work was no longer categorized as art.

However, artists who did not seek their work in the way Lux did viewed these new developments with great hostility.[16] They were now engaged on two fronts: against the customary incomprehension of the public, and against artists who designed for mass production (who were pleased that their work had a social function and that their products could not be works of art, and who were delighted that art was to be found "somewhere quite different").

The appointment of Behrens by Jordan provided a test case. Through the alliance of art and technology, it appeared that the social isolation of the artist had been done away with and that the industrial mass production of trash would be replaced by the large-scale manufacture of well-designed goods. The aim was to bring together the apparently irreconcilable spheres of art and design, technology and commerce, machine production, and economic viability to their individual and mutual advantage, and for the public good. Through the example of practical art—through a "reorganization of everything visible"[17]—the aesthetic pleasure of the individual in an exclusive "fine art" was to be transformed and extended into a cultural mission for mass education. This was not merely the utopian dream of one man, but a project conceived in conjunction with an industrial giant, with all its economic power and potential for social penetration—"only a great industrial enterprise" could "alter the general condition of society in favor of culture."[18]

By no means did the charisma of this model for the production and the sale of progress depend entirely on its ability to promote better taste. Its attraction went much further, surmounting all political contradictions. An ideal process can be defined: Platonically beautiful, good and useful objects would be mass-produced by contented workers in well-designed factories. Not only would these objects be beautiful and useful in themselves; they would also be an advanced expression of the industrial age and would be sold in well-designed stores and shops, which would act as suppliers of culture and good taste to all levels of society.[19] Depending on the political viewpoint of the interpreter, this process would promote socialism, or the spread of democracy, or the creation of the style of the age, or a strengthening of the economic competitiveness of the nation. What other productive element in Wilhelmine society could claim all this?

It is a common error in art-historical polemics to describe this concept in sweeping terms as bourgeois, or as the product of industrial capitalism. However, recent research into interest and pressure groups in the Wilhelmine period has shown that the large firms that embarked on modernization programs were attacked from all sides. Although individually powerful, these firms represented only a small part of manufacturing industry. They were attacked not only by commercial organizations representing smaller firms that were not members of the Werkbund, but also by official industrial and commercial agencies.

In glaring contrast to Behrens's AEG program and to the aims of the Werkbund, the powerful Volkskunst and Heimatkunst movements saw only "the greatest contradiction between art and business . . . between the simple pursuit of beauty and rational calculation." Volkskunst, called a "fountain of youth" that would refresh the visual culture of the nation, could only survive, it was claimed, under a "noncapitalist, semisocialist, cooperative system."[21]

The foundation of the Werkbund in October 1907 had been stimulated by dissatisfaction with the Fachverband für die wirtschaftlichen Interessen des Kunstgewerbes (Association for the Economic Interests of the Applied Arts), which, predictably enough, became one of the Werkbund's most vigorous opponent groups. At its third congress in June 1909, the Fachverband launched a savage attack against "modern tendencies in art." Director Behr observed in his speech, and not without some justification, that "the majority of housing schemes adhere to traditional forms," that "modern forms are favored only when funds are limited," and that "by advocating simplicity in its program, modernism has become the style of those of moderate means."[22] Clearly, Behr looked down on the alliance between the artist and "those of moderate means." At the 1900 Paris Exhibition, Otto Eckmann had viewed the "expensive, backward-looking junk" on display with equal contempt, comparing it with the things designed by his artist friends in Munich, which were "cheap and took their forms from the new art."

By making his lamps and kettles simple and undecorated, Peter Behrens freed these appliances from the social-status connotations of expensive exclusivity and from the ornamentation appropriate to these connotations. Using color and form as his aesthetic means, he opened the way for domestic use and mass consumption of electric machines, tools, switches, fans, and kitchen equipment. With his originality and lack of compromise, Behrens shaped a completely new sensibility and receptivity toward design that transcended mere utility and such status-bound notions as good taste or possession. "Simple form" as a "cheap" style for those of "moderate means" meant in reality that the civilizing attributes of technology were made available to new sections of the population. (Enough has already been written about the negative consequences of this optimistic starting position.)

4
Poster for electrical heating and
cooking appliances. AEG photo 8149,
15 September 1911.

Once again, we come across the correlation between technological development, an awakening by businessmen to market needs, and "simple form." It was entirely justifiable that the increased production and distribution of more useful and more attractive goods should, at the same time, have been registered by salesmen as an increase in turnover, described by the engineer as technical progress, and viewed by artists and art critics as a manifestation of the inevitable trend toward democratization.[23] The AEG concept was thus engaged at several levels in the contemporary debate on industrial and commercial policy.

Were there an architectural study of the administration buildings and production plants of the members of the industrial interest groups in the Wilhelmine period, then the fundamental contradictions of their architectural images would be very clear. On one side was manufacturing industry, export-intensive and working with "surrogate" materials. On the other side were the members of the "Bund von Eisen, Kohle und Garn mit Getreide" (Union of Iron, Coal, Yarn, and Grain).[24] (This contrast can only be mentioned here as an unresearched problem.)

Thus, in simplified terms, the Behrens-AEG experiment was an economically vital union between the work of an artist, which reached all social levels and promoted turnover, and the products of an export-intensive branch of manufacturing industry: The experiment drew fire from all sides—it was criticized by the advocates of "semisocialist" Volkskunst, by the reactionaries in the Heimatkunst movement, by the supporters of arts and crafts and of "fine art," by heavy industry and agriculture, and by the majority of the Social Democrats. The place of the artist in this process was the subject of a furious argument at the celebrated 1914 Werkbund conference at Cologne.[25]

During the war, Hermann Muthesius returned to the thoughts on the relationship between art and the machine which he had first formulated in 1902,[26] and which, in the meantime, had been adopted by Behrens. In 1917 Muthesius described the essence of mass production as the serial repetition of absolutely consistent single objects. He saw mass production as the industrial form of the future, as it reflected the contemporary trend of both products and men toward anonymity—a trend he welcomed without reservation.

A sensitive point in the history of the relationship between art and technology was thus reached. Behrens's original intention in 1907 had been to emancipate the individual from the formless, anarchic materialism of manufacturing industry by creating an atmosphere in which good design could flourish. This implied a complete visual reorganization involving the firm's products, production processes, working conditions, and housing. All of this was transformed by Muthesius's definition from a bourgeois liberating impulse into the exact opposite. Werner Sombart commented astutely that "while living practitioners in the arts were attempting, by means of good design, to free themselves from the dead matter that threatened to overwhelm them, . . . in the sphere of science, material concerns were increasingly subjugating the human element."[27] With the spread of standardization and anonymity in the world of technology and industry, the means were developed for a new subjugation of the individual. This had been the real theme of the Werkbund debate in 1914.[28] By the outbreak of the October Revolution, the Russian Constructivists had derived from it the methodology for their artistic offensive. In contrast, the bourgeois artists in the Werkbund raised the cry "Back to art as craftsmanship!" at their Stuttgart conference in 1919. In his Stuttgart address, entitled "The Tasks of the Werkbund," Hans Poelzig renounced the alliance between art and industry. Industry, he said, was concerned "simply with technical matters" and was "ruled by economic considerations." Art, however, was a "will to form," which should disclaim any connection with business. Only then, felt Poelzig, could art defend itself against fashionable exploitation by mass production and against standardization. The Werkbund, Poelzig said, should base its activity on "craftsmanship and artistic creativity," not on "technology and industry."[29]

Behrens sensed clearly that the very essence of his work for the AEG was being challenged. In 1920 he was forced to acknowledge "the collapse of a technically and economically advanced civilization," and he bemoaned the spread of "despairing resignation" and "the conscious destruction of form." "In its place," he said, "appear amorphous creations, the deformation of natural forms, disharmony and dissonance." Even before the war a "new age" had been prophesied in Expressionist art.[30] This highly subjective art was denounced at the time by the practical-minded Behrens as having no bearing on the reality of the time. His own aim, as a practical artist, had been to "ennoble" the technological civilization and to "infuse it with spiritual life." Confronted by the ruins of this civilization, he was now forced to admit that Expressionism had, after all, been the true manifestation of the age.

Behrens began to work on his design for the Memorial Hall in the administration building of I.G.-Farben at Höchst (illustration 5) in the autumn of 1920.[31] The contrast between the radically new style of the Höchst complex and, say, the administration building Behrens had designed for the AEG in 1917 (illustration A163 in catalog below) must be understood in terms of his traumatic realization.

Other influences, too, were at work. After the mechanized slaughter of the war, Behrens sought at Höchst to purge both industry and himself by invoking the spiritual help of Gothic mysticism and of Goethe's Farbenlehre. The Höchst complex stands in complete contrast to the optimistic rationalism of the offices Behrens had designed before the war for Mannesmann and for Continental. Equally striking is the range of expressive power invested in the design of an office. In an essay he wrote in 1920

Peter Behrens, IG-Farben factory at
Höchst, charcoal drawing, 1926.
Courtesy of Princess Margaret von
Hessen und bei Rhein, Schloss
Wolfsgarten.

for Hermann Graf Keyserling's Schule der Weisheit (School of Wisdom) at Darmstadt, Behrens described the essence of this architecture: "The building laws are mysterious. Multiplicity expands into the infinite and incalculable. The earth's gravity is not compensated for by statics and by piling up imposing building masses, but seems to be overcome entirely. Space does not enclose, does not confine, it leads into incalculable depths, climbs into distant heights."

Max Brod had already recognized this reversal of opinion when he commented in April 1914 that "the application of rational and seemingly rational measures has been so terribly overrated that we want now in our bad conscience to sate our spirits with a gluttonous orgy of irrationalism."[32]

In the immediate postwar years, Behrens, like Poelzig, Gropius, and Taut, believed that art had to return to its roots in craftsmanship. Yet by 1922 he was already looking for a way out of the seemingly inevitable schism between the worlds of art and technology. Behrens admitted that "at present the intellectuals in particular" viewed technology as "the expression of a calculating, analytical, capitalist and imperialist age." They desired, he said, by means of an art based on spiritualization and emotional simplicity," to "escape back to distant lands and past times." He pointed to the schism that prevented "both the engineer and the man of artistic sensibility from taking part in all aspects of our worldly existence." "Yet no one," he said, "could seriously dispense with the benefits of modern technology." Of these benefits he went on to say: "We need them today more than ever, and in the best and cheapest form. Precisely because we are economically depressed, we must make our life simpler, more practical, and more comprehensible. Only with the aid of industry can this be achieved. But those who do not want to have their life split between spirituality and technology are also right. Whether or not technology can succeed in becoming a means to and an expression of culture rather than remaining an end in itelf is therefore a question of great historical importance."[33] Behrens thereby redefined the original problem of 1907.

Behrens's pupil Walter Gropius conceived the Bauhaus as a laboratory in which this problem would be mastered. In 1907 Behrens had felt obliged in his work for the AEG "to bring art and propriety to the most distant strata of the population." With the Bauhaus at Weimar, Gropius now wanted to reach—in the language of the Expressionists—"new, intellectually untapped layers of the people."[34]

In the spring of 1934, in a paper given to the Design and Industries Association in London, Gropius described the aims of the Bauhaus and laid out a number of its main principles:

This conception of the essential unity of all creative work was what inspired me in founding the Bauhaus as a school of design. In carrying out this scheme I tried to solve the ticklish problem of combining imagination with technical proficiency, and strove to train a new and hitherto nonexistent type of collaborator who should be equally skilled in design and technical proficiency. . . . The Bauhaus accepted the machine as the essentially modern vehicle of form, and sought to come to terms with it. Its workshops were really laboratories in which practical designs for present-day goods were conscientiously worked out as models for mass production, and were continually being improved on. This dominant aim of creating typeforms to meet every commercial, technical, and aesthetic requirement necessitated a picked body of men of all-around culture who were thoroughly experienced in the practical and mechanical as well as the theoretical, scientific, and formal aspects of design, and who were well versed in the laws on which these are based. The constructors of these models had also to be fully acquainted with factory methods of mechanical mass production, which are radically different from those of handicraft, although the various parts of the prototypes they evolved had naturally to be made by hand. It is from the individual peculiarities of every type of machine that the new but still individual "genuineness" and "beauty" of its products are derived, whereas illogical machine imitation of handmade goods infallibly bears the stamp of a makeshift substitute.

The Bauhaus represented the school of thought that believes that the difference between industry and handicraft is far less a difference due to the nature of the tools employed than of the effect of subdivision of labor in the former and one-man control from start to finish in the latter. Handicrafts and industry must, however, be understood as opposites perpetually approaching each other. Handicrafts are now changing their traditional nature. In future their field will be in research work for industrial production and in speculative experiments in laboratory-workshops where the preparatory work of evolving and perfecting new typeforms will be done.

. . . Our guiding principle was that artistic design is neither an intellectual nor a material affair, but simply an integral part of the very stuff of life. Further, the revolution in artistic mentality has brought in its train that new elementary knowledge which is implied in the new conception of design, in the same way that the technical transformation of industry has provided new tools for its realization. Our object was to permeate both types of mind; to liberate the creative artist from his otherworldliness and reintegrate him into the workaday world of realities; and at the same time to broaden and and humanize the rigid, almost exclusively material mind of the businessman. Our governing conception of the basic unity of all design in its relation to life, which informed all our work, was therefore in diametrical opposition to that of "art for art's sake" and the even more dangerous philosophy it sprang from: business as an end in itself.[35]

It is clear that after 1918 Gropius's ideas had freed themselves from the philanthropic and nationalistic tendencies of Friedrich Naumann, which had inspired both Behrens and Gropius prior to 1914. The Gropius of the Bauhaus had also lost his faith in reform from above, to be brought about gradually by a handful of enlightened industrialists and artists working together in a nonpolitical pressure group like the Werkbund. Also missing was Walther Rathenau's belief in the ability of the capitalist system, when developed to its full potential, to eliminate poverty, alienation, and educational deprivation and to overcome production deficits and unprofitability.[36]

Unlike Behrens, Gropius and the Bauhaus were not attached to any firm. Gropius's work, therefore, had no advertising or publicity function. Furthermore, he did not have to demonstrate the validity of his designs through the products of a world-renowned firm in open competition with other companies. Gropius was ultimately able to see the work of his "laboratory" as that of a team of teachers and students, whereas Behrens's studio was organized in a highly efficient manner. Although Behrens very wisely kept his independence by reserving his right to work for other firms, he was nevertheless always concerned with practical commissions. He did not have the freedom enjoyed by the Bauhaus, which, as a relatively independent agency, could choose projects that would provide both prototypes for possible industrial production and teaching materials for a school of art and design.

To acknowledge the presence of Behrens's 1907 program in Gropius's 1934 paper in no way detracts from the historical importance of the Bauhaus. On the contrary, it reveals a happy and (in Germany) rare example of long-term development and continuity. In both cases one can detect the passion for the "perfection of material achievement" that had moved Max Weber, on seeing the designs of Behrens, Olbrich, and Pankok at the 1904 St. Louis World's Fair, to feel "proud of his own nation." These new German products prompted even in Weber the momentary thought that in the design of pots, glasses, chairs, and household utensils the Germans would be "the mentors of the West."[37]

Gropius's ideas provided the basis for Herbert Read's book *Art and Industry* (London, 1934). Read included the extract from Gropius's London lecture quoted above, and added "I have no other desire in this book than to support and propagate the ideals thus expressed by Dr. Gropius. . . ." As recently as 1976, Noel Carrington called Read's book "a New Testament for the whole design movement [in Great Britain]." Read's quasi-religious language, faith in the "master," and apostolic sense of mission to spread the "doctrine" all suggest a religious simile with respect to the Bauhaus: Gropius stood on the broad shoulders of Behrens as the apostles stood on the shoulders of the prophets.

Herbert Read came across the emigrant Gropius in London in 1934. Gropius was there because the authorities in Germany had begun to occupy themselves with the creation of a new "people's order . . . based on the discrimination between friend and foe, between those who conform to the people's order and those who are alien to it." Both Gropius and Mies fell into the alien and un-German category. In 1935, with the tobacco factory at Linz, Behrens composed the German swan song to architectural internationalism.

It is one of the most oppressive ironies in the history of German art that the uniquely universal impact and influence enjoyed by the two Behrens pupils, Gropius and Mies, was the result of the declaration by the German government that their work was alien to the German nation. The model for a modern existence which Naumann, Muthesius, and Behrens sought to promote and sell on the pre-1914 world market against bitter international competition now crossed the national frontiers effortlessly. Just at the time when this model was establishing itself as a universal precept and pattern, the members of the Bauhaus, who were the successors to Naumann, Muthesius, and Behrens, were robbed of their national identity and called enemies of the people.

Behrens and Messel: From the Mythology of Industry to "Art in the Industrial Process"[38]

... the true lover [of art] sees not only the truth in the imitation, but also the virtue of selection and the ingenuity of combination.
Goethe[39]

After January 1894, and possibly even earlier, the AEG used the so-called "Goddess of Light" as its trademark (illustration 6). With flowing tresses she sits sideways on a winged wheel. Her right foot rests on a globe, which emerges through the clouds in a profusion of lightning flashes. With her right hand she raises a glowing light bulb into the night sky. Compared with the bulb, the stars and the narrow crescent of the moon give out only a meager glimmer of light.

By adopting the "Goddess of Light," Emil Rathenau followed the widespread tendency of industry to portray its aims, its technological processes, and its dynamic power in mythological terms. In the case of the AEG, which was offering light and power for the common good, the mythological reference—the power of the AEG transcending the light of the heavens—was proud to the point of arrogance. In other cases it was more modest, as in the Carlsberg brewery's attempt to link its beer with Ceres, the goddess of grain. Further examples of industrial mythologizing were offered by the Flohr Elevator Company, whose advertising posters showed Sisyphus rolling his stone up the hill, and the Berliner Elektrizitätswerk (a subsidiary of the AEG), which decorated a commemorative publication in 1897 with a drawing of a dynamo inhabited by a female figure wrapped in a coil of wire (illustration 7). According to the mythology, steam power was created in Hades by giants with long beards; electric power, in contrast, was the province of innocent maidens.

Emil Rathenau would doubtless have agreed with Werner Sombart that "the only motive for economic processes is organized human trading," and that technology should be understood as "the functional arrangement of material goods for human needs."[40] There was, nevertheless, a deep-rooted need to defend, comprehend, or extol technology in terms of its mythological and symbolic origins. Sombart's more sober approach prevailed, but only very slowly. In the 1901 lecture cited above, he explained that it was absurd to declare that "steam is the driving force of our modern economic life, as one constantly reads." "Steam, gentlemen," he continued, "is the driving force of the steam engine; that which installs the engine in a particular place and for a particular purpose is the will of the industrialist." But the extent of its power to create and utilize new sources of energy made it hard for industry at that time to identify with Sombart's functionalist definition. Similarly, the revolution in Germany's social and cultural life was too obvious, the hopes attached to industry too optimistic, and the criticism of the negative effects of industrialization too menacing for Sombart's formula to gain easy acceptance.

With the advent of Jugendstil, industry's attempt to define its own image entered a second phase, and naturalistic symbolism was abandoned. The production of energy was no longer portrayed as the wonderfully effortless and pure labor of those ubiquitous goddesses who ignited arc lamps, fed power stations, and wove telephone connections out of electric wires. By commissioning Otto Eckmann, a leading Jugendstil artist, to design its contributions to the Paris World Exhibition, the AEG already demonstrated in 1900 that it saw a correspondence between its own work and that of the avant-garde. Among Eckmann's designs for the AEG was a new trademark to replace the one, probably designed by Franz Schwechten, that had first appeared in gold mosaic on the portal on the Brunnenstrasse (illustration 1). For Schwechten's three initials, composed of interlocking acanthus tendrils, Eckmann substituted three letters in his own "Eckmannschrift"—one of the first modern typefaces of the twentieth century. In the few graphic designs Eckmann produced for the AEG one can see how he used his characteristically Jugendstil curves to frame the products of the firm and thereby invest them with a certain dynamism. This dynamism, however, was Eckmann's own, and bore no specific relation to technology. Indeed, it was equally appropriate on the book jackets of the plays of Gerhart Hauptmann which Eckmann designed for the S. Fischer publishing house in Leipzig. Eckmann's graphic work deserves at best a limited acknowledgement, as proof that the AEG had turned to a modern artist of his stature. This manner of graphic design was specifically Eckmann's, however. It could not free itself from the personality of the artist or create a new and unmistakable style appropriate to an industrial concern such as the AEG.

Illustrations of industrial products, trademarks, and factories framed by ornamental borders originated in early-nineteenth-century England and became an internationally favored motif in sales catalogs, commemorative publications, and advertisements. One of the thousands of possible examples is a catalog published in 1904 by the Westinghouse Electric and Manufacturing Company of Pittsburgh (illustrations 9, 10). This differed from, say, the 1884 catalog of the Chicago firm Van de Poele—which actually showed the functional blessings of electricity in a realistic manner (illustration 11)—in much the same way as Eckmann's work differed from its predecessors. Exactly a thousand years after floriate decoration had been used in the liturgical books of the tenth century, it enjoyed a remarkable revival in the age of electrical mythology. Instead of illuminating the *sanctus* or *te igitur* in manuscripts such as Saint Gall Psalters, it was now wound around the initials of industrial firms. Rather than rely simply on photographs, the catalogs depicted electrical power with an ornamental and quasi-religious symbolism that invoked ''the sentimentalism of the allegory of power.''[41]

WAREN-ZEICHEN.

6
The trademark used by the AEG after 1894. Courtesy of H. Rogge.

7
Ludwig Sütterlin, ''Dynamo,'' 1897. Courtesy of H. Rogge.

8
Otto Eckmann, publicity card for AEG light bulbs, 1899–1900. Courtesy of H. Rogge.

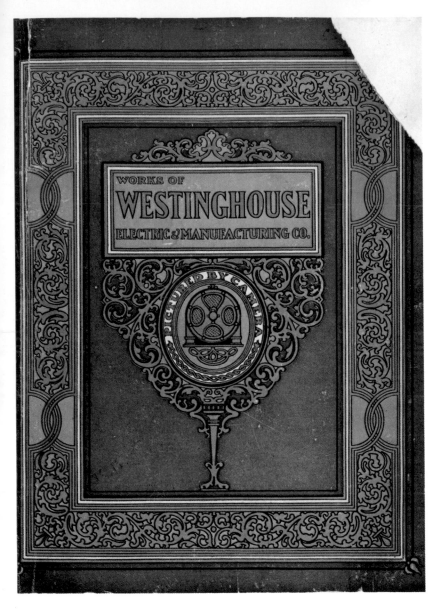

9
Title page of sales catalog of
Westinghouse Electric Company,
Pittsburgh, 1904. New York Public
Library.

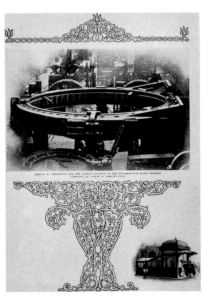

10
Page from 1904 Westinghouse
catalog. New York Public Library.

11
Title page of sales catalog of Van de
Poele Electric Company, Chicago,
1884. New York Public Library.

Yet the reality of the world of technology and the graphical attempts to dress it up stood in implacable opposition.

Although Otto Eckmann did away with the references to early-medieval book illustrations, he still attempted to draw a naturalistic analogy between linear ornament and electrical current (see illustrations 8 and 32). These nervous lines were indeed capable of portraying "power"—even technological power—but, as Henry van de Velde remarked, they did that "by borrowing energy from the one who drew them." This linear art remained the style of one individual. It did not, as Behrens was later to demand, "arrive, by artistic means, at those forms which are analogous to the machine and to machine production."[42]

Eckmann died in 1902 and was succeeded by the distinguished architect Alfred Messel. Messel designed an administration building for the AEG which was erected on the Friedrich-Karl-Ufer between October 1905 and October 1906 (illustration 12). The commission was given to Messel after an unsuccessful competition. With this project, Messel and his collaborator, the sculptor Hermann Hahn, sought to give symbolic expression to the character and principles of the AEG. They developed a symbolic language that went beyond the economic and technical rationalism of the AEG but did not fall back on the conventional naturalism of industrial mythology. The result corresponded closely to Walther Rathenau's own taste.

Messel's administration building tried to break away from the precedent set by the AEG's original main office, which had been built in 1892 in the manner of a Baroque palace (illustration 13). In his design, Messel shunned both the medieval romanticism of Schwechten's North German brick Gothic (illustration 14) and the antitraditionalism of Jugendstil. In its pilastered and rusticated grandeur, Messel's administration building alluded instead to the aristocratic palaces built by Palladio and Sanmichele in Vicenza, Verona, and Venice. With this attempt to transform a shabby arm of the River Spree into an echo of the Canale Grande, Messel created the most important office building in pre-1914 Berlin. He had achieved a similar effect with his designs for the Nationalbank and for the Berliner Handelsgesellschaft (a firm headed by Carl Fürstenberg, a friend of Emil Rathenau and chairman of the AEG's supervisory board).

Although the facade of the AEG administration building in no way shied away from grandeur, its grandeur was modest in comparison with the more obvious architectural displays of economic and industrial wealth that were being erected at the same time in Chicago and New York by the giant industrial concerns. Messel's measured and solid architectural language reflected an immense self-confidence and assurance, based equally on solidity and fantasy. It clearly differentiated itself from the parvenu architecture of the Gründerzeit,[43] which was supported by borrowed money and by the security offered by stylistic plagiarism. These charges could certainly be leveled at the old AEG main office on the Schiffbauerdamm. A contemporary critic noted how susceptible the ornamental plaster-and-stucco facade was to the severe Berlin winters. In contrast to this peeling stucco, which cannot have improved the firm's image, Messel's facade on the Friedrich-Karl-Ufer, built of Hartershofen limestone, expressed tradition-conscious, solid, genuine, and lasting standards. The facade differentiated itself not only from the many styles of the Gründerzeit, but also from the irresponsible arabesques of Jugendstil.

The relationship between the formal architectural language of the banks, offices, and factories built for Carl Fürstenberg and Emil Rathenau and the economic development of the companies involved is easier to postulate than to define. Any attempt to relate the two can, however, draw on the extraordinarily detailed testimony of Carl Fürstenberg, which has been passed on by his son:

13
Cremer and Wolffenstein, main office
of Berliner Elektrizitäts-Werke and
AEG, Schiffbauerdamm, Berlin, 1892.
From *50 Jahre BEW* (1934).

14
Franz Schwechten, AEG forge and
welding shop, Voltastrasse, Berlin-
Wedding. AEG photo 4441, 23 June
1906.

In his time even the best architects built by no means "functionally," but principally with the facade in mind. A bank facade had to display dignified columns and pilasters. The old Berliner Handels-Gesellschaft was very beautiful . . . , but an ideal office building now looks quite different. These architectural questions are very important, for they clearly show Carl Fürstenberg's intentions with regard to the bank's development. On leaving S. Bleichroeder, he first set up business in a large private house. In those days the proprietors were not only personally liable, but also had their own capital tied up in the bank. In 1900 my father emphatically turned away from his initial concept, when collaboration with other large banks changed the picture entirely. For "reasons of appearance," as one would now say, my father found that it had become necessary to give the firm the status of a major banking house. As a result of this change of attitude, spacious new premises were constructed, which were in keeping with the considerable increase in the firm's capital.[44]

The architectural language of the AEG's original administration building on the Schiffbauerdamm (illustration 13) by Cremer and Wolffenstein (a firm that was very successful with the Berlin business world and with the Wilhelmine court) expressed comparable attitudes. This intended purpose, however, could only have been inferred from the inscriptions on the facade and possibly from the shops at street level. Otherwise, the facade was entirely in keeping with the established tradition of residential architecture, and the main block made no reference to the elongated office wings at the rear. The fact that Emil Rathenau actually lived on the principal floor—the "piano nobile"—explains the building's similarity to a Neo-Baroque

palace. The predominance given on the facade to this residential role denied the building's principal function as offices. The executive offices were located on the mezzanine floor above the shops, with the boardroom at the center. Although the mezzanine seems squat and visually tied to the shops, it was as high inside as the other stories. The second and third floors, corresponding to the residential chambers in the Baroque model, dominated the floors below, where large windows were separated by narrow pillars. The top floor, according to the Berlin address book, contained two apartments which were rented after 1892 to two of the firm's directors, Felix Deutsch and Paul Mamroth. All the floors in the rear wings were used for offices. An article in the *Zeitschrift für Bauwesen* stressed the skill with which the architects had satisfied "the demands of the extensive administration without sacrificing stateliness and comfort in the apartments." The main staircase and the first hydraulic elevator to be installed in Berlin (see illustration 31) were intended "principally for access to the directors and to the apartments."

More than anything else, it was the mythological representation of the beneficial activity of the two firms that revealed the real function of the building as a joint head office. There were large escutcheons on the facade with images of city silhouettes lit by a carbon arc. The main entrance was decorated with stars and blossoming boughs. The head of Minerva framed by electrical sparks appeared in the pediments above the top row of windows, and the pediments on the principal floor had a winged dragon as the bringer of light. There were festoons made up of globes, torches, trumpets, crowns, and palm fronds. The winged helmet of Mercury, the god of trade, decorated with palms and laurels, flanked the main entrance. All these images depicted electricity as the provider of light, power, and life. The central pediment depicted the power of electricity to promote good and banish evil: Apollo, the god of light, was shown driving away the female demons of darkness.

A similar optimism about the future radiates from the Gothic portal on the Brunnenstrasse (illustration 1) built by Schwechten in 1896. The tympana of the side entrances carried the AEG trademark on a gold background, framed by light bulbs. On the pediment of the main arch the diamond quatrefoil, an early-Christian "majestas" motif, was filled not by the Pantocrator and the Evangelists but by the cogged wheel representing the new gospel of the machine. Light bulbs hung from the tree of life in the tabernacles of the twin spires, and shafts of lightning bound in sheaves appeared in the flanking panels. The spires were crowned by spheres of white glass.

The inscriptions and the display windows on the facade of the old main office on the Schiffbauerdamm pointed to the true function of the building with a reticence similar to that shown by the early AEG factories. The boardroom conformed to the traditional pattern of the "Berliner Zimmer," and the offices of the directors, executives, and staff were either hidden or subordinated to the demands of the palace facade. Only the display windows, with their nontraditional demand for uninterrupted space, began to break up the adopted proportions of the palace facade by extending above the main entrance. Nevertheless, the two residential floors still dominated the facade. A critical look at the elevation shows that the corners of the facade fell apart and broke at their joints. The pillars between the windows on the ground floor and the mezzanine had no connection whatsoever with the recessed plane of the wall above. The three bays of the central portal were squeezed from both sides, so that the portal itself looked up for help to the fanfare of the portico above. The portico itself straddled the salon in Emil Rathenau's apartment in a very ungainly manner. The attempt to accommodate the founder's apartment, administrative offices, and a retail store under one roof led to conflicts typical of the period. At Schiffbauerdamm, Cremer and Wolffenstein tried unsuccessfully to overcome these conflicts with the aid of the unifying power of the Baroque facade. The problem was ultimately solved by Messel's 1905–06 administration building.

With expansion, the AEG's administrative needs increased to such an extent that Emil Rathenau, like Carl Fürstenberg before him, was forced to move his business out of his private residence and into a large office block. The concept that linked the identity of the firm with the official residence of its founder was thus abandoned, and with it a view of work that was cosmically unbounded in its optimism. The allegorical portrayal of the firm's activity now focused on work as the performance of a duty, on science and technology, and on operational safety and reliability. This new mythology of work no longer believed in the direct relation of industrial labor to absolute goodness and to the productive forces of nature. Instead, it sought to characterize the work ethos of the firm as the specialized subdivision of clearly demarcated tasks. The formal consequence of this was the obvious relaxation on Messel's facade of those elements that sought to enforce unity. Strictly hierarchic organization was replaced by a growing awareness of the equal status of many different work processes and of their varying spatial requirements.

Behrens, in his unrealized 1917 project for an AEG administrative center at Humboldthain (illustration A163), went considerably farther than Messel in developing a standardized, anonymous language for office design. Behrens had already taken steps in this direction with his 1911–12 administration building for the Mannesmann organization in Düsseldorf[45] (illustration 17). Here all the symbols of power and dignity were definitively ascribed to the firm rather than to its owner. In recognition of this change in structure and character, Behrens firmly rejected the traditional classical formulas in the articulation of the facade. Whereas Messel had established an architectonic order on his facade with a pediment, pilasters, rustication, and dependent forms, Behrens limited the use of classical motifs to the small, strongly delineated entrance area and the stairwell. Otherwise, the building was a clear statement of equality; identical cells housing identical administrative units were lined up side by side.[46]

15
Hermann Hahn, allegorical figures, AEG main office, 1908.

16
Hugo Kaufmann, "Betriebssicherheit," clay statue, formerly in AEG main office. AEG photo 11758, 26 February 1914.

In Messel's AEG building (illustration 18), an Olympian firmament vaulted the large boardroom and Zeus and his eagles still defined the essence of electricity as a mythological power.[47] This reference was also retained on the commemorative medal Hermann Hahn designed for Emil Rathenau's seventieth birthday on 11 December 1908 (illustration 19)[48]: Like the famous Decadrachm of Agrigento, the reverse side of the medal depicted an eagle and, in addition, a sheaf of lightning flashes as the Olympian symbol of electricity. What was intended on the Greek original to be an attribute of the father of the gods now belonged to the creator of the AEG. In its simplicity, Hahn's portrait reflected Rathenau's intense dislike of arrogance and pretentiousness.[49]

The commemorative medal's contrast between the pensive portrait (which reflected Emil Rathenau's uncompromisingly Spartan sense of duty as well as his commercial imagination) and the mythological symbols of power described well the disparity that had suddenly appeared between Rathenau as an individual and the vastly greater scale of his business, which had become an "autonomous entity." As any business grows in scale and complexity, the ability of the founding entrepreneur to act or to intercede in its development decreases.[50] It was possible, however, to sublimate this conflict into the responsibility of the entrepreneur for the destiny of a growing workforce (in Le Corbusier's words, "a nation of a hundred and fifty thousand souls"[51]) and into the knowledge of the benefits the firm had brought to the community by generating power and producing appliances, tools, and machines for public and private use. The content of the Emil Rathenau commemorative medal might perhaps be understood in these terms.

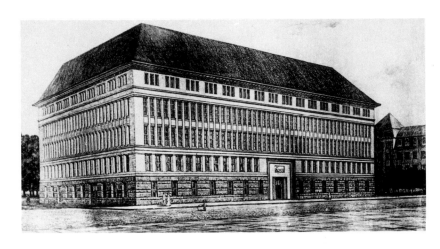

17
Peter Behrens, main office of Mannesmannröhren-Werke, Düsseldorf, 1911. Courtesy of F. Stoedtner.

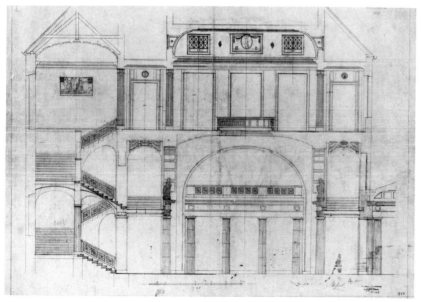

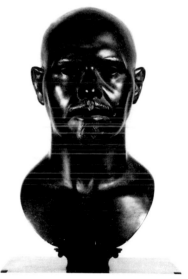

19
Hermann Hahn, silver medal
commemorating seventieth birthday of
Emil Rathenau, 11 December 1908.
Private collection, Berlin. Photo
courtesy of H. Rogge.

18
Alfred Messel, section through
entrance hall of AEG main office,
pen drawing, December 1905. Plan
collection, Technische Universität
Berlin.

20
Hermann Hahn, bronze bust of
Walther Rathenau, 1908. Märkisches
Museum, East Berlin.

It is proof of Hermann Hahn's empathy as an artist that he portrayed his friend Walther Rathenau, the heir to the achievements of Emil Rathenau, in a very different way. The bronze bust of Walther Rathenau from 1908 (illustration 20), preserved in the Märkische Museum in East Berlin, has very appropriately been called "the Caesar-like portrait of Rathenau the Younger."[52] In its frontality and its idealized nakedness, the bust recalls earlier images of Hellenistic rulers. This similarity was endorsed by Walther Rathenau himself in his oft-quoted appraisal of his economic power as successsor to his father: "Three hundred men, all mutually acquainted, control the economic destiny of the continent. . . . they belong to the rising generation of city dwellers, to the educated middle classes. They are, in short, the businessmen and managers of the second and third generation."[53] The expansion of Emil Rathenau's business empire filled his successor, the "manufacturer and businessman" Walther, with "an almost statesmanlike attitude toward his companies and his business ventures," which he had come to view "as an entity that grows of its own accord and makes its own demands upon us."[54] Whereas the Emil Rathenau medal had depicted the relationship between the entepreneur and an endlessly expanding public enterprise as a conflict, this conflict resolved itself in Hahn's bust of Walther Rathenau into a demand for an executive function based on managerial control, on "power and responsibility." This executive role went beyond the bounds of commerce and entered into the affairs of state. Hahn's portrait of Walther Rathenau did not share Emil Rathenau's astonishment at the incredible growth of the family enterprise and made no recourse to mythology as an aid to comprehension. Instead, it strove to identify commercial performance with statesmanlike power. Perhaps one could take this to be the bust's literal meaning. Walther Rathenau appeared to describe both the bust and himself when he spoke of the "aureole" that had "surrounded the businessman's head" since "the power that major industry is capable of exercising in the capitalist state" had been revealed.[55] It is not surprising, therefore, that Hermann Hahn "suppressed all the fine, individual features in favor of extreme stylistic simplification."[56] In this expressionless face Rathenau's most

intimate thoughts on the "depersonalization of possession and ownership" and on "objectification" found visible form. One could almost be eavesdropping on a conversation between Walther Rathenau and Hahn when one reads in Rathenau's book *Mechanik des Geistes* (Mechanics of the Spirit) of "the aversion of the Greeks to anything that was uniquely fortuitous . . . against the hated and despised individualization of the portrait." According to Walther Rathenau, "the differentiation among higher, nobler creatures becomes very slight. . . . It thus seems that at an important point in the hierarchy of empirical and organic existence the concept of individualization disappears."[57] Hahn's bust, like the Emil Rathenau medal, was nothing more than an attempt to explain expansion and power in mythological terms. In the bust, however, this process was no longer portrayed in the context of a private perception, but was elevated into the demand of a new elite to lead and to fulfil its mission, which was "to regulate and dominate."[58]

It was Peter Behrens's task to give form to Walther Rathenau's new conception of his own role and the role of industry. The "entire AEG organization," its "collective character,"[59] was to be given expression in the new languages of architecture, product design, and advertising.

The Olympian eagle, representing electricity, entirely dominated the view of the Oberspree cable works on the embossed plaquette (by Hermann Hahn?) that was set into the cover of the Festschrift for the twenty-fifth anniversary of the AEG on 14 April 1908 (illustrations 21 and G12). With this cover, Behrens revealed the entirely new formal means which he was to develop into a method of portraying and promoting the AEG. No longer would the industrial world of the AEG be represented by factory views or by the conventional mythological adaptations, as on the Emil Rathenau medal of 1908. Even more striking examples of the appropriation of mythological motifs can be found in the 1897 Festschrift of the Berliner Elektrizitätswerke, a subsidiary of the AEG (illustrations 6 and 22), and in the illustrations to textbooks on electricity published around the turn of the century (illustration 23). In his new graphic conception, Behrens freed the AEG's printed materials from any naturalistic, literary, or mythological function. Pictures were replaced by drawings and by lettering. For example, the system of grid and lettering on the cover of the twenty-fifth-anniversary Festschrift was in no way subservient to the pictorial impact of the plaquette, but rather laid claim to a function of its own. Behrens abandoned both symbolic representations and the illustration of industrial plants and electrical appliances and looked instead for a simple format with which to depict technology. This format would no longer call on the traditional resources of mythology in order to explain the nature of technology, but would derive its formal principles from the laws governing technical processes and industrial production. As Behrens put it, it was essential "to arrive, by artistic means, at those forms that are analogous to the machine and machine production."[60]

In this radical process of material abstraction, pictorial illustrations or symbols were replaced by a stylized typography and the rhythmic play of framed surfaces and colors. In the plaquette for the 1908 Festschrift, the eagle was superimposed on the factory as a symbol of the transcendental source of electrical power. In contrast, on the title page of the same book, Behrens offered a geometrical figure—the hexagon—as an analogy to the technological commerce of the AEG. Thus, Behrens turned radically away from the traditional manner in which industrial firms presented themselves. Instead of leading from the particular characteristics of the firm in question to the mythologically perceived sources of technology, Behrens assembled the AEG's hexagonal trademark in just the same way as the firm's products were themselves assembled. The evocatively crystalline form of this sign, composed of exactly calculated empty areas within the framed plane, conveys a profound sense of perfection. It promotes a mood of contemplation in the observer akin to that generated by "art." In this moment of artistic pleasure, Behrens did not miss the opportunity to include the name AEG, thus investing the industrial and technical associations of the firm's trademark with the aura of artistic perfection. The AEG's invitation to the Schiffbau-Ausstellung (illustration G11) can be taken as an example of this technique.

21
Hermann Hahn (?) and Peter Behrens, cover of Festschrift marking twenty-fifth anniversary of AEG. Courtesy of H. Rogge.

22
Ludwig Sütterlin, "Goddess of Light,"
1897. Courtesy of H. Rogge.

23
Cover of Multhaupt, *Die moderne
Elektrizität* (Berlin, 1901). Courtesy of
H. Rogge.

24
Peter Behrens, advertising brochure
for AEG light bulbs, 1910. Courtesy of
H. Rogge.

The entirely novel power of suggestion and association that aesthetic stimulation conferred on a trademark was especially effective in those advertisements and posters in which Behrens included AEG products within the formal design. For an example of the breadth and scope of Behrens's technique, one has only to look to his drawings and illustrations of light bulbs (illustrations 24 and G30–G37). The possibilities range from the silhouette of a bulb as a stylized source of light to realistically painted images of bulbs set in nichelike frames and suspended iconically, like an Andy Warhol soup can. Behrens also produced an early form of photorealism: In a small-format brochure the axially placed bulb took on an oversize, surreally plastic form, as if it were a real bulb viewed through a magnifying glass. Any diminution of the material character of the bulb was avoided, be it by reference to a connecting wire, to the bulb's spatial relations, to its function in a lighting scheme, or to the light it produced. In the AEG's advertisements for electrical appliances there were no users, no pictures of superior households with maids in pinafores. Through their "free" aesthetic appeal, the expensive new devices lost their luxury character and became consumer goods for all.

When this "significant aesthetic stimulus"[61] was savored to the full, an everyday product such as a light bulb gained the quality of uniqueness enjoyed by an art object. Removed from its useful value and functional context, the form of the product appeared not to have been determined by considerations of purpose or function, but to have been constructed out of the aesthetic fiction of its own purity. Behrens took, as it were, a light bulb from the production line, gave it a geometrical frame and a name, and using line and color reconstructed its technical form into an artistic form. He then presented it to the consumers and to rival firms as the precious creation of industrial art, which, for the price of a few pfennigs, delivered the beauty and perfection of an AEG product as well as the quality and efficiency of the bulb itself.

The electrical nymphs that populated technical publications around the turn of the century were international and were interchangeable from firm to firm. Even the intelligent classical allusions the Rathenaus had made through Messel and Hahn had only sought a general association of meaning that could embrace both business and technology. In contrast, the hexagon, the firm's initials, and the iconic drawings of its products stood for the AEG alone. At the same time, however, these symbols represented the emphatic affirmation by a new class of industrial leaders—in direct opposition to the taste of the Wilhelmine court—that Industriekultur expressed the style of the age.

In the light of this interpretation, an attempt should be made to describe an aesthetic concept that, in its radical negation and transformation of the function of art as naturalistic representation and its "exploration" of the elementary formal potential of art, paralleled the experiments of the international avant-garde. Unlike the "fine art" of painting, however, Behrens's graphic design was not "abstract" but concrete art. Behrens succeeded in creating a formal procedure that seemed to be analogous to the methods of technological production.

It is clear that this technique of pitching publicity material at the highest aesthetic and intellectual level could only function when the aesthetic purism of the illustrations in the firm's redesigned brochures, catalogs, and calendars did not conflict with the actual design of the products themselves. More correctly, it could only function when the products had also been completely redesigned, thus removing an already existing conflict. Only then could the truth of Behrens's basic design hypothesis—that in the context of the AEG it was fundamentally possible to draw an analogy between the processes of artistic and technical production—prove itself.

We have now arrived at the essence of Behrens's work for the AEG. It is absolutely clear that he did not merely draw up modern designs for projects that had already been defined. Rather, he subjected one product after another to his experiment with form. By reshaping the appearance of these products, Behrens stamped them first of all as creations of the AEG. At the same time, he conferred on them the honor of the first entirely modern style of industrial design. Avant-garde design thus became a reflection of the technological lead which Walther Rathenau described as "the greatest, indeed the only commercial asset." One should lead, said Rathenau, in plant and product, in industrial relations, in technical know-how, in organization, and in working methods.[62]

Behrens explained in a lecture delivered at the AEG in June 1909 that it was a "natural consequence" of his intention to create an "artistic context" for the AEG products that it should also be "carried over to their advertising."[63] The principles behind this "artistic style" for industrially mass-produced goods will be discussed later, but here we should look at an even more surprising analogy drawn by Behrens. On 26 May 1910, Behrens addressed the eighteenth annual meeting of the Verband Deutscher Elektrotechniker (Association of German Electrical Engineers) at Braunschweig. His theme was "Art and Technology." In his address he commented that "the same approach that has just been described as suitable for architecture is also valid for smaller, industrially produced objects." Behrens thereby defined an artistic method by which a plant, the plant's products, and the illustration and exhibition of the products could be designed according to the same formal principles. When designing his own house in the artists' colony on the Mathildenhöhe in Darmstadt, the young Behrens had found it difficult to integrate his life in all its manifestations into the character of the house. He was now in a position to translate this problem into a new context—that of the planning and design of a massive industrial complex. In his approach to this task, Behrens

avoided subjectivity and an "individual stylistic direction" in the sense of Olbrich, Eckmann, or van de Velde by concentrating on "forms analogous to the machine and machine production." The quantum leap that differentiates Behrens's industrial architecture and product design from all previous and similar attempts was based on this infinitely simple formula. He endowed industry—the dominant productive force of the modern age—with a genuine means of artistic expression. Behrens thus embraced industry with an affirmative enthusiasm, following the examples of Max Weber, Friedrich Naumann, and Walther Rathenau.

Differences much like those between the pre-1908 AEG letterhead shown in illustration 6 and the Behrens-designed book cover shown in illustration 21 can be seen when one compares the Riga factory of the Union-Elektrizitätsgesellschaft (illustration 25), which the AEG took over in 1905, with Behrens's AEG turbine factory in Moabit (illustrations A17–A32).

At the corner of the factory block at Riga was a stepped, arcaded facade resembling the west front of a church or an iconostasis forbidding entry to the sanctuary. It was built in a curious mixtue of styles: Prussian orderly, neo-Schinkel, and North Italian brick. The artless elongation of the machine hall, which was demanded by production considerations, was terminated at the rear by a facade similar to that at the front.

At the center of the front facade, like the saint on the facade of a church, stood a statue of the "Goddess of Light,"[64] surrounded by the tracery of a rose window and by a a large inscription (Russische Elektrizitätsgesellschaft UNION). This facade was conceived purely as a dummy wall and offered no access to the factory behind. The main gate for the firm's employees stood next to it, heavily laden with grilles and iron bars. The factory facade and the gateway shared the same front with a large administration block, which screened the factory yard and dominated all the other buildings, rather like a town hall built in the taste of late-Renaissance Paris. Still on the same front, beyond the administration block—where the main street was planted like a boulevard—stood the house of the factory director. The house was surrounded by an enclosed, almost parklike garden, and had been designed in the Schinkelesque style favored at the time for the villas around Berlin's Tiergarten.

25
Union-AEG factory, Riga, ca. 1905.
AEG photo 15006.

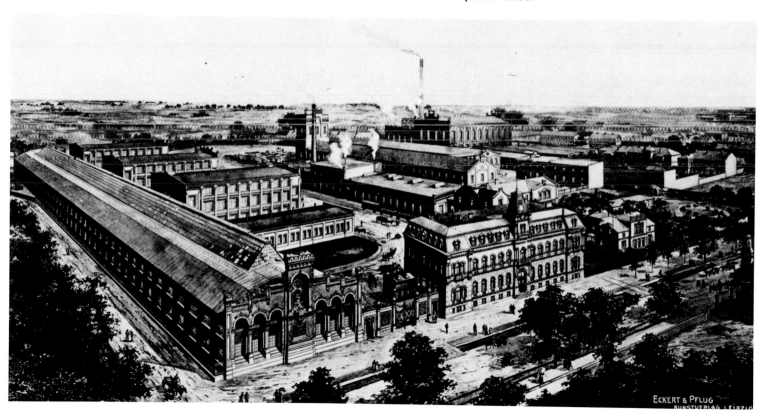

This well-considered layout followed a basic model that appeared in all industrialized countries and was variable according to production process and location. In such a layout, the tranquil hierarchy of a medieval monastery appeared to have survived. Karl Schumacher, Karl Ernst Osthaus, and other, more formidable critics had already noted that this idyllic image of industry was breaking up. In a speech at Munich in 1907, Osthaus spoke of "the dangers of alienating the spirit of production from the spirit of invention."[65] In the plan of the Riga factory this schism was extremely vivid. The very existence of the workshops was hidden behind facades specially constructed for the purpose. These facades not only masked the reality of the factory but also offered an allegorical and fictional version of their own: The production of light was achieved by a mythological goddess, with her back to the workbench. It was quite logical that the administration of such an allegorical chimera should be dressed up in a garb appropriate to preindustrial rulers and should adopt the forms of city government and aristocratic pomp.

After 1908, Behrens erected a series of factory complexes for the AEG: on the Huttenstrasse site in Moabit, on the Brunnenstrasse in Wedding, and at Oberschöneweide (illustrations 26, A17 ff., A43 ff., and A154 ff.). If one compares these with the Union factory at Riga or even with the earlier installations of the AEG itself, one can see an absolute change in the way the workplace was conceived. The production areas in Behrens's factories were not hidden behind high walls, screened by elaborate facades, or banished from the streetscape by palatial administration buildings, ornate portals, or company residences. In contrast to the Riga layout, Behrens literally turned the hierarchy of the building complex inside out. Instead of hiding them from public view, Behrens sited the workshops along and up to the street line, as the dominant spatial and visual elements. These elements were not arranged according to a mythological or ideological hierarchy, but were arranged functionally according to the demands of the production processes and of transportation. This change of viewpoint spelled the rejection of the defensive, retreating, and sublimating response to industrialization that had characterized the nineteenth century. The new, affirmative character of Behrens's architectural language

also expressed itself in the use of new materials and constructional techniques. Not only did Behrens make wide use of concrete, steel, and glass in the AEG factories, but he also exposed these materials without inhibition. His use of traditional brick was equally straightforward.

In the nineteenth century, brick was widely used to give factory buildings a decorative, gothicky cladding (see, for example, illustration 14). Behrens, on the other hand, used the individual brick as the smallest visible unit in massive buildings such as the small-motor factory shown in illustration 27 and the high-voltage factory shown in illustration A58. His regular and rhythmic use of the brick emphasized its material nature, its industrial production, and the ubiquity of its use while suppressing any pictorial, ornamental, or historicist tendencies. The gigantic half-columns on the facade of the small-motor factory did not refute this interpretation. The smooth regularity of the brickwork denied any historical antecedent and achieved exactly the degree of abstraction necessary to preclude any thoughts of traditional columniation. The decorum of the classical orders was not forgotten, but was transferred into a basic principle of Behrens's architectural syntax. According to this principle, Behrens's task was to find analogies to the world of technology by creating a "uniform series" and by "respecting the internal construction through the use of close-fitting external cladding."[66]

The fundamental artistic impact made by this street front derived from the majestic columnar facade, which acted as a unifying force without placing the building within a historical continuum. As a contemporary observer noted: "One indeed senses the link back to the classical codex, but one is still very aware of the steely present. One anticipates and looks for the machines."[67]

26
Otto Bollhagen, bird's-eye view of
AEG factories in Berlin-Wedding, ca.
1928. AEG photo 20471.

27
AEG small-motor factory, Voltastrasse,
Berlin-Wedding, 1913. AEG photo
10967.

Behrens's principles were even more valid for the concrete, glass, and iron machine halls, and in these constructions his belief in the potential of industrial architecture found even clearer expression. Here, industrially produced building materials became identified with the workplaces of technical production, and the architecture of the factory became an instrument in the work process. The long hall of the large-machine factory was the natural enclosure for the work that was done inside. The side pillars not only supported the walls and the roof, but also made up the frame on which the overhead cranes ran. The rails, brackets, and supports for the cranes and machines that directed the production process were exposed on the wall and determined its construction. The assembly shops, like the turbine factory, consisted, as chief engineer Karl Bernhard put it, of "nothing more than a frame suitable for carrying heavy crane loads." "The braces of this frame", Bernhard continued, "incidentally supported the roof and walls, which excluded the wind and weather from the working areas."[68] Behrens understood how to transform the engineer's frame into an artistic "composition." He articulated the proportions and the spacing of the iron partitions and the wall panels, and employed the various building materials in such a way that these components functioned as relatively free elements in the organization of the wall.

The actual work sequence that ran inside the large-machine hall—with the active help of the architecture—appeared on the outside, on the street front, as a rhythmic analogy to the process of mass production. The street front did not make any mythological allusions, nor did it hark back to a harmonious, preindustrial age. There was no discrepancy here between the inside and the outside, as there had been at Riga or in the older AEG factories; exactly the same elements were used both inside and outside. Behrens did not disguise his sheds, neither did he take refuge in the trite functionalism or insipid Sachlichkeit [objectivity; practicality] he later described as a "fanfare for banality."[69] Instead, he gave the building a well-fitting outer skin, a lucid wall structure, and an expressive face.

In addition to this type of factory, in which the building acted simultaneously as a gantry, Behrens was also commissioned to give architectonic form to assembly processes involving simple, constant, and uniform work and not demanding the movement of "gigantic masses." The high-voltage-equipment factory (illustration A58) and the small-motor factory (illustration 27) were typical examples. The function of this type of building was to arrange, both horizontally and vertically, "the greatest possible number of simple and identical work processes."[70] There was no need here to anchor heavy lifting gear or transmission shafts to the roof and wall supports. It was possible, therefore, to conceive the architectural envelope for the workshops as a rhythmic sequence of identical small-scale units (illustrations A54 ff.). In the small-motor factory, these repeating units were held together on the street front by the row of giant half-columns and articulated on the courtyard side by the projecting blocks and the stairwells (illustrations A85, A89 ff.). The mass assembly of small appliances from entirely prefabricated parts made relatively simple architectural demands; all that was needed was a vibration-free base for the machines and a protective shell. In the turbine and large-machine factories the fabrication process was made physically possible and was literally supported and transported by the architecture. In complete contrast, the function of the architecture in the small-motor factory was to encase the work process, often in rooms that had no auxiliary machinery and were entirely devoted to assembly work. The architecture was thus freed from any load-bearing function and simply provided a convenient and appropriate envelope. A parallel might be drawn between this architectural liberation and the emancipation of the external coverings of electrical appliances from their working parts. Once again, Behrens's architectural design created an aesthetic analogy to the process of production. The "collective essence" of the factory was created out of the structured organization and repetition of thousands of smaller units.

With Behrens's turbine factory and small-motor factory, the architectural presentation of industry was pursued for the first time with positive enthusiasm, and large-scale industry was accepted as the dominant productive force of the new era. This enthusiasm for newness, power, and scale (although not necessarily for vast external dimensions) corresponded historically to the equally passionate demands of Max Weber and Friedrich Naumann for an unequivocal acceptance of industrialization and its consequences. Behrens gave concrete form to ideas that were more or less shared by van de Velde, Muthesius, Schumacher, Endell, Poelzig, and Grenander and had been given a firm base in the program of the Werkbund. Though Behrens was the first to give form to these ideas, others were soon to follow.

In Behrens's own studio in Neu-Babelsberg an attempt was made to progress beyond the dummy facade of the turbine factory. The result was the Fagus factory in Alfeld, which was built in 1911 to the design of two of Behrens's students, Walter Gropius and Adolf Meyer. Gropius's model factory at the 1914 Werkbund exhibition at Cologne (illustrations 28–30) was a further step beyond Behrens's manner of composition, which favored large, all-enclosing forms. The asymmetrically balanced elements of the Gropius design no longer strove after a higher unity of sequence or of grouping. Widely disparate elements were assembled, loosely interconnected, fused, and forced together into a cell-like entity. Although the whole complex submitted to an axial order, the separate elements were no longer bound together into one unit. A skeptical observer commented: "If this factory is supposed to be beautiful, then its beauty lies in the ideas it conveys about the charm of clear organization."[71] At Riga, the various elements of the factory were hierarchically ordered and separated. In Berlin they were grouped according to function, assimilated, and

displayed as parts of the whole. Now, at Cologne, they were fused—one could almost say welded—together. The factory shed and the exhibition pavilion resembled tools and machines; conversely, the large armor-plate press laid claim to the aesthetic qualities of a piece of sculpture, and coexisted quite harmoniously with the surrounding architecture, gardens, and fountains. It would have been difficult, however, to realize Gropius's ideal scheme under the real conditions of industrial production. In contrast to the overdecorated and coercive industrial architecture of the nineteenth century, which used feudal symbolism to regiment the workforce, Gropius's formulation of the relationship between human labor, nature, and art was liberal and free in the extreme.

In their work for the AEG, Peter Behrens (and later his student Gropius) created a method of industrial organization that has been interpreted by some critics with a weakness for tautology as the method of developed capitalism or even monopoly capitalism. The progress of the AEG's architecture from its inception to the reforms undertaken by Behrens proceeded in such a way that it is neither possible nor desirable in this outline to consider the various aspects of art history, social history, or the history of the AEG in mutual isolation, but this much can be said: In the uncertain early years of the firm, Emil Rathenau employed the architects to the royal household and to the successful business world in Berlin—among them Schwechten and Cremer & Wolffenstein—to design prosperous-looking, conformist buildings in which to house his own residence and the firm's offices and factories. After achieving commercial success, the AEG linked itself to the architect Messel and the sculptor Hahn. Working from the sound base of the Prussian humanist tradition, Messel was not only the architect most favored by the rapidly expanding world of business, commerce and banking, but was also the guiding figure for the youthful architectural avant-garde. Messel's subsequent success and fame as the designer of the Pergammon Museum and the esteem in which he was held by the Kaiser paralleled the success and social advancement of Emil Rathenau. Such successes were grounded not on inherited wealth or capital, but on the achievements of a new class of bourgeois entrepreneurs.[72]

28
Walter Gropius, administration
building, factory, and pavilion of Deutz
Gasmotoren AG, Werkbund exhibition,
Cologne, 1914.

29
As illustration 28, with steel press.

30
As illustration 28, administration
building. Courtesy of F. Stoedtner.

When the AEG finally expanded beyond Berlin and even beyond Germany, Behrens was summoned. He was inexperienced, untried, and controversial, but full of ideas. After a successful period of probation, the AEG committed itself fully to a risky experiment with the totally new and alien style of the avant-garde. The policy of differentiating the public image of the AEG from those of its competitors—a policy made extremely clear with the AEG's distinctive pavilion at the Berlin Schiffbau-Ausstellung in 1908—brought with it both dangers and opportunities. There was the danger of isolation within the individual style of one talented designer, with the obligation to constantly readapt to the fashion of the moment. Conversely, there was a possibility that the equation between "the Behrens style and the AEG style,"[73] which had been applauded by Behrens's contemporaries, would achieve universal intelligibility, validity, and durability as an expression of the hopes for a German Industriekultur.

It should not be forgotten that no alternative of the same quality as Behrens's AEG model existed at the time, merely a choice between the prevailing uncontrolled pragmatism and a retreat into the preindustrial world.

Even the most vigorous opponents of capitalism and big business were occasionally impressed by the AEG's achievements. On 15 June 1912 the social-democratic paper *Vorwärts* described "some new factories" as "logical and spacious . . . and designed with regard to the most recent advances (baths, water closets, ventilators, electric lights, etc.), which are still lacking in the homes of millions of workers." *Vorwärts* said that these factories pointed "the way to the future," and that "in the major industrialized nations, capitalism [was] treading the path of modern proletarian architecture."[74]

It deserves to be pointed out that the "double-face of modern architecture," as Alexander Schwab dubbed it in 1930, was here given its contours for the first time. What had begun as a secession, as a protest by artists against the style of the court and the academy, became an attempt at integration by the leaders of industry, formulated in the language of architecture. As a result of its renunciation of historical legitimation, and therefore of its origins in the industrial work process itself, this language could be understood at one and the same time as "bourgeois and proletarian, capitalist and socialist."[75] Architecture thus offered the means of establishing a coalition. Such a coalition, however, did not become reality before the First World War and remained simply the dream of social idealists like Friedrich Naumann. During the Weimar Republic, the egalitarian tendencies in politics and art frequently coalesced as a social-democratic identity. Has architecture fallen behind in today's West German welfare state?

Peter Behrens and Michael von Dolivo-Dobrowolsky: The Cladding of the Standardized Component

Dans cette Europe hyperhygiénique et lavée des pâmoisons symbolistes, l'objet a été roi, et s'il fallait en choisir le symbole, ce pourrait être le petit ventilateur de Behrens, qui est une forme d'une incroyable délicatesse, papillon mécanique aussi séduisant et poétique que les 'constructions dans l'espace' qui sont les premiers chefs-d'oeuvre de Pevsner et de Gabo.
André Fermigier[76]

Hercule Poirot, sitting in front of his electric radiator (and feeling a quiet satisfaction in its neat geometrical pattern), was giving instructions.
Agatha Christie[77]

If only all the teapots from which tea is drunk in England and America were good German teapots!
Friedrich Naumann[78]

Tradurre la tecnica in metodo e la struttura in oggetto.
Giulio Carlo Argan[79]

In his 1907 manifesto, Behrens defined the task involved in redesigning some of the AEG's products:

• There must be no copying of handcraftsmanship, historical styles, or other materials.
• Mechanized production methods should not be denied, but rather stressed and implemented exactly.
• The clear construction of rational forms in the appropriate materials was not an end in itself. The aim was the artistic affirmation of technical production, which could be achieved by developing design methods that would correspond to and would appear aesthetically analogous to machine forms.
• In order to give an aesthetic dimension to technical forms, the design process must arrive at standard types complying with the laws of mass production. By this, Behrens meant that industrial products should not be decorated in a phony ornamental or handcrafted manner and presented as pseudo-unique objects. Any style of design that was particular to one artist should be avoided; rather, a firm should aim to portray itself visually in the formal expression of the standardization of all its products.
• It would then be possible to solve the conflict between the design of technical appliances and the architectural surroundings in which they were used. This would be achieved neither by matching the ornamental cladding of the appliance to the decor of its surroundings nor by artistically disguising the "disturbingly" technical character of something like a light. Instead, a fundamental equivalence should be established between the design process appropriate to technical products and architectural design.
• If a product showed "clear construction, appropriate materials, and graceful beauty," then it would transcend merely functional value and would radiate the appeal of all perfectly fashioned objects. This appeal would reach not only the artistically educated minority; as a consequence of the mass circulation and use of the product, it would reach all sections of society. At the same time, the new technical advances would not become ensnared in the net of popular taste.

This ambitious program for the design of "arc lamps, electric fans, switch panels, ovens, switches, and terminals" was confronted by entirely novel problems that had emerged from the development of electrical engineering and its tradition-free products. In a lecture delivered in 1906, Friedrich Naumann had commented on the problems that had arisen from the replacement of the hand by the machine and the substitution of machine production for handcraftsmanship.[80] Behrens, however, was confronted by a quite different problem: determining which forms and designs were suitable for entirely new electrical appliances. Confronted with the complete novelty of these machines, designers had previously turned for support to their handmade precursors. In particular, lanterns, lamps, and chandeliers governed the decorative forms of electrical lighting. When the nature and the mass production of the new appliances made it impossible for the glass blower, the bronze caster, or the tinsmith to fall back on old forms, the Werkmeister took over the job of decoration. The same was true of the electric kettle. At first, the electrical components exercised no influence on the design of the kettle, and were hidden as far from view as possible within the traditional craft forms. This gave the buyer the impression that mass production had made the charm, prestige, and efficacy of expensive, handmade silver teapots accessible to everyone. This absurd and contradictory situation caused people to scorn cheap, mass-produced electrical appliances.

A sales-intensive business producing consumer durables could not, in the long term, survive the criticism that it was making second-class goods. It was essential to find a formal language that could articulate the technical quality of the AEG's products and portray their usefulness and indispensability in both the private and the public sphere. It was not enough, however, for this language to express merely the intrinsic aesthetic qualities of a technically perfected instrument or machine.[81] A greater and deeper commitment was demanded.

It is appropriate to follow the introductory summary of Behrens's aims with an account of the technical organization of mass production. This account was given in a lecture (reprinted in this volume) delivered on 17 January 1912 in the conference room of the AEG by Michael von Dolivo-Dobrowolsky, perhaps the AEG's most outstanding engineer. Dolivo-Dobrowolsky was the director of the appliance factory on the Ackerstrasse, where the arc lamps, electric fans, and switches Behrens had redesigned were not only made but also exhibited (illustration 38). He was thus Behrens's direct technical counterpart, as were Oskar Lasche in the turbine factory and Georg Stern in the factory for high-voltage equipment.

Dolivo-Dobrowolsky began his lecture by attacking the "deeply rooted prejudice" that condemned mass-produced goods as "cheap and nasty" and as "junk." To counter this prejudice, he said, it was important to clarify the "concept of modern mass production"—a concept that "characterizes our entire age." From this position Dolivo-Dobrowolsky argued that, at a certain level of technical complication and product volume, the individual manufacture of each object—commonly seen as superior and desirable—was necessarily inferior to machine production. He insisted that in the electrical industry mass production did not mean the large-scale manufacture of cheap and carelessly made single objects, but rather "the mass fabrication of a vast quantity of different products." In each case, everything depended upon the elimination of "individual finishing" and on the "absolutely precise mass reproduction" of the prototype, using the most exact quality control. (In the electrical-appliance factory alone, twelve thousand products were listed, of which no fewer than eight hundred were various types of switches—"adapted to the diverse wishes of the international market, to the varying demands and social classes of the customers, and the different conditions under which the machines would work.")

These ideas of Dolivo-Dobrowolsky closely followed Walther Rathenau's. On the occasion of a visit to the AEG by members of the Werkbund on 11 June 1920, Rathenau made a short speech "welcoming his guests to a light buffet on the magnificent roof garden." In his speech he argued that "the establishment of a large-scale electrical industry in Berlin, a city which major industry had avoided, was only ventured and ultimately achieved in the firm and proven conviction that, by using special machinery and by mass-producing the component parts, a large industrial concern could deliver solidly made goods of a consistent quality, and could do so both cheaply and profitably." Rathenau then turned to the prejudice against the machine: "When I was young, my father never ordered a jacket from a tailor who used a sewing machine. This unfounded prejudice against the machine has been replaced by the realization that the machine alone can work faultlessly, consistently, safely, thoroughly, and cheaply. Our strength lies at all times in this realization, and this principle makes us invincible."[82]

According to Dolivo-Dobrowolsky, the problems inherent in the mass production of many diverse machines and products could be solved by standardizing the component parts of all the different variations and types within a particular range. "Standardization," he said, "forms the link between a mass of articles and the mass-produced article." Mass fabrication, therefore, was the "mass manufacture of component parts." To create a product range, one then merely had to assemble the necessary standard components in the appropriate combinations. This in turn demanded that the components be as simple as possible in order to facilitate easy, exact, and rapid assembly. It would then be possible to isolate the product almost entirely from the "participation, individuality, and arbitrariness of the workers," and, with the help of the appropriate equipment, to achieve a standard of precision unattainable with handcraftsmanship. Furthermore, it would no longer be necessary to make up components for any one particular project; the parts could be produced and kept in stock, "irrespective of whether more switches of one type are

ordered today and more of another type ordered tomorrow." As orders could be filled rapidly under this method of production, the "extremely expensive storage of finished goods" could also be eliminated. The various tools used in the manufacturing process were described by Dolivo-Dobrowolsky as aids to "part manufacture" that excluded the "arbitrariness of the worker." This description makes absolutely clear how the craft definition of the tool had been inverted, for according to the craft definition the great multitude of tools were evolved in order to realize the specific intentions of the craftsman.

In his lecture, Dolivo-Dobrowolsky referred only indirectly to the role of the designer. His comments, however, are of fundamental importance, as they make clear the conditions under which Behrens worked. Dolivo-Dobrowolsky stressed that the component parts and the function of a switch "remain the same, irrespective . . . of the height of the base and the material from which its cover is made, be it porcelain, brass, or something else." This meant nothing less than the freeing of the cover of the switch from the material, form, and function of the switch's mechanism; different types of switches could be given the same housings, or switches of the same type could have covers made in different forms and materials. Walter Benjamin characterized as "bourgeois" the sentimentally anthropomorphic nineteenth-century practice of enclosing household utensils in "cases, covers, and sheaths." Under the dictates of industrial mass production, the general separation of the external form from the internal mechanism became a normal characteristic of mechanical appliances. The external form of an appliance was only a "component" insofar as it provided some form of mounting, protection for the mechanical parts, and safety for the user. (Objects from the preindustrial era, such as clocks, also need a solid covering to protect the sensitive but harmless mechanism. Without doubt it is the combination of harmlessness and sensitivity that gives to the owners and users of these instruments a sense of warmth and affection that cannot be found in industrially made appliances. Furthermore, the danger attached to those preindustrial appliances that used fire as an energy source, for example the oven, is entirely different from the danger inherent in electrical appliances; the electrical danger is not to be found inside the appliance itself, but in invisible, nonlocalized forces flowing along wires and cables from distant power stations.)

In extreme but not uncommon cases, the divorce of the mechanism from its casing led to the complete spatial separation of the driving force, the machine being driven, and the controls. In these cases the traditional notions about the "unity" of an appliance and the identity of form and function were destroyed. Artur Fürst described this characteristic of electrical appliances vividly in 1911, using the elevator as an example.[83]

The elevator in the BEW-AEG administration building on the Schiffbauerdamm still asserted its hand-hammered autonomy as a carriage with invisible wheels (illustration 31).[84] Otto Eckmann gave independent status to his switch panel by surrounding it with a frame that looked handmade and expensive and also made a statement about one of the panel's functions: The light switch was the center of a sunburst (illustration 32). Behrens resolved the new problem of providing nonverbal operating instructions not through naturalistic representation, but by means of the organization of his console (illustration 33).

Behrens's button console might be seen as an incunabulum in a world that would be increasingly dominated by such buttons. This humble console marked the end of a period in which the function of art had been decorative and the emergence of art's new role of giving spatial organization and definition to actions, processes, and decisions.

31
Elevator in AEG main office,
Schiffbauerdamm, Berlin, after 1892.

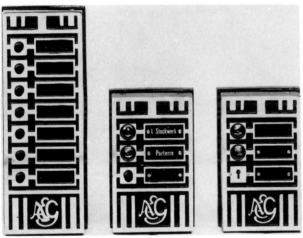

32
Otto Eckmann, AEG push-button
console, before 1902. AEG photo
2885.

33
Peter Behrens, AEG push-button
console, 1911. AEG photo 8133.

In the context of measuring instruments, Dolivo-Dobrowolsky explained the relationship between the internal mechanism and its visible skin from the engineer's viewpoint: The first task of a manufacturer with an annual turn-over of 300,000 meters in hundreds of different types was to work out the highest possible number of components that could be "manufactured commonly for a whole range of products." Standardization was to be taken to the ultimate degree: "We make all the base plates identical, and fit them with identical covers, with the same glass faces to protect the pointers and dials. As the pointer does not have to concern itself about whether the numbers to which it points refer to watts, volts, or revolutions, we use the same pointer." At this stage, however, arose the problem of the unlimited options open to the designer of the meter's external casing—a problem that Behrens's appointment was intended to solve.

All this enthusiasm for precise assembly and function, standardization of all components, and the saving of time and money was checked by the apparently simple question of cladding these complicated mechanisms. Who should design the covers, base plates and pointers, and how? No attention comparable to that given to the problems of technology and economics had been devoted to the question of design.

Before 1907, the external design of the AEG's products had been left, according to Behrens, to the taste of the Werkmeister. These foremen drew up the cases for the tubes of the arc lamps, the wire cages for the electric fans, the covers for the switches, the cases for the clocks, and the meter boxes. This practice could no longer be maintained, however, in the face of increasingly urgent economic considerations. When confronted by growing competition and a diminishing technological lead, the AEG was forced to recognize that the technical decision to use the same pointers for all meters in no way helped to determine the form or design of the pointer. It had become necessary to reconsider the firm's sales strategy.

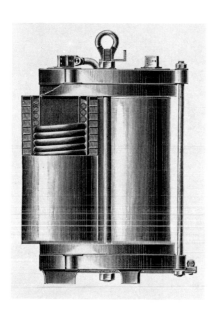

36
Peter Behrens, pamphlet for AEG
automobile speedometer, 1912.
Courtesy of H. Rogge.

34
Hugo Spindler, wood engraving
of AEG transformer. From
*Elektrotechnische Ausstellung Frankfurt
1892* (catalog), p. 826.

35
Hugo Spindler, wood engraving of
AEG motor. From *Elektrotechnische
Ausstellung Frankfurt 1892*, p. 971.

Should both the technical specifications and the design of the electrical appliances be tailored to the "widely varying demands . . . of different classes of customers"? Should the technical differences between the products in one range be matched by a differentiation in the external form, corresponding to the wishes of the customers? Did all customers really want the same pointer on their meters? What influence did the cladding of electrical appliances have on sales, especially when the competing products were of equal technical quality? Did the cladding gain in importance as the increased complexity of the goods made it more and more difficult for the consumer to judge technical quality? In short, how did such factors as trust, technical know-how, suggestivity, and the firm's prestige affect the AEG's sales?

For Dolivo-Dobrowolsky, the form-giving or artistic contribution to the manufacturing process was limited to the simple cladding and covering of the products, as demanded by the delicate nature of the complicated electrical products. Consequently, no role in the design of the technical components could be entrusted to the "artist," for the design and construction of the components were to be freed from any hint of arbitrariness and subjectivity. While both the progressive differentiation of the appliances' functions in response to the increasing demands of the customers and the equally progressive "standardization of parts" were attracting the ingenuity of the engineers, the external cladding of the same appliances was still afflicted with the tedium of fluted tubing and randomly formed boxes, frames, and covers.

Behrens had recognized in 1907 that in the future all applied art would be industrially produced, and that neither the artist nor the worker would physically make the goods. He also acknowledged that this was the unavoidable result of the highly organized division of labor. Behrens did not try to justify the new tasks of the designer in terms of traditional artistic activity, nor did he resign himself to the simple criticism of industrially produced "junk." Industry's design needs should not be left to the Werkmeister, he said, but should be seen as a challenge to the artist in the search for new and still-undefined solutions. In a lecture delivered in Dresden in 1906, Friedrich Naumann called the separation of the activities of the artist and the businessman a "great advantage," and suggested that a new artistic movement might thereby develop that could reach "the utmost in its art."[85]

It is not clear if Behrens shared his friend's view that in the "age of mechanization" great benefits would result from the unreserved acknowledgment of the need for artistic homogeneity. In 1910, while still working in Behrens's studio, Walter Gropius penned a "Program for the Founding of a General House-Building Company with Uniform Artistic Principles."[86] In this very significant sequel to Behrens's own ideas, Gropius adopted the arguments of the engineers to prove that machine-made products were not only technically but also artistically superior to their handmade precursors. According to Gropius, the undoubted and unavoidable advantages of technology and the elimination of handcraftsmanship, when coupled with mass production, guaranteed "an exemplary standard" and "superior quality." Rather optimistically, Gropius identified technical standardization with qualitative standards, and depicted industrial mass production as a vehicle for the propagation of artistic value.

Dolivo-Dobrowolsky's lack of concern for the cladding of his company's machines and appliances stemmed in part from the nature of the products, and also from the demands of the customers. Basically, the products can be divided into three categories: products that were indispensable for the functioning of other machines (meters, gauges, transformers, motors), products that had become essential to public life (street lighting, public transport, power plants), and products that brought convenience, ease, and economy to the home and the business (electric fans, household appliances, tools, lamps). Because of their indispensability, functional efficiency, and innovative qualities, the products in the first and second categories probably interested Dolivo-Dobrowolsky the most. In the third category, however, the problem of motivating the buyer had a considerable influence on the volume of turnover. After the turn of the century, the importance of advertising, packaging, and design began to be discovered.

Traditionally, a customer decided to buy a particular tool after looking into all aspects of its construction and function. At an early date, however, Paul Jordan realized that, even for technicians, it was no longer possible to make such thorough appraisals of competing technological products. Faced with the diversity and complexity of such products, buyers became increasingly dependent on emotional values such as "trust" in a particular firm, and also on the suggestive power of a product's outward appearance. What Dolivo-Dobrowolsky saw as the unimportant packaging of the real substance of the appliance became a determining factor working for or against its purchase. "Don't believe," said Jordan, that even an engineer takes an engine apart for inspection before buying it. Even as an expert, he also buys according to the external impression. A motor must look like a birthday present."[87] In order to create the impression that not only the motors but as many AEG products as possible were "birthday presents," Jordan had urged the appointment of Behrens.

In a supplement to the December 1907 edition of the *AEG-Zeitung*, Behrens outlined the principal factors involved in his remodeling of the company's arc lamps:

The lantern of an arc lamp has the technical function of protecting the conductors against dust and moisture. . . . A simple, weatherproof sheet-metal tube would suffice for this purpose. But the lantern also has an aesthetic function: It should hide the naked rods from the eyes of the viewer and cover them with the most agreeble possible form. From an aesthetic point of view, the sight of a plain tube was hardly an improvement. For this reason, decorated armatures were created by cladding the original lantern tube with rich foliate patterns. . . . The AEG was resolved to bring the design of the arc lamp into harmony with the artistic demands of the modern age. . . . Professor Behrens has accomplished this task. With simple lines he has achieved an artistic effect that is appropriate both to the function of the lantern and to the characteristics of the materials. The coloring of the new lanterns is also original. . . . Behrens uses a simple green. A more lively tone is lent by the bronze trim and by the studs in the same material, which, against the dark background, call to mind the effect of lighter-colored inlays.[88]

To give such attention to the design of a technical product was quite uncommon at the time, as was the brochure in which the product was advertised. The outward appearance of the arc lamp was suggestively presented in a color picture (illustration P15). The accompanying text began by describing the design of the casing, and only after this turned to the lamp's function. The list of the various lamps and accessories included elegant drawings, but no mention of the functional relationships of the components.

This emphasis on form went so far that, in the exhibition rooms Behrens designed for the administration building on Friedrich-Karl-Ufer and the electrical-appliance factory on the Ackerstrasse, the AEG's products (in particular the arc lamps) were not arranged according to their technical development, nor did the display consist simply of those products that were then available; instead, the aesthetic progress of the lamps was documented (illustration 38). We have here, as it were, the Hegelian certainty of a Darwinesque final victory for beauty and grace over the banal and the ugly. Who cannot but sympathize with this proof that the norm is changeable?

In June 1909, Behrens conducted the members of the Staatswissenschaftliche Vereinigung (State Scientific Union) through an exhibition of products made from his designs. The *AEG-Zeitung* reported that "almost all the artistically influenced products were clearly arranged in the conference room of the factory, and an earlier model of the same product was placed beside each new design for the sake of comparison."[89] Here, in the heart of Dolivo-Dobrowolsky's factory, the divorce of the outer casing from the inner mechanism, for which he had laid the theoretical foundation, came to pass. In Behrens's hands the formal history of the arc lamp did not dwindle into a history of the cladding of the lamp, but developed itself into an ever-more-refined thesis on the possibility of giving visual form to the priciples of technical function. The artist portrayed the simplification of the form of the object as analogous to the rationalization of its production.

The ever-increasing subdivision of the components of electrical appliances as a result of standardization gave added importance to the creation of aesthetic analogies, as the individual components no longer possessed the characteristics of primary technical forms. According to Behrens, the inner equipment of the arc lamp consisted of "cold, naked rods." In contrast, the aesthetic function of the lamp was "to hide these rods from the eyes of the viewer and cover them with the most agreeable possible form." In this definition of the role of design, Dolivo-Dobrowolsky's theory of the role of cladding was decisively altered.

To the engineer, the only function of an appliance's cover was to provide mutual protection for the delicate mechanism and for the user. Behrens rethought this negative definition. He pronounced the end result of the engineer's work—the dissembling of a mechanism's functional processes into standardized component parts—so aesthetically unsatisfactory that it was necessary to give the appliance a well-designed cover if it was to be used either in private or public places. The "stabilization of the form by means of cladding" was necessary, said Behrens in 1909, where "a sufficiently simple, calm appearance" could not be achieved through the construction alone or where the construction was "ugly."[90] This statement might be seen as the foundation of all modern design. Behrens went on to say that the pursuit of the principle of naked functionality in the cladding of something like an arc lamp had only led to equally unsatisfactory "bare metal tubes and pipes," which were not improved by the addition of "ornamental metalwork, bulges, and so on." The critic Karl Scheffler hid his face from these arc lamps, seeing in them only "the prosaic hideousness, the absolute formlessness of the naked production process."[91] A comparison between the old arc lamps and those redesigned by Behrens after 1907 illustrates Behrens's method and reveals an undeniable improvement in design.[92]

Behrens's first product designs for the AEG were for a series of special arc lamps for indirect lighting. He simplified the existing models through a more sparing use of lines and gradations and a general clarification of the form (illustration P16). The working parts of the lamp remained unaltered. Even the earlier model had no added decoration and was made up only of functionally necessary parts, such as the reflector and the cover for the regulator. The form of the reflector, however, was broken up by numerous unnecessary moldings, grooves, and bulges, which gave it an unresolved, uncertain contour. In contrast, the redesigned reflector was austerely articulated; the two matching concave curves gave it a clear, harmonious silhouette. The same restraint appeared in the hood, whose smooth outline was repeated by the bracket from which the lamp was hung. The metal clamps necessary for opening the lamp were only slightly altered, and the heavily decorated ring at the base of the reflector with which the lamp was pulled down was replaced by a knob.

37
Hugo Spindler, wood engraving of
AEG light fixtures, 1892. From
*Elektrotechnische Ausstellung Frankfurt
1892*, p. 72.

38
Exhibition of AEG products in electrical-
appliance factory, Ackerstrasse.
Courtesy of H. Rogge.

39
AEG arc lamp, old model. Courtesy of
H. Rogge.

40
Peter Behrens, AEG arc lamp, new
model. Courtesy of H. Rogge.

Even more marked than in these early designs was Behrens's impact on the lamps intended for outdoor use. Unlike its predecessor, which was broken up by several randomly grouped horizontal moldings (illustration P15), Behrens's intensive-flame arc lamp (illustrations P27, P28) was articulated only where operational and technical factors called for it. The lamp was thus clearly divided up into hanging bracket, cap, shaft, reflector, and globe. These elements no longer collided abruptly, as they had in the older model, but were sensitively related to each other. A good example of this is the way in which the projecting, eave-like tips of the lamp shaft led down to the gentler curves of the reflector.

Although the new design for the arc lamps was conceived with regard to the lamps' purpose and their mass production, it did not bow to the dictates of function and material. As Behrens himself noted, it was a "fallacy" to believe that "even the most exacting and stringent attempts to satisfy functional requirements" could, on their own, create "the moment of beauty."[93]

A comparison with the older lamps makes it clear that the sequence of single parts, which was determined by technical considerations, was subjected as a "composition" to the aesthetic principle of proportional relationship. For example, the individual elements of the economy lamp can be read as a composition of half-spheres, semicircles, cylinders, convex and concave curves, and segments of circles; this is particularly clear in a drawing published in an advertising brochure, shown here as illustration 41. In its compositional unity, which was stressed by the color-accented moldings and rims and by the highlighting of the screws, hooks, and chains, this lamp achieved the character of an art object, with its verity based on the analogy it drew with technical construction. In Behrens's interpretation, the geometric legitimacy of the composition was founded on the sequence of individual parts, which in turn were derived from the functional demands of the lamp.

41
Peter Behrens, pamphlet for AEG arc-lamp hoist. Courtesy of H. Rogge.

Although the forms of the lamp fitted closely around the internal construction, they strove to establish their own coherence and did not seek to justify their divisions and accents in terms of the mechanism. The necessary separation of the cover from the mechanism was executed, on the aesthetic level, as if it was an essential element in the design. The technical rationality of the appliance was thus translated into the sovereignty of a composition.

Behrens felt that, "in addition to the functional and material worth" of an object, there existed "another important value, namely the pleasure which it gives." Even today, Behrens's designs still radiate this aura of pleasure. Like fine antiques, Behrens's arc lamps, fans, clocks, and kettles transcend simple function or the mere curiosity value of their place in the history of technological development. In their perfection they triumph over obsolescence and the law of the rubbish tip.

A comparison between the bare or overdecorated old lamps and those of Behrens shows clearly that, since the technical requirements of the lamp remain unchanged, the autonomy Behrens gave to the external casing represented a quiet revolution of millimetric nuances and slight alterations of line and surface treatment. His designs followed their predecessors closely, but strove after rhythmic clarification, proportional purity, and a strengthening of the sculptural forms. It was not his job to abandon the old design entirely or to produce a completely new alternative. The progress made with respect to the earlier models had to be not only measurable and directly visible, but also accessible to the emotions. As the customers became less and less able to judge and compare the technical quality of an electrical appliance, aesthetic progress was substituted as an analogy to the superiority of the product in question. The outer casing did not express or explain the appliance's formless, delicate, dangerous, and incomprehensible inner mechanism; instead, it offered a visual and tactile analogy to the appliance's manufacture and function.

Whether it was to replace the gothicky dial and Renaissance housing of the wall clock shown in illustration 42, the preciously decorated and complicated constructions of the kettles shown in illustrations 43 and 44, or the ponderousness of the old electric fans, Behrens always succeeded in finding a new form that was rational, graceful, elegant, and robust. He substituted a series of variable basic forms for the handcraft pretentions of the kettles, and he endowed the bare mechanics of the electric fan with the grace of a sculpture.[94]

In his attempt to rescue the industrially made product from its position of low esteem, Behrens did not turn to painstaking handcraftsmanship, but to the logic of the series and the system. For the kettles and for the ceiling fans (which survive only in old Humphrey Bogart movies), Behrens designed systems in which a range of constant elements could be assembled in various combinations.

The kettle series (illustrations 45 and P133 ff.) consisted of three basic forms—round, oval, and octagonal—set on a molded base. Semicircular or square handles made of woven cane were fitted into a standard metal sleeve, which was attached to the body of the kettle by round lugs resembling suction caps. How good and sensible this design was can be judged from the many attempts to improve on it and to make it "more functional." The handle mountings were fixed directly onto the sloping face of the kettle between the body and the lid, so that no screws, rivets, or hinges spoiled the immaculate vessel. Apart from the junction with the kettle body, the spouts of the round and oval kettles were the same, as were the molded bases and domed lids of the round and octagonal models. From the appropriate number of identical elements, the series

44
AEG kettle catalog, old models,
ca. 1911. Courtesy of H. Rogge.

45
Peter Behrens, AEG kettle catalog,
1911. Courtesy of H. Rogge.

42
C. Closheim, wood engraving of
electric clock made by C. Theodor
Wagner, Wiesbaden, 1892. From
*Elektrotechnische Ausstellung Frankfurt
1892*, p. 838. Courtesy of H. Rogge.

43
AEG kettle catalog, ca. 1900.
Courtesy of H. Rogge.

Tee- und Wasserkessel

Ausführung: Mit leicht auswechselbarem Patronenheizkörper,
Rohrumflochtenem Griff, Anschlußstöpsel, 2 m
Schnur und Steckkontakt Nr. 725

2443 6   2433 8

P. L. Nr.	Inhalt ca. l	Watt-ver-brauch	Siede-zeit ca. Min.	Ausführung	Ge-wicht ca. kg	Preis 110 und 220 Volt
2433	0,75	275	10	Altmessing gehämmert	0,45	18,—
2434	1,25	550	14		0,80	23,—
2435	1,75	550	18		0,85	26,—
2436	0,75	275	10	Messing vernickelt gehämmert	0,45	18,—
2437	1,25	550	14		0,80	23,—
2438	1,75	550	18		0,85	26,—
2439	0,75	275	10	Messing poliert	0,50	18,—
2446	1,25	550	14		0,85	22,—
2441	0,75	275	10	Messing vernickelt	0,50	18,—
2442	1,25	550	14		0,85	22,—
2443	0,75	275	10	Messing vernickelt gehämmert	0,50	17,—
2444	1,75	550	18		0,85	24,—
2445	0,75	275	10	Messing gehämmert	0,50	17,—
2446	1,75	550	18		0,85	24,—

2439—2441   2440—2442

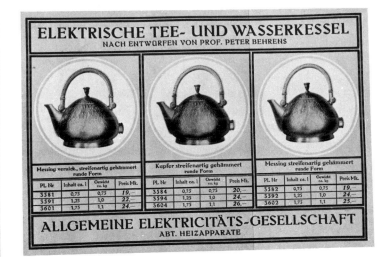

ELEKTRISCHE TEE- UND WASSERKESSEL
NACH ENTWÜRFEN VON PROF. PETER BEHRENS

Messing vernick., streifenartig gehämmert runde Form				Kupfer streifenartig gehämmert				Messing streifenartig gehämmert runde Form			
PL Nr	Inhalt ca. l	Gewicht ca. kg	Preis Mk.	PL Nr	Inhalt ca. l	Gewicht ca. kg	Preis Mk.	PL Nr	Inhalt ca. l	Gewicht ca. kg	Preis Mk.
3581	0,75	0,75	19,—	3584	0,75	0,75	20,—	3582	0,75	0,75	19,—
3591	1,25	1,0	22,—	3594	1,25	1,0	24,—	3592	1,25	1,0	24,—
3601	1,75	1,1	24,—	3604	1,75	1,1	26,—	3602	1,75	1,1	25,—

ALLGEMEINE ELEKTRICITÄTS-GESELLSCHAFT
ABT. HEIZAPPARATE

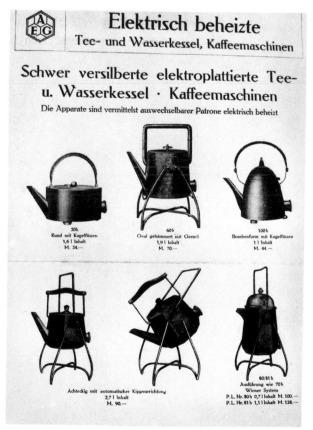

yielded a wide range of variations. The round, oval, and octagonal kettles were supplied in three materials (brass, nickel-plated brass, and copper-plated brass), three finishes (smooth, hammered, and grooved), and three sizes (3/4, 1 1/4, and 1 3/4 liters). Thirty variations were offered, although many more were theoretically possible. Dolivo-Dobrowolsky's law of production, which stated that the variability of a series should stand in an inverse relation to the standardization of the component parts, was exactly adhered to, and a calculated balance was struck among the relative freedom of design, the formal autonomy of the kettles, and the limited number of identical elements used. (At the same time, the AEG was still producing a large range of traditional kettles, and also silver-plated "artistic" kettles (illustrations 46 and 47); this added up to about 75 variations. In 1912 the average price was between 18 and 25 marks; the cheapest kettle was 13 marks and the silver-plated luxury model was 128.

As he had done with the arc lamps, Behrens drew the impetus for the redesigning of the kettles from existing AEG products. His round design clearly represented an attempt to improve upon the traditional kettle form, which had survived the introduction of electricity.[95] This traditional form was characterized by uncertain contours, the absence of a base or at best a shallow base, various profiles for the shoulder and lid, thin or plump handles, and a spout like that of a watering can, which literally grew out of the kettle. Behrens shaped all this into a smooth, rivet-free, streamlined form. In the same way, the oval kettle was related to an older AEG model.[96] As if with hedge-trimming shears, Behrens cut off the ornate forms of the original in order to create another of his variations on the theme of an electric kettle. The octagonal design also followed the lead of an older "heavy-silver-plated tea and water kettle" that cost between 90 and 128 marks and balanced like a spider on a metal frame. Behrens transformed this model into a form which iconographers of architecture should classify in the same succession as the Palatine chapel in Aachen.

46
AEG kettle catalog, old models.
Courtesy of H. Rogge.

47
AEG kettle catalog, old models.
Courtesy of H. Rogge.

In the context of the AEG and its total output, the kettles, the honeycomb trademark, and the pavilion at the 1908 Schiffbau-Ausstellung stand out as the designs with which Behrens established his basic premises for his subsequent work in product design, graphics, and architecture. The autonomy and homogeneity of Behrens's output, coupled with its technological inventiveness, mark it as a specifically modern achievement. In their imitation of the handcrafted forms of precious tableware, the early versions of electrical kitchen appliances still asserted their social status as luxury objects appropriate to grand households and the galleys of luxury yachts.[97] Behrens's complete renunciation of such historicism anticipated the transition of electrical appliances from luxury objects into goods for mass consumption whose streamlined forms and geometric structures drew a happy analogy to their abstract construction, production, and function. The advertising value of the external shell was indispensable. Walther Rathenau explained in 1907: "The creation of an applied electrical industry demanded the transformation of many aspects of modern life. This transformation was not initiated by the consumer, but was organized by the manufacturer."[98] The need to create a market gave the question of design an undeniable importance. As Rathenau had noted in 1901, "To recognize needs and to create them is the secret of all commerce."[99]

The narrative of this section began at that point when Michael Dolivo-Dobrowolsky and other AEG engineers made the mass production of electric heaters and cooking appliances both technologically feasible and commercially profitable. On 11 September 1907 the *Berliner Tageblatt* carried a report on an exhibition of industrial inventions. It commented: "The AEG demonstrates the practical application of electrical current for domestic use by exhibiting some very elegantly formed appliances for heating and cooking. . . . It is only very recently that new designs have made it possible for electricity to be used economically for cooking purposes, thus heralding a new epoch in this branch of the electrical industry." The Behrens-designed kettles of 1908 were still being made in Nuremberg by the Bing-Werke, a subsidiary of the AEG, from 1922[100] until late in the 1920s—an extremely long life for a mass-produced design.

Very little is known about the AEG's design policy after the resignation of Behrens in 1914 and the retirement of Jordan in 1920. There are indications, however, that the tradition of close collaboration with the contemporary avant-garde, which had existed from the time of Messel and Eckmann and had flourished with Behrens, was maintained until the end of the 1920s. The subsequent design history of the AEG would be a rewarding area of study, but goes beyond the scope of this book. Nevertheless, some general points and observations might be made.

The various product areas of the AEG reacted in different ways to the impulse of Behrens's work. After 1925, Bruno Salbach was the head of the exhibitions department. He recalled that after World War I some efforts were made to dissociate the firm from Behrens's work and even from his trademark. This move was resisted, however, by Salbach and by Hans Krebs, a Behrens pupil who had been appointed chief designer. Together they created the outstanding exhibitions in the 1920s and early 1930s, which had direct links to the work of the Bauhaus in the fields of typography and exhibition technique. Salbach knew Mies and Lilly Reich, and was one of the first to buy their tubular steel furniture for use on his exhibition stands. He was also in contact with Moholy-Nagy.[101] After the Behrens kettles had been discontinued, the Bing-Werke reverted straight back to the Biedermeier manner, which nevertheless managed to harmonize with Salbach's severe exhibition designs. A coffee machine from the late 1920s marked an attempt, presumably by Krebs, to improve on design in this area.

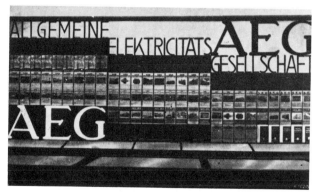

When production of the Behrens-designed fans came to an end, the AEG reverted once again to an earlier model. In contrast, Behrens's clock designs were developed in an exemplary manner. By using the basic form, the hands, and the numerals Behrens had designed in 1910, the designer of the Elektrochronus clock of 1929 achieved a timeless functionality and modernity (illustration P106). A highpoint in the whole history of the AEG's publicity material was the work done for the firm between 1928 and 1933 by the Dutch designer César Domela Nieuwenhuis, born in Amsterdam in 1900, who was a member of the De Stijl group and a friend of Piet Mondrian. Domela's 1928 pamphlet "25 Jahre AEG-Dampfturbinen," his photomontages, and his posters (illustrations 49, 50) are surely among the most beautiful graphics not only of De Stijl but of the whole of the 1920s.[102] They testify to the effortless identification of the AEG with the artistic avant-garde that distinguished the firm's collaboration with Eckmann, Messel, and Behrens.

"Only by continuously renewing its types, models and standards is industry able to create social and consumer values," said Giulio Carlo Argan, "for only in this way can industry accelerate the rhythm of progress and identify itself with the constant renewal of societal structures."[103] In the period under consideration, no other large industrial concern fulfilled this demand more completely than the AEG.

48
AEG exhibition at Leipzig Trade Fair,
1928. Courtesy of H. Rogge.

49
Cesar Domela Nieuwenhuis, cover of brochure *25 Jahre AEG-Dampfturbinen*, 1928. Courtesy of H. Rogge.

50
Cesar Domela Nieuwenhuis, advertisements for AEG, 1931. Courtesy of H. Rogge.

Peter Behrens and Karl Bernhard: The Language of the Architect and the Truths of the Engineer

The artist will let no one take away from him the scintillating and profound task of interpreting life, and defends himself against dispassionate, simplistic methods and conclusions. . . . he considers the continuance of his type of creativity to be more important than the scientific devotion to truth.
Friedrich Nietzsche[104]

The ideas of the age press for architectural expression, the monumental demands of the work process need enclosures which are able to express the intrinsic value and the working methods of the plant.
Walter Gropius[105]

In May 1908, Peter Behrens—having already designed brochures, typefaces, and electrical appliances, organized exhibitions, and built temporary pavilions to house them—turned his attention to the AEG's old railway-equipment factory (illustrations A47, A50). Although final designs for renovating the factory had been drawn up by Johannes Kraaz in 1906, Behrens completely redesigned the combined clock and water tower, turning it into a statement of his new architectural program. Against Kraaz's late Gothic, Behrens set the early Renaissance, and this with all the enthusiasm that went with a new beginning, an all-embracing method, and a reassessment of architectural values. On the tower, Behrens established an asymmetrical rhythm with stepped windows set between narrow brick ribs. This ascending rhythm was terminated by the clock, which Behrens was forced to take over from the earlier design. Above the clock, the polished stereometry of the cube of the water tank and the triangular roof echoed forms of industrial production and rejected any historical references to brick Gothic or to town hall spires. A similar stereometry, expressing architectural rationality and clarity, can also be seen in AEG products such as the electric clocks Behrens designed after 1910 (illustrations P100 ff.). As Behrens explained, "this approach, which has just been described as suitable for architecture, is also valid for smaller, industrially produced objects."

Around the time he was working on the AEG pavilion for the Schiffbau-Ausstellung and on the water tower, Behrens was also occupied on the powerhouse of the turbine factory on the Huttenstrasse (illustrations A13 ff.). In the powerhouse, Behrens translated the style of the AEG's exhibition pavilion into a new method for the permanent display of machinery.

In the exhibition pavilion, Behrens strove after coherence and formal unity. In the powerhouse, however, he clearly separated the control room from the engine room, and exposed two internal levels through the large windows. According to Artur Fürst's contemporary account, this modest building was regarded as "something quite new," and was "very widely imitated." The two 3,000-horsepower turbines on the upper level delivered power to the turbine factory and to the neighboring light bulb factory. As Fürst noted, auxiliary machines such as these were usually housed "in a damp, dark shaft in the cellar, far removed from the light of day." He wrote enthusiastically about Behrens's solution: "The AEG has, for the first time, broken with the old cellar principle, which has been passed on like an illness from generation to generation." The machines, said Fürst, were placed "in an open story clad with plain, glazed tiles and amply lit by large windows, so that one does not have to descend dark stairs into the murky depths."[106] This design set a precedent for the AEG's pioneering work in the building of power stations.

Behrens's early AEG buildings gained the approval of his immediate patrons, such as Oskar Lasche, the director of the turbine factory. Yet the exhibition pavilion, the tower on the railway-equipment factory, and the turbine-factory powerhouse remained marginal contributions. These cladding jobs did not involve Behrens in the actual production processes any more than did his graphic work and illustrations for the firm's brochures. The spatial organization of the production processes was a matter for the production engineer and the construction engineer. The results of their work, which were as functional as they were formless, were then occasionally given over to the architect, who provided portals and facades. We have seen this in the case of the AEG factory at Riga, and it was equally true of the facades of the foundry and press shop on the Voltastrasse, the railway-equipment factory, and Schwechten's facade for the appliance factory on the Ackerstrasse.

For the first time in the Ackerstrasse factory, the AEG dressed up a very normal factory with portals, projectures, scrolls, decorative brickwork, monumental inscriptions, and flagpoles, all meant to reflect the firm's ever-increasing magnitude and might. The workings of the engineer were hidden behind the art of the architect. As Paul Westheim asked, "Why *not* shelter behind soothing culisses, if freedom of action could thereby be achieved?"[107] The architect did not seek to reach an understanding with the language of the engineer who designed the factory, but with the Sebastianskirche across the street, with the Stettiner Bahnhof, and with the nearby barracks of the Fusilier Guards—buildings whose architectural language spoke of loftier things than the banal truths of industrial work. We can safely assume that Paul Jordan and the AEG board did not expect this practice to be continued when they asked Behrens to collaborate with Lasche and with Karl Bernhard (a civil engineer) on the construction of the new turbine factory on the Huttenstrasse (illustrations 54 and A17 ff.). If they had planned to pursue the facade architecture of Schwechten and Kraaz, then the AEG board would hardly have tolerated Behrens's drastic intervention in the railway-equipment factory or allowed the stroke of genius he brought to the water tower. It is clear that, from the outset, the board members were thinking of a new architectonic conception for the turbine factory.

The design of the load-bearing frame of the turbine hall and of the supports for the overhead cranes could obviously not be entrusted to an artist-architect like Behrens; Oskar Lasche's conception of the new factory demanded the skill and experience of a civil engineer. However, as Behrens was not expected to design a facade in the traditional sense, it must have been planned from the beginning that he would participate directly in the design process. This was already a departure from the usual practice, whereby the autonomous construction of the engineer was only subsequently given an appliqué decoration by the architect.

The factory was completed in October 1909 after only six months of construction. The December *Kunstchronik* said the following:

The AEG's new turbine hall is the result of a happy collaboration between artist and engineer, between functional demands and artistic design. Professor Peter Behrens drew up the plans and, it should be emphasized, conceived the basic constructional form of the whole complex. He is to be thanked for the splendid silhouette of the huge building and for the glorious, cathedral-like effect of its interior. The execution was entrusted to the engineer Bernhard, who understood how to solve the task set by the artist in a constructionally appropriate manner.

However, in January 1910, Oskar Lasche named Behrens as the creator of the new turbine factory and made no mention whatsoever of his colleague Bernhard:

With regard to the design of the hall and its artistic execution, it can be claimed that although the Huttenstrasse itself does not belong among the sights of Berlin, the massive external forms of the modern reinforced-concrete building that has been constructed to the designs of Professor Peter Behrens reflect the mighty work performed inside.[108]

A month later, Karl Ernst Osthaus spoke of Bernhard only as the inventor of the traveling crane, and said that the factory had been designed by Behrens. (See the selection reprinted in this volume.) Fürst, Mannheimer, and Gropius also named Behrens alone as the creator of the turbine hall.

In March 1910, Behrens gave a detailed account of the collaboration:

The AEG entrusted me with the design of both the external silhouette and the internal space. Inasfar as the constructional work was important for the spatial appearance, it was executed according to my instructions. The constructional implementation of this concept was put in the hands of the well-known engineer Bernhard, . . . [who] executed the technical drawings and the necessary calculations with the greatest possible understanding of all the artistic considerations involved and solved every problem with a truly remarkable inventiveness.[109]

Behrens was careful to make clear here that, as artistic adviser to the AEG, he was empowered to express his intentions and to give instructions. Bernhard's complaint that "when the author was first approached in the autumn of 1908 the wishes of the management (that is, Lasche) and of the artistic adviser made some of the preparatory work unnecessary"[110] indicates that Behrens had completed a preparatory design before the autumn of 1908, at which point Bernhard was commissioned to do the structural design work and calculations. It is for this reason that Lasche spoke of Behrens as the sole creator of the turbine hall.

In the account he published in January 1910, Bernhard referred repeatedly to Behrens's contribution and described how often the construction had to be adapted to meet the definitive instructions of the architect. This was particularly true of the form of the gable ends, which, said Bernhard, "was derived mainly from artistic considerations." The "compact, flat termination of the interior space" was intended, he said, "to enhance the external appearance of the building" and to promote "the cathedral-like sense of spaciousness."[111]

Bernhard was clearly annoyed by the lack of references to his contribution in the numerous early accounts of the turbine hall. The editors of the magazine *Industriebau* published a notice in the July 1911 edition in which "Herr Regierungsbaumeister Bernhard" stated that he was "the designer of all the steelwork . . . in the turbine hall and the high-voltage factory." This was followed up in September 1911 by an article in which Bernhard kept to his original account of the collaboration (see "The New Hall for the Turbine Factory. . . ," in this volume) and also ascribed to Behrens the idea of inclining the side walls inward. At the same time, however, he strongly criticized the end wall on the Huttenstrasse. He saw no justification for the use of concrete as a filler in the continuation of the glass panels. Bernhard would clearly have preferred to extend the glass and steel construction of the side walls right up to the front facade, and to have glazed it like the side walls. (The argument between Behrens and Bernhard over the front facade of the turbine factory, and Bernhard's unsuccessful, "honest" alternative, led directly to the four uniformly glazed walls in Gropius's Fagus factory of 1911.) Bernhard also felt that the cladding of the corners was an unsuccessful idea: "Everyone sees the gable, which consists of a thin skin of reinforced concrete in front of a steel frame, as a mighty piece of concrete construction: two corner piers supporting a high tympanum." This was "a reversion to the practice of concealing the structure of large works of engineering behind an artistic cladding;" in contrast, Bernhard continued, "the steel and glass front on the Berlichingenstrasse is genuine, and is an undisputed masterpiece of steel construction."

Justified as Karl Bernhard was in emphasizing the part he had played in the construction of the turbine factory, even such a good engineer as he was quite helpless when made to work with a mediocre architect. This occurred in 1911, when Bernhard designed a power station in Strasbourg (illustration 51) in collaboration with Alfred Löwe.[112] In this design, the exposed steel framework of the boilerhouse merely reflected accurate calculations and was of no aesthetic significance. Similarly, Löwe's design for the engine room (which Bernhard praised) could not be rescued by Bernhard's competent construction. This comparison between the Behrens-Bernhard turbine factory and the Löwe-Bernhard power station is not intended as a proof that Behrens was the inventive spirit and Bernhard the executive agent; nevertheless, the deep divide between the architect and the engineer cannot be ignored.

Behrens's turbine factory—his swan song for the facade as a vehicle for promoting the patron's public image and for delivering artistic messages to the public—came in the middle of an interesting period in the history of the development of the end facade. It followed the Anhalter Bahnhof of 1878 and the AEG stamping shop of 1900 (both by Schwechten) and Behrens's own amazing design for a railway shed at the 1910 Brussels World's Fair. It was, in turn, followed by Gropius's negation of the facade, and by the capsule-like "calming down" of the form in Gropius's factory at the 1914 Werkbund exhibition.

For Behrens, close collaboration with an engineer on the construction of a major industrial plant was a new and engrossing experience. It influenced the ideas on the relationship between art and technology with which he had been preoccupied for several years. This becomes very clear if one looks carefully at Behrens's earliest statement on this theme, the transcript of a talk he gave in the AEG lecture room on 13 January 1909 (during the planning phase of the turbine factory).[113] In this lecture, Behrens firmly rejected "the tendency in our modern aesthetics that seeks to derive all artistic forms from function and technology." It was, he said, one of the fundamental errors of the age "to believe that artistic form can be determined by or can develop spontaneously out of technology." He called

the mere pursuit of "constructive legitimacy" a "pseudo-aesthetic." Pointing out the irrefutable fact that "the most varied constructions" were appropriate "to the same purpose", he concluded that it lay "in the hands of the architect" to determine which type of construction "best suited the original artistic intentions." These artistic intentions were based on two premises.

The first premise was that technical constructions were, as a rule, "ugly" because they were motivated only by material aims and because they were overcomplicated and incomprehensible. In support of his argument Behrens cited a celebrated professor of mechanical engineering named Riedler, who recommended that "when a suitably simple and calm appearance cannot be achieved with the construction alone, then cladding should be used to give the simplest possible effect." The function of art, said Behrens, was to translate the complexity of technical appliances and buildings into an aesthetic analogy, which should not follow the materialism of mechanics but should be independently conceived, rhythmic, and well-proportioned. To Behrens, the design of buildings or technical products according to these precepts meant the creation of stereometric, smooth, and simple casings: "Although not every part of the construction should be hidden from view, there should be covering at those places where the construction is ugly. . . . it is not the job of architecture to disclose ugliness but rather to enclose space."

Does Behrens's work offer one of the greatest twentieth-century alternatives to the facade architecture of the nineteenth century, or is it only a variation on the skillful concealment of the complicated facts of the "world of mechanization"?[114] Behrens's second premise offers some help in answering this question: He presupposed that a return to earlier styles and manners would be of no use in the attempt to come to terms aesthetically with technology. Instead, Behrens and some other artists regarded the

51
Karl Bernhard and Alfred Löwe, power station, Strassburg, 1911.

52
Franz Schwechten, Anhalter Bahnhof (railway station), drawing, 1878. Courtesy of AEG.

53
Franz Schwechten, AEG stamping shop, 1900. AEG photo.

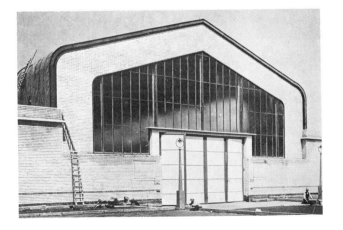

54
Peter Behrens, AEG turbine hall, 1909.
AEG photo.

55
Peter Behrens, railway shed, Brussels,
1910. AEG photo.

56
Walter Gropius and Adolf Meyer,
Fagus factory, Alfeld, 1911. AEG
photo.

57
Walter Gropius and Adolf Meyer,
machine hall, Werkbund exhibition,
Cologne, 1914. AEG photo.

new technical processes, industrially produced materials, and the changed conditions of production as a reason for paring their formal means down to the elementary, nonreferential values of linear dynamism and stereometric clarity. In this way they demolished the bridges that linked them with tradition, avoided the hopeless protest of rejecting technology, and won an independent position from which to launch attacks that would alter the world of technology, open it up, interpret it and make it understandable, clad it, criticize it, and even conceal it. In this confrontation with technology, the artists desperately defended their freedom and autonomy.

Without doubt, the most comprehensive involvement of an artist in the world of technology was that of Behrens with the AEG. It was Behrens who first conceived the method of creating artistic analogies, and he passed it on to his students as a task to be continued into the future. His intentions reached beyond the idea of appropriate materials, beyond the exposure of a constructional system. Even the mere aesthetic composition of an architectonic skin according to rhythmic principles no longer seemed a self-evident necessity to Behrens. This method was adequate only for such things as the arc lamps, the kettles, and the dentist's drill shown in illustration P86.

It was not enough for the factory halls to provide supports and anchorages for the cranes and machines according to the calculations of the engineer, for according to Behrens an "inner union" between the work of the engineer and that of the architect was achieved only when a factory communicated the material values of the industrial processes it was designed to house. The creation of these analogies demanded more than "functional form" and "truth to materials." Gropius spoke of the expression of "inner values" and of a "method" of design that would be required in industrial buildings (see note 105), and thereby invested architecture with the ability to express, in its compositional system, the methodology and value system that was common to all branches of technology.

As Karin Wilhelm's essay in this volume points out, the three exposed sides of the turbine factory are all entirely different. Facing the Berlichingenstrasse, the supporting pillars that project beyond the inclined glass wall articulate an endlessly extendable series of identical elements. On the courtyard side, in contrast, the glass and steel frame construction is entirely functional and unremarkable. With the principal facade on the Huttenstrasse, Behrens made an abrupt break with the system used on the other two sides in favor of an intricate composition that effortlessly denied the restraints imposed by the structure. The front facade used the same industrial materials that were used on the other walls (glass, steel, and concrete), but there they proclaimed more than the obvious fact of their structural reliability.

These three different ways of enclosing the interior space offer emphatic proof of Behrens's thesis that "the most varied constructions" can be used for the same purpose. The dissimilarity was not arbitrariness, but an attempt to give artistic expression to three essential elements of industrial work. The long Berlichingenstrasse wall emphasized vertical elements. The pillars here are not only the most prominent features in the design, but actually stand out from the wall. If these pillars had only the traditional function of columns—to support the building and define its physical limits—then a much lighter frame would have sufficed. But these pillars also hold up the cranes, the most powerful tools in the factory.

On the courtyard front, Behrens refrained from making a similarly demonstrative statement; he emphasized the two stories of the lower hall and did not make the crane supports nearly so prominent.

The main end wall on the Huttenstrasse shuns both the display of working methods made on the Berlichingenstrasse and the pragmatism of the courtyard front. Instead, it makes a defiant statement about the autonomy of architectural design, untrammeled by the restraints of function, structure, or convention. Behrens was striving after freedom to express a comprehensive system of values that would go beyond the promotion of the AEG and its products. The practical function of this end wall—to illuminate the interior—was denied by the gable and the corner pylons, although the structure designed by the engineer made it easy for these areas to be glazed as well. Rather than simply glaze the front, however, Behrens set the green-painted window surround on a silver-gray plinth and projected it out beyond the coarse-grained, golden-colored wall with its inlay of green bands. He thus established the window as a flat composition whose shape and size claimed the autonomous status of an easel painting. New building materials and the concealed work of the engineer were used by Behrens to demonstrate the reversibility of traditional material values; the solid-looking wall at the corners is simply cladding and the delicate, glazed panel is load-bearing. Thus, the traditional metaphors applied to "natural" building materials—metaphors of growth, load and support— became meaningless. In their place, novel means emerged with which to express the interrelationship of forces, proportions, and form—means that Behrens used to demonstrate the potential and the artistic virtues of the new, industrially produced building materials.

The design of the turbine factory represented an architect's passionate attempt to break free from the domination of technology and to depict instead the method and the ethos of the collective work which the same technology promoted. Just as Behrens transcended the laws of structure of function, so he promoted not only concrete things like turbines and the AEG but also a system of values appropriate to the nation's identity and productivity. His prime objective was, at the same time, the most transient. The formal techniques and means Behrens used to depict industrial work have, for the most part, freed themselves from this original motive. In doing so, they have left a permanent and unsurpassed public statement about the nature of industrial work.

After the fundamental debate over the turbine hall between Behrens and Bernhard, the other buildings for the AEG were clearly developed according to Behrens's ideas. With the high-voltage-equipment factory, Behrens was able to achieve the now commonplace feat of adapting one project (his 1906 design for the Tietz store in Düsseldorf, shown in illustration 58) to entirely different demands.[115] With the small-motor factory, he carefully sought to support the autonomy of the composition by using classical elements.

Besides reflecting an aesthetic tendency of the period, Behrens's inclination toward spatial clarity in the interior and smoothness and simplicity on the exterior was influenced by technical developments. A contemporary writer named Nachimson noted that "where there was previously a single large steam engine for the whole factory which delivered power to the machines via a much ramified network of transmission belts, . . . today we find electric motors spread throughout the entire factory." "The maintenance, lubrication, control, and repair of the old transmission system," he went on, "has disappeared almost entirely."[116] As illustrations 59 and 60 suggest, the interior architecture of early factories lost all meaning (apart from its pragmatic function as a shield against the weather) in a jumble of shafts and pulleys. In the early days of heavy industry (see illustration 60), the assembly work was done almost entirely by hand. Even the heaviest components were moved around by hand without any mechanical help, as if the factory was an outsized locksmith's shop. In contrast, the new, lightly built assembly shops aimed for the greatest degree of clarity and the widest possible span.

Illustrations 61–63 show how Behrens's new approach to cranes simplified the interiors of his factories. The crane supports ran the whole length of the walls and combined with them to delimit the architectural space. Aesthetics and function became one and the same.

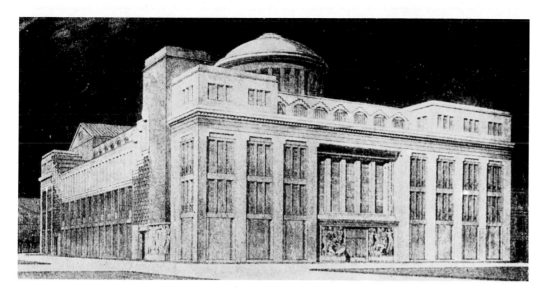

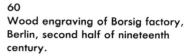

58
Peter Behrens, design for Tietz store, Düsseldorf, 1906. From Hoeber 1913.

59
Thomas Robinson's textile mill, Stockport, England, 1835.

60
Wood engraving of Borsig factory, Berlin, second half of nineteenth century.

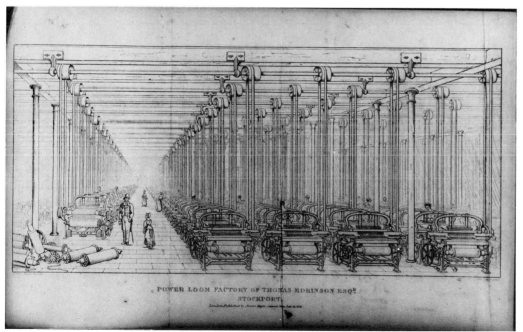

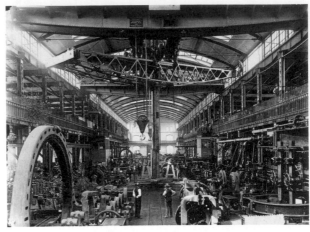

61
Old AEG machine factory,
Brunnenstrasse, 1899. AEG photo
1330.

62
Old AEG turbine hall, Huttenstrasse,
ca. 1900.

63
AEG assembly hall for large machines,
Hussitenstrasse, 1912.

Peter Behrens and Walther Rathenau: Two Forms of Classicism and Two Views on Art

Il n'est pas sûr que le monde serait sauvé s'il était transformé en une colossale AEG.
Gaston Raphael[117]

The whole world knows what Rathenau has achieved as a manager, and yet no one can mock the idea of management as caustically and effectively as he can.
Alexander Moszkowski[118]

In attempting to reconstruct the discussions that went on within the AEG about Behrens's aims and expectations, and the success or failure of his work, one is repeatedly confronted with the problem of limited sources. Both the AEG's archives and Behrens's private papers have been lost or destroyed. Behrens's plans and goals as seen through his own eyes can be partly reconstructed from the article in the *Berliner Tageblatt* as well as from his other writings, and the unprecedented publicity his work attracted—certainly a criterion of success in the eyes of the firm—has also survived.[119] Yet we know practically nothing about Behrens's actual design work in the studio, or about the part played by his immediate superior, Paul Jordan, nor are there any recorded comments on Behrens's contribution by Walther Rathenau or any other leading figure in the AEG. The only source that remains is the writings of Rathenau, whose wide learning in all aspects of the arts led inevitably to judgments on the design policy of the AEG.

In his diary, Rathenau referred three times to visits by Behrens, each time in the company of artists and art historians. On each occasion Behrens was mentioned by name as one of a large company.[120] In addition, Behrens and Rathenau had many mutual friends in Berlin society and must have met regularly in that context, and Rathenau is known to have visited the Behrens home.[121]

After the war both Rathenau and Behrens were members of the Bund der Erneuerung wirtschaftlicher Sitte und Verantwortung (Society for the Renewal of Economic Morality and Responsibility), which had been founded in July 1920. Rathenau had wanted to call it the Bund sittlicher Wirtschaft (Society for an Ethical Economy). The chairman of the Bund der Erneuerung, Karl Scheffler, had initially hoped to assimilate the Werkbund into this group.[122] Behrens was also a member of the short-lived Demokratischer Volksbund, established in November 1918 as a vehicle for "the political engagement of the leaders of the Berlin electrical industry."[123] His fellow members included Max Liebermann, Louis Tuaillon, August Gaul, Hermann Hahn, Hermann Muthesius, Werner Sombart, Gerhart Hauptmann, Richard Dehmel, Friedrich Naumann, Theodor Heuss, Georg Klingenberg, Ernst Troeltsch, Friedrich Meinecke, Albert Einstein, Graf Kessler, Franz Oppenheimer, Bruno Paul, Gustav Pauli, Wilhelm Valentiner, Alfred Weber, and Fritz Wichert. These facts seem to point to a friendly association between Behrens and Rathenau based on their work for the AEG and on a general consensus of beliefs. All this leads to a very witty satire written in 1913 by Carl Schmitt, a 25-year-old constitutional lawyer, together with his colleague Fritz Eisler:[124]

With full Germanic soulfulness Melchior Lechter[125] had formed the lofty Gothic window through which the finely filtered light and the muffled noise of the mechanical age passed ceremoniously into the private office of the bank director. No style of interior design had failed to leave its imprint on this room. A piece of furniture designed by Behrens grinned somberly from each corner; Olbrich[126] hung down heavily from the ceiling; Pankok[127] crouched in the frieze, and the eye constantly fell upon contours, objects, and vases that declared, with a shrug of resignation, that they too had been formed by the hands of an artist.

A carpet, ripe and rich as India's rice fields before the harvest, muffled the footprints of the princesses and aristocratic ladies who were wont to visit the bank director at his place of work. Like a black granite boulder, the writing desk issued a polite but energetic challenge to the advance of soullessness, lifelessness, and advanced mechanization. The quintessence of overlaid "Culture" gushed out of every chair leg, every grain in the wood was crammed with a measured sensibility; the Behrens-designed canary sang of learning from every pore, and cultivation leapt in flamed tongues from the mouth of the magnificent Scottish sheepdog like a red pennant.

A courageous Liebermann portrait[128] blinked seriously across at the two disheveled Voyous of Munch,[129] who indeed appeared to realize how unworthy they were of the balanced synthesis of Greek Sophrosyne, Roman Virtus, and Germanic inutility that teemed around them. On the long wall glowed the flat myth of a Böcklin in all its gloomy richness and controlled strangeness. One of Franz von Stuck's sumptuous fountains of colors gushed forth with a sparkling sensuality—quite apart from its intellectual content. A sandy Grunewald landscape by von Leistikow dreamed on the opposite wall and took art to such monumental heights that the bank director could never stop himself from shaking the sand out of his shoes after he had performed his devotions to it.*)

Silently beside it hung a blood-soaked still life by Corinth, and on the other side Max Klinger managed to remain philosophical. It was, however, the religious simplicity of a painting by Fritz von Unruh that rose above the surrounding conflict of religious confessions as if to say: "Lord, deliver us from evil!"

The day was notable for Walther not only for its social, literary, and cultural successes, but also as his fortieth birthday. He laid down the golden pen with which he had just written, with great elegance, a chapter on India rubber and transcendence. This article was for a widely read international journal and was composed accordingly, as the common property of all educated men.**) He then reached into the lowest drawer of the granite boulder and took out a Behrens-designed Upmann cigar, which he later

stubbed out dramatically in an onyx dish after only two pleasantly relaxed puffs. His eyes than looked for the reins that converged in his room. Seizing them, he sat again at his boulder, reins in hand, sober, iron-willed, and conciliatory.

*) Cf. Apelles. How insignificant seem El Greco and Cézanne by comparison. Or has Herr Meier-Gräfe already contracted hayfever while looking at a painting of a meadow by Cézanne? The incidental question whether Apelles's much-discussed birds were blackbirds or ducks can be rejected, as it is not yet clear what type of fruit was used to lure the above-named birds. Besides, the question has been exhaustively answered by bank director Rathenau in *Denkschrift über den Entenschnabel in Kamerun* [Memoir on the Duck Beak in the Cameroons], Vahlen, Berlin, 1912, chapter XIX passim. The duck beak does not refer to Miss Ellen Key, as the addendum "in the Cameroons" makes clear.
**) Publisher's note: This is also the intended purpose of the *Schattenrisse*.

This piece was a satire on the Jugendstil idea of the unity of decor and the personality of the individual. One should not detract from its humor by comparing it with the actual circumstances; however, there is not the slightest indication that Walther Rathenau's office, his house on the Königsallee, the floor he occupied in his parents' house on the Victoriastrasse, or his country estate contained a single object designed by Behrens. Nor was there any mention of luxurious furnishings and appointments. Without exception, eyewitness accounts recorded an impression of refined simplicity and cool elegance in the tradition of early Prussian Classicism, a manner Rathenau admired.

The question of the relationship between the cultural beliefs of Behrens and Rathenau must be answered on another level. This is not the place, however, for a discussion of Rathenau's aesthetic theories. Instead, let us consider to what extent Rathenau's writings were influenced by Behrens's basic ideas and by the example of his work.

The two shared a deep antipathy towards the pomposity and theatricality of the Gründerzeit. Rathenau's repeated condemnation of the Wilhelmine bourgeoisie's "gadget craziness" and "hunger for goods" belongs among the classic critiques of the follies of the period. In common with fellow intellectuals, he despised the "bombastic architecture" of the new state, such as Raschdorff's Berlin Cathedral or the so-called National Monument, an equestrian statue of Wilhelm I.[130] A story told by the writer Hermann Burte makes clear Rathenau's feelings on this matter. In 1912 Burte visited the Laufenburg power station together with Rathenau. They were standing on a narrow jetty high above the surging waters of the Rhine. As Burte related,

A man came onto the jetty carrying plans, and asked if the connecting bridge should have a certain sort of roof, which would be in keeping with the character of the town. "Nonsense!" cried Rathenau. "That would be exactly the same sort of kitsch as the Romanische Haus und Café beside the Kaiser-Wilhelm-Gedächtniskirche in Berlin."[131]

Both of the buildings mentioned had been designed by Franz Schwechten, who had also worked for Emil Rathenau's father and for the Kaiser. Walther Rathenau's dread of kitschy historical cladding was shared by Messel, Brehrens, Klingenberg, and Issel. On this fundamental point, therefore, Rathenau was entirely sympathetic to Behrens's approach.

Both Emil and Walther Rathenau had a profound aversion to any form of private ostentation, and this trait found an expression in their decision to employ the architect Johannes Kraaz[132] to design their own houses. Walther Rathenau had known him over many years as "a capable and dependable man" who had worked with Schwechten for the AEG. In the 1905–06 competition for the AEG administration building he was beaten by Alfred Messel, and the railway-equipment factory was taken out of his hands by Behrens in May 1908. (This was, as we have seen, Behrens's

first job for the AEG, and a few years later he went on to redesign and modernize Kraaz's original street front.[133]) The strict separation of private and business life enabled Walther Rathenau to trust to his own distinctly Neo-Classical taste rather than try to integrate his private life with the new architectural life of the AEG by commissioning a house from Behrens. (This integration was reserved for the housing estates of the AEG's staff and workers.) Nevertheless, it is remarkable that the Rathenaus chose Kraaz to design their own houses just at the time when he was being dismissed from the AEG as old fashioned. The death of Alfred Messel may, however, have played a part in this.

Behrens both knew and admired most of Walther Rathenau's sculptor friends, all of whom worked in a manner opposed to the taste of the Wilhelmine court (see note 57). He must also have had an equal sympathy for Rathenau's painter friends, who included Max Liebermann and members of the Berlin Secession.[134] Some of Rathenau's literary associates were also known to Behrens—notably Richard Dehmel, "whose view of the world placed him next to Rathenau in the eyes of their contemporaries."[135] Hugo von Hofmannsthal, Franz Blei, and Julius Meier-Graefe should also be mentioned. Behrens had first met Hofmannsthal during the preparations for "Ein Dokument deutscher Kunst," an exhibition held in Darmstadt in 1901.[136] Blei and Meier-Graefe both wrote about Behrens from 1897 on. Max Osborn's first article on Behrens appeared one year later, and he also published a piece on Rathenau's Grunewald house in 1912. Several articles devoted to Behrens's work also appeared in Maximilian Harden's magazine *Die Zukunft*.

It is clear that Rathenau enjoyed extensive social contacts and friendships with "those literary and artistic circles that had come to prominence in the bitter feud with the Kaiser over his supreme boycott"[137] and also shared their artistic convictions. However, as suggested above, his sympathy for modernism was not unconfined. Rather enigmatically, it did not extend to architecture and the applied arts, the disciplines that most directly concerned the AEG and those that were practiced by Behrens.

To understand the profound disparity between the views of the man who was to become the president of the AEG and those of the firm's artistic adviser, we must look at the apparently kindred liking for Classicism that these men shared. It cannot be denied that the same Classicism that Rathenau tried to revive so faithfully with his house in Grunewald[138] (illustration 64) also exercised a dominant influence on Behrens's work at the same time. When Rathenau moved into his new house in January 1911, Behrens was working on two projects: a villa in Dahlem for Theodor Wiegand, the archeologist and director of the Pergammon Museum,[139] and the planning stage of the German embassy at St. Petersburg—the major work of this Neo-Classical interlude.[140] The development of Behrens's work from the abstract, geometric Classicism of the Düsseldorf and early Berlin period to the more historicist manner of 1911–12 might not have occurred had it not been for the influence of Rathenau. In addition to any direct influence Rathenau might have had, there was also the version of Neo-Classicism that Messel (whom Behrens admired greatly) had developed for the AEG and its subsidiaries. This interpretation contradicts neither the general tendency toward Neo-Classicism in Germany and especially Berlin during the early years of the twentieth century nor the fundamental differences between the views of architecture held by Rathenau and Behrens. Rathenau combined his desire for an aesthetic revival of early Berlin Classicism with an unmistakable aversion to the architecture of the Gründerzeit and of his own period. The architect Fritz Schumacher claimed in January 1911, just as Rathenau was moving into his new house, that he sought, "with biting ridicule, to discredit all the architectural aspirations of the age."[141]

The house of Walther Rathenau's parents on the Victoriastrasse (illustration 65) also had the character of an aristocratic city residence of around 1800. It has been attributed to Gabriel von Seidl and to Johannes Kraaz, and dated 1903 or 1910–11. Walther Rathenau collaborated on the ground plan and had rooms in the upper story.[142]

In their direct return to the manner of Gilly and Gentz, rather than to that of Schinkel, both Emil and Walther Rathenau saw the realization of very personal ideals. For Emil it symbolized private thrift, absolute realism, and a sober work ethos. No one knew better than Walther Rathenau that such an image of elegant Prussian austerity was not to be had cheaply, or, more exactly, that it cost just as much as "cheap" ostentation. According to his definition,

Elegance means the fantastic expenditure of means and effort in order to create a relatively simple and aesthetically pleasing effect. . . . Luxury and elegance go together just like elegance and austerity. . . . Elegance is controlled extravagance."[143]

These personal ideals of the Rathenaus were elevated by Messel in his design for the AEG administration building into the firm's public image. The "imposing" facade in the style of a palace of the northern Italian Renaissance suggested solidity, power, and charisma. In contrast, Messel decorated the office interiors in a manner approaching the Prussian style of 1800, with a large added shot of Wilhelmine archeology.[144] The interior depicted the work ethic for the benefit of the firm's employees, whereas the facade offered the public a symbolic image of well-being and prosperity. In the last years of his life Messel became the principal architect to the Berlin business world, and worked for Carl Fürstenberg's Berliner Handelsgesellschaft and for Emil Rathenau's AEG. He passed on the principles of his Neo-Classicism with varying success to the younger architects. In the case of Behrens, the impetus of modernity was added to this Berlin Classicism; then the style was catapulted into the mainstream of the European avant-garde by Behrens's students Gropius and Mies.[145]

64
Walther Rathenau and Johannes
Kraaz, house at 65 Königsallee, Berlin-
Grunewald, 1911.

65
Gabriel von Seidl and Johannes Kraaz,
house of Emil Rathenau, 3–4
Victoriastrasse, Berlin, 1910.

66
Peter Behrens, Imperial German
Embassy, St. Petersburg, 1911–12.

67
Peter Behrens, design for hotel in San
Remo, 1914.

In contrast to Messel, however, Behrens was concerned in his study of Prussian Classicism with the contemporary problems of methodology and universal comprehensibility. His aim was the creation of a rationalized version of Schinkel's Classicism that could be thought of as analogous to the modern industrial world. Karl Scheffler defined the problem very accurately in 1912: "In the sense of today's practical architect, distinctly modern elements already exist in the buildings of Schinkel, the quiet beginnings of a conscious, urbane, functional architecture."[146] Behrens transformed this Schinkelesque Classicism into a new architectural language that could be used with equal facility for administration buildings, such as those of Mannesman in Düsseldorf and Continental in Hanover, or to represent the German state in the St. Petersburg embassy[147] (illustration 66). It was also appropriate for the later factories of the AEG, for exhibition halls, for the Kurhotel der Zukunft (Spa Hotel of the Future) in San Remo[148] (illustration 67), and for opulent villas such as those for Mertens in Potsdam, Kröller-Müller in the Hague, and Wiegand in Berlin.[149]

To Walther Rathenau, Prussian Classicism, and in particular its palaces and country houses, represented a very personal point of reference. It was the embodiment of his own most intimate set of values, whose modernity lay precisely in its conservatism. It symbolized for him the takeover by the new governing class of bourgeois industrialists. I have already referred to this idea in the analysis of Hahn's bust of Rathenau. It is easy to understand Rathenau's emotions on buying the Gilly-designed Schloss Freienwalde; the imminent collapse of the house could be seen to stand for "the decline of the aristocracy," which was "without support in the mechanistic society."[150] Similarly, Rathenau's expensive and exact restoration of the house could be seen as an attempt to legitimize the takeover. In his biography of Rathenau, Alfred Kerr describes this psychological condition:

"Rathenau constantly stressed his frugality (a Diogenes of big industry)—but in his head he had an ineradicable passion for country houses. This was not a general passion for the eighteenth century, but simply for the Hohenzollerns in the eighteenth century. Accordingly, when he took over his apartment in the Tiergarten he immediately arranged for the window sills to be taken out and the window openings to be extended downwards—it all seemed a bit like Potsdam-Sanssouci. With quiet, half-suppressed pride, he drew my attention to the alterations. This was long before he bought the former Hohenzollern house, Schloss Freienwalde. I said: "I really don't understand it. In almost every respect you're a modern, free-thinking man. You're even, as a true innovator, having the floors in this flat painted gray" (he was the first in Berlin to do this)—"and yet on the other hand: Sanssouci, Rococo, the past? What do you particularly like in it?"

"The Hohenzollern style."

"And what qualities in particular do you admire in the Hohenzollerns?"

"Their 'märkische' austerity, their frugality, their simplicity."

"But you aren't copying their simplicity: you're copying their palaces." He laughed, and I continued: "Do you know what it reminds me of?"

"—?"

"A farmer once decided to model himself on his neighbor. Strangely enough, the neighbor ted himself only on potatos but drank the finest of wines. The farmer wanted to imitate him exactly and . . . began to drink fine wines."

Rathenau made no angry face. "My dear Doctor," he said, "in these matters one should not only concentrate one's attention on the dynamic aspect, but also on the potential."

I was rather uneasy. He hadn't retaliated and neither could I. So we were even, "fifty-fifty."[151]

Walther Rathenau's very real contemporaneity clothed itself in the "cultivated sensibility of an epigone."[152] It was with this sensibility that he established the boundaries between the world of business and his private life and distinguished among the world of "mechanization," his own social class, and the architectural avant-garde.

Behrens, in contrast, aimed with his modern version of Classicism at a unifying and understandable architectural language. This language could be used not only for the workplaces and homes of the controlling entrepreneurs, but also for those of the managers and workers of a large company like the AEG. It would then serve to define the whole company as "a unified body."[153] Behrens's ideal offered a fascinating parallel to the liberal dream of his friend Friedrich Naumann, who advocated the social integration of all the members of the modern industrial society. With his Classicism, Behrens was trying to achieve that social quality Georg Simmel had ascribed to the art of the Greeks: It was "stylized" and appealed to the "entire social body" rather than to the "individualistic single consumer."[154] In his important article of March 1908 on the garden-city movement, Behrens described the principle of Gruppenbauweise (building in clusters) as a form of living created for "people as social beings," in contrast to the "open" manner of building in the nineteenth century, which isolated the single house with an "exaggerated emphasis on individual and anarchistic independence."[155]

In the housing estates he built for the AEG before the war, Behrens had the opportunity to implement, if only in part, his far-reaching plans for domestic housing (illustrations A184 ff.). Stylistically, these estates did not imitate rural models, but turned instead to the Classicism of the factories. Behrens said, "It would be desirable if, by sharing the same principles, these small estates were able to fuse with the industrial buildings into an organic unity out of which a new and unique sort of industrial city could develop."[156]

Never had there been a comparable attempt to design a company housing estate using the formal vocabulary of industrial architecture. Fritz Neumeyer has written of the contrast between boulevard architecture and the requirements of a workers' estate, and in this volume he singles out Behrens's adaption of industrial architecture for housing as a unique occurrence in the history of domestic architecture. Behrens applied a moderate version of the unified Classicism of the factories to the design of dwellings for the AEG's employees, from the workers to the directors—assuming that the latter were willing to join in. With the means available to him as an artist, Behrens tried to realign the inequalities of the social pyramid in the horizontal composition of pergolas and terraced houses. It would seem that this aim was successful, if one can take the social structure of 10–18 Fontanestrasse, Oberschöneweide, as typical: In 1926 the workers Lackner and Janischewski, the electrician Pietrowski, the commercial clerk Schulze, the artist Frisch, the graduate engineer Friedner, and the works director Stein all lived on this same street.

As Neumeyer notes below, the "Doric" colonnade (illustrations A193 ff.), the "entablature," the rectangular towers, and the tympana at Oberschöneweide "support the illusion that the viewer is standing in front of a row of factory halls." However, Behrens did not use these Classicist forms to follow the nineteenth-century practice of cladding working-class housing in historical forms imitative of the more middle-class apartment blocks and rejecting any modern industrial influence. Rather, he combined the serial possibilities of the Classical formal language with the industrial demand for standardization. The housing that resulted could be "built in a rational way using standard elements and serial methods of production."[157] This is a tangible example of Behrens's concept of industrial Classicism as a new style—"aspro stile nuovo"—that would fuse products, producers, housing, and factories into "an organic unity." From its inception in 1910, Behrens saw his work on housing as a part of the process of redesigning every aspect of the AEG's activity. However, only parts of his housing schemes were realized.[158]

Behrens's AEG housing designs consciously seized on the materials and the forms of the goods produced by the inhabitants and of the factories in which they worked. The axiality of the plan for a workers' town that Behrens published in 1917 in *Vom sparsamen Bauen* as the result of his planning work for the AEG cannot be included in the conventional sequence some historians have drawn from the Renaissance castle to the Baroque palace, the factories of the nineteenth century, and the parade grounds of the twentieth-century dictatorships, for Behrens's town was derived from the vision of a community in which people from all levels of the social pyramid lived and worked together. Behrens did not drive his axes through the town as a statement of domination, but offered this type of spatial organization as an analogy to Emil Rathenau's production principles. Rational and economic methods of production demanded the axiality of the assembly line, the crane track, and the overhead transporter. In his plan for an industrial town Behrens turned to pure geometric order to create a visual analogy that could embrace the factories, the smallest appliances, and the housing. Walther Rathenau's ideas on the quasi-governmental structure of large industrial organizations found here a counterpart in the residents' loyalty to the firm. The sense of group identification promoted by Behrens's design was quite different, however, from the class-specific solidarity that found expression in the suburbs built in Berlin in the 1920s by Bruno Taut and Martin Wagner. One was the response of an enlightened employer to the challenge of social democracy; the other was a model plan of social democracy itself, which could be delivered repeatedly by the same architects.

68
Berlin-Oberschöneweide, 10–18 Fontanestrasse, extract from *Berliner Addressbuch*. Courtesy of H. Rogge.

It is clear that Behrens also took the specific modernity of his Classicism as the basis for his work in product design. We have already seen that, in designing technical appliances, Behrens was not content to ignore the electrical components, but looked instead for a form in which the components and their functions could express themselves.[159] Here too he assumed a position which it would be inexact to call neutral. The difficulty and delicacy of this position stemmed from Behrens's rejection of the twin temptations of nineteenth-century product design as defined by Karl Scheffler—Behrens resolved neither to "decorate" the appliances nor to abandon them to "the prosaic hideousness, the absolute formlessness, of the naked production process." The resulting forms appropriate to the type, the series, and the standard model could get along quite happily without the help of historical retrospection or eclecticism: "Although one senses the link back to the Classical codex, one is still very aware of the steely present. One expects to find and looks for the machines."

With his epoch-making designs for the turbine factory and the arc lamps, Behrens created—effortlessly, it seemed—self-explanatory analogies linking industry, art, and Classicism. After this dazzling beginning, however, he turned increasingly to history to provide the support and the justification he needed in his difficult task. After 1913 the precarious balance between the "Classical codex" and the "present" tended to favor the consolidation of traditional values. With the factories in Oberschöneweide, the Berlin exhibition halls,[160] the Festhalle at the 1914 Werkbund exhibition,[161] the Volkshaus in Lübeck,[162] and the AEG administration at Humboldthain (illustration A163), Behrens sought to secure and promote everything of universal and binding value that he had achieved in his work for the AEG. This dream of universality was another parallel to Walther Rathenau's thoughts on the quasi-governmental structure of major firms like the AEG. World War I shattered this belief in the possibility of creating a style representative of the nation's industrial power as an alternative to the international monarchic style. The fragments Behrens produced at the end of his life now appear Expressionistic, culminating in the mysticism of the Memorial Hall at Höchst. The "steely present," which had been accepted so emphatically and endowed with the legitimacy of Classicism, had led into the catastrophe. The analogies of industrial production were replaced in the short term by the Gothic hereafter and the handcrafted past.

According to Osthaus, Behrens's prime concern was to bring art back into the production process.[163] This aggravated the disagreement between Behrens and Walther Rathenau, and extended it into another area of mutual interest: fine art. The attempt to forge an alliance between art and technology, between technical norms and aesthetic types, between industrial mass production and the universal dissemination of the collective style of a future industrial culture—in Rathenau's eyes all this represented the Fall, the moral ruin that "dragged art down into the dust and noise of everyday life."

Although he granted continued existence to all the other arts, Rathenau denied the possibility that architecture and the applied arts could recover from the ravages of the Gründerzeit. Not only did he deplore the fact that architecture had sunk "to the level of a supplier of art-historical decoration," but he saw the future of architecture as "irretrievably destroyed—in the sense of genuine creative design—by the mechanization of the production process." "Architecture", said Rathenau, "concluded the list of major victims" of mechanization. Furthermore, the "dreadful decline of the applied arts over the past eighty years, which even the most earnest endeavors have failed to halt," was a legacy, he said, of mechanization.

To Walther Rathenau, the reason for the demise of architecture and craftsmanship as true art forms lay in their servitude to functionalism, to "commercial motivation," and to the functional demands made by industry. For this reason he drew a sharp distinction between architecture and the applied arts, on one hand, and literature, music, and the plastic arts on the other: "Art does not have to fulfill any purpose whatsoever, be it decorative, representative, instructive, entertaining, morally edifying, recollective, or stimulating to the senses." Among the functions that corrupted art, Rathenau included not only such "ignoble" concerns as "advertising and business," but also "instruction, entertainment, . . . decoration, and sensory stimulation." The concept of art was thus restricted to an extreme subjectivity, which Rathenau uncompromisingly pursued. He demonstrated the private nature of his own version of Classicism with his rejection of the Clasical language Behrens had developed for the initially unsympathetic executives of the AEG. Rathenau designed his Grunewald house as a retrospective gesture, using forms taken from preindustrial architecture. Yet both Rathenau and Behrens invoked the same system of values to justify their radically different versions of Classicism. Rathenau turned to Classicism in order to make a private statement about the absolute incompatability of business, art, and individuality; Behrens used it to formulate a restorative synthesis of the three.

Although Walther Rathenau felt that technical inventions could "at no time be complete and perfect," he admitted that they could be "beautiful." However, he had reservations about the quality of this beauty which, he said, "is perceived by the engineer and affected and overrated by the aesthete":

. . . half of this beauty depends on rational understanding and is therefore ephemeral. If a machine is totally obsolete, then it might still retain a picturesque quality, . . . but the unprejudiced eye will see it as junk, as a defunct link in a scientifically interesting development . . . [without] lasting worth.

It was, according to Rathenau, "an outrageous abuse" to provide everyday appliances with a form that gave them the appearance of works of art.

On 27 November 1905, Rathenau wrote to Felix Holländer, the dramatic adviser to Max Reinhardt: "Much as I venerate art and respect commerce, I find the border areas between the two odious and suspect."[164] This maxim, which Rathenau was to repeat on other occasions, struck at the heart of Behrens's design philosophy and at the grounds for his appointment by the AEG. We are confronted here by a paradox: Rathenau could envisage a conflict-free, socially mobile future society, such as Behrens was attempting to create for the AEG, yet he had nothing but criticism for Behrens's visual reorganization, which was the first stage in this process. Clearly, Rathenau's critical comments were directed not only at the culture of the Gründerzeit but also at Behrens's work for the AEG— the most comprehensive attempt made this century to win back a place for art in the practice of industrial production, and with it a social dimension. It followed from Behrens's ideas that art should not be constrained by Rathenau's paradoxical definition; that it should not remain "free of purpose and function" merely to suit the private purposes of those who could afford it.

Detailed study of Rathenau's writings and speeches (facilitated greatly by Ernst Schulin's edition) shows that, although Rathenau was very interested in Behrens's work for the AEG and recognized it as an "earnest endeavor," he often commented on comparable reforming experiments in terms that vacillated between skepticism and irony, between sympathy and antipathy.

Already in 1912, as Behrens's newly refurbished AEG stood before him, Rathenau criticized the "hopeless" attempts to overcome "the restraints imposed by mechanistic function":

Man has the feeling that he once possessed some things that were irreplaceable; he is now artfully trying to win back what has been lost by planting little sanctuaries in his mechanized world, such as roof gardens on top of factories. Here is a nature cult dragged out of the past, there a superstition, the dream of a communal existence, a sham naivety, a false sense of jollity, a purified Christianity, an archaism, a stylization. . . . Nevertheless, this game does not deserve our contempt, for it arises out of a passionate longing. Yet it remains helpless and childish, for arcadian groves do not flourish on the shaking ground of mechanization.[165]

Here Rathenau was referring explicitly to the roof garden atop the old machine factory on the Brunnenstrasse (illustration 69) as an example of the hopelessness of all efforts to elevate aesthetics into an exclusive first principle. Behrens had redesigned and replanted this roof garden in 1910 for the guests of the AEG.

Similarly, Rathenau said that the "strident, hastily conceived" forms of technical appliances had little chance of competing with hand-produced objects developed over the centuries. With his predilection for eschatological dreams of a future which could not be rushed or hurried into existence and his belief in the continuity of the past, Rathenau repeatedly criticized "hurriedly thought-out design," "novelty," "reckless imitation," and "ephemerality."

Architecture, this "most circumspect of all the arts" was finished, said Rathenau—"irredeemably destroyed by the mechanization of production." "All attempts to invent new building regulations, styles of ornament, and art forms with pen and ink" were "doomed to pitiful failure." He deplored the fact that the Ionic capital and entablature were no longer used in architectural design and had been superseded by "a riveted construction that would be aesthetically pleasing and technically clever in the design of a lamp." It is very likely that Rathenau was referring directly here to the riveted construction Bernhard and Behrens had used in the turbine hall.

69
Peter Behrens, AEG roof garden, Brunnenstrasse. AEG photo 10514.

Rathenau uncompromisingly defended art's absolute freedom from function and its subjective nature. Any attempt to enlist the help of art to alleviate the effects of mechanization was bound to fail, for art was an unsuitable means for this purpose. Art abused in this way, said Rathenau, "extols the distorted and the false by means of sentimentality and mechanical pathos," "strives to achieve the strongest possible contrast with the previous consumer practice" (thereby "treading the path of fashion"), and "carefully assembles trash and baubles for glossy display and expensive sale." This could be seen as Rathenau's commentary on Behrens's redesigning of the AEG's arc lamps, kettles, factories, sales literature, and retail shops. One could almost think that Rathenau was making a direct reference to Arthur Fürst's *Berliner Tageblatt* article (reproduced below), which lauded in Behrens's work all the attributes Rathenau scorned. To Rathenau, such things as "daring design," "reckless imitation," the sudden arrival of "hastily conceived forms," and much-publicized breaks with earlier versions of an appliance were all "whipped up by the competition at the exhibitions."[166] The desire to exploit anything that was successful, felt Rathenau, was merely an attempt to improve on the banal, the "propping up" of that which was "distorted and false." He reacted no less angrily to those people who "weave the mean implements of modern life into their sensibilities" and "write of arc lamps and hotel gardens in rhymes of deliberate daring."[167] In 1916, one year before the publication of Rathenau's *Von kommenden Dingen*, the Inselbücherei brought out Theodor Däubler's *Das Sternenkind*. Among this collection of poems was one entitled "Diadem":

The arc lamps crown the sunset,
Their lilac rays will outlive the evening,
Spectrally they float above the noisy throng
Like vitrified fruits from other worlds.
I find it hard to comprehend the essence of these lamps.
The stars seems wise, the moon will gladly be angry,
Why do you turn pale under the starry diadem?

According to Rathenau, a poet who wrote on such themes was not a "prophet," but merely "a supplier of aesthetic diversion."

Rathenau also categorically opposed the "optimists" who "hope that every new invention, form of transportation, or occupation will produce new artistic forms." To "sing the praises of mechanization" was, he said, like "discussing with a pit pony the strangeness of its situation."[168] He cannot, therefore, have had much sympathy for the drawings and watercolors of the AEG factories done by Lovis Corinth and Hans Baluschek (illustrations 70–72),[169] and Walter Dexel's 1917 painting "Arc Lamps" (illustration 73)[170] must have received the same damning criticism as Däubler's poem.

Who did Rathenau mean when he spoke of the "insufferable boasters who extol every mechanized necessity to us as a step toward perfection"? He never tired of comparing the "old things from the age of craftsmanship" with the "mass junk of our consumer industry." Even though it is possible that he was referring here to the cheap goods sold in the department stores, his accusation that "the calculated rhetoric of machine ornament" was used to "mock the old appliances" was also applicable to Behrens's ceiling fans, to the surface decoration of his kettles, and to his electric heaters.

"We cannot take a step without being accompanied and surrounded by arty drawings. Adornments of color and form are applied to every utilitarian object; the typefaces that talk to us during the day have artistic pretensions. . . . The whole world is sweating art from every pore." This could also be an allusion to the graphic-design work Behrens did for the AEG's brochures and pamphlets. Against the "torturous" efforts of artists like Behrens, Rathenau set "true art," which made tangible "the laws of the organic world, of destiny, of the soul, and of the divine." This could best be achieved, said Rathenau, by music, "the true art of our time." By making spiritual experience accessible to us, music "is transfigured into a pure work of the spirit." The music room in his house in Darmstadt suggests that Behrens would probably have agreed with this sentiment, perhaps with the reservation that one should not see transfiguration as the only function of art.

70
Lovis Corinth, AEG machine factory,
Brunnenstrasse, charcoal drawing,
1908. Helbing auction catalog 55
(16 November 1926), plate 55.

71
Lovis Corinth, machine hall of the AEG,
Berlin, charcoal drawing.

72
Hans Baluschek, AEG assembly hall,
Hussitenstrasse, watercolor, ca. 1912.
Courtesy of AEG.

73
Walter Dexel, arc lamps, oil on
canvas, 1917. Collection of the artist.
From Werner Hofmann, *Walter Dexel*
(1972).

Rathenau was able to admit that the "mean results of utilitarian profiteering" did possess "exactness—a highly bred virtue of the innumerable generations in the lineage of the machine." But to Rathenau this too was only "the devil's beauty." He also saw that the value of the new appliances lay in the ease with which they could be replaced rather than in their durability; therein lay the profit on the turnover of this "mass junk" whose "grinning glitter leers toward the rubbish heap, on which its brief existence will end."

Rathenau brushed aside the idea that good design might increase turnover, an idea that found support within the AEG and had been a decisive factor in the appointment of Behrens. Only technical exactness could, in Rathenau's eyes, redeem an appliance from the dreariness of utility production. To Rathenau, the real benefits brought by industrially made products and the maintenance of a technological lead over the competitors offered adequate guarantees of economic success,[172] especially when reinforced by the experience possessed by a firm like the AEG. The business of designing the form of the products was a matter for misguided aesthetes.

Rathenau returned in 1919 to the question of industrially produced goods and the attempt to elevate their design to the status of an aesthetic, educational, and social imperative. In his important work *Die neue Gesellschaft* he expanded his critique into a wider attack on all bourgeois or socialist attempts at reform. Behrens was once again singled out for reproof; particular targets were his AEG roof garden, the geometry of his designs, and his then-novel use of colored concrete. Rathenau wrote:

We are dumbfounded by the educated but untested banalities of that easy schoolboy optimism that, with the flick of a wrist, conjures up for us the usual little paradise garden of rectangular factory culture and the joy of multicolored concrete. The same optimism assures us that the introduction of the six-hour working day and the abolition of private property will lead directly to the supersession of the horror of the cinema by classical concerts, liquor stores by people's libraries, gambling dens by uplifting lectures, street robberies by gymnastic exercises, detective novels by the works of Gottfried Keller, and kitsch and novelty goods by examples of chastened craftsmanship, and that out of the world of boxing, betting, hand-grenade practice, and butter swindles will blossom an era of humility and brotherly love.[173]

As admirers of Nietzsche, both Rathenau and Behrens could have appealed to him in support of their respective claims. Rathenau would have affirmed Nietzsche's definition of the artist as one who "stands for the solitary individual against the whole society," to whom "art is a means of making life possible for the many individuals,"[174] and whose real enemy since the time of Ruskin had been technology. Behrens, on the other hand, would have cited Nietzsche's scorn for the subjective artist. Like Nietzsche, Behrens would also have called "first and above all" for "victory over the subjective, release from the ego," since "the willful subject and its egoistic purposes can only be thought of as the opponent of art, not its source." In his architectural work, Behrens tried to implement Nietzsche's call for "a remodeling of the world in order to make it bearable to live in."[175] Behrens tried, as he wrote, "to go into all the demands made by a factory complex using both artistic and technical means, to endorse these demands, indeed to raise them to the level of principles and to give them physical expression."[176] This is what Manfredo Tafuri has rather unsympathetically dubbed the "parola d'ordine" not only of social democracy but also of democratic capitalism: order and planning.[177]

The debate between Rathenau and Behrens which was acted out on the sites of the AEG characterized that difficult stage of development at which the inescapable demands of mechanization could no longer simply be deplored or transformed by an act of will into the subjective ideal of traditional Prussian Classicism. Rathenau regarded Behrens's work as the creation of forms, models, and modules. He saw the "power of the designer" as something that might corrupt the authority of the planning model. Rathenau's own campaign for "spirit and vision"[178] was conducted, however, on a level at which only "pure" souls were at home. Behrens's aim was to "clad" ugliness, to bring order and "calm" to chaos, to design the outer casing as "a worthy expression of the working methods," to find external forms that would "no longer hint at the complication of the technical organism,"[179] and thus to conquer the world of mechanization with the power of artistic form and aesthetic order. Moreover, he defined his artistic activity as something that was inseparably linked to the production process and to the problem of construction. This brought with it the inevitable risks of weakness, venality, and banality.[180]

Behrens needed only three drawings in order to show how a piece of sheet metal could be pressed into 81 variations in a brilliant system of round, oval, or octagonal, nickel-plated, copper, or brass, smooth, hammered, or grooved kettles. The individual piece was ennobled and placed in a context by the system. Rathenau was probably criticizing this design too when he complained in 1912 of "the trend towards specialization and abstraction, intentional manipulation, programmed thinking, and complicated uniformity."[181] But to Behrens's triumphant command over a mass-produced object Rathenau could only offer two alternatives: the costliness of the handmade silver kettle and the dictatorship of banality.

Rathenau's friends Alfred Kerr and Franz Blei had little sympathy for this aspect of Rathenau's "critique of the age." They felt that he was only capable of seeing "modernity" in things that were "technical and mechanical," and that in doing so he encapsulated himself in a "nebulous romanticism." As a result, his taste was that of "those people who achieve dullness effortlessly." Kerr saw "this far too obvious idolization of nonindustrial craftsmanship" as rather unoriginal—a criticism that apparently left Rathenau unmoved. As Kerr commented, "It was hardly worth inflating such a truism into a vehicle for disguised Weltschmerz."[182]

Rathenau's opinions gain in pertinence and topical trenchancy if they are placed in a wider context and not regarded merely as a critique of the AEG's innovatory design program. The disagreement between Rathenau and Behrens was over the nature and the methods of art, not over the ultimate goal of human labor. Both men desired to create an antidote against mechanization, against the domination of the Wilhelmine court, and against all forms of escapism. In contrast to the world of business and industry, Rathenau saw the domain of art as something the private individual had to protect from the modern world in general and from the modern artist in particular. Behrens, in contrast, saw in art the twentieth century's last hope of making the mechanized world bearable.

Beyond the comments already cited, no more exact record has survived of Walther Rathenau's reaction to the new architecture Behrens had created for the AEG. Hans Fürstenberg recalled the special affinity Rathenau felt for Messel's administration building on the Friedrich-Karl-Ufer.[183] But Behrens represented a younger generation of architects which Rathenau looked on without the affection he had felt for Messel's work—the less so since he felt that industrialization had been responsible for the "end" of architecture. It is nevertheless impossible to believe that Rathenau, who saw himself as half architect, did not follow the progress on the new buildings exactly. Unfortunately, we know nothing of his response. It is possible, however, to trace to his father's intervention the strange break which the assembly shop for large machines in the Hussitenstrasse (1911–12) made with the earlier AEG factories, in which Behrens had used pilasters, half-columns, and towers.

Peter Behrens, assembly hall for large machines, Hussitenstrasse, 1912. AEG photo 9023 (18 May 1912).

76
Peter Behrens, drawing of assembly hall for large machines, Hussitenstrasse, July 1911. AEG photo 8244.

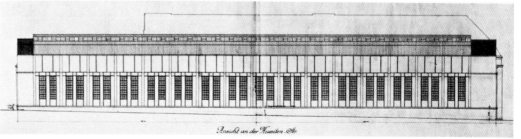

74
Peter Behrens, exhibition pavilion for Zementwarenfabrikanten Deutschlands, Berlin-Treptow, 1910. Courtesy of F. Stoedtner.

In his 1929 account of his work for the AEG ("On the Aesthetics of Factory Design," reproduced in this volume), Behrens mentioned the large assembly shop, "which in its external form is clearly an iron-frame building, a brittle building material which was chosen at the wish of the late 'Geheimrat' Rathenau." "It was certainly interesting," he continued, "to try to achieve here too, as far as possible, a sense of volume and articulation. To do this I used the vertical pillars and the projecting crane track." Behrens's specific reference to Emil Rathenau's personal intervention in the design of the most prominent factory in the new Brunnenstrasse complex implies that Behrens was forced to abandon his own intentions. Exactly what these intentions were is not known, but a design that carried on from the facades of the small-motor and railway-equipment factories would have been likely. Had the direction taken by the AEG's architecture unsettled Emil Rathenau? Was he disturbed by the physical advance along the facades of his factories of a Classicism that was entirely different from the Classicism of Messel and his own son, and that still seemed foreign in factory buildings? Did he regard the demonstrative translation of industrial work into visible performance as a contradiction of his own conception of work? Should his categorical imperatives of profitability and absolute economy be sacrificed in favor of brick quality, brick quantity, and brick coloring? We don't know. At any rate, Emil Rathenau's insistence that the large machine hall be built in iron was an expression of his desire to return to more traditional building methods. It also carried the directive that Behrens refrain from any trimmings that might transform the outside wall into a factory facade in the formal sense; that the actual construction of the hall should once again be stated, without any metaphors.

In Behrens's text the tone of lingering regret is unmistakable, as is the conviction that he had managed "here too, as far as possible" to achieve an aesthetic rendering of the exposed pillars and the bracing system of the iron frame. This depended on Behrens's ability to translate the structural demands of the large supporting pillars and the horizontal tracks of the overhead crane into a "giant order" appropriate to a wall 176 meters long. The tracks straddled sixteen bays, stood on a continuous plinth, and extended upward through the attic to the roof. The dominant pillars and trusses formed a relief frame, while the areas of glass and brick created a subtle rhythm at the window level. Within each recessed bay, the strips of glass and brick had their own plinths and attic stories made of iron-framed brick panels, which echoed the larger scheme of the wall. Even with these subdivisions, Behrens maintained the unity of the wall's frame and infill structure. The load-bearing members pushed through the wall like veins or ribs, so that the function of the machine shop was expressed in its formal structure. Like the side wall of the turbine factory, it did not simply have the traditional, static role of defining and sheltering the interior space. The rails brackets, and supports for the cranes and tools that guided the work processes inside the hall were set into the wall. Exposing the frame made the contribution of the wall to the production process visible from the street. The glazed transparency of Gropius's Fagus factory reflected more than a hint of Behrens's solid yet floating wall, in which real work and the aesthetic transfiguration of this work were joined together.

With the steelworks in Hennigsdorf (illustration 77), Behrens achieved an almost Florentine clarity in this type of iron-frame construction. The model Behrens provided here was subsequently brought to artistic perfection in Mies's designs for the Illinois Institute of Technology (illustration 78).

It was without doubt the opposition of Emil Rathenau, perhaps supported by his son, that thwarted Behrens's repeated attempts between 1909 and 1911 to redesign Gate 4 on the Brunnenstrasse site. With the Brandenburg Gate as his model, Behrens planned a triumphal arch fusing Classicism and the machine aesthetic (illustrations A74 ff.). As this scheme was not concerned with the improvement or enlargement of a factory, Paul Jordan was probably not involved. Emil Rathenau had found such a demonstrative display of pomp desirable in 1896, when Schwechten's portal was built, but by 1912 a more straightforward solution was considered quite adequate.

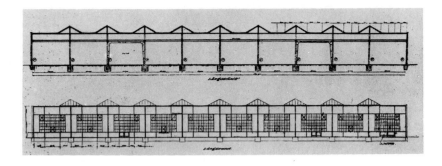

77
Peter Behrens, factory at Hennigsdorf,
1917.

78
Ludwig Mies van der Rohe, Illinois
Institute of Technology, Chicago,
1945.

From the inception of the AEG, Emil Rathenau and his three early colleagues, Deutsch, Jordan, and Mamroth, realized that the firm should make use of architectural skills wherever possible. They initially secured the services of Schwechten and the partners Cremer and Wolffenstein, two successful Berlin architects who integrated the firm's buildings into the scenery of the Berlin business world. The artists who were engaged after the turn of the century, the architect Messel and the sculptor Hahn, were required to provide more than the garb appropriate to a successful firm. Although their interpretation of the nature of industrial work was sadly inadequate, it did at least go farther than comparable attempts made at the time. In constructing a historical succession, for example, Messel delved deeper than the architects of the Gründerzeit. His search for a humanist frame of reference for the ethos of work and productivity took in Prussian Classicism, the Italian High Renaissance, Roman splendor, and Greek Classicism. To this architectural and historical legitimation, Hermann Hahn added the plastic dimension of mythology, with tasteful quotations from Attic reliefs, Roman vases, Tuscan sculpture, and Baroque putti, cartouches, and festoons.

In the same years of commercial prosperity Liebermann painted a portrait of the firm's founder, Munch one of his son, and Slevogt one of Carl Fürstenberg, the firm's banker. Hahn cast a medal for Emil and carved a marble herm of Walther Rathenau, and Corinth and Baluschek did drawings and watercolors of the firm's factories. Also at this time, Behrens illustrated commemorative addresses and designed the bindings for the firm's Festschriften, and the critics wrote enthusiastically in the art journals about the arrival of art in the AEG. Hahn's bronze bust of Walther Rathenau testified to Rathenau's claims to social and political leadership, and, at the same time, lent these claims historical and mythological legitimacy. Caesarlike, Rathenau looked to a near future in which the industrial entrepreneurs, with their quasi-governmental organizational skills, would assume the leading role previously held by the landed nobility.

In his design for the AEG administration building, Messel brought a self-conscious aura of tradition and convention to a traditionless industry. Hahn offered a mythological version of industry, with the eagle of electricity, industrial muses, and busts of the chairman. Behrens added a method of artistic planning and an organizational procedure that was aimed at both the workshop and the products. He did not clothe the collective labor of the AEG in the dignity of tradition, as Messel had done, or dress it up with the embellishments of mythology, as had Hahn; instead, he applied the principles of architecture and the new concept of serial production directly to the work process. In the same way as he drew up kettles, fans, and arc lamps, so he designed factories, housing, and railway stations, all of which expressed the special character of the AEG.

Although this search for ideal solutions was conducted in the context of one firm, Behrens conceived his work for the AEG as a pioneering model that would be applicable to all industrial communities. This model offered both commercial and artistic benefits. Although it was a powerful example, it was not a governmental dictate. It exposed itself to the criticism and competition of other firms and to the constraints of economic success. Behrens's dream of a unity of technical, artistic, and social productivity ultimately disintegrated under the growing weight of coercive economic demands. The dream vanished and was replaced by the renewed isolation of the artist and a growing schism between artistic work and industrial production—a schism that even an institution like the Bauhaus was barely able to straddle. The more powerful and better established planners of today do not make the Behrensian mistake of being artists.

Notes

1. *Werke in drei Bänden*, ed. K. Schlechta (Munich, n.d.), vol. 3, p. 526.

2. "Technische Schönheit," *Sozialistische Monatshefte* 1 (1914), p. 562.

3. Peter Behrens, "Reform der künstlerischen Erziehung," in *Der Geist der neuen Volksgemeinschaft. Denkschrift für das deutsche Volk* (Berlin, 1919), p. 95.

4. Wolf Dohrn, "The Example of the AEG" (in this volume).

5. Buddensieg 1975 (see bibliography), pp. 276 ff. See Behrens's own account in "Art and Technology" (in this volume). Karl Scheffler wrote similarly of "the bold and fortunate move of the directors Rathenau and Jordan in bringing Behrens to Berlin" ("Moderne Industriebauten," morning edition, *Vossische Zeitung*, 26 September 1912).

6. Hirschberg 1929–30, pp. 5 ff., 37 ff.

7. See Hoeber 1913, pp. 46 ff; Catalog 1966, no. 133, illustration 66; *Das deutsche Kunstgewerbe*, 1906, no. 3; *Deutsche Kunstgewerbe-Ausstellung Dresden*, official catalog (Munich, 1906), p. 195 and back cover; guide to the exhibition by Fritz Schumacher, *Das Kunstgewerbeblatt* 15 (1904), pp. 198 ff.; *ibid.* 17 (1906), pp. 177, 185 ff., 205 ff., 226 ff.; W. Niemeyer, *Dekorative Kunst* 10 (1907), pp. 137 ff.; E. Schur, *Die Rheinlande* 12 (1906), pp. 56 ff.; P. Schubring, *Die Hilfe* 12. no. 29 (22 July 1906), p. 10; W. Dohrn, *ibid.* 12, no. 46 (18 November 1906), p. 10.

8. Hoeber 1913, p. 33; Schäfer, *Die Rheinlande* 10 (1905), pp. 428 ff.; Krebs, *Dekorative Kunst* 14 (1906), pp. 77 ff.

9. *Die Rheinlande* 12 (1906), pp. 56 ff.

10. *Das neue Kunstgewerbe in Deutschland* (Leipzig, 1908), p. 177.

11. Osthaus, *Kunst und Künstler* 4 (December 1907), p. 123.

12. "A Factory Building by Peter Behrens" (in this volume).

13. Scheffler (see note 5), p. 163.

14. *Kunst und Künstler* 6 (June 1908), pp. 432 ff.

15. Lux, "Die Kunstindustrie und das Qualitätsproblem," *Die neue Zeit* 27, no. 1 (1909), p. 769.

16. See Werner Hofmann, "Luxus und Weiderspruch," *Ein Dokument Deutscher Kunst 1901* (Darmstadt, 1976), I, pp. 21 ff.

17. Fritz Meyer-Schönbrunn, *Peter Behrens* (Hagen and Dortmund, 1913), p. 3.

18. Joseph August Lux, *Das neue Kunstgewerbe in Deutschland* (Leipzig, 1908), p. 250.

19. See Gabriele Heidecker's chapter in this volume and note 23 below.

20. Hartmut Kaelbe, *Industrielle Interessenpolitik in der Wilhelminischen Gesellschaft. Centralverband Deutscher Industrieller 1895–1914* (Berlin, 1967); Hans-Jürgen Puhle, *Agrarische Interessenpolitik und preussischer Konservatismus im Wilhelminischen Reich*, second edition (Bonn, 1975); Siegfried Mielke, *Der Hansa-Bund für Gewerbe, Handel und Industrie 1909–1914* (Göttingen, 1976); Kurt Junghanns, *Jahrbuch für Geschichte* 15 (1977), pp. 329 ff.

21. Carl Johannes Fuchs, "Volkskunst und Volkswirtschaft," *Das Kunstgewerbeblatt* 18 (1907), p. 20.

22. Report of lecture, *Berliner Tageblatt*, 22 and 23 June 1909.

23. Max Osborn ["Die moderne Wohnräume im Waren-Haus von A. Wertheim zu Berlin," *Deutsche Kunst und Dekoration* (1902–03): pp. 259 ff.] wrote that "the main principle of the contemporary yearning after arts and crafts . . . is essentially democratic." Osborn called the modern department store "a significant factor in the culture of democracy." Hendrik Berlage described the arts and crafts movements as a "cry in the realm of the spirit like the labor movement in the realm of economics" and said that "the ideal of the economic equality of all men will also point to new directions in art" [*Das Kunstgewerbeblatt* 20 (1908), p. 245]. See also Wilhelm Stöffler, "Pforzheim, Kunst und Industrie, Rede auf dem 3. deutschen Kunstgewerbe-Tag," *Das Kunstgewerbeblatt* 18 (1907), p. 35 ("Art for the connoisseurs, hand craftsmanship for the exclusive circles of informed admirers, but industrial art for the people") and Robert Breuer, "Der Einkauf als kulturelle Funktion," *Deutsche Kunst und Dekoration* 21 (1907–08), p. 79; *Die Hilfe* (1913), p. 348 ("The reinforced concrete style is being developed in the containers and instruments of the new masses, in factories, bridges, stations, stores, meeting halls—concrete

and democracy belong together"). Paul Westheim [*Sozialistische Monatshefte* 1 (1914), p. 571] spoke of the "socialization of horticulture." Richard Gaul acknowledged the "machine made furniture" of Riemerschmid and the Leipziger Künstlerbund at the 1906 Dresden exhibition as an example of "the conscious democratization of modern domestic design" [*Das Kunstgewerbeblatt* 17 (1906), p. 226]. In 1909 Osthaus called the shop owner an "educator of the people" [Michael Müller, *Kunst und Industrie* (Munich, 1974), p. 118].

24. See *Die Hilfe* (19 December 1909), p. 809; Friedrich Naumann, "Industrielle Auseinandersetzung," *Die Hilfe* 17 (1911), p. 434.

25. See Joan Campbell, *The German Werkbund: The Politics of Reform in the Applied Arts* (Princeton, 1978), pp. 57 ff.

26. See Muthesius, *Handarbeit und Massenerzeugnis* (Berlin, 1917); Julius Posener, *Hermann Muthesius*, exhibition catalog (Berlin, 1977), p. 13; Muthesius, "Kunst und Maschine," *Dekorative Kunst* 5 (1902), pp. 14 ff.

27. *Die Deutsche Volkswirtschaft im 19. Jahrhundert*, eighth edition (Darmstadt, 1954), p. 417.

28. See the pointed letter of Wilhelm Niemeyer to Osthaus, 23 July 1914 (Karl Ernst Osthaus Archive, Hagen, DWK 64):

It is imperative for the whole movement, and touches on the most profound of all ethical principles, that the causal link between intellectual activity and economic consequence should not be inverted by the spiritual vulgarity of a Muthesius. If such a view were to

succeed here, then the word Americanism would gain an elevated ethical status in contrast to this form of intellectual crudeness. You have done something decisive in tackling this matter. It seems to me that what Muthesius is advocating are condensed, half-understood, and misinterpreted ideas taken from Behrens. It is the fate of Behrens's ideas, like his designs, to become strangely vulgar in the hands of lesser men.

See also the related letters of Gropius in Marcel Franciscono, *Walter Gropius and the Creation of the Bauhaus in Weimar* (Urbana, Ill., 1971), pp. 262 ff.

29. See the text of Poelzig's speech in *Mitteilungen des deutschen Werkbundes* 4 (1919), reprinted in Wend Fischer and G. B. von Hartmann, *Zwischen Kunst und Industrie, der Deutsche Werkbund* (Munich, 1975), pp. 161 ff.

30. All quotations here are from one of Behrens's most thoughtful essays, "The Ethos and the Realignment of Artistic Problems" (in this volume).

31. Documents from the Höchst Archive; "Peter Behrens schuf Turm und Brücke," *Beiträge zur Geschichte der Chemie* 4 (Höchst, 1964); Cremers 1928, pp. 2 ff.; H. Seeger, "Bürohäuser der privaten Wirtschaft," *Handbuch der Architektur* IV, no. 7, volume 1a, third edition (Leipzig, 1933), pp. 53 ff.; Paolo Portoghesi, *Controspazio* (1970), p. 20; Catalog 1966, no. 86.

32. *Weisse Blätter* 1 (1914), p. 747.

33. Behrens, "Stil?," *Die Form* 1 (1922), p. 6; Fischer and von Hartmann, *op. cit.*, pp. 181 ff.

34. Wolfgang Pehnt, in Giulio Carlo Argan, *Die Kunst des 20. Jahrhunderts*, Propyläen Kunstgeschichte, volume 12 (Berlin, 1977), p. 341.

35. Walter Gropius, "The Formal and Technical Problems of Modern Architecture and Planning," *RIBA Journal* 41, no. 13 (19 May 1934), pp. 679–694.

36. See for example Rathenau, *Die neue Gesellschaft* (Berlin, 1919), pp. 22 ff., 48.

37. Marianne Weber, *Max Weber: ein Lebensbild*, second edition (Heidelberg, 1950), p. 328; H. H. Gerth and C. Wright Mills, eds., *From Max Weber: Essays in Sociology* (London, 1948), p. 30.

38. This concept of "Kunst in der Produktion" is not taken from the many statements made by the Russian constructivists in the 1920s, such as those collected by Hubertus Gassner in the catalog *Kunst in die Produktion* of the Neue Gesellschaft für bildende Kunst (Berlin, 1977); instead, the reference is to the article by Karl Ernst Osthaus included in the present volume.

39. "Wahrheit und Wahrscheinlichkeit der Kunstwerke."

40. Gustav Kemmann, *Die Berliner Elektrizitätswerke bis Ende 1896, geplant und erbaut von der Allgemeinen Elektricitäts-Gesellschaft* (Berlin and Munich), p. 135; Werner Sombart, "Technik und Wirtschaft," *Jahrbuch der Gehe-Stiftung zu Dresden 7* (1901), pp. 53 ff.

41. Walter Fürst, *Kunst und Künstler* (6 August 1908), p. 510.

42. "Art in Technology" (in this volume).

43. Strictly, the Gründerzeit was the period of wild financial speculation between the end of the Franco-Prussian War in 1871 and the start of the depression in 1873. More generally, the term is used for the period 1870–1890.

44. Hans Fürstenberg, *Erinnerungen. Mein Weg als Bankier und Carl Fürstenbergs Altersjahre* (Wiesbaden, 1965), p. 33.

45. Hoeber, pp. 172 ff.; Hoeber, *Das Kunstgewerbeblatt* 24 (1912–13), pp. 186 ff.; Cremers 1928, illustrations 33–38; *Festschrift zur Erinnerung an die Einweihung des Verwaltungsgebäudes der Mannesmannröhrenwerke in Düsseldorf, 10. Dezember 1912; Kunst und Künstler* 9, no. 5 (1910–11), p. 256 ("It is equally welcome that Behrens is to design the extensive administration building for the firm of Mannesmann"); Müller-Wulckow, *Genius* 1 (1919), p. 100 ("Basically it is nothing but the systemization of the office building as Messel had already done for the AEG").

46. The same statement had been made much earlier in Chicago.

47. See *Berliner Architekturwelt* 9 (1907), pp. 446, 458 and illustration 539. A projected ceiling painting, for which there is a sketch in the drawings collection of the Technische Universität Berlin, was not realized.

48. Ulrike Köcke, ed., *Katalog der Medaillen und Plaketten des 19. und 20. Jahrhunderts in der Kunsthalle Bremen* (Bremen, 1975), p. 69, illustrations 57 and 58. More exact information can be found in *AEG-Zeitung* 11, no. 9 (March 1910), p. 15.

49. Two statues executed by Hahn in 1908 for the vestibule of Messel's office building (illustration 15) also strove to present administrative work in a mythological way: "Knowledge" was depicted as a clasical muse, while "Industry" (?) held a cogwheel. [See note 47; Georg Jacob Wolf, "Hermann Hahn," *Die Kunst* 15 (1914), pp. 289 ff.; Fritz Stahl, *Alfred Messel* (Berlin, 1910).] The two statues and the putti group were displayed in front of the AEG pavilion at the 1908 Deutsche Schiffbau-Ausstellung in Berlin. With his neo-Hellenistic figure "Betriebssicherheit" (illustration 16), the then-celebrated but now-forgotten sculptor Hugo Kaufmann (see Thieme and Becker, *Allgemeine Künstlerlexicon*) displayed similar daring in adapting classical models.

50. Max Scheler, review of Sombart's *Der Bourgeois, Die weissen Blätter* 1, no. 6 (February 1914), pp. 580 ff.

51. *Etude sur le Mouvement . . .* (in this volume).

52. G. J. Wolf, "Hermann Hahn," *Die Kunst* 15 (1914), p. 298; Hermann Esswein, "Hermann Hahn," *Die Plastik* 3 (1913), pp. 37 ff., plate 47; Ernst Schulin, "Die Rathenaus. Zwei Generationen jüdischen Anteils an der industriellen Entwicklung Deutschlands," in *Juden im Wilhelminischen Deutschland 1890–1914* (Tübingen, 1976).

53. "Unser Nachwuchs," *Neue Freie Presse,* 25 December 1909, and in appendix to *Zur Kritik der Zeit* (Berlin, 1912), p. 207. In contrast, Hahn's marble herm of Walther Rathenau of 1905 (illustrated in appendix A) stresses the visionary writer, with Nietzsche's distant eye and Pegasus as a guarantor of fame and inspiration, plus the unusual escort of two fauns.

54. See reference 50 and Max Scheler (after Rathenau), "Staatsgeschäfte und Privatgeschäfte gleichzusetzen," *Zur Kritik der Zeit,* appendix, p. 195. Rathenau wrote to Franz Oppenheimer on 14 March 1918: "If a factory were to be given over to me, then let it be called Germany" [Rathenau, *Briefe,* volume 1 (Dresden, 1927), p. 384]. He subsequently wrote "The work of running a large business enterprise . . . surpasses that involved in governing a small country" and, further, "Today, the large business is a factor which belongs to the entire society, . . . which has become subservient to the public interest" [Rathenau, *Vom Aktienwesen* (Berlin, 1917)]. See Golo Mann's introduction to the political writings in Walther Rathenau, *Schriften* (Berlin, 1965), pp. 259 ff., 268.

55. Rathenau, *Zur Kritik der Zeit,* appendix, p. 210.

56. Esswein, "Hermann Hahn."

57. "Von kommenden Dingen" (1917), in *Walther Rathenau–Gesamtausgabe,* volume 2, ed. Ernst Schulin (Munich and Heidelberg, 1977), "Zur Mechanik des Geistes" (1913), ibid. See also *Zur Kritik der Zeit,* p. 61: "But it depends on the conceptual ability of the bourgeois intelligentsia in Germany as to whether and when it will be called upon to assume the responsibility for cultural and political life after mechanization has run its course. In Germany at present the intelligentsia carry only a small part of this responsibility even though the most important material tasks rest on its shoulders—the maintenance and feeding of the expanding population and the management of the country's financial responsibilities."

58. Rathenau, "Zur Mechanik des Geistes," p. 271; *Zur Kritik der Zeit,* p. 171.

59. Rathenau, "Zur Mechanik des Geistes," pp. 169–176.

60. "Art in Technology" (in this volume).

61. Gert Selle, *Die Geschichte des Design in Deutschland von 1870 bis heute* (Cologne, 1978), p. 68.

62. *Reflexionen* (Leipzig, 1908), p. 97; "Von kommenden Dingen," p. 362.

63. These and the following quotations are from "Art in Technology" and "Art and Technology" (both in this volume).

64. The "Goddess of Light" might have been adopted after the takeover by the AEG, although it is not inconceivable that the Union and the AEG both used similar goddesses in their trademarks.

65. In Fischer and von Hartmann, *Zwischen Kunst und Industrie*, pp. 32 ff. See also Osthaus, *Henry van de Velde* (Hagen, 1920), p. 21; S. Müller, in *Karl Ernst Osthaus* (Recklinghausen, 1971), p. 260.

66. "Art and Technology," "Artistic Values in Factory Building as Publicity," "On the Aesthetics of Factory Design," "Prof. Peter Behrens on Aesthetics in Industry" (all in this volume).

67. Robert Breuer, "Kleinere Kunstnachrichten," *Deutsche Kunst und Dekoration* 27 (1910–11), p. 492.

68. In *Zeitschrift des Vereins deutscher Ingenieure* (1912), p. 1250.

69. Behrens on Theodor Heuss, in *Die Hilfe* (1940), p. 75.

70. Rathenau, *Zur Kritik der Zeit*, p. 42.

71. R. Gournay, *Die Weissen Blätter* 1, no. 11–12 (July—August 1914). pp. 1354 ff.

72. Hartmut Kaelbe, *Berliner Unternehmer während der frühen Industrialisierung* (Berlin, 1972). See also Rathenau's comments on this matter discussed above.

73. Anton Jaumann, *Deutsche Kunst und Dekoration* 22 (1908–09), p. 353.

74. Heinz Sperber, "Wegmarken proletarischer Kunst," *Vorwärts* 29 (15 June 1912), supplement. This article caused a vigorous controversy.

75. See Albert Siegrist (pseud. Alexander Schwab), *Das Buch vom Bauen* (Berlin, 1930), pp. 65 ff.

76. "La géometrie, mère de la Folie" (article on "Tendenzen der 20er Jahre" exhibition, Berlin, 1977), *Le Monde*, 1 September 1977.

77. *The Labors of Hercules* (1947), p. 29.

78. "Werkbund und Weltwirtschaft" (lecture, 4 July 1914), in Naumann, *Werke*, ed. H. Ladendorf (Cologne, 1964), vol. 6, p. 340.

79. *Progetto e destino* (Milan, 1965).

80. "Kunst und Industrie. Vortrag in der Dresdener Kunstgewerbe-Ausstellung," *Werke*, vol. 6, pp. 433 ff.; see especially p. 440.

81. Naumann, "Kunst und Technik" (1904), *ibid.*, p. 193.

82. "L" (pseud.), "AEG," *Berliner Börsenkurier*, 12 June 1910.

83. *Die Wunder um uns* (Berlin, 1911), pp. 58 ff.

84. It can be inferred from the city arms with electrical sparks that this AEG photograph of June 1900 shows this very elevator.

85. *Werke*, volume 6, p. 441.

86. Reprinted in Hans Maria Wingler, *Bauhaus* (Cambridge, Mass., 1969).

87. See Behrens, "On the Aesthetics of Factory Design" (in this volume).

88. See illustrations P24–P26 in catalog below.

89. "Prof. Behrens on Aesthetics in Industry" (in this volume).

90. "Kunst und Technik, Vortrag gehalten im Vortragssaal der AEG am 13. 1. 1909," *Berliner-Tageblatt* ("Zeitgeist" supplement), 25 January 1909.

91. *Die Architektur der Grossstadt* (Berlin, 1913), p. 156. See also Scheffler, "Kunst und Industrie," *Kunst und Künstler* 6 (1908), p. 431: ". . . the naked hideousness of uncultivated industrial design. The formlessness is nowhere more shocking than in those cases where the designer is called in after the engineer is finished with his calculations and with his utilitarian form."

92. This short section was originally published in Buddensieg and Rogge 1977.

93. "Art and Technology" (in this volume). See also note 115 below.

94. See André Fermigier, note 76 above, and G. C. Argan, *Die Kunst des 20. Jahrhunderts* (Berlin, 1977), p. 20.

95. See AEG lists: Hz 3, 1911³, "Elektrische Heiz- und Kochapparate," p. 14, P.-I. no. 3428-29 and 3550-53.

96. *Ibid.*, 117, P.-I. no. 3443–46; also Hz 1025.

97. See "Die Küche der Zukunft," in Fürst, *Die Wunder um uns*—a remarkably early description of the all-electric kitchen.

98. Letter to Dr. Meissner, 26 November 1907, in *Briefe*, vol. 1 (Dresden, 1927), no. 29.

99. *Impressionen*, third edition (Leipzig, 1902), p. 175.

100. *50 Jahre AEG* (Berlin, 1956), p. 227.

101. This is evident from the *AEG-Mitteilungen* and the company review *Die Spannung*.

102. The recent literature on Domela makes no mention of his work for the AEG. His cover design for the steam turbine brochure is probably the most outstanding example of applied De Stijl graphics. Two other examples of his work, from the 1931 *AEG-Mitteilungen*, are reproduced here as illustration 50. Domela had an advertising studio in Berlin until 1933 and worked for other firms, including Siemens.

103. *Progetto e destino* (Milan, 1965), p. 136.

104. *Menschliches, Allzumenschliches Werke*, ed. K. Schlechta (Munich, n.d.), vol. 1, pp. 545 ff.

105. "Industrial Building" (in this volume).

106. *Emil Rathenau, der Mann und sein Werk* (Berlin, 1915), pp. 88 ff.

107. "Technische Schönheit," *Sozialistische Monatshefte* 1 (1914), p. 563.

108. In *AEG-Mitteilungen*, January 1910, p. 4.

109. "The Turbine Hall . . ." (in this volume).

110. "The New Hall of the AEG Turbine Factory in Berlin" (in this volume).

111. "The New Hall for the Turbine Factory . . ." (in this volume).

112. P. Simon, "Das Elektrizitätswerk Strassburg," *Der Industriebau* 2 (1911), pp. 145 ff.

113. See note 90 above. The lecture was also mentioned in *Die Werkkunst* 4 (1908–09), p. 80.

114. The way Behrens decorated the National Gallery on the occasion of the 1906 Jahrhundert-Ausstellung in Berlin was described by Franz Dülberg (*Zeitschrift für bildende Kunst* 17, no. 161) in remarkable terms, making Behrens the forefather of later packaging artists like Christo: "Walls of coarse, matt linen mercifully cover up what the National Gallery used to be and, it is to be hoped, will never be again. A new branch of artistic creativity is thereby inaugurated, a sort of cladding art, which may be made use of by future generations, particularly in Berlin. Even if reverence forbids the pulling down of such buildings as Raschdorff's Cathedral and the row of monuments which cheerfully grow out of the earth in the Tiergarten, they could still be wrapped under a worthwhile, artistic outer layer."

115. Hoeber 1913, p. 58; Catalog 1966, illustration 62; Osthaus, *Kunst und Künstler* 6 (1908), p. 121 and illustration on p. 118; J. A. Lux, *Hohe Warte* 9 (1908), pp. 37 ff. (view and ground plan).

116. "Die elektrotechnische Revolution der Gegenwart," *Die neue Zeit* 27 (1909) p. 537.

117. *Walther Rathenau. Ses idées et ses projets d'organisation économique* (Paris, 1919, pp. 278 ff.

118. ("In memoriam Walther Rathenau," *Die neue Rundschau* 33 (1922), pp. 810ff.

119. See the biographical information in Hoeber 1913, and also the early reactions to Behrens's AEG work reprinted in this volume. As a first-rate art-historical source, the daily press is practically untapped. Many of the respected authors who published in the art journals also wrote for the arts pages of the newspapers.

120. Walther Rathenau, *Tagebuch 1907–1922*, ed. H. Pogge von Strandmann (Düsseldorf, 1967): "26 March 1911 (Sunday). Midday 23 people to breakfast, the Kolbes, the Hallers, the Kysers (writer), Behrens, Lepsius (painter), E. R. Weiss, Edith Andreae etc. Afterwards a walk with the Hallers. After dinner with Paul Jordan, Staudt." "11 May, Thursday. Evening at Felix Deutsch's, with Sombart, Behrens, Gnauth." "28 January 1912, Sunday. 23 gentlemen to breakfast. Wölfflin, Brahm, Grönvold (painter), Reicke (deputy mayor of Berlin), Heimann (reader in the S. Fischer publishing house), Kardorff (painter), Ewers, Loerke (writer), Collier (journalist), Harrach (painter), Gaul (sculptor), Behrens, Karl Walser (painter), Kyser etc. See also J. A. Lux, in *Rathenau*, ed. Schulin (note 57), p. 606: "Besides Peter Behrens, the only able mind in the company seemed to me to be Rathenau, who resembled Behrens in his attitude."

121. Petra Behrens, who was born in 1898, recalled Rathenau's many visits to the hospitable home of her parents in Babelsberg. Before 1950, Ernst Hauswedell auctioned Behrens's copy of the 1918 edition of Rathenau's collected writings, which carried the inscription " . . . to his dear friend Peter Behrens." [Information kindly given by Petra Behrens. See Hauswedell, auction no. 228, November 1978, lot no. 2071, Walther Rathenau, *Reflexionen* (1908), with dedication to "Peter und Lilli Behrens, in friendship."] Behrens's wife Lilli said in *Illustrierte Woche* (1955), p. 1352, that Rathenau was a regular visitor. (The author is grateful to Petra Behrens for providing a copy of this article.)

122. See *Rathenau*, ed. Schulin, p. 815. See also Rathenau, letter to Karl Scheffler, 27 November 1919, in Rathenau, *Briefe*, volume 1 (Dresden, 1927), p. 200: "I know too little about the Werkbund to form an opinion on whether it would allow itself to be transformed into a political lobby." See also Marie von Bunsen, *Zeitgenosse, die ich erlebte, 1900–1930* (Leipzig, 1932), p. 100. Behrens wrote an article on the aims of the Bund der Erneuerung in *Die neue Rundschau* 31 (1920), pp. 1051 ff.

123. On the Demokratischer Volksbund see Hans Martin Barth, in *Jahrbuch für die Geschichte Mittel- und Ostdeutschland*, 16–17 (1968), pp. 254 ff. A complete list of signatories appeared in the *Frankfurter Zeitung*, 19 November 1918, and named "Lujo Brentano, Dehmel, Einstein, Gaul, Hahn, Carl and Gerhart Hauptmann, Heuss, Kerschensteiner, Graf Kessler, Liebermann, Meinecke, Muthesius, Naumann, Oncken, Franz Oppenheimer, Bruno Paul, Gustav Pauli, Sombart, Louis Tuaillon, Wilhelm Valentiner, Alfred Weber, Fritz Wichert."

124. Johannes Negelinus, Mox Doctor (pseudonym), "Walther Rathenau," *Schattenrisse* (Leipzig, 1913), no. 2, pp. 12 ff. I am grateful to Ernst Schulin for the reference to the complete text. Carl Schmitt himself was kind enough to explain to the author the background to his Rathenau-Behrens parody: As a bored junior lawyer in the firm of Plettenberg and Loberich, Schmitt was very enthusiastic about Theodor Däubler's epic "Das Nordlicht," and wrote a letter asking Walther Rathenau to support Däubler financially. Schmitt received two aloof replies, which prompted the satire. Albert Kollmann subsequently told Schmitt that Rathenau had not been offended by it. The "informant" on Behrens was Däubler himself, who was a great admirer of Behrens, and who was driven by his rich girlfriend Ida Bienert to see almost every important new commission Behrens built in Germany. See Däubler, *Der neue Standpunkt*, ed. Fritz Löffler (Dresden, 1957).

125. Melchior Lechter, who belonged to the Stefan George circle, designed monumental windows for the Wertheim store in Berlin and for the Landesmuseum in Münster.

126. This is a reference to J. M. Olbrich. Similarly heavy lamps hung in one of his late works, the Tietz store in Düsseldorf.

127. Bernhard Pankok (1872–1943).

128. Liebermann only did a drawing of Rathenau (see appendix A).

129. Rathenau owned a double portrait by Munch of the painter Paul Herrmann and the doctor Paul Contard, dating from 1897, illustrated in *Kunst und Künstler* 11 (1913), p. 405. See Kurt Glaser, *Edward Munch* (Berlin, 1917), p. 145, illustration 32. Alfred Kerr commented on Rathenau's "emphatic esteem for the Norwegian Munch and for his fantastic-primitive painting;" see *Rathenau*, ed. Schulin, p. 631. In 1920 Marcel Ray described Rathenau's office as "a large, bare room" and sensed "a chilly environment;" see *Rathenau*, ed. Schulin, p. 811.

130. *Rathenau*, ed. Schulin, pp. 49, 185, 257, 400, 407, 484. See also Rathenau, "Die schönste Stadt der Welt," in *Impressionen* (Leipzig, 1902), p. 140: "The Lustgarten has lost its character through the building of the Cathedral in the World's Fair style." See also ibid., pp. 144, 149, 155.

131. *Rathenau*, ed. Schulin, p. 688.

132. On Kraaz see Buddensieg 1975, pp. 274 ff. and note 8.

133. See the essay by Henning Rogge and illustration A53 below. Osthaus ("A Factory Building . . . ," in this volume) pointed out that it was singularly odd to take a building that had been completed only a few years earlier and recast it in a new style: "Old factories are being remodeled in accordance with the new design standards which the firm has committed itself to provide for its employees."

134. By employing them in the interior decoration of the Imperial German Embassy at St. Petersburg (see note 140), Behrens brought great prestige and prominence to the painters of the Berlin Secession. See Karl Scheffler, *Der Profanbau* (1914), pp. 309 ff.; Alfons Paquet, *Die Rheinlande* 14 (1914), pp. 34 ff.; Hartmut Niederwöhrmeier, Die deutsche Botschaftsgebäude 1871–1945, Ph.D diss., Darmstadt, 1977, pp. 74

135. Harry Graf Kessler, *Walther Rathenau, sein Leben und sein Werk* (Wiesbaden, 1928), p. 86. Behrens had known Dehmel since the 1890s. Their correspondence is now in the Dehmel Archive in the Stadt- und Universitätsbibliothek, Hamburg. Behrens decorated two books by Dehmel and made two woodcut portraits of him.

136. Hugo von Hofmannsthal, letter to Hermann Bahr, 24 March 1900, in Hofmannsthal, *Briefe 1890–1901* (Berlin, 1935), quoted in exhibition catalog "Die Insel" (Marbach, 1965).

137. Graf Kessler, *Walther Rathenau*.

138. Max Osborn, "Das Haus Walther Rathenau in Berlin-Grunewald," *Moderne Bauform* 11 (1912), pp. 465 ff.; W. Baumgarten, "Von der Architektur Berliner Neubauten," *Deutsche Bauhütte* 17 (1913), pp. 58 ff.; Etta Federn-Kohlhaas, *Walther Rathenau, sein Leben und Wirken* (Dresden, 1927), plate 5; Alfred Kerr, *Walther Rathenau, Erinnerungen eines Freundes* (Amsterdam, 1935), pp. 25 ff. Hans Fürstenberg describes the interior in Kessler, *Rathenau*, p. 378.

139. See Heinrich de Fries, *Moderne Villen und Landhäuser* (Berlin, 1924), illustrations 62 ff.; Robert Breuer, *Innendekoration* 24 (1913), pp. 431 ff.; Fritz Stahl, *Wasmuths Monatshefte für Baukunst*, 3 (1918–19), pp. 265 ff. The building file is dated October 1910; (information from Fritz Neumeyer).

140. At the end of 1910, while still architect to the AEG, Behrens was asked to design the Imperial German Embassy in St. Petersburg. This commission may have stemmed from the intercession of Walther Rathenau, whose country estate bordered on that of the German chancellor, Theobald von Bethmann Hollweg. Behrens's design shocked the imperial authorities. It was a daring first architectural attempt to depict the German nation as a modern industrial state, using the symbology of the AEG. A comparable instance was the use of the Roman script Behrens had designed for the AEG in the official German catalog at the Brussels World's Fair, discussed in this volume by Heidecker.

141. *Stufen des Lebens. Erinnerungen eines Baumeisters* (Stuttgart, 1949), p. 370, reprinted in *Rathenau*, ed. Schulin, vol. 2, p. 670.

142. See *Berliner Architekturwelt* 15 (1913), p. 110, with subtitle "Johannes Kraaz"; Harry Graf Kessler, *Tagebücher 1918–1937* (Frankfurt, 1961), p. 130; Kerr, *Walther Rathenau*, p. 28; *Die Bauwerke und Kunstdenkmäler von Berlin, Bezirk Tiergarten*, ed. I. Wirth (Berlin, 1955) (inexact information). The building file is dated June 1910 and signed by Kraaz (information from Fritz Neumeyer).

143. *Reflexionen*, p. 254.

144. Behrens admired Messel's "imposing administration building," and especially "the wonderfully large vestibule, which receives the visitor with the persuasive power of Roman might." (See Behrens's obituary of Messel in *Frankfurter Zeitung*, 6 April 1909.) Hans Fürstenberg has kindly written to the author about the especial affection Rathenau had for Messel's administration building. Perhaps the particular taste of Walther Rathenau could be attributed to Messel's rejection of the styles of the German and Italian Renaissance and the Neo-Baroque in favor of Greek, Roman, and Prussian models.

145. The classical sources of Modernism are still given far too little attention in comparison with the view, derived from the pioneering influence of Pevsner, that sets the coordinates between William Morris and the Bauhaus. Marcel Franciscono [*Walter Gropius and the Creation of the Bauhaus in Weimar* (Urbana, Ill., 1971)] has pointed out the importance of Behrens's denial of Muthesius's thesis that the sources for the Modern Movement in Germany were exclusively English. See Behrens's contribution to the discussion following a lecture by Muthesius, *Volkswirtschaftliche Blättern* 9 (1910), pp. 265 ff. Behrens referred here to the local Munich impulses, to Fiedler and Hildebrandt, and compared the medievalism of Morris with Gedon's infatuation with the Renaissance.

146. "Moderne Industriebauten," *Vossische Zeitung*, 26 September 1912, reprinted in *Die Architektur der Grossstadt* (Berlin, 1913), p. 154.

147. The start of the planning phase for the Continental administration building has not yet been firmly established, but must have been at the end of 1911 or the beginning of 1912. On the St. Petersburg embassy, see note 140. The preliminary design was approved by Wilhelm II on 23 February 1911.

148. Frank Servaes, "Das Kurhotel der Zukunft, ein Bauplan von Peter Behrens," *Der Architekt* 1 (1916), pp. 41 ff. This scheme, representing "many years of work," got as far as the laying of the foundation stone but was abandoned as a result of the outbreak of war. In its formal language it is related to the offices of the firm Frank and Lehmann in Cologne, which were completed in June 1914. See the advertisement in the catalog to the 1914 Werkbund exhibition at Cologne.

149. Behrens did not receive the commission for the Kröller-Müller house in the Hague before March 1911. His extensions to the Potsdam house of Dr. Alice Mertens, which had originally been built by Persius, were particularly indebted to the work of Schinkel; see Hoeber 1913, pp. 115 ff., and Max Dessoir, *Buch der Erinnerung* (Stuttgart, 1946), pp. 278 ff.

150. Rathenau, *Zur Kritik der Zeit*, p. 61; *Zur Mechanik des Geistes,* pp. 169, 171, 174 ff.

151. Kerr, *Walther Rathenau*, pp. 28 ff.

152. Karl Scheffler, *Die Architektur der Grossstadt* (Berlin, 1913), p. 155.

153. Rathenau, *Zur Kritik der Zeit*, p. 61; *Zur Mechanik des Geistes*, pp. 169, 171, 174 ff.

154. Fritz Hoeber, "Der kollektivistische Charakter der griechischen Kunst," *Sozialistische Monatshefte* 2 (1910), pp. 705 ff. In this important essay on the modernist inclination towards Classicism in the early twentieth century, Hoeber refers to Georg Simmel's essay "Das Problem des Stils"

[*Dekorative Kunst* (1908), pp. 307 ff.]. For the view of Classicism held by Behrens's own circle see Wilhelm Niemeyer, "Friedrich Gilly, Friedrich Schinkel und der Formbegriff des deutschen Klassizismus in der Baukunst," *Mitteilungen des Kunstgewerbevereins zu Hamburg* (October 1912). Niemeyer, a student of Schmarzow and friend of Wilhelm Pinder, was a poet, and also taught at the Kunstgewerbeschule in Hamburg. He was an early admirer of Behrens.

155. *Die Gartenstadt* 2 (1908), pp. 26 ff.; extracts in *Berliner Tageblatt*, evening edition, 25 March 1908.

156. "The New Factory Architecture" (in this volume).

157. See the essay by Neumeyer in this volume.

158. Walther Rathenau looked on such workers' estates with the same skepticism with which he viewed all middle-class reform movements. He was probably referring to Behrens's housing schemes and his book *Vom sparsamen Bauen* (1917) when he spoke of "the simple-minded falsehood and deceit . . . of the garden city idyll, with its concert halls, open-air theatres, and entertainments in the fresh air," and viewed such plans as "an ideal which is entirely acceptable to mediocre architects, practitioners of the applied arts, and 'Kulturpolitiker' " [*Die neue Gesellschaft* (Berlin, 1919), p. 25]. He added that, even in a socialist society,

"only a few obligatory garden cities" would be built, "which, by their very nature, would be established for a few thousand favored households, and which probably would never be completed" (ibid., p. 42). See also Schulin, pp. 93, 354. It is very likely that the article by Behrens on garden cities published in the *Berliner Tageblatt* on 25 March 1908 and in *Die Gartenstadt* 4 (1908), pp. 1 ff., 44 ff., was related to the AEG housing projects.

159. See above and G. C. Argan, *Progetto e destino* (Milan, 1965), p. 143.

160. See "Die neue Automobil-Ausstellungshalle am Kaiserdamm, Berlin, 1915," *Der Industriebau* 6 (1915), p. 381. In Catalog 1966 this was incorrectly dated 1910.

161. See *Das Kunstgewerbeblatt* 25 (1913–14), p. 157; 27 (1915–16), p. 31; *Kunst und Künstler* 12 (1914), p. 617; *Profanbau* 1 (1914), p. 490; 2 (1914), pp. 479, 560; *Dekorative Kunst* 17 (1914), p. 532.

162. See *Kunst und Künstler* 12 (1913–14), p. 246; *Deutsche Bauzeitung* 47, no. 2 (1913), pp. 839, 921 ff., 935; *Sozialistische Monatshefte* 1 (1914), p. 81; Moeller van den Bruck, *Die Tat* 5 (1913), pp. 595 ff.

163. This and the following quotations are from *Rathenau*, ed. Schulin.

164. Ernst Hauswedell, Hamburg, Auction 137, 28 May 1965, lot 816.

165. This and the following quotations are from *Rathenau*, ed. Schulin.

166. Quoted from the Fürst article.

167. *Rathenau*, ed. Schulin, p. 304.

168. Ibid., pp. 263, 283.

169. I am grateful to Hans-Jürgen Imiela for both the reference to and the photograph of Corinth's drawing (illustration 70) and to Thomas Deecke for the drawing shown as illustration 71. Both drawings were probably based on photographs such as illustration 61.

170. See Werner Hoffmann, *Walter Dexel* (Starnberg, 1972), illustration 21; Walter Dexel, Kestner-Gesellschaft Hanover, Catalog 1, 1974, illustration p. 41, no. 24.

171. This and the following quotes are from *Rathenau*, ed. Schulin.

172. Rathenau, *Impressionen*, third edition (Leipzig, 1902), p. 197.

173. *Die neue Gesellschaft* (Berlin, 1919), p. 28.

174. Nietzsche, *Die Geburt der Tragödie*, in *Werke*, ed. K. Schlechta, vol. 1, pp. 36, 40.

175. *Unschuld des Werdens*, ed. Baeumler (Leipzig, 1931), no. 520, p. 195.

176. "Fabrikneu," *Das Echo, Deutsche Export-Revue*, no. 1936 (Berlin, 1919), p. 1295.

177. Manfredo Tafuri, *Progetto e utopia. Architettura e sviluppo* capitalistico (Rome, 1973), p. 65; English edition: *Architecture and Utopia: Design and Capitalist Development* (Cambridge, Mass., 1976).

178. *Die neue Gesellschaft*, p. 60.

179. Walter Gropius, "Industrial Building" (in this volume); Gropius, "Der stilbildende Wert industrieller Bauformen," *Der Verkehr, Jahrbuch des Deutschen Werkbundes 1914* (Jena, 1914), p. 31.

180. Walter Benjamin, "Der Autor als Produzent" (1934), in *Versuche über Brecht* (Frankfurt, 1966), pp. 104 ff.; Tafuri, *Progetto e utopia*, pp. 54 ff.; Herbert Marcuse, "Industrialisierung und Kapitalismus," in *Max Weber und die Soziologie heute* ed. Stammer (Tübingen, 1964), pp. 161 ff. [also in Marcuse, *Kultur und Gesellschaft 2* (Frankfurt, 1965)]; Claus Offe, "Technik und Eindimensionalität," in *Antworten auf Herbert Marcuse*, ed. J. Habermas (Frankfurt, 1968). Offe notes "an astonishing and unsettling kinship" between Marcuse's thesis on technocracy and the "conservative institutional analysis of authors like Hans Freyer, Helmut Schelsky, and Arnold Gehlen." On the renewed discussion in the 1920s on artistic work as constructive activity, see Richard Hamann, *Kunst und Kultur der Gegenwart* (Marburg, 1922), and the essays by Gropius, Riezler, Behrens, and Haring in *Die Form*, 1 (1926).

181. *Rathenau*, ed. Schulin, p. 44.

182. Franz Blei, *Männer und Masken* (Berlin, 1930), pp. 263 ff.; Kerr, *Walther Rathenau*.

183. Letter from Hans Fürstenberg to the author, 26 August 1978.

"A Motor Must Look Like a Birthday Present"

Henning Rogge

Nobody knew better than he that his father too had occasional business failures; but no one believed this was possible, for as soon as someone has the reputation of being a Napoleon, then he also wins his lost battles. To assert himself beside his father, Arnheim had never had any other option, therefore, than to put his own intellect, politics, and public life at the service of the business. Arnheim Senior seemed pleased that the young Arnheim knew and could do so much; but when an important question had to be decided—a question that had been discussed and considered for days from all angles, technical, financial, intellectual, and economic—then his father thanked him, recommended the opposite to what had been suggested, and answered all objections with a helpless, obstinate smile. Even the directors often shook their heads at this, but sooner or later it became clear that the old man, for some reason, was right. It was almost as though an old hunter or mountain guide was made to listen to a conference of meteorologists, and yet ultimately made up his mind according to the prophecy of his rheumatism.
thoughts of the celebrated author Paul Arnheim (Walther Rathenau) on the intuition of his father Samuel (Emil Rathenau), in Robert Musil's *Der Mann ohne Eigenschaften*

When Peter Behrens was appointed artistic adviser to the Allgemeine Elektricitäts-Gesellschaft in 1907, the firm had been in existence for twenty-five years. Stimulated by the industrial development of Germany, the firm had expanded during this period at an incomparable rate until it belonged with General Electric Company, Westinghouse, and Siemens and Halske among the leading industrial monopolies in the world economy. With its numerous subsidiary companies, the AEG aspired, in the words of its founder Emil Rathenau,[1] "to carry the advances of technology to the most distant corners of the earth." On the occasion of the firm's twenty-fifth anniversary, Friedrich Dessauer commented euphorically: "The influence of this organization is ubiquitous; it brings light, forces the natural power of tumbling waterfalls into the service of mankind, drives railways across the lands, spans space with telegraphy, lights beacons, and sends the power of the machine into the mineshafts."[2] The hymn of praise to the firm swells here into a glorification of the achievements of electrical technology, whose economic importance since the middle of the nineteenth century had led to the creation of a new industry just as the introduction of the mechanical loom had done at the end of the eighteenth century and the development of steam power at the beginning of the nineteenth.

With telegraph and cable installations, the electrical industry made a vigorous economic start that led, particularly in the United States and England, to a flood of projects and new companies. Even at an early stage this expansion was characterized as "electromania." After the initial low voltage phase, the electrical industry was given a powerful stimulus in the 1880s when high-voltage technology ws opened up. Werner Siemens had laid the basis for this development with his discovery of the dynamo principle in 1866. Looking ahead, Siemens said of his dynamo that "the thing really will be very important,"[3] and explained to the Akademie der Wissenschaften that "technology has at this moment been given the means to provide electrical current of limitless power cheaply and conveniently, wherever manpower is available."[4]

Electricity could be sent from a power station located on a distant coal field to Berlin and used there for lighting, in electrochemical processes, or to drive machinery. Herein lay the great advantage of electricity over steam power, for the steam engine could not be installed where required as an individual power unit, and its power output could only be transmitted mechanically over a few meters. As the production of electrical current became economically practical and electricity became established as an easily conveyable, salable commodity, high-voltage technology blossomed into a new industry. The development of the AEG was intimately linked to the growth of this new branch of industry, which not only generated the new energy but also manufactured the equipment necessary for its production, distribution, and application: turbines, generators, cables, insulators, transformers, lamps, motors, and much more.

In Walther Rathenau's judgment, this new branch of the economy was actually created in Germany, and was based on "the farsighted planning of its initiators and on the very healthy business policies of that institution in which this new development was embodied."[5] Rathenau was referring here in particular to the AEG and to its founder, his father Emil Rathenau—the most important of the "initiators."[6] Emil Rathenau had studied

1
Werner von Siemens's first dynamo-electric machine, 1867. From *50 Jahre Berliner Elektrizitäts-Werke* (1934).

engineering and then worked in England for two years in order to gain experience. Returning to Berlin, Rathenau and his friend Julius Valentin took over the M. Webers machine factory on the Chausseestrasse, in what was then the engineering quarter, near the factories of Egells, Borsig, Wöhlert, and Schwartzkopff. Under Rathenau's direction the firm prospered for ten years until, following the trend of the Gründerzeit and in spite of Rathenau's opposition, it was turned into a public company—the Berliner Union. In the general economic crisis that came shortly after, the new company went into liquidation. Emil Rathenau had already sold off his share in the company for 3 million marks and at the time of the collapse was only employed as a salaried managing director.

Thus, in 1875, at the end of the first phase of his commercial activity, Emil Rathenau was a young man of not insubstantial private means. He set about looking for new tasks and opportunities. To Rathenau the heavy mechanical engineering industry in Berlin seemed to have lost its importance, and on his visits to the World's Fairs in Philadelphia (1876) and Paris (1878) his interest shifted more and more away from traditional engineering and toward the new technology of electricity. During this transitional period, various proposals and schemes came to nothing—for example, the idea of introducing the telephone into Germany. There were, however, concrete economic reasons that spoke against this idea: The almost handcrafted production of telephones would attract strong competition, and their manufacture and distribution was limited by foreign patents. Furthermore, Rathenau viewed low-voltage electricity as strictly for the precision mechanic, whereas he, as a qualified engineer with experience in heavy mechanical engineering, was more drawn to high-voltage technology. Here he saw "the earlier technology ennobled by electricity."[7] In the fusion of mechanical engineering and the dynamo principle, Rathenau perceived the then visionary and highly significant possibility of supplying electrical current from a centralized source by means of giant turbines and generators. This could not be achieved instantly, however, and Rathenau initially concentrated on the development of electric lighting.

2
Emil Rathenau, 1880. From
Gedenkblatt zum 20. Juni 1915.

At that time, the gas light still meant "the primitive gas tap . . . with whose flickering light were associated not the most agreeable of smells."[8] As a source of illumination the yellow flame of the gas lamp left a lot to be desired. It was also a fire risk and converted a large amount of energy into heat. The electric arc light[9] offered illumination three hundred times more intense. Even though arc lighting was only to be seen in a few main streets and squares in Paris, it earned the city the name "ville lumière," which gave Rathenau the idea to install it on the Leipziger Strasse in Berlin.[10] The populace viewed the electric arc lamp as a sensation. It was noted with astonishment that with this form of lighting one could go about as if it were daytime, that one could see the facial features of the people on the opposite pavement, that the splendid white light rendered all colors as if by daylight, and that the contrast with the gas lamps in the shops only served to make the new lighting seem even more dazzling.[11] Thus the arc light, with its radiant brightness, was able to replace gas lighting in particular situations where the greatest possible intensity of light was desired: in street lighting and in the illumination of stations, factories, and theaters. The much-admired power of arc lighting proved, however, to be a disadvantage in other areas. When critics complained that "in the dazzling light it is impossible to see properly on the street"[12] and Edison opined that "the light was too bright and too big,"[13] it became clear that arc lamps were too intense for domestic use. Thus, in 1880 the engineer Hippolyt Fontaine could still insist: "For private dwellings, gas light offers the most pleasant, most comfortable and cheapest form of illumination. Perhaps the electric light will establish itself here and there in single large rooms or in especially luxuriously appointed houses, but these will be such rare exceptions, that it seems unnecessary to take them into consideration. . . . The electric light can never threaten the gas light, the oil lamp, or the candle."[14]

At the 1881 Exposition internationale d'Electricité in Paris, Thomas Alva Edison's incandescent lighting system was presented. That an electrical equivalent to the gas light had been developed for those uses the arc lamp could not cover was made clear in a *Le Temps* review which noted that Edison had forced the electric light to moderate its brilliance and to adopt the form, the manner, and even the color of the modest gas flame, and had thus made it suitable for the home.[15] The demonstration of the incandescent lamp led Werner Siemens to speculate that "the incandescent lights will soon knock everything else dead, and will open up another large domain in the use of electricity."[16] In a specific reference to the competition with the gas light, Siemens said that "at one stroke, the incandescent lamp can bring about an almost infinite expansion in electric lighting, which will result in the ousting of gas by electricity."[17]

That this prediction came true was due in no small measure to Emil Rathenau and Werner Siemens. The two men responded differently to the challenge of the new technology. Siemens, the 65-year-old inventor and head of the largest electrical firm in Germany, was among the most prominent visitors to the exhibition. At the time, he saw transportation as the most important potential area for the use of electricity and took a rather reserved and skeptical view of the new development in lighting.[18] Nevertheless, he immediately started his own tests, and was confident that his own researches would bring even greater success.[19] The reaction of Emil Rathenau, then 43, was quite different. Still looking for a new field of activity, Rathenau saw in the Edison lighting system a chance to compete successfully with the established electrical firms. He later recalled,

I was thrilled by the discovery made by the celebrated recluse of Menlo Park. . . . Every single detail in Edison's system was so brilliantly thought out and so skillfully worked through that one felt that it had been tested for decades in countless cities. Neither the sockets, the switches, the fuses and the lamp holders, nor anything else relating to the installation were lacking, and the generating of the current, together with its regulation and transmission via junctions, house connections, electrometers, and so on, had been perfectly developed with amazing understanding and incomparable genius.[20]

As well as being enthusiastic over the new technology, Rathenau also recognized the importance of planning each essential component as part of an integrated system that would be suitable for large-scale production.

The direct practical applicability of the new technology and the chance to create a market for it may have been the ultimate factors in Emil Rathenau's decision to commit himself to this new field. He was, furthermore, more convinced than almost anybody else of the future importance of incandescent lighting. Edison had made over the rights to his invention to a limited company, whose Paris branch was responsible for issuing manufacturing licenses on the European continent.[21] In order to obtain these rights, Rathenau looked for interested parties in German banking circles. For many reasons, it was not easy at that time to raise money for ventures involving electricity. The funding of new industries still did not belong to the openly accepted areas of interest for serious bankers. The bankers acquired great prestige by negotiating such things as government credits, and although they made a large amount of money out of railway construction, it was still felt that "financial involvement in iron, steel, and coal" was "speculation in the wildest sense of the word" and "not really worthy of a solid banker."[22] To this professional reticence was added a particular skepticism about electrical concerns, which was a consequence of bad experiences with the shares of cable and telegraph companies during the Gründerzeit. Rathenau's plan to add one more firm to all the others that were active in this industry, and especially one that would impinge in Berlin on Siemens's sphere of influence, must have seemed unpromising and risky to the bankers. It is not surprising, therefore, that Carl Fürstenberg, who was then working for S. Bleichröder and was later to come into close contact with the AEG through the Berliner Handels-Gesellschaft,

3
Edison's room at Exposition internationale d'Electricite, Paris, 1881. From *50 Jahre BEW* (1934).

4
Emil Rathenau and Thomas Edison (right) in the Moabit power station, Berlin, 25 September 1911. From *50 Jahre BEW* (1934).

should have recalled that for many years Emil Rathenau was thought by the majority of Berlin bankers to be "a downright fantasist."[23] In spite of all these difficulties Rathenau managed to find backers for his project, thanks largely to the support of Ludwig von Kaufmann, a partner in the banking firm of Jacob Landau. On 22 April 1882, half a year after the Paris exhibition, Rathenau's efforts led to the founding of a financial consortium made up of the Landau banking house, the Nationalbank für Deutschland, and the brothers Sulzbach. Contracts were negotiated with the Compagnie Continentale Edison,[24] and on 15 July 1882 a "Gelegenheits-Gesellschaft" was formed. That such a mutual research company should have been established with the relatively low starting capital of 225,000 marks was proof of the circumspection with which Rathenau's plan was viewed. The purpose of the company was to find out what prospects Rathenau had of introducing Edison incandescent lighting into Germany. As the company's business manager, Rathenau established his office at number 40 Unter den Linden.

In order to prove that a viable industrial and finance company could be built on the new lighting system, Emil Rathenau had begun to seek out people who were interested in the Edison system even before the contracts were signed. As the first practical trials were to be given the character of demonstration installations, Rathenau sought to test the lighting in many different situations. He tried above all to find customers who were respected as leading representatives of their particular branch of business. His first customers were the printing shop of the *Berliner Börsen Courier* and the Böhmische Brauhaus, both among the largest and most prestigious establishments in their fields. The particular characteristics of the new lighting system were appropriate to the special demands of the two companies; the spectral composition of the light was important in the printing trade, and low heat was desirable in brewing. In this way, the system gained additional valuable publicity from the testimonies of the two firms.

The installation of the new lighting in the Bankhaus Landau was even more important, for it led to a contract to design and fit a joint lighting system for the Union-Club on the Schadowstrasse and the club Ressource von 1794 on the Dorotheenstrasse. Both of these exclusive clubs were patronized by leading Berlin businessmen, and this contract was of no little significance to Rathenau's plans to introduce his new lighting in a prestigious manner. The company then gained wider publicity with a trial street-lighting scheme on the Wilhelmstrasse, and, above all, at the Internationale Elektrizitäts-Ausstellung in the Glaspalast in Munich, which had been organized by Oskar von Miller on the model of the Paris exhibition.[25] At this exhibition, which was opened on the night of 16 September 1882 in a blaze of illumination, the new company's demonstration of incandescent lighting excited such interest that it must then have become clear to the backers that the introduction of the Edison equipment would, with Rathenau's determination, be profitable.

After these promising trials, the research company was converted into a limited company, which was officially registered on 19 April 1883 as the Deutsche Edison Gesellschaft für angewandte Elektricität (DEG). The entire share capital, which by this time was 5 million marks, was taken up by the founders themselves.[26] The DEG's aim was the industrial exploitation of the Edison patents for the transmission of light and power. In exchange for the patent rights, the company paid high royalty fees on every bulb and lighting accessory sold.[27] The rights to the patent were further limited by an agreement with Siemens and Halske that delimitated the interests of the two firms in order to avoid competition. Emil Rathenau was the chairman, Oskar von Miller (who came slightly later) was the managing director, Felix Deutsch was the Prokurist (executive secretary), and Rudolf Sulzbach and Ludwig von Kaufmann were respectively the chairman and the vice-chairman of the supervisory board. The DEG's office, originally occupied by one bookkeeper and one typewriter, was set up at 96 Leipziger Strasse, and the manufacture of light bulbs began at the factory on the Schlegelstrasse at the beginning of 1884.[28]

After the contractual obligations to the Edison companies had been terminated and the arrangement with Siemens and Halske modified, the firm reconstituted itself at a general meeting on 23 May 1887 and adopted the name Allgemeine Elektricitäts-Gesellschaft.[29] In this way, the progress from a research company formed to assess market prospects to a company manufacturing lighting components under license was quickly followed by the establishment of a large business complex. In keeping with its name [Allgemeine means general], the AEG's production program embraced every aspect of the electrical industry, and it even extended into other, often unrelated fields.

Share capital, dividends, and number of employees all increased rapidly. By 1907–08 the starting capital of 5 million marks had multiplied to 100 million (plus 37 million in debentures), and by 1913–14 this figure had risen to 155 million (with 108 million in debentures). The dividend rose from 4 percent in 1883 to 13 percent in 1907–08. The total number of employees rose from 6 in 1883 to 32,035 in 1907–08 to 70,162 in 1911–12.

By preventing direct competition, buying stock in established companies, and setting up subsidiaries, banks, and holding companies,[30] the AEG developed into a concern that, at the end of the period of concentrated expansion in the German electrical industry, had, together with Siemens and Halske-Schuckert, taken a leading position. In 1903, by arrangement with the American General Electric Company, the world market was divided up among the leading firms.[31] Under this agreement, the AEG's sphere of influence took in Germany, Austro-Hungary, Russia, Finland, Holland, Belgium, Sweden, Norway, Denmark, Switzerland, Turkey, the Balkan states, and parts of South America.

5
Generators under construction in the
AEG large-machine factory, 1899.
AEG photo.

6
AEG products being dispatched to
South America on NAG truck, 1907.
AEG photo.

It is not possible here to give a comprehensive account, even in the form of a short survey, of the AEG's "almost magical growth" (Felix Deutsch), which, until his death on 20 July 1915, was essentially the life's work of Emil Rathenau. Instead, I shall focus on the characteristics of the AEG's business policy that define the context of Peter Behrens's appointment to the firm.[32]

As already explained, the development of the AEG had been based on a new technology whose potential had been quickly and fully recognized by Emil Rathenau. This was made clear in the brochure "Das Edison-Licht," which Rathenau brought out in 1882 as the company's first technical publication and which served as a vehicle for propagating the new technology. In the first part of the brochure the merits of Edison lighting were described. It was then asserted that "the Edison light is competing successfully everywhere against gas lighting." Rathenau forecast that, in the future, electricity would serve the lighting needs of many businesses "as its exclusive domain." In a cautious but firm stand against the mighty gas companies, Rathenau also correctly forecast that the pattern of use between gas and electricity would change and then be strictly demarcated. "The era of electric light and the decline of gas lighting" would then, he said, be "an accomplished fact." He added that "at that moment at which gas ceases to exist as a means of illumination, it will secure the enormous, competition-free field of heating . . . just as soon as the gas experts turn their backs once and for all on the use of gas for lighting." The section entitled "The Transmission of Mechanical Energy for Domestic Use" pointed farther into the future; what had until then only been tried by Edison in his own factory should be made generally accessible. Electricity would be "transmitted by wire from the steam-driven generator to the location of the consumer's dynamo machine." "According to need," electric current would "bring light or power, and at the same time turn on lamps in houses and machines in factories." High-voltage technology would bring the production and distribution of electric current from a network of power stations.

At the time of writing, this was a prognosis for the future whose realization seemed to be distant or uncertain; however, it clearly shows that Emil Rathenau, in contrast to the other experts, understood the full importance of the new technology at an early stage. Although this insight might be seen as a precondition of Rathenau's success, it is important to remember that the translation of this vision into reality was not merely a process of industrialization but one of creating a new branch of the economy on the basis of the new technology. This difference was stressed by Walther Rathenau, the founder's son and a member of the AEG board until 1902,[33] when he wrote,

The older industries were concerned with the manufacture of single products according to the scale of the demand created by the consumer. . . . The form of industry was the continuation of the old handwork with division of labor, large-scale fabrication, and the use of mechanical power. The creation of an applied electrical technology meant the establishment of a new economic field and the transformation of many aspects of modern life. This transformation was not initiated by the consumer, but was organized by the manufacturer, and had, to a certain degree, to be forced.[34]

This corresponded to the attitude shared by both Emil Rathenau and Felix Deutsch and expressed in the business policy of the AEG. The firm did not limit itself to production, assembly, and delivery, but also acted as an entrepreneur. In order to win acceptance for something new, the AEG had to compete against existing industries and technologies. Electric light had to compete against gas lighting, the power station against the gas works, electric railways against steam trains and horse-drawn trams, and the centralized power supply against the independent power source. As no similar development had occurred previously, the practicability of the new technology had to be proved. This took an immense expenditure of capital, for, as an innovating competitor, the AEG had to create "parallel operations, which necessitated complicated equipment, with one stroke."[35]

Emil Rathenau's business policy can be conveniently illustrated by comparing it with that of the other great German electrical tycoon, Werner Siemens. As a scientist and engineer Siemens primarily concerned himself with the development of the new technology, and as a manufacturer he tended to limit his activity to supplying the existing demand for technical products. This cautiousness showed itself in his dismissal of Rathenau's idea of illuminating the Leipziger Strasse with Siemens arc lamps as technically premature. The same cautiousness also lay behind the extreme lack of interest with which he viewed the Internationale Elektrizitäts-Ausstellung in Munich (although Siemens's judgment that this exhibition was simply another contribution to the epidemic of the age[36] is understandable when one realizes that this was the fifth such exhibition in barely three years). As the head of a family firm, Siemens discounted this exhibition in particular and similar exhibitions in general as "publicity exercises to raise the share price of the participating companies."[37] Such a reserved attitude was entirely alien to Rathenau, and therein lay his chance to build up a business in the area previously dominated by the old, established firm of Siemens. Siemens and the AEG initially strove to accommodate each other's interests, but it was inevitable that competition would arise as the firms developed.

Emil Rathenau's progressive attitude toward technology and business had a sound base. After his engineering studies, he had gained a thorough knowledge of high-quality, modern mechanical engineering in England, which was then universally recognized as the leader in this field. He applied these skills to his own production on taking over the Webers machine factory, where he was able to gather more experience in the application of modern techniques. In contrast to traditional engineering practice, he appreciated how a manufacturer could couple technical development to commercial objectives. A good example of this was his work on a standard steam engine. Rather than follow the usual procedure, whereby the customer commissioned an engineer to work out the exact amount of power needed for a particular purpose and then had an engine built to the specifications, Rathenau developed an engine that was not designed to match any single set of specifications but to match the potential needs of a certain group of customers. The emphasis in business policy thus shifted from fulfilling commissions to offering standard products.

Standardizing the engines rendered all the work previously involved in the calculation, design, and installation of each unit unnecessary. Standardization also facilitated the production, for the need to build engines to constantly differing specifications and for different tasks had precluded the replacement of hand labor by machine production. With standard designs, however, the rational use of automatic machines was made possible. As the engines could be offered at a lower price, the customers adjusted their demands to match one of the standard types, and the manufacturer gained an advantage over his competitors. Rathenau had come across these production techniques during his travels in the United States, where they had been developed to increase competitiveness and in response to high wage demands. "The study of the American methods," he recalled, "had deepened my understanding of modern manufacturing processes and served as a pointer to the direction which I was to pursue."[38] He also realized the significance of these techniques in the context of the emerging social-democratic movement in the working population.[39]

Mass production in the old small-motor
factory, ca. 1900. AEG photo.

Rathenau was not the first manufacturer in Berlin to start producing goods on the American model.[40] In his view, however, the others had not applied the method thoroughly enough.[41] Rathenau followed the American model deliberately and systematically, with a far-reaching program of standardization, by the "pursuit of the principle that limited the number and choice of products through the division of labor," and by the "replacement of physical labor by automatic machines."[42] The revolutionizing of the earlier methods of production by the new machines, which he called "tools of the future," also gave Rathenau the opportunity to demonstrate the superiority of electricity in the manufacturing field:

It is a difficult task to make it clear to the public just how willing a handmaiden electricity is, and how few people understand about making use of the services of electricity. Think of the work that is still performed in the city of brains [Berlin] using expensive sources of energy—work that could be done better and more cheaply by electricity! A careful look into the large factories of the German capital would show those responsible for them what sums of money are being thrown out of the window year in and year out. I would perhaps be accused of exaggeration if I quoted figures, or if I claimed that, with help of electricity, jobs that previously earned hardly anything for either employer or worker and had been forced out of the city can not only be done today without any of the physical labor that was formerly involved but can also yield a satisfactory profit for both parties. How is this wonder to be explained? One electric horsepower replaces eight diligent workers, costs less than one-twentieth of the cost of employing these eight, and produces the power day and night, with changing shifts of machine tenders. We are afraid of the glut of goods being produced at low cost in the Far East, yet with the right organization of labor we could manufacture the goods just as cheaply as in these countries. In the [18]40s, simpleminded men were foolish enough to burn down factories and destroy machine tools because they supposedly made workers redundant. One realizes today, however, that a reduction in the cost of production methods and of the goods produced leads to a rapid and progressive increase in the demand, which then provides the opportunity to employ more workers.[43]

It is not possible here to go into the many complex aspects of this illuminating text. Instead, it will suffice to emphasize that, at an early date and with an eye on the world market, the AEG introduced exactly worked out production methods modeled on the Taylor System, and constantly strove to perfect them. This process began in 1897, when the small-motor factory was equipped with special machine tools, each of which could be tended by one unskilled worker, whose productivity was thus increased threefold. These machines were replaced between 1904 and 1908 by automatic machines, several of which could be looked after by one person. As a result, the productivity of the individual worker rose once again by the same factor of 3, and this tendency was maintained in subsequent years with a slower progression. With this increased productivity came the lower wages paid to unskilled workers, or, when possible, the even lower rate paid to women. Although the higher investment capital for the new machines had to be set against this, it was noted at the time that "the savings were quite considerable."[44] The costs in the AEG's workshops were further reduced by replacing at an early stage the usual system of power transmission with individual power units. This brought benefits in the construction of new factories, in that workshops no longer had to be planned with regard to the transmission machinery—the traditional maze of axles, belts, and pulleys. This made it possible to use a lighter and cheaper construction and, for the first time, to create adequately lit, uninterrupted working areas. As the individual power units ran only when they were needed, great savings in basic operating costs were achieved.

8
Women winding coils, 1906.
AEG photo.

The development and application of rational methods of production was accompanied by a spatial organization of the workshops and installations which was also based on the American model and was worked out to the smallest detail.[45] To this was added division of labor, which was applied with Prussian vigor at all levels of the firm.[46] All this corresponded to the principles on which Emil Rathenau, Paul Jordan,[47] and the directors of the various factories proceeded with the expansion of the manufacturing plant. In the early period, additional buildings were rented; the time eventually came, however, when in spite of nonstop operation through the introduction of day and night shifts an expansion of the plant could no longer be avoided. Successive extensions were then added until the available land was completely built up. Only when the desired increase in production capacity could no longer be achieved in this way was a new site acquired, on which the process was then repeated. In addition, whole manufacturing processes were frequently transferred from one factory to another in order to match an optimal utilization of the plant to the prevailing market demand. The factories were thus in a state of constant change and expansion. Under this carefully restrained approach, which aimed at the highest possible profitability, the demands on production made by the orders in hand were generally greater than the capacity of the workshops. This cautiousness was characteristic of the firm even in periods of high prosperity, and it was only after the turn of the century that plans were drawn up for future expansion.

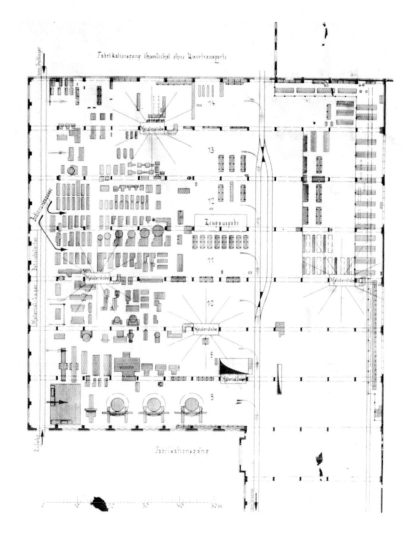

9
Plan of installations in the large-machine factory, 1900. Courtesy of AEG.

In contrast to its policy of extreme economy in the realm of production, the firm spent freely on product development and marketing. The importance of technical development had already been shown by the Deutsche Edison Gesellschaft, whose first factory on the Schlegelstrasse contained a fully equipped laboratory. As a result of the development work done in this laboratory, the general opinion of the DEG's lamps was that they were qualitatively superior, even to the original Edison products. Walther Rathenau said that the qualitative and technological lead that was a critical factor in the firm's development should be "closely bound over decades to the firm's enterprises, so that as the foreign competitors became stronger, they were still always left in a position of dependence."[48] This matched the firm's trading policy of not limiting itself to the production of goods for an existing market, which Walther Rathenau called "simply carrying goods to the market", but which rather aimed to open up new areas and "to suggest the need, and in many cases force it to a certain degree on the customer."[49] This was done without any feeling of bad conscience, as it was not seen as the suggestion to the public of absurd needs with a view to making a profit, but was programmatically defined and understood as a means of achieving civilizing progress. In this definition, electricity was cast in the role of a promoter of modern culture.[50] When inspired by national pride, a trading policy such as this would, said its promoters, help Germany achieve a leading position among the industrial nations of the world.[51]

In its model form, the sales strategy was given an exemplary trial by the research company and steadily developed in the course of the expansion of the DEG and the AEG. In its early years, the firm's publicity was essentially concerned with proclaiming the potential of high-voltage technology against the claims of other, already established systems. As a result of the firm's success in doing this, the subsequent publicity material not only had to urge the use of electricity, but also had to encourage the customers to extend their existing installations, or to exchange them for ones that were technically more advanced.

In his essay *Aufgaben der Elektrizitäts-Industrie* (Tasks of the Electrical Industry), Emil Rathenau dealt with commercial policy. He began: "After the initial need for electrical material . . . has been more or less covered, the time approaches when the worn out or old goods should be replaced by improved and more modern models."[52] The sales strategy had to be directed toward those areas in which the use of electricity was most widespread, such as lighting and, in particular, arc lighting. Although arc lamps were only one item among the thousands in the AEG catalog, the competition between the eighty or so firms producing them was extraordinarily intense. The difficult market position of the arc lamps—squeezed between gas and incandescent lighting—had led to constant technical improvements and resulting changes in form. The outcome was a multitude of models that were virtually indistinguishable from each other. Here, as with other products, an improved outward appearance, when coupled with technical quality, would certainly influence the decisions of the customers. As Paul Jordan, the director responsible for the lighting factory, lucidly put it: "Don't believe that even an engineer takes an engine apart for inspection before buying it. Even as an expert, he also buys according to the external impression. A motor must look like a birthday present."[53]

10
Preparations for lecture on high-
voltage technology at Hotel
Esplanade, 20 March 1913. AEG
photo.

In addition to the argument in favor of good design for its own sake, there was publicity value in linking the name of a well-known artist to one's products. In contrast to the usual bland brochures and instruction manuals, the AEG presented its arc lamps in a verbally and visually lavish style (illustrations G40 ff.), and connected them with name and title of the designer: "new arc-lamp fittings designed by Professor Peter Behrens"; "artistically formed to the design of Professor Peter Behrens."[54] Herein also lay another weapon in the fight to conquer the stubborn prejudice against industrially mass-produced goods. By improving quality and seeking in publications and lectures[55] to establish quality and precision as characteristics of machine production, the manufacturers tried to counter the lingering reputation German industry had gained in the 1870s for producing cheap and nasty trash. In a similar spirit, they also took measures to counter the aesthetic reservations of the bourgeoisie, in whose eyes the previous offerings of industry had either been the "undesigned" factory model or the pretentiously decorated luxury model stamped out of tin. The former was rejected as unsuitable, the latter condemned as a sham. Through the designs of a notable artist, the mass-produced goods of industry were to be freed from this aura of disrepute and made presentable.

The recognition of the effect of the outward appearance of products must logically have led to the conclusion that the reputation of the manufacturing firm and the impression given by the factory were even more important. In 1909, Wolf Dohrn said of the AEG that "they have understood best how to transfer the findings of German science, and in particular of electrical technology, into economic practice." It followed from this that it was "certainly a kindred task to utilize the artistic talents of our age in our economic life."[56] The AEG's "worthy" efforts to bring the design of its products and later of its entire business image "into harmony with the artistic demands of the modern age"[57] nourished among "the enlightened bourgeoisie of the period" the hopes, which had "arisen with the industrial boom," that "the entrepreneurs and the businessmen might gain a leading role in society and might succeed the court and aristocracy as arbiters in matters of taste and artistic policy to the general public."[58] The expression of these hopes attracted considerable public attention to the firm. Some typical comments follow.

In Berlin it will soon be better, thanks to the AEG! Saintly Behrens, have mercy upon us! (Joseph August Lux, 1908)

The AEG has understood that the exclusion of creative genius from industrial production has led to a lingering illness in our age, and that its reinstatement is an act of cultural necessity. (Karl Ernst Osthaus, 1910)

We have here a sign that the bourgeois commercial spirit, which previously was only concerned with an increase in material value, is beginning to idealize, that at last it is giving the utilitarian object an ethical quality . . . [and] thinking about its responsibility to beauty. (Karl Scheffler, 1908)

The AEG can lay claim to be the first in Germany to have demonstrated in an exemplary manner such a collaboration between engineer and artist, and it is certainly not chance that it was the AEG in particular that has brought such success to this experiment. (Wolf Dohrn, 1909)

That which the most progressive spirits hardly dared hope for ten years ago, and which the Deutscher Werkbund has recently been striving for with great energy and gradually increasing success, has been accomplished by the AEG with one bold decision: The AEG has given back to the world its right to art in the industrial process. (Karl Ernst Osthaus, 1910)

The rival firms will probably pay very close attention to this decision of the AEG, and sooner or later will certainly be forced into competition with artistic endeavors like these, which are free from all Jugendstil aberrations. (Karl Scheffler, 1908)

Aided by reactions like these, the AEG gained prestige not only in the sphere of business, but also in the cultural sphere.

The interest and approval the AEG experiment excited in informed circles can be judged by the attentive interest with which it was followed and reported on, and which was extended to each successive phase of Behrens's activity. These reports published preliminary announcements of the newly designed products and factory buildings and then presented the finished objects. The praise heaped on the experiments even extended to the "idealization" of the "bourgeois commercial spirit," and implied the hope that the AEG model would have an exemplary influence on future developments. Osthaus, Scheffler, Dohrn, and other critics created the conditions under which it was possible for Behrens's experiment to go beyond the world of business and to reach a cultural plane that was above the arguments and factiousness of economic, technical, and formal interests.

For a short period in the history of the expansion of the electrical industry, the AEG's insight into the supremacy of cultural values led to the creation of the Industriekultur that had motivated Behrens's work for the firm. This suggests a new version of "Aus Erfahrung Gut" (good from experience), the popular variant on the firm's initials: "Aus Einsicht Gut" (good from insight).

11
Peter Behrens in the study of his house in Neu-Babelsberg. Photo by W. Titzenthaler, first published in *Die Dame* in 1914.

The range and scope of Behrens's activity for the AEG in Berlin can be shown by citing a series of almost randomly chosen examples of his work. He designed an exhibition (illustration P1) from the pavilion right down to the invitation card. This work included brochures and posters for the electrical appliances exhibited (illustrations G30 ff.) and the appliances themselves, such as a dental drill (illustration P86), a humidifier (illustrations P77 ff.), and the casings for a whole series of arc lamps and electric fans (illustrations P16 ff. and P38 ff.). He also designed the factories in which these things were manufactured—for example, the highly complex factory for transformers, resistors, and high-voltage equipment (illustrations A54 ff.) and the monumental small-motor factory (illustrations A83 ff.). He was responsible for the planning of the firm's extensive housing estates (illustration A191) and for the design of two boathouses (illustrations A178 ff.), and he laid out a dignified roof garden above the factories at Humboldthain illustrations A106 ff.). Behrens's designs for the AEG are too numerous to itemize here. They extended from simple box labels (illustration G73) to a large-scale industrial town, and can be found in every conceivable area of the firm's activity. With the exception of the electrical appliances, which as a result of technical development and the pressure of consumerism have become collector's items, many of the relatively large number of works that have survived are still serving their original purposes today. This is true of the advertising graphics and, in spite of the war, of the factories. The factories, which at the time of building were among the most advanced anywhere, are still fully operational seventy years on. Behrens's typefaces are still used in the firm's signet, and set a standard against which the firm's present-day graphic material finds it hard to compete.[59]

Because the turbine hall has gained near-mythical status, any questions about the interests that led to this encounter of artist and industry or about which of the original intentions were ultimately realized tend to be answered with reference to this one example. In this way, the fame of the turbine hall has distracted attention from the enormous diversity and number of designs Behrens produced in the course of his association with the AEG. As Nikolaus Pevsner has said, however, "It seems very possible indeed that art history will accord just as much value to these smaller objects as to [Behrens's] major buildings." These less grand designs are important precisely because they were not the result of particular projects or special commissions, but because they were all under Behrens's purview as Künstlerischer Beirat (artistic adviser), responsible for all questions concerning visual and artistic matters.

Behrens was counted among that group of artists which in Germany, as in other European countries, had tried since the turn of the century, "in the midst of the witches' sabbath of sentimental formlessness and squiggle-soaked Jugendstil,"[60] to reform and ennoble all aspects of daily life according to artistic precepts. The programmatic aim of these artists was to promote a higher standard of taste and "Lebenskultur" through art education.

Behrens's first contacts with the AEG, when he was the director of the Kunstgewerbeschule in Düsseldorf, were quite unremarkable and did not attract any comment in the press. The AEG had already employed other designers on particular projects: Otto Eckmann, for example, had created all the graphic and publicity material for the 1900 Paris World's Fair, Alfred Messel had designed the administration building on the Friedrich-Karl-Ufer, and Franz Schwechten had designed the appliance factory on the Ackerstrasse and the main gate to the machine factory on the Brunnenstrasse.

Behrens's first work for the AEG was not concerned with the firm's architecture or products, but simply with graphic designs, which he executed as one-off commissions. One of the first of these was for the firm's magazine *Mitteilungen der Berliner Elektricitaets-Werke*, which between 1907 and 1909 carried Behrens's very logical, almost didactic cover designs, incorporating his own monogram (illustrations G1 ff.). Further examples from this early period are a richly illustrated, leather-bound certificate to mark the award of the Grashof Medal to Emil Rathenau (illustrations G23–G25) and a new title banner for the *AEG-Zeitung* in Behrens's own typeface (illustration G7). Also at an early date, Behrens arranged an exhibition of the firm's products at the Allgemeine Ausstellung von Erfindungen der Klein-Industrie (held in Berlin in the summer of 1907) in a pavilion that carried the new, Behrens-designed trademark (illustration A9).

Behrens was then brought in to design electrical appliances. It was announced in the June 1907 edition of the magazine *Werkkunst* that the AEG in Berlin had "commissioned Peter Behrens in Düsseldorf to design artistic forms for arc lamps and all their accessories."[61] Whereas the earlier designs had all been for single, nonindustrial, handcrafted objects, the work on the arc lamps meant the designing of the external form of a mass-produced object. The announcement only two months later that Behrens had "accepted an appointment in Berlin as artistic adviser to the AEG"[62] marked an extension of the original, restricted commission. His activity was now not limited to the arc lamps alone, but extended to include the design of all of the firm's products that were "in the broadest sense of the word related to the plastic arts." These included, as the announcement went on to say, "not only lighting fixtures, but also switch consoles, electric ovens, fans, and many other things."[63] Behrens resigned his post in Düsseldorf and moved to Berlin in the autumn of 1908.[64] His appointment to the AEG provided an almost model case for the aspirations of the Deutscher Werkbund, which was established two months later with both Behrens and the AEG as founding members. For the first time on such a scale, an attempt was made to "join aesthetic and economic needs"[65] with the aim of "bringing together for the common good the spirit of business, which is rooted in a good turnover, and the ethical values of the artist, which lay stress on quality and form."[66]

Just how the aesthetic maxims of the artist and his didactic, social, and economic ideas were to be aligned with the interests of industry emerged from the theoretical statements on the relationship between art and technology that Behrens frequently made in his lectures and publications.[67] In his essay on the aesthetics of the factories, Behrens looked back to his early work for the firm: "My work began with the design of an arc lamp. To have the chance to do such work was remarkable at that time, for who should determine the external form of technical products and draw up the designs for them was still an open question. Should it be left to the engineer or should an artist be involved?"[68] It had been the practice of industry until then to leave the external design of an appliance or machine to the engineer who had developed it, and only in a few exceptional cases were artists entrusted with this task.[69] In general, however, "artistic creation and engineering performance" were seen as "very dissimilar, if not exactly conflicting activities."[70] The choice and sequence of the concepts in this quotation—art and creation against work and performance—was a reflection of the current situation—a situation marked, said Behrens, by "the contradictory confusion of romantically inclined design on one side and the satisfaction of functional demands on the other." The latter, he said, "corresponds to today's real needs, but takes no account of aesthetic form."[71] The Kunstindustrie, as the commercial sector of the applied arts was called, occupied itself with the manufacture of luxurious consumer goods for wealthy and artistically informed private customers. Industrially made goods either were conceived as luxury models (which imitated handcraftsmanship, simulated genuine materials, adapted historical models, and were aimed at the same wealthy group as the products of the Kunstindustrie) or were relegated to the status of so-called Ingenieurform or factory goods (which were strictly utilitarian in design and without any formal or decorative pretensions).

It was in this context of a strict division between applied art and industrial production that Behrens's first designs appeared. The range of arc lamps for factory lighting, which had been on the firm's sales lists since 1905, were now brought out with redesigned casings and in new colors (illustrations P16 ff.). For the economy arc lamp, also already in production, Behrens designed a new armature that differed considerably from the original model (illustrations P24 ff.). The presentation of these lamps in a Behrens-designed brochure is most instructive on his new role as an industrial designer. As mentioned already, the brochures were entitled "New Arc-Lamp Fittings Designed by Professor Peter Behrens," and, most unusually for the period, they carried splendid color illustrations. In these brochures, the function of the armature was explained, the firm's services to culture extolled, and Behrens's contribution highlighted:

The lanterns of arc lamps have the technical function of protecting the conductors against dust and moisture; this is especially important outdoors, where the lamps would otherwise be exposed to the wind and weather. It is true that a simple, weatherproof sheet-metal tube would suffice for this purpose.

But the lantern also has an aesthetic function: It should hide the naked rods from the eyes of the viewer and cover them with a form which should be as attractive as possible. From an aesthetic point of view, the sight of a plain tube is hardly an improvement. For this reason, attempts have always been made to render the design of the lantern more attractive by adding moldings and bulges to the simple, cylindrical form. Such primitive decoration did not always satisfy the public taste, however, and for rooms that demanded a decoratively patterned light fitting the "ornamented armature" was created by cladding the original lantern tube with rich foliate patterns.

In recent years, interest in the applied arts has reawakened in Germany. Today we no longer see artistic beauty in the imitation of the style of a past epoch. Artistic form should rather illustrate the purpose of the object as clearly as possible, using expressive means that correspond to the characteristics of the given material. How unnatural and overloaded the garland of leaves on the lantern of the old style of arc lamp appears to today's better-educated eye, how inept are the efforts to reproduce the graceful forms of delicate leaves in pressed metal.

It is a worthy task to initiate a change in this area. The AEG has understood how to bring the design of the arc lamp into harmony with the artistic demands of the modern age, and commissioned Professor Peter Behrens to produce the necessary designs.

The accompanying illustration [P24 in this volume] provides an example of the way in which Professor Behrens has accomplished this task. With simple lines he has achieved an artistic effect appropriate both to the function of the lantern and to the characteristics of the material.

The coloring of the new lanterns is also original. Proceeding from the conviction that black lacquered lamps look austere to the point of ugliness in modern, artistically coordinated rooms, Behrens looked for a more friendly color that would be subtle enough to fit into any surroundings. He found this in a simple green. A more lively tone is lent by the bronze trim and by the studs in the same material, which, against the dark ground, call to mind the effect of lighter-colored inlays.[72]

On grounds of both content and style, it may be assumed that this text was written by Behrens himself. In contrast to the visual advertising material, which was full of technical details, this brochure dealt almost exclusively with design considerations. It showed how Behrens, in his search for the appropriate form, tried to satisfy the conditions imposed upon him, and it indicated what he saw as the object of his design work. The form could not be considered here (as it had been in his earlier work) as a one-off piece of studio design for a particular ambiance, or allowed to develop as the "free creation of an unfettered creative impulse."[73] Rather, it was tied to the requirements of production engineering and to the economic conditions imposed by the manufacturer and the market. These conditions considerably limited the scope for design variations. Behrens was concerned here with utilitarian objects, which, as he acknowledged, "should principally serve a practical purpose rather than beautify the surroundings."[74] As the design was intended for anonymous buyers, it could not be related to the chosen style of one particular environment, but had to be "matched to the most diverse architectural styles all at the same time."[75]

There were also technical and economic restraints. The mechanisms of the various appliances made it imperative that "the internal construction be respected." In the case of the arc lamp this meant the complicated assembly of regulating mechanism, resistor, tubes to hold the carbon electrodes, and so on, combined with the demand that the design should facilitate the regular changing of the carbon rods by hand. Large-scale manufacture also demanded economy in materials and simplification of the production process from raw material to finished product,[76] for every minute saved in the manufacture of each article was ultimately of great importance because of the sheer volume involved.

As the basis of mass production, the fabrication by more or less automatic machines of one particular component was enormously expensive in relation to the subsequent assembly work. This led to a desire to use standardized parts common to various models.[77] Such standardization kept prices down, made it possible to offer a wide range of different articles by assembling the components in different combinations, and also meant easier storage and provision of spare parts.[78] Right down to the consideration that savings could be made on space, packaging, transport, and breakage by using the already known principle of stackable goods,[79] a whole set of conditions arose that fundamentally distinguished Behrens's work for the AEG from the designs of the handcraftsmen. Design through creative fantasy—which until then could basically be realized in the satisfaction of one's own aesthetic needs—became, as Pevsner observed, a service. The artist as industrial designer was given the task and the new, socially oriented responsibility of mediating between economics and aesthetics, between art and industry.

The understanding that Behrens brought to this task can be seen in the statement on his recent appointment which he published in the *Berliner Tageblatt* in August 1907.[80] This article was based on the assumption that in the realm of the arts, too, the future would belong to industrial means of production. As Behrens put it, the spirit of the time was "pushing in the direction of Industriekunst." Inspired by the dazzling successes of technology, Behrens saw here the potential ability to translate "artistic and creative work into material assets."

To avoid the isolation of the arts in a society that had recently undergone great structural changes in the course of industrialization, Behrens felt that artistic work should establish a direct connection with industry. This would then endow the mass products of industry with the status that, in the eyes of the bourgeoisie, had previously been reserved for the fine arts. Behrens spoke of his hopes for "the initiation of a general cultural milieu in which it would be possible not only to serve those who were artistically sensitive but also to bring art and propriety to the most distant strata of the population." To Behrens, the aim of making "the benefits of creative work accessible to wider circles"[81] meant explaining to the customers, who were "for the most part indifferent,"[82] that "they should consider these mass products to be just as dignified and attractive as the very best goods previously made by the traditional craftsman."[83] This task was to be pursued as a direct challenge to "the defiant lack of taste for the immediate surroundings of our fellow men."[84] In bringing the great asset of artistic creativity to the conventional taste of the public at large, one was also serving those artistically sensitive members of society who were "searching for noble, generally more simple forms."[85] This reflected Behrens's view of contemporary buying habits, according to which "the educated public go from shop to shop in order to find better designs, while the undiscriminating public can be persuaded to do anything"[86] and would buy "whatever is available and forcefully offered."[87] By embracing the creativity of artists, it was hoped that industry would help technology to transcend the current limits of material civilization and establish itself as an autonomous cultural force. In this way, industry would find a solution to a problem of its own making: the problem of mass culture.

In a lecture delivered to the annual assembly of the Verband Deutscher Elektrotechniker in 1910, Behrens accorded his industrial art equal status with his earlier studio art and explained how forms of industrial art should be derived from the manufacturing process involved:

Particularly in electrical engineering, it is not a question of covering up the outside of the appliances with decorative trimmings. Instead, new forms should be found to match the entirely new character of this branch of technology. One should not merely allude to art and industry in each machine-made object, but should strive for an inner union of the two. This will be achieved when all imitation of old craft forms is abandoned. Instead, the opposite course should be pursued. The techniques of mechanical production should be exactly implemented and given artistic expression. Genuineness should be accentuated in every respect, and, above all, those forms that derive from and correspond to the machine and machine production should be applied in an artistic manner.

It is a matter of achieving for each single product standard types that are cleanly constructed and appropriate to the materials used. In their design, these types should not pursue anything tremendously new, but should be developed out of the current good taste of the period.[88]

In Behrens's programmatic statement on the new formal language of industrial design, the conditions imposed by machine production became determining factors in the aesthetic concept. This was made clear in the demand that, in designing for the machine and machine production, one should proceed with the intention of creating standard types suited to the materials involved and, where possible, related to existing designs. Behrens did not view products as handcrafted decorative pieces, but rather as "utilitarian objects that should principally serve a practical purpose rather than beautify the surroundings."[89] It followed that "the aesthetic design principle for all machine-made objects" consisted "not in the addition of ornamental embellishments, but in the artistic consideration of the basic form."[90] Rather than conceal their industrial provenance, the products should affirm the reality of their mechanical manufacture. In his redesigning work, therefore, Behrens did not proceed from the old decorated forms, but neither did he try at all costs to replace the old models with new ones. Instead, he took the engineering forms already in production as the starting point for his designs. By reworking them and making them more economic and logical in their use of stepped contours and moldings, he simplified and clarified these existing designs.

This can be seen in an exemplary manner in the arc lamp for indirect lighting (illustration P16). The mechanics of the lamp remained unaltered; only the metal casing, which was necessary for protection and for reflecting the light, was changed. The earlier type did not have the added vegetable decoration of the luxury model, and was thus made up only of the parts which were functionally necessary, such as the reflector and the cover for the regulator. The form of the reflector, however, was broken up by numerous uncalled-for moldings, grooves, and bulges, which gave it an unresolved, uncertain contour. In contrast, the redesigned reflector was austerely articulated. The two matching concave curves gave it the clear, harmonious silhouette of a broad, shallow dish, which was more suited to the task of reflecting the light upward than the convex form of its predecessor. The same restraint appeared in the cap, whose smooth outline was repeated by the bracket from which the light was hung. The further modifications to the bottom handle and to the metal clamps, which were used for lowering the lamp and for opening it, were slight but not without significance. Although, as explained, the aim of Behrens's redesigned forms was to "illustrate the purpose of the object . . . using expressive means that correspond to the characteristics of the given material,"[91] they were nevertheless not subservient to the dictates of function, materials, or technology. Behrens was not interested in "the mere recognition of the so-called genuine formal values of machine-produced objects," or in "the discovery of the supposedly hidden beauty and the 'rationality' of works of engineering,"[92] which could, because of their inherent physical laws, create an aesthetic impression quite by chance. According to Behrens, this was a "pseudo-aesthetic." It could therefore be no solution, he said, to tell a manufacturer to keep "solely to absolutely functional forms," for it was a "fallacy" to believe that "even the most exacting and stringent attempts to satisfy functional requirements" could, on their own, create "the moment of beauty."[93] Another quality was also important to Behrens, namely "the pleasure we take in an object, quite apart from its functional and material value."[94] The limitations imposed by the processes of construction and assembly should not be the only form-determining factors. In the tension between the traditional aesthetics of function and modern functionalism, Behrens felt that "the moment of beauty" could not be derived from technology, nor could it be achieved as the product of utilitarian purpose, materials, tools, or manufacturing techniques. Rather, it would be achieved as the consequence, to quote Riegl, of a consciously directed Kunstwollen (artistic volition) for which the technical limitations were significant as coefficients of friction   critical but not creative factors in the form-determining process.

This aesthetic principle gained the approval of Behrens's contemporaries. Karl Scheffler regarded Behrens's designs "less as the works of freely inventing artist and more as the felicitous creations of an engineer who was highly educated in aesthetics."[95] Robert Breuer saw in them a "return from folly to good-looking rationality."[96] Le Corbusier found them "modest, sober, and almost impersonal in character."[97] Behrens's simple geometric forms, lucid connections, and clear proportions were, according to Anton Jaumann, "so abstract, so functionally and mathematically comprehensible" as an expression of the industrial world that "it was unimportant if they were produced by the artist himself or by a machine."[98]

From a set matrix of forms, designs were arrived at by repeating the same or different elements, in an analogy to machine production. The models thus designed were individually different from each other, yet were linked by an all-embracing nexus of forms. Through shape, color, and the use of tombac alloy, the AEG's arc lamps were given a specific identity that distinguished them from their competitors. In the sphere of graphics, the *Mitteilungen der Berliner Elektricitaets-Werke* was published for many years in the original format laid out by Behrens. The principle of flexibility within a fixed formal matrix also found expression in the AEG's architecture. For example, the small-motor factory was originally planned as a symmetrical building some 200 meters long. After construction had begun, the plan was changed and the factory was extended, without difficulty, to a length of 330 meters.[99] This principle proved indispensable to the stated aim, which was to give the firm's image a coherent form and impact. The creation of a unified design image on such a large scale was an enormous task, beyond the power of one individual. However, the design work not executed by Behrens himself or by his own studio could be done by others under his direction in the Behrens style, which had also become the AEG style. As early as 1909, Behrens's consulting hours were announced in the AEG's house newspaper: "From now on, our artistic adviser, Herr Professor Peter Behrens, will be available every Thursday afternoon at 5 P.M. in the AEG administration building (1st floor, in the office of Herr Direcktor Zander) to offer advice on all matters concerning artistic questions."[100]

Notes

1. Speech of thanks at banquet held to celebrate his 70th birthday, reprinted in *AEG-Zeitung* (Festnummer) 11–12 (1908), p. 12.

2. "Organization technischer Arbeit. Betrachtungen anlässlich des 25jährigen Bestehens der Allgemeinen Elektrizitätsgesellschaft," *Hochland* 5, no. 2 (1908), p. 12.

3. Letter to Wilhelm Siemens, 17 January 1867. See also Conrad Matschoss, *Werner Siemens. Ein kurzgefasstes Lebensbild nebst einer Auswahl seiner Briefe* (Berlin, 1916), vol. 1, p. 261.

4. "Über die Umwandlung von Arbeitskraft in elektrischen Strom ohne Anwendung permanenter Magnete," address to Akademie der Wissenschaften, Berlin, 17 January 1867, reprinted in Matschoss (note 3), vol. 1, pp. 82 ff.

5. Letter to Dr. Meissner, 26 November 1907, in W. Rathenau, *Briefe*, fourth edition (Dresden, 1927), pp. 52–56.

6. On Emil Rathenau see Felix Pinner, *Emil Rathenau und das elektrische Zeitalter* (Leipzig, 1918); Pinner, "Emil Rathenau, der Kaufmann und das Leben," supplement to *Zeitschrift für Handelswissenschaft und Handelspraxis* (Leipzig, 1913); Artur Fürst, *Emil Rathenau. Der Mann und sein Werk* (Berlin, 1915); Alois Riedler, *Emil Rathenau und das Werden der Grosswirtschaft* (Berlin, 1916); Maximilian Harden, "Emil Rathenau," *Die Zukunft* 23, no. 40 (1915), pp. 23–30; Bernhard Dernburg, "Emil Rathenau," *Allgemeine Zeitung*, 5 December 1908; Alfons Goldschmidt, "Emil Rathenau," *März*, 5, no. 3 (1911), pp. 239–241; H. Brinckmeyer, *Die Rathenaus* (Munich, 1922); Robert Haas, "Emil Rathenau. Zur 90. Wiederkehr seines Geburtstages," *Spannung. Die AEG-Umschau*, 2, no. 3 (1928), pp. 70–73, and no. 4 (1929), pp. 108–110; Carl Fürstenberg, in *Die Lebensgeschichte eines deutschen Bankiers*, ed. Hans Fürstenberg (Berlin, 1931), pp. 169 ff.; *50 Jahre AEG*, manuscript from 1933 (Berlin, 1956), pp. 10 ff.; Harry Graf Kessler, *Walther Rathenau. Sein Leben und sein Werk* (Berlin, 1928), pp. 9 ff.; Ernst Schulin, "Die Rathenaus. Zwei Generationen jüdischen Anteils an der industriellen Entwicklung Deutschlands," *Juden im Wilhelminischen Deutschland 1890–1914* (Tübingen, 1976).

7. Emil Rathenau (note 1), p. 15.

8. According to the recollection of the banker Carl Fürstenberg (note 6), p. 173.

9. Except in a few special cases, the electric arc lamp is not used today for lighting purposes; it has been superseded by the incandescent lamp. However, the name "Bogenlamp" has survived in German, and is popularly used to refer to street lights on lamp standards. The luminous intensity of gas lamps around 1908 was about 10–16 HK (Heffner candlepower), that of the arc lamp 200–500 HK and more.

10. From the winter of 1877–78, fashionable parts of Paris, such as the Avenue de l'Opéra and the Place de la Concorde, were lit by arc lamps working on the Jablochkoff system. While visiting the 1878 Paris World's Fair, Emil Rathenau became acquainted with this system; at a subsequent meeting he tried to persuade Werner Siemens to illuminate the Leipziger Strasse in Berlin. Siemens regarded the project as technically premature and declined.

11. See Hefner-Alteneck's report to the Elecktrotechnische Verein in 1880, in Matschoss (note 3), vol. 1, pp. 89 ff.

12. C. Matschoss et al., *50 Jahre Berliner Elektricitäts-Werke 1884–1934*, p. 5

13. Conrad Matschoss, "Die geschichtliche Entwicklung der Allgemeinen Elektricitäts-Gesellschaft in den ersten 25 Jahren ihres Bestehens," *Jahrbuch des Vereins Deutscher Ingenieure*, 1909, vol. 1, p. 55.

14. A. Fürst, *Das elektrische Licht. Von den Anfang bis zur Gegenwart. Nebst eine Geschichte der Beleuchtung* (Munich, 1926), p. 79.

15. Ibid., p. 110.

16. Werner Siemens, letter to Karl Siemens, 30 November 1881.

17. Werner Siemens, letter to Karl Siemens, 11 December 1881; see Matschoss (note 3), pp. 712 ff.

18. Werner Siemens, letter to Wilhelm Siemens, 7 December 1880; see Matschoss (note 3), p. 679. "It is true, that at the moment, I attach more significance to transmitting power than to lighting. I believe, in fact, that my view will soon be proved to be correct. . . ." Siemens achieved great success with the first electric railway, which was officially opened on 12 May 1881 in Lichterfelde, as well as the railway in Paris, which ran from Place de la Concorde to the site of the electricity exhibition. See also letters of 12 May and 19 October 1881, pp. 691 and 705.

19. Letter to his brother in St. Petersburg, 19 October 1881; see Matschoss (note 3), pp. 704 ff.

20. Emil Rathenau, speech (note 1), p. 16.

21. The Edison Electric Light Co. of Europe Ltd., New York, was responsible for issuing patents throughout Europe. This company in turn founded the Edison Electric Light Co., London, responsible for the British market, and the Compagnie Continentale Edison, Paris, responsible for the rest of Europe. The latter held the rights to incandescent lights and for the construction of power stations. Individual installations were the responsibility of the Société Electrique Edison, and manufacturing licenses came under the control of the Société Industrielle et Commerciale Edison, Paris.

22. Fürstenberg (note 6), p. 175.

23. Ibid.

24. On 13 May 1882 two contracts were agreed, concerning the establishment of a research company for the introduction of the Edison incandescent lamps and the transfer to the consortium of the general agency for the building of power stations in Germany.

25. Oskar von Miller (1855–1934) made a trip to France in 1881, as a building assistant at the Kgl. Bayrisches Kanal und Flussbauamt, to study hydroelectric power. A year later he was appointed as a director of the AEG by Emil Rathenau, and he held this post until 1890. While in France he had visited the Exposition Internationale d'Electricité, on whose pattern the Munich exhibition (of which he was Secretary) was organized. He later achieved fame as the founder of the Deutsches Museum in Munich (1903) and as the constructor of the Walchensee power station (1924).

26. The minutes listed "Dr. jur. Hermann Löwenfeld, Direktor d. Nationalbank f. Deutschland; Ludwig von Kaufmann; Rudolf Salzbach, Frankf./M.; Emil Rathenau; Hugo Landau; Carl Schlesinger, Trier; Wilhelm Wolff; Julius Friedländer, Breslau; Paul Gaspard Friedenthal, Breslau; Dr. Hugo Kunheim; and Edmund Becker, Leipzig, as well as the following finance houses: Nationalbank für Deutschland; Gebrüder Sulzbach, Frank./M., Salomon Rau, Munich; and Jacob Landau."

27. For each lamp there was a license fee of 16.67 percent of the cost-price, for the generators either 16 or 12.50 marks depending on horsepower. In addition to these running license payments came the transfer of 1,500 shares and a lump-sum payment of 350,000 marks.

28. In the fiscal year 1885, 60,000 incandescent lamps were manufactured; in 1886 the figure was 90,000; in 1887–88 it was 300,000. After the turn of the century, the average yearly production amounted to 7 million.

29. The AEG's articles of association of 23 March and 27 April 1887 also defined the contractual relationship with Siemens and Halske; see 50 Jahre AEG (note 6), pp. 75 ff. Entry in the register of companies followed on 12 July 1887, the share capital increased to 12 million marks, and the seats on the supervisory board were allotted to Siemens and Halske (2), Deutsche Bank (2), Delbrück, Leo & Co. (2), Rudolf Sulzbach, Jacob Landau, Paul Gaspard Friedenthal, and Edmund Becker. The AEG monogram was first used as a trademark in 1898.

30. See J. Loewe, "Elektrotechnische Industrie," in Die Störungen im deutschen Wirtschaftsleben während der Jahre 1900ff., Schriften des Vereins für Sozialpolitik no. 107 (1903); W. Koch, Die Konzentrationsbewegung in der deutschen Elektroindustrie (Munich and Berlin, 1907); Goldschmidt (note 6); Kurt Heinig, "Der Weg des Elektrotrusts," Die neue Zeit 30, no. 2 (1912), pp. 474–485 [cf. Lenin, Der Imperialismus als höchstes Stadium des Kapitalismus (Peking, 1974), pp. 82 ff.]; E. Noether, Vertrustung und Monopolfrage in der deutschen Elektrizitäts-Industrie (Mannheim and Leipzig, 1913); Fürst (note 6), pp. 71–74; Paul Ufermann und Carl Hüglin, Die AEG. Eine Darstellung des Konzerns der Allgemeinen Elektricitäts-Gesellschaft (Berlin, 1922), pp. 22 ff.; Peter Berglar, Walther Rathenau. Seine Zeit, sein Werk, seine Persönlichkeit (Bremen, 1970), p. 272; Jürgen Kocka, Unternehmer in der deutschen Industrialisierung (Göttingen, 1975). The extent to which the firm branched out is shown strikingly by the list of addresses in AEG. Adressen-Verzeichnis (Berlin), October 1913.

31. Matschoss (note 3), p. 64.

32. The records relating to the appointment of Behrens were lost with the firm's archives, which are thought to have been removed to the Soviet Union in 1945.

33. The fact that, besides Emil Rathenau, his two sons Erich and Walther were also directors of the AEG meant that the family had a majority on the board. This attracted criticism from the shareholders, which led to Walther Rathenau's resignation from the board in 1902. He remained the owner of the Berliner Handelsgesellschaft, however, and in this capacity joined the supervisory board of the AEG two years later.

34. Walther Rathenau (note 5), p. 52.

35. From a report presented by the AEG in 1896 to the elders of the Berlin merchants' guild, quoted in Ufermann and Hüglin (note 30), p. 39.

36. "It saddens me that Munich has also succumbed to the exhibition epidemic. I thought that art ruled alone there!" W. Siemens in a letter to Prof. von Beetz, in 50 Jahre AEG (note 6), p. 32.

37. Ibid., p. 33.

38. Emil Rathenau (note 1), p. 14.

39. Recalling in 1908 the period when he was looking for a new area of activity, he commented: "An even more important factor [than the problem of location] influenced my decision to refrain from starting up a new business right away and to wait until the crisis that had claimed countless victims in the worlds of finance and industry had fully run its course. Patriotic factory owners who in spite of these difficult times still generously supported the members of their workforce who were serving in the army earned no thanks for this. Instead, they had to accept regretfully after the war that the wave of enthusiasm for the social democratic movement was even greater than before. Men like Siemens, Schwartzkopff, and I—who also had the honor of belonging to this small group—hoped in vain to contain the discontent of the workers through welfare facilities and the provision of housing. Under these conditions, a revival of the once-celebrated Berlin mechanical-engineering industry could only be expected when physical labor had been replaced by automatic machines or when the particular skill and intelligence of the Berlin workforce had been totally utilized."

40. The impetus was given in Berlin by Ludwig Loewe. In his company's annual report of 1870, Loewe gave an enthusiastic account of American production methods. He proposed to make his sewing machine factory into a "model mechanical workshop for Germany." This was to be done by building a new type of machine, whose component parts could be "calculated with scientific accuracy" so that the "exact and perfectly regular manufacture of all the parts" could be achieved, with the "complete and strict exclusion of all hand work" by "total automation." See Maria Borgmann, Arbeitsbedingungen, Probleme der Betriebsführung u. d. sozialen Frage in der Berliner Maschinenindustrie i. d. Zeit von 1870 bis 1914, doctoral dissertation, Berlin, pp. 119 ff.

41. "Intelligent factory owners had imported more or less automatically functioning machines from America, but could not achieve adequate results, for precision work was not valued highly enough, or habit too easily encouraged the return to old-fashioned tools." Emil Rathenau (note 1), p. 13.

42. Ibid.

43. Emil Rathenau, *Aufgaben der Elektrizitäts-Industrie* (Berlin, 1910), pp. 6 f.

44. Hans von Sothen, Die Wirtschaftspolitik der AEG, doctoral dissertation, Freiburg University, 1915, p. 19.

45. The detailed preparation and implementation of the workshop organization and the drawing up of the work schedules was done by Kayser, the head of the machine factory workshops. In this connection, he was sent of a long study tour to America. See O. Lasche, *Elektrischer Einzelantrieb in den Maschinenbauwerkstätten der AEG* (Berlin, 1899), pp. 29 ff.

46. See Fürst (note 6): "The AEG's operations were directed in the 'Prussian' style. This was often unwelcome to some individuals among the mass of employees, but it is impossible to achieve great results by any other means." On this question, Hans Dieter Hellige [*Geschichte in Wissenschaft und Unterricht* 19, no. 9 (1968), pp. 538 ff.] quotes a conversation between Kaiser Wilhelm II and Walther Rathenau at their first meeting on 10 February 1900:

KW II:
Rhodes has just told be about your factories. He's certainly an experienced fellow, but he was flabbergasted by them.

WR:
Your majesty, the English can learn something from our German factories. They always add one factory onto another. Here, the whole thing is projected and worked out as a unified scheme. And then there is the German public servant, with his conscientiousness and discretion, who always puts his duty before his own interests.

KW II:
Yes, we've got the material.

WR:
And finally the organization. Here we look at the Prussian state and try to copy it on a smaller scale.

KW II:
Yes, organization is the main thing. In this you should model yourself only on the state.

47. Paul Jordan (b. 1854) worked for the company from the time of the initial "Gelegenheits-Gesellschaft," and was on the board of directors of the AEG for more than 30 years. His particular responsibilities were the construction and organization of the factories. In addition, he was a member of the supervisory boards of the Deutsche Werft AG, Hamburg; the Nationale Automobil-Gesellschaft (NAG), Berlin; and Felten & Guilleaume Carlswerk AG, Cologne-Mülheim. See *Spannung. AEG-Umschau* 2, no. 10 (1929), p. 300.

48. Note 5, p. 55.

49. *Die Allgemeine Elektricitäts-Gesellschaft 1883–1908*, Festschrift (Berlin, 1908), p. 8.

50. ". . . I ask you . . . to regard this experiment favorably, as a new step on the path toward a beneficent civilization"—Emil Rathenau, concluding his address at the opening of the water-powered generating plant at the Frankfurt Exhibition of 1891. In his book on the tasks of the electrical industry (note 43), Rathenau wrote that, if it were possible, the production of cheap electricity would "transform our earning pattern and our economic life," "raise the national wealth to an undreamt-of level," and "assign to electricity the role it seems destined to claim as a promoter of modern culture."

51. ". . . we can therefore proudly claim that we march at the head of all civilized peoples. . . . We shall ensure that the leading position in electrical engineering, which Germany occupies in both hemispheres, will be maintained." Emil Rathenau at the inauguration of electric lighting on Unter den Linden, Berlin, 1888, quoted by Pinner (note 6).

52. Rathenau (note 43), p. 1.

53. Behrens, "On the Aesthetics of Factory Design" (in this volume).

54. First quotation is from the introduction of the AEG economy arc lamp in *AEG-Zeitung* 10, no. 6 (1907), suppl. 2; second is from the introduction of the high-power arc lamp, ibid. 11, no. 8 (1909), suppl. 8.

55. For example, Michael von Dolivo-Dobrowolsky, "Modern Mass Production in the Electrical Appliance Factory of the AEG" (in this volume).

56. Wolf Dohrn, "The Example of the AEG" (in this volume).

57. See note 54.

58. Tilmann Buddensieg, "Peter Behrens und die AEG. Neue Dokumente zur Baugeschichte der Fabriken am Humboldthain," in *Schloss Charlottenburg*, Festschrift for Margarete Kühn (Munich, 1975), p. 277.

59. Compare the similar judgment of Juri Soloview: "When I think that the AEG has been designing since the time of Peter Behrens, then the result is not so impressive when compared with our own Soviet design, which is only ten years old." [*Forum. Zeitschrift für Gestaltung*, no. 4 (1976), p. 54].

60. Fritz Meyer-Schönbrunn, *Peter Behrens* (Hagen and Dortmund, 1913), p. 3.

61. *Werkkunst* 2, no. 17 (1907), p. 271.

62. *Werkkunst* 2, no. 22 (1907), p. 351; see also *Berliner Architekturwelt* 10 (1908), p. 239.

63. *Werkkunst* 2, no. 24 (1907), p. 382; see also the announcement in the *Berliner Tageblatt* of 28 July 1907 and Behrens, "Art in Technology" (in this volume).

64. See Behrens's letter to Karl Ernst Osthaus, 29 August 1907: ". . . I am extraordinarily pleased that you approve of my decision. I have done a lot of work as a result of my position here in Düsseldorf, and would be glad if it could be put to the common good." (Osthaus Archive) See also F.

H. Ehmcke, *Frankfurter Zeitung*, 23 August 1907; Ernst Schur, *Dekorative Kunst* 11 (October 1907), p. 48; Robert Breuer, *Werkkunst* 3, no. 10 (1908), pp. 145–149. The official beginning of Behrens's activity as artistic adviser to the AEG was 1 October 1907 (Osthaus Archive, 28 August 1907). He moved to the Haus Erdmannshof in Neu-Babelsberg, near Potsdam, in October or November (Osthaus Archive, 1 October and 17 November 1907). He was officially employed as artistic adviser until 1914 (Akademie der Künste, West Berlin, personal file, 5 October 1936, sheet 96, no. 9b).

65. Fritz Hellwag, "Peter Behrens und die AEG," *Kunstgewerbeblatt* 22 (1911), p. 150.

66. Eugen Kalkschmidt, "Kunst und Industrie," *März* 4, no. 3 (1910), p. 144.

67. See the appendixes to this volume.

68. Behrens, "On the Aesthetics of Factory Design" (in this volume).

69. The Berliner Elektricitäts-Werke, which was owned by the AEG, had already commissioned designs for arc lamps and lamp posts from freelance artists at the end of the nineteenth century. Professor L. Schupmann of Aachen designed the lamps installed on Unter den Linden. See *Berlin und seine Bauten* (1896), vol. 1, p. 41.

70. Behrens, "On the Aesthetics of Factory Design" (in this volume).

71. Behrens, "Art and Technology" (in this volume).

72. See note 54.

73. Dohrn (note 56), p. 362.

74. "Prof. Peter Behrens on Aesthetics in Industry" (in this volume).

75. Ibid.

76. Dohrn (in this volume). In the same year, Anton Jaumann wrote of the new arc lamps: "The decisive factor was mass production. Savings were to be made in both materials and labor." See A. Jaumann, "Neues von Peter Behrens," *Deutsche Kunst und Dekoration* 12, no. 6 (1909), p. 353. Franz Mannheimer spoke of the "savings in manufacturing costs and work time that will necessarily result from . . . an engaged concern for the form of factory-made products." See Mannheimer, "Arbeiten von Professor Behrens für die AEG," *Der Industriebau* 2, no. 6 (15 June 1911), p. 124. Neither Behrens nor the AEG mentioned this aspect.

77. In the "AEG-Norms," as they were then called, fixed standards for products, individual parts, and trademarks were laid down.

78. ". . . the AEG were already endeavoring in the 1890s to standardize the numerically most important components, in order to reduce the firm's stocks of raw materials and semifinished products on one hand, and to shorten the delivery time for special orders on the other" [*50 Jahre AEG* (note 6), p. 146]. ". . . many parts are so designed, that they can be used for various models" [Jaumann (note 76), p. 353]. Michael von Dolivo-Dobrowolsky assessed the standardization of parts as follows: "This 'component economy' is so extremely important in modern mass production that an enormous amount of intellectual effort is devoted to developing it further and more fully" [Dolivo-Dobrowolsky, "Die moderne Massenfabrikation in der Apparate-Fabrik der AEG" (manuscript), p. 101.

79. Jaumann (note 76), p. 353: ". . . storage and transport were also thought of: The individual parts can be easily fitted into each other, thus saving space, packing, and transport costs, and the cost of breakages."

80. See note 63.

81. Behrens, "Art and Technology" (in this volume).

82. Behrens, lecture to Versammlung Rheinischer Handwerkskammern, 1922, quoted in W. Lotz, "Aus der Werkbund-Entwicklung," *Die Form* 7, no. 10 (1932), p. 313.

83. G. Peschken and T. Heinisch, "Berlin zu Anfang unseres Jahrhunderts," in Lucius Burckhardt (ed.), *Werkbund. Germania, Austria, Svizzera*, 1 (1977), pp. 35 ff.

84. Behrens, "Kunst und Technik," lecture given in AEG lecture room, 13 January 1909. Extracts published in *Berliner Tageblatt*, "Zeitgeist" supplement, 25 January 1909.

85. Ibid.

86. Ibid.

87. Behrens (note 82).

88. Behrens, "Art and Technology" (in this volume). See also Behrens, *Über die Beziehungen der künstlerischen und Technischen Probleme* (Berlin, 1917), pp. 18 ff.

89. "Prof. P. Behrens on Aesthetics in Industry" (in this volume).

90. Behrens, "Reform der künstlerischen Erziehung," in *Der Geist der neuen Volksgemeinschaft. Denkschrift für das deutsche Volk* (Berlin, 1919), p. 104.

91. See note 54.

92. Tilmann Buddensieg and Henning Rogge, "Formgestaltung für die Industrie. Peter Behrens und die Bogenlampen der AEG," in Gerhard Bott (ed.), *Von Morris zum Bauhaus* (Hanau, 1977).

93. Behrens, "Art and Technology" (in this volume).

94. Behrens (note 82).

95. Karl Scheffler, "Kunst und Industrie," *Kunst und Künstler* 6 (1908), p. 433.

96. Robert Breuer, "Peter Behrens und die Elektrizität," *Deutsche Kunst und Dekoration* 13, no. 10 (1910), p. 265.

97. Le Corbusier, *Etude sur le Mouvement d'Art Décoratif en Allemagne* (in this volume).

98. Jaumann (note 76), p. 352.

99. This plan was probably not executed because of the war. The shell of the third building phase—the one affected by the change in plan—was first constructed at the end of 1913.

100. *Interne AEG-Zeitung* 12, no. 5 (1909), p. 61.

The Workers' Housing of Peter Behrens

Fritz Neumeyer

Company-owned workers' housing gained in importance during the nineteenth century as a means of tying down qualified workers by linking the contract of employment and a tenancy agreement. In the boom period of German industrial expansion between 1885 and 1914, company housing developed into an indispensable component in the company policy of the giant industrial concerns. The skilled workers, the real target group of the company housing, had increased greatly in number as a result of the expansion of production and the intensification of production methods (for example, the three-shift day and the Taylor system) and had assumed an irreplaceable function in the production process. The increasing gravity of the socio-political situation was also a significant factor during this period; large regional strike movements, the elctoral successes of the Social Democratic Party, and the rapid increase in union membership made greater engagement by the employers in the realm of company welfare advisable as a means of maintaining the status quo. In the words of Carl Friedrich von Siemens, it was a prerequisite of technical progress that "the labor force, and especially the most valuable part of it" should find itself "in satisfactory circumstances"; it was "in the direct interest" of industry to tackle the housing question and "to see to it that at least some of the workers, especially those on whose performance industry is primarily dependent, can in this respect lead a contented existence."[1]

Under the influence of the enlightened bourgeoisie, a shift in political emphasis occurred during the Wilhelmine period. There was a move away from the vigorous persecution of socialists in favor of a more liberal approach to the interests of the working classes. The social policies of the post-Bismarck era no longer placed the "appeased" worker in the foreground, but rather the "contented" worker. This was a necessity for high-quality production, without which a leading position in the market was not to be achieved.

In artistic circles, too, a systematic discussion over the living conditions of the working classes was initiated. Only after industrialization had developed did the architectural avant-garde begin to occupy itself with the problem of workers' housing. In the nineteenth century, architects generally shared the view of the Berliner Architekturverein, which rejected a proposed competition for workers' housing on the grounds that such an exercise would offer too little architectonic interest.[2]

The impetus for social and aesthetic reform promoted improvements in workers' housing that paralleled the development of factory design and of production techniques. Just as spacious, well-lit workshops designed according to functional and artistic principles were intended to increase productivity, so it was felt that "men who live in fresh air and well-ordered circumstances are more able to produce the high-quality work demanded of them."[3] In addition, certain expectations about the conduct of the inhabitants were linked to the "improved" housing. The architect Richard Riemerschmid insisted that "When everything is planned and executed in this way, the result must be that the dwellings will display the same characteristics, both inside and outside, which we would like to find in their inhabitants: They will be honest, decent, simple, modest, proud, serene, self-confident, cheerful, and loyal."[4] Similarly, Karl Henrici was convinced that, "especially in times of social peace," the "sight of a prettily appointed workers' estate" had "an extraordinarily impressive quality."[5]

The association of aesthetic and social motives according to the formula "beauty = social peace" corresponded to a unified artistic and architectural treatment of the industrial world in general, which was then conceived as a collective work of art (Gesamtkunstwerk) embracing factory buildings, workers' estates, houses, and flats. But although the identification of the worker with "his" place of work could occur on a formal and aesthetic level, his legal status there was left untouched by this assimilative process.

The discussion of workers' housing was led by artists and architects, and trial schemes were promoted by some of the large industrial concerns and by rich private patrons (among them Karl Ernst Osthaus). The designs worked out for the many company estates built at this time are still regarded as models of functional architecture and town planning.

There was a desire "to bring cultural purification and enrichment to the existence of the worker," and this "within the bounds of his family circle." And insofar as this desire corresponded to those demands "which we rightly wish for the worker's family in respect of cultural sensibility," so "this moral imperative" was to be "fully expressed in the workers' housing."[6]

It was a reform from above. Hermann Muthesius described the workers'-housing movement of the period as "the efforts of the patronizing providers" and criticized the fact that "in their programs, the needs of the workers were guessed at rather than worked out from the worker's point of view."[7] It is not surprising that this reform movement made its principal impact not directly on working-class housing, but (like the garden city movement) on middle-class housing; it was thought desirable that the skilled workers be integrated ideologically, if not financially, into the ranks of the bourgeoisie.

In 1918, by which time the housing shortage had been further aggravated by the war, Peter Behrens recognized that previous housing programs had principally benefited the middle classes, and concluded that there was a need for an efficient, rationalized program for building small flats:

Everyone is talking and writing about the extraordinary social importance of the housing problem to the great multitude of the workers, . . . but almost all of the practical solutions founder on the concept of the masses who are firmly bound to the lowest income bracket. Thanks to the entirely admirable and worthwhile work that has already been done, the small terrace house and the higher-quality flat have become accessible to a much larger section of the population than previously. But in the final analysis we are still talking about a very small percentage of the working classes, for the gains that have been made are to the almost exclusive benefit of the higher-income groups. . . . It seems essential to bear such considerations firmly in mind in order to be uncompromisingly clear about what has to be done and in order to understand how imperative it is that future work should, free from any sentimental considerations, aim at the creation of a type of housing unit that, while satisfying all today's social, hygienic, and cultural demands, would still be financially accessible to the great mass of lower-paid workers.[8]

Behrens also felt that the workers' housing was modeled too closely on the norms of middle-class housing, and wanted to rid the facades of low-income housing of any formal middle-class allusions. The form of the small flat, said Behrens, should "also be considered from the worker's standpoint."[9] He first attempted to do this himself with the AEG housing on the Paul Jordan Strasse in Berlin-Hennigsdorf, which he designed in 1918. The style of this new housing was in marked contrast to the characteristically abstracted Classicism that Behrens had used in the AEG estates at Hennigsdorf (1911) and Oberschöneweide (1915).

The AEG Estates in Hennigsdorf and Oberschöneweide

The first reference to the planning of a workers' estate for the AEG is to be found in an enthusiastic article on the company's turbine factory written by Karl Ernst Osthaus in 1910: "New factories to Behrens's designs are under construction or being drawn up, and the artist is already working on the plans for a garden suburb for the firm's salaried staff and workers, which is to be built on the banks of the canal between Berlin and Tegel."[10] The plans for a workers' estate were also referred to by the young Charles Edouard Jeanneret (later called Le Corbusier) in the report on German design which had been commissioned from him by the art academy at La Chaux-de-Fonds; he must have seen them when he was working in Behrens's studio for five months in 1910–11. Jeanneret reported: "He is building extensive workers' colonies, in which the nation of 150,000 souls who win their bread from the AEG will find accommodation. Behrens is an energetic, unfathomable, earnest genius, with a profound desire to dominate, as if created for this task and this age, in harmony with the spirit of modern Germany."[11] A further reference to the AEG's plans for a large housing estate is to be found in Walther Rathenau's diary entry of 31 December 1911: "Morning visit from Franz Oppenheim. About factory and dormitory town near Berlin. I explained to him that we had pursued the idea ten years earlier but had abandoned it because of the opposition of the Social Democrats. Midday with Ernst Rathenau over the same matter. We want to look into it once again."[12] This

project, which cannot now be identified because of the loss of the firm's archives, was closely concerned with the general problem of industrial location in Berlin. The rapid increase in house building after the Gründerzeit had hemmed in the industrial concerns to such an extent that enlarging their plants was both physically and financially impossible. Several large firms, among them Borsig, Siemens, and Schwartzkopff, sold their plants in the city and used the proceeds to construct large, up-to-date factories on cheap land outside the city. In the course of this relocation satellite towns were established, and the firms played an active part in their development through the building of company estates.[13]

Unlike the other large companies that abandoned concentrated production at the old urban locations, the AEG kept to a more decentralized structure during the period of rapid expansion at the turn of the century, even though the idea of relocating into one centralized complex outside the city was considered. Indeed, the cable works was moved in 1898 to Oberschöneweide, an autonomous industrial suburb in which several small and medium firms had set up businesses after 1880. But the AEG factories in Wedding were kept in operation and, where possible, extended. Wedding was a traditional center for mechanical engineering in Berlin, and it offered an extraordinarily large pool of skilled workers and an inexhaustible supply of cheap female labor.[14]

Work was begun on the building of a company estate in 1910, when the AEG's plan to build its own porcelain factory was put into practice after the invention by the firm of a new type of high-voltage insulator. The mass production of these insulators demanded large quantities of raw materials, and a suitable location had to be found for the factory outside the city. Although Emil Rathenau did not originally want to expand to the west of the river Havel, he finally agreed to the purchase of 300 acres of land in Hennigsdorf with a 1.8-kilometer frontage on the main inland shipping route. As Rathenau said at the time, this large site was bought "so that the next fifty years will be provided for."[15] The plan for the factory also called for the construction of workers' housing. Yet by 1918 only one Behrens-designed housing block had been built, for the steady defection of the village population from agriculture to factory work prevented any shortage of labor.

Apartment Houses for the AEG in Hennigsdorf

For the land to the west of the Hennigsdorf factory site, Behrens drew up a development plan with a rectangular street layout. The first building to Behrens's design was the double-fronted block at 14–15 Rathenau Strasse, which was built in 1911. (It is not known why the development of Rathenau Strasse was not pursued beyond this single house.) If one extends this first element, the result in a stepped street line similar to that which was later used in the housing on Paul Jordan Strasse in 1918. The rhythmic alternation of open spaces and constriction was the result and also the expression of Behrens's very characteristic grouping technique, a technique he also used in estates at Merseburg (1912) and Lichtenberg (1918).[16] Paul Mebes had already used this layout as the basis for the design of the Wohnhausgruppe Charlottenburg II, a housing block which had been built by the Beamten-Wohnungs-Verein on a site in Charlottenburg bounded by Horstweg, Danckelmannstrasse, and Sophie Charlotte Strasse.

At the time, many architects adhered to the middle-class ideal of the detached family house in their plans for workers' estates. Behrens rejected this form of open planning, for he saw in it a tendency toward "anarchic independence" due to an excessive emphasis on individualism. Instead, he proposed that the buildings be arranged in groups. It appears that he consciously avoided the use of the term "row housing," as he was not content simply to line up his housing units in rows. Instead, he tried to arrive at a more sophisticated form that not only would lead to a reduction in building and maintenance costs but (more important) would give aesthetic expression to the social conditions under which the inhabitants lived.[17] In addition, this form of housing allowed for communal cooking and housekeeping.[18]

The collective-housing theories of 1908, which have been revived in an indirect way in the student communes of recent years, had direct consequences for the design of the AEG's double-fronted house. The plan of the house followed the model of French representational architecture, with a central block (*Corps de logis*) and projecting side wings (*Communs*), arranged around a front courtyard (*Cour d'honneur*). Communal facilities such as shops and a restaurant were located at street level in the two side wings.[19] Although this plan was retained, the final version differed in many essential points from the preparatory design (illustration A186). At the insistence of the planning authorities, the intended attic story was abandoned. The lowering of the roofline and the consequent loss of volume and floor area in the central block, coupled with the shortening of the side wings to half their planned length, altered the proportions of the building and detracted from its monumental impact. The powerfully rythmic dormer windows in the first version, which, with the shadows which they cast, looked like giant denticulations, were pulled back from the eaves into the roof itself, with the result that the attic windows as built looked like small, subsidiary strips. In the final version the pergolas on the flanking wings were also dispensed with, and were replaced by a fence, which ran the length of the facade and gave the central courtyard the function of a semipublic open space. The walls of the house (illustrations A187–A190) were faced with handmade red bricks, the same material used on the factories opposite. This material, considered particularly suitable for industrial locations because of the fastness of its coloring,[20] was used here with the precision and attention to detail that typify Behrens's work. The only decoration was provided by the broad window surrounds of light-colored brick. These surrounds were set back by a finger's width into the dark brickwork of the facade, and the almost imperceptible shadow gave a heightened sharpness to the contours of the surrounds. In contrast, the external windowsills were projected out from the facade by the same amount. There were hints of capitals on the brick pillars between the loggia windows, and the neat, flat, light-colored cornice strip was run around the entire block, including the gables. The walls were pointed with white mortar, and a diamond pattern was worked in to the brickwork. At the intersections of the walls the protruding bricks interlocked alternately at right angles, as if hinged around the vertical axis of the corner.

The curved walls leading to the stairwell doorways are especially interesting. With the help of these curves, the transformation from outside to inside, from the flat plane of the wall to the door opening, was made smoothly and without any abrupt changes in direction. This gave the visual impression of a solid wall that generated an inward pull. The problem of the doorway was solved here by Behrens in a startlingly simple and effective manner. Gropius and Meyer used this motif at almost exactly the same time for the entrance to the Fagus works at Alfeld (1911), their first building after leaving Behrens's office. The curved corner was later to become almost a trademark of twentieth-century architecture.

The treatment of the outer walls was extremely unusual for domestic architecture of the period, and all the more so in the context of workers' housing. Because of the abundance of openings, the wall area was reduced to a grid structure. The broad window surrounds emphasized the illusion of openness that Behrens was striving after and allowed the wall to appear as little more than a pared-down, constructional skeleton.[21] Such well-lit workers' housing had never been built in Berlin before.

In contrast to the modern and inventive treatment of the structure, the ground plan had considerable shortcomings. Because of the way the chimney flues were arranged, the flats facing the courtyard and the street could not be adequately heated. The conflict between the external design and the distribution of the internal spaces is also very disturbing. Once again as a result of the unfortunate placing of the chimneys, the band of five linked windows, which daringly opened up the upper story under the gables of the side wings, was spread across four different rooms. The two outside windows were located in the extreme outside corner of an unheatable living room, behind the middle window (rather suprisingly) was a bathroom, the next window belonged to the pantry, and the window nearest the courtyard led to a kitchen (which with three windows was probably overilluminated).

In this, his first design for workers' housing, Behrens failed to do justice to his functionalist ideas.

The Boathouse of the Elektra Rowing Club

On moving the cable works to a new site in Oberschöneweide, the AEG did not initially have to erect any housing of its own, as speculative builders had gained a footing there and had already constructed Mietskaserne (tenement blocks).[22] Instead, the AEG first built a boathouse for the company's rowing club, the Rudergesellschaft Elektra. This club, which had grown out of the Beamter-Verein (salaried-staff club) of the AEG and the Berliner Elektrizitätswerke, drew its members from the large number of engineers and clerks who worked for the two concerns. The boathouse, conceived both as a base for the rowing club and as a recreational facility for the AEG's employees, was formally opened on 18 May 1912.[23]

As viewed from the water, the boathouse's three functions were very clearly articulated. The two large doorways set into the slightly sloping wall at ground level pointed to the storage space for the boats. The arches of the enclosed veranda and the flanking pergolas suggested that pleasant hours could be spent in the public rooms. The four small, shuttered windows in the slate-clad gable led to apartments which were available on weekends to club members who lived in the city.

In fitting out the hall in which the boats were housed, Behrens clearly made use of his experience in industrial architecture. As in a factory, two traveling cranes were installed in the double-bayed hall to lift the boats, which all had names taken from the electrical industry, off the trolleys on which they were carried to the water. The traditional oarsman's method of carrying boats on the shoulders was thus made obsolete, in accordance with the principles of industrial production and of Taylorization. The aesthetic principles of the industrial world were already evoked at the door by rails, which ran into the boathouse as if into a factory shed. The design of the double portal with pilasters and an architrave was very similar in its proportions to the gates of Behrens's factory buildings. The interior of the boathouse, worked out by Behrens in the smallest detail, shows the same exactness and refinement found in the living rooms of his private houses. Clear connections can be drawn between single details; for example, the fireplace in the entrance hall of the boathouse was very similar to one in the Wiegand house of 1912,[24] and the bannisters in the entrance hall were a slimmer version of those in the garden hallway of the same house. Other such parallels are not difficult to find, for it was Behrens's intention to create typical solutions that, with small variations, could be used again and again. Rooms intended mainly for public and social functions were given timbered or coffered ceilings, irrespective of whether the building was the head office of an industrial concern, an embassy, or a boathouse.

Many of the qualities on which Behrens's architecture was based around 1910 were to be found in the boathouse. One was the often highly original treatment of materials by industrial techniques; the wood paneling in the entrance hall of the boathouse was actually sandblasted. Other typical qualities were the differentiation of the forms by means of discrete moldings, the clear and cool proportions of the rooms, and the simple and functional articulation of the whole structure. These qualities gave the boathouse, which was "in itself a characterless establishment,"[25] the status of a work of art. Sport was not depicted here as the mere exercise of the body, but as the physical expression of a modern, cultured citizen in the company of his peers.

The Design for a Housing Estate at Oberschöneweide

The AEG first considered building workers' housing at Oberschöneweide in 1914–15, presumably prompted by the boom in business that followed the outbreak of war. In addition to the scheme for row housing that was implemented in 1915, Behrens also drew up a little-known alternative plan[26] that is remarkable in several respects.

The trapezoidal site plan (illustrations A191, A192) reveals a regular and rhythmic spatial sequence made up of a series of closed blocks set along the so-called Wohnstrasse, which runs down the middle of the site. Set along the 160-meter-long Wohnstrasse is an alternating sequence of enclosed courtyards, leading to the staircases, and open spaces, which run directly onto the access road at the back. The unbroken street lines on both sides of the Wohnstrasse are penetrated at street level by the entrances to the enclosed courtyards.

The representative character of the scheme is immediately apparent in the layout. The large open spaces were intended for the common use of the residents and were to be accessible only from the rear service road—not from the Wohnstrasse, which was conceived as a pedestrian street. The block structure is broken up along the service street in order to give rhythm to the street space.

In the perspective drawing (illustration A196), the Wohnstrasse appears as a rather grand axis. A central walk runs between regularly placed flower beds and is marked at intervals by single free-standing statues. The formal and distinguished nature of this garden promenade is emphasized by the flanking Doric colonnades, which support the continuous band of the balcony parapets at the first-floor level. The entrances to the enclosed courtyards are given prominence by the addition of either a portico or a triumphal arch motif. This formal garden and the elegant facade architecture flanking it make a curious contrast to the demands of a workers' estate and to the reflections on the need for utility in garden city design that Behrens had published in 1908. Behrens clearly intended to create a distinctly urbane housing estate that, apart from the provision of accommodation, had nothing in common with the conception or the architecture of the usual workers' estates of the period.

In the schematic distribution on the site plan, 180 apartments are marked on each level; this means that the whole project comprises some 700 apartments. The majority have two rooms plus a kitchen, a bathroom, and an entrance hall. (The row-housing estate built on the site in 1915 had 160 apartments of comparable size.) On closer inspection of the design it becomes clear that Behrens had set himself the task of finding a blend between the compact structures and intensive land use of city architecture and the demands for a hygienic and healthy style of life. This duality was to become a matter of urgent interest in the 1920s to those architectural theorists who were concerned with large-scale housing complexes.

In Behrens's plan the subdivision of the ground plan is clearly articulated. The staircases, hallways, kitchens, and bathrooms are all installed in the 3.5-meter-wide zone at the rear of the block. The living rooms are located in the front section of the house, whose depth is reduced by 80 centimeters on each ascending floor so that the ground floor is 5.9 meters and the top floor is 3.5 meters deep. Two-meter-wide balconies run continuously in front of every living room and appear on the facade as stepped-back terraces. In this way, an 80-centimeter-deep strip at the front of each balcony on the three lower floors is directly open to the sky. Load-bearing walls at 3-meter intervals divide the progression of the cell-like building into segments. The ground plan is regular, apart from the complicated corners, and the blocks could have been built using a series of standardized elements.

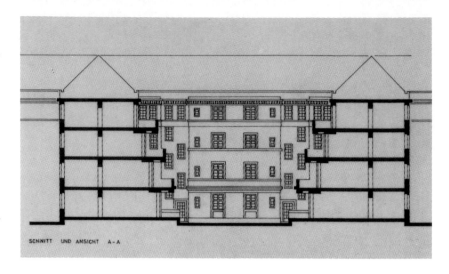

SCHNITT UND ANSICHT A-A

1
Project for stepped housing at Oberschöneweide: section through courtyard.

It is not impossible that Behrens conceived this very unusual design for mass housing with industrial prefabrication in mind. (However, it is hard to see how the cantilevered balconies could have been built without reinforced concrete, a material not generally used in domestic architecture prior to 1920.) Within the AEG, a system for industrialized house building had already been proposed by Behrens's colleague Walter Gropius.[27] Although Behrens did not publicly pursue this idea while he was working for the AEG,[28] he considered the problem very thoroughly in his book *Vom sparsamen Bauen*, which was published in 1918. In the same year, work began on the AEG's housing on Paul Jordan Strasse in Hennigsdorf.

Quite apart from the probable intention of establishing a rationalized manner of building, this design is of importance in the development of stepped apartment housing. It is unclear whether Behrens knew of Henri Sauvage's structurally similar scheme for a stepped apartment house.[29] Another possible contemporary source was the "casa a gradinata" suggested by Sant'Elia in 1914, which might have been known of in Germany through the links between the Italian Futurists and Herwarth Walden's "Sturm" group.

Behrens felt that stepped housing, by offering a bit of open air to every resident, would counter the three great enemies of public health: tuberculosis, infant mortality, and the general risk of contagious diseases. For this reason, the stepped block recommended itself particularly for apartment houses in the city.[30] This thesis had already been proposed by a doctor named Sarazon in 1906, in a scheme for a stepped hospital with an open-air terrace on each floor.[31] In the case of Behrens's design, the extent of the projection was determined by the concrete construction.[32] Behrens's extensions are clearly balconies rather than terraces, but depth of 2 meters was a considerable increase over the dimensions of the conventional balconies of the period. It was obvious to Behrens, however, that

this construction had certain weaknesses. For reasons of symmetry, balconies were also included on the north-facing side, which cut out the daylight and thus directly contradicted the health-giving intentions of the design. [It would seem that Behrens had become aware of this flaw by the time he made his drawing of the Wohnstrasse (illustration A196), for in this drawing both the north-facing balconies and the south-facing ones are bathed in sunshine.] And in a retrospective article (published, significantly, in the magazine of the German Red Cross in 1925) Behrens criticized the idea of building overhanging terraces using a simple concrete construction and said that all attempts to do this had proved inadequate. Although "the idea had been given expression" in these early projects, he said, "the cost of realizing these projects would have been absurdly high and could not have been justified from an economic viewpoint."[33]

Finally, this design deserves special attention because its particular characteristics are the direct consequence of the transference of the formal language of Behrens's industrial architecture into the realm of domestic building. The two sketches of the Zeppelinstrasse reproduced below as illustrations A193 and A194 make the industrial provenance of this architecture very clear.[34] The powerful entablature of the ground-level colonnade that divides the open courtyards from the street is very reminiscent of Behrens's design of a portal for the AEG site at Humboldthain (illustrations A75–77). Similarly, the square towers with stepped windows and the technique of flanking a gable end with a tower are equally characteristic of the AEG high-voltage-equipment factory and of this housing project. The perspectival view of the Zeppelinstrasse (illustration A194) offers striking proof of the degree to which Behrens had assimilated the lessons of industrial architecture. In this sketch the gable ends, which are separated by the 20-meter-wide courtyards, are portrayed as if through a telephoto lens, so that each pair of gables is pulled together almost as a single building unit. The floor-to-ceiling windows with grid-pattern glazing bars reinforce the illusion that the observer is standing in front of a row of factory sheds interspersed with deep courtyards. It was clearly Behrens's intention to make a formal and aesthetic connection between the world of the factory and the housing of those who worked in the factory, to find a unified language of forms appropriate to the industrial age.[35]

Row Housing at Oberschöneweide

The stepped housing project for Oberschöneweide was not implemented, presumably for economic reasons. Instead, the AEG built two-story row housing on the same site in 1915 (illustration A197). The row housing was aligned along the four streets marking the perimeter of the site, and the open space thus enclosed was divided up into gardens. The houses on the Zeppelinstrasse were single-family units, probably intended for salaried staff or foremen; the accommodations on the three other streets were smaller flats and maisonettes.

All the flats and houses were planned to meet the demands of a working man and his family, with a living room, a kitchen, an adjoining scullery which also served as bathroom, and a lavatory. Characteristic of both types of floor plan (illustrations A201, 204) is the attempt to make maximum use of the limited space.[36] The kitchen was set behind the front room on the same axis, and these two rooms took up the entire depth of the house. The "parlor" favored by the well-situated workers and middle classes was not included in the plan. Behrens also broke with the standard nineteenth-century practice of placing living rooms on the street front and kitchens facing the courtyard, a layout that was used regardless of orientation. In the houses on An der Wuhlheide, the living rooms face south toward the gardens while the kitchens and staircases are on the north side, facing the street.

The facades were uniformly treated with flat stucco and simply yet vigorously articulated. The upper edge of the facade was forcefully terminated by the square profile of the eaves. This powerful horizontal accent was extended along the whole length of the street front and was reinforced by the shadows cast by the eaves. The upper-story windows were set tightly under the eaves, and a smooth, flat band of stucco was wrapped around the house block like a frieze, with the protruding, light-colored window surrounds set into it. The unornamented walls were subdivided by a narrow relief molding running between the two stories. Wooden shutters, which were both functional and decorative, added life to the facade and accentuated the window openings.

The design of these row houses was pervaded by an inner logic that verged on abstraction. The simple organization of the structure and the tenacious repetition of the individual elements along the entire length of the facade served to increase the monumental effect. Rather than introduce small variations to avoid boredom, Behrens concentrated on a concise and controlled manner of expression. He achieved this by using simple geometric forms that articulated the building according to its inherent proportional order, encompassed the entire structure, and established clear relationships among the individual elements. In the sustained rhythms of the fenestration a system of parallel diagonals was alluded to (illustration A206). By displacing the window frames diagonally, Behrens gave tension and rhythmic liveliness to the facades.

The rhythm was developed particularly clearly on the facades facing Fontanestrasse and Roedernstrasse (illustrations A203, 208). At the outer ends of each double house unit, the facade is stepped outward with bay-like projections, which run from the ground right up to the eaves. In the context of the entire front these bays appear as pairs, giving a continuous rhythm to the horizontal accents of the facade. Here, on a small scale, Behrens achieved the same effect he had introduced with the rhythmic alignment of giant pilasters on the front of the small-motor factory.

The successful way in which geometric forms were used to impose a visual order onto the facade can be seen in the design of the main dormer gables on Fontanestrasse and Roedernstrasse. The three corners of the gable were used as the points of intersection of the diagonal grid. The actual roof lines of the gable, however, do not follow the grid exactly, but are curved inward slightly. The resulting gentle curves lead the eye downward in both directions toward the eaves and the paired bays on the facade, and then back up to the next main gable. A sense of wave-like motion is thus given to the horizontality of the row construction. The source of this effect is the geometric relationship of the dormer gables;

they follow the arc of a circle, whose center is at the intersection of a line going upward from the end wall of each double house unit and the extended diagonal of the gable itself. The formal impact of this detail can be judged by its absence from the houses in Roedernstrasse, where the gable profile was straightened out in the course of re-roofing. As a result, the subliminal, abstract Classicism of these double houses has become more apparent, with the bays echoing the Classical pilasters, the eaves the architrave, and the gables the tympanum. It would seem that Behrens had adopted here the facade of a Classical town house of 1800 as his formal model, in order to reinterpret it and reapply it to the housing of a quite different social class.

Vom sparsamen Bauen and the Workers' Housing on the Voltastrasse in Hennigsdorf

The discussion on workers' housing, in which Behrens had been actively involved since 1910, was brought to a temporary halt in 1918. The aggravation of the general housing shortage by the war made it manifestly clear that the problems involved in building mass housing had remained unsolved, in spite of the many model estates that had been established by enlightened industrialists. In 1917 and 1918 the pressure of events finally forced the state to abandon its passivity with regard to the provision of housing. The fear of social disturbances led to the promise, on paper at least, that every returning soldier would be given a small house.

The book Vom sparsamen Bauen (On Economical Housing) was written by Behrens in collaboration with Heinrich de Fries and published in 1918. In it Behrens identified the "great mass of lower-paid workers" as the target group for future house-building programs. It was for this group that an appropriate and functional housing type had to be developed: "One must realize that the way of life of the worker is different from that of the civil servant and the bourgeois, that his opinions, his habits, his desires, and his rights are specific and well-defined and put their own stamp on his social class. It is pointless to offer him a model home to which he should

then accustom himself, but which he will always regard as something strange, as something that does not match his character."[37] Behrens and de Fries insisted that the form of the worker's house should be thought out "from the worker's point of view," as a type of housing specific to that social class. The theory of small-house design they developed in Vom sparsamen Bauen was based on the ideals of cheapness and quality. In order to lower the costs of building and maintenance, a complete rationalization of methods was proposed. This process of rationalization also had consequences for the layout of the estates. Schemes that would "devour expensive land merely for streets" and thus promote high road-building costs were to be shunned. Such complex and picturesque plans were condemned as romantic relics serving only illusory market functions.

Behrens and de Fries wrote that whole streets—and, where possible, whole estates—should be made up of houses of the same type, in order to facilitate the industrial mass production of standardized building elements. Construction, they said, should follow the Taylor system. The efficiency of the individual worker was to be maximized, human labor replaced by machines, and the whole building process revolutionized. Shutter-poured concrete was recommended for the load-bearing frame; partition walls were to be constructed of breeze blocks made by machine on the site.

A reduction in the size of the rooms was also considered. This would not necessarily lessen their usefulness if supported by new designs for smaller, more practical furniture. Where possible, furniture was to be built in, for fitted cupboards were cheaper to produce than free-standing wardrobes and chests. Behrens had already taken a step in this direction in 1911 with the exhibition of furniture specifically designed for the smaller house or flat.[38] The ocean liner—considered the embodiment of the new ethos

of the machine age—served as a model. A shipboard cabin, "which in spite of its smallness provides pleasant, thoroughly adequate, comfortable accommodation for weeks on end," was cited as proof that "even under considerable spatial limitations, it is possible to live comfortably when the space available is used well and the furniture suitably designed."[39] To compensate for the smaller dwellings, communal facilities such as canteens, day nurseries, and meeting halls were planned for the estates. Writing on communal facilities in a 1908 article on the garden city movement, Behrens had already argued that it was not essential for residents to have close contacts with each other beyond those prompted by economic and practical necessity.[40] He saw the provision of such facilities as a kind of social service.[41]

Quite apart from the thoroughness with which it treated the problem of the small house, *Vom sparsamen Bauen* stood above other contemporary tracts on the same theme[42] in its uncompromising acceptance of scientific and technical production methods as a means of overcoming the antiquated practices of the building industry. The industrialization of construction methods, which was indeed to become a fundamental element in twentieth-century mass housing, was recognized by Behrens and de Fries as the necessary precondition for effective house building.

The AEG houses built in 1918–19 on Paul Jordan Strasse in Hennigsdorf (illustration A184) were a first attempt to build according to these principles. Behrens published an article in 1919 entitled "Die Gruppenbauweise" in which these houses were referred to.[43] In his brief summary of the essential arguments of *Vom sparsamen Bauen* at the start of the article, Behrens expounded the advantages of building houses in groups on high-density sites rather than in rows. In accordance with this idea, the

2
Doorway of house at 14–15 Rathenaustrasse on the estate at Hennigsdorf.

3
Henri Sauvage, apartment block, 26 Rue Vavin, Paris, 1912–13.

line of houses on Paul Jordan Strasse was made up of a series of double houses which were set back from the street line and linked by flanking house blocks aligned at right angles to the street. This created a sequence of courtyards on the street side of the housing group. The intended layout, which had already become a well-known feature of Behrens's housing estates, was once again adopted. Three double houses were aligned around three sides of a rectangular courtyard, which provided access to all six units (illustration A212). The courtyard was linked to the street by a hedged path. The layout of these simple forms produced a rhythmical sequence of double houses set back parallel to the road and four-family blocks abutting it at right angles.

By basing the four-family blocks on a cruciform ground plan, Behrens may have succeeded in using the land more economically than would have been the case with a conventional row-house layout. The benefits of this saving in space were offset, however, by the increased costs which resulted from the large number of corner constructions, the increased external wall area, and the complicated form of the roof.[44] The ground plans themselves were also far from convincing, for the flats in the four-family blocks had the disadvantage of facing in one direction only: either to the east or to the west. Partly as a result of this, they suffered from inadequate through-ventilation.[45]

In their outward appearance, the houses on Paul Jordan Strasse gave a striking indication of the frugality of their construction, which used breeze blocks according to the so-called Becher system. It was Behrens's intention to leave this new material bare, "to allow its formal and gray coloration to have its own effect."[46] The powerful, simple, and untreated walls of the cubelike blocks were bound together by the continuous horizontal band of the eaves, on which was set a low, hipped roof. As a contrast to the rough gray of the outer walls, the window shutters and the wooden boarding under the eaves were painted green. The small sheds facing the front gardens on the street side were the only parts of the structure to be given a decorative treatment; with a geometric pattern of dark wooden

bars alternating with light-colored strips of plaster, they stood out from the lifeless gray of the facade. This functionally unnecessary accentuation of the sheds can be explained by their dominant position on the plan. Like the towers of a propylaeum (not to be discounted as a formal source), they flanked the front courtyard and emphasized the rhythmic sequence of the structure. It would appear that the key to the whole design is to be found here: In contrast to the flat, monotonous impression made by a simple row-house layout, the grouped layout reflected Behrens's desire to bring more dynamic and rhythmic modeling and a greater sense of architectural substance to his housing. As an artist, Behrens's predominant interest was architectonic and spatial expression, visual form. The inevitability with which the indented ground plan was produced as the logical consequence of functional considerations tends to suggest that the theory of Gruppenbauweise was used to lend functional legitimacy to a purely aesthetic intention.

The basic ambitions that inspired *Vom sparsamen Bauen*—to create a house type tailored to the needs of the industrial worker and his family, and to develop housing typical of and specific to this class—were not pursued in this manner in the housing programs of the Weimar Republic. The development on Paul Jordan Strasse remained a one-off attempt to test the theory of Gruppenbauweise in practice. When the AEG started to build again in 1920 on the other side of the street, Behrens's layout was adhered to but the ground plans of the houses were altered substantially. There was also no longer any desire to leave the facades bare and untreated. Behrens's successor in the AEG architect's office was Jean Krämer, who had been promoted to managing architect in Behrens's own office after Mies had left. In 1920, when work began on the large-scale expansion of the AEG estate in Hennigsdorf, Krämer did not feel bound to the ideas of his master.[47]

Notes

1. "Die bedeutung der Wohnungsfrage für die Industrie," in *Grossstadt und Kleinhaus* (Berlin, 1917), p. 9.

2. F. Neumeyer, "Arbeiterwohnungen 1900–1918," *Werk und Zeit* 2 (1977), p. 10.

3. E. Haenel, *Die Gartenstadt Hellerau* (1911), quoted in S. Müller, *Kunst und Industrie* (Munich, 1974), p. 44.

4. R. Riemerschmid, "Das Arbeiterhaus," *Höhe Warte* 3 (1907), p. 141.

5. K. Henrici, "Allgemeines und Spezielles über den Bau und die Einrichtungen von Arbeiterwohnungen," *Zeitschrift des Vereins Deutscher Ingenieure* 24 (1906), p. 953.

6. F. Fammler, "Arbeiter-Wohnhäuser," *BAW* (1911), p. 41.

7. "Die Entwicklung des künstlerischen Gedankens im Hausbau," *Schriften der Zentralstelle für Arbeiter-Wohlfahrtseinrichtungen* 29 (1906), p. 9.

8. P. Behrens and H. de Fries, *Vom sparsamen Bauen* (Berlin, 1918), pp. 14 ff.

9. Ibid., p. 16.

10. "A Factory Building by Peter Behrens" (in this volume).

11. St. v. Moos, "Peter Behrens und Le Corbusier," in *Peter Behrens 1868–1940*, exhibition catalog (Kaiserslautern, Hagen, Darmstadt, and Vienna, 1966–67), pp. 21 ff.

12. H. Pogge von Strandmann (ed.), *Walther Rathenau, Tagebuch 1907–1922* (Düsseldorf, 1967), p. 153.

13. On the history of company housing in Berlin from 1848 to 1918 see Fritz Neumeyer, Der Werkwohnungsbau der Industrie in Berlin und seine Entwicklung im 19. und frühen 20. Jahrhundert (diss., Technische Universität Berlin, 1977–78). This essay is a shortened, reworked version of one chapter of the dissertation.

14. A. Riedler, *Emil Rathenau und das Werden der Grosswirtschaft* (Berlin, 1916), pp. 156 ff.; P. Czada, *Die Berliner Elektroindustrie in der Weimarer Zeit* (Berlin, 1969), p. 156.

15. At the general meeting of 1910; see R. Sprenger, "Wie Hennigsdorf wurde," *Die Spannung* 11 (1927–28), p. 328.

16. Site plan at Merseburg in Hoeber 1913, p. 209; Waldsiedlung Lichtenberg in *WMB* 5 (1920–21), pp. 320 ff.; Neumeyer (note 13), pp. 206 ff.

17. "The open style of building rightly belongs to the end of the analytical nineteenth century, to the exaggerated emphasis on individuality. In this style there is an element of anarchistic autonomy. But men are gregarious beings and depend on each other. It seems to me only right that this should also be given aesthetic expression." P. Behrens, "Die Gartenstadtbewegung," *Gartenstadt* 2 (1908), p. 27.

18. Ibid.

19. Hoeber (1913, p. 151) attributed Behrens's use of this ground plan to the influential example of the English garden city movement. Fourier's Phalanstères were a more likely source for Behrens's ideas on collective housing. The schematic ground plan of a Phalanstère, as drawn up around 1840, was composed of a front courtyard, central block, and side wings. It was palace architecture—ultimately derived from Versailles—that was to serve social purposes. See F. Bollerey, *Architekturkonzeption der utopischen Sozialisten* (Munich, 1977).

20. *Der Industriebau* 6 (1915), p. 333.

21. In a De Stijl manifesto of 1924 ["Towards a Plastic Architecture," in U. Conrads, *Programmes and Manifestos on 20th-Century Architecture* (London, 1970), pp. 78–80], Theo van Doesburg demanded that solid building forms be hollowed out, that the interior space be opened up to the outside: "The walls themselves no longer support; they merely provide supporting points. . . . The new architecture is open. The whole structure consists of one space." Behrens's 1911 design satisfied these demands in what, for a brick construction, was an exemplary manner.

22. A. Zimm, *Die Entwicklung des Industriestandortes Berlin* (Berlin, 1959), p. 96.

23. Hoeber incorrectly dated the boathouse 1910, as did H. J. Kadatz. The correct date is given in *Architekturführer DDR* (East Berlin, 1976), p. 138. A pamphlet published by the AEG to mark the opening of the boathouse in May 1912 was entitled Das neue Bootshaus der Ruder-Gesellschaft "Elektra" im Verein der Beamten der AEG und BEW.

24. On the Haus Wiegand by Peter Behrens, see the 1979 publication of the Deutsches Archäologisches Institut Berlin, ed. F. Neumeyer and W. Hoepfner.

25. AEG pamphlet (note 23).

26. The design has survived in photographs of six pages of sketches, in the archive of Dr. Stoedtner at Düsseldorf. They were first published by T. Buddensieg and H. Rogge in *Lotus International* 12 (1976), pp. 90–127.

27. S. Giedion, *Walter Gropius, Mensch und Werk* (Stuttgart, 1954), p. 74.

28. Cremers 1928, p. 24.

29. This apartment house was built in 1912–13 on the Rue Vavin in Paris. Like Sauvage's apartment house on the Rue des Amireaux (1925), this building has a concrete construction and projecting balconies. See S. Giedion, *Bauen in Frankreich* (Leipzig and Berlin, 1928), pp. 108 ff.

30. Cremers 1928, pp. 31 ff.

31. W. Hermann, *Deutsche Baukunst des 19. und 20. Jahrhunderts, Von 1840 bis zur Gegenwart* (Basel and Stuttgart, 1977), p. 61.

32. In a normal stepped block, the walls of each story are set directly above those on the story below, and each receding step makes up a terrace. In the Behrens design, however, special constructional measures are needed to support the balconies.

33. "Etagenhaus und Kleinsiedlung," *Blätter des Deutschen Roten Kreuzes* 5 (1926), p. 36.

34. According to the information in the Stoedtner archive, these drawings carry the titles "view from Wohnstrasse" and "Verkehrstrasse." Both, however, are views of the same street from two different perspectives.

35. In 1919, Behrens had suggested that workers' estates and industrial plants could, "by sharing the same principles, . . . fuse with the industrial buildings into an organic unity out of which a new and unique sort of industrial city could develop." The estates were to be established "in close contact with the industrial installations" and designed and built "in the same spirit of industrial energy." P. Behrens, "Der Fabrikneubau," *Das Echo. Deutsche Exportrevue* (16 October 1919), pp. 129 ff. See also Tilmann Buddensieg, *Peter Behrens und die AEG* (Munich, 1975), pp. 271–299.

36. Plans of these row houses are not included in the publications on Behrens's domestic architecture, nor have any original plans survived. My plans are based on my own studies of the estate, which has been preserved without major alterations. According to Prof. Dr. Kurt Junghanns, who kindly made enquiries, no official building files are extant.

37. Behrens and de Fries, *Vom sparsamen Bauen*, introduction.

38. The Kommission für vorbildliche Arbeiterwohnungen (Commission for Model Workers' Housing) held an exhibition of furniture in the Berliner Gewerkschaftshaus in 1911–12. Behrens contributed designs. After the exhibition, he was appointed by the commission to design standard furniture for a worker's flat containing one room and a kitchen. The result was praised by the commission as "an expression of the character of the modern proletariat." See: *Concordia* 19, no. 2 (1912), p. 32; R. Breuer, "Arbeitermöbel von Peter Behrens," *DKD* (1912), p. 131; S. Günther, "Arbeitermöbel: Architektenentwürfe zu Arbeitermöbel in Deutschland," *Kunst und Alltag um 1900*, Werkbund-Archiv Jahrbuch 3 (Berlin, 1978), pp. 179 ff.

39. P. Behrens and H. de Fries, *Vom sparsamen Bauen*, p. 52. The residents of an estate built according to the program outlined in the book could only be compared to third-class passengers.

40. "Die Gartenstadtbewegung" (reprint of article in *Berliner Tageblatt*, 5 March 1908), *Die Gartenstadt* 2 (1908), p. 27. See also S. Müller, *Kunst und Industrie* (Munich, 1974), p. 45.

41. Compare St. v. Moos, "Wohnkollektiv, Hospiz und Dampfer. Notizen zur Vorgeschichte von Le Corbusiers 'Unité d'habitation,'" *Archithese* 12 (1974), pp. 30–41, with extensive list of sources.

42. H. Tessenow, *Hausbau und dergleichen* (1916); F. Schumacher, *Die Kleinsiedlung* (1917); H. Muthesius, *Kleinhaus und Kleinsiedlung* (1918).

43. *WMB* 4 (1919–20), pp. 122–127.

44. Furthermore, the saving in land to be achieved through the increased depth of the houses was considerably less than was suggested by Behrens and de Fries, whose argument was based partly on incorrect calculations. Instead of the suggested 38 houses, an 11-hectare site could actually accommodate only 19.2 units. Dr. Weishaupt published a critique of the so-called Gruppenbauweise in the *Deutsche Bauzeitung* (vol. 53, pp. 130 ff.) in 1919. This careful and exact analysis uncovered the contradictions and incorrect calculations behind Behrens's proposals. In his reply (ibid., vol. 53, pp. 620–623), Behrens dismissed Weishaupt's article as "tendentious." See also G. Albrecht, "Peter Behrens Vorschläge zur Kliensiedlungsfrage," *Zeitschrift für Wohnungswesen* (1918), pp. 260–262.

45. According to Behrens's description in *Vom sparsamen Bauen*, through-ventilation was not desirable, as it only led to draughts and increased difficulty with heating. (In contrast to the four-family houses, through-ventilation is still possible in the double houses built in the grouped layout.) It was seriously suggested that adequate ventilation would be achieved by leaving open the damper on the stove. See *Vom sparsamen Bauen*, p. 40.

46. Behrens (note 43), p. 124.

47. "When the architect Jean Krämer took over the continuation of work on the Rathenaustrasse/Voltastrasse estate, which had been started before the war, the first thing he did was to change the general plan completely. Quite justifiably, Krämer could find no reason why uniform, four-house blocks on absolutely straight, uninteresting streets should have been planned and also partly constructed on an almost virgin site, for which no specific density had been prescribed." U. Dietrich, "AEG Siedlung in Hennigsdorf b. Berlin," *Bauwelt* 22 (1929), p. 1. On the completion of the Hennigsdorf estate, see also M. Osborn, *Jean Krämer* (Berlin, 1927); H. Littauer, "Industrieller Werkwohnungsbau," *Spannung, Betriebszeitung der AEG* (December 1927), pp. 72 ff.

Fabrikenkunst[1]: The Turbine Hall and What Came of It

Karin Wilhelm

They let the word *betriebstechnisch* [technological] melt on their tongues as their grandparents did *Nachtigall* [nightingale].
Kurt Tucholsky

According to Artur Fürst,

The Edison-Gesellschaft [forerunner of the AEG] . . . not only executed the contracts placed with it, but also built power stations itself in order to sell them at a later stage. The first annual report contains the principle "We intend to build power stations with our capital, and to sell them to independent companies as soon as they have been put into operation, in order to keep our capital constantly available for new undertakings." In this way, new buyers were found for each project. The decision to construct plants was facilitated, so that the number of customers would increase as rapidly as possible. A finance company was linked to the construction company.

Hartmut Pogge von Strandmann writes that there had been discussion since 1907 over "the establishment of a state electricity monopoly . . . for the generation and distribution of electric power. . . ." Walther Rathenau, Pogge says, "advocated a state monopoly, which he saw as a consequence of the development of electricity generating techniques, of the trend towards ever larger power stations, and of the need to centralize the supply of electric current."[2]

This essay discusses a few of the AEG's power stations, chosen for their architectural and technical significance.

As early as 1884 (under its old name, Deutsche Edison-Gesellschaft) the firm contracted with the Berlin city council to build a power station, which went into service in August 1885. This first public power station in Germany, built on the Markgrafenstrasse, replaced the "block stations" (small plants, usually installed in the cellars of existing buildings and supplying current for a small block of houses) that had been in use.[3] The new station initially served the inner city within a radius of 800 meters. It was followed in the same year by a power station on the Mauerstrasse. The demand for energy stimulated concentrated technical and scientific efforts, with the result that by 1888 two more power stations had been constructed in Berlin, on the Schiffbauerdamm and the Spandauer Strasse. Generating stations soon become export articles; one was planned for Barcelona in 1896 and others followed in Genoa and Sampierdarena.

In 1902, Walther Rathenau resigned from the chairmanship of the Elektricitäts-Lieferungs-Gesellschaft, a company the AEG had established in 1897 for the construction and operation of generating stations. Emil Rathenau found a successor for his son in Georg Klingenberg, who had made a name for himself as a consulting engineer. Klingenberg organized the Department for Power Stations as a powerful administrative section within the AEG management, and this department had subordinate sections for "mechanical engineering, electricity supply, switchgear, and for building and architecture."[4]

The existence of the last-named section was particularly noteworthy, for little importance was attached at the time to the architecture of generating stations; it was customary to tack a layer of historical ornament onto an iron frame (illustration 1). Klingenberg, hower, had an "artistic disposition" and "exercised a considerable influence on the artistic form of the power stations projected by the AEG at all times during the period of his association with the firm."[5] He often employed freelance architects, especially the partnership of Dr. Walter Klingenberg and Werner Issel from Berlin-Lichterfelde.[6]

When Peter Behrens joined the AEG as artistic adviser in 1907, he was asked for advice on how an elegant external appearance might be given to the Fürstenwalde power station, which was then under construction.[7] The AEG had begun negotiation with the Fürstenwalde town council in 1899 over the building of a generating station, but the council had been unable to proceed with the project because of municipal commitments. After the AEG offered concessional terms, the negotiations were resumed again in 1906, and construction was started in the following year. Between 1907 and 1908 the ownership of the installation was transferred to the Electricitäts-Lieferung-Gesellschaft. According to a contemporary report, "the building progressed only slowly as a result of the complicated foundation work, and first became operational in March 1908."[8]

1
Franz Schwechten, BEW electrical substation, 91 Alte Jakobstrasse, ca. 1900. From *Deutsche Bauhütte*.

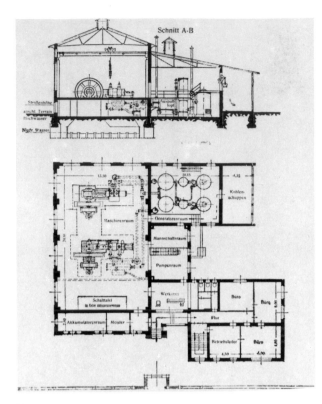

2
Ground plan and elevation of
Fürstenwalde power station, 1908.
From *Deutsche Bauhütte*.

3
Fürstenwalde power station. From
Deutsche Bauhütte.

4
Entrance to Fürstenwalde power
station. From *Deutsche Bauhütte*.

The Fürstenwalde station was made up of a turbine house and an administration building. Accommodation for the works manager was provided on the upper floor of the administration building, which was linked to the turbine house by a covered walkway. Both parts of the building were reached via a formal entrance portal. Brick construction, faced with large areas of lighter-colored stucco, was used throughout. Although it is impossible to find out exactly the extent to which Behrens was involved in the planning, his decorative touch can be clearly seen on the portal and in the single-story wing in which the storage batteries were housed. He gave a curved contour to the hipped gable of the portal and used light-colored plaster panels as a geometric ornament to contrast against the darker background. Above all, the small white squares on the three gables of the battery shed, on the entrance portal gable, and on the linking walkway are sure evidence of Behren's hand. (Behrens used exactly this type of ornament, usually in variations based on other geometric forms, to decorate and illustrate many of the AEG's products. In this way, he remained consistent to his demand that industrial design should avoid ''overelaborate ornamentation'' or, if that proves impossible, should choose an ''impersonal'' form of decoration. And, as Behrens said, ''this demand is nearest met by simple geometric ornament.''[9]) Like the AEG's electrical goods, its power stations were built from the foundation stone to the last tile on the roof by the firm itself.[10] By carrying the decorative form used on the firm's products and graphic designs over to the power station, Behrens extended his concept of an all embracing manner of design to include a building. In this way the power station too became another AEG product and part of what was seen as a unified range of goods.

The Fürstenwalde power station showed further evidence of Peter Behren's hand. It would seem that the power station was not only meant to be convincing because of its modern, high-performance technology, but—like all the firm's finished products—because of its equally modern architectonic form. Unlike the later AEG factories in Berlin, whose outer shells pointed to the quality of the goods produced within, the Fürstenwalde power station sought in its own form to offer proof and evidence of product quality. The connection between marketing strategy and the cultural responsibility of industry was clearly pointed out by a contemporary critic:

Just as one can rightly recognize someone as a tasteless primitive from the absurd and ugly details of his house and furnishings, so every sensible person today is also inclined to judge the character of a given firm by the design and finish of its buildings and factories. Crude tastelessness and coarseness are proof to the knowing eye that the managers of the firm are culturally backward, that contemporary intellectual currents flow past them without influencing their ideas, that they pay no attention to modern life. And people who are inactive and inattentive in this respect are certainly equally careless in other areas of their activity.

Every intelligent manufacturer will strive, accordingly, to give his factory buildings and workshops that character of precise, clear, and practical beauty which is being developed ever more clearly in our art and which, to the eyes of later ages, should stand as testimony to our way of thinking, as a symbol of our work.

The forms Behrens has used for [the Fürstenwalde power station] show how this requirement is to be fulfilled.[11]

In the year in which the Fürstenwalde power station went into operation, Behrens was developing the AEG's architectural image in a wide range of architectural work. The exhibition pavilion for the Deutsche Schiffbau-Ausstellung in Berlin was built to his plans in June 1908, and the powerhouse beside the turbine factory was also completed in the September of that year. During 1908 Behrens was also involved in the redesigning of Johann Kraaz's railway-equipment factory, and the new turbine hall was erected between April and October 1909. Behrens's attention was also taken up by the planning stage of the ''factory for transformers, resistors, and high-voltage equipment'' (the ''high-voltage factory,'' for short), which was built between April 1909 and July 1910.[12]

With the commission for the turbine hall (see illustrations A17–A32) Behrens had for the first time the opportunity to supervise all the phases in the construction of a large, complicated factory installation and to fully incorporate in the architectural conception the production and structural factors involved. He was thereby given the chance to go beyond the level of being merely a "facade artist," to which Hermann Muthesius had once relegated the industrial architect.[13]

Naturally, Behrens was subject to certain constraints in designing the turbine hall. It was stipulated at the outset that the building frame should be made of steel using a hinged construction, and that for the sake of lighting all nonstructural walls should be made of glass. The "basic architectural conception," however, was Behrens's own.[14]

This conception was based on the aesthetic conviction that a humane culture could be created on the basis of machine production. The development of such a culture was dependent, according to Behrens, on whether or not the technical achievments of the age were "to be given expression in a mature, noble art."[15] This implied that what Muthesius called the "inner relationship between the Zeitgeist and the engineering spirit"[16] should be given a formal, aesthetic reality, and that, in Behrens's words, "lucidity must be maintained, particularly in the structure of a building designed for industrial use, for just such a building should become the occasion for a new beauty characteristic of the spirit of our age."[17] It was not enough merely to transfer the decorative forms of industrial product design onto the building in which the products were manufactured; rather, the process of machine production itself was to be formulated in specifically architectonic terms. The fact that engineering construction remained a material precondition of the process only served to support this intention.

In his design for the turbine hall Behrens used the constructional elements in three different ways. On the front facing the Berlichingenstrasse he emphasized everything constructional (illustrations A26 ff.). The solid vertical supports of the hinged frames were exposed for the entire height of the wall and were locked powerfully into the concrete plinth; the large areas of glass between these pillars emphasized their compactness. The result was a rhythmic repetition of identical elements whose function was directly displayed in the exposed impost hinges. Like the pillars that tapered down onto them, the hinges gave the impression that they could be multiplied to any length with the same repeating cadence. The dynamic flow of identical, precise forms cast in a modern material suggested to the eye an analogy to a sequence of mechanical movements, a consistent, exact, powerful, and precise operation. The constructional abstraction of the frame was offered as an equivalent to the mechanical abstraction of the production process.[18] Concise, calculated forms were common to both interior and exterior. The sequence of these forms, in which the constructional demands of the hall were given a precise and tangible expression, created on the outside a counterpart to the factory interior, whose layout was determined by the precise movements of the machines. Karl Ernst Osthaus was almost incredulous about this: "Is it not strange, how such a logical and unified building becomes a symbol of that which it encloses?"[19]

The impact of the Berlichingenstrasse front was weakened on the other long side of the hall, the side facing the yard. In order to emphasize the main hall, Behrens set the two-story-high side hall slightly back from the street line and clad the shed in concrete to the depth of the turbine hall's first main truss. He did this, he said, in order to give "an even stronger impact to the steelwork on the sides of both halls."[20] Behind this concrete-clad bay, the rest of the wall was constructed of steel supports and wide horizontal steel beams. The panels between the window bands were filled with brick and then clad with sheet metal. The predominant feature here was the economical treatment of the materials; the architectonic impact of the wall was derived entirely from the satisfaction of functional demands, from supporting and filling in. Rather than emphasize the technical requirements of the building, Behrens used nothing that did not "result directly out of the engineering construction."[21]

On the courtyard side, the building's frame, which was displayed on the Berlichingenstrasse front, was reduced to a straightforward statement of the constructional reality of the supporting steel skeleton and the areas of infill. Whereas the process of machine production was given symbolic representation on the street front, a simple equation of function and performance was applied on the courtyard side, which was hidden from public view. The visible interpretation of the principles that determined the factory's internal layout vanished on the courtyard side, where the dominating factor was the reduction of the building's form to an abstraction of its function. In this respect, the courtyard front was the most typical expression of the characteristic of Behrens's design that Anton Jaumann described as follows: "One might say that in all his works the human hand is without importance. His lines are so abstract, so detached, so mathematically comprehensible that whether they were drawn by the artist himself or by a machine is irrelevant. . . . his hand is a machine."[22]

This confluence of machine production and architectural language made the turbine hall into a paradigm of modern industrial architecture. As late as 1933, Richard Hammann wrote the following.

A rational, functional, and yet powerful and monumental building: the factory, a utilitarian construction, is portrayed with dehumanized, objective forms which are nevertheless entirely human creations. Constructive art in the design of the factory and constructive work inside the factory, rational creativity and rational production join together here.[23]

But Hammann qualified this in his description of the gable front on the Huttenstrasse, which he felt made "too much public display," was "too temple-like, too ceremonial."[24] On the gable front, Behrens had tried to achieve a subtle interpretation of the constructive elements of the shed (illustrations A25, A30). The characteristic qualities of the end facade were rigid symmetry, spatial separation of the set-back side hall, and an exact formal treatment. The determining elements were the segmental concrete gable, the large window which ran right up to its base, and the inward-sloping corner pylons articulated by horizontal steel bands. The engineer Bernhard criticized these pylons "on the grounds of artistic truth,"[25] for they had no load-bearing function.

Thus, the end facade had the character of a show front. It seems to make a complete break with the two side fronts, but on closer examination it becomes clear that the same method of design used by Behrens on the Berlichingenstrasse front was also applied to the end facade. The powerful, projecting gable is, in the last analysis, simply another example of the intensification of the construction form used on the Berlichingenstrasse front: the roof of the main hall, which "for artistic reasons" had been given a "barrel-like vault with six faces."[26] As on the Berlichingenstrasse, the construction was taken absolutely seriously and found an expression in an autonomous form that, although it went beyond what was absolutely necessary, did not deny the roof construction. Behrens created in this way a noble and monumental form that, when contrasted against the tapering pylons, further amplified the symbolic presentation of the construction. The segmental gable which was pushed forward in this way summoned up associations with the classical and humanistic tradition, giving the building the solemn character of a temple. On the two side fronts Behrens adhered to the principle of creating constructional analogies to the machine processes going on inside, but on the end facade this principle was reduced to a single independent form heavy with associational values. The tired theme of the repetition of the same self-justifying motif was suppressed to such an extent that Franz Mannheimer could see the end facade as the symbolic expression of a single tool: "The narrow street front projects at the center, and together with the squat roof looks like a hammer with its thick handle standing on the ground."[27]

Behrens thus developed in the turbine hall three different levels of architectural and aesthetic statement: constructional veracity on the courtyard side, a representation of the manufacturing process on the Berlichingenstrasse, and symbolization and ambiguity on the Huttenstrasse. This new departure in factory design, and the concentration on genuinely architectonic factors in contrast to the earlier, decorative practices, took place in conjunction with radical changes in the realm of production engineering.

Production engineering had just gained an important new innovator in the person of Georg Klingenberg. The need to supply ever larger amounts of energy demanded economy measures in the production of electrical power, and Klingenberg felt that savings could be achieved by concentrating productive potential and defining a clear succession of processes. As a contemporary was later to recall,

The idea of the direct and continuous supply of energy led Klingenberg to arrange for the coal to run in a straight line along the axis of the boiler house, and to align the boiler house and the machine room so that the steam would be piped the shortest possible distance at the highest possible speed, with correspondingly short pipe connections. The same idea also led him to link the boiler and the economizer together as one unit, to provide for the shortest links possible between the generators and the switchgear, and to set all the subsidiary processes as near as possible to the main axis and at right angles to it.[28]

The first power station to be built according to these new guidelines was the Märkische Electrizitätswerk at Heegermühle, near Eberswalde, shown in illustration 5. This station, erected between 1909 and 1910 by a subsidiary of the AEG, was made up of a combined boiler and turbine house (linked by a bridge to a separate building housing the switchgear) and a free-standing house for the works manager, all of red brick. As Klingenberg recalled in 1913, "With the planning of the Märkische Elektrizitätswerk in 1909, I set myself the task of proving that, in comparison with the manner of construction that had been usual until then, it was possible to achieve a significant reduction in the specific costs of power stations, and

furthermore than the efficiency of the plant could be greatly increased in this way."[29] This power plant, for which Walter Klingenberg and Werner Issel acted as architectural advisers, "attracted attention over many years and became the model for many other power stations."[30] It drew interest not only because of its technical aspects, but also because of its architectural qualities.

Although the Märkische Elektrizitätswerk was of great importance to the AEG's commercial strategy, there is no evidence to suggest that Behrens was involved in it. Nevertheless, the whole complex carried stylistic marks developed in the AEG factories in Berlin and well known to the firm's design department and to the architects associated with it. Just as Behrens had emphasized the gable ends on his additions to the railway material factory and on the turbine hall, so the silhouette of the power station was similarly accentuated (illustration 8). Architectural details that Behrens was using in his contemporaneous designs for the Brunnenstrasse complex also appeared at Heegermühle. As at Brunnenstrasse, the gable ends of the turbine house and the switchgear house of the Märkische Elektrizitätswerk emphasized the roof construction. Indeed, the subsidiary block at the front of the turbine house was articulated in exactly the same way as were Behrens's railway-equipment factory and his factories at Hennigsdorf: The windows were aligned in recessed vertical panels (illustrations 6, 8, A50, A141). Like the tower of the railway-equipment factory (illustration A47), the switchgear house of the power station had a clearly molded triangular gable and a pronounced roof cornice. Even more striking, it had the faceted, protruding stairwell which Behrens had developed for the high-voltage factory (illustration A58). The linking of white-framed windows in bands and the layering of the wall in order to create axial strips of windows were also techniques Behrens had used (illustrations A47 ff., A57 ff.). Echoes of the humanist tradition in architecture, such as Behrens had

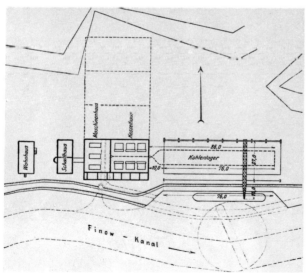

5
"Märkische" power station,
Heegermühle, 1909–10, site plan.

called up so vigorously in the end facade of the turbine hall, still lingered here, but were unmistakably united with the intention that prevailed on the Berlichingenstrasse front: to arrive at the architectural motifs by accentuating the constructive elements. But the functional objectivity of the courtyard front of the turbine factory also left its traces on the Heegermühle power station: The boiler house, with its six single chimneys, was entirely built around a steel frame construction, which was only broken up by the horizontal tie beams, between which the windows were installed.[31]

An admiring appraisal of Georg Klingenberg's achievment by a contemporary critic can be applied not only to the technical unity of the power station complex but also to its architectural unity, which also embraced the machine room: "Before he came, the architect, the boiler maker, the mechanical engineer, and the electrician were allowed to design the various separate aspects of a power station, and the intellectually quite unrelated parts were then put together as well as they could be. Klingenberg was the first to build up the power station out of one mold, as a true work of art."[32] It is clear that the idea of architectural investment in the sense of giving a public face or a representative function to a technological building was becoming redundant. As a result of the specific sequence of work operations, which determined the spatial layout, and because of the subdivision of the building into defined areas for particular tasks, the architectural construction or form of the building gained a new descriptive role: The architectural design conveyed visually the particular function of a building or part of a building.

The development initiated by the Märkische Elektrizitätswerk reached a climax with the Grosskraftwerk Zschornewitz at Golpa, near Bitterfeld. Begun in March 1915, this plant was by 1919 "the largest steam-powered generating station in the world."[33] This plant too was designed according to the Klingenberg principles.[34] The four boiler houses abutted the turbine house at right angles, and the eleven cooling towers were located on the opposite side of the machine house. A large, free-standing switch house completed the installation. Because the plant was initially planned "to supply power to industries of particular strategic importance,"[35] it was important to the war effort that it be constructed quickly. "In the interests of rapid installation,"[36] Georg Klingenberg reported, the boiler houses and the adjoining turbine house were built using an all-steel frame and panel construction. Klingenberg transformed this necessity into an architectural concept. In his 1913 book *Bau grosser Elektrizitätswerke*, Klingenberg included a chapter entitled "Architektur" in which he set down a whole catalog of demands that, in his opinion, factory architecture had to satisfy. "One should never forget," he wrote, "that a power station is nothing but an electricity factory and that, just as with other factory buildings, its industrial character should not be concealed. In reality, theatrical-looking buildings are frequently put up, especially when municipal architects have kept for themselves the job of providing the architectural design. . . . When special structural devices are used, such as a steel frame in the boiler house, steel roof trusses in the turbine house, etc., then they should be allowed to appear in an appropriately simple form on the exterior and should not be hidden behind a secondary construction." Writing of overdecorated designs, Klingenberg commented that "the impartial observer expects to find in a power station the image of a factory and not of a lecture hall in which one incidentally comes across machines."[37]

The function of an office or a switch house, however, was quite different from that of a boiler house. At Golpa these control and administrative buildings adhered to traditional architectural motifs. The exterior of the three-story office building hinted at columns and an architrave, and was fronted by a facade carrying giant pilasters. The columns on the side

8
Märkische power station. From
Klingenberg 1913.

9
Golpa power station, 1915–19, site
plan. From *Wasmuths Monatshefte für
Baukunst*.

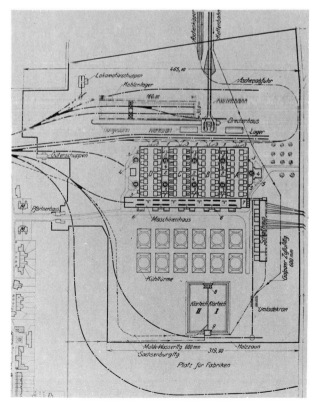

10
General view of Golpa power station.
From *Wasmuths Monatshefte für
Baukunst*.

11
Gable front of boiler houses of Golpa
power station, with coal conveyors.
From *Wasmuths Monatshefte für
Baukunst.*

12
Golpa power station. From *Wasmuths
Monatshefte für Baukunst.*

13
Office of Golpa power station. From
Wasmuths Monatshefte für Baukunst.

14
Control house of Golpa power station.
From Klingenberg 1920.

15
Turbine house of Golpa power station.
From Klingenberg 1920.

16
Workers' housing in Golpa,
1915–19, standard ground plans.
From Klingenberg 1920.

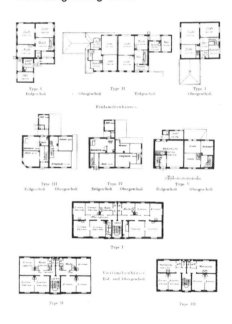

17
Peter Behrens (artistic adviser),
workers' housing in Golpa, 1915–19.
From Klingenberg 1920.

18
Peter Behrens (artistic adviser), house
of works manager and transformer
building at Golpa, 1915–19. From
Klingenberg 1920.

walls supported capitals, and a roof cornice held the whole block together. The blank walls of the three-sided rear wing were divided by pilasters into large panels, which were separated from the windows above by an ornamental string course. Even fictive architecture was allowed. On its short end the switch house had a triangular gable which was not the conclusion of a pitched roof, but was set in front of a flat roof. To identify the entrance to the switch house, a short architrave hovered above the roof line to make this part of the facade resemble a portico. In the machine house the desire to distinguish particular functions by reference to classical types was very clear. The entrance to each hall was indicated by a pillared porch which, by association with a "vestibule," further served to indicate the point of entry. Through this process of association, external architectonic expression was given to the various representative functions ascribed to each particular building or part of a building.

In comparison with the Fürstenwalde solution, the rejection of a unified formal language is quite clear in the design of the Golpa power station. The ennoblement of a factory building, such as Behrens had achieved with the classicist gable end of the turbine hall and had adapted for other buildings,[38] was rejected on principle by Georg Klingenberg. Accordingly, Walter Klingenberg and Werner Issel limited formal or historical features to the realm of management. The different buildings in the power station complex were assembled together by them according to the logic of the production process and were given a final veneer of uniformity when the same light-colored plaster was applied to the whole complex.

Behrens's pupil Walter Gropius, who had also worked on the turbine hall, tried to counteract this tendency. A year before work began on the Golpa power station, Gropius was given the opportunity to build a model factory for the 1914 Werkbund exhibition at Cologne. As the critic Adolf Behne wrote at the time, "The problem Gropius had to solve was a double one: He had not only to design a factory but a model factory which, at the same time, would also be a good exhibition building.''[39] In this double character lay both restriction and potential. On one hand, the exhibition aspect had to be taken into account: this meant that formal and representational demands had to be given more consideration than was usual in a factory. On the other hand, the nature of the commission supported all those artistic considerations whose realization did not have to be restricted by the demands of actual production processes or by the wishes of the factory owner. Gropius simply had to satisfy the set conditions, which called for a "machine factory" which was to be "modern in its components and dimensions" and "in keeping with the general character of the industrial section [of the exhibition]"[40] The factory was to be divided into "the office block, the adjoining courtyard with garage buildings, and the machine hall."[41] At its north end was to be a machine hall "connected with the special pavilion of the Deutz gas-engine factory."[42] In addition, Gropius was responsible for the "general design and layout of the buildings,"[43] and he had to incorporate in his design the so-called Maschinenhalle II introduced by the firm of Breest and Co. at the 1913 Internationale Baufach-Ausstellung at Leipzig.[44]

Within the framework of these conditions, Gropius worked out a design in which all utilitarian demands were subordinated to a radical artistic statement. Even the layout of the factory was based on a highly contrived form (illustration 19). The centerpiece of the plan was a strongly symmetrical inner courtyard with carefully recessed corners. The shape and alignment of the courtyard determined the placing of the other elements of the factory. The office block acted as a subsidiary cross-axis (illustration 20).[45] The entrance portal to the office block was set into a contrasting, darker-colored surround, and, like the machine hall, straddled the main axis. Enclosing the courtyard on both sides were inward-facing garages.

The relationship of the office block to the garages and the machine hall was thus formally established by means of the axis, so that the subordinate reference to production processes actually reflected aesthetic preference rather than a functional sequence of shorter and more economical paths. This subordination of the circulation pattern of a factory to an artificial aesthetic scheme illustrated the conception of contemporary architecture as "synthetic form-giving,"[46] which Gropius favored at the time. Like Behrens, Gropius felt that the "fundamental tone of [the] age" was set by "commerce, technology, and transportation," whose "types and expressive forms" had to be built up "from new technical and spatial preconditions,"[47] and that the new architecture had to be created on the same basis.

Gropius achieved artistic unity in the Werkbund factory by virtually isolating the productive area and by forcing it to submit to the same order as the administration block. By using a symmetrical axis,[48] Gropius ideally integrated the spatially separated work areas into one body, unifying them (as it were) by ennobling the production areas according to the example of Behrens. This unity was underlined by the use of decorative elements derived entirely from the chosen building materials. For example, the light-on-dark clinker-brick surround that framed the door leading from the back of the offices into the courtyard was a reversal of the color scheme of the main portal on the front facade of the office block. At the other end of the courtyard, the same light-on-dark combination was used for the entrance to the machine shed, but here the rails on which the shed doors were hung replaced the dark band of brickwork on the courtyard door of the office block as the horizontal termination (illustrations 21, 22). By such means, an almost reciprocating system was established among the various parts of the factory, which supported their assimilation into the whole. Gropius tried to exclude anything that contradicted this system. He even threatened to give up the commission when he was told of a plan to exhibit a large armor-plate press in the courtyard[49]—this would have destroyed his refined and balanced ensemble. (The press was finally relegated to a site at the back end of the machine hall, in front of the Deutz pavilion.) The attempt to unite the workshop and office buildings into one architectural entity also determined the design of the elevation. Here, however, the formal influence ran in the reverse direction to that already described: The design of the public building was guided by that of the functional shed.

The starting point for the Werkbund design was the steel construction of the three-bay machine hall, whose side faces were blocked in by Gropius with clinker-brick walls topped by window bands. With this combination of a steel frame, masonry, and glass he also built the striking gable end. Here, a brick band duplicated the form of the flattened arch and provided a surround for the large, steel-framed glass panel. This mixture of materials, which were all treated as equals, was repeated on the office block. Brick was used to clad the front facade, while on the rear facade, facing the enclosed courtyard, a broad glazed band was supported on brick pillars. There was no cladding or veiling of the architectural form, which was entirely developed out of the structure. Indeed, the opposite was the case: From the visibly massive block roof was suspended a glass wall, which completely enclosed the supporting columns.

With the Werkbund factory, Gropius was able to realize his artistic demands in an exemplary way. In order "to give worthy expression to the intrinsic value of the plant and its working methods,"[50] Gropius completely renounced the architectural language that had been cultivated up until that time and dispensed with all traces of the "external dignity" that "embellished conventional architecture and decoration."[51] He did not refrain, however, from using a traditional method of composition in order to gain the desired harmonious effect—an effect that was heightened by exploiting the material qualities and structural potential of the factory. This was quite new. Gropius no longer produced a unity of function and public display in one all-embracing form, as Behrens had done, but, by refusing to give one or other of the buildings a particular architectural prominence, achieved a visible external homogeneity among the parts. In each part of the complex, however, the real differences among the various work processes were at least theoretically maintained, even though these differences were no longer given architectural expression. In this, Gropius could refer back to a 1910–11 building in which he had already tried to achieve similar results.

Gropius's first commission after leaving Behrens's studio in 1910 had been for the Karl Benscheidt shoe-last factory (Faguswerk) in Alfeld an der Leine.[52] Working together with Adolf Meyer from the basis of an already-worked-out ground plan, Gropius drew up a three-story building to house both the workshops and the offices. The exterior wall was composed of brick pillars and broad, projecting bands of windows (illustration 23). By substituting glass panels for the conventional brick wall, Gropius exposed the various work processes carried out inside the building: on the ground floor the mechanical production of shoe lasts, on the middle floor the office work, and on the top floor the manufacture by hand of model lasts. The architecture refrained entirely from making interpretative statements in the form of quotations from or adaptions of classical architecture. Indeed, it negated any such claims with the all-over glass covering, which displayed the actual work processes in a completely neutral way. In the Werkbund design, the curtain wall on the courtyard front of the office block was the only evidence of this approach.

Gropius's ambition to create an architecturally homogeneous factory installation out of buildings with different functions by means of clearly defined compositional principles proved illusionary. No prototype came out of the model factory. What in 1914 was seen by Theodor Heuss as pregnant with promise ("He [Gropius] does not make declamations, is completely unrhapsodic in his nakedness, and one cannot devise any lyrics for him—but he is good"[53]) was judged useless ten years later:

19
Factory at Werkbund exhibition,
Cologne, 1914, site plan. From
Deutsche Kunst und Dekoration, 1914.

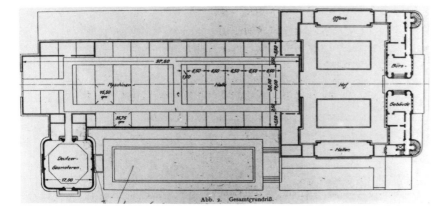

21
Inner courtyard of factory at
Werkbund exhibition. From *Deutsche
Kunst und Dekoration*, 1914.

22
Inner courtyard of factory at
Werkbund exhibition. From *Deutsche
Kunst und Dekoration*, 1914.

20
Office block of factory at Werkbund
exhibition. From *Deutsche Kunst und
Dekoration*, 1914.

23
Fagus factory, Alfeld, 1911, facade.
From W. Müller-Wulckow, *Architektur
der zwanziger Jahre in Deutschland.*

24
Machine house of Fagus factory. From
Müller-Wulckow.

Modernity should strike one in the eye. But Sachlichkeit [objectivity] is a style that does not allow itself to be exaggerated. All these dogmatic cubes, these unnecessary (and totally unpractical) glass walls, these assaults against the sense of statics are basically no more than "Architecture" all over again. These forms are just as rigidly predetermined as those on an old facade. And the effect is thoroughly romantic. It corresponds to the literary notion of technology, but not to its operation![54]

This criticism was penned by Fritz Stahl, a former member of the Werkbund, in reference to the "Grosskraftwerk Klingenberg." Stahl regarded this power station as a mature, model example of industrial architecture. It was built by the AEG for the Berliner Städtische Elektrizitätswerke Aktien-Gesellschaft, and work was begun on it in September 1925. A contemporary account explained that "the AEG undertook all the functions of an advisory engineer . . . from the preparatory work right to the stage of giving over the key to the completed plant, including the architectural design and construction, and all the mechanical and electrical installations."[55] This was a gigantic power station for the period, and it produced 192,750 million kilowatt-hours per month. Such an output was only possible as the result of further rationalization in the production process, which naturally affected the design and the layout. As Tröger noted,

The construction of a large power station calls for automation across the whole front, for the automatic supervision and control of all the operational and monitoring equipment, and thereby for the general application of the techniques which have been in use for years in electrical control systems.

The experience gained in the building of switchgear installations has taught that the introduction of automatic control fundamentally changed the general layout of the plant; the concern for a clearly arranged layout for the whole plant declined in importance and was replaced by an increased emphasis on a more sensible grouping of the various component parts of the complex according to the particular tasks they have to perform.[56]

In the face of such technical demands, an artistic concept could only be realized in a limited way; the use of a formal, architectural scheme of composition was already quite impossible. In contrast to Gropius and the Werkbund factory, Klingenberg and Issel, the designers of this power station, "were deprived of alternatives in the design of the building."[57] For the boiler house, the turbine house, and the office block they were forced to use a steel frame with tie beams running the length of the wall, as this type of construction guaranteed the shortest building time. Only the 30,000-volt switchgear house was built with load-bearing walls.

The two boiler houses (illustration 27) were independent of, but linked to, the turbine house. They were set on each side of a central axis, which was expressed on the symmetrical gable front more as a constructional statement than as a design feature. The same open display of modern constructional and material values was typical of the machine house (illustrations 28, 29). This method of deriving the architectural form of the sheds purely out of the constructional elements was developed quite systematically as the legacy of Behrens. But now the front exposed to public view was also submitted to this principle (illustration 30). With his design for the gable end of the AEG turbine hall, Behrens had given the public an ennobled image of industrial labor. The front facade of the turbine house, in contrast, was pared down to its structural reality, and nothing else was added beyond that "which derived directly from the building technology," as Karl Bernhard had said of the courtyard of the turbine factory. Constructional reality thus finally lost its "back yard" character and was accepted as an adequate expressive vehicle for industrial buildings.

The ten-story office block (illustrations 31–34) had a wide range of functions; it housed a water tank on top, a lecture hall, public rooms, and a small museum. The steel frame was hidden behind decorative brick and tile work. (The idea of a glazed curtain wall was rejected.) The design strove to differentiate between the administration building and the production areas. The use of color on the industrial sheds was not only intended

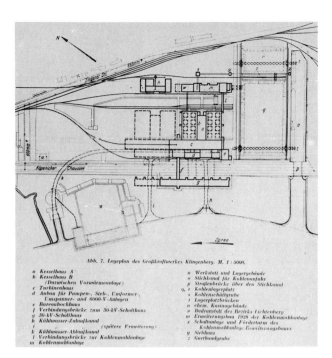

25
Klingenberg power station, Rummelsberg, 1925–26, general site plan. This and the following illustrations are from R. Laube, *Das Grosskraftwerk Klingenberg* (1927).

Abb. 7. Lageplan des Großkraftwerkes Klingenberg. M. 1 : 5000.

a *Kesselhaus A*
b *Kesselhaus B*
   (Dazwischen Vorwärmeanlage)
c *Turbinenhaus*
d *Anbau für Pumpen-, Sieb-, Umformer-,*
   Umspanner- und 6000-V-Anlagen
e *Bureauhochhaus*
f *Verbindungsbrücke zum 50-kV-Schalthaus*
g *50-kV-Schalthaus*
h *Kühlwasser-Zulaufkanal*
i *(spätere Erweiterung)*
k *Kühlwasser-Ablaufkanal*
l *Verbindungsbrücke zur Kohlenmahlanlage*
m *Kohlenmahlanlage*

n *Werkstatt und Lagergebäude*
o *Stichkanal für Kohlenanfuhr*
p *Straßenbrücke über den Stichkanal*
q, r *Kohlenlagerplatz*
s *Kohlenschüttgrube*
t *Lagerplatzbrücken*
u *ehem. Kasinogebäude*
v *Badeanstalt des Bezirks Lichtenberg*
w *Erweiterungsbau 1928 der Kohlenmahlanlage*
x *Schaltanlage und Förderturm des*
   Kohlenmahlanlage-Erweiterungsbaues
y *Siebhaus*
z *Gurtbandgrube*

26
General view of Klingenberg power station.

27
Gable end of Klingenberg power
station.

28
Turbine house of Klingenberg power
station.

30
Interior of turbine house of
Klingenberg power station.

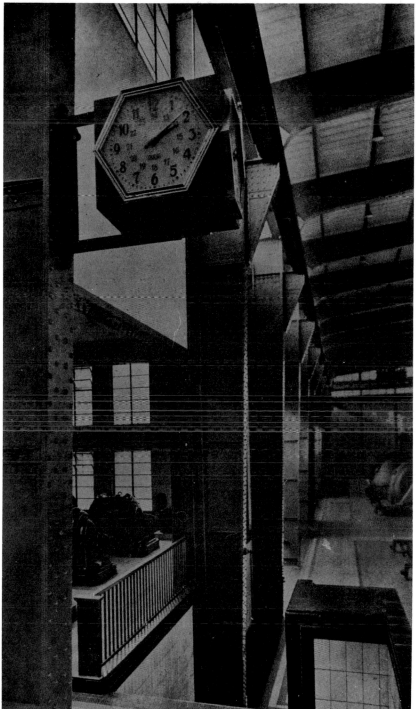

29
Gable end of turbine house of
Klingenberg power station, with bridge
to office tower.

as an embellishment, but also served "to distinguish the individual operational areas clearly from each other and to make them easily recognizable to the workers."[58] However, in spite of the luxuriousness of its coloring and detailing, the office block was also subjected to a certain form of rationalization as the center of a communications network: "Not only architectural factors were important in siting the office block; also important was an optimal location in terms of the distribution of the workforce and for overall communications."[59] It is true that by adopting a frame-and-panel construction for the office block the architects did strive for a harmony of motifs with the boiler house and turbine house; this pattern, however, was predetermined by the decision to use a block partition wall.[60]

The switchgear house was divided from the main group of buildings by a roadway, but directly linked to it by a footbridge. In this way, the switchgear house appeared to have been purposefully isolated, as if to confront the rest of the plant. Its special standing within the complex was made clear by the luxuriousness of its interior. The move from the turbine house to an autonomous building marked the growing importance of swtichgear since the time of the Fürstenwalde design. As Tröger noted, the nerve center of the switchgear house, the control room, was "responsible for the overall supervision of the individual sectors and for coherent action, particularly in cases of malfunction." He continued: "The control room, which had previously only served the electrical circuitry, was given operational control over the entire plant, and thus gained significantly in importance. With this development, the Grosskraftwerk approached an enclosed machine whose component parts worked harmoniously together and which only needed to be set in motion and attended to at one point."[61] For the switchgear house the architects produced a mixture of regal pomp in the powerful architrave and technological splendor in the illuminated, steel-framed ceiling. With its steps and coffers, the ceiling transcended its simple functional purpose of providing adequate lighting and became a sweeping, illuminated vault.

31
Office tower of Klingenberg power station.

34
Control house and office tower of Klingenberg power station.

35
Switchgear house of Klingenberg power station.

32
Detail of brickwork on office tower of Klingenberg power station.

33
Reception hall of Klingenberg power station.

36
Main control block of Klingenberg
power station.

This totally new world of automation marked the historical end of Behrens's attempt to free a simple factory hall from the prevailing function-profit relationship by investing it with the power of culture. However, in the three representational levels he gave to the turbine hall, Behrens had created the preconditions for the development of a modern industrial architecture. The three methods could be used at will according to the nature and function of the particular building. It was these design principles rather than the concrete architectural forms that were to have a lasting influence. In their attempts to achieve the combination of multiplicity and overall unity that Behrens had given to an industrial complex, his followers tended toward exaggeration. In doing so, they were in striking opposition to the enthusiasm for uniformity vigorously propagated in the 1920s by Gropius. Although Behrens's successors were doubtless still able to give architectural articulation to real functional and representational differences, they did so in a language that was becoming more and more obsolete. In contrast, Gropius and his fellow compaigners radicalized the design method itself. By renouncing a narrative architectural language, their simple, plain, and stereometric volumes could claim to be an egalitarian system of design. The egalitarian stereometry of the Gropius group seemed to offer the chance to create a new industrial style, a goal that Behrens had hoped to achieve through the ennoblement of all types of technical products. The abandonment of the direction followed by Behrens cleared the way for the success of the new style—a success that led Behrens in 1932 to draw the following conclusion:

It would appear that the resources of technology in the widest sense are being employed to promote values such as physical health, comfortable living, the effortless execution of social affairs, and everything else that belongs to an urban existence. It could follow from this that the forms of architecture, perhaps unconsciously, will approach the forms that are specific to technology.[62]

37
Ceiling and Behrens-designed clock in
main control block of Klingenberg
power station.

Notes

1. This title was chosen in reference to an article written by Franz Mannheimer: "Fabrikenkunst," *Die Hilfe* 16, no. 18 (1910), pp. 289–290.

2. See Hartmut Pogge von Strandmann, "Widersprüche im Modernisierung Deutschlands. Der Kampf der verarbeitenden Industrie gegen die Schwerindustrie," in *Industrielle Gesellschaft und politisches System* (Bonn, 1978), pp. 231–232; Georg Klingenberg, *Bau grosser Elektrizitätswerke*, first edition (Berlin, 1913), I, pp. V–XII. In Berlin, electricity was provided by private companies until 1915, and then by a municipal company, the Berliner Städtische Elektrizitätswerke AG.

3. The Städtische Elektrizitätswerke (founded by Emil Rathenau), which later became the Berliner Elektrizitäts-Werke, was the company responsible for these block stations.

4. W. Majerczik, "Elektrizitätswerke vom AEG-Typ," *AEG-Zeitung* 16, no. 9 (1914), p. 19.

5. R. Laube (ed.), *Das Grosskraftwerk Klingenberg* (Berlin, 1927), p. 15.

6. It has not been possible to find out anything about this firm of architects. It may be surmised that Walter Klingenberg was related to Georg Klingenberg, whose father was a practicing architect in Berlin. In the partnership, it would seem that the drawing work was done by Issel. Walter Klingenberg and Issel worked for the AEG until 1928 at the latest.

7. In addition to the clear stylistic attribution, Behrens's collaboration is confirmed in an account of the Fürstenwalde power station in the architectural magazine *Deutsche Bauhütte*: R. Rose, "Ein Elektrizitätswerk," *Deutsche Bauhütte* 14, no. 19 (1910), pp. 162–163.

8. G. Siegel, "Das Elektrizitätswerk Fürstenwalde," *AEG-Zeitung* 12, no. 9 (1910), p. 1. This author makes no mention of Behrens, but it was unusual for individuals to be mentioned in the *AEG-Zeitung*. Furthermore, the information on the opening of the power station is inconsistent. On page 6 of the article, the author writes that "in the autumn of 1908 the power station was put into service with a connected load of approximately 1,300 incandescent bulbs, 80 arc lamps, and 50 motors with around 135 horsepower." An exact dating has not yet been possible, but this power station must certainly be regarded as one of Behrens's first architectural works for the AEG.

9. "Art and Technology" (in this volume).

10. "The individual components of the AEG power stations, the machines, cables, insulators, and so on, were manufactured almost entirely in the AEG's own factories. The AEG power stations took on a very individual character through the use of these much-patented components. . . ." (Majerczik, note 4, p. 16). Of course, the building materials were supplied to the AEG by contractors, but the planning of the plants was done entirely in the offices of the AEG.

11. Rose, note 7, pp. 162 ff.

12. See appendix C.

13. Hermann Muthesius, "Das Formproblem im Ingenieurbau," *Jahrbuch des Deutschen Werkbundes 1913* (Jena, 1913), p. 23.

14. Karl Bernhard, "Die neue Halle für die Turbinenfabrik der Allgemeinen Elektrizitätsgesellschaft in Berlin," *Zeitschrift des Vereins Deutscher Ingenieure* 39 (1911), p. 1627. This article contains an exact description of the turbine hall.

15. Behrens, "Art and Technology" (in this volume).

16. Hermann Muthesius, "Die ästhetische Ausbildung der Ingenieurbauten," *Zeitschrift des Vereins Deutscher Ingenieure* 53, no. 31 (1909), p. 1226.

17. "Art and Technology" (in this volume).

18. In his book on the architecture of the French and Russian revolutions, Adolf Max Vogt has identified three ways in which "work" was given architectural expression. At least one of these, the description of "building work or constructional work," is applicable to the forms developed by Behrens: "This means that the supporting, load-bearing and bracing elements are as clearly recognizable and differentiated as possible. . . . When a construction can exactly express itself in its total economy and the deliberateness of its means, as well as in its simple, measured proportions, then the 'work' of the structural parts is also accentuated and given expression, both hierarchically and mutually. Work, understood here simply in the physical sense, becomes a visual event." Adolf Max Vogt, *Russische und französische Revolutionsarchitektur, 1917, 1789* (Cologne, 1974), p. 159.

19. "A Factory Building by Peter Behrens" (in this volume).

20. "The Turbine Hall . . . " (in this volume).

21. Bernhard, note 14, p. 1630. Bernhard went on to say that, for this self-imposed restraint, "the engineer must give his most sincere thanks [to Behrens]."

22. "Neues von Peter Behrens," *Deutsche Kunst und Dekoration* (1908–09), p. 352.

23. *Geschichte der Kunst. Von der altchristlichen Zeit bis zur Gegenwart* (Berlin, 1933), p. 866.

24. Ibid.

25. Note 14, p. 1682.

26. Note 14, p. 1628.

27. "Factory Art" (in this volume).

28. M. Radt, "Klingenberg als Erbauer grosser Kraftwerke," in *Zum Gedächtnis an Georg Klingenberg* (Berlin, 1926), p. 17. A complete account is given in Georg Klingenberg, *Bau Grosser Elektrizitätswerke* (Berlin, 1913, 1920).

29. Klingenberg, note 28.

30. W. Lulolfs, "Zum Gedächtnis Dr. G. Klingenbergs," in *Zum Gedächtnis an Georg Klingenberg* (Berlin, 1926) [reprinted from *Sterkstroom, Zeitschrift für Elektrotechnik im Haag* (27 January 1926)]. See also "Das Märkische Elektrizitätswerke," *AEG-Zeitung* 11, no. 12 (1909), pp. 8 ff.; "Das Märkische Elektrizitätswerk," *BEW-Mitteilungen* 12, no. 9 (1916), pp. 131–134; R. Laube, "Die Architektur von Elektrizitätswerken," *AEG-Mitteilungen* 13, no. 8 (1917), pp. 111–119.

31. The windows were installed in a similar way in Behrens's porcelain factory near Hennigsdorf (1910).

32. Radt, note 28, p. 17.

33. "Die Elektrizitätsversorgung Berlins aus dem Grosskraftwerk Zschornewitz," *AEG-Mitteilungen* 15, no. 6 (1919), p. 61. See also H. de Fries, "Industriebaukunst," *Wasmuths Monatshefte für Baukunst* 5, no. 5–6 (1920–21), pp. 130 ff.

34. Behrens was also employed at Golpa. As there were no towns or villages near the site of the power station, the AEG had to build housing for those employed at the plant. Design work on the housing was begun in July 1915, and the first construction followed in August. "At the beginning of 1917, 195 single houses, 16 four-family houses, and 3 eight-family houses were completed. The design work was assigned to Professor von Mayenberg, Dresden, and Dr. Klingenberg and W. Issel, Berlin-Lichterfelde. Professor Behrens from the electricity works was consulted as artistic adviser." (Klingenberg, note 28, p. 102) It would seem that the AEG continued to engage Behrens for jobs like this even after he had left the company. Although the provision of housing was relatively new for the firm, it had to be done well, and Behrens guaranteed this, even though he was only involved at the very last stage of the design. At Golpa, too, there were large, molded gables and windows strung together in bands—the accentuation of the structural elements, just as in Behrens's industrial buildings.

35. "Die Elektrizitätsversorgung Berlins . . ." (note 33), p. 61.

36. Klingenberg, note 28, vol. 3, p. 56.

37. Klingenberg, note 28, p. 51.

38. Tilmann Buddensieg has described how this process of ennoblement became a self-conscious expression of industrial might, and, on the other hand, how it sought to establish contact with points of reference in the existing city fabric: "Even large-scale industry understood, although admittedly only in specific areas, how to integrate itself into the wider life of the city. The buildings of the AEG shows how the originally defensive architecture from the end of the nineteenth century became increasingly self-assured and communicative." ["Strassenraum und Stadtbild in Berlin," in Festschrift Wolfgang Braunfels, ed. F. Piel and J. Traeger (Tübingen, 1978), p. 38].

39. "Die Fabrik," *Die Umschau* 18 (1914), pp. 86 ff. In this article Behne occupied himself with superfluous figurative sculpture, which he did not think appropriate to a model industrial plant. He forgave Gropius, however, and ascribed this lapse to the nature of the exhibition, as was confirmed by Osthaus. Behne did not go into this problem any further.

40. *Deutsche Werkbundausstellung Cöln 1914* (official catalog); p. 316.

41. Ibid.

42. Ibid.

43. *Zentralblatt der Bauverwaltung* 102 (24 December 1913), p. 711.

44. This standard shed was praised by Adolf Behne ["Die Leipziger Baufach-Ausstellung," *Die Tat* 5, no. 5 (1913–14), p. 506], and Gropius called it "outstanding, and decidedly suitable for the purpose of an exhibition" [quoted in Peter Stressig, "Walter Gropius," in *Karl Ernst Osthaus. Leben und Werk* (Recklinghausen, 1971), p. 465]. "In formal terms," Gropius continued, "it represents the best example of its type that I know of."

45. Gropius told Osthaus that he regretted this handicap, but had nevertheless tried to achieve a unified layout by setting at the front a symmetrical block containing "a decent staircase and offices" (Walter Gropius, quoted by Stressig, note 44, p. 465).

46. Walter Gropius, "Der stilbildende Wert industrieller Bauformen," *Jahrbuch des Deutschen Werkbundes 1914* (Jena, 1914), p. 31. In all his pre-1914 publications, Gropius's line of argument was almost identical to that of his teacher, Behrens. This influence, however, is more noticeable in Gropius's theoretical statements than in his contemporary buildings.

47. Gropius, ibid., p. 30.

48. As Julius Posener has noted, "Symmetry is not simply a method of composition which one can use at will; symmetry means public display" ["Muthesius als Architekt," *Werkbund Archiv* 1 (Berlin, 1972), p. 63].

49. See Stressig, note 44, p. 466.

50. Gropius, "The Development of Modern Industrial Architecture" (in this volume).

51. Behne, note 44, p. 505.

52. See Helmut Weber, *Walter Gropius und das Faguswerk* (Munich, 1961).

53. Theodor Heuss, "Die Architektur (Von der Werkbundausstellung)," *Die Hilfe* 27 (2 July 1914), Bauhaus Archive, no. 22/298.

54. Fritz Stahl, introduction to *Das Grosskraftwerk Klingenberg*, R. Laube, ed. (Berlin, 1927), pp. 5 ff.

55. R. Tröger, "Die Richtlinien der Anlage," in "Das Grosskrafterk Klingenberg," *Zeitschrift des Vereins Deutscher Ingenieure* 71, no. 53 (1927), p. 1834. See also *Das Gross-Kraftwerk Klingenberg, Beschreibung der Anlagen und Beiträge von am Bau beteiligten Firmen, bearbeitet von der Abteilung für Zentralstationen der Berliner Städtische Elektrizitätswerke Act. Ges.* (Charlottenburg, 1928); Deutscher Stahlbau-Verband, *Berliner Stahlhochbauten* (Berlin, 1936); Helmut Kreidt, "Industriebauten," *Berlin und seine Bauten* (Berlin, 1971), IX, pp. 72, 74, 102 ff.

56. Tröger, note 55, p. 1837.

57. R. Laube, "Die Bauanlagen des Grosskraftwerkes Klingenberg," in "Das Grosskraftwerk Klingenberg," note 55, p. 1854: "The ground plan was worked out according to functional and technical demands, and produced a building volume to which the architect was tied. Alterations could only be made with a view to the practical utilization of the building or to reducing costs."

58. Stahl, note 54, p. 6.

59. Laube, note 54, p. 22.

60. Laube, note 54, p. 1854: "The pattern of the paneled walls resulted from the block partition construction, which was specified for reasons of economy."

61. Tröger, note 55, p. 1837.

62. Peter Behrens, "Zeitloses und Zeitbewegtes," *Zentralblatt der Bauverwaltung* 52, no. 31 (1932), p. 364 (reprint of a speech of 22 March 1932 to the Preussische Akademie des Bauwesens, Berlin).

Peter Behrens's Publicity Material for the AEG

Gabriele Heidecker

The source of monumentality never lies in physical size. Works of art with not exactly large dimensions can be very monumental and give the impression of magnitude. They can be so formed that they appeal not only to one particular, stylistically sensitive viewer, but can justifiably claim to appeal to a wider circle.
Peter Behrens, 1908[1]

The AEG's Pavilion, Catalog, and Advertisements at the Deutsche Schiffbau-Ausstellung, Berlin, 1908

The AEG's advertisement (illustration G11) in the official guide to the Deutsche Schiffbau-Ausstellung [German shipbuilding exhibition], held in Berlin in June 1908, referred the reader to a "distinctive building opposite the Kaiser Wilhelm Gedächtniskirche [memorial church]" in which the firm's exhibit was to be seen. Exactly what was on display there was not revealed, however, and the reader's gaze was not attracted to the advertisement by ornamental graphics, technical information, pictures of the firm's products, or views of its factories. It was the absence of these traditional motifs and the unusual design of the advertisement that gave it its impact: A hexagon is set in a rectangular frame with its horizontal and vertical axes on the center line of the rectangle. Three smaller hexagons in a honeycomb pattern frame the initials AEG in Roman capitals. This unit of three hexagons is placed under a block of writing almost like a plinth or pedestal, under which, in the center of the page, is set a thick rule which gives the whole block a floating character. The functional and geometric layout of the column of print produce a clear and interesting impression, the more so as the text is printed in a particularly rhythmic Roman script. In their power and precision, the capital letters in both signet and text are reminiscent of the classic Roman lapidary script, whose characteristics were derived from the techniques of stone carving. Peter Behrens admired these same characteristics in the modern version of the Roman script, which he described as "one of the most beautiful of all common scripts"[2] and which he favored in all his graphic work. In its strong functionality, expressive power, and elegance, Roman seemed to Behrens an appropriate script with which to devise a new, "distinctive" graphic image for the AEG.

The AEG's pavilion (illustrations 2 and A1–A8) followed the same principle. In its rejection of conventional exhibition techniques, it distinguished itself clearly and strikingly from its neighbors. This pavilion, Behrens's first architectural commission for the AEG,[3] was based on an octagonal ground plan and was 20 meters high in the interior and 18 meters in diameter.[4] According to Adolf Behne,[5] its form, construction, and proportions had something in common with the Baptistery in Florence. The two different levels and the high side wing served to increase the effect of monumental solemnity. While the upper level corresponded to the tribune in the apse of a basilica, the lower level had a precursor in the mausoleum of Galla Placidia in Ravenna (ca. 440 A.D.). From the outside, the upper story appeared to recede behind the strongly molded cornice that ran around the octagon at two-thirds of its height. The entrance faced the main exhibition halls and was made up of a small porch with a pediment and a high entrance arch, into which were set double swinging doors topped by an inscribed architrave (illustration A3).[6] The pieces of sculpture, by Hermann Hahn, came from the AEG's administration building on the Friedrich-Karl-Ufer.

1
The original design for the AEG trademark, photographed 23 June 1908. AEG photo.

4
Peter Behrens, design for Evangelical Church at Hagen, 1906. From Meyer-Schönbrunn 1913.

5
Peter Behrens, AEG pavilion at 1908 Deutsche Schiffbau-Ausstellung. From Meyer-Schönbrunn 1913.

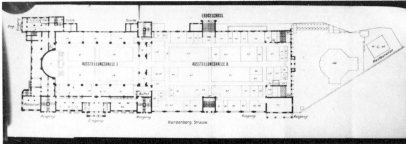

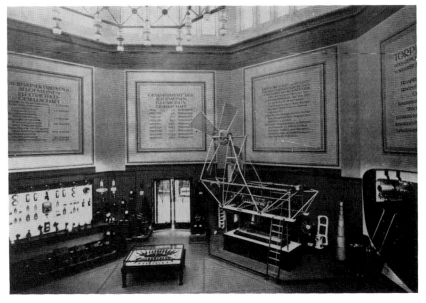

2
View into Hall 1 of 1908 Deutsche Schiffbau-Ausstellung, Berlin.

3
Site plan of 1908 Deutsche Schiffbau-Ausstellung. *Berliner Architekturwelt*, 1907.

In spite of all the direct appeals to classical precedents,[7] forerunners of this design could also be found in the earlier work of Behrens (see, for example, illustration 4). What was new, however, was the reinterpretation of these motifs for a building designed to publicize a commercial undertaking. As an attempt at "binding aesthetic and economic demands together," this building stood as a symbol of the commencement of Behrens's activity for the AEG. At the same time, it was the first successful attempt "to reduce opposing (and, until recently, apparently irreconcilable) endeavors to the most simple formula."[8] On the other hand, these linear and slightly Schinkelesque references to both sacred and profane sources not only "put the pretentious Romanesque of the Gedächtniskirche utterly to shame,"[9] but also confronted it with the modern age. Against the ethos of the Gedächtniskirche, Behrens set the characteristics of a modern industrial firm, whose organizational structure and qualitative standards were given physical expression and symbolic accentuation in the lucid composition and smooth, almost undecorated walls of the pavilion.

The design of the pavilion was developed from two viewpoints. As the AEG catalog explained, since "the space has simply to form a suitable context for the industrial products on display, decorative effects have been dispensed with in the interior"[10] (illustrations 5 and A4). On the walls, the right angle dominated; every profile was a demonstration of functionality, every line and uninterrupted plane a statement of order. As on the exterior, the upper story was demarcated on the inside by a pronounced cornice   a dark band dividing the artificially lit area from the area lit by daylight. A large chandelier hung down as the only decorative element and as the focus of the room (illustration A5). This chandelier was made up of two octagonal lattice frames, the upper one double and the lower one single, held together by vertical chains. Small spheres decorated these chains, and electric wires ran down them to the arc lamps that hung from them. The intention was to combine a specially made frame constructed out of prefabricated parts with mass-produced arc lamps in a striking way.

On the floor, inset linoleum strips repeated the octagonal plan of the light and the general plan of the building. The central octagonal pattern was framed by a rectangle, which was then extended further to form another octagon. The floor was thus divided up into triangular and rectangular compartments, in which the exhibits were painstakingly installed.

It was felt desirable that "specially selected, characteristic objects" should "strike the visitor individually, so that his interest would not be distracted by a mass presentation." The AEG's products stood on plinths like pieces of sculpture, either singly or in groups, or were arranged in symmetrical groups in frames on the wall. The smaller objects, jewels of precision, lay under glass on heavy tables with square, polished legs, which were typical of Behrens's exhibition furniture. For the more complex assemblies displayed in their actual settings (such as the interior of a torpedo boat or a ship's bridge), individual display areas were developed out of specific elements of the pavilion, which were inventively interpreted as nautical structures. The part of the exhibit that depicted the interior of a submarine looked like a church nave from the street.[11] Similarly, the high, tribunelike niche framed and illuminated the mockup of a ship's bridge as if it were an organ loft or a high altar. This large piece with its steps and handrails not only projected out into the central space, but also included an elegantly furnished cabin set below the level of the pavilion floor. Wherever Behrens installed a room in the interior of the pavilion, he made the installation visible from the street as an annex to the main building.

On the ground floor a direct visual contact was set up between the visitor and the machines on display. The impact the technical precision would have on the observer was calculated carefully, and the identification of this fine workmanship with a superior firm was given visible expression in the exhibition techniques used. Six large, inscribed panels set on the next level up presented the machines, numbered and anonymous, as the products of a large international company. Here the AEG sought to impress with statistics. The 5-meter-high wall panels, with their ornamental borders and their Roman script, had a clear function as a mediating and dividing strip, a third level between the display area and the upper band of windows. The panel texts clarified the relationship between product volume and product value as an index of the firm's rank,[12] and described the nature and function of the instruments on display. (They were much more, therefore, than "tales of great industrial feats."[13]) The presentation and enumeration on the panels showed the same self-confidence as the display of the machines below. The machines themselves did not shrink from the light that shone copiously down on them; their quality "justified the artistic effort"[14] that had been devoted to their presentation.

The garden of the pavilion (illustrations A6–A8) played an important role in the overall conception of the AEG's publicity image and as a vehicle for Behrens's ideas on design. The effect of monumentality and solemnity, clarity, order, and system was increased by the addition of a festive element: the play of light and water in the garden arbors. Particularly at night, the magic of the lighting, as a symbol of both the firm's massive energy resources and its technical ability, made a bright futuristic contrast to the princely mosaics on the Kaiser Wilhelm Gedächtniskirche. The effect of the light-colored geometric frame was particularly impressive, for this insubstantial architecture of light, together with the cofferlike rectangles of the flower beds, surrounded the pavilion like a net with its own illuminated laws of construction. The fact that one is reminded of the lines and dotted patterns on the poster and the catalog cover Behrens designed for the exhibition (illustrations A1, G30) shows that the magic of the 35,000 light bulbs succeeded in portraying Behrens's design principles in a most charming and effective manner.

In the many gardens Behrens designed for exhibition sites, the lattice frame played an important part in propagating his new ideas on architecture.[15] He used this tangibly geometric system to demonstrate his views on the aesthetics of proportion. To Behrens, proportion was the first essential for unified design, the sole binding and linking element between the parts and the whole. Proportional harmony had been achieved, he felt, when the impression had been created "that nothing can be added or taken away" without detriment, that "every part is of great significance."[16]

Proportional relationships can be established in rectangles, but not in squares. Behrens, therefore, took the rectangle as the basic unit of his grid. The rectangle can express harmony through its proportions and stimulate different responses in the viewer according to its location and alignment. In Behrens's catalogs and posters, rectangles were used to create architectonic relationships. The square appears in his designs only as an ornament—not in the sense of something added on, but as a symbol of calm and static permanence. When coupled with the circle, the square is aligned concentrically (as in a ground plan), or superimposed axonometrically, or arranged in a sequence of squares and circles as a means of suggesting rhythmic movement.[17] Finally, the combination of circle and square can suggest three-dimensional movement either into or out of the flat plane. In the lattice frame in the garden of the 1908 Berlin pavilion, as well as in his 1905 pavilion at Oldenburg,[18] Behrens preferred a horizontally accented rectangle rather than the small, upright version which he had used at the 1907 Kunst und Garten-Ausstellung at Mannheim. The precise, clear, cubic forms that had been evolved for the Oldenburg pavilion probably seemed appropriate to Behrens for the definition of a general design structure for the AEG. His conception of the firm as "a place from which power emanates . . . deserving our respect" determined the monumental character of the proportions. This character was reflected in the firm's advertising graphics and buildings, and particularly in the factories, which had a specific publicity function.[19]

The cover of the AEG's guide to the Schiffbau-Ausstellung (illustration A1) depicted the street side of the pavilion in a stylized drawing set in a rectangular frame. This frame, together with the inscription "Allgemeine Elektricitaets Gesellschaft," was in turn enclosed within a larger and heavier frame, which was punctuated with white dots.[20] On the back cover, the name and the image were fused together as the firm's trademark. The horizontal row of three identical squares placed between two sets of three vertically aligned rectangles is a system that can be extended at will to create an ordered sequence. The central square is placed in such a way that a higher form—a cross—becomes prominent. The timeless modernity of these cover designs marks a high point in Behrens's work in this field. The two covers brought together two aspects of his AEG graphics: the simplified drawing within a frame and the abstract architectonic composition of planes. Both types were used according to the occasion and were sometimes superimposed upon each other.[21]

Behrens had already used the elevation of a building as a pictorial symbol in his poster for the Deutsche Jahrhundert Ausstellung (illustration 7) and later in the Anker Linoleum Company's catalog for the Dritte deutsche Kunstgewerbe-Ausstellung (Buddensieg essay, illustration 3). Common to these designs is the vigorous separation of the plane areas by a strong lineation that is characteristic of Behrens's analytic treatment of architectural elements and can also be found in his buildings of the period (see, for example, illustration 8).[22]

6
The powerhouse of the AEG turbine factory on a brochure.

7
Peter Behrens, poster for Deutsche Jahrhundert-Ausstellung, 1906. Courtesy of H. Rogge.

8
Peter Behrens, exhibition pavilion,
Dresden, 1906. Two views of inner
courtyard. Courtesy of F. Stoedtner.

9
Peter Behrens, room in Schede house,
1904. Courtesy of F. Stoedtner.

In 1901, Behrens had taken the opportunity to combine architectural and graphic design in the booklet describing his own house at Darmstadt. This publication introduced the Behrens script to the public for the first time. With the Anker pavilion he had developed this idea by designing the pavilion, the catalog, and the firm's trademark all according to the same aesthetic principles. The balancing of the schematic image of the pavilion on the front cover against the anchor trademark on the back cover corresponded to the later Berlin guide, but the division into four stepped blocks was abandoned in the Berlin version in favor of a grander surround. The characteristics of Behrens's new style of graphic design for the AEG were strongly pared-down forms; the avoidance of an overly obvious grid system; light set against dark; contrast between smaller repeating elements and a larger, more complicated whole; and powerful lettering set against empty frames. Behrens clearly rejected some of the more individualistic traits of the earlier, more analytical style, and concentrated on the new technique as a means of creating impressive and characteristic symbols, thus "intensifying" the expressive power of image, form, lettering, and "tangible forms of . . . exactness" in the products.[23]

A high point in the "intervention on behalf of art"[24] was the public introduction in the catalog to the Schiffbau-Ausstellung of the new Behrens Roman script, first offered for sale in October 1908 by the Klingspor type foundry in Offenbach.[25] On the catalog cover, handwritten classical Roman script was used as an expression of tradition-consciousness and timelessness (see illustrations G15–G17). In contrast, the title page (illustration G9) was set in Behrens Roman, with standard frames and borders. These borders were immediately used on the AEG's leaflets and catalogs by the compositors, who achieved in this way the anticipated typical and "tasteful" AEG layout without any direct intervention by Behrens.

Showrooms and Shops

But this mystery of the marriage of the customer to the goods demands concentration. Every means possible must be used to isolate the goods. Above all, the window needs a framework.
Karl Ernst Osthaus, 1913

A year after the Schiffbau-Ausstellung, the products that had been remodeled to Behrens's designs were exhibited in the conference hall of the AEG. For comparison, an example of the same product in its old form was displayed beside each new design. In the showroom that was subsequently installed in the electrical appliance factory (illustration P13), the same contrasting technique was used to stress the aesthetic improvements that had been made to the mechanically unaltered arc lamps, and the old models were actually labeled as such. Beneath a whitewashed ceiling, with small incandescent bulbs in each coffer, hung phalanxes of arc lamps and ventilators, while on the walls were geometric displays of plugs, fuses, electric clocks, and meters (illustration P14). The various categories of product were separated by screens and accompanied by wall panels with framed titles in Grotesque lettering. The smallest articles were spread like pieces of jewelry across heavy Behrens-designed tables like those used in the 1908 pavilion (illustrations 5 and A4).

The spatial impact of the showroom was enhanced by a novel cladding of the pillars. The row began with a broad pilaster, whose dark edging matched the wall, and was continued by a polygonal pillar, which was enclosed by a glass display case set on a high plinth. On the inside of the case the faces of the pillar were given a new function as supports for the catalogs and brochures on display. The coffers on the ceiling, the framed panels that divided up the walls, and the showcases, wall displays, pillars, and partitions that articulated the room itself were all strictly interrelated. A system of coordinates determined the location of everything in the room, even the chairs (illustration P13); this technique was long established in Behrens's interior design work (see, for example, illustration 9).

The AEG's new sales strategy was aimed at the "interested customers."[26] As Fritz Hoeber commented, "the fact that the AEG wishes to sell its attractively redesigned products, made in equally modern and attractive factories, in exquisite showrooms" was "not only the logical extension of its earlier policy;" it also represented an attempt "to make direct contact with the large, highly receptive buying public, which could be influenced not only technically but also artistically by the firm as a creative force."[27] Hoeber continued: "In Peter Behrens, the company now possessed an architect to whom the artistically perfect styling of a salesroom was nothing new. He had already realized his theories of shop design in the conversion for the Joseph Klein, later Becker carpet company in Hagen" (illustration 10). Undoubtedly, Behrens worked with direct reference to the AEG's many retail outlets and to the "customer service" program that had been initiated by Felix Deutsch.[28]

The shop-window exhibition held in Berlin in the autumn of 1909 made it clear that the display window could exercise an extraordinary attraction. Behrens described the exhibition as "a new and most original idea, devised to promote dignified sales promotion," and added that "one can measure the amount of interest it attracted by the curiosity of the general public, which almost held up the traffic," and by the turnover, "which was so high in some cases as otherwise only in the pre-Christmas period."[29]

Karl Ernst Osthaus had accused some earlier competitions of having the "hypertrophic atmosphere" of exhibitions which in reality "refrain from displaying sellable goods" and sought merely to "attract, amaze, and set the town buzzing at an unprecedented wonder of decorative art."[30] Such displays, he said, "lack the principle of functionality which we regard as the unmistakable criterion of artistic achievement." In contrast, he admired the "new form of window" in which "the display is content to be a display." In spite of all this, however, Osthaus did not want to do without the "mystical magic" that expensive materials and dazzling light gave to the goods on display: "Anything presented in this way glitters like a king with gems shining on his crown, to whom dancing girls offer dishes laden with golden fruits. The passerby is spellbound. . . ." Osthaus missed this quality of fantasy ("the trader's truest helper") in some of "those practical displays with which we are bored by people who cannot comprehend that art is based on feeling and not on adherence to a set thesis!"

The exhibitions and the constantly changing displays in the shops "gave rise among the city population to a new social habit, window shopping."[31] In the case of the AEG, the "important publicity value of the shop window"[32] did not have to be exploited by means of fashionable gimmicks. Instead, the firm concentrated on a new style of display that emphasized the product, presenting it as solid, timelessly beautiful, and yet contemporary. Captivating displays worked all the better for the AEG, since Behrens in his "all-embracing activity" had achieved "a unified style of customer publicity" and had succeeded in "portraying the character of . . . the AEG and its products in convincing and memorable forms."[33]

An important part in this self-presentation was played by the AEG's shops, which provided the perfect context for the display of the goods. The two shops on the Königgrätzer Strasse and the Potsdamer Strasse, which Behrens fitted out for the AEG in 1910, offered direct competition to other shops in the city center, and were intended to attract customers who had not necessarily set out with the intention of buying AEG products. In this way, the talents of sales representatives or middlemen could be dispensed with.

10
Peter Behrens, Klein carpet showroom,
Hagen, 1906. Courtesy of F.
Stoedtner.

These shops were intended for the sale of "smaller appliances (some of which were still available in hand-finished versions) produced by the electrical industry or related to it." These included both utilitarian objects, such as lamps, and luxury goods such as electric fires, fans, and kettles. Although according to Behrens the same principles were to be applied to product design as to the design of the firm's factories, it was particularly important that these smaller products should in their "beautiful form" clearly differentiate themselves from rival products, as they came "into direct contact with a wide public."[34] The purpose of the shops was to make contact with the customer on the street via an unmistakable AEG style, free from the capricious taste of the individual shopkeeper.

Osthaus's 1913 demand[35] that shop windows needed a framework was certainly a reference to Behrens, who had already created such a system for the above-mentioned AEG shops.[36] Behrens devised two variations in which an asymmetrical arrangement of a wide window and a door with a fanlight was composed as a unit, which was then related to the remaining wall area. Visually the entire storefront was reinterpreted as a framed display window (illustration P7).

The courtyard of the Königgrätzer Strasse shop (illustration P4) was clearly meant to be understood as the anteroom to the salesroom. It was divided from the bustle of the street by an iron railing, whose decorative pattern echoed the firm's brochures. Access to the shop was only through two narrow openings. The passerby, who saw the goods beckoning from afar, was thus induced to enter the courtyard, where he was held captive both by the physical constraints and by the visual stimulus of the display. The green window frame[37] containing Behrens's "exhibition of appliances for home and workshop" projected out from the light-colored passe-partout of the wall[38] and the hammered[39] sheet-copper surround. The entire composition of window, door, frame, and surround was strikingly contained and contrasted against the wall by an astragal frieze.[40]

The height of the backing screen and the depth of the window display case were determined by the height of the door and the depth of the entrance porch between the street door and the double swinging doors in the interior. In the tripartite fanlight the three large golden initials AEG in Grotesque script were set at the same height as the three lines of inscription on the showroom window, and together they created a compositionally necessary and decoratively highly effective upper termination. As Behrens insisted that lettering was the "principal motif in all advertisements," it was not surprising that he devoted "particular artistic attention" to the "tasteful positioning" of the inscriptions, which could only serve "to support the commercial purpose" behind the shop.[41] The balanced division of the frame, the precise arrangement of the metal rails and shelves, the marbled paper in the delicately framed panels of the backing screen, and the silk curtains created the atmosphere of a costly and elegant stage set in which were displayed the "technically superior household goods of the AEG." This theatrical image was reinforced at night by the lighting, done "principally by footlights," which was able "to bring a particularly elegant appearance to the gently gleaming appliances."[42]

Behrens was particularly fond of diffused light,[43] and he used it not only in the shop window but also in the interior. In the vestibule (illustration P5) the soft light given out by the matte glass globes of the two low lamps set on the marble fireplace in front of a broad mirror[44] gave the room a comfortable air of "calm practicality."[45] The complete fireplace composition, including the internally illuminated AEG clock that stood between the lamps, had already been exhibited and offered for sale in March 1910 in the reception room of the Keller and Reiner Gallery on the Potsdamer Strasse.[46]

The AEG gave an example of how its standard domestic products might be appropriately incorporated into the home by displaying them in the Königgrätzer Strasse vestibule alongside pieces of widely available furniture. In the salesroom (illustration P6), the counter stood in front of built-in cupboards. The wall was divided up by pilasters, the lower parts of which were glass showcases with "polished bronze frames" and dark plinths. In the niches between the pilasters, mirrors reflected the shining appliances. The dark, padded armchairs extended from the niches into the showroom. Amid the contrast between light and dark, between the heavy leather armchairs and the shimmering, transparent showcases, stood three-legged oval tables, which looked as exposed in their delicacy as the goods on display. The back room (illustration P9) was divided up into several sections by free-standing partitions with built-in cupboards. Each section acted as a display area for a particular category of appliances. Simple dark wooden chairs stood in each section and between the high, narrow windows on the corridor side. The atmosphere here was more prosaic than in the other room; the motors and meters stood on open shelves, not in glass cases.

The Potsdamer Strasse shop (illustration P2) stood out from the ugly shops and the grayness surrounding it. Although smaller than its neighbors, the AEG shop put them in the shade with the "luminous power" of its portico-like marble frame. The white-marble-clad pilasters and architrave were strictly related to the shop window and the door, both of which were deeply recessed as if in a niche. Green granite was used for the plinths and the narrow cornices of the pilasters, and the metal door and window frames as well as the larger frame around both were painted green. On the left side of the frame and running to three quarters of its height was the door opening. The structure of the frame, like the whole composition, looked like the title page of an AEG brochure. The foot of the window was protected by a square metal coffer. Into the fanlight, which was also square, was set a lattice pattern made up of the familiar Behrens combination of superimposed squares and circles, which enclosed a circular extractor fan. The show window had a deeply set backing screen, three display levels, and silk curtains. It also used a "hidden lighting" technique, with which Behrens anticipated Endell.[47] The principal impact of the shop front, however, was achieved by the carved inscriptions that gave the architrave and the pilasters the character of antique stelae. Behrens's predilection for classical scripts, which were originally chiseled into stone and applied principally to architecture, found a meaningful expression here. Behrens's 1902 comments on antique inscriptions can also be applied to the decoration on the plain rectangular panels on this shop front: "The antique script carved into the stone ashlar of Roman monuments often seems, even when we do not concern ourselves with the sense of the words, to be the final artistic requirement for the perfect completion of a work of art."[48]

The interior of the Potsdamer Strasse shop (illustration P3) was dominated by the customary elegant sense of order. A brown leather three-seater sofa was set into the dark wooden paneling on the left wall. On the wall above the sofa was a glass showcase with sliding doors in which the complete new range of teakettles was displayed. The delicately patterned green wallpaper and the round electric clock on the wall above made a lively color contrast to the whitewashed ceiling, which had a light bulb mounted in each of its deep coffers. The modesty of the decoration was matched by a certain luxuriousness in the use of traditional materials such as marble, leather, and wood. This feeling of luxury enveloped the appliances on display with such natural and effortless elegance that the buyer of a kettle might optimistically believe that he had also acquired some of this elegance for his own home.

Typefaces of the AEG

Do not think that any book, or anything printed at all, is too trifling to be examined for traces of beauty. The smallest leaflet, visiting card, or business card, the advertisement and the newspaper are set either tastefully or without taste. By trying to promote beauty in simple things, you provide in the best way possible for the artistic education of the public! And do not hide behind the argument that good taste in typography costs more than no taste.
Peter Jessen, 1900

Behrens's first work for the AEG was the development of a new, exclusive typeface for all the firm's printed material. It is necessary, particularly in considering the beginning of Behrens's activity for the firm, to differentiate between two different script forms and the uses to which they were put. One was a classic, widely varying Roman script (illustrations 15 and G23–G25) which was always written by hand (usually in capitals) and was used only within the AEG. The other was the so-called Behrens-Antiqua [Behrens Roman], initially used only by the AEG under the name Deutsche Antiqua but later employed much more widely. The handwritten title pages of the AEG brochures were gradually replaced by the latter (illustrations G56, G57).

Three considerations governed the design of the new script:

- Like the redesigning of the plant and the products, the AEG's refusal to use an existing typeface contributed to its differentiation from other firms.
- The particular characteristics of the new AEG script (and thus the firm's image) could not be based on the individual style or the calligraphic capriciousness of one artist.
- The desire to avoid individualistic traits in the new script led at first to a "fifth Behrens script" based on the surviving variations of the classic Roman script. The aim was to invoke the dignity of this script, which had been developed out of the antique monumental script, so that the architecture, the general form, and the sequence of these newly redesigned

letters summoned up the image of work and performance. Like the products and the factories, the lettering was to achieve this directly, concretely, and in a modern manner that, at the same time, was to be exclusive to the AEG. In the resulting Behrens Roman script, the designer avoided, as he had done in his first Darmstadt typeface of 1901, any suggestion of an individual "poetic flourish."

The avoidance of individualism put the new script in marked contrast with the Eckmann script—"the most original and individual of script forms"[49]— which at the turn of the century reflected the inclination toward (in the words of the title of a 1902 book by Willy Hellpach) "nervosity and culture." The AEG had exploited that fashion by commissioning Otto Eckmann to design the firm's catalog for the 1900 Paris World's Fair (illustration 11). With a new trademark, a new script, and uniform decorative motifs, Eckmann had created the beginnings of a unified publicity style for the AEG. But the result was so typical of Eckmann that in the long run it was impossible to fuse it with any subsequent AEG style. One of Behrens's achievements was to combine as a unity the AEG style and that of the Behrens Roman. At the beginning, the title pages of the AEG's brochures were all hand-lettered,[50] presumably by Behrens himself, and in this way the regularity of printed script was consciously avoided. The hand lettering contributed to the extraordinary appeal and the amazing diversity of the Behrens-designed publicity material.

Characteristic of the new Roman script were strong and rhythmically formed diagonal strokes—especially the leftward-sloping serifs of the A and the G (illustration 12). Yet in both the final trial designs and the finished brochure titles (illustrations G15–G17, G19, G20) there are letters whose direct forebears can be found in the classical Roman and medieval scripts that had been revived and put back into use by the Leipzig printing firm of Poeschel and Trepte.[51] Very striking is the way Behrens frequently altered the strength, direction, and form of the serifs (for example, in the E and the C) and completely reformed some letters (such as the G). He also changed the general contouring of the script, which with the passage

11
Otto Eckmann, AEG catalog, Paris
World Exhibition, 1900. From Meyer-
Schönbrunn 1913.

12
Peter Behrens, calendar, 1910. From
Meyer-Schönbrunn 1913.

of time gradually but clearly evolved away from a sharp rectangularity toward a softer and more rounded profile. (Compare the trademark in illustrations G79 and G80 with the names of the months in illustrations G20–G22.) Some of these variations can be attributed to the occasion and the nature of the publication; for example, a more static alignment of the lettering was used in the official announcement shown in illustration G11, whereas a more individual style, with the contraction of A and E and with oblique serifs, was used to characterize the AEG's own catalog to the 1908 Schiffbau-Ausstellung (illustration A1).

With his upper-case script, Behrens sought to integrate into one version all the current variations on the classical Roman script. The result was a flexible script whose weight and rhythm could be elegantly adapted to suit the particular task. For example, in 1907 Behrens redesigned the title banner of the *AEG-Zeitung* (illustration G7) using an expansive, relaxed script that corresponded to the curvaceous form of the initials. Similarly, the blocklike letters on the cover of the 1907 *Mitteilungen der Berliner Elektricitäts-Werke* (illustration G2) were compressed together and governed by the rigorous structure of this composition. The many designs by Behrens and his colleagues show how much a line of print is able to respond to the given proportions without losing its typical characteristics. As a vigorous handwritten script, the Behrens Roman was chosen wherever an official or formal design was needed for a cover or a similar purpose. These covers were generally printed on colored, heavy paper boards to heighten the impression of value and craftsmanship.[52]

The initial D in the 1907 Rathenau address (illustration G24) and that in the special edition of the *AEG-Zeitung* published on 11 December 1908 on the occasion of Emil Rathenau's seventieth birthday (illustration G8) mark the beginning and the end of the development of a calligraphic script into the AEG's anonymous house typescript, Behrens Roman.[53] There is only one piece of evidence to suggest that Behrens had worked

13
Klingspor catalog showing Behrens Roman script and decorative elements. Courtesy of F. Stoedtner.

14
Page from official German catalog, 1910 Brussels World Exhibition. Courtesy of F. Stoedtner.

on this script at an earlier date: the poster to the 1906 Deutsche Jahrhundert-Ausstellung in Berlin (illustration 6). This poster carried an elongated, rather heavy capital script. Although the serifs were all triangular, this script can be counted as a forerunner to Behrens Roman. This is made clear by the unusual form of the N, with two heavy vertical strokes of the same width and an unstressed diagonal.[54] The most striking characteristics of Behrens Roman are the absolutely vertical ductus and the use of two different serifs.[55] The linear serifs begin with their point at the top left and end by being drawn out of the downstroke toward the right. This gives a sense of progression, especially to the larger letters. The exact, triangular serifs on (for example) the horizontal strokes of E and T reinforce the angular appearance of the script, and this angularity is not affected by the rather ornate hooks on G, W, V, and C. Only the Q dances out of line on its curving tail stroke.

Some of Behrens's contemporaries were upset by the "steely, rectangular, rigid" quality of the letters.[56] Although a "concrete relationship" can be noted between the script and the world of "materials and technology,"[57] its impact was governed by strictly rational factors. Typography has been described as "nothing other than two-dimensional architecture,"[58] and it is clear that there was a conscious relationship between Behrens's monumental lettering and his architecture, which was dominated at the time by the elongated rectangle, the square, and the circle and which was determined ever more strongly by the principle of the rhythmic sequence. The strong architectonic interdependence of the individual forms and the varying width of the large letters, which were further enriched by an additional round E, made possible an "unfettered rhythm" at the expense of "the earlier stylistic demand for regularity in the dimensions of each letter."[59] This was in accordance with Behrens's conception of rhythm as the essence of the modern age. It followed that this rhythmic quality should also find expression in a typeface; "after architecture," Behrens said, print should give "the most characteristic picture of an age."[60] He did not, however, follow Larisch's[61] recommendation that the spaces between letters be constant. The alternation of circles with self-contained rectangular forms points to an architectural motif which belongs as a decorative element to the Behrens Roman script: the abstracted frieze of astragal or triglyph and metope (illustration 15).

15
Peter Behrens, crematorium, Hagen, 1906–07.

Unlike William Morris, who based his Golden Type on "the Roman script of the Italian Renaissance," Behrens began his studies with the ninth-century Carolingian capital and uncial script.[62] (This script was modeled on Roman inscriptions, and also used the "early medieval semi-uncial."[63]) By adopting this source, Behrens united his fondness for the antique spirit as expressed in the Roman lapidary script with the "Germanic cultural sphere." According to Rodenberg, Behrens's direct model was the fifth-century Codex Argenteus in Upsala. "The uncial model," Rodenberg noted, "can be seen in the capitals D, F, P, U, and the round E."[64] The particular beginning to the hair stroke and the form of the N was also "taken from the old scripts."[65] The introductory brochure to the Behrens Roman script (see note 53) said the following:

The similarity in character between this Roman script and the early-medieval semi-uncial and Carolingian script shows the lasting power of a genuine tradition. This is still the mark of a mature artistic achievement.

Out of this tradition developed the search for a rhythmical and lively script form based on the succession of narrower and broader capital letters: the narrow P and R, the broad G, O, and D. In contrast to the preference in the scripts of recent years for uniform, equally weighted capitals and regular spacing, a well-thought-out and rhythmical alteration in the spacing is, without doubt, an artistic enrichment.

It is to be hoped that, in its imitation of the Roman script of the Germanic culture, the Behrens script will assist the task of reviving the Roman script in the German spirit . . . and will point to a solution. . . . Let us hope that a further valuable example will be added to this homogeneous and German graphic style, let us hope that the foundation has been laid for a DEUTSCHE ANTIQUA [German Roman script]!"

The Behrens Roman script has been described as "the maturest product"[66] of the calligraphy course organized by Behrens (as director of the Düsseldorf Kunstgewerbeschule), Anna Simons, and F. H. Ehmcke on behalf of the Prussian Ministry of Commerce and offered to teachers at colleges of art and technology.

At the Paris fair of 1900, the individualistic style of Eckmann's AEG publicity represented an avant-garde departure from the more conventional form of the official catalog.[67] Now, at the 1910 Brussels World's Fair, everything in the official German catalog,[68] including the individual advertisements of the various exhibiting firms, was printed in Behrens Roman, and the script originally designed for the AEG was displayed as a typeface appropriate for the new industrial Germany. Not only did the "Behrens style" establish itself as identical with the "AEG style," but the "AEG style" was also the "national style" of typography. The unique quality of this style was its ability to unite Germanic and classical elements in a script of modern proportions and impassive clarity. The development from the original monogram of the firm into the abstract AEG trademark was a search for graphic anonymity, conducted within the bounds of the firm. The circular signet of 1907 (illustration G77) was very similar to the ER monogram which Behrens stamped into the binding of the Rathenau address of the same year (illustration G23). It is probable that these last vestiges of a personal handwriting were consciously applied to the trademark to emphasize the personal relationship between the founder and the firm. A stylistic unity was created between Emil Rathenau's monogram and that of the AEG.[69] The oval signet of 1908 (illustration G78) also had this monogram character, but did not suggest the same sense of dignity.

With the hexagonal symbol shown in illustrations 1 and G79, the AEG trademark was launched on its publicity campaign. Each item produced by the firm carried the same stamp. According to Wolf Dohrn,[70] it was "a symbol of the prevailing spirit of labor" and was used enthusiastically by the Werkmeister, who "saw the new mark as the true symbol of their work." The development of an entirely abstract symbol—three letters in a rectangular frame (illustration G80)—was to follow. The rectangular-framed version, which first appeared in 1912, conformed to the general trend toward a softer contour, which was also evident in the Behrens Roman script. But something else was different, too. In the hexagon, as in the script, the emphasis had been vertical, with elongated, sharp-edged letters. Suddenly the horizontal axis was dominant, and the letters no longer strained upward but were heavy and squat. Lanzke (1958) felt that specific reasons had also led Bernhard, Hohlwein, and other graphic artists to "heavy lettering, suitable for poster design." For this reason, the AEG trademark that is still in use today can be seen as typical of the period in which it was created. More striking, however, is its origin in the "spiritual type font" of Behrens, whose predilection for the triangle, the rectangle, and the square can still be seen particularly clearly in the three initial letters. Even in the unframed version there exists an architectonic system of order, for the three initials are consciously played off against each other in their differing forms yet held together by the power of their individual and mutual proportions.

The decorative borders for Behrens Roman and for the slightly earlier cursive version appeared in the AEG's newspapers as well as in its decorative addresses (illustrations G23–G29) and in literary collectors' items.[71] The uncial version had been developed out of the cursive, and the two could be used together. Forerunners of these decorative patterns could be found in Behrens's interiors. Some had appeared in the designs for carpets and wall and floor inlays incorporating astragal, metope, and triglyph motifs,[72] which had been developed in the Düsseldorf period (see illustration 8). The models for these were Tuscan incrustation motifs such as those at San Miniato in Florence. Similar motifs were also used on lamp holders, carved furnishings, and decorative latticework,[73] and in AEG advertising material (illustrations G31, G52).

The decorative border surrounding the text of the Rathenau address (illustrations G16 and G24) suggests the splendid manuscripts of the court school of Charlemagne (for example the Godescalc Gospel Lectionary) and the St. Gereon Evangelium,[74] with its many framing bands and rows of dotted decoration. The same dotted motif was also used by Behrens on the wall panels of the 1908 Schiffbau-Ausstellung pavilion (illustration 5) and, in a reduced form, in some AEG publications (illustration G14). These dotted borders were either drawn up individually each time or assembled out of elements in the Behrens Roman font (illustration G44). The models for the wider borders with single decorative elements were ornamental manuscripts and—appropriately—decorative ironwork, enamelwork,[75] and filigree.

Behrens's ornamental technique and his method of interpreting his sources are demonstrated especially well by the capital D in illustrations G26, G27, and 13. In assembling the decorative collage, which is made up of Irish and pre-Carolingian elements, Behrens proceeded according to a principle that, although derived from the models themselves,[76] is incomprehensible without an exact knowledge of Alois Riegl's book *Die spätrömische Kunstindustrie nach Funden in Österreich-Ungarn*.[77] Riegl's account of the artistic methods of the "advanced Roman imperial age" had a great appeal to Behrens. These included the theories of motif and complementary motif and the techniques of achieving a coloristic effect in openwork and in chiseled bronzes with the help of "reciprocal patterns" and of "the continuous rhythmic alternation of light and dark." Behrens developed a method of ordering his late-Roman-enriched repertoire of "contrasting curves," "angular forms," and "complementary positive and negative motifs"[78] and of developing them in conjunction with kindred types of ornament.[79] The initial D stands in a free relationship with the surrounding ornamentation. The letter itself is edged by a lighter contour which responds to the decorative pattern. The ornament never touches the lettering, but reacts to the architectural form of each initial as support, brace, or load, and sometimes responds with a dynamic flourish of its

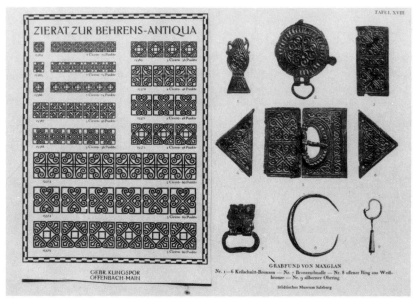

own. The ornament is made lighter and darker according to the "temperament" of the initial, which it frames in an almost imperceptible rectangle. The lighter, complementary ornament only follows the contours of light and gold-colored initials, like the D in the Rathenau address, giving them a shimmering appearance. Otherwise, it abuts the white edging band of the dark letter without being developed out of it.

Behrens's treatment of the large tendril motif is an example of the way in which he gave a unified, "organic" form to one larger motif made up of a multiplicity of single elements. The small spiral tendril contained within the D is taken out, enlarged, and unfurled down the page. In the course of this unwinding, all the smaller elements are hierachically ordered and molded to conform to the curl of the tendril. At no point is this principal form firmly delineated; rather, it is defined as the trace of a movement that starts out as a curve complementary to that of the letter D and pulls all the subsequent influences together into one formal statement. This large curve represents the portrayal of individual formal elements "by means of a rhythmic composition on the picture plane."[80] In contrast, the decorative pattern stamped into the leather cover of the Rathenau address (illustration G23) is much closer in spirit to industrial practice.

From the repertoire of late Roman decorative elements, Behrens chose exactly the one whose simplified form made it particularly suitable for endless repetition. In order to create large forms in series, it is necessary to break the form down into the simplest elements, which can then be combined in many different ways and reproduced endlessly. Such simple motifs were favored in the chisel technique by which bronze jewelry was embellished between the third and sixth centuries A.D. (illustration 16). The motifs Behrens derived from this model were based on the square and on a corner element that produces small "hearts" (see illustration G69). By

16
Peter Behrens, Rathenau address,
1907. Marburg photo.

17
Behrens decorative elements and late
Roman chiseled bronze. From A. Riegl,
Spätrömische Kunstindustrie (1927).

developing the play of light and shadow in the original jewelry, Behrens arrived at four basic ornamental patterns. As a decorative principle, such a regular sequence of variations on one theme stands in total opposition to the organic unity of the letter and the dominant tendril motif. The late Roman practice, according to Riegl, was based on the "leveling of the basic form and the individual elements," and led to "mass composition." The "isolation of the single element" that led to a "uniform sequence of the same form," the "objectivity of appearance," the "resultant *typical* character," and the "anonymity that is always inseparably bound to such an anti-individualistic manner of artistic creation" (all mentioned by Riegl[81]), together with the interdependence of all the motifs on the picture plane, are equally characteristic of Behrens's decorative style. Behrens—"an attentive reader of Alois Riegl"[82]—utilized Riegl's concept of Kunstwollen, adopted the late-Roman principles of design, and translated Riegl's "Kunstindustrie" into his own "Industriekunst."

All the Behrens scripts were manufactured by the Klingspor type foundry in Offenbach. Some were used in trial editions before being officially introduced. The first publication set in Behrens Script, which was introduced officially in October 1902, was *Festschrift der Künstlerkolonie: Ein Dokument Deutscher Kunst* (1901). According to Rodenberg, the Behrens Cursive introduced in 1907–08 was arrived at by the circuitous route of cursive script. Behrens Roman first appeared in the AEG's guide to its exhibition at the Schiffbau-Ausstellung of 1908.[83] Behrens Medieval, officially introduced in 1914, underwent a trial printing in 1913. The decorative embellishments that went with Behrens Roman were put into production by the Klingspor company and enjoyed the same wide success as the typeface itself.

The Advertising Graphics

The realm of art begins at the point where an object that has been simplified into a sovereign form becomes the universal symbol for all similar objects.
Peter Behrens, 1900

The various phases in the development of Behrens's graphics can be seen as a historical sequence; the phases, however, often overlapped. The geometric phase was characterized by the conspicuous system of framing that appeared, for example, in the Kunsthalle in Oldenburg (illustration 18).[84] According to Behrens, his intention was "to isolate the walls and make them independent by means of the framing," in order to demonstrate the "self-assurance of the individual form."[85] This system is clearly evident in the poster for the 1906 Deutsche Jahrhundert-Ausstellung (illustration 6). In the 1908 brochure for the AEG arc lamp factory (illustration G40), the separation and enclosure of the triangular panel no longer serves to clarify the content but is a decorative end in itself. In 1906, Behrens developed a decorative repertoire out of the architectural motifs he had employed in the crematorium at Hagen (illustration 15) and the Tonhaus der Flora in Cologne. This new repertoire embraced both the ornamental elements of the Behrens Roman font (for example, the "metope frieze" seen in illustration 19) and abstract expressions of Behrens's design principles. The circle and the square in numerous combinations make up one of the basic themes.[86] Although used mainly as a single motif, it was also multiplied in endless sequence in linoleum patterns, in the manner of Vasarely.

19
Peter Behrens, brochure for AEG steam turbines, 1908. Courtesy of F. Stoedtner.

20
Anker linoleum, 1906, designed by Peter Behrens. Courtesy of F. Stoedtner.

18
Peter Behrens, Kunsthalle, Oldenburg, 1905. From Hoeber 1913.

This geometric formula was applied in the most memorable way by Behrens in his first graphic composition for the AEG, the cover designs for the 1906–1909 editions of *Mitteilungen der Berliner Elektrizitätswerke* (illustrations G1–G3). The 1908 cover is the most striking because of the way in which the central motif is accentuated; the complementary spandrel forms create a spatial echo effect around a motif that to this day has lost nothing of its modernity.[87] The first cover design of 1906–07 also achieves a spatial effect in spite of the rather precious scrolls; the dots in the corners of the frames increase in size and lead the eye progressively outward from the center. In Behrens's metal-filament-lamp poster of 1907 (illustration G30), probably his first poster design for the AEG, unifies the two main aspects of this phase in his work: the principle of framing, which analytically divides up the picture plane by ascribing more or less importance to the various parts, and the geometric system of ordering, which coordinates these frames into a pictorial image. The subject of the poster is thus isolated by the framework, and attention is focused toward it by the geometric structure. The symmetrical layout also embraces the dots that radiate out from the lamp with ever-decreasing intensity. A comparable poster by Eckmann (illustration 8 in Buddensieg's essay above) portrayed the same situation as an eruption of light. Although both posters have a certain symbolic content, only the Behrens version, thanks to its "basic mathematical harmony," identified the "absolute precision of all the elements" in the picture with the product on display and with the firm that made it. Through the "unity of all the assembled parts"[88] and the surrounding triangle, the intrinsic form of the light is highlighted.[89] This is particularly clear in the negative version of the poster which was included in the brochure for the lamp (illustration 22). The principle of Behrens's poster design, reduced to a formula, is that the geometry on the picture plane serves to accentuate the form of the object.

21
Peter Behrens, staircase of Schröder house, Hagen, 1908. Courtesy of F. Stoedtner.

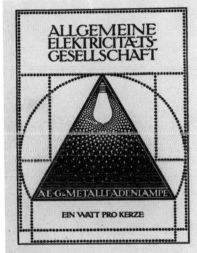

22
Peter Behrens, brochure for AEG metal-filament lamps, 1907. This and the following illustrations courtesy of Kunstbibliothek, Berlin.

A similar system lay behind the composition of the title page of the 1908 catalog of Christmas tree lights shown in illustration G38. Here, however, the visible "guidelines" have disappeared, the lettering stands—rather exceptionally—in place of the surrounding arc, and the focus on the lights delineating the tree is intensified.

According to Gagel,[90] "the most important stylistic prerequisite for the development of the descriptive poster [Sachplakat]—and also for the functional style [Sachstil]—was geometric purism." The gradual recession of this interpretative scheme in favor of a "rigorous articulation of the planes" according to architectural principles and a "wonderfully harmonious distribution of the lettering" were to characterize the subsequent phases in the development of Behrens's graphic art. However, the "mathematical exactitude" and the preference for symmetry remained, as the basis of the individual character of the AEG house style.[91]

What Gagel[92] called the "tectonic or architectonic" style of advertising graphics in the pre-1914 period found its clearest expression in the work of Behrens. As the graphic vehicle for his architecturally derived aesthetic program he used the frame.[93] Although all the graphic designs of this period followed the same principle, not all of them portrayed the frame as symbolic architecture. The majority, however, did, and the frame was composed of pilasters, architraves, and sills. The aim was to produce a standard format to which each new hand-drawn composition would conform. The format could then be reproduced at will from the existing printing blocks, and the drawings, product illustrations, lines and columns of print, numbers, specifications, and title banners could easily be related to each other (see illustrations G43, G44, G56, G57).

Behrens worked according to the theory of the interrelationship of concept and scale; proportion was to him *the* force of order, and not only in the subdivision of the picture plane. He also understood proportion in the figurative sense as the relationship between pictorial display and intended effect, between the object depicted and its intrinsic qualities. Even when, for reasons of pictorial content, Behrens abandoned the formal layout of pilaster and architrave, an invisible framework still remained to give a sense of order to the composition (see illustration G61).

In contrast to the two-tone, decorative splendor of the cover of the arc-lamp-factory brochure (illustration G40), the title page (illustration G41) carries a framed composition reminiscent of the facade of the AEG shop on the Potsdamer Strasse. The enclosed circle carrying the date and the block of lettering in the "architrave" are part of the "building," whose proportions and formal, hierarchic composition are presented in a monumental manner. In this AEG proscenium arch, products or drawings could be displayed at will. The framework was adjusted to suit the dimensions of the object on display, and additional pilasters or sills could be added to reduce the pictorial area (see illustrations G48, G49).

In the arc-lamp brochure, the lamps are reproduced in the most direct manner. This clarity set a pattern for a whole series of brochures. The layout, with a delicate frame surrounding the picture of the lamp (illustration G42), was clearly meant for a small format. The high-quality color print presents the lamp in an illusionistic context, as if it were floating in the ether. The surrounding space is indeterminately gray and shadowless (compare illustration P15). In its surface attraction and exquisite coloring, the beauty of the lamp casing is presented as the beauty of the simple object. Comparison with this makes it clear that in the 1909 silhouette presentation of the arc lamp (illustration G43) the message to be conveyed was the unique and unmistakable form of the lamp. Here the form was abstracted from the object as a combination of elegant two-dimensional elements derived from the simple outlines of sphere, cone, and cylinder. The form of the arc lamp was thus given the character of a trademark (see illustration G44); like a signet it dominates the surrounding framework.

Behrens created another type of abstract image in his design for the quartz-lamp brochure of 1908 (illustration G39). The lamp was portrayed neither in its spatial actuality nor in its pure two-dimensional form. Instead, two curving lines were offered by Behrens to symbolize the radiating light. The enclosure of this symbolic form within a rigidly symmetrical frame, with a capricious Roman script, freed the double curve of any concrete designation.

The framed presentations described above are found almost exclusively in small-format works. An exception, however, is the metal-filament-lamp "icon" shown in illustration G30 (clearly a later poster that should be considered with the next group). The arched frame, decorated with the splendid ornament of the Behrens Roman script, intensifies the impact of the isolated, free-floating bulb.

The more pictorial manner of poster design, which was also adopted for small-format publicity material such as leaflets and stamps (illustration G74), falls into two phases. Common to both is the copying of photographs of the product; this graphic presentation, however, differed in the two phases.

The first phase can be characterized as the painterly phase. In illustration G55 (cf. illustration P37), the electric fan is shown in three-quarter view—an angle Behrens otherwise avoided, as it went against his belief that static and symmetrical views were the most striking. The schematicized effects on the fan of light and shadow are analyzed in delicate shades of gray. Although this does not correspond to the original color scheme, it gave the picture of the fan an artistic quality in its own right. It also gave the poster, with its midnight-blue background, a greater impact than any photograph could have achieved, especially from a distance. The isolation of, say, the image of a light bulb in front of a strongly colored but completely flat background recalls the techniques of commercial photography.

This alienation heightened the plasticity of the lamp image, which when juxtaposed with the firm's initials and the title achieved an almost iconic quality. This tendency was developed further in the second type of presentation.

In the second technique of reinterpreting photographic images there are no longer any illusionistic shadows. The poster and prospectus for the metal-filament lamp (illustrations G32–G37) show how the graphic quality of the shadow was transformed into strongly defined dark areas set in a complementary relationship with the lighter half of the screw fitting. The contour of the bulb is taken directly from the real bulb and yet emancipates itself as an autonomous graphic image. This image, freed from reference to any external factors, is responsible only to the proportional system established by the frame and the lettering. The graphic form itself is given the character of a signet. The 1907 metal filament lamp poster shown in illustration G30 creates spatial references through the framework of lines, but quite different are the lamp posters shown in illustrations G32–G37. Compositionally, these aim inward toward the subject of the poster, and according to Behrens they were not conceived as "an architectural detail, through which a spatial idea could be realized." Characteristic of this type of poster is the way in which the object "stands out from the uniformity of its surroundings." "Herein," said Behrens, "lies not only its commercial success, but also its artistic originality."[94]

The technique of focusing on the simply drawn light bulb, without any reference to its functional context, also appeared at this time in the work of other graphic artists who were active in Berlin.

This "Schlagschattengrafik" [heavy-shadow graphics] technique, which was used principally for depicting technical objects and machines, had two roots: the traditional woodcut and the retouched photograph which had taken its place in technical publications. In order to clarify the general relationships between the parts, both techniques used an intensified contrast of light and dark. Illustration G63 shows a combination of both techniques.

In the process of transformation from object to photograph to graphic image, only the full tones and hard contrasts were retained in the graphic material showing the metal-filament lamp. To maximize the effect of the poster at a distance, Behrens simplified the forms and eliminated all the half-tones.[95] Behrens's contemporary Lucian Bernhard had already used this method in 1907–08 in his poster for Adler typewriters (illustration 23), and in doing so had established his own poster style. Particularly in his industrial graphics, Bernhard was to perfect a presentation based on pure contrasts. This technique was also to appear in some of the AEG publicity material. Leaflets with interpretations of Behrens's framing system in the style of Bernhard,[96] as well as many brochures showing factory silhouettes,[97] support the supposition the Bernhard worked with Behrens.[98] (On Behrens's advice, signatures were dispensed with in brochures and posters.) Among the AEG designs in this style were the publicity seals shown in illustration G74 and the graphics in the 1908 steam-turbine catalog (illustrations 19 and G59). However, the dominating diagonal that was so typical of Bernhard's compositions never gained the upper hand over Behrens's principles of axiality and symmetry. Bernhard's dynamic method of composition and the easy appeal of his graphics stood in direct opposition to Behrens's architectonic and symbolic conception of design. There were, nevertheless, technical similarities, such as the double border around the trademark.

23
Lucian Bernhard, poster for Adler typewriters, 1907.

24
Lucian Bernhard, poster, 1907.

25
Lucian Bernhard, poster for Vertex light bulbs, ca. 1912.

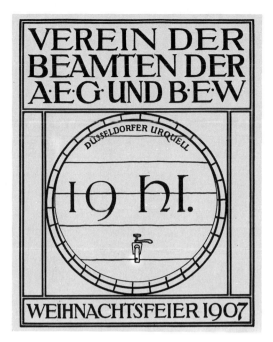

26
Verein der Beamten der AEG und
BEW, *Bierzeitung* (1907), cover, title
page, p. 10, p. 11.

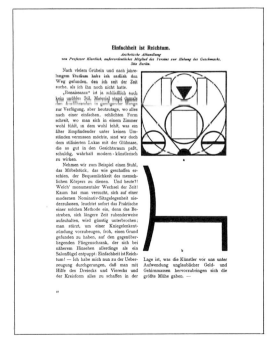

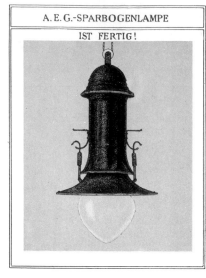

27
Magazine "Vielharmonische Mitteilungen des Vereins der Beamten der AEG und BEW" (December 1909), pp. 4, 5.

28
Magazine "TfSt!!!," p. 2: "Art in the AEG. Remodeling of the turbine factory facade in 1907."

29
Magazine "TfSt!!!," p. 2: "Even more art in the AEG. The remodeling of the turbine factory facade planned for 1908."

Throughout the period of Behrens's activity for the AEG, other graphic designers and agencies also produced advertising material for the company, occasionally supplying rather old-fashioned reinterpretations of Behrens's models (see, for example, illustration G70[99]). For many of the other designers, however, Behrens's layouts, script forms, and graphic techniques provided the framework within which they could realize their own ideas in a more or less uniform manner. Furthermore, so much everyday and humdrum printed material was produced to Behrens's design that the penetration of his graphic manner could be felt everywhere, and was influential even outside the AEG. Yet toward the end of Behrens's activity in the firm a new trend gained the ascendancy over his variable system of standard layouts and led to an uncontrolled multiplicity of styles such as had been usual before 1907. The appearance of the artist's signature on brochures marked the end of the anonymous company style. In 1916, Behrens was on the jury that selected designs for postcards portraying the nitrogen lamp (illustration G86). These designs make clear the move toward the figurative poster.

Behrens's unique ability to find symbols for technical appliances and their functions, and to set them in a suggestive balance against the accompanying text, may also be illustrated by one more striking example. Just as the quartz-lamp brochure took a particular place in the group of framed designs, so the searchlight brochures of 1909 and 1911 (illustrations G50, G51) were exceptional examples within the second category of illustrated designs. Not only do they have the usual three elements of illustration, lettering, and background, but the searchlight itself is reduced to a signet.

Characteristic of all the different types of advertising graphics produced by Behrens is the abstraction and reduction of both the diverse and the systematic down to a typical symbol. Form here was that quality which was propagated by the spirit of the modern age. Form stood above—or, better, embraced—the material around which it was pounded into shape. But, according to both Behrens and Riegl, form is dominant over material. As the physical embodiment of an idea, form is independent of material, although material considerations can give substance and direction to the idea. Behrens's graphic works illustrated this physical embodiment of an idea. The process of abstracting an unmistakable type out of the unique qualities of a particular form corresponded to the stated aim of creating types that would be not only universally valid, but also generally understandable.

With so much abstraction and so little room for individuality, the artists in Behrens's studio might have found working for the AEG tedious and stultifying. Yet writing the same titles to order again and again, never being allowed a private flourish, constantly having to repeat the same layout, and loading every page with the message of Behrens's "beautiful new form" and the weight of the firm's pretensions did not lead to the standardization of their brains. This is shown by the AEG's Bierzeitung (beer newspaper). (The Bierzeitung, a comic or satirical magazine, had its origin in the German student custom of the Kneipe.) Besides publishing the first example of the brochure design that would be used for the arc lamps (illustration G40) and the first evidence of the collaboration of Louis Oppenheim (illustration G58), the *AEG-Bierzeitung* also rolled a beer barrel into Behrens's sacred framework and spoofed Behrens's factory windows (illustration 29). That the critical fantasy of the Bierzeitung's contributors was contained within Behrensian proportions and did not spill over like foaming beer can probably be ascribed to the master's omnipresent influence.

Notes

1. "Was ist monumentale Kunst?," *Kunstgewerbeblatt* 20, no. 3 (3 December 1908), p. 46.

2. "Rudhard'sche Giesserei in Offenbach a. M.," *Behrens Schrift und Zierrat* (October 1902), pp. 4 ff.

3. The AEG had already commissioned Behrens to design a small pavilion for the Allgemeine Ausstellung für die Erfindungen der Klein-Industrie, held in Berlin in September 1907 (illustration A9). The result was a small, lattice-clad building on which the new company monogram (illustration G77) was to be seen alongside the old one. There was also a "splendidly produced catalog," probably from Behrens's hand (see Fritz Stahl's article on the exhibition in *Berliner Tageblatt*, 29 June 1907). The NAG exhibition stand at the 1907–08 Internationale Automobil-Ausstellung in Berlin was decorated by Behrens with the trademark NAG in Grotesque lettering set on a scroll-like gable bordered by light bulbs. Beneath the gable was a columnar facade. This stand was the immediate forerunner of the pavilion at the Schiffbau-Ausstellung of June 1908. Behrens's first permanent building for the firm, the powerhouse for the turbine factory (illustration A13), followed in September 1908.

4. For the dimensions see *AEG-Ausstellungsführer zur Schiffbau-Ausstellung Berlin 1908*.

5. "Peter Behrens und die toskanische Architektur des 12. Jahrhunderts," *Kunstgewerbeblatt* 23 (1912), pp. 45, 48–50.

6. This minimally decorated portal, a small porch with a high arcade and a triangular gable, also had precursors in the early Italian Renaissance—for example, the portal of San Domenico, Urbino, and the front of San Bernardino, Perugia.

7. For example, the windows in the upper light of the lantern of the Royal Palace, Berlin.

8. Hellwag 1911, p. 150.

9. Scheffler 1908, p. 433.

10. *AEG-Ausstellungsführer*, note 4.

11. Translator's note: Schiffsraum = ship's interior; Schiffe = nave.

12. The panels gave the correlations between products and factory space in square meters of built area, and capital reserves and assets in "marks, employees and horsepower," "track length," and "sales organizations."

13. Jaumann 1909, p. 10.

14. Scheffler 1908.

15. See M. Osborn, "Die Düsseldorfer Ausstellung," *Kunst und Künstler* 11, no. 12 (September 1904), p. 501; P. Behrens, "Der moderne Garten," in Hoeber 1913, p. 227; Hoeber 1913, p. 72.

16. P. Behrens, motto, in B. Scheja and E. Hölscher, *Die Schrift in der Baukunst* (Berlin, 1938), p. 35. In a similar vein, Alberti [*Zehn Bücher über die Baukunst*, second edition (Vienna and Leipzig, 1912), VI C, p. 293] defined beauty as "a certain rational relationship of all the parts."

17. See illustrations 15, 19–21, and G2.

18. For the Kunsthalle in Oldenburg (1905) Behrens developed a formal purism based on a simple pattern of squares, diagonals, and triangles. This pattern was used on all the buildings and in the garden layout, and provided the basis for the technique of abstraction that crystallized in the Berlin pavilion. Reduced to the most basic forms, the outline and image of the Berlin pavilion are as clear as a drawing. In contrast, the garden layout uses different basic forms: the square, the sphere, and the pyramid. Similar design techniques are to be found in Behrens's ornamental graphics.

19. Compare A. Behne, "Fabrikbau als Reklame," *Das Plakat* 6 (June 1920).

20. Very striking is the hierarchically organized system of framing, which the exhibition guide shared with the poster for the 1906 Deutsche Jahrhundert Ausstellung in Berlin (illustration 7) and which gives a more than merely decorative function to the successive frames. A simpler version of this architectonic framing system had been used by Behrens in 1901 as a wall decoration in his own house in Darmstadt, and in 1904 on the cover of the official German guide to the St. Louis World's Fair. The same means of dividing up the flat plane was also used on the cover of the Festschrift produced for the 25th anniversary of the AEG (illustration G23).

21. These two characteristics also appear in the designs for the two shop fronts (illustrations P2, P7).

22. Compare the Hagen crematorium of 1906–1907 (Hoeber 1913, illustrations 65–70) with the courtyard at the 1906 Deutsche Gewerbeausstellung at Dresden (illustration 8).

23. Wolf Dohrn, "The Example of the AEG" (in this volume).

24. Le Corbusier, *Etude sur le Mouvement dÁrt Décoratif en Allemagne* (in this volume).

25. Prior to this, the Behrens-Roman had become *the* AEG script; later, it was to become the company's house style. A precursor of the initial D on page 4 of the exhibition catalog (illustration G9) was the handwritten address presented to Emil Rathenau on 17 June 1907, one of Behrens's first commissions for the AEG (illustrations G23–G25). The same script appeared as a typeface slightly less than a year later in the Festschrift marking the 25th anniversary of the founding of the AEG (illustrations G12, G13). The Behrens Roman script was probably designed entirely within this ten-month period.

26. "Prof. Peter Behrens on Aesthetics in Industry" (in this volume).

27. Hoeber 1913, p. 155.

28. See appendix A.

29. "Die Wirkung des elektrischen Lichtes bei dem Schaufenster-Wettbewerb in Berlin," *AEG-Zeitung*, November 1909, pp. 5–7. The exhibition was organized by the Verband der Berliner Spezialgeschäfte and the Zentralstelle für die Interessen des Berliner Fremdverkehrs. E. Oppler-Legband [*Die durchgeistigung der deutschen Arbeit, Ein Bericht vom Deutschen Werkbund* (Jena, 1911), pp. 51–52] saw in its popularity "the best proof of the practical success of the movement aimed at the improvement of taste."

30. "Die Schaufenster," *Jahrbuch des Deutschen Werkbundes* [*JDW*] 1913, pp. 60–63.

31. C. Friemert, "Der 'Deutsche Werkbund' als Agentur der Warenästhetik in der Aufstiegsphase des deutschen Imperialismus," in W. F. Haug (ed.), *Warenästhetik* (Frankfurt, 1975), p. 202.

32. Behrens, "Die Wirkung des elektrischen Lichtes . . ." (note 29), p. 7.

33. H. Weidenmüller, "Die Durchgeistigung der geschäftlichen Arbeit," *JDW* 1913, pp. 71, 73. The general demands made here by Weidenmüller sound like descriptions of Behrens's work for the AEG.

34. "Art and Technology" (in this volume).

35. "Das Schaufenster," *JDW* 1913, p. 62.

36. A similar border with a broad shell-limestone frame was used shortly after by Bruno Paul in his shop on the Potsdamer Strasse for the Werkstätten für Friedhofskunst. See K. Pallmann, "Künstlerische Ladengestaltung als Aufgabe des Architekten," *Deutsche Bauhütte* 18 (1914), p. 122, illustration 127.

37. F. Mannheimer 1911, p. 136.

38. Pallmann (note 36), p. 110: ". . . which, set deeply into the marble facing, framed the large display window like a picture." Pallmann was mistaken here. Either he was confusing the two shops (for in the Potsdamer Strasse shop the frame was actually set deeply into the marble facing) or he had misread the projection of the frame in the Königgrätzer Strasse shop as a recession.

39. H. Mannheimer, "Die AEG-Bauten," *JDW* 1913, p. 41.

40. The molding on the main entrance to the Mannesmann administration building of 1911–12 had the same section. There, however, it was used in the reverse direction, it led into the building and demarcated the doorway from the endlessly extendable rhythm of the facade. In this, it recalled Messel's door in the Nationalbank building in Berlin.

41. "Prof. P. Behrens . . ." (in this volume).

42. Pallmann, note 36, p. 110.

43. Behrens, "Die Wirkung des elektrischen Lichtes . . ." (note 29), p. 6.

44. Hoeber 1913, p. 158.

45. Pallman, note 36.

46. Keller and Reiner, *Mitteilungen der Berliner Elektricitäts-Werke* 6, no. 3 (March 1910), pp. 39–40 and illustration on p. 43.

47. Osthaus, "Das Schaufenster," *JDW* 1913: "Endell had found the best solution for the lighting. Others had anticipated him in doing away with the external arc lamps, which dazzle rather than illuminate. Concealed lighting had already appeared in shop windows as a legacy from the stage."

48. Behrens, note 2, p. 4.

49. O. Grautoff, *Die Entwicklung der modernen Baukunst* (Leipzig, 1901).

50. Illustration 5 is an example.

51. An undoubted model was the Aldus Antiqua, a script designed by Francesco Griffo, used in the *Hypnerotomachia Poliphili* (Venice, 1499), and brought to international recognition by the publisher Aldus Manutius. In Behrens's papers there is a sheet of his script with the annotation *poliphil* beside letters of the sort shown in illustration G19. The Tiemann-Roman of 1907 and the Medieval of 1909 were both produced by Klingspor and, as reworked versions of classical models, have a lot in common with this fifth Behrens script. See Hans Loubier, *Die neue Deutsche Baukunst* (Stuttgart, 1921), illustration 141 (script 41) and illustration 132 (scripts 5–8).

52. The value Behrens put on the color and structure of these boards can be seen in the case of the 1913 Behrens monograph by Meyer-Schönbrunn, in the letters from Behrens to the Ruhfus printing works in Dortmund (Karl-Ernst-Osthhaus-Archiv, Hagen, FV 6, 7a, 7b; especially the letter of 24 January 1912).

53. The initial D (from the Behrens Roman script) in the 25th-anniversary Festschrift of 1908 (illustrations G12, G13) is, apart from the border, the same as the one in the AEG's guide to the Schiffbau-Ausstellung (illustration G10)—the first publication to use Behrens Roman. The same initial was also printed in the June edition of *Kunst und Künstler* at the beginning of an article by Karl Scheffler, "Neues von Peter Behrens." As the Festschrift was published on 14 April, the earliest date for the final design of the capital D in the Behrens Roman script is thereby established. The handwritten initial in the Rathenau address of 17 June 1907 is, with minor variations, the direct predecessor. Behrens was apparently still working on the initial letters in December 1907; this is documented by the first publication of the initial A (perhaps a preparatory version) in K. E. Osthaus, "Peter Behrens," *Kunst und Künstler* 4, no. 4 (December 1907), p. 116. The copy deadline for this edition was 3 December 1907. The slightly altered final version appeared officially in October 1908 in the Klingspor version, complete with the accompanying decorations. An introductory brochure was also published at the same time.

54. The form of the letter N appears in Franz Delaville's 1907–08 poster design for the Wiener Werkstätte, "Es war einmal ein Königssohn." The primitive sans-serif script is related in character to the Behrens Roman. See *Katalog Darmstadt*, 1977, vol. 2, pp. 184–186, no. 373.

55. There are four families of rounded scripts, differentiated by the serifs: triangular or medieval, linear or didot bodoni, square or medieval, and sans serif or grotesque. The rhythm of the hair strokes and the ground strokes determines the character of the script. Behrens Roman has triangular and linear serifs.

56. J. Poppenberg, "Buchkunst," in Richard Muther (ed.), *Die Kunst* (October 1908), p. 140.

57. Hoeber 1913, p. 75.

58. Hermann Zapf, in K. G. Schauer, "Graphologie der Lettern," *Der weisse Turm, eine Zeitschrift für den Arzt* (5 July 1965), p. 6.

59. H. v. Trenkwald, "Schriften der Giesserei Gebr. Klingspor, Offenbach a.M.," *Kunstgewerbeblatt* 20, no. 3 (December 1908), p. 54.

60. Behrens, note 2.

61. Note 49, p. 186.

62. Behrens ["In Erinnerung an gemeinsame Arbeit," F. H. Ehmcke and Anna Simons, *Schriften der Corona VIII* (Zurich, 1938)] acknowledged his debt to Anna Simons for her "many-sided stimulation," her knowledge of the calligraphic revival in England under Morris, and her understanding of Edward Johnston's method of revitalizing "antique and medieval calligraphy."

63. Note 59, p. 54.

64. J. Rodenberg, *In der Schmiede der Schrift* (Berlin, 1940), p. 50.

65. Ibid.

66. Loubier, note 51, p. 45.

67. Eckmann's AEG catalog for the 1900 Paris World's Fair was of the same high printing quality as the official German catalog, which was published in Georg Schiller's Neudeutsche script, with graphic design by Bernhard Pankok. The Neudeutsche script was used here for the first time.

68. *Weltausstellung Brüssel, 1910, Deutsches Reich, Amtl. Katalog.* "Published by the Reichskommissar with Verlag Georg Stilke, Berlin. Typesetting and printing by the state publishing house, artistic control of printing Prof. Walter Tiemann. Catalog typeface by Gebr. Klingspor, Offenbach am Main." There is no mention of the name Behrens Roman.

69. There is no firm evidence to confirm H. Lanzke's suggestion ["Von der Hausmarke zum Warenzeichen," *Deutscher Drucker* 2 (1953), p. 8] that the monogram was a compromise solution, influenced by the company management.

70. "The Example of the AEG" (in this volume).

71. See, for example, "Die Gedichte Walters von der Vogelweide," *Kunstgewerbeblatt* 20, no. 3 (December 1908), p. 52.

72. Behrens applied Riegl's concept of Kunstwollen in a thoroughgoing manner. Compare the decorative motifs of the cursive script with the entrance to the 1910 Mairowsky house at Cologne-Lindenthal with the magazine title *Neudeutsche Bauzeitung* in Hoeber 1913 (pp. 28, 134) and with illustration 10 of the present essay.

73. See illustration 65 in *JDW* (1912).

74. See Schnitzler-Bloch, *Die ottonische Kölner Malerschule*, vol. 1, plates 22, 24.

75. The decorative pattern on the cover of the Echternach Gospel and the decorative borders of the Lorsch Gospel are typical of the Egbert workshop in Trier around 1000 A.D.

76. See the initials in the Book of Durrow, ca. 700 B.C. [folio 3V in A. Aston Luce (ed.), *Evangeliorum Quattuor Codex Durmachensis* (Olten, Freiburg, 1960)]; the Book of Kells, 800 B.C. [folios 29 recto and 34 recto in *The Book of Kells* (London, New York, 1952), plates VI, IX]; the Lindisfarne Gospels, 710–720 A.D. [folio 139 recto in T. D. Kendrick (ed.), *Evangelium Quattuor Codex Lindisfarnis* (Olten, Lausanne, 1956), p. 208, illustration 46].

77. The first part of this book appeared in 1901.

78. Riegl, *Die Spätrömische Kunstindustrie* (Vienna, 1927), pp. 293 ff.

79. How thorough Behrens was in applying the principle of the equal value of reciprocal areas of light and dark can be seen in the ease with which light and dark values were reversed in his graphic designs. Compare illustrations G30 and 22.

80. Riegl, note 78, p. 390, plate XX, numbers 1–3 (Keilschnittbroncen, Linz Museum). The patterns here correspond to those of the decorative elements of the Behrens Roman script (illustration 17).

81. Note 78, p. 391.

82. T. Buddensieg, "Riegl, Behrens, Rathenau," *Kunstchronik* 3 (October 1970), pp. 282 ff.

83. See note 53.

84. The style of framing is a sign of Viennese influence (Hoffmann, Olbrich).

85. Behrens, "Umlagerung der Probleme," in *Der Leuchter* (Darmstadt, 1920), p. 325.

86. The coupled square-and-circle motif appeared in series in the coffered ceilings of the Katholisches Gesellenhaus at Neuss (1908–1910) and the German embassy at St. Petersburg (1911–1913), and painted on the dome of the lecture room in the Folkwang Museum at Hagen (1905). As a single motif it appeared on the gable of the crematorium at Hagen (1906) and in the fanlight of the AEG shop in Potsdamer Strasse, Berlin (1910). As an inlay the same motif appeared in the Obenauer house (1910) and the Mairowsky house at Cologne (1913). See Hoeber 1913, illustrations 38, 70, 71, 109, 145, 146, 225.

87. The "echo effect" of the circle-and-square motif is still used today—for example, in the logo of the television station Sender Freies Berlin.

88. W. Niemeyer, "Die Harmonie der Behrens'schen 'Raum-Mathematik,'" quoted in Hoeber 1913, p. 224.

89. In contrast to the title of the Anker catalog (illustration 3 in Buddensieg's essay above), which has a similar composition, the content stands out more strongly here. Nevertheless, the framework and the lamp still dominate.

90. H. Gagel, Studien zur Motivgeschichte des deutschen Plakats, Ph.D diss., Freie Universität Berlin, 1971, p. 41.

91. J. Schinnerer, "Moderne Reklamekunst," *Zeitschrift für Bücherfreunde* 2 (1910), pp. 122–123.

92. Note 90, p. 217.

93. It is a characteristic of Behrens's graphic design that the content was, without exception, held within a frame. These frames usually have an architectonic quality, for architecture, to Behrens, was an expression of order and proportion. Proportion, he felt, was the highest design principle, and was symbolized by the frame.

94. Behrens, "Bahnhofsarchitektur und Eisenbahnreklame," in *Die Eisenbahnreklame* (Berlin, 1922), pp. 8–9.

95. This simplification also conveyed "the longed-for tranquility" (L. Nachtlicht, "Dresden 1906, Einleitendes und Aussenarchitektur," *Werkkunst*, 1905–06, p. 292). The universal need for calm was described by Deipyros in *Moderne Reklame* (1904), pp. 10 ff.: "The eye should not be offered nervosity but tranquility: a point to which it can hold, in which it can take refuge from all the tumult presented to it."

96. AEG measuring instruments and projection lamp, *AEG-Zeitung* 11, no. 1 (July 1908).

97. For example, *JDW* 1912, illustration 97V.

98. On Bernhard's use of Behrens's ornament, compare illustration G40 with illustration 11 of M. Hildebrandt, "Bernhard," *MdVDR* 1910–11 (p. 4). Behrens employed Bernhard-influenced designers like Louis Oppenheim, and occasionally he even worked with Bernhard. Compare Oppenheim's clock design using Behrens lettering (illustration 53) with the Bernhard poster in illustration 24 here.

99. This leaflet for one of the AEG's subsidiary companies shows a fundamental misunderstanding of Behrens's principles, in spite of the Behrens Roman script and the proportional layout. The tubes are given an associational similarity to organ pipes, which would be unthinkable in the posters of either Behrens or Bernhard as the image does not show the suitability of the means to the desired ends. Compare illustration 83 in note 90.

Peter Behrens and the AEG's Railway Projects

Sabine Bohle

During his employment with the AEG, Peter Behrens had several opportunities to work on the problems of rapid-transit railway systems. He designed a railway viaduct and a station, and also the internal layout and fittings of railway carriages—then, as now, an unusual job for an architect. The railway designs Behrens created in connection with the AEG's rapid-transit project of 1907 count without doubt among the most notable of his works. Because of the many time-consuming difficulties encountered in the planning phase, the project was never implemented; as a result, it has been given little attention until now.

In 1907 the AEG presented a plan for a railway from Gesundbrunnen to Neukölln. This plan was based on preparatory studies going back to 1891,[1] and was an alternative to the suspended-railway project of the Continentale Gesellschaft für elektrische Unternehmungen, based in Nuremberg.[2] Although the proposed routes were almost identical, the AEG's design had certain advantages from the outset over the suspended railway. One disadvantage of the latter was its unusual basic principle, which made it extremely difficult to integrate into the existing railway network. An even more serious factor was the general antipathy of the authorities toward any form of overhead railway.[3] The AEG proposal also failed to gain the immediate approval of the authorities, for, with the exception of a 2.4-kilometer underground section between Invalidenstrasse and Spree, it too called for an overhead railway. Before a contract could be made with the city of Berlin, the AEG was forced to make extensive changes to its program.

New plans presented in July 1909 proposed that the track be taken underground from Humboldthain to Urbanhafen. Economic considerations mitigated against putting the entire line underground. As the city insisted that the track be underground as far as Hermannplatz, it offered after lengthy negotiations to carry some of the additional costs that would result. The contract between the city of Berlin and the AEG was signed on 18 March 1912, and with that the idea of a suspended railway was finally rejected. Planning permission for the AEG line was granted on 4 July 1914.

In addition to the two driving positions and the engine room, the interior of the car was divided into three third-class compartments totaling thirty seats and one second-class compartment with ten seats. The two classes were divided by a partition with a door in it. The second-class section was entered via the rear driving position, and the third-class section via a gangway located between the rear driving position and the engine room.

The interior layout and fittings, described by Georg Königshagen[11] as "eigenartig" (singular; original), clearly revealed Behrens's personal style and his preference for clear, lucid forms. Königshagen confirmed that the interior design was carried out according to the instructions of Behrens.[12] Very striking was the subdivision of the third-class compartments by panels, with strongly molded frames and inclined edges, which ran to half the height of the car and looked almost like extended seat backs. This daring method of dividing the compartments anticipated today's express cars and made a marked contrast to the then-customary method of separating the compartments by roof-high partitions. In the absence of such partitions, a new place had to be found for the luggage racks. Behrens set them along the side walls above the windows, thus achieving an even stronger impression of spaciousness and clarity in the interior.

Dark-stained oak was chosen for the wall paneling in the third-class section and in the entrance gangway. The seats were painted black and had simple wooden backrests. The floor was covered in green linoleum, and the roof was painted white.

2
AEG diesel-electric rail car, 1914–15.
Cremers 1928, p. 76.

3
AEG diesel-electric rail car
photographed in 1964. Courtesy of
Sigurd Hilkenbach.

4
Section and floor plan of AEG diesel-
electric rail car. *Organ für die
Fortschritte des Eisenbahnwesens*, N.F.,
54 (1917).

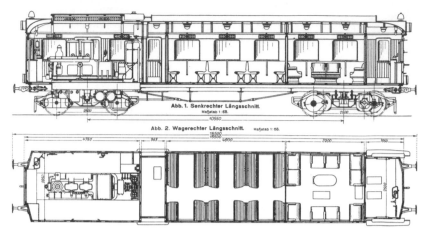

5
Third-class accommodations in AEG rail
car. Cremers 1928, p. 76.

6
Second-class accommodations in AEG
rail car. *AEG-Mitteilungen* 1917, p. 90.

In the second-class section, comfortable seats covered in striped plush were arranged around the walls facing a swiveling oval table. As was customary in second-class compartments, the walls were clad in mahogany. The ceiling was painted white, and the floor was of heavy linoleum with a black and white pattern. All in all, the interior fittings of the second-class section gave a very dignified and stylish impression. The salon style in which the seats were arranged was reminiscent of privately owned luxury carriages such as those the AEG had built in 1914 for the Khedive of Egypt.[13]

Behrens's railway designs are only one stone in the extensive mosaic of his work. In their clear and precise formal language they reveal a sure understanding of technical and constructional considerations. These qualities found particularly lucid expression in the railway-car design of 1914–15. Some of the ideas that first appeared in the 1910 designs for an elevated railway station were to be given form almost twenty years later in the U-Bahnhof Moritzplatz in Berlin, Behrens's only underground-station design and one that is still valid today.

Notes

1. On the 1891 plans for a rapid transit railway, see R. Kolle, "Der Entwurf einer elektrischen Untergrundbahn für Berlin," lecture delivered to the Verein für Eisenbahnkunde, 8 December 1891, published in *Glaser's Annalen für Gewerbe und Bauwesen* 29, no. 11.

2. On the design for a suspended railway, see *Zum Entwurf einer Schwebebahn in Berlin* (Nuremberg, 1905).

3. Their experience with the underground railway built in Berlin by Siemens and Halske had been positive, although before the very successful construction of the Siemens underground railway the authorities had strictly rejected the idea of such railways. (The unsuitable Berlin soil and the new drainage system were given as reasons.)

4. The constructional work was carried out by the AEG-Schnellbahn AG. This company was founded in 1913 as a subsidiary of the AEG specifically for the purpose of building and operating the Gesundbrunnen-Neukölln railway line. It went into liquidation in 1923.

5. The model was published in *Mitteilungen der Berliner Elektricitätswerke* 11 (1915), p. 165. Although there was no direct reference to Behrens, his manner can be detected in certain details, such as the hexagonal station signs and the deeply recessed advertising panels surrounded by heavily molded frames.

6. Similar panels were also used on the overhead railway in Hamburg, which was built in partnership by Siemens and the AEG and opened in 1912. They also appeared on the section of the Berlin overhead railway running along Schönhauser Allee, opened in 1913.

7. Paul Wittig, *Die Architektur der Hoch- und Untergrundbahn in Berlin* (Berlin, 1922), p. 9, illustration 15.

8. Tilmann Buddensieg and Henning Rogge, "Peter Behrens e l'architettura della AEG," *Lotus International* 12 (September 1976), p. 127.

9. Compare also the photograph taken on 26 August 1911 of Behrens's watercolor design for the AEG entrance gates at the corner of Hussittenstrasse and Gustav-Meyer-Allee [Tilmann Buddensieg, "Peter Behrens und die AEG, Neue Dokumente zur Baugeschichte der Fabriken am Humboldthain," in *Festschrift für Margarete Kühn* (Berlin, 1975), p. 295].

10. *AEG-Mitteilungen* 13, no. 6 (1917), p. 88. See also *Glaser's Annalen für Gewerbe und Bauwesen*, 963 (August 1917), p. 37; Paul Joseph Cremers, *Peter Behrens, Sein Werk von 1909 bis zur Gegenwart* (Essen, 1928), p. 76; W. Franz, "Peter Behrens als Ingenieur-Architekt," *Dekorative Kunst* 20 (1917), illustrations 150 and 151; *Peter Behrens 1868–1940*, exhibition catalog (Kaiserslauten, 1966–67), no. 139, illustration 50.

11. Georg Königshagen, "90 PS-Öltriebwagen mit elekrischer Kraftübertragung," *Elektrische Kraftbetriebe und Bahnen* 15 (1917), p. 146.

12. Ibid.

13. On the carriage for the Khedive of Egypt, see *AEG-Mitteilungen* 13, no. 3 (1917), p. 37.

BEHRENS ON ART AND TECHNOLOGY

writings selected by
Tilmann Buddensieg

with editorial and bibliographic
assistance from
Henning Rogge and
Christiane Klebe

In their scope, importance, and impact, the writings of Peter Behrens remain an untapped source. A complete edition is in preparation, but this task is complicated by the remote places of publication, the numerous reprints, and the constant modification of the author's ideas. In the following section only the earliest and most important texts on the question of art and technology are reproduced; these offer indispensable insight into Behrens's thinking in the period 1901–1929.

The Peter Behrens House

introductory comments, exhibition catalog, Darmstadt, May 1901

Architecture is called Baukunst and brings together in its name . . . the art of knowledge, the command of the practical, useful discipline of building, and the art of the beautiful. There is a liberating quality in this, when one sees the two concepts of practical utility and abstract beauty united in one word. For often, in our age regrettably often, these two concepts stand in hostile opposition to each other. We have been through a period in which they almost became opposites. This period is now behind us, and we can claim with some satisfaction that the signs of reconciliation are becoming ever more discernible. The practical object no longer appears prosaically to us as something that merely serves its purpose, but as something that combines with its use a sense of satisfaction. Efforts were also made previously to enliven the soberness of everyday utilitarian objects by adding decoration and ornament in order to conceal their crude, workaday purpose. The object was loaded with unnecessary, purposeless decoration, and thus became even more worthless. The additions had a negative effect in another respect: The functional qualities of the object could no longer be seen, and the desire to use it was thus unconsciously depressed. Then came the recognition of the psychological delight in the useful and functional. One wanted to see the use, to recognize the function. This desire was carried over to the production of the object, and value was placed on its material and construction. One went even further, and stressed the function and the design, exposed the construction, and created forms that invited use. The point was then reached at which the artistic aspect of design was seen to exist in this logical development. For this logical development of an artistic perception, coupled with the progress of technology and the discovery of new materials, guarantees the fertility and legitimacy of the modern style. Through the unification of the two artistic concepts, therefore, we can now talk with justified conviction of a truly contemporary style of architecture.

Art in Technology

Berliner Tageblatt, 29 August 1907, evening edition

As we have already announced, Herr Prof. Peter Behrens has been persuaded to accept the post of artistic adviser to the Allgemeine Elektricitätsgesellschaft in Berlin. In response to our enquiry, he has given us the following account of the problems he will tackle in his work for the company.

For some time, I have been commissioned by the Allgemeine Elektricitätsgesellschaft, Berlin, to produce new designs for the products manufactured by the company. The company probably proceeded from the following considerations: In the manufacturing process until now, the emphasis has been laid simply on the technical aspects. The determining factor in the matter of the external form has been the taste of the individual Werkmeister, and this was true of all firms concerned with the production of technical goods. From now on, however, the tendency of our age should be followed and a manner of design established appropriate to machine production. This will not be achieved through the imitation of handcraftsmanship, of other materials and of historical styles, but will be achieved through the most intimate union possible between art and industry. This could be done by concentrating on and implementing exactly the technique of mechanical production in order to arrive by artistic means at those forms that derive directly from and correspond to the machine and machine production.

It is well known that the Allgemeine Elektricitätsgesellschaft manufactures the most diverse products related to electricity, such as arc lamps for direct and indirect lighting, electric fans, switchgear, heaters, and all manner of small articles like circuit breakers, contacts, etc. For these products, the attempt should now be made, using standard types, to achieve a graceful beauty that is cleanly constructed and appropriate to the materials used. On no account, however, should an individualistic style be established. As all products of society have a more or less close relationship to architecture, this design aim is of general significance. For the new approach will make it possible for the three-dimensional artist and the architect to reintegrate those objects whose technical character previously upset the artistic layout of a room into the all-embracing artistic order.

There is no longer any doubt that the future of industry also has an artistic dimension, and that our age calls for the type of product that is most responsive to this dimension. In the realm of the applied arts, our age calls for *Industriekunst*.

Two benefits will accrue from the practical realization of these ideas. First, the conversion of artistic and creative work into material assets will be promoted, as it is in the field of technology. Second, the way will be prepared for a general improvement in public taste, making it possible not only to satisfy the artistically sensitive but also to bring art and propriety [Anstand] to the most distant strata of the population.

In the logical application of these intentions, the company also attaches great importance to the artistic and typographic design of all its publications. The layout and arrangement of the exhibitions organized by the company will also be governed by the principles outlined here.

It is a matter of great credit that one of the leading industries has seen it as its duty to establish contracts with art.

Prof. Peter Behrens on Aesthetics in Industry

text of a lecture, *AEG-Zeitung* 11, no. 12 (June 1909), pp. 5–7

Members of the advanced training course run by the Staatswissenschaftliche Vereinigung recently met in the electrical-apparatus factory of the AEG in order to study the products and the manufacturing methods of this factory and subsequently those of the machine factory. Before touring the factories, the group visited an exhibition of products manufactured to the designs of the artistic adviser to the AEG, Professor Behrens. Almost all the artistically redesigned products were clearly arranged in the conference room of the electrical-appliance factory. An earlier model of the same product was placed beside each new design to serve as a contrast.

Professor Behrens himself acted as a guide through this exhibition and made the following comments:

"It must be stressed from the start that with all these things—arc lamps, electric fans, and so on—we are not concerned with arts and crafts products, but with utilitarian objects that are intended less to beautify the surroundings than to serve a practical purpose. For this reason alone, the accent should be placed on good proportions rather than on enriching the form of the objects, which would obscure their character. Thus, a simplification that promotes the clear proportional articulation of the various parts is more desirable than a rich ornamentation. In addition, the way in which the outer shell is fitted should show respect for the internal construction. For just this reason, the contrast between the dark green of the armature and the lighter, polished brass of the bands and rivets was chosen for the standard arc lamp and the fan. Only by following such principles can one arrive at a form that can adapt itself to fit in with all the diverse architectural styles of our individualistic age. In addition to the standard models, however, there is in many cases a demand for a slightly more luxurious version using better materials (such as tombac), on which a degree of ornamentation is more justified. But here, too, excessively rich ornament should be avoided, for it would be incompatible with the mechanical process by which the tombac version too is manufactured. The contrast between simple machine production and florid design would be very disturbing. The ornament, therefore, should always have a rather impersonal character. The so-called geometric manner of ornament comes nearest to this requirement.''

The lecturer illustrated these principles with various types of arc lamps for both direct and indirect illumination, with electric fans, resistors, winches, etc., and pointed out that until now only a small part of the firm's products had been redesigned from an artistic viewpoint. He added, however, that it was the intention of the management to give the same careful attention to other products, like electrical components, electric cooking pots, teapots, kettles, and heaters. As these are mass articles in the fullest sense of the term, used today in every household, a highly developed technology can be placed at the service of art. Through the mass production of utilitarian objects of refined design, it is possible to bring good taste to the most distant strata of the population.

The lecturer then showed a large number of publications, posters, price lists, brochures, and the like, adding that, if the attempt was made to give the products themselves an artistic form, then it followed naturally that the same should be done to the accompanying publicity material. As in all advertising, the most important feature of a poster is the lettering. The lettering, therefore, should be the dominant feature in the artistic layout, and should be incorporated in the design wherever possible—on the machines themselves, in the publicity material, and even in letterheads—but always with the proviso that legibility should not suffer. Also in exhibitions that are intended to draw attention to the firm's products and to their qualities, the commercial intention can be only be helped by a tasteful layout, as was the case at the AEG display at the Schiffbau-Ausstellung in the summer of 1908.

A number of photographs were displayed which gave a picture of the exhibition pavilion beside the exhibition halls at the Zoological Garden, as well as views of its interior and surroundings. In conclusion, Professor Behrens showed colored renderings of his large-scale designs for the turbine hall and the machine factory. He ended his lecture by pointing out that the general improvement of taste was also an economic necessity, for this brought the possibility of converting intellectual work into material assets. Artistic work, in particular, is not something that anyone can do, but demands a high level of discrimination. A nation cannot be indifferent to whether it is merely very productive, as are many other nations, or whether it creates something that cannot be imitated as it stems from the nation's own culture. In the last analysis, a feeling for good taste that permeates a whole nation is a testimony to its productivity.

The example of the French is proof enough. For centuries, and right up to the present day, they have been able to derive benefit from their aesthetic and cultural domination. Particularly as Germany's geographical situation makes it dependent on the world market, the AEG's commendable decision to give full attention to the question of taste is something of far-reaching and symptomatic importance to our age.

The Turbine Hall of the Allgemeine Elektrizitätsgesellschaft zu Berlin, designed and described by Professor Peter Behrens, Neu-Babelsberg

Mitteilungen des Rheinischen Vereins für Denkmalpflege und Heimatschutz 4, no. 1 (1 March 1920), pp. 26–29

With minor variations this same text also appeared in *Deutsche Techniker-Zeitung* 27, no. 6 (12 February 1910), pp. 87–90. In 1917 a modified description of the gable front of the turbine hall was added as a footnote, in response to the growing criticism of the younger generation of architects. See "Über die Beziehung der künstlerischen und technischen Probleme," *Technische Abende im Zentralinstitut für Erziehung und Unterricht,* vol. 5 (Berlin, 1917). A shorter version with some changes in the text appeared in Dutch in *Wendingen* 3–4 (March–April 1920), pp. 4–20, and in Czech in J. Krejcar (ed.), *Zivot, L'art nouveau-construction-activité intellectuelle contemporaine* (Prague, 1922), pp. 54–62.

The turbine hall of the Allgemeine Elektricitätsgesellschaft, which has recently been completed to my designs, is located on the corner site bordered by the Huttenstrasse and the Berlichingenstrasse in the north of Berlin. The ground plan was so arranged that it not only took the existing railway tracks into account, but also made the fullest possible use of the limited space available within the confines of the building lines. It was nevertheless possible to accentuate the main hall by setting the side hall back slightly. The dominant architectural idea in the design of the main hall was to pull the steel components together, and not, as is characteristic of normal lattice construction, to spread them out. The internal volume thereby was to be contained on all sides within closed, flat planes in order to create the clarity of architectonic proportions, which alone can promote the sense of spaciousness. To achieve the same effect externally, a solid, hinged-fram construction was chosen. This was particularly important because the design intention was to construct the building as far as possible only out of steel and glass. Where these two materials were inadequate, then infilling walls were to be built out of well-finished concrete.

Unlike masonry walls, however, these concrete infills should not give a load-bearing impression, but should leave this entirely to the steel frame. In support of this principle, the windows facing the Berlichingenstrasse are also inclined backward, parallel to the inner edge of the heavy steel pillars, so that the lintel running along the side elevation creates a deep shadow over the top of the long front. The lintel works like a steel cornice, and together with the front gable heightens the impression of the volume of the roof. The roof itself rests on the side pillars and on the window frame in the front facade. The curved corners of the building are made of concrete and are divided up by iron tie beams, which emphasize the contrast between the infill nature of the concrete pylons and the structural nature of the vertical supports on the long side. On the front facade the static element finds aesthetic expression in the large steel-frame window, which for this reason is made up throughout of repeating steel elements. In order to make the entire window an expression of the load-bearing frame, it is set flush to the plane of the gable, and this impression is heightened by the glass panes, which also lie flush to their steel frames. [Footnote: A flat, flush plane was called for the large window on the front facade, as this window is the structurally supportive element on which the seven-cornered gable sits. The two corner pylons only have a linking and enclosing function. Precisely for this reason, they are made of another material—namely concrete—and stand with their horizontal articulation in intentional contrast to the verticality of the structural frame. As the pylons do not add stability, they are also given the inclined plane of the side windows.]

The smaller, attached hall is constructed entirely out of concrete on the front facade and also to a depth of 4 meters on the courtyard side (as far as the first pillar on the main hall), in order to increase the impact of the steel work on the sides of the two halls. The courtyard facade of the side hall reveals a row of steel supports between broad horizontal tie beams in the same material. The windows, too, are set flush to the load-bearing frame. By doing this, it was intended to give a sense of volume to a building principally constructed out of glass and steel. In their outward appearance, both steel and glass lack the voluminosity of a pile of masonry. The impression of spindliness and fragility can only be countered by setting these materials flush on the same plane and giving them, by artistic means, the appearance of volume and stability. For these qualities remain hidden from the eye, in spite of the mathematically demonstrable strength of the steel. Both sculptural and ornamental decoration have been dispensed with, first because the character and function of a factory hall demand simple forms, and also because decoration would not have aided the desired sense of proportional volume but rather detracted from it.

The hall is 207 meters long on the Berlichingenstrasse and 39.3 meters wide on the Huttenstrasse. The building has a volume of 151,500 cubic meters. The whole complex is made up of a main hall with a span of 25.3 meters and a two-story side hall with a cellar. The heights of the separate spaces were determined by the positioning of the cranes, and this was determined by the production process. The constructional elements were designed to match the unusual static demands of the plant. The traveling cranes in the main hall have a load-carrying capacity of 50 tons at a speed of 2 meters per second, so that the cranes' four coupled wheels each carry 40 tons. In the upper story of the side hall are located traveling cranes with a capacity of 10 tons. The floor of this upper story has a normal loading of 2,000 kilograms, increasing in places to 3,000 kilograms per square meter, while the traveling cranes in the lower story

have a capacity of 40 tons and the floor a loading of 10,000 kilograms per square meter. The supporting system of the main hall is made up of 22 steel frames at intervals of 9.22 meters. This distance was determined by the need to lead the railway tracks into the hall. Subsidiary tie beams are incorporated into the side wall.

Running along the center of the main hall's roof is a raised skylight, which also acts as a ventilator. As the elevation shows, the roof of the upper story in the side hall is vaulted and reinforced longitudinally by a reinforced concrete joist, in order to decrease the span of the patented Bernhard shearing beam.

The reinforced concrete work on the hall (which was initially only 123 meters long) was done by the firm of Czarnikow and Co., Berlin, and the Union Company of Dortmund was responsible for the steelwork. The structural work was completed in five months, a phenomenal performance when one thinks that over 2,000 tons of steel alone were needed. At present, the hall is the longest steel-frame building in Berlin.

The AEG entrusted me with the design of both the external silhouette and the internal space. Inasfar as the constructional work was important for the spatial appearance, it was executed according to my instructions. The constructional implementation of this concept was put in the hands of the well-known engineer Bernhard. In its technical and structural aspects, therefore, the building is the product of the most modern know-how. Bernhard executed the technical drawings and the necessary calculations with the greatest possible understanding of all the artistic considerations involved, and solved every problem with a truly remarkable inventiveness.

Art and Technology

lecture delivered at the 18. Jahresversammlung des Verbandes Deutscher Elektrotechniker, Braunschweig, May 26, 1910

This was reprinted in *Elektrotechnische Zeitschrift* 31, no. 22 (2 June 1910), pp. 552–555, as "Bericht über die Jahresversammlung des Verbandes Deutscher Elektrotechniker am 26. und 27. Mai 1910 in Braunschweig" in *Elektrotechnische Zeitschrift* 31, no. 27–32 (1910), in *Der Industriebau* 1, no. 8 (15 August 1910), pp. 176–180, and ibid. 1, no. 9 (15 September 1910), pp. 80–85, and with minor variations in *Deutsche Wirtschafter-Zeitung* 6, no. 20 (15 October 1910), columns 919–932. Behrens had already delivered a shorter paper on the same topic on 13 January 1909 in the AEG lecture room; the "important passages" of this were published under the title "Kunst und Technik" in the weekly "Zeitgeist" supplement to the *Berliner Tageblatt*, 25 January 1909.

Even when compared with the outstanding eras of the past, the products of the human creative urge in our own age are not to be ignored as proof of our intellectual energy. For it must be admitted that even if they are of a different nature, the products of our age are in no way inferior to their predecessors. The most impressive manifestations of our ability are the products of modern technology. The progress of technology has created a more highly developed civilization than has ever been achieved before. But only a civilization has been created and not a culture—at least not yet if, like [Houston Stewart] Chamberlain, one understands civilization as progress in our material civilization gained through reason and enlightenment, and culture as the intellectual and spiritual values created by philosophy and art.

A life without the civilizing benefits and the indefatigable progress of modern technology is unthinkable. And although it might seem that the spiritual impulse of our age is purely civilizing, another aspect of our existence shows, nevertheless, how much we are dominated by the need for culture. Especially in the realm of art there is the most enormous demand for education, active participation, and development. Certainly no previous age had so much opportunity to attend concerts or had as many art collections, theaters, and art societies as there are today. And among all the branches of the arts, the leading position is held by the fine arts, including architecture and applied art. One among many proofs of this is the huge number of art exhibitions and journals. Yet in spite of this our public life does not bear the marks of a mature culture, for the two spheres of technology and art do not come into contact with each other. This is especially so in that area where they should join most, namely in architecture and in industrial production.

The architect looks for aesthetic content solely in the treasure trove of past centuries and ignores the promising indications that modern construction also gives with regard to form. In contrast, the engineer is interested only in the construction of his steel buildings, and believes that in reaching a result by means of calculation he has also achieved his goal. Nor with the products of industry, which are becoming a part of our surroundings in increasingly large measure, is the form anything more than the result of the cheapest production methods, determined by the taste of the Werkmeister. Thus, in both our immediate and our wider surroundings, our eyes fall everywhere on disharmony, which reveals itself on one hand in the pretentious chaos of romantic form and on the other in utilitarian design that corresponds to our real contemporary needs regardless of aesthetic content.

Over the last ten years a new industrial art has been developed in Germany, an art whose seriousness and quality cannot be doubted. In buying up almost all our exhibits at the 1904 St. Louis World's Fair, the Americans recognized the excellence of German design. This revival of the applied arts is one of the most welcome signs of the aesthetic productivity of our age. It is all the more regrettable, therefore, that two such important areas as art and technology should exist in mutual isolation. Through this dualism, our age is failing to achieve the sense of visual unity that is both precondition and testimony of a true style. For by style we mean the unified means of formal expression, which in the past was the product of the entire intellectual life of an epoch. The determinants in such a style are those elements that are common and uniform, not the exceptional or the peculiar. The tendency toward such a unity has emerged in the revitalized applied arts, where the impulse derived from the construction of each object is valued as a form-giving quality. Perhaps it is exactly this fact that has contributed in part to the blossoming of the applied arts over the last decade.

Since the time of his first great achievements, in contrast, the engineer has turned away increasingly from the artistic tendencies of the age. This is both understandable and justifiable, for the enormous development of technology and transportation over the last fifty years had made such demands of the engineer that his inventiveness was occupied exclusively in this task. The result was that he was unable to give any thought to the aesthetic appearance of his inventions.

In spite of this legitimate preoccupation, it was still observed that the creations of the engineers were also not without a certain sort of beauty. One has only to think of the great iron halls, which certainly make an aesthetic impression with their broad, sweeping roofs. We also cannot deny the aesthetic attraction of those small, simple buildings constructed by the engineer, or, above all, the attraction of the daring and logical construction of the machines themselves. In both these instances, there is no prevailing artistic conception, and the aesthetic success is quite fortuitous. This fact can be explained in that the products possess an inherent pseudo-aesthetic, for they embody a natural law, namely the law of mechanical construction. It is the law of organic being, which nature also reveals in all her works. But just as nature is not culture, so culture cannot be created merely through the accomplishment of utilitarian and material intentions. And it is entirely natural that, for all our sincere and enthusiastic recognition of the achievements of technology and transportation, the desire for absolute beauty should still break through. For we are not prepared to believe that from now on the new values of exactitude and extreme functionality will take the place of those values that previously delighted and ennobled us.

It is true that the engineer is the hero of our age, and that it is to him that we owe our economic position and our international standing. If other nations look at us enviously, then the reasons for this envy are our German industry, our engineering, and our organizational ability. They would not begrudge us our great musicians, poets, and philosophers. But it cannot be claimed that the creations of the engineers are in themselves already elements of an artistic style.

A certain modern school of aesthetic thought has promoted this misconception by wishing to derive artistic form from utilitarian function and technology. This view of art stems from the theories of Gottfried Semper, who defined the concept of style by demanding that the work of art should be the product first of its function and second of its materials and the tools and procedures involved. This theory comes from the middle of the last century, and should, like many others from this period, be seen as one of the dogmas of Positivism (Riegl).

Admittedly, when one recalls the "artistic" goods produced by industry over the last decades, one can understand how Semper's view could have been seen as a new truth. For without exception these were badly made machine products ("factory ware," as it was then censoriously dubbed). The bad workmanship and cheap materials of these products were covered up by as rich a decoration as possible, as it was the principle of this branch of industry to copy handcraftsmanship and real materials with counterfeit imitations. But these times are past—praise the Lord!—and our industry is today capable of manufacturing technically perfect products. But even now, the standard of design can satisfy discriminating taste in only a few cases. I am convinced that this shortcoming cannot be overcome by instructing the manufacturers to keep only to the most functional form. On the contrary, it seems to me much more important to try to understand the essential nature of art.

Art originates as the intuition of powerful individualists and is the free fulfillment of a psychological need, untrammeled by material conditions. It is made not by chance, but is the creation of the fervent and deliberate will of the free human spirit. It represents the satisfaction of psychological intentions; that is, intentions translated onto a spiritual plane, such as are most clearly revealed in music. The musical element, the simple rhythmic element, is the essential factor in artistic creation. Or, as the Viennese scholar Riegl has put it, "Semper's mechanistic view of the nature of the work of art should be replaced by a teleological view in which the work of art is seen as the result of a specific and intentional artistic volition that prevails in the battle against functional purpose, raw materials, and technology." These three last-named factors lose, thereby, the positive role ascribed to them by the so-called Semper theory, and take on instead an inhibiting, negative role: ". . . they constitute, as it were, the coefficient of friction within the overall product."

In the process of creating artistic form, therefore, technology is not a creative but rather a critical factor, although clearly one of great importance. It was acknowledged at the beginning of this lecture that both the new constructional techniques and the new materials, iron and steel, are also important factors in the artistic context and should be evaluated as such. But no new beauty can be developed out of these things alone. Just as there are physical laws, so there are artistic laws. And these laws, which have remained valid as a continuing tradition since the beginning of human civilization and which became the spiritual property of Goethe and Lessing, cannot and should not be abandoned. They are real, and retain equal rights beside the demands of technology.

The fundamental laws of the arts do not necessarily have to be expressed in the time-honored materials of stone and wood; they can also be transferred to the new, modern materials. Just as it seems false and contradictory to clad daring steel constructions with stone in order to turn them into romantic knights' castles, as has been done with many of the great German bridges, so it is equally wrong not to recognize the need to subordinate constructional questions to the natural laws of art, principally the demands of proportion. Certainly, modern technology has given us new and important values, and has produced the greatest achievements of our age. Consequently, the techniques and research methods of the engineer should not be disturbed. But to us there is a difference between the ability to make theoretical discoveries based on mathematical thought and practical production, which has the task of transforming the received abstract knowledge into a multiform national asset by giving it plastic form. It seems important to differentiate between these two areas of activity within the discipline of technology. It will then be conceded that, in those instances where one is concerned not with entirely novel problems but with well-tried techniques and approved materials, one should use forms that create an aesthetic impression. In the very fact that there are several constructional solutions to one and the same problem—in the fact that one has a choice—already lies the invitation to choose according to one's taste; that is, according to the laws of beauty. And when this happens, it is exactly the same process as has occurred in cultural history since the earliest times, namely a manifestation of man's inherent urge to pursue beauty. This process also occurs in technological activity, and it is principally a matter of recognizing this. Presupposing his willingness to value beauty, it is the task of the engineer to recognize which forms are truly beautiful and to apply them according to aesthetic rules.

The request that one should wherever possible take beauty into account may appear to be self-evident, and aesthetically pleasing form should certainly be derived from the engineer's own activity and not sought in appliqué decoration. However, the creation of artistic forms either in simple or complicated sequence is not a task in which one can succeed simply on the basis of good intentions and good taste. For in the realm of technology too, such creation is an aspect of the highest manifestation of human life, namely art. While dilettantism stands opposed to all serious intentions and skills, it has a particularly pernicious influence on art, especially when art is a manifestation of the power that gives our age its character. It is a question of the greatest importance, and one with a bearing on the history of human culture, whether or not the great technological achievements of our age will succeed in becoming the expression of a mature culture—in other words, whether the external manifestations of our existence will achieve the uniformity necessary to create a style.

One often hears that we are approaching an iron and steel style. But, as already noted, no style derives from construction or materials alone. There is no materialistic style, and there never has been. The all-embracing unity of an age stems from a much broader complex of conditions than can be represented by these two factors alone. Technology cannot permanently be understood as an end in itself, but gains in value and significance just at that point at which it is recognized as the most refined means of achieving a culture. A mature culture, however, speaks only through the language of art.

From the side of the art lover, there are great hopes of achieving a style linked to the highly individual development of the applied arts as they have evolved in Germany since the end of the 1890s. And although the talent behind these most diverse artistic statements should in no way be underestimated, it must nevertheless be asserted that there can be no individual style. An individual and personal artistic inclination cannot create the all-embracing unity of forms that in history has made an exact and eternal monument to a particular age. This formal unity will rather be derived from the preconditions of our age, among which technology and economics are the most important. Our most serious task, therefore, is to help technology to achieve artistic quality, at the same time helping art to great achievements through contact with technology.

I have tried to indicate that, by their very nature, art and technology are very different forms of intellectual expression, and that it is an aesthetic fallacy to believe that beauty can be derived solely from technical principles, from the exact fulfillment of function. Accordingly, I have just put forward the demand that art and technology should be fused together into one activity. I don't believe that this is a contradiction. For it seems necessary to me to separate the two intellectual activities clearly from each other, but to lead them toward a mutual goal—the goal I described at the outset as culture, which in history has found tangible expression in the concept of style. We can recognize in history how the combination of great technological skill and a deeply felt art produced the style of an epoch. We only have to think of the Egyptian pyramids, which were counted in the later ages of Greek and Roman antiquity among the wonders of the world. They prove that the Egyptian people must at that time already have had considerable knowledge of practical mechanics. Only with this knowledge could such edifices have been built, which demanded that great weights be lifted and moved around using limited resources of power.

The buildings of the Romans offer us the same proof. They created the architectual form of the arch and consequently the vault, something of great importance for the following epoch. On the basis of this new constructional principle, the Romans became magnificent architects. In the same way, we admire equally the gracious beauty of Gothic architecture and the audacity of the construction. The best example, finally, is provided by the Renaissance, the period that shows most clearly a simultaneous blooming of technical skill and a new style of art.

Now, it is certainly true that all the buildings of earlier periods were the work of one hand, that the architect devised and implemented both the artistic expression and the constructional system at the same time. Thus, the artist Leonardo also built fortifications and machines of war. But our age is different. Today, neither the artist nor the engineer can combine specialized disciplines. Whereas in the time of Leonardo the encyclopedia of knowledge was comprehensible to one man, today it is specialization that creates our enormous productive power.

Engineering is a difficult, scientific occupation that, with today's demands, calls for total dedication. But artistic creation is itself also a full-time occupation that completely absorbs one's thoughts and feelings and, like any other occupation, requires many years of study and continuous undivided interest. Yet it is from the engineer, who takes his work more seriously than anyone else, that a full recognition of the new creative ideas and

aims is first to be expected. We are certainly all united in the conviction that the industrial architecture of the future as well as the products of industry must, in addition to their high practical utility, also be given a more finished appearance. We all regard it as wrong when an industrial building is suddenly put up in a beautiful piece of landscape, especially if it is built in a style that would insult even an industrial town or suburb. We feel that it is necessary, therefore, that artistic attention be devoted to such buildings. This, however, does not imply a rich or expensive design, but rather one that conforms to artistic rules. But the question then arises: Who should design such buildings? It is unlikely that a special profession, which one could call engineering-architecture, will develop. Rather, I believe that the future will require the close collaboration of engineer and architect. In this, neither the architect nor the engineer will be subservient to the other. Although it upsets us when a factory hall destroys the rhythm of line and materials in a well-articulated street front through its naked functionalism, it is just as wrong when an architect clads the intelligently worked out construction of an industrial building and introduces something entirely alien to the function and the internal layout of the building. In particular, the internal structure of an industrial building must be kept clear, and it is just this sense of structure that should become the basis of a new type of beauty typical of our age. Nothing of any significance in life is the product of a particular profession, but can be ascribed to the energy and enterprise of great, powerful personalities. It is all the same to me whether the conception for important contemporary projects should come from a farsighted and technically gifted architect, or from a rhythmically sensitive, artistically gifted engineer, or even from a farsighted organizer who defines the basic idea and then persuades the artist and the constructor to realize it. The main thing is that the nature of contemporary design should be recognized and implemented, and that those engineers and architects should be employed who have the necessary design ability and sure sense of taste.

If the talk up to now has been mainly about structural engineering, this can be explained by the importance this branch of engineering has for our period, which calls for large-scale industrial complexes. The large, functional buildings serving transportation, which call for engineering construction, are now appearing in such large numbers and on such important sites that they are beginning to dominate the cityscape. When the theme of art and technology is under discussion, these buildings in particular should not go unmentioned.

What upsets us in the existing buildings of this type is the impression that the architectural aspects of the materials and design are treated as secondary considerations. They look as though they were constructed simply for their practical purpose and then given a facade in any old historical style, designed by a third- or fourth-rate architect without regard to the internal structure. When, however, an engineering building of this type remains free of second-hand architectural additions, it then contrasts strongly against the neighboring buildings because of its lack of substance. A good example of the immateriality of steel construction is the Eiffel Tower in Paris, which was admired so much when it was built. Today, it is impossible to regard it as a beautiful monument when we compare it with the noble buildings of antiquity. One gains no other impression apart from that of a naked skeleton—although it should be added that, according to an informed expert, more material was added for reasons of aesthetics than was strictly necessary on purely constructional grounds. Without doubt, the success of structural design lies in establishing the minimum amount of material for a given construction, and the beauty of iron and steel lies partly in their rigidity without volume. In a

certain way they have a dematerializing character. This character, admittedly, is only revealed when the iron and steel are openly exposed. When this is done, however, the spatial conception of architecture should not suffer. For architecture is the creation of volumes, and its task is not to clad but essentially to enclose space. If it were now said that the beauty of pure iron or steel construction lies in line, then I would repeat that line has no substance and that architecture exists in volume and substance. The practical needs of industry as well as our present-day need for air and light demand large openings. But that is no reason for all architecture to give the impression of a thin, wiry skeleton or of a threadbare framework. By their very nature, both steel and glass lack in their appearance the voluminosity of layered masonry. But, through a well-thought-out distribution of areas of light and shadow on the facade, the building can be helped to achieve substance and can thereby be given an aesthetic feeling of stability, which without this arrangement would remain hidden from the eye regardless of the building's mathematically demonstrable stability. This sense of visual stability can be achieved by pulling large areas of glass and their vertical supports together onto one plane, from which the horizontal tie beams are allowed to project powerfully. The constructions of the engineer are the result of mathematically ordered thought. No one would doubt their structural stability, but it is a different matter whether or not this is given a dynamic visual expression, thus fulfilling the aesthetic demand (as a Doric temple, for example, does perfectly). We have already become accustomed to some modern forms of construction, but I do not believe that mathematically worked out stability will ever achieve a suggestive impact on the eye. For this would mean that an art form would be given a purely intellectual basis, which is a contradiction in itself. Furthermore, the principle of rhythm is of great importance, as it has been in the architecture of all ages. It is really a rhythmic interpretation when we say that our age goes faster than that of our fathers. Our age has been seized by a haste that has no time for details. When we race through the streets of our city we are no longer able to notice the details of the buildings. In the same way, the images of the city that flash past the traveling railway carriage can only have an impact through their silhouettes. The individual buildings no longer speak for themselves. Such a view of our surroundings has already become commonplace to us, and the only sort of architecture that corresponds to it is one that is as compact as possible, with undisturbed planes whose conciseness precludes any visual obstacles. When any particular feature is given prominence, it should be placed in the direction of the goal toward which we are moving. The articulation of large areas, a lucid contrast between prominent features and widely stretched flat planes, and a unified repeating sequence of essential features—these are all essential techniques.

In fact, the same approach that has just been described as suitable for architecture is also valid for smaller objects produced by industry or related to it in some way. Of course, the things that most demand artistic treatment are those that come into contact with a wide public, such as industrially produced goods. Indeed, a striking example is provided by the complete range of products manufactured by the electrical industry. The extent and diversity with which electricity has been profitably introduced into our business and domestic life is admirable. We constantly come upon machines, appliances, tools, and luxury goods of all sorts that stand in the service of electricity. They, too, are all new and functional, but, like the industrial buildings, they either state their purpose or are covered over by an artistic form from an earlier age that bears no relation to the product. Particularly in electrical engineering, it is not a question of covering up the outside of the appliances with decorative trimmings. Instead, new forms should be found to match the entirely new character of this branch of technology. One should not merely allude to art and industry in each machine-made object; one should strive for an inner union of the two. This will be achieved when all imitation of old craft forms and historical styles is abandoned. Instead, the opposite course should be pursued. The techniques of mechanical production should be exactly implemented and given artistic expression. Genuineness should be accentuated in every respect, and, above all, those forms that derive from and correspond to the machine and machine production should be applied in an artistic manner. It is a matter of achieving for each single product standard types that are cleanly constructed and appropriate to the materials used. In their design these types should not pursue anything tremendously new, but should be developed out of the current good taste of the period. In the manufacture of simple appliances of less intrinsic importance, such as the components of an electrical installation, all obtrusive ornament should be avoided. Here, the intention should merely be to design them in such a way that their presence is neither disturbing nor offensive. However, objects that are installed in our direct surroundings, in rooms in which we live, may perhaps be permitted a rather more rich decoration. This is especially true when expensive materials are used, for the materials justify a discreet application of ornament. Overly rich ornamentation, however, should always be avoided in machine-made goods, for it disturbs our sense of good taste when we keep on finding the same pretentious forms repeated in great numbers. The contrast between the richly ornamented form and the simple, mechanical means of production would be too disturbing. The ornament, therefore, should always have a rather impersonal quality. Simple, geometric ornament comes nearest to this requirement.

How much electricity immediately demands a new manner of formal expression, which could promote a contemporary style has not yet fully come into our consciousness. For example, the electric light fixture still resembles the old candelabrum. Not only is the shape retained, but sometimes there are even imitation candles made of porcelain—all this in spite of the fact that the electrical engineer knows that the light of the incandescent bulb has a different diffusion pattern than the light of a candle, and that for this reason the bulbs should hang down. The artistic advantage of the electric light lies principally in the fact that it is not dependent on a heavy fixture, but can be distributed around the room without any constraints. Rather than take over the form of the candelabrum for the new type of light, we should regard the new light as a stimulus for a new form. Without doubt, a candelabrum carrying many wax candles gives a particularly festive impression, even to our modern, pampered taste for lighting effects. The mood created by the Christmas tree in both grownups and children has the same origin. It lies in the fact that the main source of light is not concentrated in a few points, but rather distributed among a large number of low-intensity sources across a large area, so that the light is very diffused. The effect is the exact opposite of that of an arc lamp suspended in a room. More attention should be given to this principle in internal lighting, and it would better reflect the nature of electric lighting if one were to do away with the central light fixture. In its place the lights could either be spread across the ceiling or, as one sees quite often these days, hidden behind a high, molded cornice to reflect off a white-painted ceiling. I have experimented with miniature lamps, using the well-known two-candlepower bulbs attached at 10-cm intervals to a rubber-coated cable. I then strung up this light garland under the ceiling to make a many-stranded illumination scheme. In this way I achieved the diffuse lighting effect of a candelabrum. Although this first attempt looked rather primitive, perhaps because of the lack of metal components, I still believe that similar attempts in this direction using a large number of low-power lamps could prove to be appropriate to the principle of electric lighting and its inherent stylistic demands.

Industry has the power to create culture by bringing together art and technology. Through the mass production of utilitarian objects of aesthetically refined design, not only would a service be rendered to the artistically sensitive, but art and propriety would also be brought to the most distant strata of the population. It would be possible to make the high values of intellectual work accessible to wider circles, following the example of the art of printing. Ultimately, the general improvement of taste is also an economic question. It becomes possible to convert intellectual work into material assets. This work is valuable, discriminating, and individualistic, and it is not something that just anyone can do.

A nation cannot be indifferent to whether it is merely productive, as are many other nations, or whether it creates something that is individual and that cannot be imitated because it stems from the nation's own culture. In the last analysis, a feeling for good taste that permeates a whole nation is a testimony to the nation's ability. The example of the French is proof enough. For centuries, and right up to the present day, they have been able to derive benefit from the dominance of aesthetics in their culture. It is particularly important for Germany, which has now achieved political power, also to win power in artistic areas. In Germany, industry is more dominant than agriculture. As a result of its geographical situation, Germany is dependent on the world market. Therefore, Germany should strive to win a leading position in the world market, not only through purely technical performance, but also through the artistic quality of its products.

Even though it must be conceded that, by their nature, art and technology are quite different, this in no way lessens the legitimacy of the view that they still belong together. Art should no longer be regarded as a private matter in which one indulges at will. We do not want an aesthetic system that looks for its rules in romantic dreaming, but one that is based on the full legitimacy of bustling life. Nor, however, do we want a technology that goes its own way, but one that is receptive to the artistic will of our age. In this way, German art and technology will work toward one goal: toward the power of the German nation, which reveals itself in a rich material life ennobled by intellectually refined design.

Conclusion of speech at opening of new AEG administration building, Mannesmannröhren-Werke, Düsseldorf, 10 December 1912

Zur Erinnerung an die Einweihung des Verwaltungsgebäudes der Mannesmannröhren-Werkes in Düsseldorf, 10. 12. 1912 (Düsseldorf: Mannesmannröhren-Werke, 1913), pp. 70–85

. . . There is no longer any doubt that the housing in our modern cities is being relocated in healthy and pleasant surroundings on the periphery of the city and in the green suburbs. As a result, the inner city is increasingly becoming a business area.

In this situation, the most appropriate course would seem to be to consciously pursue the goal of creating a proud commercial city, rather than to merely accept the inevitable with a more or less heavy heart. Every measure that appears to support the interests of the city should be introduced in order to stress this commercial character as strongly as possible. In terms of planning, the city should be conceived as a uniform architechtonic entity, and one could think of nothing more magnificent than constructing an entire city with a unified architectural character and style.

Basically, it is incomprehensible that a building that serves a serious purpose should not reflect this seriousness in its outward appearance. Instead, these buildings are still burdened with bay windows, little gables, and the well-known surfeit of cheap sculptural decoration. Why are the demands made by such a building not adopted as an artistic motif and then given the most noble expression possible, both internally and externally, by means of carefully worked out proportion? Proportion is the alpha and omega of all artistic creation!

It seems that, in spite of their logical consistency, energy, and dependable efficiency, which we can thank for the rapid economic development of our nation, industry and commerce have not always recognized clear and logically developed ideas on artistic form. Instead, they fell victim to dilettantish tendency toward romanticism and ostentatiousness. In certain towns, however, such as Düsseldorf, there are buildings that can be seen as serious artistic works, committed to the creation of a new type.

I feel strongly bound to say here that in my ideas on the architecture of a modern commercial building I received from Herr Erich, the managing director of the Mannesmannröhen-Werke, not only understanding but many invaluable suggestions. To Herr Erich and to his colleague, Herr Bungeroth, I would like today to express my sincere thanks for their enthusiastic collaboration and their support for all my suggestions. Modern progress, which threatens to plunge everything from the small-town idyll to the major city into chaos, sets for architecture new tasks that can only be fulfilled in the spirit of industry and commerce. The development of monumental art has always been the expression of the current nexus of power. If in this sense one can speak of the art of the Church in the Middle Ages, of the art of kings in the Baroque era, and of bourgeois art around 1800, then I believe that our richly flourishing industry today constitutes a center of power that cannot remain without influence on our culture.

The New Factory Architecture

Das Echo. Deutsche Export Revue, no. 1936 (16 October 1919), pp. 1294–1299

The text of this article was repeated in a wider context in the 1929 article "On the Aesthetics of Factory Design" (see below) except for the following important passage on workers' housing, which is therefore reprinted here.

. . . Finally, the small estates should be mentioned; their increasing importance in this age, particularly for industry, cannot be ignored. At the moment they are linked very closely to the industrial plants, and they should therefore be constructed and designed in the same spirit of industrial vigor. We shall increasingly be obliged to take a successful house type and construct it repeatedly as a terrace row.

It would be desirable if these small estates could be amalgamated with the industrial plant into an organic unity based on the same ideas. Out of this unity could develop a new and characteristic type of modern industrial city.

Artistic Values in Factory Building and their Effect as Publicity

Das Plakat 11, no. 6 (June 1920), pp. 269–273

Apart from the conclusion, which is printed below, this article is substantially similar to "The New Factory Architecture" and "Industrial Architecture and Urban Design."

. . . And industry too has occasion these days to consider the impression made by its factories and administration buildings. It has been known for a long time, and not only on emotional grounds, that more and better work is performed in well-lit and friendly factory halls impeccably designed according to the basic laws of health than in constricted and smoky sheds. The spirit of the plant and the buildings communicates itself to the work. This fact is particularly important because we have to concentrate today more than ever on high-quality work if we hope to compete at all in the world market. But it is also necessary for another reason for industry to consider the impression it makes. If someone is looking for quality, then he will look for it where the manufacturing process seems to him to guarantee it. It is a well-known fact that when products are bought they are principally judged not on their technical qualities, which are often difficult to assess, but on their external appearance. Furthermore, the impression made by the place of manufacture and by the company as a whole is a decisive factor in the decision. It cannot be denied, therefore, that architecture and engineering aesthetics are of considerable importance as publicity.

The Ethos and the Realignment of Artistic Problems

in *Der Leuchter. Jahrbuch der Schule der Weisheit*, Hermann Graf Keyserling, ed. (Darmstadt, 1920), pp. 315–340

This short passage (pp. 324 ff.), which is not without self-criticism, is taken from one of the best literary pieces of the "Expressionist" Behrens. Much of the article "Stil?" [*Die Form* 1 (1922), pp. 5 ff.] is based on this piece.

The art of this prewar period found appropriate expression in the monumental and the decorative. To such an age, monumentality represents material greatness, the proportion of quantities rather than the concentration of quality. Monumental art, aesthetic imperialism. Single details, which stand in a relationship to each other in which they mutually outdo each other, are made to appear bigger and more powerful; intensification up to the prevailing dominants. Piling up of preciousness of materials and indulgence in handcraftsmanship. Decoration that forces the arts together, which adds them up to create the whole. Sovereign domination of technology. Virtuosity as overbearing possession of acquired skill. Self-confidence of the single form. The individualization of each part of a building through the accentuation of its static or constructional purpose. The surfaces isolated and made independent within frames.

The spiritual art of earlier times and distant lands clearly gives us proof of the opposite sort of art, offers strong symbols of the spiritualization of moving innocence and primitive greatness. The spiritual sincerity develops the form, uninfluenced by materials or format. This might be small or large; it is of no consequence. Even the untouched, natural qualities of the material and the clumsiness of the maker's hand make us happy, in contrast to mechanical exactitude and the emptiness of technical know-how.

The work is self-impression, devotion, giving, is honor and worship. For this reason, the art is symbolic, only hints, simplifies, in order to say only what is essential, sacrificed out of the inexhaustible wealth of the endless abundance of forms. The building laws are mysterious. Multiplicity expands into the infinite and incalculable. The earth's gravity is not compensated for by statics and by piling up imposing building masses, but seems to be overcome entirely. Space does not enclose, does not confine; it leads into incalculable depths, climbs to distant heights. The movement and stretching through space occurs by means of the rhythmic sequence of the parts of the building in endless repetition of similar forms. The basic law of this art is not the monarchical principle of the subordination of the parts in respect to their tasks and mutual relationships under a dominant principal form, but is constructive ornament, geometric speculation, number mysticism.

This art is not flattering, it is severe. It is not intoxicated with the rosy appearance of the outside world, with the reflection, the shine, or the velvety darkness of alluring objects. This art, too, stands opposed to the Impressionism of our age. Clues for the development of our art can perhaps be most easily gained from painting. Impressionism is superficial art. The shadows, reflections, the silvery atmosphere and all the accidents of nature are intrinsically valuable particles and elements, and are joined together by a painting technique appropriate to the subject to make a complete picture, an independent organism, a self-contained microcosm. In contrast, the nature of the new art, similar to primitive art, is symbolic. It offers abbreviations, indications of what an object is in general, not under special lighting or special circumstances. It portrays the object as one would reproduce it from memory. The simplification toward the essential goes back to the basic forms (sphere, cube, cylinder) out of which the objects are made up. To these are added symbols, which clarify the forms and introduce concepts.

This art, therefore, is an art of concepts, not painterly but formalistic. But the forms are not the forms of convention, but of the consciousness of a great unity of all existence with the universe.

In this interpretation lies, once again, the ethical destiny of the new art. From it emerges the necessary understanding of a new and higher set of fundamental laws, for what moves us most profoundly is the amazement and awe with which we view the incomprehensible higher order of the world. There are already signs in all areas of the arts that a new harmony is establishing itself. It is an unmistakable fact that a certain type of contemporary plastic art is looking for ulterior laws. Yet it seems as if the basic idea of this painting is to give rhythmic articulation to the picture plane by means of lines and areas of color, and through these symbolic forms to express the actual artistic ideas. Just as sculpture first creates its masses, so the modern painting first seeks the formal elements that lead to a new type of harmony, before it puts these elements at the service of the subject matter. Certainly these methods of creation are also related to the new architectonic spirit of our age. For with architectural forms, too, it is actually no longer a question of creating a flattering appearance of practicality in the materially perceived sense, or of simulating constructive necessities, but simply a matter of giving symbolic representation to spatial concepts using abstract methods—rhythm, the play of lines and planes. The aim is to allow the space to become active, like the Gothic nave, which is said to be the mirror image of a procession.

Architecture too strives toward infinity; but more than any other art it is the art that, because of its techniques and purpose, remains bound to tangible materials. For this reason, it cannot carry itself off into the spheres of a transcendental world in which it metamorphoses into an idea. It remains tied to the earth, but it seeks a spiritual link with the universe, with the natural law that dominates the world and gives substance its prismatic incarnation in polymorphous forms.

This is the struggle for the whole, for totality. Architecture is the art of forming space. In its original sense, space is infinite and inconceivable. We are now accustomed to understanding it by enclosing it. For us, space is made tangible by that which provides a resting place for our senses, a place our senses can comprehend as coordinates of our mental world. Enclosure, therefore, should be understood as an ideal notion rather than as a material or tangible quality. And for this reason, spatial enclosures are not the closed walls of a prison, but precursors, promises of redemption. This task will be achieved when the spatial enclosures establish their legitimacy through their relationship to the wider surroundings, or depict themselves as part of a larger unity.

Industrial Architecture and Urban Design

Der Neubau 7, no. 8 (24 April 1925), pp. 97–102

The text is substantially similar to "The New Factory Architecture," "Artistic Values . . . ," and "On the Aesthetics of Factory Design," except for the passage below, which reveals a remarkable deviation by the "Expressionist" Behrens from the principles of his pre-1914 industrial architecture.

. . . In this way, the form of the industrial building should be accentuated against the building's innate functionalism. It seems, however, as if only the functional aspects of industrial buildings have been recognized until now. Urban design has suffered under these buildings, and simply put up with them wherever they were necessary. Many theories have already been put forward about the mechanistic spirit that determines the design vocabulary of our age. These theories, however, were derived themselves from the mechanistic spirit, and claimed that artistic forms should be evolved out of functional demands. In building, this resulted in the tendency to temper the newness and strangeness of coolly calculated technical forms on the exterior, to make them fit in with traditional forms, to adapt them to the taste of the philistine, and to make the construction "respectable"—all this instead of recognizing that the romanticism of our age lies precisely in the technology we come up against everywhere; it lies in the attempt to break out of the earth's gravity, in the daring flight into unexplored areas, in the adventurous urge to achieve the impossible. There have been hardly any attempts to take the grotesque elements of the often bizarre forms of technology as a leitmotif and to accentuate the fantasy quality. But only in this way is it possible in the urban design context to give a cityscape accents that heighten its importance and character. This was done in the Middle Ages by the churches, which were never matched to the houses. A new spirit cannot establish itself from one day to the next.

Although there are already examples in large cities that promise a move in this direction, true success can only be hoped for when the engineer and the urban designer begin to work closely together. From such a collaboration one might expect the emergence of a discipline that would signify a new school of urban design.

I have tried to produce a stimulus in this direction in my master class in Vienna.

On the Aesthetics of Factory Design

Gewerbefleiss 108, no. 7–9 (July–September 1929), pp. 125–130

This article brings together all Behrens's ideas after 1919, and adds some brief biographical information.

. . . While an inclination toward art cannot be entirely denied today, the real interest of the age is nevertheless directed at technology. It would seem as if technology lays claim to our instincts and aspirations for everything else, as if mechanical forces aspire to replace the artistic values through which our lives were previously enhanced and ennobled, as if reproduction will take the place of production. Instead of the theater there is the cinema; for the concert there are the gramophone and wireless. For lack of recognition of the fact that technology cannot be an end in itself but only a means, we sometimes still find today that in some places it is aggressively obtrusive. It is tiresome to be everywhere surrounded by levers, buttons, switches, and tubes, for we are only reminded thereby of the physical comforts and necessities of life. This obtrusive technology must be overcome, and in its place we must find the redeeming forms in which the products of technology themselves become the expression of a mature culture. If this search for form is part of the mission of modern industry, then it cannot fail to find expression and influence in the realm of industry itself. It is unthinkable that someone who understands the technical spirit of our age could be receptive to culture and the fine arts in his private hours but against mixing art and technology during his working day at the head of a large corporation. Such a view would be in opposition to the character of our modern life, and for just this reason it would not say much for the industrialist's understanding of the economic tendencies of the age. He would also be misunderstanding the artistic development of our epoch and failing to recognize that hygienic and social demands, and even technical achievements, lead to a manner of design whose formal language corresponds closely to contemporary aesthetic ideas in all branches of the arts.

When I look back twenty years or so, it seems to me that these or similar ideas had already stirred in some minds, but had not been able to exert any influence, as the impetus to set them in motion on a large scale was lacking. For this reason, I still look gratefully upon my appointment as artistic adviser to the AEG as a lucky chance that came my way. The AEG was a genuinely large-scale industrial concern that manufactured the most diverse products and had factories whose necessary expansion and enlargement set great building tasks. My work began with the design of an arc lamp. To have the chance to do such work was nevertheless remarkable at that time, for who should determine the external form of technical products and draw up the designs for them was still an open question. Should it be left to the engineer, or should an artist be involved? Today the question has been resolved. It is of no importance whether the design comes from the hand of a rhythmically sensitive, artistically gifted engineer, or from a technically educated artist or architect, or whether it is initiated by a farsighted organizer who employs both the engineer and artist to work on his project.

Such a wide-ranging and many-sided activity as I pursued over many years in the AEG was only possible because just such an organizer was at hand in the person of Paul Jordan. It does not seem anything special today to look for functionally appropriate, discreet, and practical design in industrial products or to give an expressive and yet dignified appearance to printed material, labels, and catalogs. Nor is it particularly new today to create functional factory types that reflect the purpose of the building, serve the social and health requirements of a large working community, and reflect the greatness and dignity of the entire company. At that time, however, none of this was at all appreciated. Precisely because it was new, it first had to be fought for and won. Even the collaboration between my employer and friend Jordan and me did not always proceed without differences of opinion. But particularly on those occasions when he did not give way to what I wanted, and when I too was not especially compliant, the result came out more clearly than either of us had initially hoped, precisely because of the mutual stimulation. And if I have been fortunate enough to have succeeded in producing something useful, then I owe it to him to say that I learned a lot from our collaboration, especially things that later proved to be of great value in the large projects I built for other companies and firms.

In designing industrial installations of all sorts, the only method of proceeding is to derive the forms out of the character and the intended purpose of the planned building. This means that the demands made by the plant should be gone into by all the artistic and technical means available; that the demands and requirements should be elevated into leitmotifs and these motifs given visual expression.

In factory design, this can be done initially through the siting of the individual buildings with respect to each other. They have to follow the pattern of the manufacturing process. The paths of the railway tracks are a determining feature of the ground plan, in that the plan must follow the curves of the tracks. By offsetting the buildings, the tracks can easily be led through the doorways of the halls. This, at the same time, provides for large storage yards. With such large-scale courtyards, which can be surrounded by high or low buildings according to need, spaces are created which, in the urban design sense, can be of the greatest artistic importance. This is especially true if the offset pattern, which is functionally necessary, is given a powerful silhouette based on the stair and lift towers. If one has had the chance to compare plants laid out according to such practical considerations with ones that have grown up over the years according to need but without a set program, one is amazed that such enormously different results can be achieved with the same building costs and the same materials.

Similar considerations are also decisive in the design of the factory itself. The way in which the production process is organized dictates the layout of spaces. Clarity, easy handling of the products, and mobility of the tools, machines, or goods demand open, unobstructed, well-lit workshops. The workplaces should be as light as possible, and the workshops and halls should be large, unobstructed, and without dividing installations. For this reason, it is advisable to set the staircases and the lifts on the outside, in specially projecting structures. In this way, the clarity of the workshop's long building line is not interrupted. In the machine factory at Humboldthain I gave the projecting stairwells an octagonal form for the first time. These stairwells are so spacious that it is possible for the entire workforce to leave the building through them at the same time. They can also be used for the removal of large loads. The octangular form of staircase has the advantage over the rectangular version that, in spite of its spaciousness, it obstructs only one window axis, as only the narrow face of the octagonal touches the facade, and the angle of the octagon allows the neighboring windows to receive full daylight. The architectural impact of the building is heightened, furthermore, by the prominent stairwells and by the lift towers, which are extended up above the ridge of the roof. Bright, well-lit rooms are a condition of productivity. The factory, therefore, must be given large windows, and the character of the building demands that the windows be more dominant than the areas of wall and should establish the prevailing character of the building volume. The windows should not interrupt the planes of the building, but should rather support their volumetric effort. They should not, therefore, sit in the walls like large holes, but by standing flush to the outer wall should give it a smooth, shining, and cheerful appearance. One might also apply another principle, however, as I did on the small-motor factory on the Voltastrasse. Here I sought to achieve a rhythmic effect through the color, the rounded form, and the extensive repetition of a row of pillars clad with blue ironbricks . . . .

. . . The turbine hall on the Huttenstrasse and the buildings at Humboldt-hain seem to be suitable illustrations of the principles that determined not only these designs but also those of many other large buildings for the AEG. A similar spatial arrangement is to be found, therefore, in the large assembly shop, which in its external form is clearly an iron-frame building, a brittle building material that was chosen at the wish of the late Geheim-rat Rathenau. It was certainly interesting to try to achieve here too, as far as possible, a sense of volume and articulation. To do this I used the vertical pillars and the projecting crane track. The turbine hall and the assembly shop are almost exactly the same size; both have a roofline height of 25 meters and are 80 meters long. The interval between the trusses is 9 meters in the turbine hall and 11 meters in the assembly shop. The proportions of the locomotive factory in Hennigsdorf are different. The shed is 16 meters high and has a span of 25 meters. The trusses are spaced at 20-meter intervals in order to give the greatest freedom of movement possible for the large, crane-carried loads.

I shall refrain from going into further details about these or other buildings, which today are either well-known, or no longer of interest.

The age of progress is constantly creating new demands, and, if Jordan's dictum is correct, will always find new solutions. For as Jordan said: "Don't believe that even an engineer takes an engine apart for inspection before buying it. Even as an expert, he also buys according to the external impression. A motor must look like a birthday present."

What is true for appliances and machines is equally true for buildings, for here in particular a well-thought-out construction can create an impression of obvious order and thus one of calm and even great beauty. This, however, should not be achieved by methods that lead to high expenditure. Buildings that serve the purpose of maximizing all the means and power of the productive process should not indulge in any sort of luxury. There should be no room for even the smallest extravagance, either in the construction or in the choice of building material. But when the importance of such buildings to the cultural structure of our age is recognized, then it does no harm to bestow on them the due care and the refined, intellectual attention through which works of aesthetic value can be created. Materials in themselves can never determine aesthetic values. In the middle of the last century, Schinkel constructed buildings that may be regarded as the ultimate manifestation of the style of the age, even though he had to limit himself to the most simple materials. It is a question of technical and artistic ability. . . .

CONTEMPORARY REACTIONS TO THE AEG'S DESIGN POLICY

selected by Tilmann Buddensieg

These chronologically arranged articles give an indication of contemporary reactions to Peter Behrens's work for the AEG. They were written by Behrens's close technical collaborators (Bernhard, Dolivo-Dobrowolsky), by art historians, architectural critics, and fellow members of the Deutscher Werkbund (Wichert, Frankl, Fürst, Mannheimer, Osthaus, Dohrn), and by Behrens's pupils (Gropius, Le Corbusier). Not included are the critiques of Breuer, Hellwag, Hoeber, Jaumann, Lux, W. Schäfer, Scheffler, and Schur, which are more easily accessible to scholars and which only expand on the basic ideas found in the following extracts. The authors of these texts approach Behrens's pioneering collaboration with the AEG from an extraordinarily wide range of viewpoints and suggest various possibilities for further development.

Airship Travel and Architecture
Fritz Wichert

Frankfurter Zeitung, 21 March 1909

Wichert (1878–1951) received his doctorate in 1906 under the supervision of Heinrich Wölfflin. From 1907 to 1909 he was assistant curator at the Städel and at the Städtische Galerie, Frankfurt, under Georg Swarsenski, and from 1909 to 1932 he was director of the Kunsthalle in Mannheim. Between 1923 and 1933, Wichert, together with Ernst May, pursued a model career in Frankfurt as the organizational head of the Frankfurter Kunstschule and as artistic adviser to the city council. The outlines of Wichert's activity in Frankfurt have been reconstructed on the basis of detailed archival research in Rolf Bothe's article "Frankfurter Kunstschule 1923–1933," in *Kunstschulreform 1900–1923*, ed. H. M. Wingler.

An interesting story is attached to the article quoted here. Reporting on the Kunst- und Gartenbauausstellung held in Mannheim in the summer and autumn of 1907, Fritz Hoeber noted the following: ". . . two such discriminating visitors as Heinrich Wölfflin and Fritz Wichert agreed, when they came across to Mannheim from the art historians' congress in Darmstadt, that these buildings were the best on view. Wölfflin added, very correctly, that Behrens would have the greatest prospects as an architect if he could add to his rhythmic play of lines and planes the cubiform beauty that makes the Palazzo Strozzi in Florence a great building. One might claim that Wölfflin was anticipating here the work of Behrens's Berlin period."

In March 1908, Wölfflin wrote to his parents that Behrens had paid him a visit "out of simple sympathy for my kind of art history", and suggested that "the students should be given two hours of drawing each week, linked to the content of my lecture." [See Joseph Gantner, *Frankfurter Allgemeine Zeitung*, 16 June 1962. This drawing course is also mentioned in *Die Werkkunst* 3 (June 1908), p. 268. See also the comments of Paul Frankl below.] It would be a worthwhile task to investigate how far Behrens's own interpretation of the turbine hall (see "The Turbine Hall. . . ," above) was influenced by Wölfflin.

. . . the idea that we shall soon be able to fly—indeed, that we can fly already—has given many people occasion to imagine the consequences of the new discovery. . . . The fetters of gravity are loosening.

This fact promises to bring about a formal revolution in our architectural ideas. When we move our imaginary streets from the earth into the sky—this will suffice as an interim example—the roof of the house gains a totally new significance. We see it from a new angle, and it achieves the importance of a facade. Roofs become facades, even if not every owner can decide to install one of the main entrances on the roof. The consequence of this radical change will be that our gravitational architecture, with its cornices, turrets, and roofline features, will seem absolutely senseless if not positively annoying. For this resigned display of the downward thrust of gravity will be an irritating reminder that, in spite of everything, we continue to be earthbound.

If the roof, the upper horizontal termination, is given something like equal importance to the vertical front, then an inevitable consequence will be that the buildings will have to be both designed and understood in a much more stereometric manner. No longer will they be able to root so firmly in the ground when the verticals lose their impact and the horizontal roof is accentuated. The result is the stereometric system: Architecture will no longer grow out of the earth, but will simply rest on it. Architectural composition will then mean stereometric combination, grouping, connection, and interconnection. The concept of top and base is losing its importance, which was derived from an earthbound viewpoint.

This will all happen when the vertical and horizontal planes are given roughly equal worth, and this evaluation will occur at the moment when we start to see the world from above. Architecture will then finally take up an absolutely contradictory position to all natural growths, in that the last analogy of roots in the earth and organic development will collapse into nothingness. . . .

With all this, it cannot be emphasized enough that our visual perception is undergoing a change as a result of the progress of technology. Seeing from above, at a greater distance from the object, is only one example of such a change. Other factors that have brought about changes in our consciousness are the speed of locomotion (and our perception of it) and the great distances that tend to traverse our thoughts. These factors will help to fashion the style of the future and have already influenced the style of the present. We think straight, systematically. But we also think in an extraordinarily "tidy" way. Using our perceptive faculties, we want to create space in the overcrowded world, to compress all essentials together into the most practical forms. In this way, lucid, clear-cut, cubiform volumes are created; everything will seem more pared down and more basic. Human life moves out of architecture and back into us! We need it ourselves. No longer do we want to lose ourselves emotionally in magnificent, succulent Baroque volutes, balustrades, and so on every time we set eyes on them. No more do we want to sit transfixed in the ecstasy of an irregularly composed gothic pattern, dreaming and removed from the realm of clear, powerful emotion! We shall be more ourselves, but perhaps slightly different, less artistically pretentious.

It has been claimed that our architecture has already developed a style appropriate to the age of airship travel. In fact the creation of the style began at the time when the simple, straight line reappeared—as a result of modern achievements in transportation. Messel and the Viennese, Olbrich and the Darmstadt group, Billing, Endell, and many others realized that the future belonged to geometric forms, forms that existed in straight lines and flat planes. But none of them thought as far ahead as Peter Behrens. He reached farthest into the future! Peter Behrens discovered the principles of an architecture that is conceived from two directions, that rests on the ground but does not grow out of it, that does not relate to the earth on only one axis but forms stereometric volumes. Quite logically, pointed towers are of no value to him, and the concepts of top and bottom are of little consequence. The roofs and horizontal planes in general have the status of facades. The spaces he creates are wonderfully lucid, with the most noble feeling of expansiveness. One understands in his work what it means to compress the structure together in order to win space in the world. Faced with this great achievement, one is inclined to forget that Behrens has not yet found his direction in all respects. Why, for example, does he give an angular form to a sauce boat, when he understands so well how to create a rounded casing for an electric fan? Why does he also design glasses, knife handles, and other things with faceted forms? He really is not so flexible after all. Rectilinearity brings him into contact with the sacred and with the style of the kitchen furniture, but not to where he is needed; there must also be a bourgeois version of rectilinearity! But all these shortcomings, which are partly the result of too much rationalization with the intellect (instead of with the visual sense), do not throw a shadow on the brilliant achievement of defining the stereometric principle for the architecture of the future. The criterion for judging the creations of Peter Behrens must also be derived from this principle, and not from the rules of other types of architecture.

The Example of the AEG
Wolf Dohrn

März 3, no. 17 (3 September 1909), pp. 361–372

Dohrn (1874–1914), the son of a famous Naples zoologist, was, like Alfons Paquet, a student of the political economist Lujo Brentano in Munich. It was in the circle of Brentano's students that Theodor Heuss met Dohrn. [See Theodor Heuss, *Vorspiele des Lebens* (Tübingen, 1953), pp. 240, 269 ff.; *Erinnerungen* (1963), pp. 109 ff.; *Friedrich Naumann* (Berlin, 1937), pp. 298 ff.] Between 1907 and 1910, Dohrn was the business manager of the Deutscher Werkbund, and during the same period he played an important part in the establishment of the Gartenstadt Hellerau. [See Kristiana Hartmann, *Deutsche Gartenstadtbewegung* (Munich, 1976), pp. 48 ff.] Dohrn belonged to Friedrich Naumann's closest circle of friends, and many of his articles on the border areas between art, politics, and economics were published after 1907 in Naumann's journals *Die Hilfe* and *Die hohe Warte*. Naumann's obituary for Dohrn was published in *Die Hilfe* 20, no. 7 (1914), and reprinted in *Naumann, Werke*, ed. Ladendorf (Opladen, 1964), IV, pp. 553 ff. Ernst Jäckh (Dohrn's successor in the Werkbund), on p. 92 of *Jahrbuch des Deutschen Werkbundes 1914* (Jena, 1914), refers to the obituaries by Naumann and Paul Claudel. [See also Joan Campbell, *The German Werkbund* (Princeton, 1978), p. 20.] From the outset, Dohrn had identified the buildings of the AEG with the aims of the Werkbund. As well as in the article reprinted below, Dohrn discussed this connection in "Die Turbinhalle der AEG in Berlin," *Der Industriebau* 1, no. 6 (15 June 1909), pp. 132 ff., and "Eine Ausstellung architektonisch guter Fabrikbauten," ibid. 1, no. 1 (15 January 1910), pp. 1 ff. In the latter he wrote: "For the industrialist the prospect opens up of no longer having to regard his factories as a necessary evil, but as the concentrated expression of the best forces of the age, as buildings whose artistic importance not only equals the tortured monumentality of our public buildings, but deservedly exceeds it." Dohrn was writing here of the exhibition whose organization was subsequently taken over by Gropius (see Gropius's "Industrial Buildings" below).

The Allgemeine Electricitäts-Gesellschaft builds dynamos, turbines, small motors, and electrical power plants for cities, factories, ships, and airships. It manufactures telegraphic and telephone equipment, arc lamps, incandescent lamps, and all the small components of an electrical system—fans, switches, push buttons, and much more. In the diversity of its production, the AEG is one of the most interesting of all large corporations.

Two years ago, the AEG appointed Peter Behrens as its artistic adviser. On hearing of the appointment, many people must have wondered what Behrens would do in the AEG. Anyone, however, who is acquainted with the nadir of taste reached by electrical installations for both private and public spheres, and anyone who has experienced the helplessness of our architects in the use of these things, will be able to imagine that some of them, even in the AEG, might be responsive to artistic treatment. The first results of Peter Behrens's intervention are new arc lamps, electric fans, covers for resistors, price catalogs, the firm's monogram, and more of the same. But other important tasks still lie ahead: the redesigning of the external form of various machines and motors and the creation of a new and artistically improved style of architecture for the factories. This alone shows that the work of Peter Behrens within the massive productive output of the AEG is not thought of merely as an episode. Close inspection reveals that the relationship between artist and firm is closer, more significant, and more successful than would seem possible when viewed from the outside.

The nature of Behrens's contractual relationship with the AEG is not known to me. It is clear, however, that he could not do his work unless he were integrated into the running of the firm like any other engineer or manager. He would then be able to develop the forms of the lamps, fans, and so on from an intimate knowledge of the production processes involved. Nothing can be achieved here with a simple studio design. Although Behrens does not conceive form merely as functional form or as the product of materials and technology, these machine-made engineering products are still more influenced by these factors than are other branches of design. Here, design is not and never can be the free creation of an independent artistic volition. Rather, the form must be developed organically out of the given manufacturing process, and the artist gets the most important stimulus for the design from the need to economize on materials and to simplify as far as possible the whole work process, from raw materials to finished product. Therefore, the more deeply the artist goes into the production process, the better will he understand its technical and economic characteristics, and his fantasy will be all the more strongly nourished. Furthermore, his understanding of the production process will stimulate the realization that the solution to design tasks such as these is not a matter of documenting the reponse of an interested artist, nor of adapting traditionally loved notions of form. Rather, it is purely and simply a matter of developing to the full the intrinsic potential of the task itself—it demands, in other words, highly objective, self-disciplined artistic work aimed at creating standard and typical forms.

In this sense, Peter Behrens's collaboration with the AEG cannot be described intimately and painstakingly enough, and it is certainly worthwhile considering in this way the fundamental significance of the collaboration between one of our leading artists and one of the world's largest companies. It indicates the direction in which architecture and the applied arts must go if they want to achieve their current goals. What induced the AEG to engage Behrens? I use this business language intentionally, in order to measure this appointment against the most stringent yardstick we possess—namely, commercial reality, the limits of which are firmly defined by the laws of profitability. From this viewpoint, the significance of Behrens's engagement is quite clear.

From the outside, one might think that it is simply a matter of deciding on the salary of the artist concerned—a minor decision in a giant concern like the AEG, akin to appointing an assistant department head in the Ministry of the Interior. But it does not end with the salary. At the same time, the engagement signifies the decision to redesign all the firm's products, to make up new molds, to renew and change the tools, and to design and set up the machines for each new form. In many respects it means comletely reequipping the workshops. With this the risk factor grows, for with mass production one cannot experiment with all sorts of designs or try out which design is most successful with the customers. The AEG makes motors, arc lamps, and electric fans in much the same way as the baker makes rolls. If the recipe is good, the sales go well. If the recipe is bad, however, the AEG, unlike the baker, cannot try a new one, for each experiment costs thousands, and a few failures give the advantage to the competition. Now, admittedly, the arc lamp principally has to satisfy technical and economic demands. But there is still a risk. And because of the scale of the operation, this risk is much greater than one would be inclined to associate with the simple engagement of an artist.

What, therefore, prompted the AEG to this engagement?

Professor Groves—the constructor of our most attractive locomotives, the Bavarian express models—once defined a perfect machine as follows, in the course of a lecture at the Munich Polytechnikum: "A machine must first be correctly *calculated*; that means that all the parts must be given adequate strength. Second, it must be properly constructed; that means it must be the best product available. Third, it must be cheap; that means as economical as possible in materials. Fourth, it must be attractive, for if a machine possesses only the first three qualities and another version comes onto the market that is, in addition, attractive, then this version will be bought." These words have programmatic importance for the development of our manufacturing industry, for this is how it actually works. In the same way, it was explained to me in the AEG that in five to ten years other nations will have learned from our technical know-how and will perhaps be able to supply an almost equivalent product. By then we must have got so far that foreign customers, who are among the best customers, still buy from us because the visual design of our product is superior to that of the others. And it is obvious that the more nearly equal the products become in technical respects, the more important the design becomes to the sales. Commercially, then, the AEG is quite correct in guiding the current movement toward the artistic improvement of industrial products in its own direction at a timely moment. No doubt the AEG will soon be emulated. The concise, exact form of the arc lamp is so convincing that the models of the other firms will soon be obsolete. The AEG has the advantage of being the pioneer. And they have no need to fear their imitators. On the contrary; the higher the general standard, the greater the impact of the best. If German design conquers the world markets, then the richest harvest will go to the firm that first brought it to classical perfection.

The commercial considerations that led to the appointment of Peter Behrens may well have been these or similar ones. After the decision to improve the design of the products had been made, it was characteristic of the AEG that it did not employ a skillful imitator or a bustling dilettante, but an artist.

This decision was also commercially correct, particularly for the following reasons:

Although a perfected form may appear to be simple, even simplified, one cannot imitate it as easily as a mediocre form. The more exactly, regularly, and rigorously it is developed, the more sensitively will it react against any coarsening through clumsy or inexact design. The impact here is decided by the millimeter—not only in the original drawing, but also in the technical realization. And the fact that such attention is paid to millimetric exactness in all phases of production is what quite properly differentiates a high-quality firm from an average one. The inimitable and

irreplaceable performance of a company is contained in this one millimeter. It is this quality that gives the company its personal stamp, even when in other respects it is an impersonal monster with a share capital of millions. In the millimeter is to be found the soul of the company, which works imperceptibly in all its workshops and rhythmically determines its output. Immaculate form thus becomes an inimitable (and, in the most rigorous sense, personal) achievement, not only in design but equally in the many stages of production. Only a company that is immaculate in all details can attempt to give immaculate form to its mass-produced goods. Such perfection, of course, creates an obvious demand for meticulously neat work, and develops naturally and spontaneously out of the spirit of such work as, so to speak, its simple psychological consequence. Besides the commercial considerations, perhaps nothing was more decisive in the appointment of Peter Behrens than the AEG's concern for perfect workmanship. Nobody seemed more likely to achieve this than Behrens. One might say that his concise, exact manner of design is the visible artistic expression of the discipline that exists within the AEG, the rigid spirit that holds together the giant body of capital and labor as a particularly vital organism.

In fact, the AEG is a creature of flesh and blood, like someone who one believes to be capable of anything as he has never failed. Whoever has the good fortune of visiting the firm gains the strongest impression of the highly personal working spirit of the many-faceted, giant organization. Opening a door from the factory office, one of the technical directors showed me the large factory hall from an elevated gallery. He led me into the enormous hall as if inviting someone into his parlor. The workshop looked so well-ordered, so clean and festive. One could look into the most distant parts of the hall: no corner, no dividing walls, no enclosures.

To the left and right of the scrupulously clean gangways are the work positions, like the trees in an avenue. At each position are the tools and the dynamos, turbines, and other machines under construction. Transportation through the hall is provided by traveling cranes running on overhead tracks. They carry the completed machines to the test bed below the gallery on which we were standing. After testing, the giant crane picks up the machine again and takes it through the hall to the exit. No transmission shafts hinder the movement of machines anywhere in the hall. Only individual power units are used, which means that every tool has its own motor. Thus each tool can be moved to the object being worked on. In this way, the work itself follows the old craft principle whereby the tool was taken to the object being made rather than the object dragged to the tool. Admittedly, the tools have developed beyond the scale of hand tools; they are not craft tools but machine tools. But in the work process the old principle is again being implemented. Thanks to the individual drive, made possible by small motors, the clarity and the mobility of the production process are greatly increased. Both these factors represent savings, even if such savings cannot be calculated exactly. As nine-tenths of all German factories have not yet introduced individual drive, our electrical industry can reckon on large and consistent sales of power units over the coming years. The AEG is already manufacturing and marketing a range of such motors.

The AEG will also be able to consult Peter Behrens over the construction of large industrial plants. Think what can be made of these factory halls when the artist and engineer work hand in hand! There is such an enormous, concentrated, and powerful atmosphere in these halls that one can hardly think of a more attractive job for an architect than giving expression to this atmosphere by the simple means of forming and articulating the space in the right way. It is a good thing that the AEG entrusted the design of a new factory building right from the outset to Behrens and the engineer Bernhard. Berlin will gain a factory hall that will be a monument to the technological spirit of our age.

Contrary to what might be thought from a superficial judgment, it is not a luxury to devote such meticulous attention to the design of a factory, for this care exercises a suggestive influence on all the work done in it. It is worthwhile examining this connection more closely, for it gives the psychological explanation of the appointment of Behrens to the AEG.

It is amazing how much work carrying personal responsibility still exists in this giant company. Equally amazing is the exactitude with which the work is done under the prevailing piecework system. This is essentially an organizational success, or, more exactly, a success of the spirit that exists in the company and among its employees. This spirit manifests itself for the most part through a meticulously maintained sense of order—"Sauberkeit," as the North Germans call it. It is said of the successful politician that he distinguishes himself in that he knows to evaluate the imponderable correctly. The same faculty was shown by the brilliant administrator who correctly recognized this significant stage in the evolution of a working community and turned it to use as a form-giving impulse. Through order, tidiness, and discipline he created an invisible, ubiquitous focus; something that functions so naturally that the outsider thinks that the work gets done "by itself." The administrator makes use thereby of the psychological fact that nine-tenths of all men are unconsciously searching for just such a focus, and become more productive the more rigidly they can identify themselves with it. Such a focus is provided by that quality Berliners call "Sauberkeit," which pervades the whole company. Indeed, the Berliners actually speak of "sauber" work when they mean exact work. In the Berliner's idealistic conception of work, "sauber" is synonymous with "classical"—that is, absolutely exemplary or ideal.

One need not pursue this working spirit in all its various manifestations in order to see how the employees of a company in which it exists gain an almost personal understanding for exact design. The work produces the form, and the form influences the work. The fact that the new, Behrens-designed trademark is used with great enthusiasm in the workshops is not, therefore, a matter of chance, but is a significant indication of the prevailing working spirit. The workers want nothing more to do with the old, conventional trademark, for they regard the new one as the true symbol of their labor. It may be that the foremen do not know this themselves, but the fact that they have such a special liking for the new trademark is more important than what they have to say about it. In this way, something is developed that I have also seen in other firms: company loyalty. This form of loyalty sets demands for quality, and then stimulates the fulfilment of these demands. Let me give an example. After Behrens had redesigned the external form of the arc lamps, various commercial travelers and salesmen employed by the AEG suggested that the small wheel assembly inside the lamp also be redesigned, simplified, and made more clear in order to match the simplified, more concise form of the lamp itself. In this instance, the improvement of the external form led to the improvement of the actual mechanism. One can see how beneficial this working spirit is, when given, so to speak, tangible symbols of its own exactness. The working spirit is reinforced by the sight of a perfected example of its own prowess. And it is important to point out that the improvement of the form rarely leads to an increase in the price of the product, and has sometimes resulted in the price being lowered.

It would seem that the relationship between Peter Behrens and the AEG is not only commercial or formal, but is, in spite of the enormous size of the AEG, personal in the highest sense. It is to be hoped that not only the market production of the AEG (the arc lamps, electric fans, motors, and so on) will come under Behrens's influence, but that the visual design of the large electrical installations will also be entrusted to him. For it could be that street lighting, tramways, industrial plants, and the like are not only technical but also artistic phenomena. The spirit of our age gives monumental expression to these phenomena at just that place at which this spirit is itself monumental: the workplace! At the moment, it is being simulated in places where, in all good faith, it is not to be found: in public buildings, for example. Peter Behrens's concise and energetic style matches the products of the AEG perfectly, and also corresponds to the firm's intellectual discipline. That his style is also appropriate to the technical character of electric lighting and the arc lamp is shown by a glance at the illustrations, and is made even more clear by the lamps themselves when one sees them hanging in a room. And when one compares the new models with the earlier ones, in particular the so-called "luxury lamp," one realizes how much more the new lamp reflects the spirit of technology. In both its form and ornamentation, the "luxury lamp" is an example of "plumber's craftsmanship" with its sundry leaf decorations and highly polished absurdities. The new lamp is what it should be: a no-nonsense object, a standard type both in its form and in its technology.

This lamp deserves note as a model for further industrial development. It is the result of a collaboration in which the engineer had to become half artist and the artist half engineer in order to complement each other in their work. We are not primarily concerned here with an artistic, but with an industrial achievement, and Behrens would be the first to accept that his own contribution is valid only in this wider context. For itself, the AEG can claim to have been the first in Germany to demonstrate, and in a model fashion, such a collaboration between engineer and artist. It is certainly not by chance that the AEG in particular has been so successful in this experiment. It is said of the AEG that, until now, they have understood best how to transfer the findings of German science and in particular of electrical technology into economic practice. It is certainly a kindred task to utilize the artistic talents of our age in our economic life, and it is a testimony both to the company's flexibility and to the farsightedness of its management that this problem was recognized and tackled at the right moment. In industry too there are classic achievements. We are dealing with one of them here, and look forward to more.

A Factory Building by Peter Behrens
Karl Ernst Osthaus

Frankfurter Zeitung, 10 February 1910

The industrialist, art collector, and patron Karl Ernst Osthaus (1874–1921) lived in Hagen, Westphalia. With his Folkwang Museum and the Deutsche Museum für Kunst in Handel und Gewerbe, he became a central figure in promoting the new movements in art and art education. He supported van de Velde, Behrens, Lauwericks, Riemerschmid, Gropius, and Taut, to name only the architects. Osthaus was acquainted with Behrens when the latter was in Darmstadt, and their friendship developed after Behrens moved to Düsseldorf in 1903. [See Herta Hesse-Frielinghaus, *Peter Behrens and Karl Ernst Osthaus* (Hagen, 1966), and Herta Hesse-Frielinghaus et al., *Karl Ernst Osthaus. Leben und Werke* (Recklinghausen, 1971).] Behrens thanked Osthaus for the article reprinted below in a letter of 16 February 1910. At the time, it was the best piece that had been written on the turbine hall.

The newly built turbine factory of the Allgemeine Elektricitäts-Gesellschaft in Berlin is a remarkable building even from the technical point of view. Mobile cranes with a lifting capacity of 50 tons at a speed of 2 meters per second present very unusual structural demands. For this reason, engineer Bernhard's construction has attracted an understandable interest in technical circles.

What distinguishes this building from all other similar factories, however, is the fact that it was designed by one of our leading architects. When Peter Behrens joined the AEG two years ago, one felt that only a reform of the firm's products was intended. It is now clear that greater things were planned. Just as a few years ago Alfred Messel elevated the department store to an artistic problem, so Peter Behrens has created with the AEG turbine factory a work that from now on will impose artistic responsibilities on every industrialist who plans to build.

We know Behrens as the most convinced advocate of primary values in architecture. He has pleaded vigorously against the picturesque inclinations of our architects and for the importance of simple lines and proportions. With his view that a complete basis for artistic form is not to be found in function and technology alone, he has long stood alone in the camp of the moderns. The fact that we know today how to assess visual and rhythmic values independent of stylistic considerations is in great part due to him.

It is strange enough that this man who scorns the functional should have been employed to solve a problem that, according to past interpretations, had no substance apart from function. And yet no other combination could produce such a clear image of the relationship of art to function. By going back entirely to first principles and to basic, nonstylistic demands, Behrens has created something that definitively points the way forward. He abandoned all detail and devoted his attention to the *spaces* and the *volume*. His significant contribution to the steel construction was the incorporation of latticelike rafters in the flat, volume-defining planes of the walls. The seven-pointed trusses that make up the basic building frame are spanned only by narrow tie beams. The fact that one could go farther in this direction by applying this principle to every detail in no way detracts from Behrens's basic achievement. The way has been shown, and it is now up to our engineers to draw the conclusions for the various different forms of steel construction. "Only a completely enclosed, plane-sided volume can guarantee the clarity of architectural proportions that first gives the chance of achieving an artistic effect." This is how the architect himself formulated his principles. Similar considerations led to the full-height portal frame construction on the outside wall of the building. Here the pillars are exposed on three sides, and the spaces between are filled in with glass walls. Behrens inclined the glass panels so that a powerful contrast is established between the flat plane and the pillars, and a strong band of shadow created under the roof. In this contrast of planes the opposition of construction and infill is made manifest. The concrete corner pieces are also inclined back toward the top and set behind the plane of the gable. The constructional relationships are further underlined by the horizontal steel bands that are wrapped around the corner pieces. A large window at the center of the end front is placed vertically under the gable and flush to it, so that its steel frame corresponds to the pillars on the side wall. The six-sided roof, supported only by the window frame and the side pillars, reaches out powerfully beyond the inclined planes of the walls and squats above the whole building as an entirely resolved, self-contained volume. The only decoration on the gable end is formed by the Behrens-designed AEG signet and the word "Turbinenfabrik" engraved in enormous letters into the concrete.

Adjoining the main hall is a lower, two-story side hall with a flat roof. The facade of the side hall is set back and clad in concrete, and this change of material makes manifest a certain sense of contrast and hierarchy. The long front of the side hall, facing the courtyard, has a steel frame construction with flush glass infill panels, following the principle of flat planes. The whole building is an expression of power and splendor. The vigorous modernity of the design and the materials is not impaired by any flirtation with ornament. We can feel the powerful rhythms of energy restrained by intelligence. In the interior we are able to detect the potential superiority of future creations. The exterior is perfect and definitive, like a Doric temple. We sense the possibility of making a variation but not an improvement; every single form is subservient to the design concept of the whole.

Is it not strange how such a logical and unified building becomes a symbol of that which it encloses? If anything makes the international standing of the AEG comprehensible, it is the absolute clarity and lucidity of its organizational structure. Anyone who goes into a technical office after twelve noon will not find any paperwork left unattended to on the desks. The enormous factory halls can be completely surveyed from one point; the view is not hindered by partitions behind which the foremen have their afternoon nap and where they hide botched work. Everything is open to the controlling eye. Seen in this way, the impressive logic of the turbine factory almost seems to be the impersonal achievement of the AEG. Personal contributions seem to be so perfectly fused into the intellectual makeup of the whole concern that people forget, especially in Berlin, to ask after the architect.

And yet it is precisely its respect for individuality that has given the AEG the distinction of being the creator of the first artistically significant factory building. Peter Behrens is the firm's artistic adviser, but his position is so informal that the AEG does not prevent him from doing the same work for anyone else as he does for his own firm. On the other hand, the AEG has hardly brought out one product suitable for artistic treatment that has not been improved by Behrens's skill. There are no uncertain gropings here, no half-measures and nervous questions about what the *public* might say about such innovations. The AEG has understood that the exclusion of creative genius from the process of industrial manufacture is an illness of our age, and that its reinvolvement is a matter of cultural necessity. That which our most progressive spirits hardly dared hope for ten years ago, and which the Deutscher Werkbund has recently been striving for with great energy and gradually increasing success, has been accomplished by the AEG with one bold decision; the AEG has given back to the world its right to art in the industrial process.

The value of this great example does not lie solely in the existence of the turbine hall or in the artistic improvement of lamps and electrical appliances, for other firms have anticipated the AEG in making single experiments of this kind. The value of the AEG's example, however, lies in the totality of the firm's efforts, in the *unity* of the artistic approach, with permeates right through the giant concern. New factories to Behrens's designs are under construction or being drawn up, and the artist is already working on the plans of a garden suburb for the firm's salaried staff and workers, which is to be built on the canal between Berlin and Tegel. Old factories are being remodeled in accordance with the new design standards the firm has committed itself to provide for its employees. Outside the realm of the applied arts, this standpoint is as unique as it is new. It is the ultimate consequence of a way of thinking that combines social sensitivity with the highest level of education, and is a guarantee of the cultural advancement of our age.

Those thousands of ifs and buts behind which factory owners are wont to shelter their products from the demands for artistic intervention have been dismissed by the example of the AEG. As a result of redesigning its products, the AEG is working more economically today than previously. The company also had the courage to burn all its bridges; its old models have been destroyed, and whoever wants arc lamps in the rococo style must go to a rival. In industry as in all spheres, half-measures are the surest instruments of failure. Anyone who wants something new must want it *completely*. As long as our industrialists look on the collaboration of an artist as an exception, this relationship will be incapable of creating an economic success. Only when such a collaboration becomes the rule, the sine qua non, will it become clear that cultural commitment offers a guarantee of further economic development.

Sheet Metal, Concrete, and Art
Artur Fürst

Berliner Tageblatt, 17 February 1910

Artur Fürst became known as a historian of technology and as the biographer of Emil Rathenau (see bibliography). Fürst's knowledge of the AEG was unrivaled. In the extract reprinted here he discusses the firm's products. The same article was reproduced in parts of Fürst's monograph on Emil Rathenau (Berlin, 1915) and in full in his book *Die Wunder um uns* (Berlin, 1911).

. . . Until recently, the arc lamp was an out and out example of clumsiness whose every line showed that it was a mass-produced article, a product of the machine's infamous indifference to all things artistic.

The Allgemeine Elektricitätsgesellschaft in Berlin recognized the need to make changes here. It was the first firm to give an artist the job of creating the exterior designs for its appliances. The first product to be tackled by this artist was the arc lamp. Previously, the external cladding of the lamps had been worked out by the electrical engineer and the Werkmeister. Both had no other responsibility beyond covering the regulating mechanism with sheet metal and the flame with glass. The result was a bulky, black cylinder, out of which an enormous glass bulb swelled quite unexpectedly and unnaturally. This glass sphere, in particular, had been passed on for decades by generations of manufacturers. It was felt that no other solution was possible. Someone who is unable to comprehend a purely mathematical concept always imagines a point in space as being spherical, and as a result the engineer and the Werkmeister thought that the point source of the arc lamp's light could only be clad in a sphere. Then Peter Behrens came along and broke completely with this worthless tradition. In place of the globe he set a most agreeable elongated glass housing, which curved cheekily toward the bottom. The design of the arc lamp was already changed fundamentally for the better. However, the ugly, black cylinder still remained above the glass. Neither its diameter nor its length could be altered, for the regulating mechanism needed room inside. Yet Behrens's arc lamps look much slimmer and smaller. The artist was able to give the previously bulky metal housing a form that seems to taper slightly toward the top. He scrapped the "decorative" rings stamped out of the metal, which were so loved by the Werkmeister, and substituted a plain sleeve that curves out carefully toward the main part of the lamp—the light source. The instant result is a beautiful arc lamp.

The task was far more difficult than many seemingly more grandiose problems in the realm of fine art, for the arc lamp is a mass article produced in the thousands to the same pattern, and even such an attractive design as Behrens's would be unacceptable to the firm if it were to cost only a few pennies more than the old, ugly model. But Behrens's beautiful, sleek lamp cost no more to manufacture than the richly ornamented model of the Werkmeister. This provides a classic proof that the concepts of beauty and expensiveness are by no means synonymous, and that the artist can also find a place in the world of mass production, whose watchword and battle cry is the word "cheap!"

After his considerable success with the arc lamp, the AEG allowed Behrens to design new forms for many more of its products. The firm was fortunate in finding in the artist from Düsseldorf a man who was able to go deeply into the specific features of the task. Even for Behrens, it was certainly not easy at the beginning to work in a manner so different from that to which he had been accustomed, for in general true art, like true science, must be "free of preconceptions," and in this respect the artist was constantly restrained by the characteristics of the existing machines and by the manufacturing costs. Professor Behrens correctly recognized, however, that this was a particularly attractive task, precisely because of the difficulties that would crop up everywhere. He saw that a narrow catwalk had to be crossed, which was not passable to everybody. He also understood that it was no less worthy to give artistic form to a small electric switch that would be manufactured in the hundreds of thousands and would soon sit on every wall than to design Gothic pews for the chapel of a remote castle. In this spirit, he designed the beautiful little desk fan, which, in its simple roundness, is an ornament to the most embellished writing desk. In contrast, the old model with its countless flutings, decorations, and buttons can barely be looked at. The most modest objects were gradually brought before the artist's forum. A tin cover for a simple resistance coil was shown to me with particular pride. Previously, a number of unspeakably bright stars had been stamped into the cover in very complicated combinations as a decorative motif. In their place Behrens set two rows of simple rectangles, and the tin cover is now a capital success. The punch for the rectangles is doubtless cheaper to make than the complicated star-shaped punch.

Behrens's influence on the AEG not only makes the products more attractive, but also affects the workforce. Previously, each Werkmeister to whom the manufacture of a new product was entrusted was happy when the appliance had been developed to the point where it functioned perfectly. He never thought of it as an object that could also be pleasing to the eye. Today it is no rare occurrence for such a man to go to the supervising engineer and say: "Here is the new machine, it works very well, but it can't be put on the market looking like it does now. Herr Professor Behrens must definitely make it a bit prettier first." This is an educational consequence of great significance. The concept of beauty has been brought here to circles that are not normally very accessible to such ideas. Without intending to, the artist has established a practical school of art and design whose success surpasses that of many formally established institutions. . . .

(There follows an account of the turbine hall, the water tower at the railway-equipment factory, and the high-voltage factory.)

Factory Art
Franz Mannheimer

Die Hilfe, 16, no. 18 (May 1910), pp. 289 ff.

We are unable to provide biographical details about Dr. Franz Mannheimer. That he was a close associate of Behrens, the Naumann circle, and the Werkbund is established by his bibliography, which does not go beyond 1914. His writings include the most complete contemporary account of the AEG's buildings: "Arbeiten von Professor Behrens für die AEG Berlin," *Der Industriebau 2*, no. 6 (15 June 1911), pp. 122 ff.; "AEG-Bauten," in *Die Kunst in Industrie und Handel. Jahrbuch des Deutschen Werkbundes 1913* (Jena, 1913), pp. 33–42; "Die deutschen Hallen der Brüsseler Weltausstellung," *Der Industriebau 1* (1910), pp. 194 ff.

The contrast between "Fabrik" (Factory) and "Kunst" (art) seems at first to be even greater than the contrast contained in the related word "Kunstindustrie." Art is freedom, individuality—industry is compulsion and mass; art is the unique and eternal—industry the thousandfold and ephemeral. Consider factories—boring spaces filled with chaotic, discordant machines, the bearers of things that are very useful, but are alien (even antagonistic) to beauty. And yet a Fabrikenkunst has recently appeared, which, like the more-established Kunstindustrie, no longer has to use the word art as a mere front for barbaric bad taste. That this Fabrikenkunst has developed can be attributed to the nature of contemporary fine and applied art. The dominating principle of *Sachlichkeit* provided the bridge—the bridge between Peter Behrens and the Allgemeine Elektrizitätsgesellschaft of Berlin.

There were probably many different motives that first led the AEG to commission the artist to improve the appearance of its arc lamps. When this attempt was successful, he was then allowed to restyle the electric fans and other products and to redesign the firm's typescript, printed material, and monogram. Later he was entrusted with the design of a water tower and stairwell, a machine hall, and ultimately a whole factory. Perhaps the concrete motives mentioned above were less decisive than the more abstract consideration that an applied art concerned with function rather than decoration must also promote the functional design of machines and workshops. Behrens's style seems particularly suited to this task. In marked contrast to the more popular styles that adapt themselves passively to the object with only a superficial concern for function, the Behrens style seeks to mold the object and is much more responsive to mathematical and constructional ideas. It is a style of *exact fantasy*, appropriate to a machine *artist*. In any case, the appointment showed a sure instinct for all these things and for the purely commercial consideration that an increase in artistic quality is an important factor in the firm's competitiveness. This holds not only for the products themselves, but also for the firm's factories and installations. If there is no difference in price, the customers will tend increasingly to favor new, pleasing forms to old, ugly ones. Furthermore, the pleasure, the competence, and consequently the efficiency of the firm's employees is increased when they work in well-lit, spacious rooms, using well-proportioned machines.

An entirely new set of interests has thus been defined. This also brings new difficulties, for a machine is not like a table, a fireplace, or a staircase. Not only is it endlessly complex, but it is also a quasi-organic construction that breathes and moves, conceives and gives birth. An artist can design a table, a fireplace, or a staircase himself, but to design an accumulator he needs, at least at the outset, an engineer's drawing or model. With his fantasy, the artist cannot willfully alter the engineer's design; at most he can give more rhythm here and there to the proportions and make the outward appearance of the object more pleasing. And just as a physical education teacher cannot make an imposing figure out of someone born ugly, or make an ill-proportioned person look good, even in specially chosen clothing, so is it equally impossible to give style to a factory building that is unaesthetic from the outset. Only technical development can help here, by gradually replacing excessively ugly forms with neater alternatives, thus preparing the way for art like a second, wiser version of nature. It is significant that the connection between art and the factory was first achieved in the electrical industry, in which the *concentration of standard machine types* first became conspicuous. On the other hand, the connection was first made through such relatively simple objects as arc lamps and electric fans.

Previously, the usual form of the arc lamp was a bulbous white sphere, topped by the metal housing of the regulating mechanism. The form was extremely unrhythmical; only the radiating light was given a sort of expression in the balloon of glass. Instead of this shape, however, Behrens took the vertical lines of the regulating mechanism as the leitmotif. The metal tube covering the mechanism was given an almost smooth profile, and the glass element was treated as its direct, rather tapering continuation. Compared with the normal lamp, Behrens's version has the advantage of tectonic compactness, and is no longer swathed in artificial and unnecessary ornament. The only characteristic one misses with initial regret is the sense of flooding light. Nevertheless, the harmonious design of the lamp is a significant advance, which will be followed by even more refined versions, such as the lamp for indirect lighting that is already available. In this design, the artist avoided the exclusively vertical form of construction; the source of light lies in a deep, funnel-shaped bowl, out of which the bright light swells upwards and spills over as if out of a chalice. No less attractive are some of the electric fans. Here, the sham bronze plating of the motor housing has been replaced by simple metal bands. In addition, the fact that the much less striking cover for a resistor now has an effective striped motif rather than the conventional and boring star pattern is another accomplishment that deserves to be mentioned, for it is essential to start with small (indeed, the smallest) details.

Externally more significant, however, is Behrens's work as a factory architect. The idea of designing factories is more exciting than detailed work on machines to an artist who thinks on a large scale. But here too he is much more restricted by the specification of the engineer than he is by the wishes of a client in the building of a house. On the other hand, the commission itself has a larger, more generous format.

Behrens's first commission from the company was for the missing corner tower of an existing building. The tower was to serve as a combined water tower and stairwell, and now stands there massively like the tower of a castle or the belfries found in most northern cities. Then he built a turbine hall on the company's site on the Huttenstrasse. Here, the previous style of workshop has been completely abandoned. This occurs already on the outside with the walls and colors. Instead of ugly red bricks and small windows, there is a roughly finished gray-white concrete plinth, on which stand the steel pillars that carry the roof. Between the pillars the glass panes are joined together into enormous panels. Nothing is nervously covered up here. Rather than hide the beauty of the forms, the dull green color of the steel and the dark green of the glass accentuate their natural beauty and unite them with the beauty of the stone. The narrow street front projects at the center and together with the squat roof looks like a hammer with its thick handle standing on the ground. In the interior the materials and colors are the same—concrete, steel and glass, white and green. Coupled with the simple and generous proportions and the high roof, two-thirds of which is also glazed, this scheme gives an extraordinary bright and warm, almost serene impression. This is amplified when one stands on the short side of the gallery. One feels that one is looking at a *steel church*, divided into a broad nave and a small side aisle with an upper story. At the first-floor level, the underside of the exposed concrete floor appears to be shaped into a series of circular and oval arches. The pillars and the free arches, the vertical and horizontal supports do not match here quite uniformly. This, however, is the only shortcoming of this building, the first machine hall in which one can breathe. This would seem to be true not only at the present, when the hall is mainly taken up with the peaceful work of machining and assembling large castings, but also when one imagines it tightly packed with busily working machines.

In the meantime, a whole *factory* has been built to Behrens's design at another AEG complex on the Brunnenstrasse. The center section of the facade is made up at ground level of two high, broad masonry doorways, crowned by triangular gables and giving easy access to the wide storeroom. Above the storeroom on the first floor are located the offices, which have this level to themselves. Access to the offices is via a separate stair tower at the rear, while to the left and right the actual workshops abut the central block and run to several stories. When it is completed, this will be the first factory whose artistic appearance is determined by the practical demands of the moment.

Time will tell what is to follow. Just as the aesthetic progress of the machines is closely related to their technical progress, so the style of the factories is partly dependent on the economic system. Here too an increasingly massive concentration of capital will also provide the chance for the right man to achieve great things. When the legal controversy over the available land is finally resolved, it will be possible to replace the crowded workshops, those prisons of labor, with spacious halls that will express on their exteriors the endless activity flowing through them.

Meanwhile, not only has a new area been opened up to art, but an interest in beauty has been taken to circles in which it had previously been quite alien. The engineer and the Werkmeister are becoming conscious of the fact that it is not enough for machines and appliances merely to "go" perfectly, but that it is also important to design them attractively. Indeed, they are gradually being taught to look for an attractive form right from the outset. At the moment, the Allgemeine Elektrizitätsgesellschaft is putting no new models into production that have not been given their final form by Behrens. In the future, when this principle has been generally established, this process of artistic improvement will begin increasingly with the engineer himself. The aesthetic receptivity both of the buying public and of the employees working in the new factories will increase in equal measure, and in this way the rift between the taste of an elevated minority and the mass of the people—a rift that is typical of our age alone—will be lessened. Only contact with *living* beauty can help to do this, more than all public information and more exhibitions in a hundred museums— only contemporary design experienced daily, a silent teacher but one certain to succeed.

Architecture Commentary: The Factory Buildings of the AEG in Berlin
Paul Frankl

Allgemeine Zeitung, 8 October 1910, pp. 772–773

Frankl (1878), called "one of the giants of German Kunstwissenschaft" by Nikolous Pevsner, was trained as an architect in Munich and at the Technische Hochschule at Charlottenburg. He was later a student of Wölfflin, to whom he dedicated his important book *Die Entwicklungsphasen der neueren Baukunst* (Berlin and Leipzig, 1914). This survey went right up to his own period, with a thoughtful study of Messel's Wertheim store. As Frankl studied in Berlin under Wölfflin at the right time, he may have attended Behrens's drawing course (mentioned above in the introduction to the Wichert excerpt).

Two weeks ago, the AEG factory in Brunnenstrasse was completed. The clearest view of the large-scale plant can be gained from one of the four corner towers.

Three rectangular four-story wings join together to make a long, U-shaped ground plan; the courtyard they enclose holds two long, parallel halls, which only extend to the second-floor level and are lit by skylights. The double format of these halls and the depression their roofs make at the center determine the composition of the facade on the narrow fronts. The facade facing the Brunnenstrasse shows the architect's intentions absolutely clearly: The sectional form of the courtyard halls appears as a pair of wide, flat gables set on broad pillars. The gray-violet color of the bricks used in this central section sets it apart from the red brick of the flanking wings, which push up energetically on both sides. These wings contain staircases, which climb symmetrically to the left and the right and are recognizable by the regular groups of three windows rising with the stairs. The upper terminations of the stair towers look themselves like staircases, with three large steps corresponding to the landings and stairs. Beside these powerful forms rises the abrupt rectangular top of the tower. It would seem as if the architect's starting point was the deep depression between the gables, which was then obscured by the transverse office wing stretched across above it. The gables are retained from the initial concept and now pierce the facade in a way that is not immediately understandable.

This impression of adherence to an underlying and fanatical desire for absolute symmetry and conciseness is reinforced when one studies the building more closely. The rear front, facing the Hussitenstrasse, is based on exactly the same design as the main front. But as there is a railway track here which runs diagonally into the courtyard, one side of the U could not be extended as far as the other. The facade recedes in three steps. The stair tower on the left projects the farthest; the broad double gable of the low central hall is stepped back on a second plane, and the right-hand stair tower on a third. The receding steps are achieved without any transitions, and are as rectangular as the building's silhouette. The elements are conceived in *one* plane, and then broken up into three layers. Thus the rigidity of the facade is dissolved in a painterly manner. One can only understand this facade when one has first understood the others.

The long side elevations are also rigidly symmetrical. Stair towers soar up at the center of both, giving a heavy accentuation to the center point of the long glass walls. The walls themselves are articulated only by the simplest of pillars, the necessary supports for the floors and the roof.

A second factory building, the turbine hall on the Huttenstrasse, was designed at the same time but was already completed by 1909. It is so different in its general appearance that one would not immediately guess that the same architect had worked on it. The main building, a single, unusually high hall, is topped by a double-folded mansard roof. There is ample light from above, and full-length windows on three sides. The great height is necessary because large machine components must be transported through the hall over the tops of other machines. Along one of the long sides runs a lower, two-story wing.

The heavy gable of the mansard roof gives expressive form and a sense of repose to the narrow street front. The originality of the facade lies in the fact that the wall is slightly inclined inward, distantly reminiscent of an Egyptian temple. Admittedly, the material is very un-Egyptian: concrete, divided into horizontal stripes by inset bands of steel. Only the wall itself is inclined. The enormous central window rises vertically from the granite plinth to the gable. As an extension of the vertical plane of the window, the gable projects out a long way over the inclined wall. The long side is made up only of steel supports, interspersed by panels of glass. Here, the pattern is reversed; the plane of the windows is inclined and the supports are vertical.

The artistic quality common to both this hall and the other factory lies in the unusual combination of rigid forms and the painterly technique of trusting the eye to register several spatial layers at the same time. The novel aspect of the buildings, then, does not lie *only* in the rejection of standard motifs. Powerful fantasy and a clear sense of direction have combined here to lift the factory building out of the realm of clumsy tastelessness and elevate it into a work of art. The individual style of the architect, Peter Behrens, is characterized by rigidity and conciseness in the general concept, austerity and inflexibility in the details, and a painterly displacement of the planes. It is his own individual, legitimate manner, and one must value his achievement.

Academic architecture will hardly be challenged or even affected by this step toward a new architectural category, the artistic factory building. But the aesthetic stock and the culture of the nation will be increased. Not only do the several thousand people who work in them find brighter, more pleasant workspaces here, but the buildings themselves also work to improve the general level of taste. For this reason, successors must be found. This step by the AEG and its architect, Peter Behrens, should be judged as an act of aesthetic enlightenment. The higher one values this, the more one appreciates its consequences: The nation will be enriched,

the number of sensitive people will be increased, and their receptivity to the fine arts heightened. One must hope all the more, therefore, that Behrens will devote himself even more intensively to this task in his future buildings. This means that he should not merely add the facades at the right places, but should develop the elevation *and* the plan as one, on the basis of a fully worked out building program that needs no subsequent additions or alterations. He should also be involved in the technical construction of the building and in the details of the steel frame, and should not simply entrust this work to the structural engineer.

One should be thankful for every artistic achievement and not find fault, but one might warn the artist—who sees his work as a sacred obligation—that the more progress he makes, the more he must shoulder this obligation himself.

Industrial Buildings
Walter Gropius

Catalog to traveling exhibition of Deutsches Museum für Kunst in Handel und Gewerbe, 1911; reprinted in *Der Industriebau* 3 (15 February 1912), pp. 46 ff.

Gropius (1883–1969), who worked in Behrens's studio from June 1908 until March 1910, concerned himself with the topic of industrial buildings at the instigation of Osthaus. The exhibition may have been the outcome of two lectures given by Gropius at the Folkwang Museum in Hagen in 1911: "Monumentale Kunst und Industriebau" and "Industriebau." Gropius also used many of the ideas contained in this essay in "Sind beim Bau von Industriegebäuden künstlerische Gesichtspunkte mit praktischen und wirtschaftlichen vereinbar?," *Der Industriebau* 3, no. 1 (15 January 1912), pp. 5 ff.

. . . The encouragement of the Deutscher Werkbund is to be thanked for this exhibition of modern industrial buildings. It is hoped that these carefully selected examples will give industrialists an insight into the successes that have already been achieved in establishing a union of art and industry through the collaboration of factory owners and architects. These successes should also promote justifiable hopes for the future.

Only recently, and in isolated cases, have factory owners consulted artistically trained architects about building their factories. In the previous decades of technical development, the manufacturer had no time for aesthetic considerations; he was first and foremost an engineer and businessman who had to concentrate on practical matters, on technology and profit. Art, to him, was a luxury. Perhaps he looked everywhere to buy works of art, but not in the sphere of his work. The factory remained a makeshift scene of dirt and misery. But with increasing prosperity came the demand for better lighting, heating, and ventilation. Occasionally an architect was called in to add irrelevant decoration to the naked form of the utilitarian building. Points of conflict were concealed on the exterior, and because one was ashamed of it the true character of the building was hidden behind a sentimental mask taken from an earlier age according to the whim of the owner. This is still the usual procedure today; the shortsighted owner forgets that such a masquerade offends the dignity of his business.

Furthermore, he will never solve his difficulties in this way. Our modern life demands correspondingly new building types. Stations, stores, and factories require their own, modern style, and cannot be built in the style of earlier centuries without lapsing into empty formalism. Instead of a superficial, external formulation, an inner comprehension of the new architectural problems is necessary. Intellect instead of set formulas, a basic artistic re-evaluation of the basic forms, no applied decoration. The proportioning of the building volumes will always remain the most fundamental task of architecture; ornamental decoration is only a final touch. Overdecoration and false romanticism can never disguise the lack of good proportions and practical simplicity. New forms, however, can never be consciously invented, but emerge of necessity from the life of the age. Some sort of form borrowed from the Rococo or Renaissance no longer corresponds to the terseness and conciseness of our technological and modern life, nor to the appropriate utilization of materials, finance, and labor. The energy and economy of modern life must exercise a determining influence on design. Exactly worked out form devoid of any element of chance, clear contrast, the ordering of structural members, the sequence of similar parts, and the unity of form and color make up the rhythm of modern architectural creation.

But it takes more than good intentions of finding new formal expression to create a monumental office building or a well-proportioned workshop. For this reason, the industrialist or businessman is dependent upon the help of the architect. It would be shortsighted of an owner who was planning a modern factory to view the engagement of an architect merely as an unnecessary burden on his budget, for through the artist's work standards are established that are of obvious importance to the whole business. More subtle calculation will lead the owner to employ all means to increase not only the volume of work done, but also its intellectual worth, which is the only decisive factor in the battle with the competition. Today, the idea of aiming productive output at the world economy is to be found everywhere. We have indications that an age of spiritualization [Verinnerlichung] is going to follow the great age of technology and science. The social question has become the great universal problem, to which art must also apply itself. The ideas of the age press for architectonic expression. The monumental demands of the work process need enclosures that express the intrinsic value and the working methods of the plant. If the factory worker is to find any pleasure in taking part in the creation of great wealth, then it is not enough to offer him light, air, and cleanliness. The fundamental feeling for beauty, which every uneducated worker possesses, also demands its rights. Only an artist, however, is able to satisfy this demand, and if he succeeds in his goal, then the contentment of the individual worker and the morale of the workforce will grow, increasing the overall productivity of the business.

There is another reason for involving an architect in the building of a factory. Whereas the artist has long been regarded as indispensable in the realm of the poster, the publicity value of the architect's collaboration has not yet been appreciated. But architectural design in particular should be welcomed by the farsighted manager, for it gives the factory installation a dignified external appearance that allows conclusions to be drawn about the character of the whole firm. The attention of the public will certainly be held more strongly by a beautiful and original factory building than by a profusion of advertisements and name signs tacked onto the building, which only serve to blunt already weary eyes even more.

From the side of the architects, the needs of industry have been recognized and taken up with interest. The completely new formal character, the power and conciseness inherent in the nature of industrial buildings must certainly stimulate the artist's lively imagination. It is to be hoped that interest will grow in industrial circles, and that the right architect will be able to find the right patron. Given the range of specialist occupations, the division of labor is now the norm. The power of the modern age is based on the correct distribution of roles, and there are signs that, by bringing together many skills, industry will exercise as strong an influence on the development of a new culture . . . as was formerly wielded by the dynastic will of a monarch.

The Development of Modern Industrial Architecture
Walter Gropius

Die Kunst in Industrie und Handel, Jahrbuch des Deutschen Werkbundes 1913 (Jena, 1913), pp. 17–22

The short extract reprinted here is a generous tribute to Behrens from the architect who was to continue his work.

The first and greatest step was made by the Allgemeine Elektricitäts-Gesellschaft in Berlin when it appointed Peter Behrens as its artistic adviser for the entire sphere of its industrial activity. Through the most fortunate union between generous management and great artistic ability, works have been created over the last five years that are, at the moment, probably the strongest and purest testimony to a new philosophy of European architecture. They testify to the ability to revalue and give new form to the changed or entirely new ideas of the age. Buildings of a truly classical character, which effortlessly dominate their surroundings, have been created by the simple means of elementary tectonics. With these buildings, the AEG has created noble and powerful monuments which one cannot pass without feeling an emotional response. The AEG has given an exemplary lead to all industry, and others have not been slow to follow.

The New Hall of the AEG Turbine Factory in Berlin
Karl Bernhard

Zentralblatt der Bauverwaltung 30, no. 5 (15 January 1910), pp. 25 ff.

Bernhard (born 1859) worked as an engineer in the government civil engineering department in Berlin. After 1898 he taught at the Technische Hochschule at Charlottenburg, and he had previously been assistant in Berlin to Prof. Müller-Breslau, the celebrated structural engineer. Bernhard also practiced as a thoroughly conventional architect. A résumé of his most important works is to be found on p. 173 of the official German catalog to the 1910 Brussels World's Fair. For the catalogs to both the 1900 Paris Exhibition and the 1904 St. Louis World's Fair, Bernhard wrote the chapters on engineering. The collaboration with Behrens also prompted him to formulate some ideas on the aesthetics of steel buildings, which were published in shortened form in *Deutsche Bauzeitung* 47 (1913), pp. 171 ff., and *Die Bauwelt* 4 (1913), pp. 35 ff. His lecture "Moderner Industriebau in technischer und ästhetischer Beziehung" was delivered at the fifty-third general meeting of the Verein deutscher Ingenieure at Stuttgart in 1912, together with Behrens's lecture "Art and Technology." On Bernhard's lecture, see *Deutsche Bauzeitung* 46 (1912), pp. 355 ff.: "Ultimately, a workshop is nothing more than a strong steel framework that accommodates the many conveying mechanisms that are necessary in a modern plant. Similar mechanisms are necessary on the slipway, but without walls and a roof, for the mounting of the overhead cranes used in building large ships. . . . The architects are unable to cope with the static and constructional demands of heavy industry. . . . The genuine and good solution results from intelligent design work; beauty develops out of the thing itself, aided only by a controlling sense of good taste. . . . This control must be exercised by the engineer himself; without a knowledge of structures and engineering design, it would lead to half-measures."

The new hall was designed by the author in collaboration with Professor Peter Behrens, who produced the artistic concept. . . . The articulation of the gable wall was derived mainly from artistic considerations, to which the construction had to adapt. The wall is made up of a steel framework, part of which supports the window and part the concrete cladding.

For artistic reasons, and at the suggestion of Professor Peter Behrens, the main hall is accentuated by setting the side hall slightly back, which also helped the engineer in his attempt to pull the steel masses together, in order to avoid the tangled net appearance of normal girder constructions. In this way a compact, flat termination of the interior space was achieved, which enhances the external appearance of the building and promotes the cathedral-like sense of spaciousness. The solid construction of the foot of the frame greatly enhances the external impact.

The building's intended function required as much light (that is to say, as large an area of glass) as possible. As a result, glass and steel were used exclusively on the long front and concrete was only used on the short sides. The windows on the Berlichingenstrasse are 14.4 meters high, and are inclined inward parallel to the inner edges of the heavy steel pillars, so that a deep shadow is cast over the windows by the lintel. This horizontal steel beam acts as a cornice, and together with the front gable gives a feeling of volume and solidity to the roof, which sits on the side pillars and the window frame on the gable end. The rounded corners are made of concrete and are subdivided by steel bands, so that they appear as covering shells, in contrast to the vertical supports on the long front. Again in contrast to the long Berlichingenstrasse front, the large window on the Huttenstrasse is vertical and the panes of glass are flush to the steel construction, which is reinforced as a wind brace by a gallery on the inside at the height of the upper floor of the side hall. The front facade of the side hall is made entirely of concrete, in order to emphasize the enclosed character of this hall. On the courtyard side, the ceiling beams of the upper story are exposed between the vertical steel supports. The beams are 2.1 meters high and extend from the lower edge of the crossbeam flanges to the height of the railing. Here too the windows are set flush to the supporting steel frame. The generous proportions coupled with the smooth skin of steel and glass are developed fully here, in order to heighten the impact of volume and materials. Sculptural decoration and ornamentation have been entirely dispensed with, because the character of a factory demands formal simplicity and also because unnecessary ornament would detract from the sense of volume and the proportional relationships the artist has sought to create.

The New Hall for the Turbine Factory of the Allgemeine Elektricitäts-Gesellschaft in Berlin
Karl Bernhard

Zeitschrift des Vereins deutscher Ingenieure 55, no. 39 (30 September 1911), pp. 1625–1631 and 1673–1682

In this later account, Bernhard describes his collaboration with Behrens in rather more critical tones.

The new hall for the turbine factory of the Allgemeine Elektricitäts-Gesellschaft, whose structure was designed by the author following the basic architectonic concept of Professor Peter Behrens, is located at the corner of Huttenstrasse and Berlichingenstrasse in Berlin and has received much attention as a typical building for heavy industry. Both the function of the hall and its architectural and structural design merit detailed description.

The length of the hall, which runs along the entire length of the street block, is an imposing 207 meters, and the width is 39.3 meters. The volume enclosed is 151,500 cubic meters. Originally, the hall was only to be built to a length of 127 meters and put into service at the beginning of October 1909. The Allgemeine Elektricitäts-Gesellschaft erected the hall for the production of turbodynamos, in order to keep pace with the great advances in turbine construction. This is seen as the most important area for development in the immediate future. The technical operations of the new hall were planned by factory director O. Lasche. According to his information, the AEG turbine factory in 1904 had produced or had orders in hand for machinery amounting to only a few thousand horsepower. By October 1909, after barely five years of expansion, the total horsepower of the machines completed already exceeded one million. In spite of the only moderately favorable market, 2,600 men were employed at this time in the factory on the manufacture of turbines. The importance of the AEG turbines, that is the turbodynamos and also the marine turbines, lay in

their low steam consumption and their dependability. The previous hall, which was 18 meters wide and had traveling cranes with a capacity of 25 tons, was no longer able to keep up with this rapid expansion. The overhead cranes in the new hall can master loads of up to 100 tons, and the span of the main hall is 23.65 meters. In accordance with the specified spatial requirements, the plant is made up of a main hall with a width of 25.73 meters and a two-story side hall (with cellar) with a span of 12.93 meters. The heavy machinery, consisting of lathes, milling machines, and drills, is installed on the ground floor. The height from the ground floor of the side hall to the floor of the upper story is 9.07 meters, which allows enough room for railway wagons to pass below the crane supports. The height of the upper story to the level of the cranes, 4.9 meters, is determined by the height of the coil-winding ovens which are accommodated on this floor. Thus the side hall is 16 meters high to the level of the eaves and 17.5 meters to the ridge of the roof.

The main hall must be even higher than the side hall so that the crane tracks can be set 15.31 meters above the floor in order to satisfy not only the structural but also the technical demands of the plant. With this height, it is possible for even the largest components and assemblies to be lifted and carried freely above the fixed cranes, the heavy machinery, and the partially assembled machines.

To these considerable spatial demands are added unusually high structural demands. Two traveling cranes serve the main hall, each with a lifting capacity of 50 tons. When coupled together they can carry 100 tons, and can travel at a speed of 2 meters per second. The braking mechanism can achieve a retardation of 1.5 m/sec². There is a necessary margin of 0.45 meter on each side of the 23.65-meter supporting span of the crane. Slewing cranes are also mounted here on both sides, attached to the columns which are spaced at intervals of 8.0 meters. Each crane has a lifting capacity of 3 tons and a swing of 5 meters. The installation of these slewing cranes makes it possible to move smaller loads in the side areas of the main hall, independent of the main overhead cranes. So that the slewing cranes do not take any usable floor space away from the production process, they are mounted at the bases of the vertical pillars, with a pivot point approximately 3 meters above the floor of the hall.

In the upper story of the side hall are two overhead cranes, each with a lifting capacity of 10 tons, or 20 tons when coupled together. The supporting span of the cranes here is 11.78 meters, with a clearance of 0.30 meter to the inner face of the structure. The speed and the retardation of the cranes are 1.10 m/sec and 1.00 m/sec². The two cranes in the lower story have a lifting capacity of 40 tons, and thus of 80 tons when coupled. Their supporting span is 11.44 meters, with a side clearance of 0.30 meter. Once again, the speed and the retardation of these cranes are 1.10 m/sec and [1.00] m/sec². . . .

A cellar runs the entire length of the side hall, and in front of it is set a continuous row of 2.2-meter-wide light wells, which are covered with glass prisms between iron supports. The large cellars are used for the storage of unused coils, presses, and machine tools, and also as storerooms, changing rooms etc. . . .

The floors are covered with wooden blocks, 8 centimeters thick, which are laid in the side hall directly onto the reinforced concrete ceiling of the cellar. In the main hall, where there is no cellar, the wooden blocks are embedded in a 2.5-centimeter-thick concrete base. In addition to the unusually high demands with regards to loading, great value was placed on satisfying the extensive lighting requirements. . . . All areas of wall that are not directly essential to the structure are made of glass, and almost a third of the roof area is taken up by skylights. Only on the gable end walls are the areas of glass limited, for specific reasons. The skylights belonging to the side and main halls also play a role in the ventilation. They can be reached for cleaning and repairs from maintenance trolleys. For this purpose, tracks are fitted along the entire length of the skylights. On the outside, the skylights are provided with narrow, boarded catwalks. The short ends of the skylights are fitted with large ventilation flaps, which also give access to the maintenance trolleys, while the external faces of the roof are accessible from the gable front on the Huttenstrasse via ladders fitted especially for this purpose. The overhead crane tracks can be reached by means of ladders fixed at suitable points, and the narrow walkways to the sides of the crane tracks are shielded by corrugated plate and surrounded by railings.

The fireproof covering of the roof is composed partly of roofing felt and partly of grooved tiles on 5-centimeter-thick pumice-concrete planks. Reinforced concrete is used for the wall infills, and it is treated to resemble freestone on the exterior.

The main structure of the hall is made up of steel frames set at regular intervals of 9.22 meters. This distance was determined with regard to the access of existing railway tracks and by the general spatial arrangement of the hall. Load-bearing supports could not be placed between these main frames. Heavier foundations were necessary for the side hall because of the cellar, the unusually high ground-floor loading of 10 tons per square meter, and the need to support the ground floor of the main hall and the soil underneath. For this reason, it was considered advantageous for the steelwork of the side hall to be anchored with a fixed-end construction into the heavy foundations which were already necessary. But in order to implement the heavily loaded side-hall construction, which is independent of the frame of the main hall, the foot of the main frame on this side is hinged above the ground floor frame of the side hall. In contrast, there were no other reasons for building heavy foundations for the outer supports of the main hall. On this side, it was merely necessary to mount the feet of the frames as low as possible on hinges, without incurring any large costs for foundations. In this way the constructional system of the main hall was developed, with a three-hinged arch and a tie member. On one side, the impost hinges sit on the side-hall frame, and on the other side they sit approximately 1.80 meters above the floor to maximize the floor space. On this side they are entirely exposed at approximately 1.00 meter above the highest point of the slope along the Berlichingenstrasse. For artistic reasons, the roof of the main hall is a six-sided barrel vault. The faces of the roof lie in section within an arc with a radius of 15 meters, as is clearly expressed in the architecture of the gable end. The center of this arc is approximately 10 meters above the ridge of the roof, and therefore approximately 25 meters above the floor. The upper flange of the roof truss follows the contour of the gable end exactly. As the hinges are weaker at the apex than at the eaves, the corners at the lower chord of the roof frame are set on an arc with a smaller radius. The roof trusses are doubled for lateral rigidity and internal strength. The roof sections of the frames are trussed arch girders, while the pillars on the Berlichingenstrasse are solid. The round tie rods are 18.70 meters above the floor, directly above the supports for the traveling cranes, and are barely visible, so that the compact impression given by the arched girders is not affected. The demand for the structural system to be given aesthetic expression is taken into account in the tapering junction of the two halves of the roof truss, which terminate in a visible hinge at the apex. As well as facilitating the maximum usage of the floor space, the tapering pillars on the Berlichingenstrasse are also particularly effective from an aesthetic viewpoint. . . . Corresponding to the solid pillars, the vertical members supporting the cranes are also inclined toward the hinge point and are attached to the pillars by diagonal braces to increase rigidity. This inclination of the inner face of the main frames, which on the outside are vertical, gave Prof. Behrens the idea of setting the large, 14.4-meter-high window panels at the same angle, parallel to the inner edge of the main frames. This idea led to the magnificent impact that is achieved by the long side on the Berlichingenstrasse. The solid pillars stand out like columns and are joined by the L-beam lintel, whose vertical face is flush to the pillars and whose horizontal face recedes 1.1 meters as a window reveal without affecting the usable internal space in any way.

Through the inclination of the windows, the lintel projects powerfully between each pillar. The direct connection between this lintel, the heavy supporting pillars on the long side, and the high-vaulted roof construction produces aesthetic confirmation of the solidity of the heavy, load-bearing parts of the structure.

A 9-meter-wide wired-glass skylight is fitted above the center section of the roof arch. The two steeply sloping side faces are covered with tiles, and the remaining, flatter faces with a double thickness of roofing felt.

The load-bearing structure of the roof is made up of a solid intermediate joist located between each pair of main frames. The joist rests on the outside on the L-beam lintel, and on the inside on longitudinal beams that run between the frames specifically for this purpose and carry the purlins and the steel rafters. These steel rafters are spaced at 0.60-meter intervals, and the pumice-concrete planks that carry the roof covering lie directly on them. Above the floor of the hall to a height of around 3 meters there is a 23-centimeter-thick concrete outer wall. Above this wall rises the already mentioned 14.4-meter-high glass wall. The window-frame construction is made up of horizontal lattice girders set between the supporting frames, which transmit the wind forces onto the pillars. The spacing of the lattice is so calculated that a narrow roll-formed section is adequate for the window bars. The horizontal girder grid also serves to reinforce the pillars and the crane supports.

The main frames of the side hall are set at 9.22-meter intervals and are made up of solid double frames with fixed ends at both sides and two hinges in the upper framing posts. . . . As in the main hall, the roof joist is a trussed girder, but here a single-web girder is used. The rest of the frame is solid and, with the exception of the upper framing posts, double-walled. Above the center of the roof is a 6.20-meter-wide skylight made of wired glass.

As in the main hall, the roof covering is doubled roofing felt on pumice-concrete planks. The direct supporting system of the roof is made up of steel rafters at 0.60-meter intervals on longitudinal purlins made out of simple roll-formed bars. To support the purlins, a subsidiary joist is located between each pair of main beams. These joists rest on one side on the 2.10-meter-high plate girder that runs along the entire courtyard front of the side hall and on the other side on the double-walled lattice-frame joist located between the frame supports. For every 9.22-meter-wide bay there is an I-beam cap vault support between the horizontal lower frame tie beams that carries the gallery floor. The I beam is riveted to the spandrel supports on the outside and to the longitudinal lattice reinforcing framework on the inside, where it projects out beyond this framework and carries the vaulted floor panels. At those places where heavier loads amounting to 3.5 tons per square meter are to be found, a tripartite system is necessary, with two I-beam cap vault supports for each bay. With this system the load is distributed evenly over all the I beams, which are constructed as riveted, double-walled plate girders. The mezzanine floor itself is made out of vaulted reinforced concrete panels with spans of approximately 4.5 and 3.0 meters, respectively. By means of a construction patented by the author, the vault thrust is transmitted to the long walls. When the loading is irregular, the thrust is transferred to unloaded floor panels via shearing beams designed especially for the purpose. In order to reduce the effective span of these shearing beams and to add stiffness to the reinforced concrete panels, a horizontal tie member in a heavy concrete beam runs the entire length of the hall, set into the mezzanine floor.

The cellar roof is also made of reinforced concrete vaults, which are stretched between heavy reinforced concrete beams. The beams rest with fixed ends on the frame foundations and the intermediate columns. In plan they are arranged so that they do not lie on the same axis as the frame, but are offset by a quarter of the frame interval. This results in the broad foundation piers that alternate in the cellar with the light openings. The reinforced concrete retaining wall that holds the lateral thrust from the courtyard is built on a shared reinforced concrete foundation and supported at the top by the already mentioned floor beams. A 0.80-meter-deep channel for piping is let into the air ditch sill in front of the wall. Here too, as on the upper floor, the lateral thrust is transmitted to the main foundations by means of reinforced vaults. Also as on the upper floor, a rigid reinforced concrete beam runs along the entire length of the cellar at the center of the ceiling in order to reduce the span of the shearing beams and, at the same time, to add stiffness to the structural system.

Whereas steel and glass predominate elsewhere in the building, concrete has been used quite unjustifiably as a filling material for large areas of the gable wall facing the Huttenstrasse. The last bay at the gable end of the long wall is constructed entirely out of concrete, and the corner pylons are given the inward inclination of the windows on the long front merely to avoid the appearance that these wall areas are load-bearing corner piers. At the suggestion of the author, the concrete surfaces are broken up by horizontal steel bands, so that the steel construction is not entirely suppressed. In spite of this arrangement and in spite of the generous architectural effect of the gable, the intended impression of cladded corners has not on the whole been successful. Everyone sees the gable, which consists of a thin skin of reinforced concrete in front of a steel frame, as a mighty piece of concrete construction: two corner piers supporting a high tympanum. This effect, which was not intended by Prof. Behrens, has gone so far that Oberbaurat Erhard from Vienna has described the AEG turbine hall in an article entitled "Die neuzeitige Tektonik" as a "reinforced concrete building" and cites it as a characteristic example of the "Materialistil" [a style derived from the materials used]. This is a reversion to the practice of concealing the structure of large engineering works behind an artistic cladding. . . . In contrast, the iron and glass front on the Berlichingenstrasse is genuine and is an undisputed masterpiece of steel construction—an artistic success which is denied to the gable front.

For operational and fire-safety reasons, a connecting bridge with a span of 18.4 meters leads from the upper story across the courtyard to the stairwell of the factory opposite. . . .

Characteristic of the artistic direction represented by Behrens is the fact that from the various suggestions put forward he chose solid plate girders with arched lower flanges, the form that best meets the structural demands. The outline of the arch is a flattened circle. . . .

Here [on the Berlichingenstrasse front], as on the entire courtyard front, the artistic effect is sought through the purest simplicity of geometric lines and proportions, and in the display of only two building materials, glass and steel. The architect prevented the engineer from creating anything other than that which derived directly from the building technology. For this self-imposed restraint, the engineer must give his most sincere thanks to Prof. Behrens, regardless of the differences of opinion over the gable. . . . The gable front on the Huttenstrasse was intentionally planned so that the steel construction could be erected on its own, independent of the concrete work. Thus the steel gable truss is strong enough to support its own weight, and the necessary reinforcement for the other loads is produced by the concrete encasing and infilling. This arrangement made possible the independence of the steel and the concrete work, which was necessary for rapid construction, without subsequently sacrificing the combined structural effects of the two materials.

Work was begun on the construction in the spring of 1909. The very extensive foundation and reinforced-concrete work took only three months, while the steel work was completed in the very short time of five months. For the design work, too, only the most limited time was available, so when the author was first approached, in the autumn of 1908, the wishes of the management and of the artistic adviser made some of the preparatory work unnecessary.

After the machines had been installed, the building was put into full operation at the beginning of last year, although it had already been in partial use three months earlier, immediately after the roof had been completed.

All the reinforced-concrete work was executed by Czarnikow and Co. of Berlin, and the steel constructional work by the Dortmunder Union. Considering the shortness of the building time and the enormous masses that had to be handled, the constructional work was an outstanding accomplishment. Even the originally planned 127-meter-long hall needed over 2,000 tons of steel. In these terms, it is the largest steel building in Berlin.

Operationally, the building has totally satisfied the high demands made of it. The systematically designed rigidity of the longitudinal and lateral axes and the correct choice of supporting structure for the hall have given the desired operational safety to the cranes, which run constantly at high speeds. When all the cranes are working, no vibrations, which could disturb precision work, are to be felt. The unusually massive dimensions of the structural members, which are due to the high loads, in no way conflict with the effective subdivision of the space. The means and the ends stand without constraint in the correct relationship to the tasks which the building has to accomplish.

. . . The collaboration of the constructional engineer with the production engineer on one side, and with the artist on the other, has given the building its character. Many modern artistic ideas are given expression here—in particular the abolition of nonconstructional trimmings, so-called, through the combination of glass and steel. Although it has attracted much comment in the world of art, the author condemns the use of a reinforced concrete casing on the gable ends for reasons of artistic truth.

Etude sur le Mouvement d'Art Décoratif en Allemagne
Le Corbusier

Essay (La Chaux-de-Fonds, 1912), pp. 43–44

Le Corbusier (1887–1965) worked in Behrens's studio between the summer of 1910 and the following Christmas. More exact dates are not known. In August 1910, the high-voltage factory had just been completed and work had begun on the first stage of the construction of the small-motor factory. While in the studio, Le Corbusier might also have come to know the first plans for the Villa Wiegand and the Mannesmann administration building. After the end of November he may also have seen the first plans for the German embassy in St. Petersburg. At Neu-Babelsberg he must have come into daily contact with such current problems as architectural "geometry," standardization, and mass production. The commonly repeated story that Le Corbusier is to be seen in the famous photograph of the Babelsberg studio (see appendix A) is incorrect, for Gropius, who left in March 1910, is pictured in the foreground. See also Stanislaus von Moos, *Le Corbusier* (Frauenfeld and Stuttgart, 1968), pp. 35 ff., and Herta Hesse-Frielinghaus, *Osthaus und Le Corbusier* (Hagen, 1977).

At the center of these developments, Germany plays the most active role in the realm of the applied arts. One simply has to think of the persuasive German offerings at the exhibitions at Turin (1902), St. Louis (1904), Milan (1906), Brussels (1910), and finally at the Autumn Salon in Paris of 1910. Peter Behrens's work for the AEG is a particular case.

I do not know anything about the beginnings of this colossal firm, which employs 60,000 workers. In June 1910 I visited the factories with members of the Werkbund, and while subsequently studying for five months with Peter Behrens I had the opportunity to become acquainted with those aspects of the AEG that are relevant to this study.

The AEG supplies electric machines, arc lamps, and all manner of electrical equipment to the whole world. The firm's management has found a way of exploiting the current architectural revival: Its products are given a completely functional character, governed by the rules of taste. This creates welcome competition against the deplorable repoussé or cast-iron ornament that, on the pretext of beautifying, has until now disfigured such things as lights, ovens, and the machines. Even the meters, manometers, and countless appliances whose names I do not know look like leprous furuncles in the home and disfigure the workshops. The management looked for the man who was capable of creating a perfectly adequate, perfectly proportioned, and perfectly useful form out of the inherent plastic potential of the materials.

They chose Peter Behrens and appointed him artistic adviser to the AEG. From them on, one could marvel at electric power stations that are consummate architectural creations of our age—rooms of wondrous calmness and cleanness whose centers are accented by splendid, solemn, magnificent machines. And the arc lamps, light bulbs, electrical sockets, stoves, and various lighting and heating units which modern comfort demands were also given a modest, simple, almost impersonal character. They are now discreet objects, whereas they previously disfigured their surroundings. Peter Behrens has designed the forms of all these things, for no visible part of a building or an electrical appliance leaves the AEG without his approval.

This authoritarian intervention from the side of art could have had deplorable consequences had not exactly the right man been found for the job.

But there is more to be said about the role of Peter Behrens. The countless new factories built by the AEG all come from his hand, and the critics have been unanimous in their praise. His most recent factory, the turbine hall, has even been described as a "cathedral of labor." He is building extensive workers' estates, in which the nation of 150,000 souls who win their bread from the AEG will find accommodation. Behrens is an energetic, unfathomable genius, with a profound desire to dominate, as if created to this task and this age, in harmony with the spirit of modern Germany.

Modern Mass Production in the Electrical Appliance Factory of the AEG
Michael von Dolivo-Dobrowolsky

lecture delivered in AEG conference hall, 17 January 1912

A short report of this lecture appeared in the *Vossische Zeitung* of 18 January. The manuscript of the lecture and two copies are in the von Dolivo-Dobrowolsky papers in the Deutsches Museum in Munich (StdNo 1977/26,27). This excerpt is based on the second, corrected copy.

Ladies and gentlemen! When I undertook to give a lecture on the theme of modern mass production in our electrical-appliance factory, I realized that it would not go without a battle against certain deeply rooted prejudices. "Massenfabrikat" and "Massenware" have become catchwords for goods manufactured according to the recipe of cheap and nasty. The market is flooded by this "junk," as the people are wont to call it. How can I dare to speak seriously abut "junk," and how can a firm like the AEG allow a public lecture about its mass-produced goods? I do not intend, however, to speak about "junk" at all, but will attempt instead to clarify thoroughly the concept of mass production. This concept, which characterizes our entire age, is as much abused as certain others, for example the concepts of "art" and "artist." The essentially noble content of the term often becomes discredited through usage, and sometimes even gains a quite different meaning that obscures the true sense almost entirely. Shortsighted shopkeepers often intentionally denigrate the wares of their rivals as "mass produced," in contrast to their own, individually made offerings. When the public's inadequately developed powers of discrimination are abused in this way, the argument is distorted in order to baffle and exploit the customers. And people fall for this in the thousands. They curse the so-called "mass-produced goods," but still buy them, knowingly or unknowingly.

Ladies and gentlemen! You too have certainly described things disparagingly as "mass produced." I would venture to question, however, whether you have any idea what "mass goods" and "mass production" really are. One can manufacture things individually, in smaller or larger numbers, by hand, with the help of tools, or by machine. In the process, one can employ skilled or unskilled hands, and skilled or unskilled machinery. It is a matter of matching the means and the ends. If it is desired that the object should never be made in exactly the same way again, that it should be unique and individual, then handcraftsmanship is certainly the most suitable means of making it. But should the object be the same as another in some or all respects, and should it be unnecessary to match each one to the particular wishes of each user, then machine production is appropriate, as handcraftsmanship implies the opposite of uniformity. One could perhaps also differentiate between these two categories of goods by asking whether or not the mark of an individual creator is desirable. The first category is concerned with something like "art," or even "art itself," whereas in the second we have monotonous but desired "uniformity," which can be taken as far as "exactitude" or even "precision."

In my opinion, the objections that could be made against this division of the products of human labor are based on a misunderstanding of the issue, or are attributable to the imperfection of the equipment (that is to say the machines). We often forget that, although a man can be a fairly good machine, and must often function in this way, he is in no way a real machine, and certainly not a very precise one. The need for human involvement ends at the point where repetition makes further intellectual effort unnecessary. Then the man must gradually give way to the machine—not because the machine is cheaper, but because it is more regular and more

exact and therefore performs this particular task better. The much-praised handcraftsmanship is justified where artistic goods with an individual character are to be produced. It is also justified when the different characteristics of the raw materials can only be compensated for through human intervention. But after the intellectual work of creating the prototype has already been completed and it is a matter of manufacturing further exact copies, then "individual craftsmanship" should be seen only as an expedient and not as a virtue. In response to the need, it is necessary for human hands to help only temporarily, until they can be replaced by "copying machines" of advanced design. It is fundamentally wrong to boast of individual "reproduction," for this is a contradiction in terms. Rather, one should be proud to have created the equipment that does away as completely as possible with "individual work" in the manufacturing process. The "individual model" is not something to be produced in the workshop or factory hall, but is the concern of the inventor or designer who creates the prototype. What would you say, ladies and gentlemen, if every sewing needle and every pen nib you used had an "individual character" and could never be replaced satisfactorily by another? What would our army do with cartridges that carried all the marks of the individual contribution of the men or women who had made them? The fewer the better! Especially as this individual participation would seldom have positive results! Remove the product as far as possible from the arbitrariness of the worker and you will get "precision"—assuming the equipment is suitable to the task. The more perfect the equipment, the less necessary is the intervention of the worker. And further, the fewer workers (or, more exactly, working hours) that are necessary to manufacture an object, the fewer *trained* workers are needed. For it is much better to remove the man and his brain from where he does not belong, and to send him to the place where he can exercise his true skills of thinking and controlling. Unfortunately, we are still a long way from reaching this ideal; yet considerable progress has been made in the conscious effort to reduce the human contribution in the "reproduction" of industrial products. As a reward, so to speak, for identifying and following this correct course, our products are now being manufactured faster, more cheaply, and more exactly. We have a "mass production" that achieves incomparably more in terms of exactness and quality than "individual" handcraftsmanship could ever do. Incidentally, you will see in the examples later that modern techniques of mass production can consciously correct and control their own working. Not only does mass production have to follow an exact model, but because of the necessary sequence of different operations its very existence depends on absolutely precise work.

After this general introduction, kindly allow me to go on to describe our electrical-appliance factory. This should give you a picture of mass production as it is practiced today. I am not taking you now into some sort of pin or pen-nib factory, where millions of tiny, simple objects are made in a small range of types, but into a factory where relatively complicated machines and products, which often have to satisfy stringent scientific demands, are made in large numbers. And all this not with a small range of products or with a restricted choice, but with a range adapted to the diverse wishes of the international market, to the varying needs and social classes of the customers, and to the different conditions under which the machines work. As examples, I can tell you that we manufacture hundreds of different models of electricity meters, and that our price list contains around eight hundred sorts of the small rotary light switches known to you as Knipser.

I have arranged for some particularly typical products from the series made in the appliance factory to be exhibited here in the hall. Each one stands only for its respective category of product, and, like the meters and the switches, is made in many variations. The sum total of the products made in the appliance factory, the price-list number as we call it, amounts to over 12,000! And yet this enormous number can be broken down and comprehended according to a relatively uncomplicated system of groups, subgroups, etc. But what is more interesting is that these objects, which are made in so many different types, are nevertheless "mass-produced articles" in the true sense of the world. When you consider that we manufacture, for example, several million of the already-mentioned switches each year, or that the annual output of such complicated things as electricity meters, costing 25–75 marks, at the moment exceeds 300,000, then you really have to use the term "mass-produced."

How does the mass production of a vast quantity of different products work, and how is it possible in a single factory? Although the AEG's factories may be extensive, we are talking here about only one of them. From every row and corner of this lecture room I hear just this question. Ladies and gentlemen, there is a single key to this puzzle. This key is called the *standardization of components*! Standardization forms the connecting link between the volume of goods and the mass-produced article. For the many hundred different types of switch we only have a few sorts of bases, and so on. Whether the switch, to use technical language, has one, two, or three poles, whether it is a so-called changeover switch, a multicircuit switch, or a simple on-off switch, it still needs the same spindle inside. The same is true for the contact springs, the curved, springy strips stamped out of brass sheet. Although the number of these springs varies from switch to switch, the springs themselves are for the most part exactly the same. Similarly, the specially formed brass connectors that lead the current into the switch from the supply wire remain the same for many of the different switch types, irrespective, for example, of whether the switch is intended for surface or flush mounting, or the height of the base, and of the material from which the cover is made, be it porcelain, brass, or something else, or wherher two or three or even more cables are led into the switch via the necessary connectors. You can see from this simple example that, in order to manufacture a large quantity of dissimilar switches efficiently, we have introduced the *mass production of component parts.* The number of different parts, however, is nowhere near as large as the number of switch models in our lists, which is the result of combining the parts in various combinations. Each part is used so often that it can be produced economically in enormous quantities by fully automatic machines and tools. These parts are all stored, and one then only needs to bring them together in special workshops in the desired combinations in order to assemble them. Thus, the factory's central supply sections, for example the stamping shop, the draw shop, etc., work quite irrespective of whether more switches of one type are ordered today and more of another type tomorrow.

Some other examples: Take an electrical measuring device; there are many similar instruments to measure amps, volts, or watts and direct, alternating, or three-phase current, and often at a point quite distant from the meter itself. Naturally, it is impossible to keep the internal mechanism of the instrument the same in all cases. So we make the base plates identical, and fit them with identical covers, with the same glass faces to protect the pointers and dials. As the pointer does not have to concern itself about whether the numbers it points to refer to watts, volts, or revolutions, we use as far as possible the same pointer in all cases, merely shortening it slightly for some sorts of instruments. In this way we arrive at different electricity meters with the same counter-gear assembly. No matter if the meter is for direct, alternating, or three-phase current, and regardless of the size of the actual mechanism, the same counter-gear assembly is always used. With an annual turnover of 300,000 meters in hundreds of

different types, we have only around one or two dozen base plates, and many of these differ from each other only in the location and number of screw holes. However complicated the task is, the trained and ingenious mind can always work out components that can be manufactured together and used on a whole range of designs, for example single cog wheels, power-supply clamps, brake pulleys, bolt assemblies, and the like. The greatest attention must be paid to such "standard" components in the design of new appliances, for only in this way can mass production be sustained, and profitable, more or less automatic machinery introduced. Existing orders can then be executed more quickly, without increasing the need for the extremely expensive storage of finished goods. This "component economy" is so extremely important in modern mass production that an enormous amount of intellectual effort is devoted to its further and fuller development. There is great scope for human initiative both here and in the development of tools and machines, and it is on this area that we should concentrate rather than on propagating individual craftsmanship. Turning the tables now, we mass producers look on hand production with derision and pity.

To my description of the nature of component-based mass production I should add that the precondition that makes it possible is extraordinary precision—the highest degree of exactitude. When the boxes of components arrive from the various workshops in the assembly halls to be put together in the appropriate combinations, there is neither the space, nor the time, nor the personnel to correct the parts that do not fit properly. This would also be a break with the principle of abolishing the "individual" object. We would abhor this mixture of the old and new methods of production, for the only outcome of such a hybrid would be that the disadvantages of both methods would fuse together and be magnified. No, nothing may be reworked or corrected in the assembly shops—only assembled! The need for exactitude in the components is self-evident, as is the perfect matching of one to the other, be they the cruder parts of a switch or the delicate spindles and jeweled bearings of the measuring instruments and meters. We have progressed so far, for example, that we can, without difficulty, strip down several meters of the same type into their smallest parts, mix these parts up, and then reassemble the meters using only a screwdriver. This experiment on an appliance that does not have the simplest of constructions has already convinced some of the supporters of "individual" production techniques where the greater precision and exactitude is to be found, and has won us many customers. We are endeavoring to bring all our products, large and small, to such a level of perfection that spare parts can be supplied and installed without being reworked or specially fitted. This is something of inestimable value in the case of foreign and overseas deliveries, for many of the customers in these distant parts of the world take little pleasure in "individual" craftsmanship.

Perhaps some of you are wondering by what means the exactness necessary for modern mass production is achieved. It is clearly impossible to stand behind every worker and factory girl, to measure and check each one of the thousands of tiny parts. But, ladies and gentlemen, we do not need to do this. For we are not in a factory where drawings and tables are to be found in every workshop, against which the goods being made are measured and marked. Here, only the so-called templates and calibres are made from drawings, as well as special tools like the cutters and punches for the stamping machines, presses, drilling templates, and so on. All these installations serve the purpose of excluding the worker entirely from the question of measurements; not the worker but the toolmaker is responsible for the right measurements. And the machine, in turn, is checked as meticulously as possible before it is installed in the workshop. The toolmaking shop, therefore, is equipped with the most exact measuring equipment; it is regarded as the most important part of the factory and tended accordingly. The components produced by fully automatic or semiautomatic machines as well as those made by simpler equipment are often spot-checked to make sure that the cutting edges, templates, etc. of the machines have not gone out of true through gradual wear.

For some products the "tool" (that is, the total number of mechanisms that exclude the arbitrariness of the worker and aid partial fabrication) is so expensive that its portion of the final price is not only higher than the labor costs, but also higher than the material costs. Such investments can only be written off very slowly. When one considers that progress often demands that the production be changed, which results in the premature replacement of some or even all of the expensive machine tools, then one can see that modern mass production is not always a bed of roses; the roses also have thorns.

While the regularity and exactness of the components is thoroughly provided for through the template and calibration work and by the continuous checks on the tools, the control of the manufactured products goes even farther.

Certainly, the most effective control for the components is, as already mentioned, their assembly in special workshops where corrective work is excluded through the lack of the appropriate tools. The piecework system of payment also means that the worker immediately rejects any part that does not fit exactly, rather than struggle with it any further. It is easy for him to do this, as the parts come from totally different workshops, and he does not know whose hands a part has passed through. The finished appliances go to so-called "final control checks," where, according to their type, they are inspected by special controllers, sometimes while running. Special books or marks give proof of these checks, so that in the case of a complaint it can quickly be established which controller should be held responsible. Some of the appliances (for example, meters, measuring instruments, and automatic switches) have to be calibrated, or adjusted to particular current levels. The calibrating process provides the most effective and most natural control of the correct assembly of the parts. Previously, calibrating rooms looked like physics laboratories, but today they are fitted out in a manner appropriate to modern mass-production methods. Only true exactness in the adjustments counts here, and there is little scope for "individual" measurement. At the workbench of each calibrater there are the most exactly prepared measuring devices, each limited to a narrow range suitable to the product in question so that only a few manipulations are necessary. The calibrater does not have to think about much and can hardly make mistakes. He is also very aware that his calibration is followed by a control calibration at another bench. To combat boredom and carelessness with these control calibrations, traps are set from time to time! Not only mass production, therefore, but also mass control. With a daily output of over 1,000 electricity meters and around 300 ammeters, voltmeters, and other measuring instruments, a different, laxer approach would be impossible. In addition, special, scientifically equipped laboratories look after the firm's good reputation by means of spot checks on all of the factory's individual product ranges. These checks are made on appliances drawn directly from the dispatch warehouse.

Having described the main features of our production to you, and hopefully raised your faith in our goods, I shall now attempt to give you a more tangible picture of our operations with a series of lantern slides showing our products and statistics about the factory. The electrical appliance factory is one link in the AEG factory chain. Together with a few separate workshops it covers an area of approximately 20,000 square meters. As a result of the relatively compact construction and the division into several stories, a working area of around 60,000 square meters remains after the many offices and storage rooms have been subtracted. We employ around 7,500 workers here, of whom approximately 3,500 are women. . . .

[There follows a guided tour of the various assembly sections, but only the account of the arc-lamp section is reproduced here. The illustrations are missing from the manuscript.]

We now want to take a look at the arc-lamp section. You will know what arc lamps look like from the outside, and can also see some examples hanging here in the hall. Illustration 13 shows some in cross section together with some of its small component parts. The outer shell of the arc lamp, the so-called armature, is generally made from strong sheet steel, preformed partly in extrusion presses and partly in compressing machines. The armature pieces are neither brazed, screwed, nor riveted here, but are joined together by arc welding. Illustration 15 shows these arc-welding machines being operated by girls. The work is done remarkably quickly, and a stronger joint is achieved than by any other method. The painting and lacquering are done using the "spray method," whereby lacquer or paint is sprayed by compressed air in a finely atomized jet onto the relevant object. This method gives an extraordinarily regular coat that reaches into all the grooves and hollows. A fully developed spraying installation with several phases and an automatic feeding mechanism is shown in illustration 17. The lacquered armatures and other parts are then loaded into special steam-heated cabinets, where the drying temperatures can be adjusted to suit the various types of paint and finish.

Illustration 19 depicts a typical assembly hall, in which arc lamps are put together from their components; while illustration 20 shows the room in which the individual arc lamps are tested and adjusted to burn correctly with the specified type and strength of electric current. There is also a roof station, which is used to test various lamp systems and new constructions under the most realistic conditions possible—for example, their resistance to various types of weather. With the observation that we deliver 50,000 arc lamps and related accessories annually, let us leave this section and proceed to the one for installation equipment.

The electrical-appliance factory manufactures only some of those products that could, in the widest sense of the word, be understood as installation equipment. Particularly noteworthy because of the quantities involved are fixtures for incandescent bulbs, fuses, and the plugs and switches that you all know.

. . . While the minute components are produced in large numbers in the central supply section, the assembly work is performed in especially large halls, in which there are hardly any machine tools.

CATALOG OF WORKS

All works are attributed to Peter Behrens except where another designer is named, where a design is identified as an earlier model or a precursor, or where the date of the work is omitted below the heading. Unless another designer is named, the presence of a date below the heading indicates that the work is attributed to Behrens. Occasionally Behrens's name is given below the heading to avoid possible ambiguity or to indicate attribution without dating. The glossary of abbreviations explains the shortened references used in this catalog.

Architecture

Henning Rogge

AEG Pavilion, Deutsche Schiffbau-Ausstellung [German Shipbuilding Exhibition], Berlin
1908

The AEG did not display its products in the official halls at the Zoological Garden like the other exhibitors, but at a separate exhibition in the firm's own pavilion on Auguste-Victoria-Platz.

Building
Exhibition pavilion with octagonal ground plan, interior height 20 meters, diameter 18 meters, set in garden with pergolas. The four pieces of sculpture at the entrance came from the administration building on the Friedrich-Karl-Ufer.

Dating
Erected for the exhibition, which was opened in June 1908 and ran for four months.

Literature
Deutsche Schiffbau-Ausstellung 1908 (AEG exhibition catalog); *ZdVDI* 52, no. 25 (20 June 1908), pp. 1015 ff.; *Wk* 3 (1907–08), p. 336; "Aus der Deutschen Schiffbau-Ausstellung," *MdBEW* 4, no. 8 (August 1908), pp. 114–117 and illustration p. 119; Scheffler 1908, pp. 432 ff. and illustrations pp. 430, 432; F. Poppenberg, *JbK* 7 (1908–09), pp. 72 ff.; *DKD* 22 (1908–09), pp. 346 ff.; Jaumann 1909, pp. 343–349, 354, and 356; *AEG-Ztg* 11, no. 12 (June 1909), pp. 6 ff.; Adolf Behne, "Peter Behrens und die toskanische Architektur des 12. Jahrhunderts," *KGB* 23 (1912), pp. 45 and 48–50; Meyer-Schönbrunn 1913, illustrations pp. 46–48; Hoeber 1913, pp. 108 ff. and illustration 121; Peter Behrens, "Neue Sachlichkeit in der Gartenformung," *Jahrbuch d. Arbeitsgemeinschaft f. dt. Gartenkultur* 1 (1930), pp. 15 ff.; Anderson 1969, p. 76, illustration 19, p. 77, illustration 22; Buddensieg and Rogge 1976, pp. 92 ff.

A1
Covers of AEG's exhibition guide (Behrens, 1908; see also ill. G9).

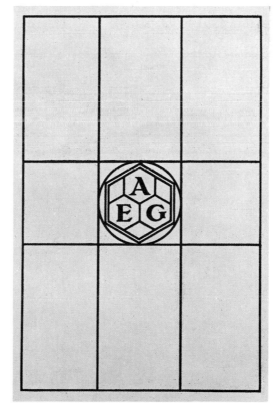

A4
Interior of the pavilion, with ship's
bridge installed in window bay.

A2
The pavilion.

A3
Front entrance of the pavilion.

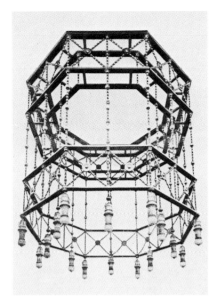

A5
Light fixture in the pavilion, carrying
16 high-power arc lamps. From
MdBEW.

A6
The garden.

A7
The illumination of the exhibition halls
facing the front entrance of the AEG
pavilion.

A8
The illumination in the garden of the
AEG pavilion.

• A9

AEG Pavilion, Allgemeine Ausstellung von Erfindungen der Klein-Industrie [General Exhibition of Inventions of Light Industry]
1907

Wooden pavilion with white lattice construction, similar to the pergolas at the Kunstausstellung at Oldenburg, 1908, and the Kunst- und Gartenbauausstellung at Mannheim, 1907. The circular version of the AEG monogram (see G77) was probably used here for the first time.

Literature
MdBEW 3, no. 9 (September 1907), illustrations pp. 130–135.

• A10

Neue Automobil-Gesellschaft Stand, Internationale Automobil-Ausstellung, Berlin
1907

Literature
MdBEW 4, no. 2 (February 1908), pp. 19–22. On the garden furniture, see Rheingauer Gartenmöbel catalog, Bank- u. Stuhltyp Nr. 904.

A10
From MdBEW.

A9
From *MdBEW*.

• A11, A12

AEG Pavilion, Ausstellung für soziale Fürsorge [Social Welfare Exhibition], Brussels
1916

Building
Temporary exhibition building with square ground plan and octagonal, pyramidal roof.

Exhibition
The side galleries housed an exhibition on the theme of accident prevention, showing machinery with safety devices, models, and diagrams. In the central space stood models of Behrens-designed factories, which were offered as examples of "dignified and functional workplaces, incorporating wideranging health precautions against all types of harmful influences in factory work" (*MdBEW*). The sculpture by Hugo Kaufmann exhibited in the middle of the room was entitled "Betriebssicherheit" [operational safety].

Dating
Constructed for the exhibition in 1916.

Literature
MdBEW 12, no. 10 (October 1916), pp. 157 ff.; Peter Behrens, *Das Plakat* 11 (1920), pp. 271 ff.

A11
AEG pavilion at Social Welfare Exhibition. From *MdBEW*.

A12
Central room of the pavilion, with models of high-voltage factory and large-machine assembly hall. From *MdBEW*.

•A13–A16

Powerhouse for AEG Turbine Factory

1908–09

Location
Berlin-Moabit, Huttenstrasse 12–16, at the northern end of the former Union-Elektricitäts-Gesell-schaft site, between the old and new turbine halls and linked to the eastern side of the boiler house.

Building
Brick construction with rectangular ground plan, 17.14 meters long and 10.88 meters wide, with a low, projecting, polygonal block on the long front for the switchgear room.

Dating
Planning application 4 July 1908. Building permission granted 20 August (Bauschein no. 1752). Beginning of construction September 1908; completion prior to beginning of work on new turbine factory on 30 March 1909.

Building Contactor
R. Guthmann, Berlin.

Literature
O. Lasche, "Das Kraftwerk der AEG-Turbinenfabrik in Berlin," *ZdVDI* 53, no. 17 (24 April 1909), pp. 648–655; Lasche, "Die Turbinenfabrik der AEG," ibid. 55, no. 29 (22 July 1911), p. 1199; Hoeber 1913, p. 116 and illustration 126; Fürst 1915, pp. 88 ff.; *AEG-Taschenbuch 1919*, p. 34; Buddensieg and Rogge 1976, pp. 72 ff.

A13
Powerhouse for turbine factory, seen from the northeast, 8 April 1913.

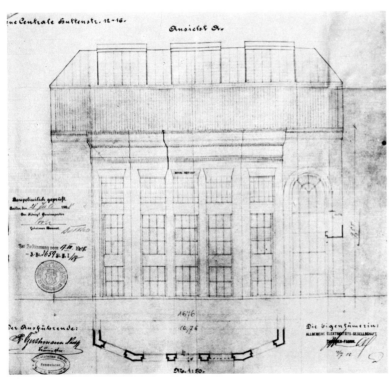

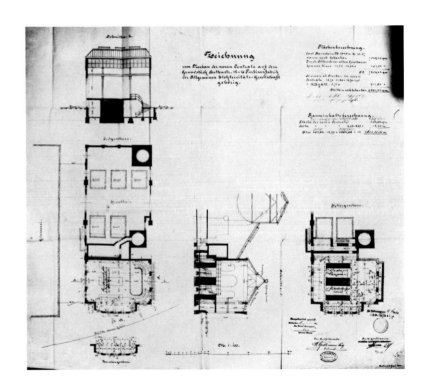

A14, A15
Drawings for the powerhouse, June
1908.

A16
Eastern end of the powerhouse, with
switchgear room, 11 January 1912.

• A17–A32

Assembly Hall of AEG Turbine Factory
1909

Location
Berlin-Moabit, Huttenstrasse 12–16, site of former Union-Elektricitäts-Gesellschaft, on corner of Huttenstrasse and Berlichingenstrasse, parallel to the old turbine hall.

Building
Main hall: 123 meters long, 25.60 meters wide, ridge height approximately 25 meters; structure of three-hinged frames with tie member. On Berlichingenstrasse front: solid steel pillars with impost hinges set on a concrete plinth approximately 1.50 meters above ground level; infilled with concrete and glass; saddle-shaped skylight in ridge of roof; two overhead cranes, each with a lifting capacity of 50 tons. On courtyard side: two-story side hall with cellar, length same as main hall, width 12.50 meters; load-bearing system of double frame with fixed ends; in lower story two 40-ton cranes, in upper story two 10-ton cranes; saddle-shaped skylight.

Structural Engineer
Karl Bernhard.

Dating
Signed and dated sketch 1908, plans 16 September 1908, planning application 17 December 1908, building permission 17 March 1908 (Bauschein no. 4709); building commenced 30 March 1909, completed October 1909.

Building Contractors
Czarnikow & Co., Berlin; Union, Dortmund.

Literature
Dohrn 1909, pp. 367 ff.; O. Lasche, "Die neue Turbinenhalle der AEG," *AEG-Ztg.* 12, no. 7 (January 1910), pp. 1–4; Peter Behrens, "Die Turbinenhalle der AEG zu Berlin," *Deutsche Techniker-Zeitung* 27, no. 6 (12 February 1910); Behrens, *Mitteilungen des Rheinischen Vereins f. Denkmalpflege u. Heimatschutz* 4, no. 1 (1 March 1910), pp. 26–29; DBH, *Der Betonbau* 14, no. 16 (1910), p. 2; Karl Bernhard, "Die neue Halle der Turbinenfabrik der Allg. Elektricitäts-Ges. in Berlin," *ZdB* 30, no. 5 (1910), pp. 25–28; Bernhard, *ZdVDI* 55, no. 39 (30 September 1911), pp. 1625–1682 and illustration 28; Karl Scheffler, *KuK* 8 (1910), p. 419; Wolf Dohrn, "Die Turbinenhalle der AEG in Berlin," *IB* 1 (1910), p. 132; ibid. 2 (1911), p. 126; Karl Ernst Osthaus, "Ein Fabrikbau von Peter Behrens," *Gartenstadt* 4, no. 8 (August 1910), pp. 89–91; Osthaus, *Frankfurter Zeitung*, 10 February 1910; Walter Gropius, *Industriebauten* (catalog to traveling exhibition of the Deutsches Museum für Handel und Gewerbe, Hagen); H. Weber, *Walter Gropius und das Faguswerk* (Munich, 1961); O. Lasche, "Die Turbinenfabrikation der AEG," *ZdVDI* 55, no. 29 (22 July 1911), pp. 1198 ff.; *KGB* 22, no. 8 (1911), pp. 149 ff.; Hoeber 1913, pp. 108–116 and illustrations 122–125; Walter Gropius, "Die Entwicklung moderner Industriebaukunst," *JDW* 1913, pp. 17 ff.; *Bau-Rundschau* 4 (1913), pp. 86 ff.; Fürst 1915, pp. 83 ff.; Peter Behrens, "Über die Beziehungen der künstlerischen und technischen Probleme," *Wendingen* 3–4 (March–April 1920), pp. 4–20; Heinrich de Fries, "Industriebaukunst," *WMB* 5 (1920–21), pp. 127 ff.; Behne 1926 (1964), pp. 31 ff.; Heinrich Hirschberg, "Bau-Entwicklung der AEG-Fabriken," *Spannung, AEG-Umschau* 3 (1929–30), pp. 38–40; Gerhardt 1929–30, pp. 496–497; Rave and Knöfel 1963, object 211; *BusB* 9 (1971), pp. pp. 50–52; Müller 1974, pp. 46 ff.; Buddensieg and Rogge 1976, pp. 92 ff.

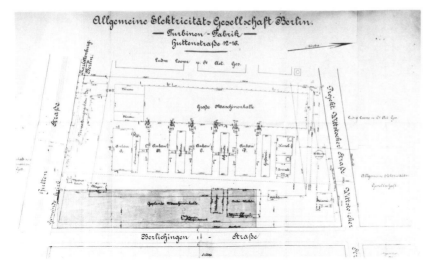

A17
Site plan of turbine factory, with
projected assembly hall drawn in.

A18
Unexecuted design for turbine hall in
sketch by Behrens, signed and dated
1908.

A19
Variation of the design, 1909.

A20
Section through main and side halls of
turbine factory.

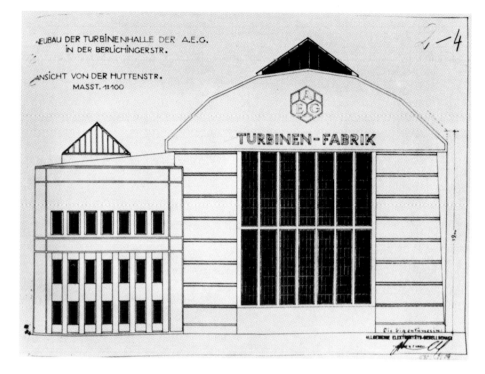

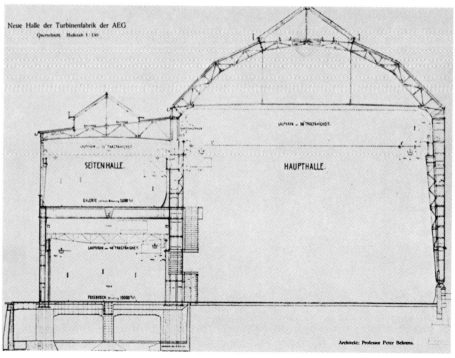

A21
Watercolor of turbine factory on Huttenstrasse.

A24
Windows on Berlichengenstrasse front
and original north end of hall.

A22
Entrance gate and new hall of turbine
factory on Huttenstrasse.

A23
Interior view of the hall, looking
toward Huttenstrasse.

A25
The turbine hall at the corner of
Huttenstrasse and Berlichingenstrasse
shortly after its completion.

A26
The turbine hall in its present condition.

A27–A32
Details of the hall in its present condition.

A33–A37
Extension to Annex A of Turbine Factory
1913–14

Location
AEG turbine factory site, Huttenstrasse 12–16, Berlin-Moabit, behind administration building and between old and new turbine halls.

Building
The existing Annex A (cellar, ground floor, and two upper floors) was to be enlarged by the addition of two floors plus two attic stories to serve as storage rooms. The large scale of this extension gave it the character of a new building. According to Behrens's plans of August–September 1913 and the structural calculations of O. Leitholf, a completely new building was to be placed on top of the existing factory annex, as if on stilts. The outer walls of the new stories were to be made up of a lattice steel construction, resting via long supporting pillars on special foundations without loading the walls below. The gables at the east and west ends of the roof were to be topped by towerlike constructions (eaves height of building 22 meters, height of towers 32.50 meters), in which the lift and paternoster mechanisms were to be installed. In this way, the lifts could be brought up into the two new attic stories. Only the gable tower at the east end was built.

Building Contractors
Actien-Gesellschaft für Bauausführungen, Berlin W. 57, Bülowstrasse 90.

Dating
Planning permission applied for 19 September 1913. Provisional permission granted 17 October. Final permission granted 4 November (Bauschein no. 3399). Existing walls reinforced November 1913. Extension completed by beginning of April 1914 and put into use 24 April 1914.

Sources
Building files.

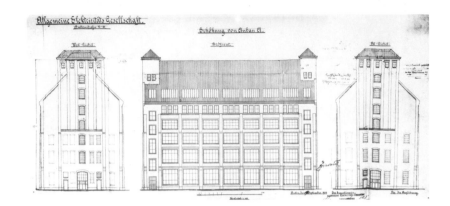

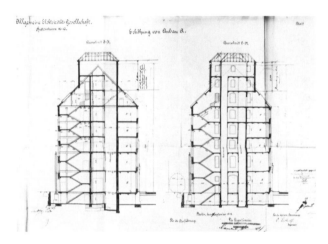

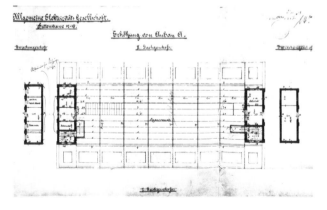

A36
The eastern gable in its present condition.

A37
View of the building in its present condition from the southeast.

A33
Elevations of the planned remodeling of Annex A, drawn 10 September 1913.

A34
Sections through the gable tower fronts.

A35
Plan of the upper attic story.

•A38–A42
AEG Munitions Factory
1916

Location
On site of turbine factory, Hutten-strasse 12–16, Berlin-Moabit, at corner of Berlichingenstrasse and continuation of Wittstocker Strasse.

Building
The urgent contracts from the army ministry for artillery shells made it necessary to build a munitions factory at the end of 1915. Behrens was employed as architect and O. Leitholf as structural engineer. To use the site to the maximum, a small hall 35 meters long and 13.98 meters wide was planned to fit between the existing workshops. At a right angle to this small hall was set a larger hall measuring 37.56 by 19.61 meters, with a side hall and an adjoining pump-house. Work was begun at the turn of the year 1915–16, and before the factory was completed in March a further extension was planned, using the same truss construction. This extension, comprising two large halls, each with a side hall, was for the manufacture of hand grenades.

Building Contractors
G. Guthmann Nachf. I. Schultz, Berlin C 19, Wallstr. 25 (building work); Karl Spaeter GmbH, Berlin W 9, Linkstr. 20 (steelwork).

Dating
First planning application submitted 15 December 1915; foundation work begun at turn of year 1915–16. Constructional drawings for munitions factory submitted 17 January 1916; further drawings submitted 11 February for the extension (double hall). Official building inspection 9 February, approved 29 February (Bauschein no. 1398). Extension inspected 25 February, approved 24 March 1916 (Bauschein no. 1505). First delivery of raw materials 24 March 1916.

Sources
Building files.

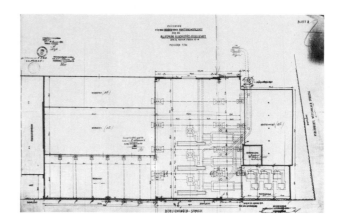

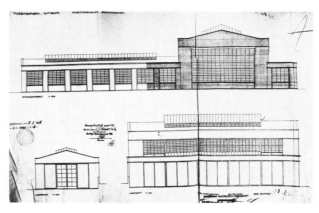

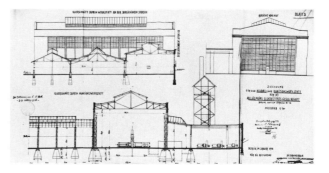

A38
Site plan of projected munitions factory on site of turbine factory on Berlichingenstrasse, January 1916.

A39
Elevations of munitions factory from Berlichingenstrasse (above) and from courtyard in constructional drawing signed by Behrens.

A40
Section and view from courtyard.

A41
Perspective view of the double hall extension to the munitions factory, drawn February 1916.

A42
Elevations of extension to munitions factory, drawn 9 February 1916.

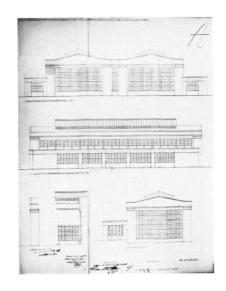

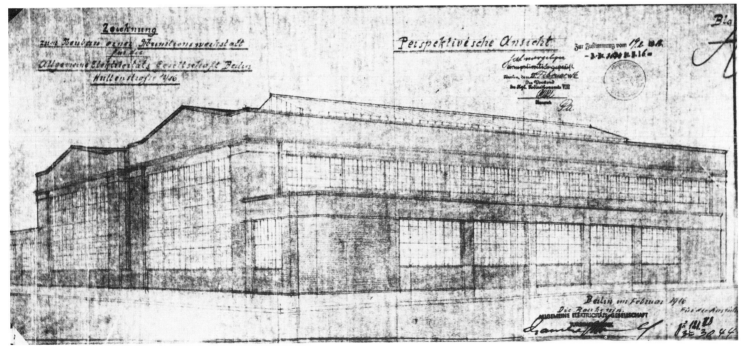

Old Factory for Railway Equipment (AEG)

Johann Kraaz, from 1905; alterations and additions by Peter Behrens, 1908

Location

Berlin-Wedding, on site of AEG machine factory, Brunnenstrasse 107a, facing Voltastrasse, between buildings of the Berliner Elektricitäts-Werke and foundry.

Buildings

Plans by Johann Kraaz 20 October 1904; building permission granted 21 August 1905 (Bauschein no. 2581). First building phase: front block, right-hand central wing, transverse block, and courtyard with cellar completed in rough state on 5 December 1906; building first used on 24 June 1907. Second building phase: excavation work for western central wing, water tower, and cellar under large courtyard in May 1908; rough shell completed 7 September 1908; put into service 26 April 1909.

Literature

Industriebau 2 (1911), p. 131; Hoeber 1913, p. 136; Buddensieg 1975, p. 278; Buddensieg and Rogge 1976, pp. 95 ff.

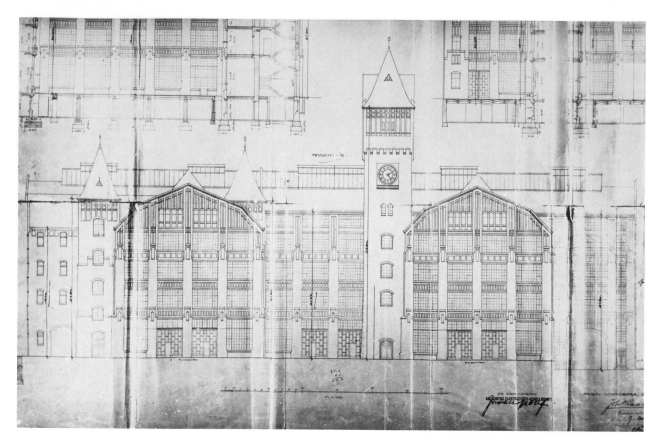

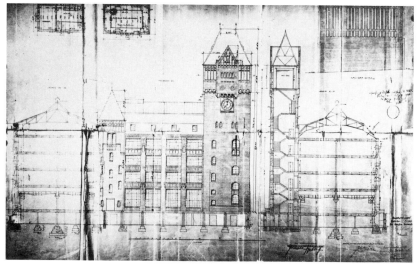

A43
Design for old factory for railway
equipment by Johann Kraaz; elevation
of courtyard side and section from
drawing of 20 Octobor 1904.

A44
Design with elevation of courtyard
side and sections, drawn 20 October
1904.

A45
Bird's-eye view of Brunnenstrasse
complex from south.

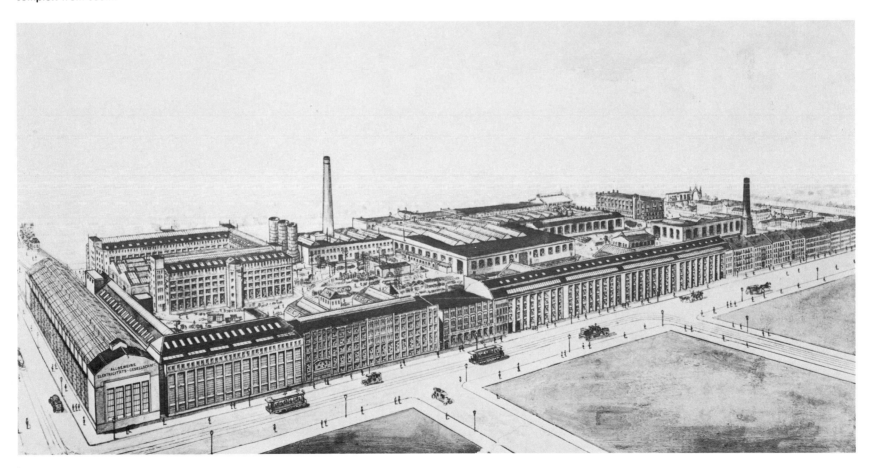

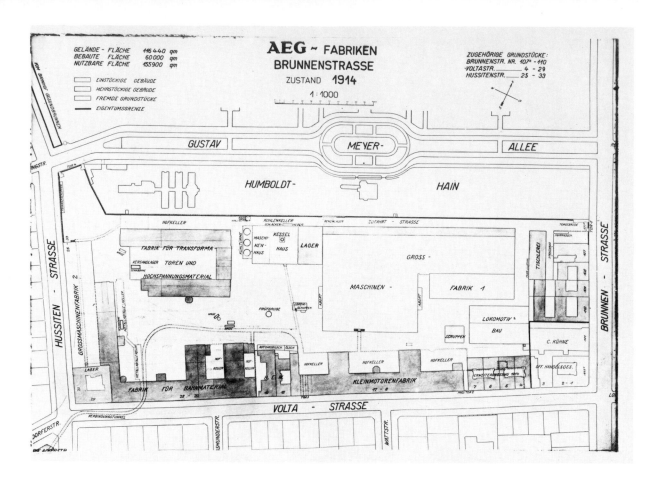

A46
Layout of Brunnenstrasse complex
in 1914.

A47
Courtyard side of old factory for
railway equipment, 1 July 1909.

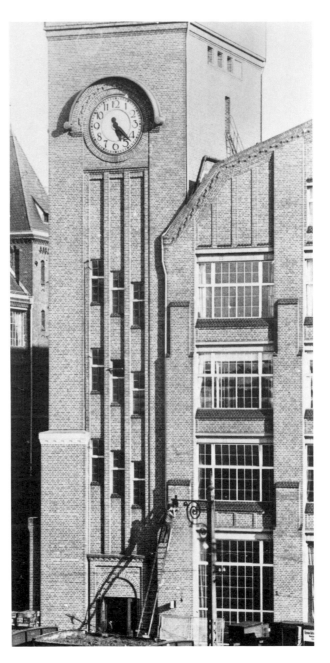

A48
Early work on second building phase,
28 May 1908.

A49
NAG trucks standing in front of old
railway-equipment factory, 24 July
1910.

•A51–A53

Alterations to Facade of Old Factory for Railway Equipment
1911

When the new factory for railway equipment was projected to re-place the foundry, Behrens stripped the Gothic decoration from the facade of the old railway-equipment factory in order to achieve an architecturally unified relationship between the old and new factories.

Dating
The alterations to the facade, which was then only three years old, were completed before work was begun on the new factory and were photographed on 3 May 1911.

Literature
Karl Ernst Osthaus, ''Ein Fabrikbau von Peter Behrens,'' *Frankfurter Zeitung*, 10 February 1913, p. 136; Buddenseig and Rogge 1976, p. 99.

A51
Kraaz's design for the old factory: elevation of Voltastrasse front, drawn 19 May 1906.

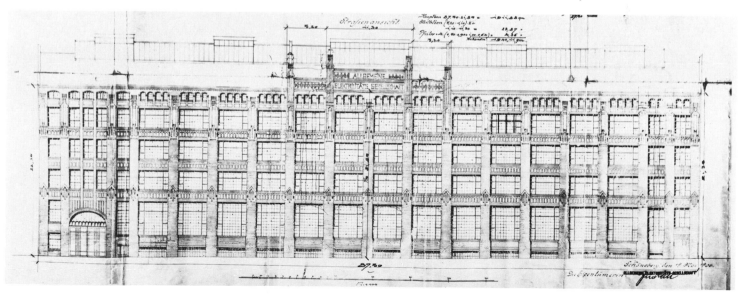

A52
Facade of old factory, designed by Kraaz, photographed 27 May 1907.

A53
The facade after remodeling by Behrens, photographed 22 August 1911.

• A54–A73

AEG Factory for Transformers, Resistors, and High-Voltage Equipment ("High-Voltage Factory")
1909–10

Location
Berlin-Wedding, in AEG machine-factory complex on Brunnenstrasse, at south end of Humboldthain, on site of the former storage sheds I–IV.

Buildings
Two parallel main wings, six stories high: north wing 25.5 meters high, with ground area of 2,335.86 square meters; south wing same height with ground area of 1,875.7 square meters. Between the two wings a double hall with a glazed roof, 11.7 meters high with an area of 3,963.77 square meters. Both wings are linked by a transverse four-story block covering 490 square meters, in which the offices are housed. The ground area of the entire complex is 8,600 square meters, with a total usable area of 33,300 square meters.

Dating and Progress of Construction
Nondefinitive constructional drawings signed by Behrens and Bernhard 27 February 1909. Planning application March 1909; building permission granted 25 May 1909 (Bauschein no. 723). Supplementary application 24 March 1910, approved on 7 May 1910. Building work already begun in April 1909.

First phase: Construction of south wing, intended for the production of high-voltage equipment. Excavation work in May, building shell completed in September, wing put into service on 18 October and 4 November 1909.

Second phase: Construction of double hall, intended for manufacture of transformers. Work begun in September 1909, halls put into service 6 January and 10 March 1910.

Third phase: Construction of transverse block. Building shell completed 14 April 1910, put into service 19 May.

Fourth and final phase: Construction of north wing (warehouse and resistor factory). Work begun at the beginning of 1910; eastern end completed May 1910, western end July 1910.

Building Contractors
Boswau & Knauer GmbH, Berlin W8, Mohren Str. 49; Thyssen & Co., Berlin NW7, Dorotheenstr. 36.

Literature
Brussels 1910, illustrations 104 and 105 (model); Mannheimer 1910, plate 24; *MBF* 9 (1910), illustrations 406 and 407 (model); Mannheimer 1911, pp. 122 ff.; *DBH* 16 (1912), pp. 210–212; *AEG-Führer*, 1912, pp. 15 ff. and 23–25; Hoeber 1913, pp. 108 ff. and 137 ff.; *AEG-Ztg* 15, no. 11 (May 1913), pp. 9–11; *JDW* 1913, illustrations 3 and 5–8; Mannheimer 1913, pp. 37 ff.; Scheffler 1913, pp. 159 ff.; *Die Kunst* 28 (1913), pp. 573 ff.; *KGB* 27, no. 2 (1915–16), p. 31; *AEG-Taschenbuch* 1919, pp. 19–21; Müller-Wulckow 1925, pp. 7 and 27 ff.; Platz 1927, pp. 260–264 and 514; Cremers 1928, p. 8, plates 26 and 29–31; *GBK* 1928, nos. 2023 and 2024; Hirschberg 1929–30, pp. 40–41; Anderson 1968, pp. 295 ff.; *BusB* 9 (1971), pp. 52 ff.; Buddensieg 1975, pp. 280–287; Buddensieg and Rogge 1976, pp. 96 ff.

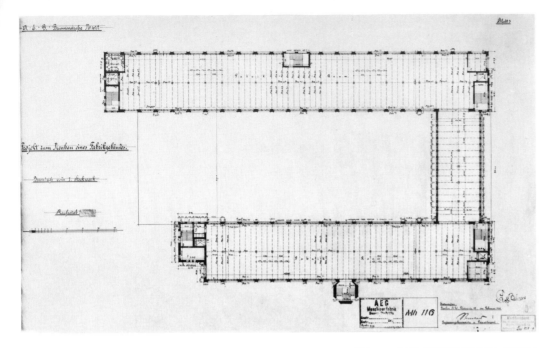

A54
The high-voltage factory: ground plan
of first floor in the original plan of
27 February 1909.

A55
Section in drawing of 27 February
1909.

A56
Drawing of east side of high-voltage
factory, photographed 11 March
1909.

A57
Drawing of west side of high-voltage
factory.

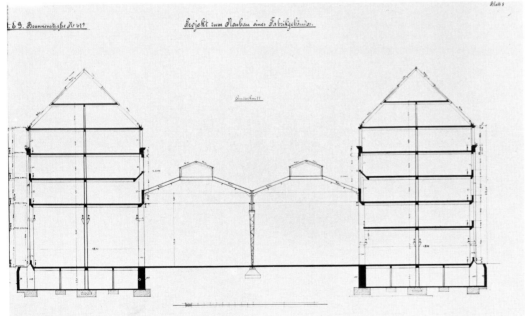

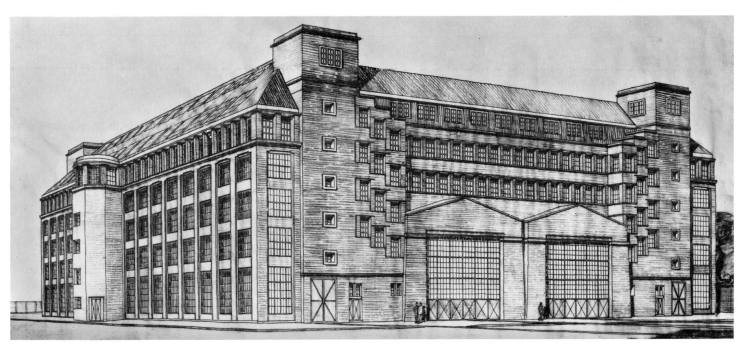

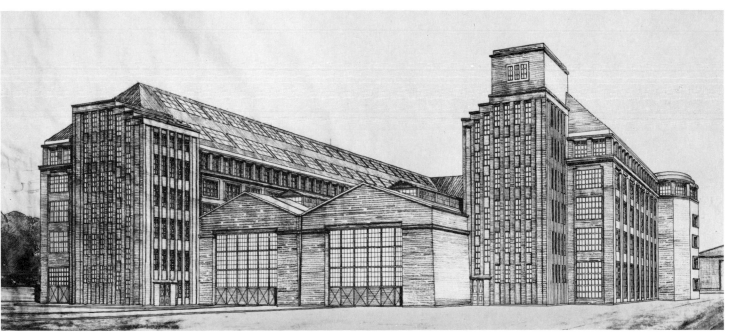

A58
Watercolors of the high-voltage
factory, photographed 10 June 1909.
From *Der Industriebau*.

Catalog • 296

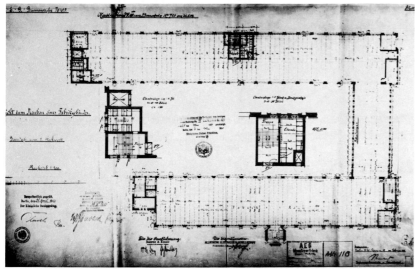

A59
Plan of first floor in original version of 27 February 1909, with additions from 24 March 1910.

A60
Elevation of west front in supplementary drawing of 24 March 1910.

A61
Elevation of north front in supplementary drawing of 24 March 1910.

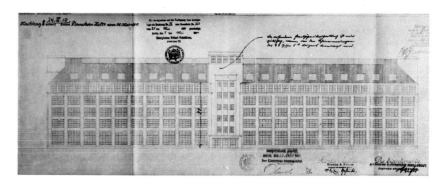

A62
State of construction on 1 June 1909

A63
State of construction on 1 July 1909.

A64
State of construction on 1 April 1910.

A65
State of construction on 1 June 1910.

A66
North and west fronts of high-voltage
factory, 11 January 1912.

A67
Stair tower on the north front,
17 September 1910.

A68
Interior view of window in high-voltage factory.

A69
Staircase in high-voltage factory.

A70
Workshop in high-voltage factory.

A71
Interior view of double hall.

A72
South and east fronts of high-voltage
factory, 19 September 1913.

A73
The high-voltage factory at night,
illuminated by arc lamps, 28 December
1910.

• A74–A78
Design for a Portal
(Gate 4)
after 1909

This design, consisting of a formal entrance arch with double openings, a gatekeeper's room, and other rooms, was for the entrance to the AEG's Brunnenstrasse site at the corner of Gustav-Meyer-Allee and Hussitenstrasse. The location was determined by existing railroad tracks. None of the designs was executed.

Literature
Mannheimer 1911, p. 122; Hoeber 1913, p. 144 and illustration 164 (variation on second design); Buddensieg 1975, p. 298; Buddensieg and Rogge 1976, pp. 96 ff.

A74
Watercolor of design for Gate 4 on Gustav-Meyer-Allee, photographed 1 October 1909. This first design was marked in on the 1909 general plan of the Brunnenstrasse site (ill. A46).

Catalog • 304

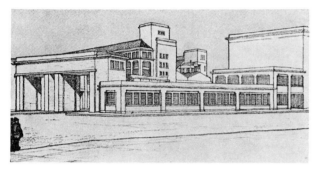

A75
Sketch of second design for Gate 4,
1910–11.

A76
Variation on second design. From
Hoeber 1913.

A77
Watercolor of third design for Gate 4,
photographed 26 August 1911.

A78
Watercolor of the third design as
viewed from inside the factory site,
photographed 26 August 1911.

A79–A82
Entranceway to Factory Area (Gate 4)
1912

After the earlier designs for a formal portal (illustrations A72–A76) were abandoned, a comparatively modest entrance was constructed at the same site, comprising two gatehouses (each 6.4 meters long, 2.90–4.67 meters wide, and 3.9 meters high) and the enclosing walls. The wall on the Hussitenstrasse was 69.7 meters long, and that facing the Humboldthain was 53.6 meters long.

Dating
Planning permission applied for 29 April 1912, building permission granted 26 July (Bauschein no. 1992). Essentially completed in August 1912.

Literature
Buddensieg 1975, p. 298; Buddensieg and Rogge 1976, pp. 97 ff.

A79
Workers leaving Brunnenstrasse site through Gate 4, 9 October 1912.

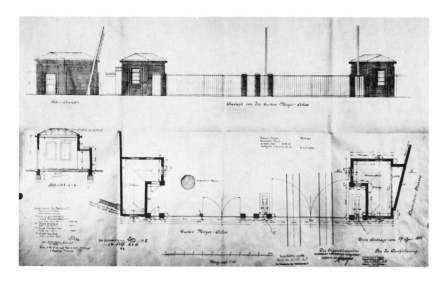

A80
Drawing for entrance gate on Gustav-
Meyer-Allee, 29 April 1912.

A81
Gate 4, at corner of Gustav-Meyer-
Allee and Hussitenstrasse, 23
September 1912.

A82
At gate 4.

Architecture • 307

AEG Small-Motor Factory
1910–1913

Location
Berlin-Wedding, in Brunnenstrasse complex, facing Voltastrasse on site of old small-motor factory.

Building
The building is clad with ironbricks. The Voltastrasse front has five stories (the lower two sharing their windows), and is articulated by a row of giant columns. Each set of seven half-round columns is followed by a square pier. Behind the Voltastrasse block (which is 195.66 meters long, 22.60 meters wide, and 22 meters high) are a side wing (23.97 meters long, 9.61 meters wide, and 10.60 meters high), two middle wings (each 23.97 meters long, 23.47 meters wide, and 22 meters high), and a stair tower (17.13 meters long, 7.76 meters wide, and 22 meters high). On a built area of 5,700 square meters, a usable area of approximately 35,500 square meters was achieved.

Dating and Progress of Construction
Preliminary project submitted 18 February 1910; planning application made 14 June and 18 August; building permission granted 20 September 1910 (Bauschein no. 2986).

After provisional approval had been given on 13 August, building began on 6 September 1910. The first phase included 66 meters of the front block, the side wing, and one of the middle wings. These were completed in rough form in February 1911 and put into service on 18 September 1911.

In the second phase, the front block was extended from 66 to 111.42 meters. This extension was completed by November–December 1911.

In the third phase, the entrance gate originally planned for the east side was abandoned and the stair tower set on the outside of the facade. These deviations from the plan were approved in December 1912 and on 22 August 1913 (Bauschein no. 2315). This phase was completed in rough form in September 1913 and put into service in February 1914.

Building Contractors
Aktiengesellschaft für Bauausführungen, Berlin W.; Thyssen & Co., Berlin N 39; Boswau & Knauer, Berlin W 8.

Literature
Mannheimer 1911, pp. 123 ff.; Pallmann 1912, pp. 210–212; *AEG-Führer*, 1912, p. 29; Hoeber 1913, pp. 140 ff.; *AEG-Ztg.* 15, no. 11 (May 1913), pp. 9–11; Mannheimer 1913, pp. 40 ff.; Hilberseimer 1927, p. 56; *GBK* 1928, nos. 2025–2027; Cremers 1928, pp. 9 ff. and plates 30 ff.; Hirschberg 1929–30, p. 41; Rave and Knöfel 1963, object 93; Rave and Knöfel 1968, object 214; Anderson 1968, pp. 298 ff.; *BusB* 9 (1971), pp. 54 ff.; Buddensieg 1975, pp. 287–290; Buddensieg and Rogge 1976, pp. 97 ff.

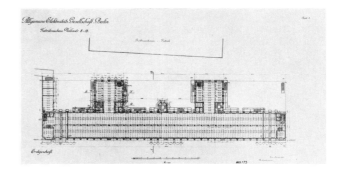

A83
Original plan of ground floor of small-motor factory.

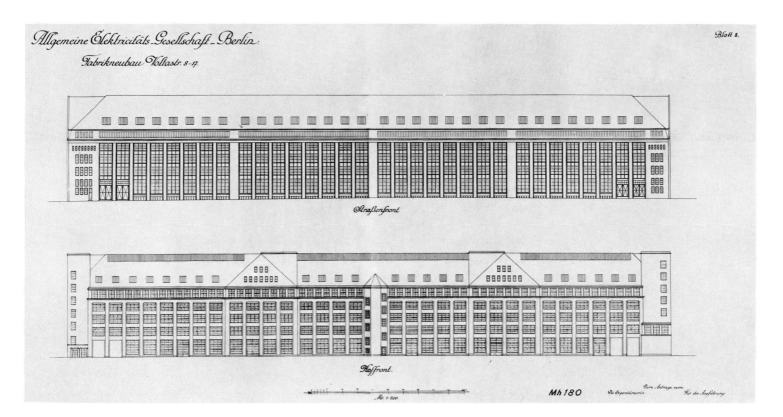

A84
Elevations of street and courtyard
fronts.

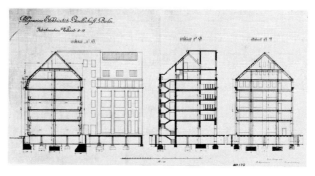

A85
Three sections.

A86
Excavation work for small-motor
factory, 1 September 1910.

A87
State of construction during first phase,
November 1910.

A88
The Berliner Elektrizitäts-Werke
building and the house at 18
Voltastrasse between the old railway-
equipment factory and the small-motor
factory.

A90
Courtyard side of small-motor factory during first building phase, 1 March 1911.

A91
Small-motor factory during second building phase, 2 October 1911.

A89
Facade of first completed phase, 22 August 1911.

A92
The two middle wings on the courtyard side, 12 December 1913.

A93
State of work on third phase, late June 1913.

A95
Double doors on stair tower, 11 March 1914.

A96
Large entrance doors, 11 March 1914.

A94
State of work on Voltastrasse front, 1 August 1911.

A97
Western end of Voltastrasse front.

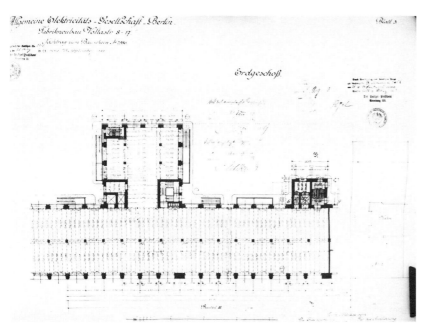

A98
Plan showing alterations at eastern end of small-motor factory (cf. ill. A83).

A99
Amended elevations of street and courtyard fronts (cf. ill. A84).

A100
Elevations of stair tower on courtyard side.

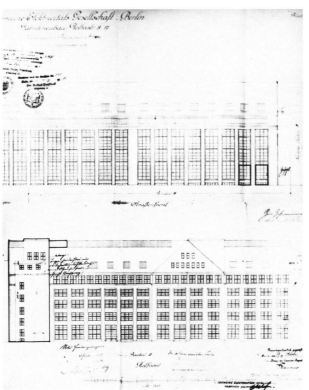

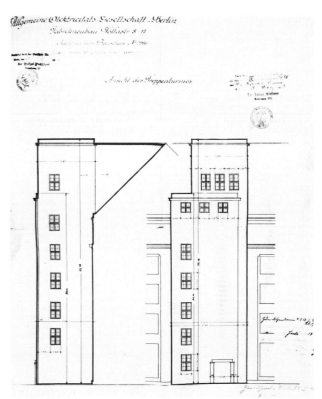

A101
Courtyard side with stair tower at
eastern end of small-motor factory,
25 October 1913.

A102
Eastern end of Voltastrasse facade,
25 October 1913.

A103
Complete Voltastrasse front of small-
motor factory as seen from southwest,
13 October 1913.

Architecture • 317

A104
Detail of facade in present condition.

•A106–A111
Redesign of Roof Garden
1911

This roof garden was located on
top of the AEG's administration
building and large-machine hall on
the Brunnenstrasse in Berlin-Wedding. There had been a simpler
layout on this roof since May–June
1906, probably constructed for the
reception held on 12 July 1906 to
mark the fiftieth anniversary of the
Verein Deutscher Ingenieure. The
earliest photograph of the redesigned roof garden dates from 1
July 1907.

Literature
AEG-Führer, 1912, pp. 33–35;
Fürst 1915, p. 98; Buddensieg
1975, p. 279; Buddensieg and
Rogge 1976, pp. 97 ff.

A106
Buffet held on old roof garden to mark
fiftieth anniversary of Verein Deutscher
Ingenieure, 12 June 1906.

A107
Garden furniture by Peter Behrens on
old roof garden, 26 August 1909.

A109
The roof garden as laid out by
Behrens, photographed 4 October
1913.

A110
Guests on the roof garden.
Dr. Hamburger, Brussels.

A111
The AEG trademark used as a floral
decoration on the roof garden.

•A112–A121
New Factory for Railway Equipment (AEG)
1911–12

Location
Berlin-Wedding, in Brunnenstrasse factory complex, facing Voltastrasse, on site of foundry and stamping shop, connecting with the neighboring building of the old railway-equipment factory.

Building
The factory is made up of a block facing the Voltastrasse (street front 72.68 meters long; courtyard front 61.63 meters long, 21.9 meters wide, and 20.86 meters high); a courtyard wing 131.51 meters long, 22 meters wide, and 22 meters high; two stair towers, each 10.64 meters long, 7.8 meters wide, and 22 meters high; and a third stair tower in the corner of the yard, 6.53 meters long, 6.55 meters wide, and 22 meters high.

Planning
This factory was planned at the same time as the adjoining assembly hall for large machines (illustrations A121 ff.). The two, linked sites were at 25–31 Hussitenstrasse and 23–28 Voltastrasse. The preliminary project was submitted on 29 April 1911; the watercolor was photographed on 29 June and the working drawings in July. The factories were added to the general plan in August–September. Provisional building permission was granted on 4 September and final permission on 28 October 1911 (Bauschein no. 3987).

Construction and Dating
Construction begun in September 1911. First phase: Block on Voltastrasse and connection to old factory. Shells completed 11 January and 21 February 1912, fitted out at beginning of March, and put into service on 15 April. Second phase: Courtyard wing at eastern end of machine hall. Shells completed 29 August and 16 September 1912, fitted out in September, and put into service on 25 February 1913.

Building Contractors
Boswau & Knauer, Berlin W 8

Literature
DBH 15 (1911), pp. 234 and 238; Hoeber 1913, pp. 144 ff.; Mannheimer 1913, p. 39; Hirschberg 1929–30, pp. 42 ff.; Banham 1960, pp. 82 ff.; Anderson 1968, pp. 300 ff.; *BusB* 9 (1971), p. 55; Buddensieg 1975, pp. 290–292; Buddensieg and Rogge 1976, pp. 99 ff.

A112
Building fronts on Voltastrasse. Left to right: new factory for railway equipment, old factory for railway equipment, Berliner Elektrizitäts-Werke, dwelling, small-motor factory. 1 April 1912.

A113
Facade of new factory for railway
equipment on Voltastrasse, beside old
factory (cf. ill. A53), 1 May 1912.

A114
Courtyard front of new railway-
equipment factory, 30 September
1912.

A117
Sections through the projected buildings.

A115
Detail of northern end of courtyard wing, 15 July 1913.

A116
Ground plan of assembly hall for large machines and new railway-equipment factory, drawn July 1911.

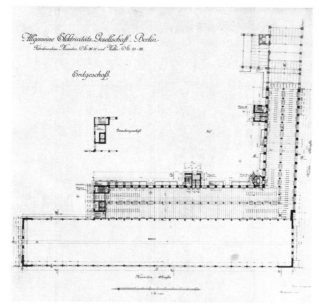

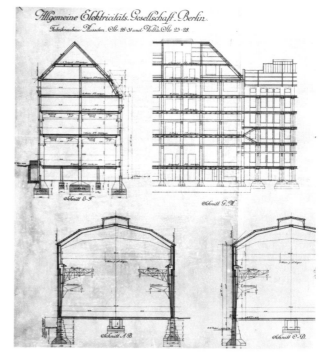

A118
Work on courtyard wing of new railway-equipment factory, 29 June 1912.

A119
Roof cladding and skylights, 5 June 1914.

A120
Elevations of courtyard, drawn July 1911.

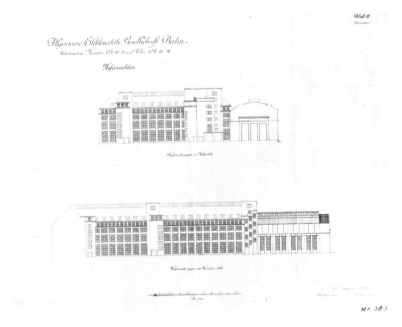

A121
Watercolor of new factory for railway
equipment and assembly hall for large
machines, photographed 29 June
1911.

• A122–A137
Assembly Hall for Large Machines (AEG)
1912

Location
Berlin-Wedding, in Brunnenstrasse factory complex, at 25–31 Hussitenstrasse and 29 Voltastrasse. Although the plot directly on the corner of Hussitenstrasse and Voltastrasse did not yet belong to the AEG, it was incorporated in the plans from the outset.

Building
A large hall, 138.88 meters long (later extended to 180 meters), width 33 meters and 30.94 meters respectively, height 24 meters, area 5,400 square meters. Steel skeleton filled in with brick and glass; roof originally covered entirely with glass. Inside, three different crane installations set one above the other: on a 15-meter-high track, two traveling cranes, each with a lifting capacity of 75,000 kilograms; below, bracket cranes, each with a lifting capacity of 5,000 kilograms, and slewing cranes with a lifting capacity of 2,000 kilograms.

Planning
The hall was planned in conjunction with the new factory for railway equipment (illustrations A112 ff.). Alterations to the plan to increase the height and width of the three windows and the doors in the north end gable wall were submitted in drawings dated 2 May 1912.

Construction and Dating
Construction begun in January 1912. First phase: Hall at 26–31 Hussitenstrasse. Shell completed in July 1912, taken over in rough form on 16 September, put into service on 5 December 1912. Second phase: Extension of the hall by four bays on the newly acquired corner site. Planning permission applied for 31 October 1928, official building inspection on 9 November 1928. Project architect: Ernst Ziesel.

Building Contractors
First phase: Deutsch-Luxemburgische Bergwerks u. Hütten AG, Abt. Dortmunder Union, Dortmund; large door in north end gable wall by Firma R. Blume, Kunst- u. Bauschlosserei, Berlin-Charlottenburg. Second phase: Dortmunder Union and Held & Francke, Berlin W, Knesebeckstrass 59/60.

Literature
Hoeber 1913, pp. 144 ff.; *IB* 6, no. 9 (1915), pp. 411 ff.; Fürst 1915, pp. 96 ff.; Behne 1920, p. 275; de Fries 1920–21, pp. 127 ff.; Behne 1926 (1964), pp. 37 and 76; Cremers 1928, plates 28 ff.; Hirschberg 1929–30, p. 41; Gerhardt 1929–30, pp. 495 ff.; Hamann 1933, pp. 887 ff.; Banham 1960, p. 83; *BusB* 9 (1971), pp. 55 and 97; Buddensieg 1975, pp. 292–296; Buddensieg and Rogge 1976, pp. 99 ff.

A122
Scaffolding being erected at beginning of construction of assembly hall for large machines, 3 January 1912.

A123
Erecting the steel frame, 9 March 1912.

A124
Filling in the steel skeleton, 23 March 1912.

A125
State of construction on 27 April 1912.

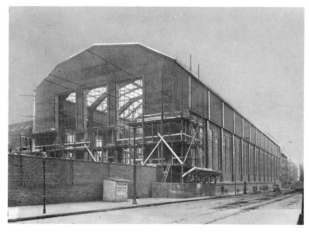

A128
The hall with the completed north front.

A126
State of construction on 11 May 1912.

A127
Installing a traveling crane, 15 May 1912.

A129
Assembly hall for large machines on completion of first phase, 6 July 1912.

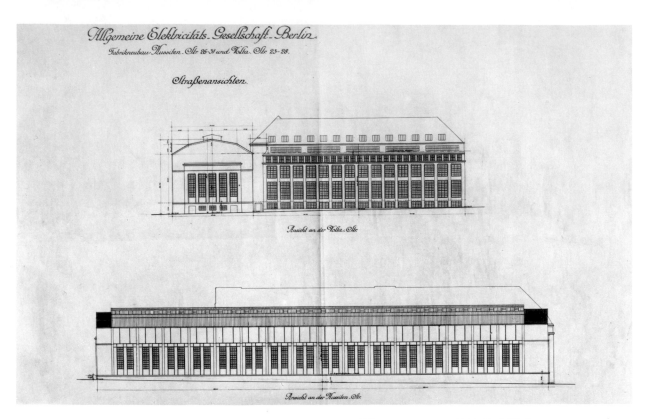

A130
Street front of assembly hall, drawn
July 1911.

A131
Sections through assembly hall.

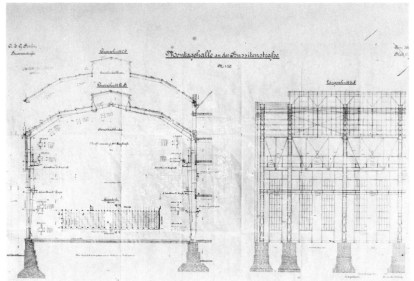

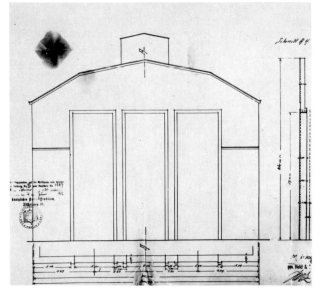

A132
Subsequent drawing of alterations to
north-end gable wall.

A133
Assembly hall with flanking courtyard wing of new factory for railway equipment, 10 May 1913.

A134
Hussitenstrasse front of assembly hall, 7 May 1912.

A135
Glass roof of assembly hall.

A136
Crane lifting casing of a three-phase generator, 1 October 1912.

• A138
AEG Factory at Riga
1913

Literature
Cremers 1928, p. 25.

A138
The AEG factory at Riga, 1913.

• A139–A142
AEG Porcelain, Oilcloth, and Paint Factories
1910–11

Location
AEG site at Hennigsdorf, near Berlin.

Buildings
Porcelain factory: five linked halls, 135 meters long and 100 meters wide (three halls for porcelain manufacture, one for heating appliances, and one for the production of Mikanit insulating material). Oilcloth and paint factories: two- and three-story brick buildings, respectively, both cubelike in form with flat roofs.

Planning
The plans for the Hennigsdorf factories had been drawn up by 1910.

Dating
Porcelain factory: Excavation work begun and foundation stone laid 2 January 1911; production commenced in the summer of 1911; one hall added in September 1911. Oilcloth factory: Put into service in September 1911. Paint factory: Drawing of elevation dated 14 February 1911; factory put into service in September 1911.

Literature
Hoeber 1913, pp. 147 and 150 and illustrations 169–171; *JDW* 1913, p. 9; *IB* 1915, pp. 396 ff.; Fürst 1915, p. 92; *ZdtB* 17 (1918), pp. 142 ff.; *AEG-Taschenbuch* 1919, pp. 36–38; R. Sprenger, "Wie Hennigsdorf wurde," *Spannung. AEG-Umschau* 11 (August 1928), pp. 326 ff.; Lindner 1927, illustration 436; Cremers 1928, p. 163; Hirschberg 1929–30, p. 42; Neumeyer 1977, pp. 210 ff.

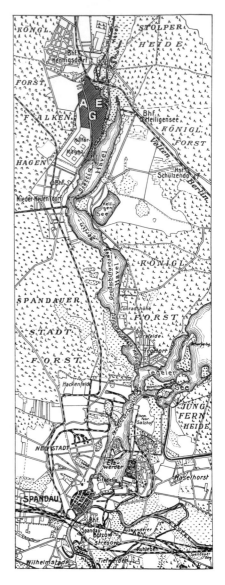

A139
Site of AEG factory complex at Hennigsdorf, on main waterway from Berlin to Stettin.

A140
The porcelain factory, 10 September 1912.

A141
The oilcloth factory.

A142
Sketch with side elevation and section of paint factory.

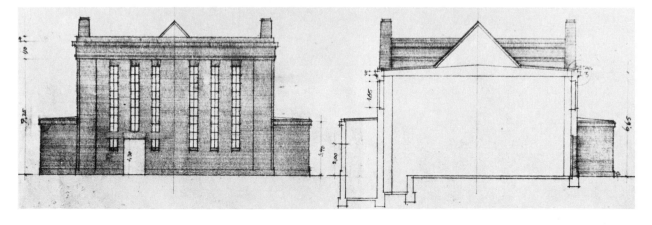

• A143–A150
AEG Locomotive Factory
1913

Location
AEG site at Hennigsdorf, near Berlin.

Buildings
This was a factory complex made up of several buildings: the main halls, a boiler-making shop, a forge, offices, and storehouses. The main building consisted of three (later four) identical halls, each 100 meters long, 26 meters wide, and 21 meters high, constructed in an impressively simple form with steel frames and brick and glass infills. Each of the halls was fitted with a traveling crane with a lifting capacity of 25,000 kilograms. In the third hall, which was used for assembling the locomotives, there was also a crane with a capacity of 50,000 kilograms. This crane could lift a completed locomotive over others still being built and place it on a particular track. A turntable with a carrying capacity of 120,000 kilograms linked the halls.

Slightly removed from the main halls was the shop where the boilers for the steam locomotives were made. Its two halls were similar to the main halls, and were both 100 meters long, 50 meters wide, and 20 meters high.

The forge was lower than the other buildings and occupied an area of 125 × 43 meters. The individual parts were formed here using hydraulic presses, compressed-air and drop hammers, and forging presses.

Offices and storerooms were housed in the production halls and also in separate buildings.

Dating
Construction was begun in the autumn of 1913. The steel skeleton of the three large halls was completed in November, and the infilling walls and glazing were finished by the end of 1913. The fourth hall, the office buildings, the boiler-making shop, and the forge were added later; these were photographed in August and November 1918.

Literature
Fürst 1915, pp. 89 ff.; *AEG Taschenbuch*, 1919, pp. 39 ff.; Hirschberg 1929–30, pp. 42–43; Gerhardt 1929–30, p. 500.

A143
The AEG locomotive factory, 19 May 1915.

A144
The steel skeleton of the three halls,
24 November 1913.

A145
The interior, 24 November 1913.

A147
The first building phase of the
locomotive factory, 16 January 1914.

A148
The office building of the locomotive factory, 13 August 1918.

A149
The boiler shop and the forge of the locomotive factory, 12 September 1918.

A150
The locomotive factory, with the fourth
hall, 13 August 1918.

•A151–A153

Halls of AEG Aeronautical Department
1915

The airplane factory, founded in 1910, was expanded during the war to an area of approximately 70,000 square meters. The factory made military planes during the war and commercial planes afterward.

Location
Southern part of AEG site at Hennigsdorf.

Buildings
Four wide adjacent halls with steel skeletons and brick and glass infilling, the roofs entirely glazed. Linked to the factory were plants making oxygen, acetylene, and tubing.

Dating
Construction was begun at the start of 1915; the steel skeleton was completed by the beginning of February and production was underway in the summer.

Literature
Fürst 1915, p. 92; *AEG-Taschenbuch*, 1919, p. 41.

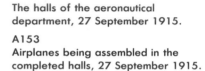

A152
The halls of the aeronautical department, 27 September 1915.

A153
Airplanes being assembled in the completed halls, 27 September 1915.

A151
The steel skeleton for the halls of the aircraft factory, 3 February 1915.

• A154–A162
Nationale Automobil
Aktien-Gesellschaft
(NAG), Berlin-
Oberschöneweide
1915–16

These were new buildings of the former Neue Automobil AG, whose name was changed on 1 April 1915.

The seven-story main building, with a tower 70 meters high, was wrapped around the large machine hall like a horseshoe. Beside the main hall were repair shops. The forge and the chassis works also had large buildings of their own. The front of the main building had a total length of over 1,000 meters and an area of 54,180 square meters. The internal layout of the factory reflected the latest technical advances; there were ten stair towers plus paternosters and 18 sets of double lifts, four of which each had a lifting capacity of 6,000 kilograms and could transport heavy trucks to the roof.

The large machine hall was 100 meters long and 60 meters wide; in addition the repair department occupied 4,500 square meters and the forge 6,000 square meters. The total usable area of the factory was around 70,000 square meters. Up to 1,100 building workers were employed on its construction, and 12 million bricks were laid. The planning was done in 1915 and the construction in 1916, and the factory was put into service in 1917.

A154
The main building. This and ills.
A155–162 are from *Wasmuths Monatshefte für Baukunst.*

A155
Entrance.

A156
Staircase.

A157
Courtyard between double hall and
main building.

A158
Courtyard front of main building.

A159
Corner, stair tower, and outer front of double hall.

A160
Overall view of NAG complex.

A161
Facade of double hall between the
two wings of the main building.

A162
View of the courtyard with the
machine hall during construction.

Architecture • 349

•A163, A164
Designs for Administration Building on Humboldthain
1917

A design for a monumental administration building has survived in photographs of two perspective drawings. The more sketchy drawing measured 10 × 23 centimeters and was on a paper board measuring 18 × 31 centimeters. It shows the administration building flanked by two separate blocks on a site beside the Humboldthain. The second, more detailed drawing is dated "Neub. 24.VIII.17" [Neu-Babelsberg, 24 August 1917].

A163
Perspective drawing of projected administration building at Humboldthain, photographed 27 August 1917.

A164
The projected administration building, drawn 24 August 1917.

• A165–A170

Project for Rebuilding and Extending Turbine-Factory Administration Building

1916

At the beginning of May 1916 a plan was drawn up to add three stories to the administration building of the AEG's turbine factory on the Huttenstrasse in Berlin-Moabit (illustration A21), to increase its height to seven stories. The four lower stories were to be integrated into the new building. When this scheme was turned down by the planning authority, Behrens worked out an alternative plan for extending the old building, which appears in a perspective sketch dated 4 (illustration A169). In this new plan, only the rhythm of receding and protruding bays hinted at the integration of the existing structure. A subsequent scheme (illustration A168) called for a completely new seven-story extension, 25 meters long, 17.52 meters wide, and 22 meters high, directly linked to the east end of the old administration building.

Because of the war no building materials were allocated to this project, and after tireless efforts over many years to have the building permit extended the plan was abandoned in 1924.

Dating
Application to add stories to administration building submitted 12 May 1916 and subsequently rejected. Alteration of plan in favor of extending the block laterally submitted 4 and 13 July, with supplementary applications. Approved on 10 July and 26 September (Bauschein nos. 393 and 732, respectively). Repeated applications for extensions to building permit until 10 April 1923. Project abandoned when building permit expired, 11 April 1924.

Sources
Building files.

A165
Perspective view of proposed further stories for administration building, drawn 12 May 1916.

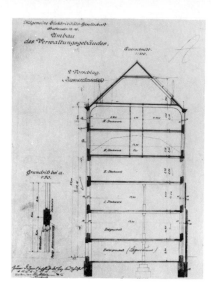

A166
Section through administration building,
drawn 25 February 1916.

A167
Elevations of street and courtyard
fronts.

A168
Elevation of street front of new block
abutting the existing administration
building, drawn 12 July 1916.

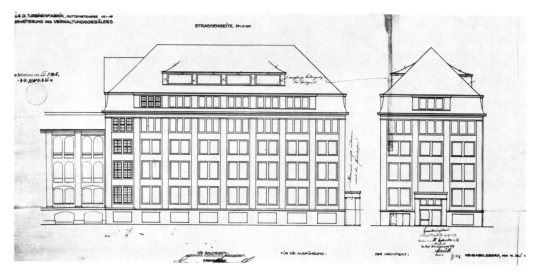

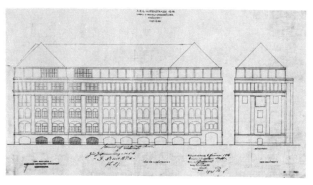

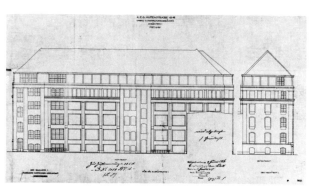

A169
Elevation of courtyard front of new block, drawn 12 July 1916.

A170
Perspective view of remodeled and extended administration building, drawn 4 July 1916.

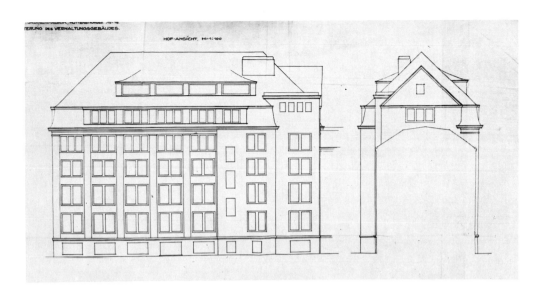

• A171–A174

Design for a Main Administration Building for the AEG

Peter Behrens and Eugen Himmel, 1939

The planned head office of the AEG was to be built in between Lutzowstrasse and Ludendorff-strasse in Berlin. The design, by Behrens in collaboration with the architect Eugen Himmel, had to conform to the existing planning regulations, which aimed to create a complete and unified streets-cape. A monumental office building with a main front 225 meters long was proposed. A dominant central block housing the main entrance was to be flanked by two 100-meter wings. A total usable area of 80,500 square meters was to be achieved with a ground plan covering 12,500 square meters. The office complex was to contain work spaces for around 4,000 workers, conference rooms, salesrooms, and exhibition areas. The planning was completed before October 1939, but the project was never implemented.

Literature

G. Troost (ed.), *Das Bauen im Neuen Reich*, third edition (Bayreuth, 1941), pp. 58 and 78; *Zweite Deutsche Architektur- und Kunsthandwerkausstellung im Haus der Kunst*, exhibition catalog, Munich, 1938–39, nos. 193 and 194 and p. 10; H. Wolff, "Der Neubau des Hauptverwaltungsgebäudes der AEG in Berlin," *Die Baukunst* (October 1939), pp. 447–454; Lanzke 1958; Albert Speer, *Erinnerungen*, seventh edition (Berlin, 1970), p. 159.

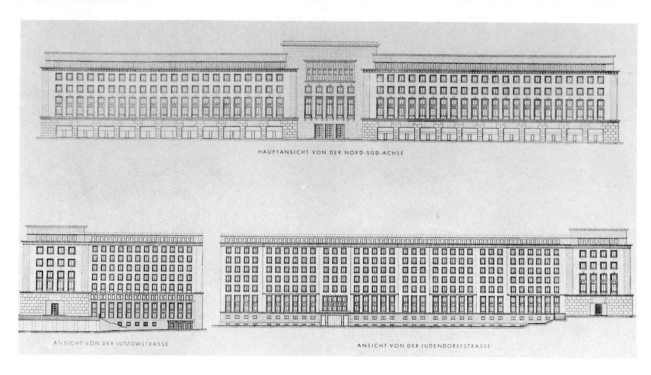

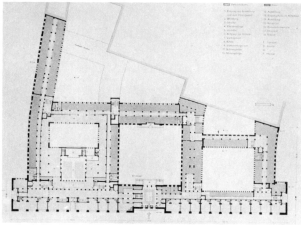

A171
Drawings of planned main office. From *Die Baukunst*, 1939.

A172
Ground plan. From *Die Baukunst*, 1939.

A174
Corner detail. From *Die Baukunst*,
1939.

A173
Detail of main entrance. From *Die
Baukunst*, 1939.

•A175–A177
Designs for Rapid-Transit Line from Gesundbrunnen to Neukölln
1911–12

The AEG railway line from Gesundbrunnen to Neukölln was planned principally as an underground railway, with short elevated sections. For the elevated sections, Behrens designed steel viaducts resting on single-pillar supports (illustration A176) and an overhead station with a covered central platform and entrance staircase. The station design has survived in photographs of two slightly varying drawings. The plan to build the railway was abandoned after the war on economic grounds.

Literature
Wittig 1922, p. 9; Buddensieg and Rogge 1976, p. 102; Sabine Bohle-Heintzenberg, *Architektur der Berliner Hoch- und Untergrundbahn* (Berlin, 1980).

A175
Design for elevated station at Gesundbrunnen (?).

A176
Variation of station design. From Wittig 1922.

A177
Design for viaduct on single supports. From Wittig 1922.

Boathouse for Elektra Rowing Club
1912

This boathouse-clubhouse, on the banks of the River Spree at Berlin-Oberschöneweide, was built for the AEG and BEW staff members who had established the Elektra Rowing Club. The design and the internal fitting were designed to the smallest detail by Behrens. The large, three-story building occupied a ground area of over 300 square meters, with a boathouse (10 × 20 meters), a workshop, and a kitchen on the ground level and clubrooms and single bedrooms on the upper floors. The boathouse was particularly noteworthy for its sensitive external color scheme, with gray-blue slate facings on the walls and roof, white painted woodwork, gray stucco, and violet ironbrick. The colors and fittings for the interior were chosen with equal care. The boathouse was opened formally on 18 May 1912.

Literature
Elektra Ruder-Gesellschaft im Verein der Beamten der AEG und BEW, AEG brochure about the new boathouse (no date); *KGB* 24, no. 10 (1912–13), pp. 192 ff.; Hoeber 1913, pp. 152–155 and illustrations 176–183 (wrongly dated 1910); Mannheimer 1913, p. 41; R. Breuer, *WMB*, 1915–16, pp. 220 ff.; *BM* 14 (1916), plate 104; Müller-Wulckow, *Bauten der Gemeinschaft* (1929), p. 38; *Architekturführer DDR* (1974), object 221.

A178
Elektra boathouse, river front.

A179
Plans of the three floors of the boathouse.

A180
The clubroom, looking toward the veranda.

A181
Street front of boathouse.

A182
First-floor landing. From Hoeber 1913.

•A183
Boathouse in Hennigsdorf
1912

A183
Boathouse in Hennigsdorf,
10 September 1912.

• A184–A190
Workers' Housing on Rathenaustrasse, Hennigsdorf
1910–11

Location
At 14–15 Rathenaustrasse, on the AEG housing estate in Hennigsdorf, opposite the factory site.

Owner
Industriegesellschaft Hennigsdorf am Grossschifffahrtsweg Berlin-Stettin, Bau- und Grundstücksgesellschaft mbH, Berlin (a subsidiary of the AEG).

Building
A three-story double-fronted block, with the central section set back to form a courtyard. All walls built of white-pointed red brick, with white clinker-brick window surrounds. Carefully detailed brickwork, included dentilated frieze under the eaves, dovetailed corners, and curved walls leading into doorways. The block originally contained 34 flats, with a shop and a restaurant on the ground floor.

Dating
This first workers' housing project by Behrens was built in 1910–11, at roughly the same time as the construction of the porcelain factory at Hennigsdorf.

Literature
Karl Ernst Osthaus, *Frankfurter Zeitung*, 10 February 1910; Hoeber 1913, pp. 150–152 and illustrations 172–175; *AEG-Ztg* 15, no. 11 (May 1913), pp. 9–11; "Arbeiterhäuser bei den AEG-Fabriken in Hennigsdorf," *JB* 6, no. 4 (April 1915), pp. 332 ff.; U. Dietrich, "AEG-Siedlung in Hennigsdorf bei Berlin," *BW* 22 (1929), p. 1; *Hennigsdorfer Siedlungsgemeinschaft mbH*, no date (1925?); Kadatz 1977, p. 43, illustration 51, pp. 52, 55; Neumeyer 1977, pp. 216–227, 328; Neumeyer, "Werkwohnungsbau um 1900," *Werkbundjahrbuch* 3 (Berlin, 1978).

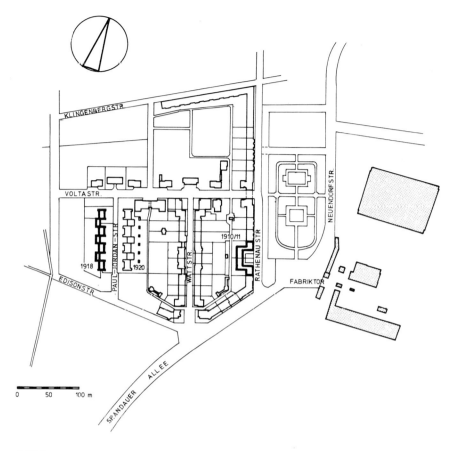

A184
Site plan.

A185
Floor plans.

A186
Preparatory sketch of housing block.
From Hoeber 1913.

A187
The completed block on
Rathenaustrasse.

A188
The open courtyard facing the street, with entrance to staircase.

A189
Present-day view from street.

A190
Present-day view from garden.

• A191–A209
AEG Estate, Oberschöneweide
1915

Location
Berlin-Oberschöneweide, on site bordered by Roedernstrasse, Zeppelinstrasse, Fontanestrasse, and An der Wuhlheide.

Owner
Gemeinnützige Baugesellschaft mbH Oberschöneweide (founded by AEG in 1914).

First Project (Unrealized)
The original housing project for Oberschöneweide was designed by Peter Behrens between 1911 and 1914 as an unusually large scheme on an urban scale, with around 700 dwellings.

Second Project (Realized in 1915)
Two-story row housing, built around perimeter of site, with entrances on Zeppelinstrasse and An der Wuhlheide giving access to the interior (which was divided into tenants' gardens). The estate contained some 170 dwellings, of which 31 were one-family houses on Zeppelinstrasse. The houses on the remaining three streets were divided up into four- to six-family flats.

Literature
WMB 5 (1920–21), illustrations on pp. 329 and 330; Cremers 1928, p. 128 (wrongly called "Siedlung Lichtenberg") and p. 164; Müller-Wulckow 1928, p. 63; *BusB* 5a, p. 365, object 221; *Architekturführer DDR* (1974), p. 138, object 219; Neumeyer 1977, p. 43 and illustrations 47–49; Buddensieg and Rogge 1976, pp. 99 ff.

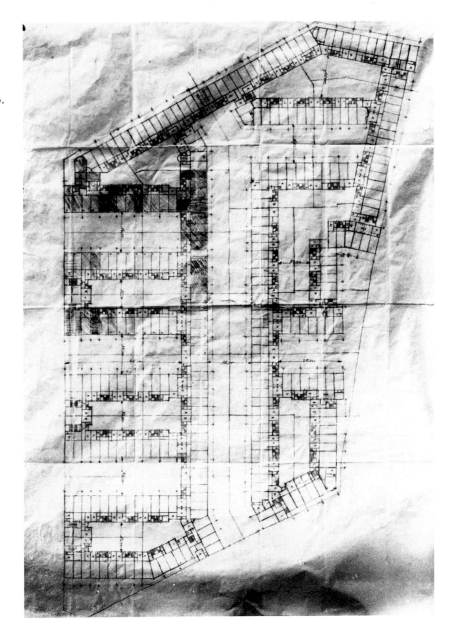

A191
Site plan of projected AEG estate at Oberschöneweide, 1915.

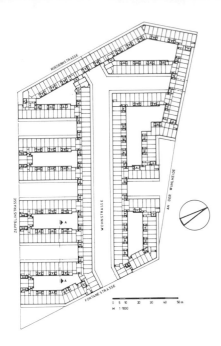

A192
Copy of 1915 site plan.

A193
Sketch of Zeppelinstrasse front.

A194
Sketch of view along Zeppelinstrasse.

A195
Sketch of view of street front on An der Wuhlheide.

A196
Sketch of view along Wohnstrasse.

A197
Site plan of estate built at
Oberschöneweide.

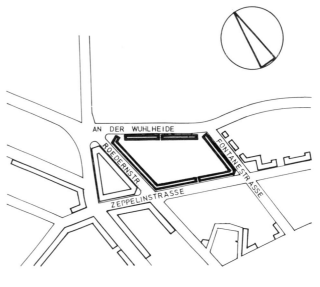

A198
Interior of site bordered by
Roedernstrasse, Zeppelinstrasse (right),
Fontanestrasse (opposite), and An der
Wuhlheide (left) in present condition.

A199
Row housing in the Oberschöneweide estate: corner of Roedernstrasse (left) and Zeppelinstrasse in present condition.

A200
Row housing on Zeppelinstrasse.

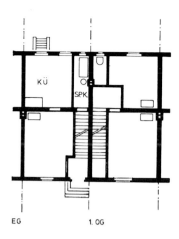

KÜ OI SPK.

EG 1. OG

A201
Plans of ground and first floors of one-family house on Zeppelinstrasse.

A202
Doorways on Zeppelinstrasse in present condition.

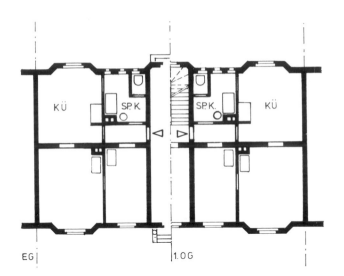

A204
Reconstruction of plans of ground and
first floors of row house on
Fontanestrasse.

KÜ SP. K. SP. K. KÜ

EG 1. OG

A203
Row house, 12a Fontanestrasse.

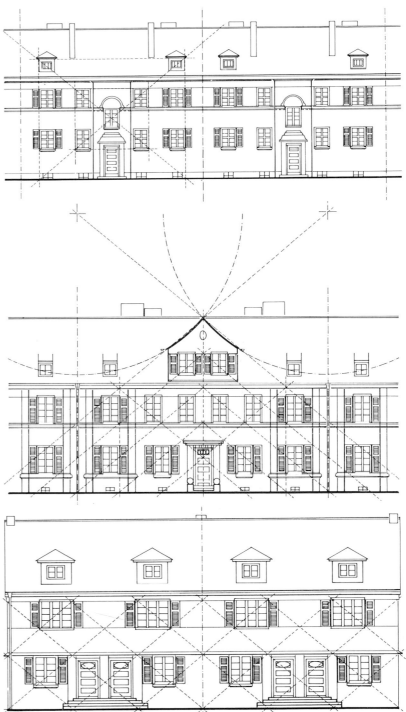

A205
Row housing, An der Wuhlheide.

A206
Studies on proportions of house facades on An der Wuhlheide, Fontanestrasse, Roedernstrasse, and Zeppelinstrasse.

A207
House at corner of An der Wuhlheide
and Fontanestrasse.

A208
Row housing on Fontanestrasse.

Workers' Housing on Paul Jordan Strasse, Hennigsdorf
1918–19

Location
Paul Jordan Strasse, on the AEG housing estate in Hennigsdorf, near the factory site; see illustration A183.

Owner
Hennigsdorfer Siedlungsgemein-schaft, a subsidiary of the AEG founded in 1919 as the successor to the Industriegesellschaft Hennigs-dorf am Grossschifffahrtsweg Berlin-Stettin, Bau- und Grundstücksgesellschaft mbH Berlin).

Buildings
The houses on Paul Jordan Strasse were laid out according to the principle of Gruppenbauweise (cluster building), which had been expounded by Peter Behrens and his collaborator Heinrich de Fries in their book *Vom sparsamen Bauen* (1918). Accordingly, every third unit in the row of two-story houses was set back from the street line to create front courtyards, each giving access to six single-family dwell-ings. The houses were constructed out of untreated breeze blocks, whose grayness was relieved only by the woodwork, such as the win-dow frames, the boarding under the eaves, and the garden sheds. The row housing opposite was built in 1920 to a different design.

Literature
See above, illustrations A183 ff.; Peter Behrens, ''Die Gruppenbau-weise,'' *WMB* 4 (1919–20), pp. 122–127; *Hennigsdorfer Sied-lungsgemeinschaft mbH*, no date (1925?); Cremers 1928, illustration 130; Neumeyer 1977, pp. 251–255, 329, illustrations 117, 118; Kadatz 1977, p. 43, illustra-tions 53, 54 (wrongly dated ''1910–11'').

A210
Row housing on Paul Jordan Strasse. Courtesy of Hennigsdorfer Siedlungsgesellschaft mbH.

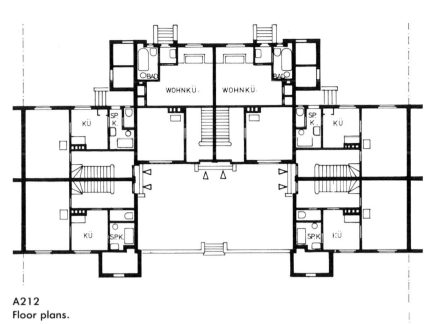

A212
Floor plans.

A211
View into a courtyard.

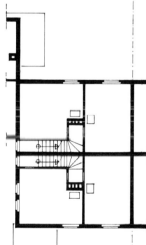

Products

Karin Wilhelm

Invitation Card to Exhibition of Tools and Appliances
1910

This invitation was sent out by the AEG to publicize its newly opened exhibition of electrical tools and household appliances in the shop at 4 Königgrätzer Strasse. The text, in Behrens Roman script, was printed in black on an ivory-colored background. The initial D was decorated in gold (cf. G24), and the border of double volutes in gold was framed by a black line. The size of the frame was 22.1 × 15.3 cm.

References
AEG-Ztg. 13, no. 6 (December 1910), suppl. 10; Buddenseig and Rogge 1977, p. 5, illustration 6.

Ausstellung der AEG
für Haushalt und Werkstatt

Telephon: Amt VI, 4646   Berlin, Datum des Poststempels

Die Anwendung der Elektricität in Haushalt und Werkstatt ist in stetiger Steigerung begriffen, hat aber noch keineswegs den Umfang erreicht, der ihrer Nützlichkeit entspricht. Kleinmotoren und Heizapparate leisten wichtige Dienste, von denen wir durch Vorführung im Betriebe weiteren Kreisen Kenntnis zu verschaffen wünschen. Diesem Zweck soll die dauernde

Ausstellung
Königgrätzerstraße 4

dienen, die wir neu eröffnet haben. Wir laden zum Besuch derselben ergebenst ein.

Allgemeine
Elektricitäts-Gesellschaft

• P2, P3

West End Salesroom, 117 Potsdamer Strasse, Berlin
1910

The door and window surrounds of the salesroom were white marble panels inside dark frames. The window shelves were arranged according to the products on display, with a three-sided backing screen (sometimes with a poster in the central panel) (see *JDW* 1913, illustration 93). The door had a honeycomb AEG trademark on glass (see G75 ff.), and the square fanlight contained a circular extractor fan set in a geometric framework. The interior walls and ceiling were geometrically articulated, with wood and stucco coffering and moldings.

References
Stoedtner photos 71976 (shopfront), 72522 (interior); Mannheimer 1911, illustration p. 137; *JDW* 1912, illustration 64; Hoeber 1913, pp. 155 ff. and illustrations 187 and 188; *JDW* 1913, illustration 93; Meyer-Schönbrunn 1913, illustrations 49 and 51; *Deutsche Bauhütte* 18 (1914), illustrations pp. 110, 114, and 127; *MdBEW* 11, no. 11 (November 1915), p. 176.

P2

P4–P9
Salesroom,
4 Königgrätzer Strasse,
Berlin
1910

The windows and door of this salesroom were framed by a protruding dark frame, which contrasted with the outer surround of white marble (cf. Mannesmann-Werke administration building, Düsseldorf, 1911–12).

References
Stoedtner photos 72517 (shopfront), 72520 (vestibule); Hagen photos 42517 (shopfront) and 42520 (vestibule); announcement of showroom opening, *AEG-Ztg.* 13, no. 6 (December 1910), suppl. 10; *MdBEW* 6, no. 12 (December 1910), pp. 178–184; "Weihnachtsmarkt und Elektricität," showroom advertisement, *AEG-Ztg.* 13, no. 7 (January 1911), p. 13; *MbBEW* 7, no. 3 (March 1911), pp. 33–40; Mannheimer 1911, pp. 136 ff.; *MdBEW* 8, no. 3 (March 1912), pp. 34 ff.; Meyer Schönbrunn 1913, illustrations on pp. 50 and 52–54; Hoeber 1913, pp. 155 ff. and illustrations 184–186; *JDW* 1913, illustrations 80 (upper) and 93 (lower); *MdBEW* 9, no. 11 (November 1913), p. 168; *MdBEW* 10, no. 11 (November 1914), p. 146.

P4

P5
Vestibule. Courtesy of Karl Ernst Osthaus Museum, Hagen.

P6
Reception room. Courtesy of Karl Ernst Osthaus Museum, Hagen.

P7

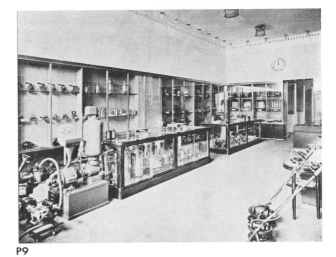

P9

P8

• P10–P12

Exhibition in Administration Building, Friedrich-Karl-Ufer, Berlin

The basement of the administration building, originally planned by Alfred Messel as a canteen (see plans, TU Berlin, inventory nos. 12057 and 12067), was converted in 1908 to house a permanent exhibition of AEG products. Behrens was probably involved in the conversion.

References
MdBEW 4, no 7 (July 1908), pp. 105–110; 5, no. 3 (March 1909), pp. 45, 46; 6, no. 2 (February 1910); 8, no. 11 (November 1912), pp. 171 ff.; 12, no. 9 (September 1916), p. 143; 12, no. 11 (November 1916), p. 175.

P10
From *MdBEW*.

•P13

Exhibition Room in Electrical-Appliance Factory, Ackerstrasse, Berlin

Products were displayed in glass cabinets and on the walls. Under the deep coffers of the ceiling the new, Behrens-designed arc lamps hung beside the older models, which were marked "ÄLTERE AUSFÜHRUNG."

References
Hoeber 1913, p. 104; *JDW* 1913, illustration 80; Meyer-Schönbrunn 1913, pp. 55 and 56; Buddenseig and Rogge 1977, p. 125.

P13
From Meyer-Schönbrunn 1913.

P11
From *MdBEW.*

P12
From *MdBEW.*

•P14
Earlier Arc Lamps, and Flammeco and High-Intensity Lamps by Behrens

Reference
P. Schmit, "Aus dem historischen Museum der AEG," *Spannung. Die AEG-Umschau*, 1927–28, no. 5 (February 1928), pp. 148–149. See also illustrations P27 and P31.

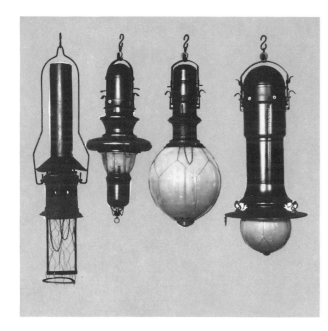

P14

•P15
Prospectus for Earlier High-Intensity Arc Lamp

P15

•P16
Arc Lamp
1907

Differential AC arc lamp designed to produce shadowless, nondazzling, indirect illumination for interiors. The light was thrown up onto the ceiling by the larger reflector and from there shone down diffusely into the room.

Types
Two different types with varying burning times of approximately 8–10 and 13–16 hours were offered: length 820 mm, reflector diameter 750 mm, 68 marks (1909), PL no. 68216; length 1,000 mm, reflector diameter 750 mm, 74 marks (1909), PL no. 68218.

Finish
Reflector: sheet metal, painted light green with bronze trim.

References
AEG-Bogenlampliste, no. 7 (1909), pp. 10–11; Stoedtner photo 49383; Scheffler 1908, p. 433; Monasch 1909, p. 14; *AFG-Ztg.* 11, no. 12 (June 1909), p. 6; *MdBEW* 7, no. 7 (July 1911); Pudor 1911, p. 297; Hoeber 1913, p. 106, illustration 111; *Casabella* 1960, p. 24 (lamp illustrated upside down); *T.M. AEG-Telefunken* 60, no. 3 (1970), p. 194; Buddensieg and Rogge 1977, p. 127, illustration 7, p. 138 (with earlier model).

LAMPE P.L.Nr. 67216 MIT LATERNE P.L.Nr. 68216

11

P16

Arc Lamp
1907

Differential DC arc lamp with inverted rods (positive rod below) for interior lighting. The small reflector bounced light off the ceiling.

Types
Two different types were offered, with burning times of approximately 10 and 16 hours: length 820 mm, reflector diameter 600 mm, 64 marks (1909), PL no. 68220; length 1,000 mm, reflector diameter 600 mm, 70 marks (1909), PL no. 68222.

Finish
Lamp painted light green with bronze trim, opal-glass reflector.

References
AEG-Bogenlampliste, no. 7 (1909), pp. 8–9; Stoedtner photo 49383; Scheffler 1908, p. 433; Monasch 1909, p. 14; Pudor 1911, p. 297; Buddensieg and Rogge 1977, p. 128, illustration 11, p. 138 (with earlier model).

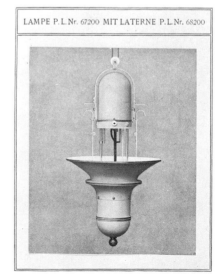

LAMPE P.L.Nr. 67200 MIT LATERNE P.L.Nr. 68200

P17

•P18
Arc Lamp
1907

Differential DC arc lamp for interior lighting, particularly intended for precision work such as that done in a print shop. Semi-indirect illumination was achieved through reflecting the light off the ceiling and also through the direct but diffuse light shining through the opal-glass reflector.

Types
Two different types were offered, with burning times of approximately 10 and 16 hours: length 820 mm, reflector diameter 600 mm, 64 marks (1909), PL no. 68220; length 1,000 mm, reflector diameter 1,000 mm, 70 marks (1909), PL no. 68222.

Finish
Lamp painted light green with bronze trim, opal-glass reflector.

References
AEG-Bogenlampliste, no. 7 (1909), pp. 8–9; Stoedtner photo 49383; Scheffler 1908, p. 433; Monasch 1909, p. 14; Pudor 1911, p. 297; Buddensieg and Rogge 1977, p. 128, illustration 11, p. 138 (with earlier model).

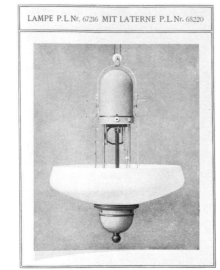

LAMPE P.L.Nr. 67216 MIT LATERNE P.L.Nr. 68220

P18

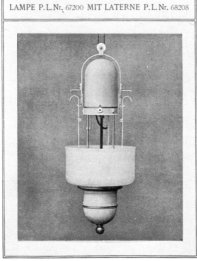

LAMPE P.L.Nr. 67200 MIT LATERNE P.L.Nr. 68208

P19

•P19
Arc Lamp
1907

Differential DC arc lamp with inverted rods (as P17) for interior lighting. Particularly suited for workshops. Semi-indirect illumination was achieved by the same means as in P18.

Types
Two types were offered, with burning times of approximately 10 and 16 hours: length 820 mm, glass globe diameter 320 mm, 51 marks (1909), PL no. 68208; length 1,000 mm, glass globe diameter 320 mm, 57 marks (1909), PL no. 68210.

Finish
Lamp painted light green with bronze trim, matte-glass globe.

References
AEG Bogenlampenliste, no. 7 (1909), pp. 4–5; Hagen photo 13124; Scheffler 1908, p. 433; Widmer 1908, p. 50; Pudor 1911, p. 297; Hellwag 1911, p. 152 (with earlier model); *JDW* 1912, p. 67; Buddensieg and Rogge 1977, p. 129, illustration 12, pp. 138–139.

•P20
Arc Lamp
1907

Arc lamp (AC or DC) for indirect lighting with inverted rods (as P17), small reflector, and glass cover. Lamps with exposed arcs could not be used in rooms containing easily inflammable materials, for example in spinning or weaving mills. It was necessary, therefore, to enclose the entire lamp.

Types
Two types were offered, with burning times of approximately 10 and 16 hours: length 820 mm, reflector diameter 350 mm, 68 marks (1909), PL no. 68228; length 1,000 mm, reflector diameter 350 mm, 74 marks (1909), PL no. 68230.

Finish
Sheet-metal reflector painted light green with bronze trim, clear glass shield between armature and reflector.

References
AEG-Bogenlampenliste, no. 7 (1909), pp. 14–15; Pudor 1911, p. 297; Buddensieg and Rogge 1977, p. 129, illustration 12a, p. 139.

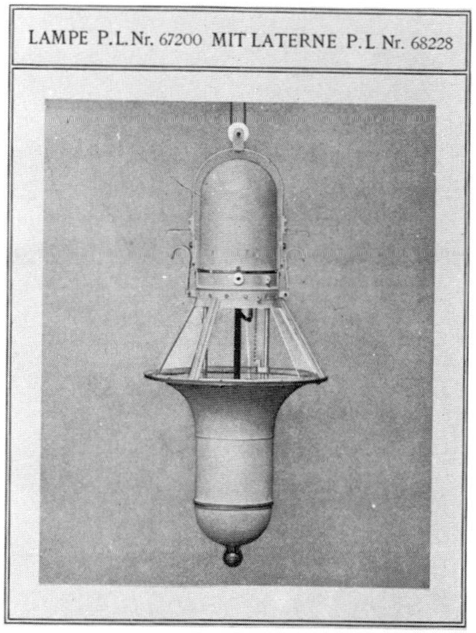

P20

• P21
Arc Lamp
1907

Arc lamp (AC or DC) for semi-indirect lighting with inverted rods and spherical glass globe (see G37). The matte-glass lower half of the globe reflected most of the light upward. The same model was available with normal rods. Both types were intended, like P20, for use in flammable surroundings. The burning time was around 10 hours. Length 820 mm, globe diameter 430 mm, 68 marks (1909), PL no. 68212.

Finish
Painted light green with bronze trim and cap. Glass globe: upper half clear, lower half matte.

References
AEG-Bogenlampenliste, no. 7 (1909), pp. 13–14; Buddensieg and Rogge 1977, p. 129, illustration 12b, p. 139.

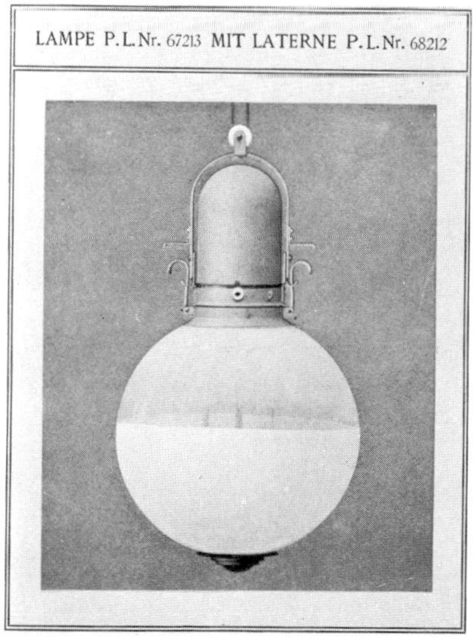

P21

• P22, P23
Arc Lamp
1907

Arc lamp (AC or DC) with inverted rods for semi-indirect lighting, with small matte-glass shade (as P19) and undulating diffuser (P22). In rooms that were too dark, too high, or not painted white, the reflection of the light had to be aided by a platelike reflector mounted on the upper part of the lamp. The plate was either flat or given concentric undulations to create a particularly effective diffuse light. In addition to this model, the following lamps were also available with upper reflectors or diffusers: PL no. 68200 (see P17), PL no. 68212 (see P21), PL no. 68228 (see P20), and PL no. 68212 for alternating current (P23).

Types
Two types were offered, with burning time of approx. 10 and 16 hours: length 820 mm, globe diameter 320 mm, 72.50 marks (1909), PL no. 68208 D; length 1,000 mm, globe diameter 320 mm, 78.50 marks (1909), PL no. 68210 D. Diffuser diameter 1,000 mm, upper reflector diameter 860 mm.

Finish
As P19; diffuser white enamel.

References
AEG Bogenlampenliste, no. 7 (1909), pp. 16–17; Stoedtner photo 49388; Monasch 1909, p. 14; Pudor 1911, p. 297; Mannheimer 1911, p. 140; Pevsner 1957, p. 115 and illustration 82 (wrongly described as a street light); Buddensieg and Rogge 1977, p. 129, illustration 14; p. 139 (with earlier model).

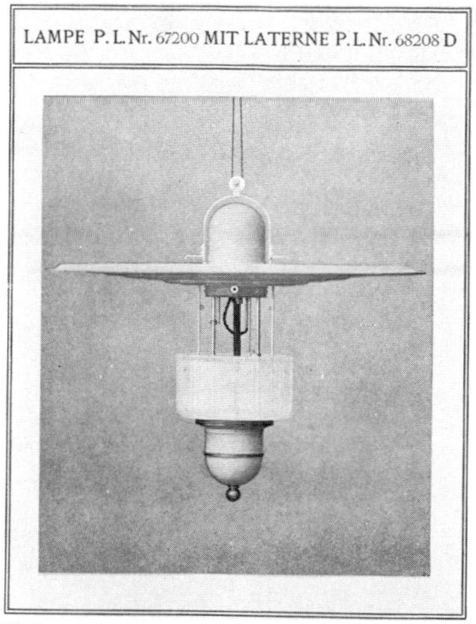

P22

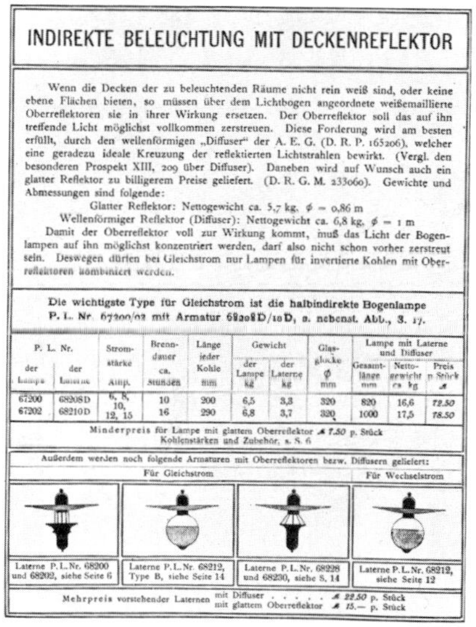

INDIREKTE BELEUCHTUNG MIT DECKENREFLEKTOR

Wenn die Decken der zu beleuchtenden Räume nicht rein weiß sind, oder keine ebene Flächen bieten, so müssen über dem Lichtbogen angeordnete weißemaillierte Oberreflektoren sie in ihrer Wirkung ersetzen. Der Oberreflektor soll das auf ihn treffende Licht möglichst vollkommen zerstreuen. Diese Forderung wird am besten erfüllt, durch den wellenförmigen „Diffuser" der A. E. G. (D. R. P. 165206), welcher eine geradezu ideale Kreuzung der reflektierten Lichtstrahlen bewirkt. (Vergl. den besonderen Prospekt XIII, 209 über Diffuser). Daneben wird auf Wunsch auch ein glatter Reflektor zu billigerem Preise geliefert. (D. R. G. M. 233060). Gewichte und Abmessungen sind folgende:

Glatter Reflektor: Nettogewicht ca. 5,7 kg. ϕ = 0,86 m
Wellenförmiger Reflektor (Diffuser): Nettogewicht ca. 6,8 kg. ϕ = 1 m

Damit der Oberreflektor voll zur Wirkung kommt, muß das Licht der Bogenlampen auf ihn möglichst konzentriert werden, darf also nicht schon vorher zerstreut sein. Deswegen dürfen bei Gleichstrom nur Lampen für invertierte Kohlen mit Oberreflektoren kombiniert werden.

Die wichtigste Type für Gleichstrom ist die halbindirekte Bogenlampe P. L. Nr. 67200/02 mit Armatur 68208D/10D, s. nebenst. Abb., S. 17.

P. L. Nr. der Lampe	P. L. Nr. der Laterne	Stromstärke Amp.	Brenndauer ca. Stunden	Länge jeder Kohle mm	Gewicht der Lampe kg	Gewicht der Laterne kg	Glasglocke ϕ mm	Lampe mit Laterne und Diffuser Gesamtlänge mm	Lampe mit Laterne und Diffuser Nettogewicht ca. kg	Lampe mit Laterne und Diffuser Preis p. Stück ℳ
67200	68208D	6, 8, 10, 12, 15	10	200	6,5	3,3	320	820	16,6	72.50
67202	68210D		16	290	6,8	3,7	320	1000	17,5	78.50

Minderpreis für Lampe mit glattem Oberreflektor ℳ 7.50 p. Stück
Kohlenstärken und Zubehör, s. S. 6

Außerdem werden noch folgende Armaturen mit Oberreflektoren bezw. Diffusern geliefert:

Für Gleichstrom:
Laterne P. L. Nr. 68200 und 68202, siehe Seite 6
Laterne P. L. Nr. 68212, Type B, siehe Seite 14
Laterne P. L. Nr. 68228 und 68230, siehe S. 14

Für Wechselstrom:
Laterne P. L. Nr. 68212, siehe Seite 12

Mehrpreis vorstehender Laternen mit Diffuser . . . . . ℳ 22.50 p. Stück
mit glattem Oberreflektor ℳ 15.— p. Stück

P23

• P24–P26

Economy Arc Lamp
1907

Arc lamp with downward-facing reflector for direct lighting in rooms with low ceilings. Like that of the long-life arc lamp, the air intake of the economy lamp was smaller than that of an open lamp, so that the carbon rods burned more slowly. But the economy lamp was brighter than the long-life lamp, as it used thinner rods.

Types
Two different types were offered: length ca. 675 mm, diameter max. 350 mm (the so-called large economy lamp, model a); Length ca. 530 mm, diameter max. 250 mm (the so-called small economy lamp, model b). The lamp was also supplied with an automatic resistor mounted above the cap (model c) and with a matte-glass globe for semi-indirect lighting (model d) (see P25, P26).

Finish
Painted dark green, with gold rims and rivets.

References
Stoedtner photo 49365; Hagen photos 12693 (model a), 12694 (model b); *MdBEW* 3, no. 9 (September 1907), p. 130; ibid. 3, no. 10 (October 1907), p. 159; *AEG-Ztg.* 10, no. 6 (December 1907), suppl. 2; *MdBEW* 4, no. 3 (March 1908), p. 41; *AEG-Ztg.* 10 (April 1908), suppl.; *AEG-Preisliste* (January 1909), p. 69; *AEG-Bogenlampenliste*, no. 7 (1909), p. 18 (see G42); *AEG-Kalender für das Jahr 1910*, August, illustration 1; Monasch 1909, pp. 2 ff.; Pudor 1911, p. 298; *JDW* 1912, p. 67; *Int. AEG-Ztg.* 15, no. 3–4 (September–October 1912), suppl. 10 (models c and d); Hoeber 1913, p. 106; Lanzke 1958, illustration 3; Casabella 1960, p. 24; von Moos 1967, illustration 12; Anderson 1968, illustration 98; Müller 1974, p. 186; Buddensieg and Rogge 1977, p. 123, illustration 2, p. 130, illustration 16, pp. 139–140 (with earlier model).

P24

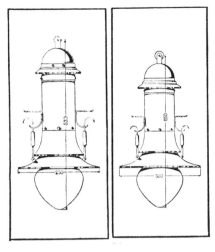

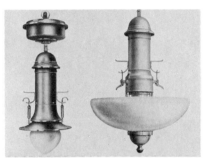

P25

P26

• P27

High-Intensity Arc Lamp
1908

High-intensity arc lamp with reflector and glass globe for direct lighting out of doors (model a). In contrast to the normal, vertical alignment, the rods in this lamp were mounted diagonally with the points down. The increased illumination achieved by this arrangement could be further improved by adding luminous salts to the rods. The resulting steam made the lamp suitable only for very large rooms or for external use. Model b, without a reflector and with a prismatic, flashed glass globe, was offered for indoor use (see P28). Length ca. 825 mm, diameter max. 240 mm.

Finish
Painted dark green, with gold rims.

References
Stoedtner photo 49210 (model b); *AEG-Ztg.* 10, no. 9 (March 1908), suppl.; *MdBEW* 4, no. 8 (August 1908), p. 116; *Int. AEG-Ztg.* (January 1909), pp. 1–3 (model b); *AEG-Ztg.* 11, no. 8 (February 1909), suppl. 9; Dohrn 1909, p. 362; *AEG-Kalender für das Jahr 1910,* August; *Int. AEG-Ztg.* 13, no. 2 (August 1910), suppl. 4, p. 5, and suppl. 5, p. 2 (model b); ibid. 13, no. 10 (April 1911), suppl. 5, p. 12. illustrations 5 and 6; ibid. 15, no. 5 (November 1912), suppl. 7 (model b); *JDW* 1912, p. 67; Franz 1917, p. 149; Lotz 1932, p. 310; *Enciclopedia universale dell'arte*, 1958, vol. 7, plate 290; Catalog 1966, illustration 52, catalog no. 198; Catalog Darmstadt 1976, vol. 2, no. 365 (model b); Buddensieg and Rogge 1977, p. 131, illustrations 20 and 21, p. 140 (with earlier model).

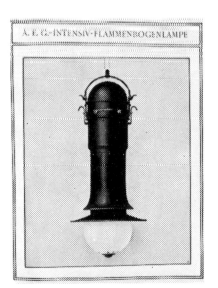

P27

• P28

High-Intensity Arc Lamp
1908

This high-intensity arc lamp, without reflector and with prismatic, flashed glass globe, was offered in the same types and finish as P27. For references, see those given for model b of P27.

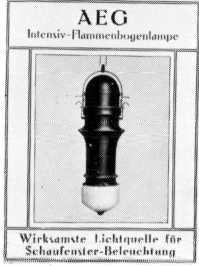

P28

•P29
Triplex Arc Lamp
1908

Triplex arc lamp for direct illumination through a cylindrical, flashed opal-glass globe (model a). As in P27 and P28, luminous salts were added to the vertically aligned carbon rods, so that the lamp could only be used outdoors or in large internal spaces. This lamp was also available with a spherical opal-glass globe (model b).

Types
Length ca. 925 or 1,076 mm, diameter max. 270 mm (model a); length ca. 1,040 mm, diameter max. 350 mm (model b).

Finish
As P27.

References
Hagen photo 13780; Stoedtner photo 49365 (model b); *AEG-Bogenlampenfabrik*, catalog (1908); *MdBEW* 4, no. 8 (August 1908), p. 116; *AEG-Ztg.* 11, no. 12 (June 1909), p. 6, figure 2; *Int. AEG-Ztg.* 12, no. 3 (September 1909), suppl. 8, p. 2, illustration 1 (model b); *Int. AEG-Ztg.* 12, no. 5 (November 1909), suppl. 5, p. 1; ibid. 12, no. 7 (January 1910), suppl. 4, p. 8, illustrations 3 and 4; *Casabella* 1960, p. 24 (dated 1907); Buddensieg and Rogge 1977, p. 133, illustrations 25 and 26, p. 141 (models a, b, with earlier model).

A. E. G.-TRIPLEX-FLAMMENBOGENLAMPE

P29

•P30
Arc Lamp
ca. 1908–09

This differential arc lamp for direct lighting had a simple mechanism, burned almost silently, and could be connected singly or in series.

Types
Model a: length ca. 970 mm, diameter max. 400 mm, spherical glass globe. Model b: length ca. 780 mm, diameter max. 258 mm, cylindrical cover.

Finish
As P27.

References
Stoedtner photo 49210 (model b); *Int. AEG-Ztg.* 13, no. 11 (May 1911), suppl. 5, p. 8, illustration 3 (model a); ibid. 14, no. 7 (January 1912), suppls. 6 and 7, p. 9, illustrations 3 and 4 (models a,b), p. 6, illustration 2 (model b); Müller 1974, p. 186; Buddensieg and Rogge 1977, p. 133, illustration 28, p. 141 (with earlier model).

P30

•P31
Flammeco Lamp
1910

Flammeco lamp with flat reflector for direct external lighting in stations, factory halls, and other places where continuous illumination was required. This was a long-burning model, and was available for factory halls with a deeper reflector (model a; see G45).

Types
Two types were offered: length ca. 985 mm, diameter 400 mm (for alternating current); length ca. 840 mm, diameter 400 mm (for direct current).

Finish
As P27.

References
K. Norden, "Langbrennende Flammenbogenlampen der AEG," *Mitt. d. Vereinigg. d. Elektrizitätswerke* 9, no. 8 (1910); *MdBEW* 7, no. 1 (January 1911), p. 7; *AEG-Ztg.* 14, no. 5 (November 1911), suppl., pamphlet; *Int. AEG-Ztg.* 15, no. 7 (January 1913), suppl.; ibid. 16, no. 6 (December 1913), suppl.; Catalog 1966, illustration 51, catalog no. 198; Selle 1973, illustration 15; P. Schmit, "Aus dem historischen Museum der AEG," *Spannung. Die AEG-Umschau*, no. 5 (February 1928), pp. 148 ff., illustration p. 149; Catalog Darmstadt 1976, vol. 2, no. 364; Buddensieg and Rogge 1977, p. 134, p. 135, illustrations 29 and 31, p. 141.

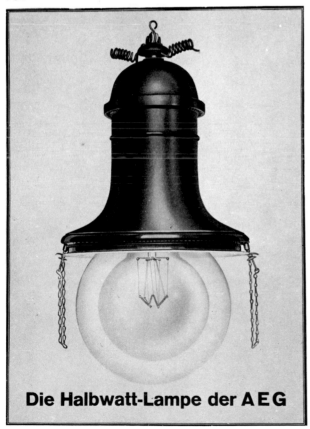

Die Halbwatt-Lampe der AEG

• P32

Nitralamp
1913

Nitralamp or half-watt lamp without reflector for direct external and internal lighting. This technically superior incandescent lamp replaced the arc lamp in many places, particularly in street lighting, shop-window illumination, and floodlighting. It provided powerful illumination at low cost. The tungsten wire filament was encased in a nitrogen-filled globe. The lamp was also offered with a reflector (see P33 and G47).

Types
Two different types were offered: length 540 mm, diameter max. 270 mm; length 650 mm, diameter max. 345 mm.

Finish
Painted black, with an opal-glass globe.

References
Int. AEG-Ztg. 16, no. 4 (October 1913), suppl.; *MdBEW*, 9, no. 10 (October 1913), pp. 152 ff.; ibid. 9, no. 11 (November 1913), pp. 167–169; ibid. 10, no. 3 (March 1914), p. 36 (special armature); ibid. 10, no. 11 (November 1914), p. 160; Buddensieg and Rogge 1977, p. 135, illustrations 32 and 33, p. 142.

• P33

Nitralamp with Reflector
1913

See P32 for description and references. Two types were offered: length 670 mm, maximum diameter 450 mm; length 670 mm, maximum diameter 550 mm.

Die Halbwatt-Lampe der AEG mit Außenreflektor

Pulley Assemblies for Arc Lamps
ca. 1908–09

Two models of pulley assemblies were offered, one for all types of arc lamps and the other for the "small economy arc lamp." PL no. 68925, with cable lengths of 13, 19, 25, and 31 m, sold for 72 marks in 1909; PL no. 68921, with cable lengths of 9, 10, 11.5, and 13.5 m, sold for 32 marks. The construction was brass, painted dark green.

References
Int. AEG-Ztg. 12, no. 4 (October 1909), suppl. 6; Buddensieg and Rogge 1977, p. 131, illustration 22.

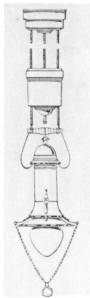

P34
From *Interne AEG-Zeitung.*

High-Intensity Arc Lamp, Installed
1908

This photograph (AEG photo no. 7279, 17 September 1910) shows the high-intensity arc lamp for external illumination (P27) mounted outside the AEG high-voltage factory at the Brunnenstrasse site in Berlin-Wedding (see A54–A73). The supporting brackets were also designed by Behrens.

P35

• P36

Lighting Scheme for Ceiling of Keller & Reiner Gallery, Berlin
1910

Incandescent bulbs and crystal glass prisms were strung together in chains here. The miniature lamps were originally used only for decorative lighting, and this scheme was intended to prove that they could also be used for continuous illumination. The diffuse lighting, stemming from many separate points, was further reflected and refracted by the prisms. By freeing the lamps from any constructional framework, Behrens enhanced the impression of insubstantiality and the ornamental character of the scheme.

References
Stoedtner photos. 71973, 72521; *MdBEW* 6, no. 3 (March 1910), pp. 40–43; *AEG-Ztg.* 12, no. 9 (March 1910), p. 7; Michel 1910, pp. 130–131; Dettmar 1911, pp. 17–18, illustration 11; Hoeber 1913, pp. 130–131, 142–143.

P36

·P37
Cover Design for Fan Brochure
ca. 1908

This cover illustrates the direct-current table fan shown in P38. For a description of the graphic work and references see G54.

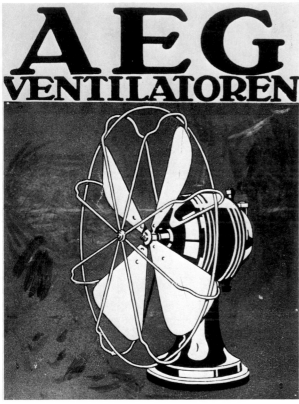

P37

·P38, P39
Table Fan
1908

Variations of this model were available on a pivoting stand (see P45), with a wall mounting (P48), and as an ozone ventilator (P39). All could be supplied for direct, alternating, or three-phase current. Four different motors were offered.

GBO: 15-watt motor, height 235 mm, blade diameter 200 mm, guard diameter 220 mm, 1912 price 23.50 marks, PL no. 66001
GB1: 25-watt motor, height 290 mm, blade diameter 250 mm, guard diameter 270 mm, 1912 price 31 marks, PL no. 66011

GB2: 45-watt motor, height 360 mm, blade diameter 300 mm, guard diameter 340 mm, 1912 price 33.50 marks, PL no. 66021

GB3: 70-watt motor, height 420 mm, blade diameter 360 mm, guard diameter 400 mm, 1912 price 44 marks, PL no. 66031.

Finish
The cast-iron motor housing was painted green, with tombac bands, and the blades were of polished brass.

References
AEG photos 14376, 14433 (Hygiene Museum), 13968; *AEG-Ztg.* 11, no. (June 1909), p. 6; Dohrn 1909, p. 368; *Int. AEG-Ztg.* 12, no. 11 (May 1910), suppl. 6; *AEG-Ztg.* 12, no. 5 (June 1910), p. 11; *MdBEW* 7, no. 5 (May 1911), p. 80 (back cover); *Int. AEG-Ztg.* 13, no. 12 (June 1911), suppl. 14; Hellwag 1911, pp. 53, 154–155; Czech 1911, p. 140; *Int. AEG-Ztg.* 14, no. 11 (May 1912), suppl. 8; *JDW* 1912, p. 66; Hoeber 1913, p. 106; *MdBEW* 10, no. 6 (June 1914), p. 88; ibid. 11, no. 5 (May 1915), p. 80; ibid. 12, no. 7 (July 1916), p. 112; Lotz 1932, p. 310; Pevsner 1968, p. 172; Anderson 1968, illustration 102b.

P38

P39

Table Fan, Earlier Model

References
Dohrn 1909, p. 369; Czech 1911, p. 140; Hellwag 1911, p. 153.

P40
From Dohrn 1909.

Table Fan, Earlier Model

This fan, which could be supplied on a fixed base or with a wall fitting, had nickel-plated blades and a black-lacquered motor casing with gold lines. More elegant models were nickel-plated or galvanized in a bronze color.

Reference
AEG photo 14426.

P41

P42, P43
Table Fan
1908

This model differed from P38 because it was designed specifically for alternating current. The speed could not be regulated, and the motor had a flatter profile. The simple forms of the casing and the base were retained. Four different motors were offered.

WBO: 25-watt motor, height 235 mm, blade diameter 200 mm, guard diameter 220 mm, 1912 price 23.50 marks, PL no. 66301

WB1: 35-watt motor, height 290 mm, blade diameter 290 mm, guard diameter 270 mm, 1912 price 31 marks, PL no. 66311

WB2: 70-watt motor, height 415 mm, blade diameter 300 mm, guard diameter 340 mm, 1912 price 52 marks, PL no. 66321

WB3: 85-watt motor, height 445 mm, blade diameter 360 mm, guard diameter 400 mm, 1912 price 78 marks, PL no. 66331.

The finish was the same as that of P38.

References
AEG photo 14445; Hagen photos (unnumbered); AEG photo 14178 (preliminary drawing); *Int. AEG-Ztg.* 14, no. 11 (May 1912), suppl. 8 (price list and preliminary drawing).

P42

P43
Courtesy of Karl Ernst Osthaus Museum, Hagen.

P44
Drawing for Fan P42
1908

Reference
AEG photo 14178.

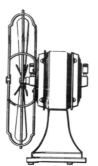

P44

P45
Table Fan
ca. 1908

This pivot-mounted version of P38 is decorated with a cube with three stepped planes on its four outer faces, which acts as a visual connection between the base and the forks holding the motor.

Reference
AEG photo 14463.

P45

• P46
Table Fan with Stylized Guard
ca. 1908

The stylized struts of the guard echoed the turning motion of the fan. Models with this type of guard were also made for wall mounting. The cast-iron motor housing was painted green, with tombac bands, and the blades were of polished brass.

References
Hagen photo (no number); Scheffler 1908, p. 434 (wall-mounted model); Widmer 1909, p. 51 (wall-mounted model).

P46
Courtesy of Karl Ernst Osthaus Museum, Hagen.

• P47
Wall-Mounted Fan with Flexible Motor Mounting
ca. 1908

The special feature of this general-purpose DC fan was the flexible mounting of the motor, which could be swiveled through 90 degrees on its bracket and tilted through 60 degrees on its pivots. To the molded cube was added a tombac-plated ferrule, which, as both decorative element and connector, linked the motor and the bracket. The cast-iron motor housing was painted green, with tombac bands, and the blades were of polished brass.

References
AEG photos 14377, 13966, 14464; Hellwag 1911, p. 155 (with illustration of an earlier model).

P47

• P48
Wall-Mounted Fan
ca. 1908

This AC fan was wall-mounted on a fixed bracket. In contrast with P47, the cube on this model has molding with a circle superimposed on a square, and a cylindrical tombac ferrule. The cast-iron motor housing was painted green, with tombac bands, and the blades were of polished brass.

References
Hagen photo 12520, unnumbered Hagen photo (front view); *JDW* 1912, p. 66; Pevsner 1968, pp. 172–173 (wrongly identified as a table fan).

P48
Courtesy of Karl Ernst Osthaus Museum, Hagen.

• P49
Low-Speed Ceiling Fan, Earlier Model

This DC fan was also available with four blades and a hanging rod.

References
AEG photo (unnumbered); AEG-Telefunken archive.

P49

• P50
Low-Speed Ceiling Fan, Earlier Model with Light Fixture

Reference
AEG photo 16602.

• P51
Rheostat-Controlled Ceiling Fan
ca. 1908

This DC fan was suitable for living rooms, restaurants, libraries, ships' cabins, etc., and was supplied with hanging rods of various lengths. It was available with four blades and a guard and with two blades and no guard. Blade diameters ranged from 300 mm to 800 mm. The cast-iron motor housing was painted green, with tombac bands; the blades were polished brass plate.

References
AEG photo 14059; AEG photo 14058 (with hanging rod and without guard).

P51

P50

•P52
High-Speed Ceiling Fan with Hanging Rod
ca. 1908

This fan had the flat motor housing of an AC motor (see P42) and the same construction and finish as P51.

References
AEG photo 14067; AEG photo 14064 (for direct mounting and with wire guard).

P52

P53

•P53
Low-Speed Ceiling Fan
ca. 1908

In this two-blade DC fan made for direct ceiling mounting, the molded cube once again acted as the connection between the mounting plate and the motor (see P51).

Types
Two types were offered: height 325 mm, blade diameter 1,090 mm, mounting plate diameter 200 mm; height 375 mm, blade diameter 1,240 mm, mounting plate diameter 250 mm.

Construction and Finish
Cast-iron casing painted green, with tombac bands; wooden blades.

References
AEG photo 13768; *MdBEW* 6, no. 5 (May 1910), p. 68 ("from a special list, appearing soon, modern form of the very latest design by Professor Peter Behrens").

•P54
Preparatory Drawing for P53
ca. 1908

Reference
AEG photo 13687.

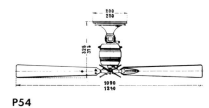

P54

•P55
Low-Speed Ceiling Fan with Hanging Rod
ca. 1908

Construction and Finish
As P53

Reference
AEG photo 14045.

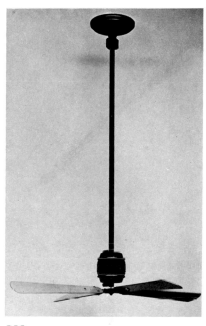

P55

•P56
Low-Speed Ceiling Fan
ca. 1908

As P53, with the addition of a hanging rod and with the alterations necessary for an AC motor.

Construction and Finish
As P53.

References
AEG photo 14056; AEG photo 14060 (for direct mounting).

P56

•P57
Low-Speed Ceiling Fan
ca. 1908

These fans had a plain, undecorated motor casing. A dignified appearance was given to the fan by encasing the motor completely and by adding a simple pommel. With these models, Behrens gave more emphasis to the cladding of the fan than to its mechanics.

Finish
Painted green with tombac bands, wooden blades.

References
AEG photo 13163; AEG photo 14036 (with light bulbs); AEG photo 14066 (as P58); Hellwag 1911, p. 156.

P57

•P58
Ceiling Fan
ca. 1908

In this version of P57, four curved metal tubes fixed to the pommel led down to lamp holders.

Reference
AEG photo 14066; see also P57.

P58

• P59

Ceiling Fan

ca. 1908

In this version of P57, the decorative character of the design was further heightened by cladding the motor casing with tombac. This model too was available with four lamp bulbs mounted on a plate under the pommel (see P60).

Finish

Motor casing, hanging rod, lamp mounting plate all tombac, wooden blades.

References

AEG photos 13564, 14061 (with lamp bulbs mounted on plate), 14315 (as P60); Hagen photo V 236/2; *Int. AEG-Ztg.* 12, no. 11 (May 1910, suppl. 6; *AEG-Ztg.* 12, no. 12 (June 1910), p. 11 (with lamp bulbs mounted on plate); *Int. AEG-Ztg.* 13, no. 12 (June 1911), suppl. 14.

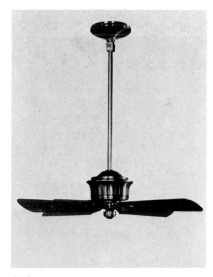

P59

• P60

Ceiling Fan

ca. 1908

Two-bladed, low-speed ceiling fan on a hanging rod with four incandescent bulbs mounted on a plate set below the pommel.

Finish

As P59.

References

AEG photo 14315 (AEG-Telefunken archive; *AEG-Ztg.* 12, no. 12 (June 1910), p. 11.

P60

• P61

Ceiling Fan

1908

Two-bladed, low-speed ceiling fan for direct mounting with a simple motor casing onto which the blades were directly attached.

Finish

As P57. Also available with tombac casing (see P62).

References

AEG photos 13164 (18 January 1915), 13565 (as P62); Scheffler 1908, p. 431; Widmer 1908, p. 49; *MdBEW* 6, no. 5 (May 1910), p. 69 (with tombac casing); Hellwag 1911, p. 153; *JDW* 1912, p. 66; Hoeber 1913, p. 107, illustration 114 (dated 1908); Lotz 1932, p. 310.

P61

• P62, P63
Ceiling Fan
1908

In this version of P61, the motor casing was decorated with geometric patterns (P62) which varied slightly from model to model. Another version had six light bulbs attached to the outer edge of the casing, under the blades (P63).

Finish
Tombac casing and hanging rod, wooden blades.

References
AEG photos 13565, 14313, 14505, 14226 (with light bulbs); *MdBEW* 6, no. 5 (May 1910), p. 69.

• P64
Ceiling Fan
ca. 1908

Two-bladed, low-speed ceiling fan for direct mounting, with tombac motor casing. The small patterns on P62 were replaced here by larger oval and oblong forms.

Finish
As P62.

References
AEG photos 14057, 14055; *MdBEW* 6, no. 5 (May 1910), p. 69; ibid. 10, no. 6 (June 1914), p. 91.

• P65
Ceiling Fan
ca. 1908

Two-bladed, low-speed ceiling fan with hanging rod. In contrast to P51–P57, the motor cover was more compact, and this was emphasized by the deep chamfers at top and bottom. The hanging rod was curved like a spout at the point where it met the top of the motor casing, and the blades did not go into a cube at the center but were mounted on a small stud.

Finish
As P57.

Reference
AEG photo 13162 (18 January 1915).

P62

P64

P63

P65

• P66
Ceiling Fan
ca. 1908

Two-bladed, low-speed AC ceiling fan for direct mounting. The broad, deep groves cut into the ceiling rose join together in the pommel under the motor. Unlike P57–P60, the blades were not attached to the pommel but fixed directly to the motor casing via angle brackets. Variations on this design were available with hanging rods, light bulbs below the motor, and four-bladed fans.

Finish
Painted green. Tombac decorative bands were available. Wooden blades.

References
AEG photos 13732, 12826 (with hanging rod), 14062 (with tombac bands, hanging rod, and four light bulbs mounted on a plate under the motor—see P60), 14062a (as P67), 14316 (with tombac bands, blades set above motor, and four light bulbs mounted on motor casing, 14065 (with tombac bands and five light bulbs set in cluster below motor—see P68, 14038 (as P68); *MdBEW* 6, no. 5 (May 1910), p. 70 (as AEG photo 14316).

• P67
Ceiling Fan
ca. 1908

Two-bladed, low-speed AC ceiling fan with hanging rod and four light bulbs hung on curved metal tubes.

Finish
Painted green with tombac bands. Wooden blades.

Reference
AEG photo 14062a (as P66).

P67

• P68
Ceiling Fan
ca. 1908

Four-bladed, low-speed AC ceiling fan for direct mounting. Blades attached to motor casing by four angle brackets. Five light bulbs mounted under casing in cluster pattern.

Finish
As P67.

Reference
AEG photo 14038 (as P66).

P68

P66

• P69
Wall Ventilator, Earlier Model
(ca. 1903)

Eight-bladed, high-speed wall ventilator with slightly curved, square-ended blades.

References
AEG photos 3156 Kf 157 (9 September 1903), 2422 Kf 169 (with modifications to motor casing and mounting), 2430 Kf 168 (with same motor and blades but for a different installation), 2429 Kf 167 (with propeller blades).

P69

• P70
Wall Ventilator, Earlier Model

Five-bladed, high-speed wall ventilator with broad, slightly curved blades.

Reference
AEG photo 14432.

P70

• P71
Wall Ventilator
ca. 1908

Four-bladed, high-speed DC wall ventilator with two concentric steps on mounting plate and circle and square motif around bolt holes. This fan, which was also supplied in a six-bladed version, was intended for large rooms such as cafés, offices, and factory halls, and was installed in the outside wall or in the upper part of a window, so that the subtleties of design were barely visible. Three different motors were offered.

Types
GB1 (25 watts): mounting plate diameter 330 mm, blade diameter 250 mm, 1912 price 30 marks, PL no. 66017.

GB2 (45 watts): mounting plate diameter 390 mm, blade diameter 300 mm, 1912 price 33.50 marks, PL no. 66027

GB3 (75 watts), mounting plate diameter 460 mm, blade diameter 360 mm, 1912 price 43 marks, PL no. 66037.

Finish
Painted green with tombac rims. Green-painted sheet-steel blades. Also supplied in gray or with tombac plating.

References
AEG photos 14430, 13166 (tombac-plated version); *Int. AEG-Ztg.* 12, no. 11 (May 1910), suppl. 6; *AEG-Ztg.* 12, no. 12 (June 1910), p. 11; *Int. AEG-Ztg.* 13, no. 12 (June 1911), suppl. 14; ibid. 14, no. 11 (May 1912), suppl. 8 (with price list and drawing); ibid. 16, no. 10 (April 1914), suppl.; *Elektrizität in Haushalt und Gewerbe*, AEG brochure (1914), p. 62.

P71

P72

• P72
Wall Ventilator
ca. 1908

Four-bladed, high-speed AC wall ventilator with iris diaphragm mechanism. The mounting plate had three concentric steps with three protruding bolt lugs decorated with a square motif. The diaphragm served to alter the size of the vent and worked on the same principle as the aperture diaphragm on a camera. It was operated by cords running over pulleys. Three different motors were offered.

Types
WB1 (35 watts): mounting plate diameter 330 mm, blade diameter 250 mm, 1912 price 30 marks, PL no. 66317

WB2 (70 watts): mounting plate diameter 390 mm, blade diameter 300 mm, 1912 price 54 marks, PL no. 66327

WB3 (85 watts): mounting plate diameter 460 mm, blade diameter 360 mm, 1912 price 80 marks, PL no. 66337.

Finish
As P71.

References
AEG photo 14443; *Int. AEG-Ztg.* 14, no. 11 (May 1912), suppl. 8 (with design drawing); ibid. 16, no. 10 (April 1914), suppl.; *MdBEW* 10, no. 6 (June 1914), p. 91; *Elektrizität in Haushalt und Gewerbe*, AEG brochure (1914); p. 62; Scheibe 1965, p. 203 (dated around 1912).

• P73
Wall Ventilator
ca. 1903

Four-bladed, high-speed DC wall ventilator with self-acting louver shutter. As a result of their lightness, the mica louvers opened and closed according to the stream of air passing through the ventilator. Louver shutters were available for all the AEG wall ventilators and were mounted on a ring which fitted over the body of the ventilator.

Types
As P71.

Finish
As P71.

References
AEG photo 16390 (AEG-Telefunken Archive); *Elektrizität in Haushalt und Gewerbe*, AEG brochure (1914), p. 63.

P73

• P74
Table Fan and Centrifugal Fan
ca. 1908

The table fan (left) was designed to such in and disperse smoke. The centrifugal fan (right) pumped a small volume of air at a relatively high pressure, so that it was particularly suitable for supplying air along pipes or tubes or for cleaning air containing steam or dust. Both types were DC.

Finish
Painted green with tombac bands.

References
AEG photo 13528; *MdBEW* 6, no. 5 (May 1910), pp. 68, 70.

P74

• P75
Humidifiers, Earlier Models

Prött-system electric water atomizers to humidify the air, mounted on fixed stands and with wire guards. These models, with simple or decorative motor casings, could also be hung from the ceiling.

References
TM AEG-Ztg. 8, no. 2 (August 1905), suppl., p. 3.

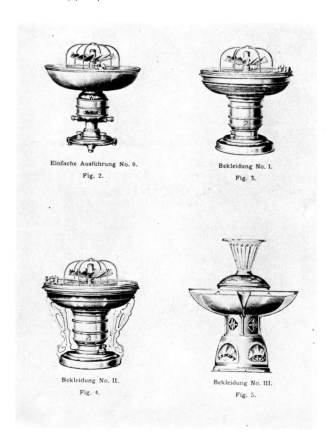

Einfache Ausführung No. 0.
Fig. 2.
Bekleidung No. I.
Fig. 3.
Bekleidung No. II.
Fig. 4.
Bekleidung No. III.
Fig. 5.

P75

• P76
Humidifier, Earlier Model

As P75, figure 2.

References
MdBEW 1, no. 4 (April 1905), p. 60; *AEG-Ztg.* 10, no. 10 (April 1908), suppl.

Allgemeine Elektricitäts-Gesellschaft, Berlin.

Elektrische Flüssigkeits-Zerstäubungsapparate.

LUFTBEFEUCHTER
(System Prött)
für Gleichstrom und Wechselstrom
zum Zerstäuben von Wasser und Medikamenten.

Patentiert in allen Kulturstaaten.

Patentiert in allen Kulturstaaten.

Tisch-Luftbefeuchter
für Gesundheitspflege und medizinische Zwecke.

Preise und Näheres auf Anfrage.

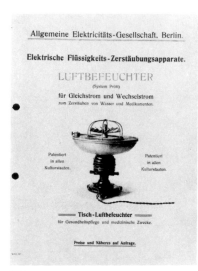

P76

• P77
Humidifier
ca. 1909

Electric water atomizer to humidify the air, mounted on fixed stand. The wire guard was dispensed with on this model, as the moisture was propelled through the jets at the center of the machine as a fine mist, without forming drops. The design stressed the technical aspects of the humidifier; the moldings on the stand and motor casing and the tombac bands were the only decorative features (see P79). This humidifier was offered in AC and DC models, at a 1911 price of 80 marks.

Finish
Painted green with tombac banks.

References
AEG photos 16690, 16684; *Int. AEG-Ztg.* 14, no. 2 (August 1911), suppl. (with price list); *MdBEW* 11, no. 7–8 (July–August 1915), p. 128 (announcement).

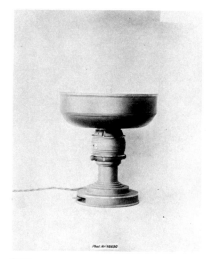

P77

• P78
Humidifier
ca. 1909

As P79. The bowl and motor casing had a decorative tombac cladding.

References
Hagen photo 14340; Breuer 1910, p. 266; *JDW* 1912, p. 66 (described as fan and illustrated upside down); Lotz 1932 (described as fan and illustrated upside down).

P78
Courtesy of Karl Ernst Osthaus Museum, Hagen.

• P79
Humidifier
1909

Sprayer to humidify the air, mounted on a fixed stand and with a wire guard. An electrically driven cone rotated inside the bowl. The resulting centrifugal force threw the water up onto the fins, where it was atomized by the draft from the rotating fan blades attached to the cone. A simple, grooved motor casing supported the wide bowl, which held the safety guard. This appliance was intended for dry, dusty rooms or for disinfection purposes.

Finish
Painted green with tombac bands.

References
AEG photo 14339; Hagen photo V 236/2; *AEG-Ztg.* 12, no. 2 (August 1909), pp. 2–3; *MdBEW* 6, no. 12 (December 1910), p. 182; Breuer 1910, p. 266; Hoeber 1913, p. 108, illustration 118 (dated 1909).

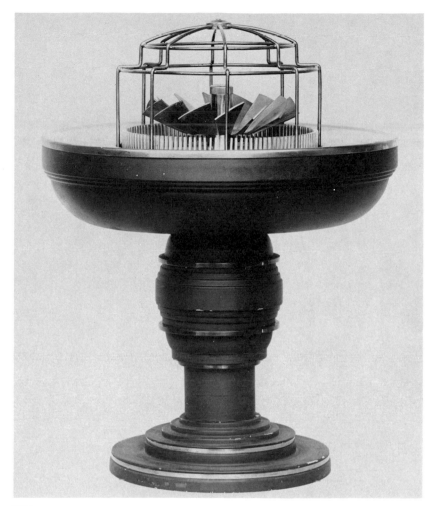

P79

•P80
Grinding and Polishing Motor, Earlier Model

Suitable for all three current types, this motor was available mounted on a high stand or on a bench bracket.

Reference
AEG-Ztg. 8, no. 7 (January 1906), suppl. 8.

P80

•P81
Grinding and Polishing Motor
ca. 1908–09

Sealed motor with dustproof bearings mounted on a fixed stand with taper spindles at both ends of the drive shaft for the grinding and polishing attachments. The machine was principally used by watchmakers, jewelers, and goldsmiths. The DC model had shunt winding, so that the speed of the motor could be regulated.

Finish
Painted green with tombac bands.

References
AEG photo 13860; *AEG-Ztg.* 11, no. 8 (February 1909), suppl. 9, p. 2; ibid. 11, no. 11 (May 1909), p. 6; *MdBEW* 10, no. 2 (February 1914), p. 32 (announcement).

P81

•P82
Grinding and Polishing Motor
ca. 1908–09

This motor was available for AC and for three-phase current. The speed of the "squirrel cage" motors could not be regulated.

Finish
As P81.

References
AEG photo 13861; *AEG-Ztg.* 11, no. 8 (February 1909), suppl. 9, p. 2; ibid. 11, no. 11 (May 1909), p. 6; *MdBEW* 6, no. 12 (December 1910), p. 182; ibid. 10, no. 2 (February 1914), back cover (announcement).

P82

• P83–P85

Kitchen Motor

ca. 1911

This electric kitchen motor was mounted on a broad base plate. An adjustable driveshaft could be attached to various kitchen appliances via a spring-loaded clutch, so that the motor could be used to cut bread and salami, stir mayonnaise, or mince meat. The simple form of the casing amplified the mechanical qualities of the appliance and was reminiscent of the polishing machine shown in P81 and P82.

Finish
As P81.

References
AEG-Telefunken photo ZWA/Fo R 1045 (dated 1911); *MdBEW* 7, no. 4 (April 1911), pp. 51–54; ibid. 10, no. 1 (January 1914), back cover; ibid. 11, no. 3 (March 1915), back cover.

P83
From *MdBEW*.

P84
From *MdBEW*.

Elektrische
Kraft im Küchenbetrieb

ist immer arbeitsfertig,
unermüdlich und absolut
zuverlässig.

P85
From *MdBEW*.

• P86, P87
Dental Drill
1908

The electric wire was led over two pulleys along a pivoting arm attached to a wooden mounting plate. The square-circle-square motif and the stepped cube used on the fans and ventilators also appeared here as decorative elements (see P45, P47, P48), and the casing of the small electric motor was given a harmonious, spherical form.

References
AEG photo 14083; *MdBEW* 4, no. 6 (June 1908), pp. 89 ff.; ibid. 8, no. 8 (August 1912), pp. 119–121 (modified version, probably not by Behrens); ibid. 9, no. 9 (September 1913), p. 141.

P86

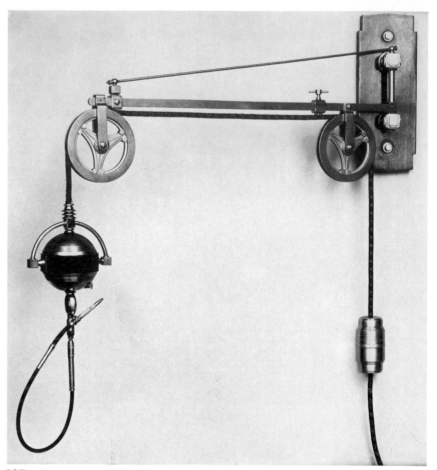

P87

• P88

Push-Button Switch, Earlier Model

(ca. 1903)

Reference
AEG photo 2907 (11 June 1903).

P88

• P89

Switch Button and Panel, Earlier Models

(ca. 1903)

References
AEG photo 2885 (19 May 1903);
MdBEW 3, no. 10 (October 1907), p. 154.

P89

• P90

Rotary Light Switch

References
AEG-Schalter-Flugblatt, 1912 (source of this advertisement); *Int. AEG-Ztg.* 15, no. 9 (March 1912), suppl.

P90

• P91

Button and Key Switches
ca. 1909

These pushbuttons and key switches were used in lift installations. Each button was clearly isolated in a light decorative frame on a dark background.

References
AEG photo 8133 (8 September 1911); AEG photo 6571 (with modified script); *Int. AEG-Ztg.* 15, no. 5 (November 1912), suppl. 2.

• P92

Transformer Covers
ca. 1908

Protective housings for transformers, made of punched sheet metal.

References
Dohrn 1909, pp. 361–372; Jaumann, *DKD* (1909), p. 351.

• P93, P94

Control Panels, Earlier Models
(ca. 1906–07)

References
AEG photos 5088 (12 September 1907), 10157, Af332. For technical details see P95 and P97.

P93

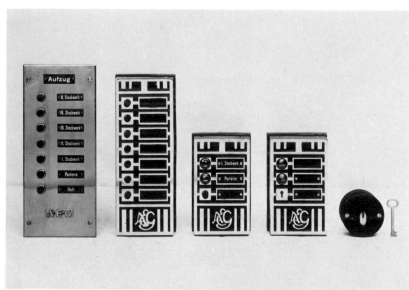

P91

P94

P92

• P95
Standard Control Panel
(Frame, ca. 1907–08)

Control panel for one three-phase, low-voltage generator and ten circuits, with clock mounting and clock (not by Behrens). These control panels were made up of several vertical bands, each for one circuit or one group of circuits. The bands were made of three sections and were 650 mm or 750 mm wide. Each band comprised an upper panel with meters; a middle panel with switches, fuses, and regulators for that particular circuit; and a lower panel to serve as a base, or to carry controls that rarely had to be attended to. This layout could be extended at will, and the marble plates were cut from one block to obtain the same pattern and coloring. In spite of this visual attentiveness, only the design of the wooden frame can be definitively ascribed to Behrens.

Materials and Construction
Front side: highly polished marble panels. Back side: unpolished marble panels. Enamel varnish; connections of tin-plated copper (all water-resistant materials).

References
AEG photos 7204 (13 August 1910), 8609, 8795 (18 March 1912–a smaller, modified version built for the Technische Hochschule, Charlottenburg); *Deutsche Schiffbau-Ausstellung, 1908*, AEG exhibition catalog (see A1–A8); *MdBEW* 5, no. 3 (March 1909), p. 46, illustration; ibid. 7, no. 7 (July 1911), p. 107 (without clock); *Elektrizität in Haushalt und Gewerbe*, AEG brochure (1914), p. 87; AEG Eisenbahn Abteiling, *Elektrische Stellwerke für Winden und Signale*, 1910 edition, p. 10; *Int. AEG-Ztg.* 14, no. 12 (July 1912), suppl. 3, p. 21; *Enciclopedia universale dell'arte*, vol. 7 (1958), plate 290.

P95

• P96
Standard Control Panel
(Frame, ca. 1907–08)

Control panel for three-phase, low-voltage generator.

Reference
Int. AEG-Ztg. 14, no. 12 (June 1912), suppl. 3, p. 11. For technical details see P95.

P96

• P97
Standard Control Panel
(Frame, ca. 1907–08)

Control panel without clock, made of metal components which could be easily assembled with clamps, screws, etc. The two upper panels in the marble version were replaced here by one panel of sheet metal. Marble could not be used in dusty surroundings such as mines, and slate or sheet metal had to be substituted. The influence of Behrens at least appears in the wooden molding between the metal plates.

Finish
Iron plate.

References
AEG photo 8609; *MdBEW* 12, no. 9 (September 1916), pp. 136–137.

P97

• P98
Instrument Column
ca. 1908–09

Column supporting five measuring instruments. There were three basic types, with scope for individual variations: Model GSA was for a maximum of five instruments. It was also possible to extend the head-piece, especially for use with generators, with a switch built in at the top of the column. This switch was also available on models GS and R. Model GS, without crossbar, was intended for transformers and the like. Model R was a simple design for a maximum of three instruments. Behrens's influence was limited to the design of the column. A large cube carrying the AEG trademark formed the connection between the column and the instrument mountings, and two smaller cubes linked the crossbar to the voltmeters and ammeters on each side. There is no evidence that Behrens was involved in the design of the instruments.

Construction
Gas pipe.

References
AEG photo, unnumbered (AEG-Telefunken archive); *MdBEW* 5, no. 3 (March 1909), p. 46 (column with switch, installed in AEG administration building, Friedrich-Karl-Ufer); *AEG-Ztg.* 13, no. 8 (February 1911), suppl. 5; Franz 1917, p. 149.

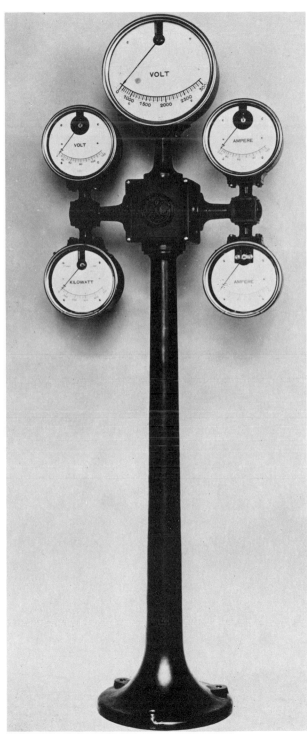

Advertisement for Slave Clocks

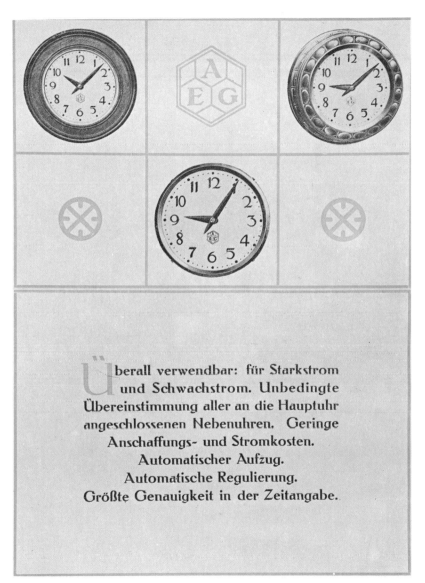

Überall verwendbar: für Starkstrom und Schwachstrom. Unbedingte Übereinstimmung aller an die Hauptuhr angeschlossenen Nebenuhren. Geringe Anschaffungs- und Stromkosten. Automatischer Aufzug. Automatische Regulierung. Größte Genauigkeit in der Zeitangabe.

P99

• P100, P101
Pendulum Clocks
1910

These electric master clocks were especially accurate, and were used to set other clocks by or to control a series of slave clocks. The master clock had a second pendulum, which completed 60 swings per minute and was linked to the clockwork by an endless chain. The long pendulum, visible through the three glass panels on the front of the wooden case, guaranteed accuracy. Behrens stripped the housing and the clock face of all unnecessary ornament, and removed the customary arrow-head pointers from the hands.

Types
N2: low-voltage wall clock, 1912 price 250 marks, PL no. 4011
SN2: low-voltage standing clock, 1912 price 485 marks, PL no. 4012
N1: high-voltage wall clock, 1912 price 212 marks, PL no. 4036
SN2: high-voltage standing clock, 1912 price 415 marks, PL no. 4035.

References
Stoedtner photo 71996; AEG price list ''Auszug aus den Spezial-listen'' (January 1912), p. 93; ibid. (July 1912), p. 205.

P101

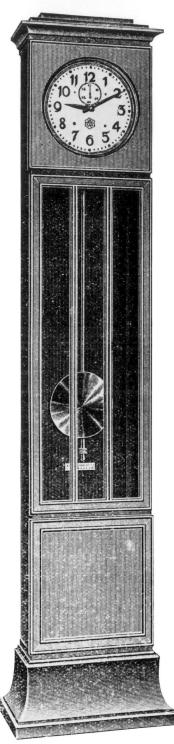

P100

•P102
Slave Clock
ca. 1910

In the low-voltage version, the slave clock was driven directly by the electrical impulses received from the master clock, which were transmitted to the hands via a coil assembly and a gathering click. The high-voltage version had an independent clockwork mechanism with a self-acting electric winder, and was automatically regulated every hour by the master clock. Both models were also supplied with outer casings (see P103–P105).

Types, with 1912 Prices
Low voltage

SU: face 200 mm, 36 marks, PL no. 4002.

SU: face 250 mm, 42 marks, PL no. 4007.

SU: face 300 mm, 48 marks, PL no. 4003.

SU: face 400 mm, 64 marks, PL no. 4006.

SU: face 500 mm, 90 marks, PL no. 4004.

High voltage

FKU: face 200 mm, 90 marks, PL no. 4032.

FKU: face 250 mm, 99 marks, PL no. 4031.

FKU: face 300 mm, 105 marks, PL no. 4033.

FKU: face 400 mm, 114 marks, PL no. 4037.

FKU: face 500 mm, 120 marks, PL no. 4034.

References
Int. AEG-Ztg. 12, no. 9 (March 1910), suppl. 8; *AEG-Ztg.* 12, no. 9 (March 1910), p. 11; *MdBEW* 2, no. 3 (1910), p. 90, fig. 35; AEG price list "Auszug aus den Spezial-listen" (January 1912), p. 94; ibid. (July 1912), p. 206; *MdBEW* 8, no. 10 (October 1912), pp. 154–155; *Int. AEG-Ztg.* 16, no. 8 (February 1914), suppl.

P102

•P103
Slave Clock
ca. 1910

Slave clock for high and low voltage with tombac casing (see P102).

Types
As P102. Three different casings were offered. Tombac casing, face as P103: 1912 prices 6, 7, 8, 9.50, 11.50 marks. Wooden casing, face as P104: 1912 prices 4.25, 5, 6, 8, 10 marks. Waterproof metal casing, face as P105: 1912 prices 8.25, 9.50, 10.50, 15.50, 21 marks.

References
As P102.

P103

•P104
Slave Clock
ca. 1910

Slave clock for high and low voltage with wooden casing (see P102).

Types
As P102, P103.

References
As P102.

P104

•P105
Slave Clock
ca. 1910

Slave clock for high and low voltage, with waterproof metal casing (see P102).

Types
As P102, P103.

References
As P102.

P105

•P106
Synchron Clock
Peter Behrens

This AC clock was to be mounted on or set into a wall. Metal or wooden cases were also available, costing between 9 and 16 marks.

Types
At least five different types were offered. The prices given are from 1931.

FU: face 200 mm, 44 marks, PL no. 290406.

FU: face 260 mm, price unascertainable, PL no. 290407.

FU: face 300 mm, 55 marks, PL no. 290408.

FU: face 400 mm, 66 marks, PL no. 290409.

FU: face 500 mm, 75 marks, PL no. 290410.

Finish
Metal casing. White face with black outer numbers and inscription "Electronos/AEG", red inner numbers.

References
Private collection, Berlin; *AEG-Mitteilungen* 1928, 1931.

P106

•P107
Outdoor Clock
ca. 1910

Model a of this clock had two faces and was intended for outdoor use on a bracket, also designed by Behrens. The same clock was also available in hanging and standing versions, and in a one-sided model (b) for wall mounting, AC and DC versions were made.

Types, with 1912 prices
a: face 500 mm, 360 marks, PL no. 4184.

a: face 600 mm, 400 marks, PL no. 4185.

b: face 500 mm, 265 marks, PL no. 4199.

b: face 600 mm, 300 marks, PL no. 4200.

Finish
Metal casing painted pale green, metal face painted white.

References
AEG price list "Auszug aus den Speziallisten" (January 1912), p. 96; ibid. (July 1912), p. 208; *MdBEW* 8, no. 10 (October 1912), p. 156; *Int. AEG-Ztg.* 16, no. 8 (February 1914), suppl., p. 19.

P107

•P108
Earlier AEG Clocks

Three electric clocks for houses and small offices. Types A, E, G, and H were fitted with a striking mechanism.

Types, with 1912 prices
Low voltage

FKR, forms A, B, D, H: 45 marks, PL nos. 4162, 4047, 4167, 4164.

FKR, forms C, E, F: 50 marks, PL nos. 4163, 4166, 4161.

FKR, form G: 55 marks, PL no. 4165.

High voltage

FKR, forms A, B, D, H: 50 marks, PL nos. 4161, 4048, 4156, 4153.

FKR, forms C, E, F: 55 marks, PL nos. 4152, 4155, 4150.

FKR, form G: 60 marks, PL no. 4154.

The additional charge for the striking mechanism varied from 16.50 to 24 marks.

Finish
Forms A–H: oak or walnut housing, stained in nine different colors. Form G in mahogany only.

References
AEG price list "Auszug aus den Speziallisten" (January 1912), p. 95; ibid. (July 1912), p. 207; *Int. AEG-Ztg.* 16, no. 8 (February 1914), suppl., p. 11 (form E); *MdBEW* 10, no. 8 (August 1914), p. 118 (form E).

P108

•P109
Alarm Clock
ca. 1910

Electric clock with alarm device for houses, factories, and schools. The clock could also be coupled with separately installed alarms, such as one for domestic servants.

Types
Low-voltage model: PL no. 4060, 1912 price 80 marks
High-voltage model: PL no. 4061, 1912 price 85 marks

Finish
Oak housing.

References
AEG price list "Auszug aus den Speziallisten" (January 1912), p. 96; ibid. (July 1912), p. 208.

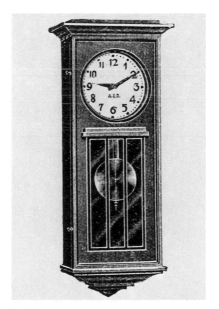

P109

•P110
Clock with 24-Hour Time Switch
ca. 1910

White-painted face, black lettering "Zeiger nur vorwärts drehen/AEG", oak housing; height 760 mm, face diameter 160 mm.

Reference
Private collection, Berlin.

P110

•P111
Time Clock for Workplaces
ca. 1910

This clock could work independently or be controlled by a master clock. The clockwork and the stamping mechanism were linked by a drive shaft.

Types and 1924 prices
Two different types were offered, with the same dimensions: height 916 mm, width 380 mm, depth of clock unit 175 mm, depth of base 260 mm.

K1, with independent mechanism and one-color ribbon: 680 marks.

K1, with master-clock control and one-color ribbon: 700 marks.

K2, with independent mechanism and two-color ribbon: 750 marks.

K2, with master-clock control and two-color ribbon: 770 marks.

Finish
Wooden or sheet-metal housing.

References
Int. AEG-Ztg. 15, no. 8 (February 1913), suppl. *MdBEW* 10, no. 8 (August 1914), p. 118; ibid. 11, no. 12 (December 1915), pp. 185–186; *AEG-Ztg.* 5 (May 1924), pp. 73–77; Prospectus "AEG Registrier-Uhren für Handel und Industrie" (no date).

BERLIN | **AEG** | 1913

Arbeiter-Kontroll-Uhren

Allgemeine Elektricitäts-Gesellschaft

P111

•P112
Independent and Master Clocks
ca. 1910

Two independent clocks (a and d; see P108) and two pendulum master clocks. The independent clocks could be supplied to order as table or mantelpiece models, like d. Behrens exhibited this model in the reception room he designed for the Keller and Reiner Gallery in Berlin. While P112b was the same as P100, the octagonal housing of the face gave an added elegance to P112c.

Types
See P100 and P108.

Finish
See P100 and P108.

References
Stoedtner photo 71996; Michel 1910, p. 131.

P112

•P113
Convection Heater
1909

Portable AC heater with two settings, in ornamental cast-iron housing. In contrast to the filament heaters, which were intended for use over brief periods in small rooms, the convector heaters were intended for constant use.

References
Stoedtner photo 71989 (right); *MdBEW* 6, no. 10 (October 1910), p. 160 (drawing of oven in advertisement on back cover); Breuer 1910, p. 266; Hoeber 1913, p. 108, illustration 120; Anderson 1968, illustration 99b.

P113

•P114
Convection Heater
1909

As P113, with different ornamentation.

P114

•P115
Convection Heater
1909

As P113, with different ornamentation.

Reference
Stoedtner photo 71989 (left).

P115

•P116
Electric Fire
(Bing-Werke, Nuremberg, ca. 1920)

The triangular housing stood on two spherical feet and a rear support. The central heating element was surrounded by a reflector bowl. Height 700 mm, depth 550 mm. AC or DC.

Finish
Hammered sheet metal.

References
RfF photo VI/964 (dated around 1907); Lanzke 1958, p. 15, illustration 15d (dated 1908); Catalog 1966, catalog no. 205, illustration 54; Anderson 1968, illustration 100b; Herwin Schaefer, *Nineteenth Century Modern, the Functional Tradition in Victorian Design* (New York and Washington, 1970), p. 191, no. 281 (dated 1906).

P116

Electric Fires
ca. 1908 (?)

The models with two and three lamps cannot definitely be ascribed to Behrens, in spite of their considerable similarity. AC and DC versions were made.

Types, with 1912 prices
At least nine types were offered.

PL no. 12h: height 550 mm, width 465 mm, depth 160 mm, 48 marks (P117).

PL no. 10h: height 510 mm, width 370 mm, depth 95 mm, 24 marks (P118).

PL no. 11h: height 550 mm, width 425 mm, depth 170 mm, 48 marks (P119).

PL no. 13h: height 700 mm, width 480 mm, depth 140 mm, 42 marks (P120).

PL no. 14h: height 450 mm, width 460 mm, depth 220 mm, 42 marks (P121).

PL no. 15h: height 680 mm, width 450 mm, depth 100 mm, 60 marks (P122).

PL no. 16h: height 660 mm, width 450 mm, depth 100 mm, 76 marks (P123).

PL no. 17h: height 570 mm, width 470 mm, depth 130 mm, 82 marks (P124).

PL no. 18h: height 555 mm, diameter 240 mm, 90, 96, and 114 marks (P125).

Finishes
PL no. 12h: polished copper.

PL no. 10h: matte-black iron grip and feet, copper reflector.

PL no. 11h: polished copper.

PL no. 13h: matte-black iron sheet, copper reflector.

PL no. 14h: antique copper with brass columns, polished copper reflector.

PL no. 15h: brass, copper reflector.

PL no. 16h: silver-oxidized copper, bronze surround, copper reflector.

PL no. 17h: hand-hammered antique copper.

PL no. 18h: model M, polished brass; model K, polished copper; model S, heavy matte-silver plate.

References
AEG-Ztg. 11, no. 6 (December 1908), suppl. 4; AEG price list "Elektrische Öfen, Heiz- und Kochapparate" (1911), pp. 3–10; AEG price list "Auszug aus den Spezialisten" (July 1912), p. 204; *MdBEW* 8, no. 9 (September 1912), p. 135 (illustration of PL no. 18h); AEG price list "Elektrische Öfen, Heiz- und Kochapparate Heizregister, Fusswärmer" (October 1912), pp. 3–7; *MdBEW* 8, no. 12 (December 1912), p. 178 (illustration of PL no. 12h—"We see in the AEG showroom at number 4 Königgrätzer Strasse a whole row of electric heaters with enticing forms designed by Professor Behrens"); ibid. 12, no. 12 (December 1916), p. 185.

P117

P118

P119

P120

P121

P122

P123

P124

P125

• P126–P132

Convection Heaters
ca. 1908 (?)

The AEG price lists of 1911 and 1912 contained convection heaters that cannot definitely be ascribed to Behrens. His involvement can be conjectured, however, on the grounds of the close similarity with P113–P115.

Types, with 1911–12 Prices
At least seven different types were offered, in AC and DC.

PL no. 3529: height 650 mm, width 550 mm, depth 300 mm, 112 marks (P126).

PL no. 3668: height 700 mm, width 460 mm, depth 219 mm, 77 marks (P127).

PL no. 3664: height 670 mm, width 455 mm, depth 180 mm, 93 marks (P128).

PL no. 3669: height 660 mm, width 480 mm, depth 210 mm, 100 marks (P129).

PL no. 3530: height 665 mm, width 450 mm, depth 220 mm, 80 marks (P130).

PL no. 3665: height 705 mm, width 510 mm, depth 265 mm, 160 marks (P131.)

PL no. 3666: height 715 mm, width 535 mm, depth 280 mm, 180 marks (P132).

Finishes
PL no. 3529: hand-hammered cast iron,

PL no. 3668: hammered sheet iron,

PL no. 3664: tombac,

PL no. 3669: hammered tombac,

PL no. 3530: hammered sheet iron,

PL no. 3665: bronze sheet.

PL no. 3666: bronze sheet.

References
AEG price list "Electrische Öfen, Heiz- und Kochapparate" (1911), p. 16; AEG price list "Elektrische Öfen, Heiz- und Kochapparate Heizregister, Fusswärmer" (October 1912), pp. 10–12; AEG price list "Auszug aus den Spezialliste" (July 1912), p. 202 (PL no. 3530); MdBEW 8, no. 9 (September 1912), p. 135 (PL no. 3665).

P127

P128

P129

P130

P126

P131

P132

• P133
Electric Kettles, Earlier Models

This advertisement (graphic design by Behrens, ca. 1910) shows models that were still produced after 1909 in addition to those designed by Behrens.

Reference
Meyer-Schönbrunn 1913, p. 25.

P133

• P134–P137
Round Electric Kettles
1909

These electric kettles had a rounded form, a rounded handle clad with woven cane attached to circular lugs, and a short, broad spout set low on the body. The increasing girth of the knob on the lid contrasts directly against the taper of the kettle. This model was also supplied without an electric heating element (see G53).

Types, with 1912 Prices
PL no. 3580: 0.75 liter, nickel-plated brass, smooth, 18 marks (a).

PL no. 3590: 1.25 liters, nickel-plated brass, smooth, 21 marks (a).

PL no. 3600: 1.75 liters, nickel-plated brass, smooth, 23 marks (a).

PL no. 3583: 0.75 liter, matte brass, smooth, 18 marks (a1).

PL no. 3593: 1.25 liters, matte brass, smooth, 22 marks (a1).

PL no. 3603: 1.75 liters, matte brass, smooth, 23 marks (a1).

PL no. 3581: 0.75 liter, nickel-plated brass, grooved, 19 marks (a2).

PL no. 3591: 1.25 liters, nickel-plated brass, grooved, 22 marks (a2).

PL no. 3601: 1.75 liters, nickel-plated brass, grooved, 24 marks (a2).

PL no. 3584: 0.75 liter, copper, grooved, 20 marks (a2).

PL no. 3594: 1.25 liters, copper, grooved, 24 marks (a2).

PL no. 3604: 1.75 liters, copper, grooved, 24 marks (a2).

PL no. 3582: 0.75 liter, brass, grooved, 19 marks (a2).

PL no. 3592: 1.25 liters, brass, grooved, 24 marks (a2).

PL no. 3602: 1.75 liters, brass, grooved, 25 marks (a2).

References
RfF photos R 1551 A (dated 1908), R 1551 B (dated 1908); AEG "Werkfoto" ZWA/Fo V/957 (with different knob on lid, dated 1908); Hagen photo 14999 (a,b,c); Marburg photo 618938 (a,b); *MdBEW* 6, no. 2 (February 1910), p. 32 (b with drawing); Breuer 1910, p. 266 (a,b,c); *MdBEW* 6, no. 12 (December 1910), p. 183 (a,b,c); *Int. AEG-Ztg.* 14, no. 7 (January 1912), suppl. 4 (a,b,c); AEG price list "Elektrische Heiz- und Kochapparate" (July 1912) (a,b,c); *JDW* 1912, p. 68 (a,b,c); *Int. AEG-Ztg.* 16, no. 4 (October 1913), suppl. (a,b,c); Hoeber 1913, p. 107, illustrations 115–117 (a,b,c; dated 1909); *MdBEW* 11, no. 1 (January 1915), p. 16, advertisement; *JDW* 1915, p. 68; Lanzke 1958, p. 12 (dated 1910); *Enciclopedia universale dell'arte*, vol. 7 (1958), plate 290 (a,b; dated 1908); von Moos 1967, illustration 15 (a, dated 1909); Catalog 1966, illustration 53, cat. no. 205 (b); Catalog Darmstadt 1967, vol. 2, no. 212 (a, dated ca. 1908); Pevsner 1968, p. 172, illustrations 172 and 173 (a,b); Anderson 1968, illustration 101b (a,b); Hans Eckstein, *Die neue Sammlung* (Munich, no date), illustration 83 (dated ca. 1908).

P134

P135

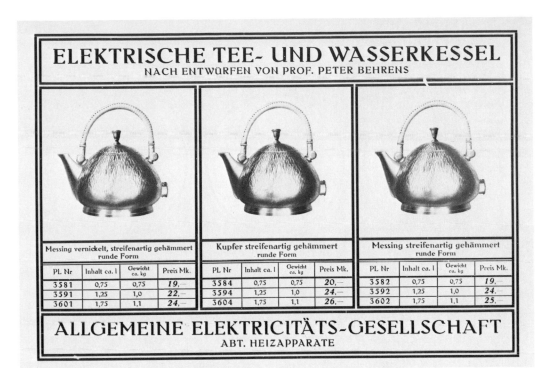

ELEKTRISCHE TEE- UND WASSERKESSEL
NACH ENTWÜRFEN VON PROF. PETER BEHRENS

Messing vernickelt, streifenartig gehämmert runde Form				Kupfer streifenartig gehämmert runde Form				Messing streifenartig gehämmert runde Form			
PL Nr	Inhalt ca. l	Gewicht ca. kg	Preis Mk.	PL Nr	Inhalt ca. l	Gewicht ca. kg	Preis Mk.	PL Nr	Inhalt ca. l	Gewicht ca. kg	Preis Mk.
3581	0,75	0,75	19,—	3584	0,75	0,75	20,—	3582	0,75	0,75	19,—
3591	1,25	1,0	22,—	3594	1,25	1,0	24,—	3592	1,25	1,0	24,—
3601	1,75	1,1	24,—	3604	1,75	1,1	26,—	3602	1,75	1,1	25,—

ALLGEMEINE ELEKTRICITÄTS-GESELLSCHAFT
ABT. HEIZAPPARATE

P136

ELEKTRISCHE TEE- UND WASSERKESSEL
NACH ENTWÜRFEN VON PROF. PETER BEHRENS

Die Kessel werden auch ohne elektrische Heizung und Rohre geliefert und erhalten dann zum Unterschied von Obigen als Zusatz den Buchstaben „n", also z. B. 3580 n. Die Preise betragen ohne Heizung Mark 8,— weniger.

Messing vernickelt, glatt runde Form				Messing glatt, matt runde Form			
PL Nr	Inhalt ca. l	Gewicht ca. kg	Preis Mk.	PL Nr	Inhalt ca. l	Gewicht ca. kg	Preis Mk.
3580	0,75	0,75	18,—	3583	0,75	0,75	18,—
3590	1,25	1,0	21,—	3593	1,25	1,0	22,—
3600	1,75	1,1	23,—	3603	1,75	1,1	23,—

ALLGEMEINE ELEKTRICITÄTS-GESELLSCHAFT
ABT. HEIZAPPARATE

P137

• P138–P140

Octagonal Electric Kettles
1909

These kettles had a square-formed handle and a long spout set low on the body.

Types, with 1912 Prices

PL no. 3587: 0.75 liter, nickel-plated brass, smooth, 19 marks (b).

PL no. 3597: 1.25 liters, nickel-plated brass, smooth, 22 marks (b).

PL no. 3607: 1.75 liters, nickel-plated brass, smooth, 23 marks (b).

PL no. 3588: 0.75 liter, matte brass, smooth, 20 marks (b1).

PL no. 3598: 1.25 liters, matte brass, smooth, 22 marks (b1).

PL no. 3608: 1.75 liters, matte brass, smooth, 24 marks (b1).

PL no. 3589: 0.75 liter, hammered copper, 22 marks (b2).

PL no. 3599: 1.25 liters, hammered copper, 24 marks (b2).

PL no. 3690: 1.75 liters, hammered copper, 26 marks (b2).

References
AEG ''Werkfoto'' ZWA/Fo VI/ 956; AEG ''Fachgebiet'' ZWf/Fo VI/955; as P135–P137.

P138

P139

ELEKTRISCHE TEE- UND WASSERKESSEL
NACH ENTWÜRFEN VON PROF. PETER BEHRENS

Messing glatt, matt achteckige Form				Kupfer flockig gehämmert achteckige Form				Messing vernickelt, glatt achteckige Form			
PL Nr	Inhalt ca. l	Gewicht ca. kg	Preis Mk.	PL Nr	Inhalt ca. l	Gewicht ca. kg	Preis Mk.	PL Nr	Inhalt ca. l	Gewicht ca. kg	Preis Mk.
3588	0,75	1,75	20,—	3589	0,75	0,75	22,—	3587	0,75	0,75	19,—
3598	1,25	1,0	22,—	3599	1,25	1,0	24,—	3597	1,25	1,0	22,—
3608	1,75	1,1	24,—	3690	1,75	1,1	26,—	3607	1,75	1,1	23,—

ALLGEMEINE ELEKTRICITÄTS-GESELLSCHAFT
ABT. HEIZAPPARATE

P140

• P141

Oval Electric Kettles
1909

These kettles had a square-formed handle clad with woven cane, delicate fluting at the top of the body, and a round knob on a flat lid.

Types, with 1912 Prices
PL no. 3585: 0.75 liter, nickel-plated brass, smooth, 19 marks (c).

PL no. 3595: 1.25 liters, nickel-plated brass, smooth, 21 marks (c).

PL no. 3605: 1.75 liters, nickel-plated brass, smooth, 23 marks (c).

PL no. 3586: 0.75 liter, matte brass, smooth, 19 marks (c1).

PL no. 3596: 1.25 liters, matte brass, smooth, 22 marks (c1).

PL no. 3606: 1.75 liters, matte brass, smooth, 24 marks (c1).

References
As for P135–P137.

ELEKTRISCHE TEE- UND WASSERKESSEL
NACH ENTWÜRFEN VON PROF. PETER BEHRENS

AUSFÜHRUNG:

Leicht auswechselbare Patronenheizkörper, komplett, mit Anschlußstöpsel, 2 m Litze und Stecker PL Nr 725

Die 0,75 l Kocher haben einen Stromverbrauch von 275 Watt, die 1,25 und 1,75 l Kocher einen Stromverbrauch von 440 Watt

Messing vernickelt, glatt
ovale Form

PL. Nr	Inhalt ca. l	Gewicht ca. kg	Preis Mk.
3585	0,75	0,75	19,—
3595	1,25	1,0	21,—
3605	1,75	1,1	23,—

Messing glatt, matt
ovale Form

PL. Nr	Inhalt ca. l	Gewicht ca. kg	Preis Mk.
3586	0,75	0,75	19,—
3596	1,25	1,0	22,—
3606	1,75	1,1	24,—

ALLGEMEINE ELEKTRICITÄTS-GESELLSCHAFT
ABT. HEIZAPPARATE

P141

Graphics

Gabriele Heidecker

• G1–G3

Cover Design and Title of *Mitteilungen der Berliner Elektricitäts-Werke*
1906–07

This magazine appeared in Behrens's cover design with volume 2 (1906) and volume 3, no. 1 (January 1907). In the volumes covering 1907–1909, one design was adhered to throughout the year and only the color was changed for each issue.

Common to all the designs is the basic geometric composition of the front cover and of the calendar on the back cover. The decorative contents of the framework varied from year to year: volume 3 (1907) has black circles, stylized scrolls and a square signet (G1), volume 4 (1908) has a pattern of superimposed circles and squares arranged concentrically around a square signet (G2), and volume 5 (1909) has four rings with a zigzag motif set concentrically around a circular signet (G3). The last issue to appear in the Behrens format was volume 3, no. 11 (November 1909).

Technique
Letterpress printing. Cover: Buchbinderei Wübben & Co., Berlin, Wilhelmstrasse 9.

Colors
Cover: gray-blue ground, black script and border, beige frame. Title page: white ground with black script and border; various colors.

References
Original: AEG-Telefunken, Berlin; title page: Meyer-Schönbrunn 1913, illustrations on pp. 22–24; von Moos 1976, illustrations 13, 14; Catalog Darmstadt, 1976, vol. 2, no. 363; Buddensieg and Rogge 1977, p. 5, illustration 2. Cover: *MdBEW* 4, no. 12 (December 1908), illustration on p. 189; ibid. 5, no. 12 (December 1909), p. 190.

G1
Cover of *MdBEW*, 1907.

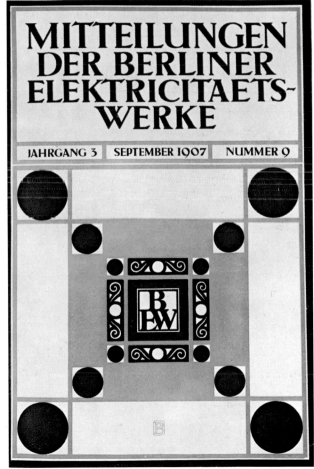

G2
Cover of *MdBEW*, 1908.

G3
Cover of *MdBEW*, 1909.

JUNI

MITTEILUNGEN
DER BERLINER
ELEKTRICITAETS-
WERKE

JAHRGANG 4   JULI 1908   NUMMER 7

S	◉	7	14	21	28
M	1	8	15	22	29
D	2	9	16	23	30
M	3	10	17	24	◉
D	4	11	18	25	◉
F	5	12	19	26	◉
S	6	13	20	27	◉

FEBRUAR

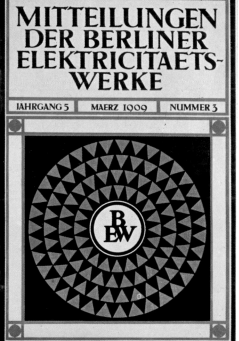

MITTEILUNGEN
DER BERLINER
ELEKTRICITAETS-
WERKE

JAHRGANG 5   MAERZ 1909   NUMMER 3

S	•	7	14	21	28
M	1	8	15	22	•
D	2	9	16	23	•
M	3	10	17	24	•
D	4	11	18	25	•
F	5	12	19	26	•
S	6	13	20	27	•

• G4, G5

Cover of *Mitteilungen der Berliner Elektricitäts-Werke*, Precursors and Successors

Even before the Behrens layout, *MdBEW* appeared each month in a different cover design and color, and with a calendar on the back cover [G4—designed by Emil von Doepler; signature E.D.; see Goldstein, *Monogramm-Lexicon* (1964), p. 167]. Photographs of AEG products on the back cover and of AEG buildings on the title page first appeared with volume 7 (1911). Although this format was pursued in the following years, only volume 7 had a cover design with script, decoration, and signet in the Behrens manner.

Technique
As G1–G3.

Colors
Various.

Reference
Original: AEG-Telefunken, Berlin.

G4
Cover of volume 2 (1906). The covers of volume 5, no. 12 (December 1909) and volume 6, nos. 1–12 (January–December 1910) appeared with illustrative graphics by L. ten Hompel [signature: L.t.H.; see Uebe, *Künstlerzeichen* (1919), no. 237]. For the design of the back cover see G67.

G5
Cover of volume 7, no. 6 (June 1911).

•G6
Title Page of *AEG-Zeitung*, Precursor to Behrens's Design

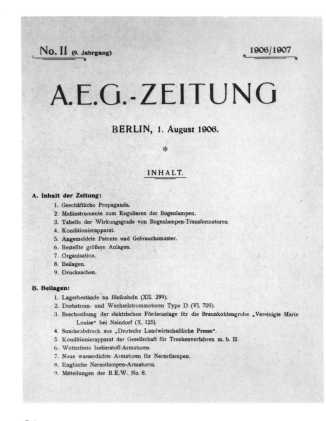

G6

•G7
Title Page of *AEG-Zeitung* 1907

Handwritten Behrens Roman script. The first issue in the new format was volume 10, no. 1 (July 1907). This format was retained until March 1909. Some alterations then appeared as a result of the change of the title to *Interne AEG-Zeitung*, but the script remained unchanged. A special edition of the *AEG-Zeitung* printed in Behrens-Antiqua was "AEG-ZEITUNG/ BERLIN/ XI. JAHRG. N°. 10-APRIL 1909." The same script was also used for the English language version, entitled AEG-JOURNAL.

Technique
Letterpress printing.

Dimensions
26.8 × 20.3 cm.

Colors
Light gray card; black print.

Reference
Original: AEG-Telefunken, Berlin.

G7

•G8
Cover of Special Edition of *AEG-Zeitung* 1908

This special edition, marking the seventieth birthday of Emil Rathenau, had 24 pages with 8 illustrations, including a photograph of Rathenau.

Technique
Letterpress printing.

Dimensions
25 × 19.4 cm.

Colors
Cream-colored card; black and green printing.

Reference
Private collection, Berlin.

A.E.G.-ZEITUNG
FESTNUMMER: 11. 12. 1908

G8

• G9, G10
AEG Exhibition Guide to Deutsche Schiffbau-Ausstellung
1908

This catalog to the AEG's special exhibition at the 1908 Schiffbau-Ausstellung had 15 pages with 7 illustrations. The covers are shown above as illustration A1. Title page (G9): Text as on front cover, each block of text in its own frame. Lower frame decorated with a diamond motif which emphasizes the central axis of the page ["Behrens Roman" decoration, as used on the back cover of *AEG-Ztg.* 11, nos. 10 ff. (April 1909–October 1909]. Text: Yellow frame around every page. Ornament on p. 3 made up of six identical elements. Decorated initial D on p. 4 at start of description of exhibition (G10). The same D also appeared with a different border in the Rathenau address of 1907 (G24), the 25th-anniversary Festschrift, 1908, and the invitation card of the AEG salesroom in Königgrätzer Strasse, 1910 (P1).

Technique
Letterpress printing, Georg Büxenstein und Comp., Berlin.

Typefaces
Cover: Roman, handwritten by Behrens. Text: first known example of the Behrens Roman typeface, with accompanying ornament, introduced October 1908.

Dimensions
17.7 × 12.4 cm. Frame on front cover 16.2 × 11 cm, on title page 14.2 × 4.9 cm, on text pages 14 × 9.4 cm.

Colors
Cover: chamois-colored ground with black lettering, graphics, and inner frames; outer frame yellow. Text pages: black lettering and yellow frames.

References
Peter Behrens, letter of 23 September 1909, KEO Archive, Hagen (Kü 418/120); Stoedtner photo 69 161; *Zeitschrift für Bücherfreunde* 2 (1910), illustrations 2, 122; Buddensieg and Rogge 1976, p. 113, nos. 14, 15; Buddensieg and Rogge 1977, p. 4.

DEUTSCHE SCHIFFBAU-AUSSTELLUNG 1908

ALLGEMEINE ELEKTRICITÆTS GESELLSCHAFT

II. 884.

G9

Der Blick des Besuchers fällt zunächst auf den in natürlicher Größe und bordmäßig gehaltenen vorderen Maschinenraum eines Torpedobootes. Es ist mit Dampfturbinen und, dem Kolbenmaschinen - Betrieb analog, nur mit zwei Wellen und Propellern ausgerüstet. Wenn auch die entsprechend große Kolbendampfmaschine zum Vergleich fehlt, so erkennt man doch an der einfachen Bauart die Vorzüge des neuen Motors für Fahrzeuge, auf denen jeder Kubikmeter Raum ausgenutzt, der Maschinendienst im Interesse der aufs äußerste angestrengten Mannschaft möglichst vereinfacht werden muß.

Der Beschauer sieht die Steuerbord-Turbine links, den zugehörigen Kondensator rechts, während der dahinterliegende Raum die Backbord-Turbine mit ihrem Kondensator in umgekehrter Anordnung enthält; die Schraubenwelle der ersten Maschine läuft also unter dem Kondensator der zweiten hindurch. Jede Turbine leistet bei 600 Umdrehungen i. d. Minute 6000 bis 7000 PS und treibt ihre Welle vollkommen unabhängig von der anderen Maschine. Das ist ein Vorteil des hier angewandten Turbinensystems, der sich namentlich beim Manövrieren dadurch geltend macht, daß für den Uebergang vom Vorwärts- zum Rückwärtslauf keine komplizierten Zwischenrohrleitungen, die den

G10

•G11
Announcement in Official Schiffbau-Ausstellung Catalog
1908

Page 303 from *Amtlicher Führer für die Deutsche Schiffbau-Ausstellung Berlin 1908*. Handwritten Roman.

Technique
Letterpress printing.

Dimensions
15 × 8.7 (frame).

G11

•G12, G13
AEG Twenty-Fifth Anniversary Festschrift
1908

Cover (G12): like the square plaquette with the eagle (by H. Hahn?), the title "AEG/ 1883–1908" is firmly placed within a rigid framework, which stands on the cover like a rectangular block. (The same plaquette appeared in an embossed version on the brown pasteboard cover of a volume of anniversary songs: "12 Dezember 1908".) Title (G13): handwritten Roman. A narrow, two-banded frame set well in from the edge of the page surrounds the text and the illustrations throughout the Festschrift, and the paper is cream-colored. Page 7 (not shown): Apart from the border, the Behrens Roman initial D is the same as those shown in G10 and P1.

Dating
As the anniversary of the company's founding fell on 14 April 1908, the Festschrift must have been completed by this date.

Technique
Brown cloth cover with embossed script and fine lines. Plaquette held by four clasps stamped out of zinc sheet.

Dimensions
Outer edges 37 × 33 cm; frame 35.6 × 31.8 cm; plaquette 12.5 × 12.5 cm (pamphlet 24 × 16 cm).

References
Original: private collection; Berlin; "Die AEG 1883–1908," *MdBEW* 4, no. 5 (May 1908), pp. 66–73.

G12

G13

Commemorative Publication on the Death of Emil Rathenau
1915

Commemorative publication brought out by Verein der Beamten der AEG und BEW. No date; 62 pages with illustrations.

Technique
Letterpress printing.

Dimensions
Frame 27.9 × 20.8 cm.

Colors
Lettering and borders in gold and dark gray on light-gray ground. Photographs of Rathenau and of Rathenau Medal (back cover) overprinted in gold.

Reference
Original: Kunsthistorisches Institut der Freie Universität Berlin.

G14
Front cover of Emil Rathenau commemorative publication.

• G15–G17

Three Sheets with Various Scripts

Peter Behrens

Script designs for titles, for use in brochures, pamphlets, price lists, etc. As the letters did not exist in print form and had to be adjusted to fit the differing formats of the publications, they were written out by hand each time. Discrepancies in the spacing and form of the lettering were a natural consequence. However, intentional alterations in the serifs and a tendency in G17 toward gentler, more rounded contours can also be observed. (In G15 and G16 the horizontal and vertical strokes form a perfect right angle; in G17 the angle has been rounded off by subsequent correction.) The numbers in G16 were used by Behrens on his clock faces; see P106.

Technique

Pen, ink, and zinc white on card strips.

Dimensions

Average length of line 23 cm; letters of varying heights; numbers in G16 1.9 cm.

Reference

Private collection, Berlin.

G15

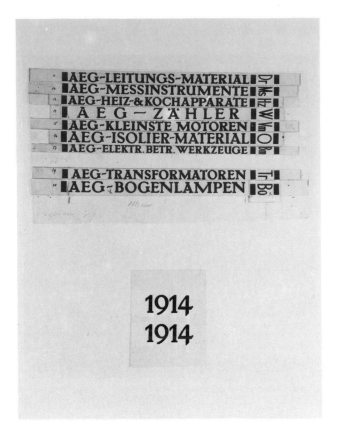

G16

Design for Sans-Serif Script

Peter Behrens

This sans-serif script is lighter and more closely spaced than the standard script in the *AEG Normalien* (1916), no. 120, pp. 89/90. The lower-case S is narrower, and the lower-case R has a rolled-up hook. Compare the upper-case letters with the inscription on the window of the Königgrätzer Strasse showroom (P7).

Technique
Pen and black ink, with corrections with zinc white, on lined parchment paper.

Dimensions
15 × 46 cm; height of letters 2 cm.

References
Original: private collection, Berlin; *AEG-Normalien* (1916), no. 120, pp. 89/90.

G17

G18

•G19

Design for Alphabet
Peter Behrens

Upper-case alphabet in Roman script, with the words "diese machen Worte zeichnen" underneath in Behrens's handwriting. The initials for the AEG trademark were taken from this alphabet (see G80), and it was used in numerous versions in brochures, posters, advertisements, and inscriptions. (A page of pencil sketches in the Behrens papers show early studies, and the note "poliphili" points to the model for this script: the "Hypnerotomachia Poliphili" of Aldus Manutius, Venice, 1499.

Technique
Pencil on parchment.

Dimensions
19 × 26.5 cm; height of letters 2 cm.

Reference
Original: private collection, Berlin.

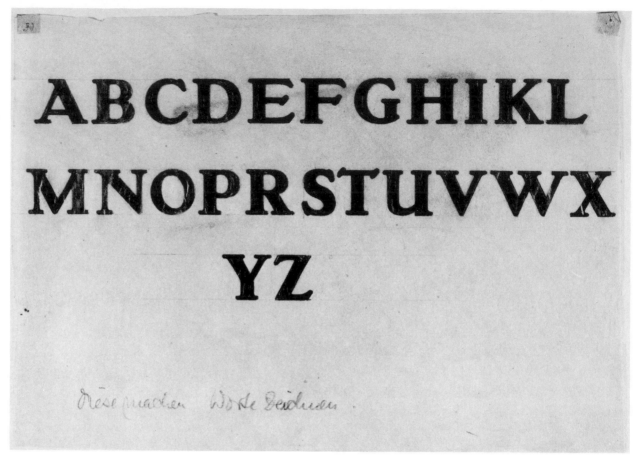

G19

G20

•G20
Script Design for Names of Months
Peter Behrens

Technique
Black ink over pencil preliminary drawing; corrections in white paint.

Dimensions
First page 17.8 × 26.8 cm, second page 19.2 × 26.3 cm; height of letters 2.6 cm.

Reference
Original: Pfalzgalerie, Kaiserslautern.

•G21
AEG Calendar for 1910
Peter Behrens

Below the title, two photographs of AEG products flank a photograph of a workshop. The name of the product is set under the workshop (in this case, Bogenlampen), and a different product is shown for each month.

Technique
Letterpress printing.

Dimensions
60 × 45 cm.

Colors
Background white; illustrations and script black, except for Sundays and holidays, which are printed red.

References
Stoedtner photo 72399 (pages for March, June, July, cutting off border); Meyer-Schönbrunn 1913, illustration on p. 12 (August); Wember 1910, no. 22 (March, with central illustration of switchgear).

G21
From Meyer-Schönbrunn 1913.

•G22
AEG Calendar for 1913
Peter Behrens

Technique
Letterpress printing.

Colors
White background, upper part gray. Lettering, numbers, and outer frames black; double frame and numbers for Sundays and holidays red.

Reference
Meyer-Schönbrunn 1913, illustration on p. 13 (January).

G22
From Meyer-Schönbrunn 1913.

• G23–G25

Certificate to Mark Award of Grashof Memorial Medal to Emil Rathenau

Peter Behrens

Two parchment sheets bound in punched, colored leather, with handworked inscription, initials, and ornamentation and gold leaf decoration.

References

Original, according to information received from AEG-Telefunken Archive, disappeared in Braunschweig. Marburg photos 616435 (front cover); 616436 (inside pages); *MdBEW* 3, no. 1 (January 1908), illustration on p. 9, pp. 10 ff.; *Kunst und Künstler* 6, no. 10 (June 1908); Gustav E. Pazaurek, "Moderne Ehrenurkunden," *Dekorative Kunst* 14, no. 1 (October 1910), pp. 25 ff., illustration 32; Meyer-Schönbrunn 1913, illustration on p. 35; Deutsche Werkbundausstellung, Basel, 1917.

G23
Leather cover of certificate. The initials are comparable to the AEG signet; see G78. The ornamentation in the spandrel-shaped corners and the rectangular pattern filling the rest of the frame belong to the decorative elements that went with the Behrens Roman script, introduced in 1908. Marburg photo.

G24
First inside page of certificate. With slight variations, the initials D and H and the decorative elements are all taken from the Behrens Roman repertoire, although the lettering is Didone with ligatures. Marburg photo.

G25
Second page. Marburg photo.

• G26

Congratulatory Address from BEW on Twenty-Fifth Anniversary of AEG
1908

Two parchment sheets bound in dark blue leather, with handworked inscription, initials, and ornamentation and gold leaf decoration. The initials E, A, and M, the decorative elements, and the pattern used to fill the last line of the address all correspond substantially to the Behrens Roman typeface and decorations, introduced in October 1908.

Colors
Apart from the introductory sentence and the initials, the script is black, framed with violet and with green ornamentation. The initials are either all gold, gold and blue, or gold and red.

References
MdBEW 4, no. 5 (5 May 1908), p. 73 (announcement); ibid. 4, no. 6 (June 1908), illustration on p. 82; Jaumann 1909, illustrations on pp. 352 (script) and 353 (front and back covers); Gustav E. Pazaurek, ''Moderne Ehrenurkunden,'' *Dekorative Kunst* 14, no. 1 (October 1910), pp. 25 ff., illustration on p. 32; Meyer-Schönbrunn 1913, illustration on p. 36; Hoeber 1913, illustration 79, p. 75; Internationale Ausstellung für Buchgewerbe und Graphik, Leipzig, 1914, *Katalog der Abt. Neuzeitliche Buchkunst u. angew. Graphik*, illustration on p. 25.

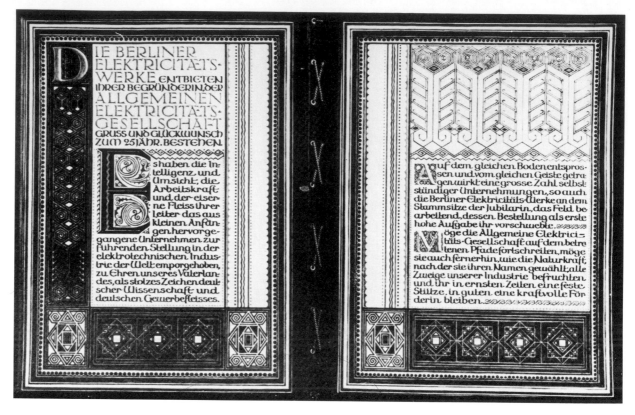

G26
From Meyer-Schönbrunn 1913.

Congratulatory Address
1913

Parchment sheet bound in leather,
with decorated text, gold initials,
and signatures.

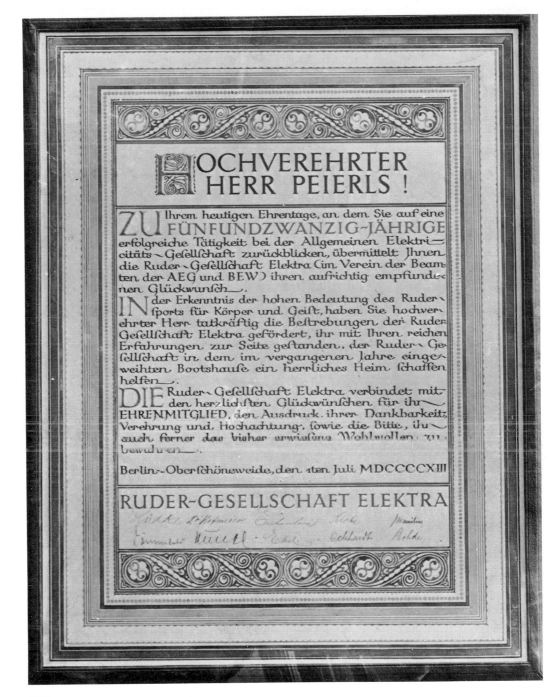

G27

**AEG Address on
Hundredth Anniversary of
Founding of Friedrich
Krupp AG.**
1912

Two parchment sheets bound in
leather, with handwritten text, initials and ornamentation, some in
gold leaf.

References
There is no trace of the address in
the Krupp company archives.
Meyer-Schönbrunn 1913, illustrations on pp. 38, 39.

G28
Inside pages. From Meyer-Schönbrunn
1913.

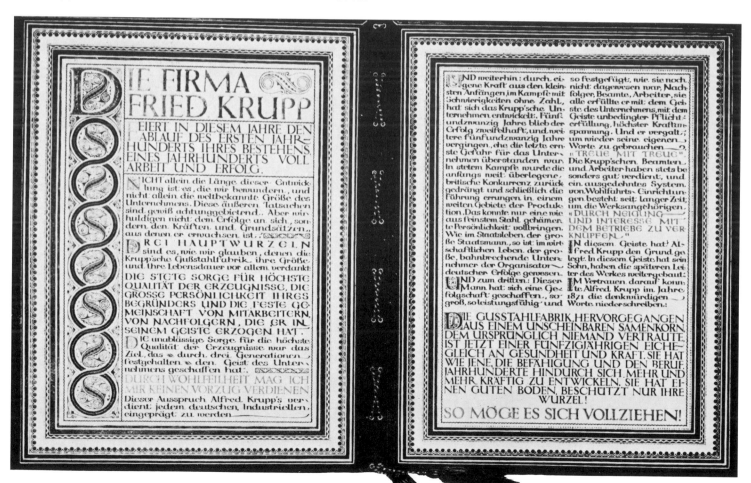

DIE
AEG
DER
FIRMA
FRIED.
KRUPP

• G30
Poster: "AEG-Metallfadenlampe"
1907

Technique
Lithograph, printed by Hollerbaum & Schmidt, Berlin.

Dimensions
67 × 52 cm.

Colors
Black and white.

References
Original: Kunstbibliothek, Berlin; Peter Behrens, letter of 23 September 1909, KEO Archive (Kü 418/120); *Graphische Werkstatten*, no. 1 (1909–10), p. 150; Hollerbaum & Schmidt (Berlin, 1910); Meyer-Schönbrunn 1913, illustration on p. 8; Wember 1961, no. 23; Weber 1961, no. 60; Schreyl 1967, no. 2; Gallo 1975, color plate on p. 165; Catalog Darmstadt, 1976, vol. 2, no. 297; *MdBEW* 3, no. 12 (December 1907), p. 178 (in negative version with slight variations).

G30

• G31
Poster: "AEG Metalldraht-Lampe"
1910

This same motif was used in a calendar illustration and on a publicity seal (see G74).

Technique
Color lithograph.

Dimensions
58 × 48 cm.

Colors
Ground dark blue-violet; lettering gold; ornament green; lamp white.

References
Original: Kunstbibliothek, Berlin; *AEG-Ztg.* 13, no. 4 (October 1910), title page; ibid. 13, no. 6 (December 1910), p. 17; ibid. 13, no. 8 (February 1911), title page; ibid. 13, no. 12 (June 1911), title page; *MdVDR* no. 30 (1912), p. 9 (publicity seal); Meyer-Schönbrunn 1913, illustration on p. 9; Klingspor, Offenbach (calendar illustration).

G31

G32

Poster Design: "AEG Metalldraht-Lampe" (Fair Copy)

Peter Behrens

This design was used again for a publicity seal (see G74).

Dimensions
Outside measurements of card 22.7 × 18.7 cm; drawing with border 20 × 16 cm.

Colors
Lamp and text "Metalldraht-Lampe" in white on midnight blue ground. "AEG" initials in vermilion with black border. Lamp holder in yellow ochre, light brown, and black, with white highlights. Filament and AEG trademark in black. The whole drawing is framed by a narrow black and a broad vermilion border.

References
Original: Pfalzgalerie, Kaiserslautern.

G32

G33

Poster Design: "AEG" with Filament Lamp (Fair Copy)

Peter Behrens

Dimensions
Outside measurements of card 14.5 × 11.5 cm; drawing 6.9 × 5.3

Colors
Black and white.

Reference
Original: Pfalzgalerie, Kaiserslautern.

G33

Dimensions
Outside measurements of paste-board 25.8 × 16.9 cm; drawing 19.0 × 19.1 cm.

Colors
Black and white.

Reference
Original: Pfalzgalerie, Kaiserslautern.

G34

● G35

**Design (for Prospectus?):
"AEG Metalldraht-
Lampe"**
Peter Behrens

Penciled Comments
Above: "Rand genau wie auf
Druck." Beside text: "1/1". Beside lamp: "vergrössern 10 cm
hoch." Below: "1/1" (crossed
out), "14,9 cm breit, 21 cm
hoch."

Dimensions
Outside measurements of card 18
× 22 cm; frame 12.1 × 16 cm.

Colors
Black and white.

Reference
Original: Pfalzgalerie,
Kaiserslautern.

G35

Design (for Prospectus?):
"AEG" with Metal-
Filament Lamp
Peter Behrens

Dimensions
Outside measurements of card 16
× 18.5 cm; frame 10.3 × 14.4
cm.

Colors
Black and white.

Reference
Original: Pfalzgalerie,
Kaiserslautern.

• G37
Prospectus for AEG Spiraldrahtlampen and AEG Metalldrahtlampen
Peter Behrens

Technique
Letterpress printing (color lithography?).

Dimensions
11.2 × 15.5 cm (double page).

Colors
Outer border red; inner border, outline of text, and drawing black; lamp white; thread of lamp holder yellow; ground blue-violet; text dark yellow ochre.

Reference
Original: Klingspor Museum, Offenbach; *JDW*, 1912.

• G38
Catalog Title: "Christbaumbeleuchtung" 1908

Technique
Letterpress printing.

Dimensions
Frame 24.6 × 19 cm.

Colors
Ground black; text dark gray-yellow; Christmas tree rich dark green with white lamps.

References
AEG-Ztg. 11, no. 5 (November 1908), suppl. 11; *MdBEW* 4, no. 12 (December 1908), advertisement on p. 178; Peter Behrens, letter of 23 September 1909, KEO Archive (Kü 418/120).

G38

G37

• G39
Brochure Cover: "Die Quarzlampe"
1908

Technique
Letterpress printing.

Dimensions
13.6 × 10.5 cm (frame).

Colors
Gray-green card; matte red printing; negative framework and lettering.

References
Original: private collection, Berlin; Buddensieg and Rogge 1977, p. 4, plate 4.

G39

• G40–G42
Designs for Arc-Lamp Catalogs
1908, 1909

After 1908 the same cover design (G40) was used for all the arc-lamp brochures. While the gray-green of the card and the black graphics remained constant, the colors were changed from product to product.

References
Cover: original in Deutsches Museum, Munich; Behrens, letter of 23 September 1909, KEO Archive, Hagen (Kü 418/120); Stoedtner photo 69 116; Meyer-Schönbrunn 1913, illustrations on pp. 17, 18; Casabella 1960, illustration on p. 24 (with additional text in central triangle). Title page: Hagen photo V 247e; Meyer-Schönbrunn 1913, p. 18; Hoeber 1913, p. 107 and illustration on p. 77; Pevsner 1968, p. 174 and illustration on p. 177. Catalog illustration: original in Deutsches Museum, Munich, *Int. AEG-Ztg.* 12, no. 5 (November 1909) (with alterations).

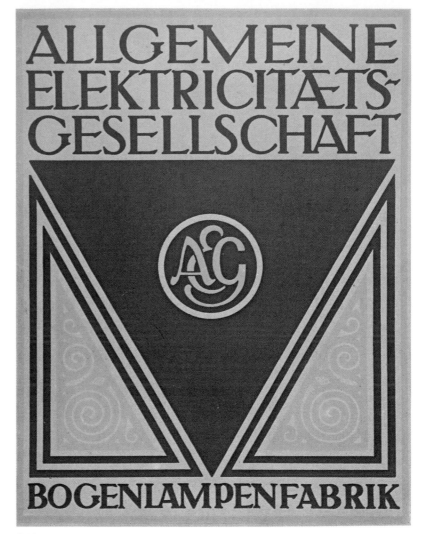

G40
Cover, 26.1 × 20.4 cm, letterpress.
Original in Klingspor Museum, Offenbach.

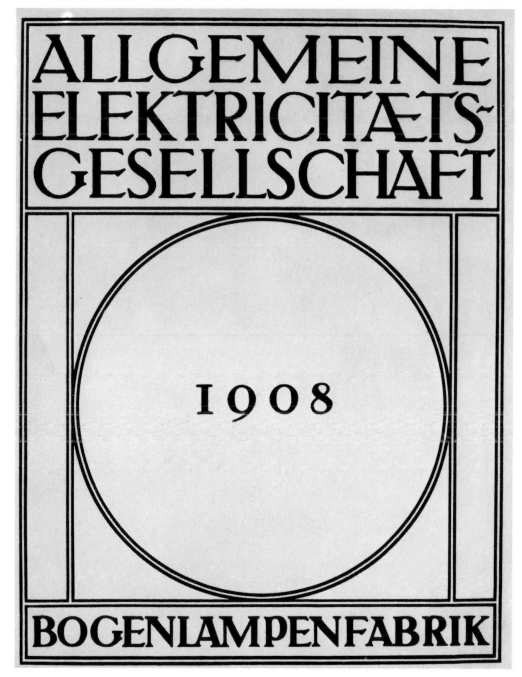

G41
Title page. Karl Ernst Osthaus Museum,
Hagen.

G42
Illustration from p. 13 of 1909 catalog.

LAMPE P.L.Nr. 67213 MIT LATERNE P.L.Nr. 68212

Pamphlet: "AEG Bogenlampen-Aufzug"
1909

Technique
Letterpress printing. Sans-serif lettering, Roman capitals, pen drawing.

Dimensions
Frame ca. 25.5 × 18.7 cm.

Colors
Rectangular framework and lamp olive green. Script, oval, and dots black on brilliant white ground.

References
Original: *Int. AEG-Ztg.* 12, no. 4 (October 1909), suppl. 6; Buddensieg and Rogge 1977, p. 130, illustration 18.

G43

- G44

Pamphlet: "AEG Intensiv-Bogenlamp für Farbenunterscheidung"
1911

Technique
Letterpress printing in Behrens Roman.

Dimensions
Frame 24.4 × 18.2 cm.

Colors
Broad frame and lettering black; dots, narrow frames, and lamp olive green.

References
Original: *Int. AEG-Ztg.* 13, no. 10 (April 1911), suppl. 4; Anderson 1968, illustration 93b.

G44

Brochure Cover: ''AEG Flammeco-Lampen''

This 1913 brochure cover, which depicts an arc lamp and the turbine hall illuminated at night, was probably designed by Lucian Bernhard, using Behrens's script, architecture, and product design .

Technique
Color lithography.

Dimensions
26.8 × 20.3 cm.

Colors
Brown card; frame, silhouette, and lamp dark brown; yellow light in hall. Highlights on lamp and hall, including trademark on gable end, gray and brown. Additional white highlights and black shadows on lamp. Lettering and background red-brown.

References
Original: *Int. AEG-Ztg.* 16, no. 6 (December 1913). For the arc lamp see P31.

G45

• G46, G47
Brochure: "Die Nitralampe der AEG"
1913

Technique
Letterpress printing.

Dimensions
28 × 20.5 cm.

Colors
Text, frame, and photograph black; ground ivory.

References
Original: *Int. AEG-Ztg.* 16, no. 4 (October 1913); 16, no. 6 (December 1913); as G47 with additional title "Allgemeine Elektricitäts-Gesellschaft" in *Int. AEG-Ztg.* 16, no. 4 (October 1913), suppl. 6; suppl. 5, price list with title page "AEG Nitra-Lampe;" Buddensieg and Rogge 1977, p. 135, illustrations 32, 33.

• G48
Catalog: "Elektrische Einrichtungen im Theater"
1908

Technique
Letterpress printing.

Dimensions
Frame 26.1 × 19.5 cm.

References
Original: *AEG-Ztg.* 11, no. 4 (October 1908), suppl. 1; Peter Behrens, letter of 23 September 1909, KEO Archive, Hagen (Kü 418/120).

G48

G46
Front page of brochure.

G47
Back page of brochure.

• G49
**Catalog:
"Bühnenbeleuchtung mit
indirekten Bogenlicht"**
1908

Graphic design as G48; handwritten Roman script.

Reference
Stoedtner photo 69115.

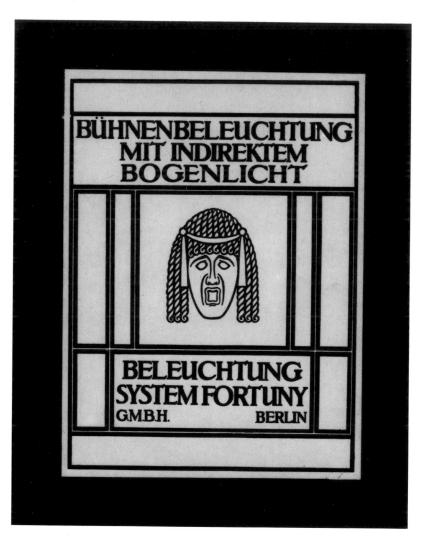

G49

• G50
**Brochure: "A.E.G.-
Scheinwerfer mit Zeiss-
Spiegel"**
1909

Technique
Letterpress printing.

Dimensions
Cover 26.9 × 20.5 cm; frame
25.3 × 19.5 cm.

Colors
Ivory-colored ground on card; lettering red; frame and searchlight symbol black.

Reference
Original: *Int. AEG-Ztg.* 11, no. 10
(April 1909), suppl. 3.

G50

• G51

Brochure: "AEG-Scheinwerfer mit Zeiss-Spiegel"
1911

Technique
Letterpress printing.

Dimensions
Cover 26.7 × 20.4 cm; frame 25.4 × 19.6 cm.

Colors
Ground red-brown on coarse linen pattern; lettering gray; frame and searchlight symbol ivory.

Reference
Original: *Int. AEG-Ztg.* 13, no. 7 (February 1911), suppl. 3.

G51

•G52

**Catalog:
"Ventilatorenfabrik"**
ca. 1908

Technique
Handwritten Roman capitals; letter-press printing.

Reference
Stoedtner photo 69115 (e.).

G52

•G53

**Price List: "Elektrische
Tee- und Wasserkessel"**
1913

Illustrated above as P136, P137, P140, P141.

Technique
Letterpress printing.

Dimensions
18.5 × 25 cm; frame 16.3 × 23 cm.

Color
Cream-gray ground; yellow stripe inside black bands of frame; letter-ing black; outside band, first stripe, and medallions white; kettles var-ious colors according to material, sometimes overprinted with red or yellow tones. Yellow overprinting on handles.

References
Original: *Int. AEG-Ztg.* 16, no. 4 (October 1913), suppl.; Catalog Darmstadt 1976, vol. 2, no. 368; Sell 1978, p. 64, illustration 44.

•G54

**Original Design for
Catalog Cover: "AEG
Ventilatoren"**
1912

The drawing, which was refined into the price list G55, shows some perspectival inaccuracies. For illus-tration see P37 above.

Dimensions
Pasteboard 28.5 × 22.5 cm; illus-tration 26.0 × 19.4 cm.

Colors
Blue lettering on white ground. Fan white; outline of fan, motor casing, and base black with strong white highlights. Ground dull blue.

References
Original drawing: Pfalzgalerie, Kaiserslautern.

• G55
Price List: "AEG Ventilatoren"
1912

The mistakes in the original design (G54, P37) have been corrected here. The same motif was also used for a publicity seal (see G74), but with a green fan on a red ground.

Technique
Letterpress printing.

Dimensions
28.4 × 22.4 cm.

Colors
Ground dull dark blue. Heading blue on white ground. Fan black to silver gray and white.

References
Original: *Int. AEG-Ztg.* 14, no. 11 (May 1912), suppl. 8; *JDW* 1913, illustration 93 (top); Catalog Darmstadt 1976, vol. 2, no. 367.

• G56
Pamphlet: "Elektrische Uhren"
1910

This front page of a clock supplement to the *Interne AEG-Zeitung* depicts the master clock illustrated above as P101.

Dimensions
Frame 25.4 × 18.9 cm.

Technique
Text in Behrens Roman; letterpress printing.

Reference
Original: *Int. AEG-Ztg.* 12, no. 9 (March 1910), suppl. 8.

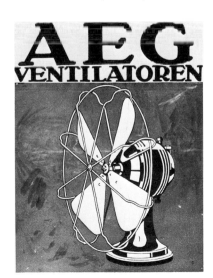

G55

G56

• G57

Prospectus: "Elektrische Uhren"

Peter Behrens

This design may have preceded G56, as the text here is handwritten whereas that in G56 is typeset.

Technique
Letterpress printing. Lettering in negative frames and clock in positive relief printing.

Dimensions
Card 25.7 × 24.6 cm; frame 19.2 × 18.8 cm.

Colors
Brown relief card; broad frame, rectangle containing oval frame and outline of clock black; dots and inner frames gold; medallion light violet; clock gray-green; clock face white with numbers and AEG signet designed by Behrens.

Reference
Original: Kunstbibliothek, Berlin.

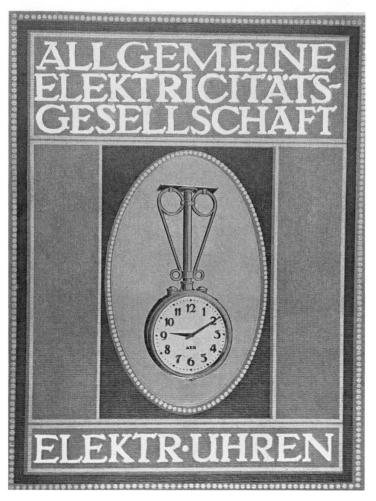

G57

• G58

Supplement: "Elektrische Uhren"
Louis Oppenheim, 1913, using forms designed by Behrens

Representation of a clock at night. Illuminated numbers and clock hands taken from a Behrens-designed clock. The same motif also appeared as a publicity seal (see G74) and as the title illustration of the brochure "Abbildungen ausgeführter Uhren-Anlagen" [Int. AEG-Ztg. 16, no. 8 (February 1914), suppl.]. The latter brochure bore the monogram "LO."

Technique
Letterpress printing.

Dimensions
26.5 × 20.8 cm.

Colors
"AEG" white, with dark blue edging; lettering white with black hatching, border and clock hands blue; numbers green; ground blue-black.

Reference
Original: *Int. AEG-Ztg.* 14, no. 11 (May 1912), suppl. 9; *MdVDR*, no. 45 (October 1913), p. 341 (small illustration with monogram "LO").

G58

Catalog: "Die AEG-Dampfturbine . . . "
1908

This catalog cover has heavy Behrens Roman ornamental bands and a strong diagonal emphasis. Behrens, in a letter to Karl Ernst Osthaus, referred to the perspective drawing of a turbine (a black-and-white full-tone rendering of a photograph) as "one of my graphic designs."

Technique
Letterpress printing.

Dimensions
26.7 × 20.5 cm.

Colors
Cream-colored ground; frame yellow ochre; lettering and drawing black.

References
Original: *AEG-Ztg.* 11, no. 5 (November 1908), suppl. 1; Stoedtner photo 69–115 (right); Behrens, letter of 23 September 1909, KEO Archive, Hagen (Kü 418/120); drawing in different frame in *AEG-Ztg.* 11, no. 11 (May 1909).

G59

• G60
Brochure: "Die Turbinenfabrikation der AEG"
1909

Cover design: recessed rectangular panel containing photograph of steam turbine (compare drawing in G59).

Technique
Letterpress printing, handwritten Roman type.

Colors
White impressed lettering on smooth, dark gray card. After 1909 a series of brochures on turbines appeared in the same design and format, some in English.

References
Originals: Deutsches Museum, Munich. Originals in English: Public Library, New York.

G60

Catalog Cover: "AEG Beleuchtung"
1910

Technique
Behrens Roman; letterpress printing.

Dimensions
Frame 25.6 × 19.3 cm.

Colors
Outer border, "AEG", outline of glass bulb, and transformer housing dark green; screw of lampholder and cable yellow; lettering, frame and shadows black.

Reference
Original: *Int. AEG-Ztg.* 12, no. 12 (June 1910), suppl. 5.

Catalog: "Schaltsäulen"
Peter Behrens (?), 1911

Technique
Letterpress printing.

Dimensions
Frame 25.2 × 18.6 cm.

Colors
Ground olive green; lettering, faces of meters, and highlights of drawing white; drawing and frames black.

References
Original: *Int. AEG-Ztg.* 13, no. 8 (February 1911), suppl. 5.

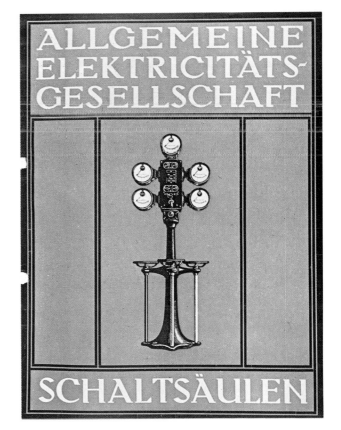

• G63

**Poster: "AEG
Geschwindigkeitsmesser
für Kraftwagen"**
1912

Technique
Color lithography.

Dimensions
60 × 40 cm.

Colors
Gray-yellow ground; lettering and
border dark gray; ground in center
circle muted orange-red; speedometer gray-brown-black. Similar
color scheme in brochure, with little
variation.

References
Original poster: Kunstbibliothek,
Berlin; *Int. AEG-Ztg.* 14, no. 10
(April 1912), suppl. 12 (as cover il-
lustration, but trimmed at the sides);
AEG-Ztg. 15, no. 10 (April 1913),
p. 17 (only the drawing of the
speedometer in black and white);
Meyer-Schönbrunn 1913, illustration
on p. 10.

G63

•G64
Pamphlet: "AEG-Tachometer"
1910

Technique
Hand lettering; letterpress printing.

Dimensions
25.2 × 18.6 cm (frame on title page).

Colors
Ground white; lettering and illustration black; frames and border light brown-gray.

References
Original: *Int. AEG-Ztg.* 12, no. 10 (April 1910), suppl. 3; Meyer-Schönbrunn 1913, illustration on p. 19.

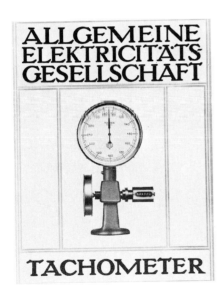

G64

•G65
Pamphlet: "AEG-Schalter"
1912

Illustrated as P90 above.

Technique
Letterpress printing.

Dimensions
Frame 22.7 × 16.4 cm.

Colors
Black and white.

Reference
Original: *AEG-Ztg.* 15, no. 9 (March 1912), suppl.

•G66
Pamphlet: "Isolierrohr Gesellschaft"

Technique
Behrens Roman; letterpress printing.

Dimensions
26.7 × 20.5 cm.

Colors
Lettering, border, and shadows in drawing black; tubes yellow ochre and yellowish green.

Reference
Original: *Int. AEG-Ztg.* 11, no. 11 (May 1910), suppl.

G66

G67

Announcements for AEG Products

Peter Behrens (?), 1909–10

This series of announcements appeared in various borders on the back cover of the magazine *Mitteilungen der Berliner Elektricitäts-Werke*. The series began with *MdBEW* 5, no. 12 (December 1909) and ran regularly on the next twelve issues [6, nos. 1–12 (1910)].

Technique
Handwritten italic type; letterpress printing.

Dimensions
Frames ca. 23.5 × 15.5 cm.

Colors
Black and white. Only in first announcement (December 1909) is the illustration in red.

G67

• G68

Brochure Cover: "AEG Zähler 1909"

1909

Technique
Text stamped into cover.

Dimensions
26.7 × 20.3 cm.

Colors
Silver lettering and frame on soft, silver-gray card.

Reference
Original: *Int. AEG-Ztg.* 12, no. 2 (August 1909), suppl. 4.

G68

• G69

Back cover of *AEG-Zeitung*, October 1909

This layout, using Behrens script and ornaments and the Behrens-designed hexagonal trademark, was used after October 1909 for the front and back covers of the *AEG-Zeitung*, with various texts.

Technique
Letterpress printing using standard type.

Dimensions
Frame 25.7 × 78.2 cm.

Colors
Black and white.

Reference
First appearance: *AEG-Ztg.* 11, no. 4 (October 1909), back cover.

G69

G70

Business Card of AEG Showroom, Königgrätzer Strasse
1910

Technique
Border in one of the Behrens Roman decorative elements; handwritten text in Roman and italic; letterpress printing.

Dimensions
7.6 × 4.3 cm.

Colors
Black script and gold ornament on white ground.

Reference
MdBEW 7, no. 3 (March 1911), illustration on p. 2; Meyer-Schönbrunn 1913, illustration on p. 29.

G71

Catalog: "AEG Elektrischer Antrieb"
1912

Technique
Handwritten Roman type; letterpress printing.

Dimensions
Frame 26 × 19.6 cm.

Colors
Outer frame, text, and medallion black; inner frames, ornamentation, and medallion cream-gray. Ground ivory-colored card.

Reference
Original: *Int. AEG-Ztg.* 15, no. 2 (August 1912), suppl. 1.

G71

G72

Advertisement: "Elektrische Kochgeräte"
Peter Behrens

Colors
Black and white.

Reference
Meyer-Schönbrunn 1913, illustration on p. 34.

G72
From Meyer-Schönbrunn 1913.

G70
From Meyer-Schönbrunn 1913.

• G73
Packing-Case Label

Technique
Handwritten Roman script.

Colors
Black and white.
No. 4

Reference
AEG photo 9734 (18 November
1912).

G73

• G74
Publicity Seals

These designs can be ascribed to Behrens with certainty only where they can be related to his poster, pamphlet, or brochure illustrations: on "Metalldraht-Lampe" see G31 and G32; on "Ventilatoren" see G55; on "Elektrische Uhren" see G58; on "Nitralampe" see G46 and G47.

Dimensions
Rectangular seals 6 × 4 cm; hexagonal seal 8 cm high and 6.5 cm wide, with 3.8-cm sides.

References
Originals: Sammlung Kourist, Bonn; "Heissluftdusche" in same format in prospectus in *Int. AEG-Ztg.* 16, no. 7 (January 1914), suppl. The model for the hexagonal seal, a demonstration panel with sets of fuses, was photographed in the exhibition room of the electrical-appliance factory (P13) and in the AEG display at the 1911 Munich exhibition [see *MdBEW* 7, no. 7 (July 1911), pp. 99 ff., illustration 2].

• G75
AEG Trademark
Franz Schwechten, 1896

Copyright applied for 11 June
1898, registered as no. 34660 in
class 42 on 6 December 1898. In-
laid into "management gate" at
107a Brunnenstrasse, built to
Schwechten's design in 1896. Also
used concurrently with new, Behrens-designed versions, for example in the AEG pavilion at the
Allgemeine Ausstellung von Erfindungen der Klein-Industrie in 1907.
See *MdBEW* 3, no. 9 (September
1907), illustrations on p. 132
(Schwechten trademark), pp. 130,
131, 135 (Behrens trademark).
See also A9.

References
AEG photo 3066 (18 August
1903); AEG photo 2704 (31 January 1903); Lanzke 1958, p. 7, illustration a; Anderson 1968,
illustration 88; Catalog Darmstadt
1976, vol. 2, no. 403 (with artist
"unknown" and dated 1895)

G75

• G76
AEG Trademark
Otto Eckmann, before 1900

Designed for AEG catalog at Paris
World Exhibition, 1900.

Reference
Original: catalog and color design
for cover, Kunstbibliothek, Berlin.

G76

G77
Courtesy of Karl Ernst Osthaus
Museum, Hagen.

• G77
AEG Trademark
Peter Behrens, 1907

Registered trademark since 1910,
although already used in 1907.
Comparable in character to G23;
E and G similar to Bohrons Italic
type.

References
Used in AEG pavilion at Allgemeine
Ausstellung von Erfindungen der
Klein-Industrie [see *MdBEW* 3, no.
9 (September 1907), illustrations on
pp. 130, 131, 135; see also G75
and A9]; AEG photo P1 51407/
08 (1 May 1908); AEG photo
8133 (8 September 1911); *DKD*
23 (1908–09), illustration on p.
82; Hellwag 1911, illustration 156
(design signed "Prof. Behrens"
and "Jordan"); KEO Museum,
Hagen (VI 313); Meyer-Schönbrunn
1913, illustration on p. 34 (lower);
Lanzke 1958, p. 7. illustration b;
Catalog Darmstadt 1976, vol. 2,
no. 410 (?), not illustrated.

• G78

AEG Trademark
Peter Behrens, 1908

Registered as trademark since
1908; E and G similar to Behrens
Italic script.

References
AEG photo, 1 December 1908
(trademark on voltmeter); Scheffler
1908, illustration on p. 434
(lower); *DKD* 23 (1908–09), illustration on p. 82; Meyer-Schönbrunn 1913, illustration on p. 34
(lower); Lanzke 1958, p. 7, illustration c; Catalog Darmstadt 1976,
vol. 2, no. 361.

G78

G79

• G79

AEG Trademark
Peter Behrens, 1908

Copyright applied for 31 January
1908; registered as no. 110446 in
class 22b on 10 September 1908.
International registration as no.
84280 on 18 October 1933.

References
AEG photo 5549 (23 June 1908,
original design); AEG photo 5550a
(23 June 1908, original design);
AEG photo 5550b (23 June 1908,
original design); AEG photo 5550c
(see A111); *MdBEW* 4, no. 5
(May 1908), p. 66; "Deutsche
Schiffbau-Ausstellung" (AEG exhibition guide), back cover (see A1);
MdBEW 4, no. 8 (August 1908), p.
117; "Amtlicher Führer für die
Deutsche Schiffbau-Ausstellung Berlin 1908" (official exhibition guide),
p. 303 (see G11); *Die Allgemeine
Elektricitäts-Gesellschaft 1883–
1908* (Berlin, 1908), p. 1, gable
end of turbine factory (see A26);
Hoeber 1913, p. 107; Meyer-
Schönbrunn 1913, illustration on
p. 34 (lower); Lanzke 1958, p.
7, illustration d; Anderson 1968, illustration 88b; Buddensieg 1975,
p. 271, illustration 1; Catalog
Darmstadt 1976, vol. 2, no. 362.

•G80
AEG Trademark

Peter Behrens, ca. 1912

Registered as a trademark since 1914. Softer contours generally, with rounded inner forms, corresponding to the script in G73.

References
AEG photo 5321 (14 February 1908, housing of trip switch); Meyer-Schönbrunn 1913, illustration on p. 34; Lanzke 1958, p. 7, illustration f (dated 1914); Catalog Darmstadt 1976, vol. 2, no. 366 (dated ca. 1912).

•G81
Neue Automobil-Gesellschaft Trademark

Peter Behrens, before 1910

References
MdBEW 6, no. 5 (May 1910), p. 76; *Int. AEG-Ztg.* 12, no. 11 (May 1910), suppl. 12; Meyer-Schönbrunn 1913, illustration on p. 34.

•G82
Neue Automobil-Gesellschaft Trademark

Peter Behrens, before 1911

References
B.Z. am Mittag, 19 October 1911 (in sports supplement, in conjunction with a drawing by Louis Oppenheim); *AEG-Mitteilungen*, no. 9 (September 1937), p. 324.

G80

G81

G82
From Meyer-Schönbrunn 1913.

•G83
Gummiwerke Oberspree Trademark
Peter Behrens, 1910

Technique
Behrens Roman script; letterpress printing.

Colors
Black and white, with red frame.

References
Original: *Int. AEG-Ztg.* 13, no. 1 (July 1910), suppl. 14; Meyer-Schönbrunn 1913, illustration on p. 21.

G83

•G84
Monograms for Berliner Elektricitätswerke
Peter Behrens, 1906, 1909

A "BEW" monogram in a square, black frame appeared for the first time in the *MdBEW* in 1906, and after the edition of 1 January 1907 was used on the title page of each issue (see G1). A circular version appeared in 1909, with the fifth volume of the *MdBEW*. A circular version with three lightning flashes on a black ground appeared in *MdBEW* 5, no. 12 (December 1909), and in each issue of volume 6 (1910); see G72.

G84

•G85
Monogram for Maschinenfabrik
Peter Behrens

Reference
DKD 23 (1908–09), illustration on p. 82.

G85
From *Deutsche Kunst und Dekoration* 1908–09.

• G86

Winning Entries in AEG Poster Contest

Eight postcards showing the prize-winning designs. The open competition for a poster advertising the AEG nitra lamp was announced in *Kunstgewerbeblatt* 27, no. 7 (1915–16), p. 140. The members of the jury were named as Peter Behrens, Curt Herrmann, Emil Orlik, E. R. Weiss, Paul Mamroth, Walther Rathenau, and Ernst Salomon. The results and illustrations of the winning entries were published in *MdBEW* 12, no. 6 (June 1916), pp. 87–90.

Technique
Letterpress printing.

Dimensions
10 × 7.5 cm.

Reference
Originals: private collection, Berlin.

Max Schwarzer 1. Preis

Max Schwarzer 2. Preis

Professor Nigg 3. Preis

Gustav Schaffer 2. Preis

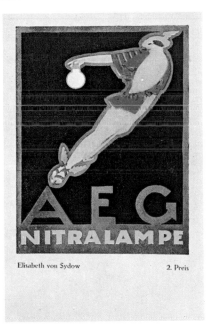

Elisabeth von Sydow 2. Preis

Ludwig Hohlwein
1. Preis

G86

APPENDIXES

A Leading Figures of the AEG, 1883–1928

Tilmann Buddensieg

In the following section are assembled portraits and short biographical details of the men who determined the technical, commercial, and financial policies of the AEG in the period 1883–1928. Owing to the lack of information and of preliminary studies, this list cannot claim to be complete or exhaustive. Also included are portraits of Peter Behrens between 1906 and 1928.

Emil Rathenau
Berlin, 11 December 1838–Berlin, 20 June 1915

See the essay by Henning Rogge earlier in this volume.

An AEG executive (Emil Rathenau?) being greeted by a porter, 13 November 1913. AEG photo 11131.

Emil Rathenau. From *Das goldene Buch des Deutschen Volkes an der Jahrhundertwende* (Leipzig, no date—1901?), p. 39.

Oil sketch of Emil Rathenau by Max Liebermann (study for following illustration).

Oil portrait of Emil Rathenau by Max Liebermann, probably painted to mark Rathenau's seventieth birthday on 11 December 1908. Subsequently lost. From Pinner, *Emil Rathenau* (Leipzig, 1908), frontispiece. The preliminary study is mentioned in Hancke, *Max Liebermann* (Berlin, 1913), p. 543; see also Nationalgalerie Berlin catalog 1249.

Silver medal by Hermann Hahn, cast for Emil Rathenau's seventieth birthday.

Portrait of Emil Rathenau by C. J. von Duren, Berlin, ca. 1915. From Fürst, *Emil Rathenau* (Berlin, 1915), frontispiece.

Sitting statue of Emil Rathenau by Hermann Hahn, cast iron, life size, 1917. Formerly displayed in the AEG administration building. Information from Andrea Volwahsen.

Emil Rathenau. From *Spannung* (1928).

Emil Rathenau standing at entrance of tunnel leading to Ackerstrasse. AEG photo 19.

Felix Deutsch
Breslau, 16 May 1858–Berlin, 19 May 1928

In the winter of 1882–83, Deutsch met Emil Rathenau; on 19 April 1883 the Deutsche Edison-Gesellschaft für angewandte Elektricität was founded. The company began business at 94 Leipziger Strasse with one book-keeper and one typewriter. In 1915, Deutsch succeeded Emil Rathenau as chairman of the managing board of the AEG. See Wenzel, *Deutsche Wirtschaftsführer* (Berlin, 1929); Felix Pinner, *Emil Rathenau* (1918), p. 397; Felix Pinner (Frank Fassland), "Felix Deutsch," *Deutsche Wirtschaftsführer* (Berlin, 1924), pp. 197 ff. The last-named article gives a detailed account of Deutsch's responsibilities as the initiator of the customer-service department, which employed Peter Behrens to design products, shops, pamphlets, and sales catalogs:

It is well known that Rathenau was a rare mixture of engineer, business-man and financier. His roots as a businessman were not to be found in the commercial sphere, but in industry, which meant that he was less inter-ested in selling the products as such and in sales techniques and more interested in manufacturing a product in such a way that it could be sold easily. The product, he felt, should be able to stimulate market demand, to satisfy existing needs or promote the needs of the future. But the tech-nically successful manufacture of a satisfactory or even superior product was not enough on its own to stimulate a new area of demand, and the sales of an innovative product could not be left to conventional marketing techniques. It was essential to display the new goods and describe them in such a way that their merits were made clear to the individual customer. This propaganda for new ideas and products belonged—at least at the beginning—to the branch of industry in which Emil Rathenau was ac-tive. . . . The marketing of standard products and mass articles, of the ma-chine-made goods that made up the largest part of a firm's turnover, was another matter. . . . But the fact that the AEG also pursued new directions in this area as well can be ascribed to the influence of Felix Deutsch, who was with the firm from its inception. Deutsch's commercial talent effectively complemented the abilities of Rathenau, which lay more in the direction of production engineering. When faced with a question he could not solve in his own individual way, Rathenau had a certain admiration and predilection for American solutions. The American marketing system was based on private sales representatives, commission agents, and electricians, who were responsible for selling the standard, mass-produced goods to the customers. In this respect, Deutsch was more logical and farsighted than Rathenau himself. . . . The three hundred technical and sales bureaus Deutsch opened in central locations both at home and abroad developed into the main supports of the sales organization and made it possible to bring all the new products onto the market by the most direct route. The bureaus were staffed by salesmen and engineers, who not only installed the equipment supplied by the AEG but also serviced it regularly and suggested possible additions and improvements to the plant. In short, the bureaus provided the customers with the same service that would otherwise have been given by so-called "consulting engineers."

See also Hermann Bücher, in *Deutsches Biographisches Jahrbuch* 10 (1928); *Spannung—Die AEG-Umschau* 1 (1928), special edition, with Deutsch's reminiscences.

Paul Mamroth
Breslau, 20 September 1859–20 November 1938

Mamroth was intimately linked with the firm from 1887 on. He was Director and a member of the managing board until 1928, then a member of the supervisory board. Pinner [*Emil Rathenau* (1918), p. 397] gives an account of Mamroth's responsibilities: "wholesaling, retailing, accounting, cashier's department, financial planning, supervision of subsidiaries—a Minister of the Interior, so to speak." Information on Mamroth was kindly given by Hans Fürstenberg.

Paul Mamroth (detail from group photograph), ca. 1910–12.

Paul Mamroth. From *Reichshandbuch der Deutschen Gesellschaft*, vol. 2 (Berlin, 1931), p. 1184.

Paul Jordan
Berlin, 26 May 1854–Berlin, 1 May 1937

The engineer Paul Jordan, who joined at the founding of the Deutsche Edison Gesellschaft in 1883, was another of Emil Rathenau's longest-serving associates. Jordan had worked in the Patent Office and was initially head of the AEG's patent department. He was later responsible for all the AEG factories in Germany (except for the cable works), and for the factories that were linked to foreign subsidiaries. See Pinner, *Emil Rathenau* (1918), p. 398. Jordan was a member of the AEG's managing board until his retirement in 1920. In 1911 he was given the honorary title of Baurat (government surveyor of works). According to Edmund Schüler, "Behrens and Jordan were similar in their boundless, domineering energy. Their powerful figures attracted attention wherever they went." (Schüler was then a legation councillor in the Foreign Ministry, and was Behrens's "client" for the embassy in St. Petersburg. His memoirs are in the Foreign Ministry Archives, Bonn.) Among other positions, Jordan was on the supervisory board of the Deutsche Werft AG, where he met and became friendly with Paul Reusch of the Gutehoffnungshütte, Oberhausen [see Erich Maschke, *Es entsteht ein Konzern. Paul Reusch und die GHH* (Tübingen, 1969), pp. 45, 55, 209 ff.]. Jordan also recommended Behrens to Reusch to design the new buildings of the GHH in Oberhausen, which were begun in 1921. [This information was kindly supplied by Herr Bodo Herzog, the archivist of the GHH. See also *Spannung—Die AEG-Umschau* 2 (July 1929), p. 300] Petra Behrens has kindly confirmed that Jordan appears on the left of illustration 11, in front of Paul Mamroth.

Walther Rathenau
Berlin, 29 September 1867–Berlin, 24 June 1922

See essay by Tilmann Buddensieg earlier in this volume.

Paul Jordan. From *Spannung* 2 (1929), p. 300.

A group of executives on the AEG roof garden, ca. 1910–12. AEG photo.

Another group of executives on the AEG roof garden, ca. 1910–12. AEG photo.

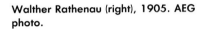

Walther Rathenau (right), 1905. AEG photo.

Marble herm of Walther Rathenau by Hermann Hahn, 1905. Present location unknown.

Bronze bust of Walther Rathenau by Hermann Hahn, 1908. Märkisches Museum, East Berlin.

A group on the AEG roof garden, ca. 1911–12. AEG photo. In addition to Walther Rathenau and Paul Mamroth, the following can be identified: Friedrich Naumann (front row, second from right), Oskar Lasche (?) (right, behind Mamroth), Artur Fürst (front row, extreme left), and Georg Stern (beside Fürst).

Walther Rathenau (detail from group photograph).

Oil painting of Walther Rathenau by Edward Münch, 1907. Märkisches Museum, East Berlin.

Crayon drawing of Walther Rathenau by Max Liebermann, 1912. F.-J. Kohl-Weigand collection, St. Ingbert. From H.-J. Imiela, *Max Liebermann als Zeichner* (Mainz, 1970), no. 70, ill. 13.

Drawing of Walther Rathenau by Arnold Busch, 31 December 1916. From Hermann Schmitz, *Schloss Freienwalde* (Berlin, no date; 1927?), facing p. 44.

Carl Fürstenberg
Danzig, 28 August 1850–Berlin, 9 February 1933

As Managing Director of the Berliner Handelsgesellschaft, Fürstenberg played an important role in the initial financing of the AEG. In 1887 he was made a member of the supervisory board; in 1896 he became deputy chairman, and later he was chairman. He was a friend of Emil and Walther Rathenau and Felix Deutsch, all of whom were on the governing board of the Berliner Handelsgesellschaft. See Wenzel, *Deutsche Wirtschaftsführer* (1929); Carl Fürstenberg, *Die Lebensgeschichte eines deutschen Bankiers* 1930; second edition, ed. Hans Fürstenberg, 1968. See also *Neue Deutsche Biographie*, 5 (1961), s.v. Hans Fürstenberg.

Oil painting of Carl Fürstenberg done by Max Slevogt in April–June 1923 for the fortieth anniversary of the Berliner Handelsgesellschaft. The fee, during the inflation period, was initially set at 2 million marks and then increased to 3 million. See Hans-Jürgen Imiela, *Max Slevogt* (Karlsruhe, 1968), p. 433. The only known photograph is in the *Berliner Illustrierte Zeitung* of 20 May 1923. A copy of this photograph and the information above were kindly provided by Hans-Jürgen Imiela. There is no trace of a second portrait.

Drawing of Carl Fürstenberg done by Fritz Grossmann in 1930 for Fürstenberg's eightieth birthday. From the collection of Hans-Jürgen Imiela, Mainz, who kindly provided the photograph and information.

Photo of Carl Fürstenberg. From *Reichshandbuch*, vol. 1, p. 511.

Georg Klingenberg
Hamburg, 28 November 1870–Berlin, 7 December 1925

Klingenberg, a lecturer at the Technische Hochschule in Charlottenburg, was a member of managing board of the AEG from 1902 to 1925. More than seventy power stations were built to his plans. Among other things, Klingenberg wrote *Der Bau grosser Elektrizitätswerke* (three volumes, 1913–14, 1920; second edition 1924; reprint 1926) and "Das neuzeitliche Elektrizitätswerk," *Zeitschrift des Vereins Deutscher Ingenieure* 65 (1925). See also *Gedenkschrift Georg Klingenberg* (Berlin, 1925).

Georg Klingenberg. From *Gedankschrift Klingenberg* (1925).

Michael von Dolivo-Dobrowolsky
St. Petersburg, 2 January 1862–Darmstadt, 15 November 1919

See "Modern Mass Production . . ." (translated in this volume).

Michael von Dolivo-Dobrowolsky. From *Das goldene Buch des Deutschen Volkes an der Jahrhundertwende* (Leipzig, no date; 1901?), p. 37.

Oskar Lasche
Leipzig, 22 June 1868–Berlin, 30 June 1923

Lasche studied mechanical engineering at the Technische Hochschule in Charlottenburg. In 1889 he became assistant to Riedler, and from there he went to the AEG as head engineer in the AEG drafting office. In 1902 he became director of the machine factory in Brunnenstrasse. From 1903 until his death he was director of the turbine factory in Huttenstrasse and in 1912 he also became a deputy member of the managing board. Lasche wrote several articles on the turbine-factory powerhouse and the new turbine hall, on which he collaborated at the planning stage with Bernhard and Behrens. He later described the turbine hall as a "complete success." See "Das Kraftwerk der AEG Turbinenfabrik in Berlin," *Zeitschrift des Vereins Deutscher Ingenieure* 53 (21 April 1909), pp. 648 ff.: "The relatively small powerhouse is notable for its simplicity and clarity. . . .". See also ibid., pp. 699 ff.; "Die neue Turbinenhalle der AEG," *AEG-Zeitung* 12 (January 1910), pp. 1 ff.; "Ein gang durch die AEG-Turbinenfabrik," *AEG-Zeitung* 14 (July–September 1911), pp. 1 ff.; Walter Kieser, *Deutsches Biographisches Jahrbuch* (1923), pp. 240 ff.; AEG Berlin, *25 Jahre AEG Dampfturbinen* (Berlin, 1928); *50 Jahre AEG* (Berlin, 1956), index.

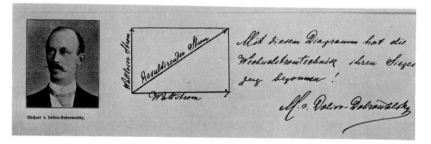

Michael von Dolivo-Dobrowolsky. Deutsches Museum, Munich.

Georg Stern
Königsberg, 11 June 1867–?

Stern was the head of the testing and meter-construction department of the Union Elektricitäts-Gesellschaft. When this firm was taken over by the AEG, he became the head of the testing department and the laboratories in the machine factory. In 1908 he became manager of the high-voltage factory, in 1921 director of the transformer factory in Oberschöneweide, and in 1926 a deputy member of the managing board (later he was a full member). See Georg Wenzel, *Deutsche Wirtschaftsführer* (1929); J. Biermanns and O. Mayr (eds.), *Hochspannungsforschung und Hochspannungspraxis, Georg Stern zum 31. März 1931* (Berlin, 1931).

Karl Bernhard
born 1854

See "The New Hall of the AEG Turbine Factory in Berlin" (translated above) and the essay by Buddensieg.

Michael von Dolivo-Dobrowolsky. From *Elektrotechnische Zeitschrift* 41 (1920), p. 12.

Oskar Lasche. From *25 Jahre AEG Dampfturbinen* (Berlin, 1928).

Georg Stern. From a Festschrift. See also *Reichshandbuch*, vol. 2, p. 1844.

Peter Behrens
Hamburg, 14 April 1869–27 February 1940

Lithograph of Peter Behrens by Max Liebermann, 1911. From Fritz Hoeber, *Peter Behrens* (Munich, 1913), frontispiece (signed by Behrens in complimentary copies).

Oil painting of Peter Behrens by Max Liebermann, 1913. Kunsthalle, Hamburg. See E. M. Kraft and Carl-Wolfgang Schümann, *Katalog der Meister des 19. Jahrhunderts in der Hamburger Kunsthalle*, no. 1595, p. 196. A preliminary study for this portrait is in a private collection in Germany.

Oil painting of Peter Behrens by Emil Rudolf Weiss, 1906, Essen, Folkwang Museum. Marburg photo.

Peter Behrens. From Artur Fürst, *Die Wunder um uns* (Berlin, 1912).

Peter Behrens. From *Zentralblatt für das deutsche Baugewerbe* 17 (1918), p. 152.

Peter Behrens, ca. 1916.

Peter Behrens is third from right in this
1910 photograph.

Etching of Peter Behrens, by Max
Oppenheimer, 1925. Private collection,
Berlin. See Stix, *Max Oppenheimer*,
no. 47.

B The Behrens Studio in Neu-Babelsberg

This photograph must have been taken before 1910, as the figure in the foreground at the extreme left is Walter Gropius, who worked in Behrens's studio from June 1908 until March 1910 (see "Industrial Buildings," translated above). The standing figure in the back cannot, therefore, have been Le Corbusier as is often supposed, for he first came to Behrens in the summer of 1910. Besides Gropius, one can recognize Adolf Meyer, Ludwig Mies van der Rohe, and perhaps Jean Krämer and Peter Grossman. The two last named were the outstanding talents in the studio [see Max Osborn, *Jean Krämer* (Berlin, 1927), p. VIII; Werner Klinski, *Peter Grossman* (Berlin, 1973), p. 1]. Grossman worked in Behrens's studio from 9 November 1908 until 30 October 1914. In April 1913, Schulenberg, the District President of Potsdam, reported in a letter to the Ministry of Public Works that Behrens ran "an important studio . . . which employs around thirty people, some at considerable salaries" (files on the St. Petersburg embassy, Foreign Ministry Archives, Bonn).

Work for AEG	Work outside AEG	Exhibitions	Lectures, articles, writings
1907			
Cover design for *Mitteilungen der Berliner Elektricitäts-Werke* (ills. G1–G3)	Redesign of shop of Josef Klein carpet firm (later Becker), Hagen, winter 1906–07	Interior at Düsseldorf (Hoeber 1913, pp. 73 ff.)	Contribution to questionnaire by Karl Scheffler, "Das Problem der Kunstschulen," *Kunst und Künstler* 5, no. 5 (Feb.), p. 207
Decorated address to mark award of Grashof Memorial Medal to E. Rathenau [*MdBEW* (4 June 1908), p. 82; ills. G23–G25 above]	Second calligraphy course, Düsseldorf (Osthaus Archive, 31 July)	Room and garden with open-air theater, Kunst- und Gartenbau-Ausstellung, Mannheim (*MBF* 6, pp. 218 ff., 248 ff., 261 ff.)	Outline of program to reform the stage, in article by Karl Scheffler, *Kunst und Künstler* 5, no. 6 (March), pp. 236 ff.
Commission to redesign arc lamps [see *Werkkunst* 2, no. 17 (June), p. 217]	Prospectus for Anker linoleum factory (Kunstbibliothek, Berlin)	Ausstellung für christliche Kunst and Handwerksausstellung, Aachen [*BM* (Oct. 1907), p. 38]	"Mein Sondergarten," in *Offizielle Ausstellungs-Zeitung*, Internationale Kunst- und Gartenbau-Ausstellung, Mannheim
Trademarks for AEG and (see ill. G84) BEW	Behrens italic script [*Werkkunst* 3 (1907–08), pp. 145 ff.]		
Title page of *AEG-Zeitung* (ill. G7)	Crematorium at Delstern almost completed (Osthaus Archive, 19 June); earliest plans May 1905 [*KGB* 20 (1907), p. 38]	Neue Automobil-Gesellschaft stand, Internationale Automobil-Ausstellung, Berlin (ill. A10)	"Kunst in der Technik," *Berliner Tageblatt*, evening edition, 29 August
Poster "AEG Metallfadenlampe" (ill. G30)	Typeface and layout for Richard Dehmel's book *Zwei Menschen*	Allgemeine Ausstellung von Erfindungen der Klein-Industrie (see "Work for AEG" column)	Announcement of lecture on calligraphy at Württembergischer Kunstgewerbeverein, winter 1907–08 [mentioned in *Werkkunst* 2 (1906–07), p. 367]
Pavilion at Allgemeine Ausstellung von Erfindungen der Klein-Industrie (ill. A9)	Site plan for villa estate in Eppenhausen [*Neud. BZ* (1914), pp. 401 ff.]		
	Redesign of own house at Neu-Babelsberg, 1907–08		

July–August 1907: Behrens appointed artistic adviser to Allgemeine Elektricitäts-Gesellschaft [*Werkkunst* 2, no. 22 (August 1907), p. 351; Osthaus Archive, 31 July 1907]

1 October 1907: Official beginning of Behrens's work as artistic adviser. (Osthaus Archive, 28 August 1907)

October–November: Behrens moved from Düsseldorf to the Erdmannhof house at Neu-Babelsberg, near Potsdam (Osthaus Archive, 1 October and 17 November 1907)

1908

Work for AEG	Work outside AEG	Exhibitions	Lectures, articles, writings
Fürstenwalde power station [*AEG Ztg.* 12, no. 9 (March 1910), pp. 1–6] *Die Allgemeine Elektrizitäts-Gesellschaft 1883–1908* [*MdBEW* 4, no. 5 (May), pp. 66–73] (ills. G12, G13 above) Congratulatory address from BEW [*MdBEW* 4, no. 5 (May), p. 73 (ill. G26 above) AEG trademark (honeycomb form), original design (ill. G79) AEG trademark (oval form) (ill. G78) Prospectus "Allgemeine Elektrizitäts-Gesellschaft Bogenlampen-Fabrik" (ills. G40–G42) Designs for high-intensity and triplex lamps Designs for electric fans (ills. P38 ff., G52, G54, G55) Pavilion and formal roof garden, Deutsche Schiffbau-Ausstellung, Berlin (ills. A1–A8) Building of powerhouse for turbine factory on Hussitenstrasse (ills. A13–A16) Advertising brochure "Die Quarzlampe" (ill. G39) First preparatory sketches for turbine hall (see Buddensieg and Rogge 1977 and ill. A18)	Design of monument to Bismarck (Hoeber 1913, pp. 92 ff. and ill. 100) Design of cover and title page for Joseph August Lux's *Das neue Kunstgewerbe in Deutschland* (Leipzig: Klinkhardt & Biermann) Schroeder house, Eppenhausen, 1908–09 Behrens Roman typeface and decorative elements introduced by Klingspor in October Elementary drawing classes at Berlin University in conjunction with Wölfflin's lectures in art history [*Werkkunst* 3 (1907–08), p. 268] Home for Catholic order, Neuss am Rhein, 1908–10 (Hoeber 1913, pp. 94 ff.)	Deutsche Schiffbau-Ausstellung, Berlin	"Die Gartenstadtbewegung," *Berliner Tageblatt*, evening edition, 25 March; *Gartenstadt* 2, no. 4, pp. 26–28 "Vom Kirchenbau," lecture, 7 April, Kunstgewerbeverein-Museum für Kunst und Gewerbe, Hamburg [*Werkkunst* 3, no. 2 (Oct. 1907), p. 32; ibid. no. 15 (May 1908), p. 240; extracts published as "Was ist monumentale Kunst," *Kunstgewerbeblatt* 20, no. 3 (Dec. 1908), pp. 46–48, and in *Weserzeitung*, 15 Dec. 1908. Lecture reported by Anton Lindner, "Peter Behrens in Hamburg," *Neue Hamburger Ztg.*, 9 April

Work for AEG	Work outside AEG	Exhibitions	Lectures, articles, writings
1909			
Commission to redesign courtyard wing and tower of old factory for railway equipment (ills. A43–A50)	Inscription on pediment of Reichstag building, Berlin: "Dem deutschen Volk"	Living room for exhibition at Wertheim store, Berlin (Hoeber 1913, pp. 129 ff.)	Lecture "Kunst und Technik" given on several occasions; extracts in *Berliner Tageblatt* "Zeitgeist" supplement, 25 January
Electric kettles (ill. G53)	Title page for *Neudeutsche Bauzeitung* 43 (Catalog 1966, p. 43)	Contribution to special exhibition at Frankfurter Kunstgewerbemuseum (Hoeber 1913, p. 221)	Lecture "Kirchenbau und -Ausstattung" to Kunstgewerbeverein Magdeburg; mentioned in *Werkkunst* 4, no. 14 (April)
New assembly hall for turbine factory (ills. A17–A32)	Wine labels for Wilhelm Gerstung. Offenbach (Catalog 1966, p. 43; Kunstbibliothek, Berlin)	Behrens exhibition at Folkwang Museum, Hagen (*Rhein.-Westf. Ztg.*, 6 April)	
High-voltage factory (1909–10) (ills. A54–A73)	Stage sets for O. E. Hartleben's *Diogenes*, Stadtgartenhalle, Hagen	Ausstellung für christliche Kunst, Düsseldorf (*MBF* 8, pp. 386, 415)	Note of protest on dismissal of Herwerth Walden as editor of *Der neue Weg*; see *Der neue Weg der Genossenschaft deutscher Bühnenangehöriger*, Berlin (March), p. 4
Electric heater in cast iron [*MdBEW* 5, no. 12 (Dec.), p. 192]	Third calligraphy course, Neu-Babelsberg		
Design for formal portal on Gustav-Meyer-Allee (Gate 4) (ills. A74–A78)	Cuno house, Eppenhausen, 1909–10 (Osthaus Archive, 24 November 1909)		"Alfred Messel. Ein Nachruf," *Frankfurter Ztg.*, morning edition, 6 April
Calendar for 1910 (ill. G20)	Annex with stable and garage, and layout of tennis court, for Frau Dr. Martens, Potsdam, winter 1909–10 (Hoeber 1913, pp. 115 ff.)		"Die Zukunft unserer Kultur," *Frankfurter Ztg.*, first morning edition, 14 April
Prospectus "AEG-Scheinwerfer mit Zeiss-Spiegel" (ill. G50)	Congratulatory address for Dr. Hans Bunte from Deutscher Verein von Gas- und Wasserfachmännern (Meyer-Schönbrunn 1913, p. 37)		Quoted in "Professor Peter Behrens über Asthetik in der Industrie," *AEG-Ztg.* 11, no. 12 (June), pp. 5–7
	Cover of *Kunstgewerbeblatt* 20		"Die Wirkung des elektrischen Lichtes bei dem Schaufensterwettbewerb in Berlin," *AEG-Ztg.* 12, no. 5 (Nov.), pp. 5–7

1910

Work for AEG

Design work for porcelain, oilcloth, and paint factory, Hennigsdorf

Small-motor factory (ills. A83–A105)

Königgrätzerstrasse showroom (ills. P4–P9)

West End salesroom (ills. P2, P3)

Clocks (ills. P100 ff., G56, G57)

Workers' housing, Rathenaustrasse, Hennigsdorf, 1910–11 (ills. A184–A190)

Work outside AEG

Ceiling illumination with miniature lamps, Keller & Reiner Gallery, Berlin [*AEG-Ztg.* 12, no. 9 (March), p. 7]

Design of silver bowls for P. Bruckmann und Sohne, Heilbronn (Anderson 1968, p. 473)

Sketches for housing estate at Neuss am Rhein (Hoeber 1913, p. 222)

Stone bench in Schlosspark von Ahlsdorf, near Herzberg (Kadatz 1977, p. 135)

Color lithograph "Rixdorfer Linoleum" (Kaiser Wilhelm Museum, Krefeld)

Interior design for house of Max Meirowsky, Cologne-Lindenthal (Hoeber 1913, pp. 130 ff.)

Cover design of congratulatory address for Emil Mosse (*KGB* 21, p. 101)

Leather furniture and light fixtures for Anker Linoleum exhibit, Brussels World Exhibition [*Wohnungskunst* 3 (1911), p. 87 and plate opposite p. 88]

Exhibitions

Contribution to show of living rooms at Keller & Reiner Gallery (Hoeber 1913, p. 221)

Living room at Gewerbeausstellung, Hagen

Model of Delstern Crematorium shown in Königsberg and at Städtebau-Ausstellung, Düsseldorf (Anderson 1968, p. 475)

Exhibition buildings at II. Ton-, Zement- und Kalkindustrieausstellung, Treptow (Hoeber 1913, pp. 123 ff.)

Railway shed, engine hall, hall of Deutscher Ingenieurverein, Anker Linoleum pavilion, and press room and library of Vereinigte Verleger illustrierter Zeitung, Brussels World Exhibition [*Weltausstellung Brüssel 1910. Deutsches Reich, Amtl. Katalog* (Berlin)]

Lectures, articles, writings

Comments on design of Catholic home at Neuss, in J. Geller, *Festschrift zur Einweihung des kath. Gessellenhauses zu Neuss* (Neuss, 1910), pp. 18–21

"Die Turbinenhalle der A.E.G. zu Berlin," *Deutscher Techniker-Ztg.* 27, no. 6 (12 Dec.), pp. 87–90, and in *Mitteilungen des Rheinischen Vereins für Denkmalpflege und Heimatschutz* 4, no. 1 (1 March), pp. 26–29

"Über die Kunst auf der Bühne," *Frankfurter Ztg.*, morning edition, 20 March

"Peter Behrens Ausstellungsbauten," *Zement und Beton* 9, no. 31 (29 July), pp. 472–474

"Kunst und Technik," lecture at 18th annual conference of Verein deutscher Elektrotechniker, Braunschweig; published in *Elektrotechnische Z.* 31, no. 22 (2 June) and elsewhere

Contribution to discussion on the place of art in the national economy, *Volkwirtschaftliche Blätter* 9, no. 15–16 (27 August)

Work for AEG	Work outside AEG	Exhibitions	Lectures, articles, writings

1911

Work for AEG	Work outside AEG	Exhibitions	Lectures, articles, writings
Porcelain, oilcloth, and paint factory built (ills. A140–A142)	Design for suspension bridge across Rhine at Cologne [*Zentralblatt der Bauverwaltung* 35 (1913), pp. 278 ff.]	Contribution to traveling exhibition "Metall," 1911–12	Lecture in Cologne, 15 March (Anderson 1968, p. 478)
Redesign of roof garden on administration building (ills. A106–A111)	Design of country house for Kröller-Müller family at the Hague (Osthaus Archive, 23 Feb. and 9 March)		"Kunst und Technik," lecture to Verein für Deutsches Kunstgewerbe, Berlin, 5 April, *Werkkunst* 6 (1910–11), pp. 124–125, 131–133
Alterations to facade of old factory for railway equipment (ills. A51, A52)	Goedecke house, Eppenhausen, 1911–12 (Osthaus Archive, 3 May 1911)		"Der moderne Gartenbau," *Berliner Tageblatt*, evening edition, 10 June
New Factory for railway equipment planned and built, 1911–12 (ills. A112–A121)	Interior design for Dr. Ruge, Berlin (Hoeber 1913, p. 133)		Extracts from "Kunst und Technik," *Innendekoration* 22, no. 7 (July), p. 294; *Deutsche Kunst und Dekoration* 28, p. 264
Brochure "AEG Scheinwerfer mit Zeiss-Spiegel" (ill. G51)	Design for water tower at Bocholt (Hoeber 1913, p. 167)		Comments on German script, in "Den Gegnern der deutschen Schrift, eine deutsche Antwort," ed. F. Seeselberg, *Werdandi* 4, no. 8
Designs for overhead and underground railway, Gesundbrunnen–Neukölln, 1911–12 (ills. A175–A177)	House for Dr. Theodor Wiegand, Berlin-Dahlem, 1911–12		Lecture to Gesellschaft für Literatur und Kunst, Bonn, 2 Dec. (Hoeber 1913, bibliography, no. 153)
	Office building and factory hall for T-Z-Gitterwerk, Berlin, 1911–12 (Catalog 1966, p. 29)		
	Factory buildings for Frankfurter Gasgesellschaft, 1911–12 (Hoeber 1913, pp. 162 ff.)		
	Administration building for Mannesmannröhren-Werke, Düsseldorf, 1911–12 [*KuK* 9, no. 10 (1910–11), p. 256]		
	Construction and interior of Imperial German Embassy, St. Petersburg, 1911–12		
	Remodeling of Delstern Crematorium, 1911–12		

Work for AEG	Work outside AEG	Exhibitions	Lectures, articles, writings
1912			
Assembly hall for large machines (planned 1911, built 1912) ills. A116, A117, A121–A137)	Alterations and new interiors for country house of Frau Dr. Martens, Potsdam (Hoeber 1913, p. 222)	Two-room workers' apartment at 2. Muster-Ausstellung von Arbeiter-Möbeln, Gewerkschaftshaus, Berlin	"Der moderne Industriebau in technischer und ästhetischer Beziehung," *Berliner Tageblatt*, 19 June
Gate 4 built (ills. A79–A82)	Design of factories and workers' housing for C. W. Julius-Blancke-Werke AG, Merseburg a.d. Saale (Hoeber 1913, p. 203)	Catalog design for and contribution to traveling exhibition of Deutsches Museum für Kunst in Handel und Industrie in United States (Anderson 1968, p. 481)	Lecture, "Ästhetik und Industriebau," Verein deutscher Ingenieure, Stuttgart 10–12 June [*Neudeutsche Bauzeitung* 8 (1912), pp. 369–370]
Elektra boathouse (ills. A178–A182) opened	Design for tomb of Bruno Schmitz		Contribution to questionnaire on architectural development in central Berlin, "Berlins Dritte Dimension," *Berliner Morgenpost*, 27 Nov.
Boathouse at Hennigsdorf (ill. A183) (year uncertain)	Design for administration building of Continental Rubber Co., Hanover		Speech at opening of new administration building of Mannesmannröhren-Werke, Düsseldorf [*Zur Erinnerung an die Einweihung des Verwaltungsgebäudes der Mannesmannröhren-Werke in Düsseldorf* (Düsseldorf, 1913)]
Trademark (ill. G80)			
Krupp congratulatory address (ills. G28, G29)			
Design for 1913 calendar (ill. G21)			

Work for AEG	Work outside AEG	Exhibitions	Lectures, articles, writings

1913

Work for AEG	Work outside AEG	Exhibitions	Lectures, articles, writings
Casings and advertisements for Nitra lamps (ills. P32, G46, G47) Factory at Riga (ill. A138) Locomotive factory, Henningsdorf, 1913–14 (ills. A142–A150) Anniversary certificate for member of Elektra Rowing Club (ill. G27) Alterations to shed A at turbine factory, 1913–14 (ills. A33–A37)	Construction of Continental Rubber administration building begun (Hoeber 1913, pp. 176 ff.) Design for hotel in San Remo [Cremers 1928, p. 164; F. Servais, "Das Kurhotel der Zukunft," *Der Architekt* 1 (1916), pp. 41–57] Design for Volkshaus in Lübeck [*KuK* 12 (1913–14), p. 246; *Sozialistische Monatshefte* (1914), pp. 80 ff.]	Contribution to Ghent World Exhibition [*KGB* 24 (1912–13), pp. 216 ff.]	Lecture at Hamburg, 19 Feb. (Osthaus Archive; Anderson 1968, p. 481) "The Aesthetics of Industrial Buildings: Beauty in Perfect Adaptation to Useful Ends," *Scientific American* (suppl.) 76 (23 Aug.), pp. 120–121 "Kunst und Technik," *Rheinisch-Westfälishche Ztg.*, 25 Nov. "Über die Zusammenhang des baukünstlerischen Schaffens mit der Technik," paper at Kongress für Ästhetik und allgemeine Kunstwissenschaft, Berlin, 7–9 Oct. [report (Stuttgart, 1914), pp. 251–265] "Kunst und Technik," *Hamburger Nachrichten*, 26 Nov.

Work for AEG	Work outside AEG	Exhibitions	Lectures, articles, writings

1914 and later

1914: End of Behrens's official activity as artistic adviser to Allgemeine Elektricitäts-Gesellschaft (personnel file, 5 October 1936, sheet 96, no. 9b; in Akademie der Künste, Berlin)

Work for AEG	Work outside AEG	Exhibitions	Lectures, articles, writings
Halls for aeronautical department, 1914–15 (ills. A151–A153)	Design of administration building for Daimler, Vienna, 1914 (Cremers 1928, p. 164)	Festhalle at Werkbund exhibition, Cologne, 1914 (*JDW* 1915, ill. p. 36) and exhibition poster [*KGB* 21 (1912–13), p. 219]	"Vom Rhythmus unserer Zeit," *Innendekoration* 25 (1914), p. 472
Commemorative publication on death of E. Rathenau, 1915 (ill. G12)	Office building for Frank & Lehmann, Cologne, 1914 (Cremers 1928, p. 164)	Address books, book covers, and typefaces at Internationale Ausstellung für Buchgewerbe und Graphik, Leipzig, 1914	"Die Zusammenhange zwischen Kunst und Technik," *Dokumente des Fortschritts* 7 (1914), pp. 134–141; also in *Kunstwart* 27, no. 16 (1914), pp. 216–223
Housing estate at Oberschöneweide, 1915 (ills. A191–A209)	Behrens Medieval type		
Factory and administration building for Nationale Automobil AG, 1915–16 (ills. A154–162)	Housing estate at Berlin-Lichtenberg, 1915 [*WMB* 5 (1920–21), pp. 320 ff.]	Contribution to Neues Bauen exhibition, Kunsthalle, Mannheim, 1914 [Sozialistische Monatshefte (1914), p. 466]	"Einfluss von Zeit- und Raumausnutzung auf moderne Formentwicklung," *Jahrbuch des Deutschen Werkbundes 1914* (Jena, 1914)
Pavilion at Social Welfare Exhibition, Brussels, 1916 (ills. A11, A12)		Social Welfare exhibition, Brussels (see "Work for AEG" column)	Contribution to debate at 1914 Werkbund conference at Cologne [see Hermann Muthesius, "Werkbund Arbeit der Zukunft," *Jahrbuch des Deutschen Werkbundes 1914* (Jena, 1914), pp. 56 ff.; Julius Posener, *Anfänge des Funktionalismus* (Berlin, 1964), p. 489]
Alterations and extensions planned for administration building of turbine factory, 1916 (ills. A165–A168; cf. A21)		Contribution to exhibition "Kunst im Kriege," Berlin, 1916	
Munitions factory, Berlin-Moabit, 1916 (ills. A38–A42)			Lecture tour of Sweden for Deutsch-Schwedischen Verein (Schiller-Nationalmuseum, Marbach, 38746)
Design for administration building at Humboldthain, 1917 (ills. A163, A164)			
Workers' housing, Paul Jordan Strasse, Hennigsdorf, 1918–19 (ills. A184, A210–A212)			
Plan for administration building on North-South Axis, Berlin, 1939 (ills. A171–A174)			

Glossary of Abbreviations

AEG	Allgemeine Elektricitäts-Gesellschaft	**BusB**	*Berlin und seine Bauten*
AEG photo	Photograph from the archives of the AEG at 107a Brunnen-strasse, Berlin-Wedding; now in the archives of AEG-Telefunken at Braunschweig and in the collection of the Department of Art History at the Freie Universität Berlin	**BW**	*Bauwelt*
		Catalog 1966	*Peter Behrens (1868–1940)*, exhibition catalog (Kaiserslautern and other cities, 1966–67)
AEG-Ztg.	*AEG-Zeitung*	**DBH**	*Deutsche Bauhütte. Zeitschrift der deutschen Architektenschaft*, Hanover
AR	*Architektonische Rundschau*, Stuttgart (later: *Wasmuths Monatshefte für Baukunst*)	**DBZ**	*Deutsche Bauzeitung. Organ des Verbandes Deutscher Architekten- und Ingenieure-Vereine*, Berlin
AREV	*Architectural Review*, Boston	**DEK**	*Dekorative Kunst. Illustrierte Zeitschrift für angewandte Kunst*, Munich
AW	*Architektur und Wohnform*		
AZJ	*Die Architektur des zwanzigsten Jahrhunderts. Zeitschrift für moderne Baukunst*, Berlin	**DIDK**	*Deutsche Industrie. Deutsche Kultur*
		DK	*Die Kunst. Monatshefte für freie und angewandte Kunst*, Munich
B 11	Preussischer Kulturbesitz, Staatliche Museen, Kunstbibliothek, Berlin		
BAW	Berliner Architekturwelt	**DKD**	*Deutsche Kunst und Dekoration. Illustrierte Monatshefte für moderne Malerei, Plastik, Architektur, Wohnungskunst und künstlerische Frauenarbeiten*
Bewag	Berliner Kraft- und Licht AG		
BF	*Bauforum*	**GBK**	Grosse Berliner Kunstausstellung
BM	*Der Baumeister. Zeitschrift für Baukultur und Bautechnik*, Munich		
Brussels 1910	Brussels World Exhibition, 1910		

Hagen photo	Photograph in the archive of the former Deutsches Museum für Kunst in Handel und Gewerbe; now the Karl Ernst Osthaus Museum, Hagen
IB	*Der Industriebau. Monatsschrift für die künstlerische und technische Förderung aller Gebiete industrieller Bauten*, Leipzig and Berlin
ID	*Innendekoration*
Int. AEG-Ztg.	*Interne AEG-Zeitung*
JBK	*Jahrbuch der bildenden Kunst*, Berlin
JDW	*Jahrbuch des Deutschen Werkbundes*, Jena
KEO Museum	Karl Ernst Osthaus Museum, Hagen
KGB	*Kunstgewerbeblatt. Organ der Kunstgewerbevereine in Berlin, Dresden, Düsseldorf, und Leipzig*
KHI	Department of Art History, Freie Universität Berlin
KuH	*Kunst und Handwerk. Zeitschrift des bayerischen Kunstgewerbevereins zu München*
KuK	*Kunst und Künstler. Illustrierte Monatsschrift für Kunst und Kunstgewerbe*, Berlin
KWU	Kraftwerk Union Aktiengesellschaft, Berlin
MBF	*Moderne Bauformen. Monatshefte für Architektur und Raumkunst*, Stuttgart
MdBEW	*Mitteilungen der Berliner Elektricitätswerke*, Berlin
MdVDR	*Mitteilungen des Vereins Deutscher Reklamekünstler*
Neud.BZ	*Neudeutsche Bauzeitung. Organ des Bundes deutscher Architekten. Wochenschrift für Architektur und Bautechnik*, Leipzig
P. B.	Peter Behrens
Photo Marburg	Photograph in picture archive of Research Institute for Art History, Philips-Universität, Marburg
PL no.	AEG price-list number
RfF	*Rat für Formgebung*, Darmstadt
RHL	*Die Rheinlande. Vierteljahrsschrift des Verbandes der Kunstfreunde in den Ländern am Rhein*, Düsseldorf
Studio	The Studio, London
Stoedtner photo	Photograph from the archive of the former Institut für wissenschaftliche Projektionsphotographie Dr. Franz Stoedtner, Berlin, NW 21 (now Dr. Franz Stoedtner Lichtbildverlag, Düsseldorf)
TM AEG-Ztg.	Technical information from *AEG-Zeitung*
TM AEG-Telefunken	Technical information from AEG-Telefunken
WK	*Die Werkkunst. Zeitschrift des Vereins für deutsches Kunstgewerbe in Berlin*, Berlin
WMB	*Wasmuths Monatshefte für Baukunst* (after 1933 *Wasmuths Monatshefte für Baukunst und Städtebau*), Berlin
ZdB	*Zentralblatt der Bauverwaltung*, Berlin
ZdtB	*Zentralblatt für das deutsche Baugewerbe. Offizielles Verkündigungsblatt des deutschen Arbeitgeberbundes für das Baugewerbe*, Berlin
ZdVDI	*Zeitschrift des Vereins Deutscher Ingenieure*

Bibliography

General Literature

"AEG." *Berliner Börsenkurier*, 12 June 1910, p. 7.

AEG. *Fabrik Neubauten, Hennigsdorf Süd, Johannisthal. Erbaut vom Baubüro DJ in den Jahren 1916–1918*. Berlin, no date.

Anderson, Stanford Owen. Peter Behrens and the Architecture of Germany 1900–1917. Ph.D diss., Columbia University, 1968.

Anderson, Stanford Owen. "Behrens' changing concept." *Architectural Design* 39, no. 2 (1969), pp. 72–78.

"Arbeiterhäuser bei den AEG-Fabriken in Hennigsdorf. Architekt Prof. P. Behrens, Berlin-Neubabelsberg." *Der Industriebau* 6, no. 4 (April 1915), pp. 332–333.

Argan, Giulio Carlo. *Progetto e Destino*. Milan, 1965.

Argan, Giulio Carlo. *Walter Gropius e la Bauhaus*. Turin, 1951.

Banham, Reyner. *Theory and Design in the First Machine Age*. London, 1960.

Banham, Reyner. *The Architecture of the Well-Tempered Environment*. Chicago, 1969.

Behne, Adolf. "Peter Behrens und die toskanische Architektur des 12. Jahrhunderts." *Kunstgewerbeblatt* 23 (1912), pp. 45, 48–50.

Behne, Adolf. "Die ästhetischen Theorien der modernen Baukunst." *Preussische Jahrbücher* 153 (1913), pp. 274–283.

Behne, Adolf. "Romantiker, Pathetiker und Logiker im modernen Industriebau." *Preussische Jahrbücher* 154 (1913), pp. 171–174.

Behne, Adolf. *Der moderne Zweckbau*. Munich, 1926; Berlin, Frankfurt, and Vienna, 1964.

Benevolo, Leonardo. *History of Modern Architecture*. Cambridge, Mass., 1971.

Berglar, Peter. *Walther Rathenau, Seine Zeit, sein Werk, seine Persönlichkeit*. Bremen, 1970.

Berlin und seine Bauten. Berlin, 1877, 1896, 1970, 1971, 1974.

Bernhard, Karl. "Die neue Halle für die Turbinenfabrik der Allgemeinen Elektricitäts-Gesellschaft in Berlin." *Zeitschrift des Vereins Deutscher Ingenieure* 55, no. 39 (30 September 1911), pp. 1625–1631, 1673–1682.

Bernoulli, Hans. "Architektur und Raumkunst in der Deutschen Werkbundausstellung." *Illustrierte Zeitung zur Deutschen Werkbund-Ausstellung*, Basel, 1917.

Blake, Peter. *The Master Builders*. London, 1960.

Blei, Franz. "Die Aufgabe des Publizisten." *Summa, eine Vierteljahresschrift, herausgegeben von Franz Blei* 1 (1917), pp. 1 ff.

Bonus, Arthur. "Friedrich Naumann und die Kunst." *Der Kunstwart* 14 (1901), pp. 341 ff.

Branchesi, Lida. Peter Behrens. Ph.D diss., University of Rome, 1965.

Breuer, Robert. "Peter Behrens." *Die Werkkunst* 3, no. 10 (9 February 1908), pp. 1–5.

Breuer, Robert. "Kunst und Technik." *Reclams Universum* 25, no. 46 (2–8 August 1909), p. 1108.

Breuer, Robert. "Druckschrift von Behrens." *Neue Revue*, no. 2 (1909).

Breuer, Robert. *Deutschlands Raumkunst und Kunstgewerbe auf der Weltausstellung in Brüssel 1910*. Stuttgart, 1910.

Breuer, Robert. "Peter Behrens und die Elektrizität." *Deutsche Kunst und Dekoration* 27 (1910–11), p. 492.

Breuer, Robert. "Kleine Kunst-Nachrichten." *Deutsche Kunst und Dekoration* 13, no. 10 (July 1910), pp. 264–266.

Breuer, Robert. "Arbeitermöbel von Peter Behrens." *Deutsche Kunst und Dekoration* 15, no. 8 (May 1912), pp. 131–133.

Breuer, Robert. "Neue Arbeitermöbel von Peter Behrens." *Reclams Universum* 28, no. 36 (25 May–2 June 1912), pp. 250–251.

Buddensieg, Tilmann. "Peter Behrens und die AEG. Neue Dokumente zur Baugeschichte der Fabriken am Humboldthain." In *Festschrift für Margarete Kühn*. Munich, 1975.

Buddensieg, Tilmann. "L'architecture." In *Jugendstil*, Europalia, exhibition catalog. Brussels, 1977

Tilmann Buddensieg and Henning Rogge. "Peter Behrens e l'Architettura della AEG / Peter Behrens and the AEG Architecture." *Lotus International* 12 (September 1976), pp. 90–127.

Tilmann Buddensieg and Henning Rogge. "Formgestaltung für die Industrie. Peter Behrens und die Bogenlampen der AEG." In Gerhard Bott (ed.), *Von Morris zum Bauhaus. Eine Kunst gegründet auf Einfachheit*. Hanau, 1977.

Tilmann Buddensieg and Henning Rogge. "Nicht nur Architekt bei der AEG—Peter Behrens." *AEG-Telefunken Report* 9 (September 1977), pp. 4 ff.

Casabella 240 (June 1960), edition dedicated to Peter Behrens. Contributions from Ernesto N. Rogers, Vittorio Gregotti, Silvano Tintori, and Aldo Rossi.

Catalog: *Peter Behrens (1868–1940)*. Kaiserslautern and other cities, 1966–67. Cited as Catalog 1966.

Catalog: *Ein Dokument Deutscher Kunst. Darmstadt 1901–1976*. 5 vols. Darmstadt, 1976. Cited as Catalog Darmstadt.

Cremers, Paul Joseph. *Peter Behrens. Sein Werk von 1909 bis zur Gegenwart*. Essen, 1928.

Cremers, Paul Joseph. "Peter Behrens. Zum 60. Geburtstag des Künstlers." *Die Pyramide* 14 (1928), pp. 30 ff.

Dietrich, Ulf. "AEG-Siedlung in Hennigsdorf bei Berlin, Architekt Jean Krämer, Berlin." *Bauwelt* 22 (1929), pp. 1–4.

Dohrn, Wolf. "Das Vorbild der AEG." *März* 3, no. 17 (3 September 1909), pp. 361–372.

Dohrn, Wolf. "Die Turbinenhalle der AEG in Berlin." *Der Industriebau* 1, no. 6 (15 June 1910), pp. 132–140.

Dürks, Wilhelm. *Urkundliche Geschichte der Landgemeinde Hennigsdorf*. Hennigsdorf, 1931.

Ehmcke, Fritz Helmuth. "Peter Behrens." In *Neue Deutsche Biographie*, vol. 2. Berlin, 1955.

Franciscono, Marcel. *Walter Gropius and the Creation of the Bauhaus in Weimar*. Urbana, Ill. 1971.

Frankl, Paul. "Architektur-Glossen. Fabrikbauten der AEG in Berlin." *Allgemeine Zeitung*, 8 November 1910, pp. 772–773.

Franz, W. "Die Architektur im Industriebau." *Die Bauwelt*, art supplement (1913), no. XVa, pp. 113a–118a.

Franz, W. "Peter Behrens als Ingenieur-Architekt." *Die Kunst* 20, no. 36 (February 1917), pp. 145–158.

Freyer, Hans. *Theorie des gegenwärtigen Zeitalters*. Stuttgart, 1955.

de Fries, Heinrich. "Die werdende Form. Zur Entwicklung der modernen Baukunst." *Die Rheinlande* 26 (1916), pp. 121 ff.

de Fries, Heinrich. "Industriebaukunst." *Wasmuths Monatshefte für Baukunst* 5, no. 5–6 (1920–21), pp. 127–129.

Fürst, Artur. *Die Wunder um uns. Neue Einblicke in Natur und Technik*. Berlin, 1911.

de Fusco, Renato. *Storia dell'Architettura contemporanea*, second edition, 2 vols. Rome and Bari, 1977.

Gestechi, Th. "Eiserne Hallenbauten in konstruktiver und ästhetischer Beziehung." *Zentrallblatt für das deutsche Baugewerbe* 17 (1918), pp. 142–145.

Giedion, Sigfried. *Mechanisation takes Command, a Contribution to Anonymous Architecture*. Cambridge, Mass., 1947.

Giedion, Siegfried. *Space, Time and Architecture*. Cambridge, Mass., 1941.

Gmelin, Leopold. "Vom 'Kunstgewerbe' zur 'Sachkunst.' Eine entwicklungsgeschichtliche Studie zur Ausstellung 'München 1908.'" *Hochland* 5, no. 8 (1908), pp. 129–144.

Grautoff, Otto. *Die Entwicklung der modernen Buchkunst in Deutschland*. Leipzig, 1901.

Gregotti, Vittorio. "Peter Behrens," *Casabella* 240 (June 1960), pp. 5 ff.

Gropius, Walter, "Die Entwicklung moderner Industriebaukunst." In *Jahrbuch des Deutschen Werkbundes 1913*. Jena, 1913.

Gropius, Walter. "Industriebauten." In catalog to traveling exhibition no. 18 of Deutsches Museum für Kunst in Handel und Gewerbe, Hagen; probably written in July 1911.

Gropius, Walter. *Scope of Total Architecture*. New York, 1955.

Hamann, Richard, and Jost Hermand. *Stilkunst um 1900*. Berlin, 1967.

Hamann, Richard, and Jost Hermand. *Geschichte der Kunst von der altchristlichen Zeit bis zur Gegenwart*. Berlin, 1932.

Hellpach, Willy. *Nervosität und Kultur.* 1902.

Hellwag, Fritz. "Peter Behrens und die AEG." *Kunstgewerbeblatt* 22, no. 8 (May 1911), pp. 149–159.

Hellwag, Fritz. "Arbeitermöbel. 2. Musterausstellung im Berliner Gewerkschaftshause." *Kunstgewerbeblatt* 24 (June 1912), pp. 179 ff.

Hellwag, Fritz. "Peter Behrens 70 Jahre." *Die Kunst für Alle* 53 (May 1938), suppl., p. 8.

Hellwag, Fritz. "Peter Behrens †." *Die Kunst für Alle* 55 (April 1940), suppl. p. 7.

Hennigsdorfer Siedelungsgesellschaft (no date; 1925?).

Hensler, Erwin. "Peter Behrens." *Mitteilungen der Gesellschaft für Literatur und Kunst in Bonn* 3 (23 November 1911).

Hesse-Frielinghaus, Herta. *Peter Behrens und Karl Ernst Osthaus. Eine Dokumentation nach den Beständen des Osthaus-Archivs im Karl-Ernst-Osthaus-Museum, Hagen.* Hagen, 1966.

Hesse-Frielinghaus, Herta, August Hoff, Walter Erben, et al. *Karl Ernst Osthaus, Leben und Werk.* Recklinghausen, 1971.

Heuss, Theodor. "Brüssel III." *Die Hilfe* 16, no. 25 (26 June 1910), suppl., p. 399.

Heuss, Theodor. "Das Hausrat des Proletariers." *Die Hilfe* 17 (1911), pp. 318 ff.

Heuss, Theodor. *Friedrich Naumann.* Stuttgart, 1937 (second edition 1949).

Heuss, Theodor. "Zu Peter Behrens 70. Geburtstag." *Hamburger Fremdenblatt*, 12 April 1938; *Neue Freie Presse*, Vienna, 13 April 1938; *Frankfurter Zeitung*, 14 April, 1938.

Heuss, Theodor. "Zum Tode von Peter Behrens." *Die Hilfe*, no. 5 (1940), pp. 74 ff.

Heuss, Theodor. *Lust der Augen. Stilles Gespräch mit beredtem Bildwerk.* Tübingen, 1960.

Heyden, Gerhard. "Vom neuzeitlichen Fabrikbau." *Deutsche Bauhütte* 15 (1911), p. 234.

Hilberseimer, Ludwig. *Grossstadtarchitektur.* Stuttgart, 1927.

Hirschberg, Heinrich. "Bau-Entwicklung der AEG-Fabriken." *Spannung—Die AEG-Umschau* 3 (1929–30), pp. 5–11, 37–43, 68–74.

Hirschfeld, Paul, and R. Jannasch (eds.). *Berlins Grossindustrie. Geschildert von Paul Hirschfeld.* 3 vols. Berlin, 1897–1904.

Hitchcock, Henry-Russell. *Architecture in the 19th and 20th Centuries.* Harmondsworth, 1963.

Hoeber, Fritz. *Die Kunst Peter Behrens.* Offenbach, 1909.

Hoeber, Fritz. "Peter Behrens Verwaltungsgebäude der Mannesmann-Röhren-Werke in Düsseldorf am Rhein." *Kunstgewerbeblatt* 24 (1913), pp. 186–189 and ills. p. 191.

Hoeber, Fritz. "Peter Behrens." *März*, 2 August 1913, p. 172.

Hoeber, Fritz. "Deutsche Buchkünstler der Gegenwart: Peter Behrens als Buch- und Schriftkünstler." *Zeitschrift für Bücherfreunde* 2, no. 5 (1913), pp. 257–268.

Hoeber, Fritz. "Neue Bauten von Peter Behrens für die AEG." *Kunst und Künstler* 11 (1913), pp. 262–266.

Hoeber, Fritz. "Peter Behrens Gartenstadt Lichtenberg bei Berlin, eine gute Lösung des Kleinwohnungsproblems." *Kunstgewerbeblatt* 28 (1917), pp. 105–118.

Hoeber, Fritz. "Das Kulturproblem der modernen Baukunst." *Zeitschrift für Ästhetik und allgemeine Kunstwissenschaft* 13 (1918), pp. 1 ff.

Hoeber, Fritz. "Die Stellung der Baukunst in der Kultur unserer Zeit." *Die neue Rundschau* 31 (Berlin, 1920), pp. 227–246.

Hoff, August. "Der gute Industriebau." *Hellweg* 5, no. 32 (12 August 1925), pp. 591–594.

Hoff, August. "Peter Behrens." *Die neue Saat* 3 (May–June 1940), p. 104.

Hofmann, Werner. *Grundlagen der modernen Kunst.* Stuttgart, 1966.

Hood, Fred. "Die Ton-, Zement- und Kalkindustrieausstellung in Berlin." *Allgemeine Technische Korrespondenz. Berlin* 7, no. 177 (10 July 1910), p. 1.

Jacques, Norbert. "Anmerkungen zu Brüsseler Weltausstellung." *März* 4, no. 2 (1910), pp. 482–488.

Jaumann, Anton. "Neues von Peter Behrens." *Deutsche Kunst und Dekoration* 12, no. 6 (March 1909), pp. 343–361.

Jeanneret, Ch.-E. *Etude sur le Mouvement d'Art Décoratif en Allemagne.* La Chaux-de-Fonds, 1912.

Imbert, José. "Peter Behrens." *L'architecture d'aujourdhui*, fourth series, 5, no. 2 (March 1934), p. 30.

Kadatz, Hans-Joachim. *Peter Behrens. Architekt, Maler, Grafiker und Formgestalter. 1868–1940.* Leipzig, 1977.

Kalkschmidt, Eugen. "Kunst und Industrie." *März* 4, no. 3 (July–September 1910), pp. 140–147.

Kalkschmidt, Eugen. "Peter Behrens und die AEG. Ein Beitrag zur Kunst in der Industrie." *Die Grenzboten* 69, no. 27 (6 July 1910), pp. 24–30.

Kalkschmidt, Eugen. "Industriebauten von Peter Behrens." *Dekorative Kunst* 16, no. 12 (September 1913), pp. 573–576.

Kalkschmidt, Eugen. "Deutsches Kunstgewerbe und der Weltmarkt." *Dekorative Kunst* 14, no. 10 (July 1911), pp. 481–504.

Kammerer, O. *Die Technik der Lastenbeförderung einst und jetzt.* Munich and Berlin, 1907.

Graf Kessler, Harry. *Walther Rathenau: His Life and Work.* London, 1929.

Kissner, Franz, and E. Reich. *Das Arbeitermöbel. Sonderschrift zur Ausstellung vorbildlicher Arbeiterwohnungen im Berliner Gewerkschaftshause.* 1912.

Klingenberg, Georg. *Bau grosser Elektrizitätswerke.* 3 vols. Berlin, 1913, 1920.

Das Grosskraftwerk Klingenberg, Beschreibung der Anlagen und Beiträge von am Bau beteiligten Firmen, bearbeitet von der Abteilung für Zentralstationen der "Berliner Städtische Elektrizitätswerke Act. Ges." Charlottenburg, 1928.

Klopfer, Paul. "Peter Behrens einst und jetzt." Der Kunstwart, no. 22 (December 1909), pp. 46 ff.

Klopfer, Paul. "Von der Seele der Baukunst." Bauwarte 2, no. 34 (1926), pp. 553–555.

Koch, Alexander (ed.). Grossherzog Ernst Ludwig und die Ausstellung der Künstler-Kolonie in Darmstadt von Mai bis Oktober 1901. Darmstadt, 1902.

Koch, Alexander (ed.). Deutsche Werkkunst. Arbeiten Deutscher und Österreichischer Künstler auf der Werkbund-Ausstellung Cöln a. Rh. Darmstadt and Leipzig, 1916.

Koch, H. 75 Jahre Mannesmann. 1965.

Kölitz, Karl. "Die Mannheimer internationale Kunstausstellung 1907." Die Kunst für Alle 22, no. 1 (1 August 1907), pp. 500, 504.

Kofler, Leo. Der asketische Eros, Industriekultur und Ideologie. Vienna, Frankfurt, and Zürich, 1967.

Kreidt, Hermann. "Industriebauten." Berlin und seine Bauten, part 9. Berlin, 1971.

Lanzke, Hermann. Peter Behrens. 50 Jahre Gestaltung in der Industrie. Berlin, 1958.

Lanzke, Hermann. Industrielle Formgestaltung und Formentwicklung. AEG information folder 99. Berlin, 1954.

Lasche, Oskar. "Das Kraftwerk der AEG-Turbinenfabrik in Berlin." Zeitschrift des Vereins Deutscher Ingenieure 53, no. 17 (1909), pp. 648–655.

Lasche, Oskar. "Die neue Turbinenhalle der AEG." AEG-Zeitung 12, no. 7 (January 1910), pp. 1–4.

Lasche, Oskar. "Die Turbinenhalle der AEG." Zeitschrift des Vereins Deutscher Ingenieure 55, no. 29 (22 July 1911), pp. 1198 ff.

Leti Messina, Vittorio. Il centenario della nascita di un Maestro: Peter Behrens. Reprint from L'ingegnere. Organo uffiziale dell'assoziazione nazionale Ingegneri e Architetti Italiani, no. 4 (1968).

Lindahl, Göran. "Von der Zukunftskatnedrale bis zur Wohnmaschine." Idea and Form (Uppsala Studies in History of Art) 1 (1959), pp. 226–282.

Lindner, Werner. Bauten der Technik. Ihre Form und Wirkung. Werkanlagen Berlin, 1927.

Lorenz, Detlef. "Peter Behrens zum 30. Todestag." Technische Mitteilungen der AEG-Telefunken 60, no. 3 (1970), pp. 192–198.

Lotz, W. "Aus der Werkbund-Entwicklung. Arbeiten und Gedanken aus den ersten zwanzig Jahren zusammengestellt." Die Form 7, no. 10 (15 October 1932), pp. 300–324.

Loubier, Hans. Die neue deutsche Baukunst. Stuttgart, 1921.

Lux, Joseph August. "Der soziale Gedanke im modernen Kunstgewerbe." Die neue Gesellschaft, Sozialistische Wochenschrift 4 (1907), pp. 133 ff.

Lux, Joseph August. Das neue Kunstgewerbe in Deutschland. Leipzig, 1908.

Lux, Joseph August. Geschmack im Alltag. Ein Lebensbuch zur Pflege des Schönen. Dresden, 1908.

Lux, Joseph August. "Peter Behrens." Hohe Warte 4 (1908), pp. 37–46.

Lux, Joseph August. "Das Schriftwesen." Hohe Warte 4 (1908), pp. 163–168.

Lux, Joseph August. "Die Kunstindustrie und das Qualitätsproblem." Die neue Zeit. Wochenschrift der Deutschen Sozialdemokratie 27, no. 1 (1909), pp. 767 ff.

Lux, Joseph August. "Peter Behrens. Eine Künstlercharakteristik." Die Propyläen (Munich) 7, no. 23 (9 March 1910), pp. 357 ff.

Lux, Joseph August. "Peter Behrens zum 60. Geburtstag." Die Baugilde 10, no. 11 (5 June 1928), p. 762.

Lux, Joseph August. "Ingenieur-Ästhetik" (review). Der Industriebau 1 (1910), p. 150.

Mannheimer, Franz. "Fabrikkunst." Die Hilfe 16, no. 18 (8 May 1910), pp. 289 ff.

Mannheimer, Franz. "Arbeiten von Prof. Peter Behrens für die AEG." Der Industriebau 2, no. 6 (15 June 1911), pp. 121–138 and ills. pp. 139 ff.

Mannheimer, Franz. "AEG Bauten." In Jahrbuch des Deutschen Werkbundes 1913. Jena, 1913.

Mannheimer, Franz. "Die deutschen Industriehallen von Prof. Peter Behrens auf der Brüsseler Weltausstellung 1910." Der Industriebau 1, no. 9 (15 September 1910), pp. 194–207.

Meyer, Peter. "Architektur als Ausdruck der Gewalt. Überlegungen zum Stil von Peter Behrens." Das Werk 27, no. 6 (1940), pp. 160–164.

Meyer-Schönbrunn, Fritz (ed.). Peter Behrens. Monographien Deutscher Reklame-Künstler 5. Hagen and Dortmund, 1913.

Michel, Wilhelm. "Neue Tendenzen im Kunstgewerbe." Innen-Dekoration 21 (March 1910), p. 130.

Moos, Stanislaus von. "Die Erneuerung." Werk 54, no. 4 (April 1967), pp. 211–215.

Müller, Sebastian. Kunst und Industrie. Ideologie und Organisation des Funktionalismus in der Architektur. Munich, 1974.

Müller-Wulckow, Walter. Bauten der Arbeit und des Verkehrs aus deutscher Gegenwart. Königstein and Leipzig, 1925.

Müller-Wulckow, Walter. Wohnbauten und Siedlungen. Königstein and Leipzig, 1929.

Muthesius, Hermann. "Kunst und Maschine." Dekorative Kunst 5 (1902), pp. 141 ff.

Muthesius, Hermann. " 'Kunst' im Gewerbe," Kunstwart 17, no. 9 (February 1904), pp. 530–535.

Muthesius, Hermann. *Kultur und Kunst.* Collected essays. Leipzig and Jena, 1904.

Muthesius, Hermann. "Diskussionsbeitrag." In *Die Veredelung der gewerblichen Arbeit im Zusammenwirken von Kunst, Industrie und Handwerk. Verhandlung des Deutschen Werkbundes zu München, 11. und 12. 7. 1908.* Leipzig, 1908.

Muthesius, Hermann. Die ästhetische Ausbildung der Ingenieurbauten, Vortrag in der 50. Hauptversammlung des Vereins deutscher Ingenieure in Wiesbaden 1909. Reprinted in *Zeitschrift des Vereins deutscher Ingenieure* 53, no. 31 (31 July 1909), pp. 1211–1217.

Muthesius, Hermann. *Handarbeit und Massenerzeugnis.* Berlin, 1917.

Naumann, Friedrich. "Kunst im Zeitalter der Maschine." *Kunstwart* 17, no. 20 (July 1904), pp. 317–327.

Naumann, Friedrich. "Kunst und Industrie." In *Das deutsche Kunstgewerbe 1906. III. Deutsche Kunstgewerbe-Ausstellung, Dresden, 1906* (Munich, 1906); also in *Kunstwart* 20, no. 2 (October 1906), pp. 66–73, and no. 3 (November 1906), pp. 128–131.

Naumann, Friedrich. *Ausstellungsbriefe.* Berlin-Schöneberg, 1909.

Naumann, Friedrich. *Schriften,* ed. Heinz Ladendorf (vols. 1,2,4–6) and Wolfgang Mommsen (vol. 3). Cologne and Opladen, 1971.

Neumeyer, Fritz. Der Werkwohnungsbau der Industrie in Berlin und seine Entwicklung im 19. und frühen 20. Jahrhundert. Ph.D diss., Technische Universität Berlin, 1978.

Niemeyer, Wilhelm. *Schriftschönheit im Druck. Ein Flugblatt. Gedruckt bei Anlass einer Ausstellung im Landesgewerbemuseum zu Stuttgart 1908.*

Osborn, Max. "Das Haus von Walther Rathenau in Berlin-Grunewald." *Moderne Bauformen* 11 (1912), pp. 465 ff.

Osborn, Max. "Bei Prof. Peter Behrens." *Die Dame* no. 13 (1914), pp. 12 ff.

Osthaus, Karl Ernst. "Peter Behrens." *Kunst und Künstler* 4, no. 3 (December 1907), pp. 116–124.

Osthaus, Karl Ernst. "Ein Fabrikbau von Peter Behrens." *Frankfurter Zeitung,* 10 February 1910. Also in *Gartenstadt* 4, no. 8 (August 1910), pp. 88–92.

Osthaus, Karl Ernst (ed.). *Wanderausstellung des Deutschen Museums für Kunst in Handel und Industrie, Hagen i. W. Unter Mitwirkung des österreich. Museums f. Kunst u. Industrie in Wien, Newark, Chicago, Indianapolis, Pittsburgh, Cincinnati, St. Louis. 1912–1913.*

Ostwald, Hans. "Das Schablonenhaus." *Hohe Warte* 4 (1908), pp. 331 ff.

Pallmann, Kurt. "Neuzeitlicher Backsteinbau." *Deutsche Bauhütte* 16 (1912), pp. 210–212.

Paquet, Alfons. "Eine Ausstellung vorbildlicher Fabrikbauten." *Frankfurter Zeitung,* 1 October 1909.

Pazaurek, Gustav E. "Moderne Ehrenurkunden." *Dekorative Kunst* 14, no. 1 (October 1910), pp. 25–34.

Pehnt, Wolfgang. *Expressionist Architecture.* London, 1973.

Pevsner, Nikolaus. "William Morris, C. R. Ashbee und das zwanzigste Jahrhundert." *Deutsche Vierteljahrschrift für Literaturwissenschaft und Geistesgeschichte* 14 (1936), pp. 536–563.

Pevsner, Nikolaus. *Pioneers of the Modern Movement.* London, 1936.

Pevsner, Nikolaus. *Pioneers of Modern Design. From William Morris to Walter Gropius.* New York, 1949.

Pevsner, Nikolaus. *Studies in Art, Architecture and Design.* 2 vols. London, 1968.

Pevsner, Nikolaus. *An Outline of European Architecture.* London, 1943.

Pevsner, Nikolaus. *Wegbereiter moderner Formgebung. Von Morris bis Gropius.* Hamburg, 1957.

Pevsner, Nikolaus. *The Sources of Modern Architecture and Design.* London, 1968.

Platz, Gustav Adolf. *Die Baukunst der neuesten Zeit.* Berlin, 1927.

Plischke, Ernst A. "Gedanken zu Peter Behrens," *Bauforum,* no. 5–6 (1968), pp. 15–17.

Poelzig, Hans. "Die architektonische Entwicklung des Fabrikbaus." *Beihefte zum Zentralblatt für Gewerbehygiene und Unfallverhütung* 18 (1930), pp. 31–40.

Pogge von Strandmann, Hartmut. "Widersprüche im Modernisierungsprozess Deutschlands. Der Kampf der verarbeitenden Industrie gegen die Schwerindustrie." In *Industrielle Gesellschaft und politische System.* Bonn, 1978.

Posener, Julius. "L'oeuvre de Peter Behrens." *L'architecture d'aujourdhui,* series 4, 5, no. 2 (March 1934), pp. 8–29.

Posener, Julius. *Anfänge des Funktionalismus. Von Arts and Crafts zum Deutschen Werkbund.* Vienna and Berlin, 1964.

Pudor, Heinrich. "Erziehung zur Eisenarchitektur." *Hohe Warte* 4 (1908), pp. 339 ff.

Pudor, Heinrich. "Die Schönheit der Bogenlampe." *Berliner Architekturwelt* 13 (1911), pp. 295–298.

Pudor, Heinrich. "Beleuchtungskörper und Beleuchtungseffekte." *Technische Monatshefte* 11 (1910), pp. 286–291.

Rathenau, Walther. *Gesamtausgabe,* ed. Hans Dieter Hellige and Ernst Schulin, vol. 2; *Hauptwerke und Gespräche,* ed. Ernst Schulin. Munich and Heidelberg, 1977.

Rave, Rolf, and Joachim Knöfel. *Bauen seit 1900. Ein Führer durch Berlin.* Frankfurt and Berlin, 1963); second edition Berlin, 1968.

Redslob, Edwin. *Gestalt und Zeit. Begegnungen eines Lebens.* Munich and Vienna, 1966.

Rogers, Ernesto N. "Behrens, architetto tedesco." *Casabella* 240 (June 1960), p. 3.

Rossi, Aldo. "Peter Behrens e il problema dell'abitazione moderna." *Casabella* 240 (June 1960), pp. 47 ff.

Scheffler, Karl. "Ein Weg zum Stil." *Berliner Architekturwelt* 5 (1903), pp. 293 ff.

Scheffler, Karl. "Kunst und Industrie." *Kunst und Künstler* 6, no. 10 (July 1908), pp. 430–434.

Scheffler, Karl. Short, untitled report on the turbine factory. *Kunst und Künstler* 8, no. 8 (May 1910), pp. 419–421.

Scheffler, Karl. *Die Architektur der Grosstadt.* Berlin, 1913.

Scheffler, Karl. "Moderne Industriebauten." *Vossische Zeitung,* morning edition, 26 September 1912. Reprinted with minor variations in *Die Architektur der Grosstadt* (1913).

Scheja, Georg, and Eberhard Hölscher. *Die Schrift in der Baukunst.* Berlin, 1938.

Schinnerer, Johannes. "Moderne Reklamekunst." *Zeitschrift für Bücherfreunde* 2, no. 4 (July 1910), pp. 115–117, 122.

Schüler, Edmund. "Peter Behrens †." *Kunst im Deutschen Reich,* edition B (Die Baukunst), 4 (1940), pp. 65 ff.

Schulz, Joachim, and Werner Gräbner. *Architekturführer DDR. Berlin. Hauptstadt der DDR.* Berlin, 1973.

Schur, Ernst. "Maschine, Publikum, Fabrikant. Aphorismen von E. S." *Dekorative Kunst* 10, no. 8 (May 1907), pp. 337–344.

Schur, Ernst. "Kunstgewerbe und Industrie." *Berliner Architekturwelt* 13 (1911), pp. 254–258.

Schur, Ernst. "Peter Behrens und Berlin." *Dekorative Kunst* 1 (October 1907), p. 48.

Scully, Vincent. *Modern Architecture. The Architecture of Democracy.* New York, 1965.

Selle, Gert. *Ideologie und Utopie des Design. Zur Gesellschaftlichen Theorie der industriellen Formgebung.* Cologne, 1973.

Selle, Gert. "Zwischen Kunsthandwerk, Manufaktur und Industrie. Rolle und Function des Künstler-Entwerfers um 1898 bis 1908." In Gerhard Bott (ed.), *Vom Morris zum Bauhaus. Eine Kunst gegründet auf Einfachheit.* Hanau, 1977.

Selle, Gert. *Die Geschichte des Design in Deutschland von 1870 bis heute. Entwicklung der industriellen Produktkultur.* Cologne, 1978.

Selle, Gert. "Über bürgerliche Reformversuche der Produktkultur zwischen 1889 und 1912." In *Kunst und Alltag um 1900. Drittes Jahrbuch des Werkbund-Archivs, 1978.* Lahn-Giessen, 1978.

Siepen, Bernhard. "Peter Behrens, 50 Jahre Formgebung in der Industrie. Ausstellung Neue Sammlung München." *Die Innenarchitektur* 5, no. 10 (April 1958).

Simmel, Georg. "Das Problem des Stils." *Dekorative Kunst* (1908), pp. 307 ff.

Simmel, Georg. *Brücke und Tür. Essays zur Geschichte, Religion, Kunst und Gesellschaft.* Stuttgart, 1957.

Simon, Hans-Ulrich. *Sezessionismus, Kunstgewerbe in literarischer und bildender Kunst.* Stuttgart, 1976.

Simons, Anna. "Der staatliche Schriftkursus in Neubabelsberg." *Kunstgewerbeblatt* 21, no. 6 (March 1910), pp. 101–103.

Speer, Albert. *Inside the Third Reich.* London, 1970.

Tafuri, Manfredo. *Architecture and Utopia.* Cambridge, Mass., 1976.

Taut, Bruno. *Bauen. Der neuen Wohnbau.* Leipzig, 1927.

Tintori, Silvano. "Tecnica ed espressione nell'opera di Behrens." *Casabella* 240 (June 1960), pp. 21 ff.

Weber, Marianne. *Max Weber. Ein Lebensbild.* Tübingen, 1926.

Wehler, Hans Ulrich. *Modernisierungstheorie und Geschichte.* Göttingen, 1975.

Weidenmüller, Hans. "Die durchgeistigung der geschäftlichen Werbearbeit." In *Jahrbuch des Deutschen Werkbundes 1913* (Jena, 1913).

Westheim, Paul. "Zwei neue Antiquaschriften." *Die Werkkunst* 4 (1908–09), pp. 209–215.

Westheim, Paul. "Die Drucksachen der technischen Industrie." *Schweizer graphische Mitteilungen* 30 (1910–11), p. 37.

Westheim, Paul. "Technische Schönheit?" *Sozialistische Monatshefte,* no. 1 (1914), pp. 561 ff.

Westheim, Paul. "Anpassung oder Typenschöpfung? Entwicklungsperspektiven des Kunstgewerbes." *Sozialistische Monatshefte,* no. 2 (1914), pp. 980 ff.

Whittick, Arnold. *European Architecture in the Twentieth Century.* London, 1950.

Wichert, Fritz. "Luftschiffahrt und Architektur." *Frankfurter Zeitung,* 21 March 1909, p. 1.

Widmer, Karl. "Handwerk und Maschinenarbeit." *Kunstgewerbeblatt* 20, no. 3 (December 1908), pp. 49–51.

Wittig, Paul. *Die Architektur der Hoch- und Untergrundbahn in Berlin.* Berlin, 1922.

Wittig, Paul. *Führung der Berliner Hoch- und Untergrundbahnen durch bebaute Viertel. Vom technischen und städtebaulichen Standpunkt.* Berlin, 1920.

Wolff, H. "Der Neubau des Hauptverwaltungsgebäudes der AEG in Berlin, Architekt Peter Behrens." *Die Kunst im Deutschen Reich,* edition B (Die Baukunst) (October 1939), pp. 447–454.

Literature on the AEG

Die Allgemeine Elektricitäts-Gesellschaft. 1883/1908. Berlin, 1908.

AEG-Zeitung, anniversary edition, 1908.

50. Jahre AEG, manuscript of Festschrift planned for 19 April 1933.

75 Jahre AEG. Berlin and Frankfurt, 1958.

AEG. Fabriken Brunnenstrasse. Grossmaschinenfabrik. Fabrik für Bahnmaterial. Fabrik für Hochspannungsmaterial. Lokomotivfabrik. Kleinmotorenfabrik. Widerstandsfabrik. Berlin, ca. 1912.

AEG. Ansichten aus den Fabriken Brunnenstrasse. Berlin, after 1913.

AEG. Zur Besichtigung von AEG-Fabriken. Berlin, 1914.

AEG. Zum Gedächtnis an Georg Klingenberg. Berlin, 1926.

AEG Taschenbuch. Den Besuchern der technischen Messe Leipzig. Berlin, 1919.

Antz, E. L. "Zur Geschichte der elektrischen Strassenbeleuchtung in Berlin." In VDI, Beiträge zur Geschichte der Technik, no. 20 (1930).

(BEW). "Zum 25jährigen Bestehen der B.E.W." Mitteilungen der Berliner Elektricitäts-Werke 5, no. 5 (May 1909), pp. 66–73.

Berglar, Peter. Walther Rathenau. Seine Zeit, sein Werk, seine Persönlichkeit. Bremen, 1970.

Biermanns, J., and O. Mayr (eds.). Hochspannungsforschung und Hochspannungspraxis. Georg Stern, Direktor der AEG-Transformatorenfabrik zum 31. März 1931 gewidmet. Berlin, 1931.

Brinckmeyer, H. Die Rathenaus. Munich, 1922.

Czada, P. Die Berliner Elektroindustrie in der Weimarer Zeit. Berlin, 1969.

Dernburg, Bernhard. "Emil Rathenau." Allgemeine Zeitung, Munich, 5 December 1912.

Dessauer, Friedrich. "Organisation technischer Arbeit. Betrachtungen anlässlich des 25jährigen Bestehens der Allgemeinen Elektricitäts-Gesellschaft." Hochland 5, no. 2 (1908), pp. 288–305.

Deutsch, Felix. Meine Eindrücke in Amerika. Lecture given on 14 December 1927 in the large conference hall of the AEG (printed text).

Dolivo-Dobrowolsky, Michael von. Die moderne Massenfabrikation in der Apparate-Fabrik der AEG. Manuscript in Dobrowolsky papers, Deutsches Museum, Munich.

"Das Märkische Elektrizitätswerke." AEG-Zeitung 11, no. 12 (June 1909); see also BEW-Mitteilungen 12, no. 9 (September 1916).

Fasolt, Friedrich. Die sieben grössten deutschen Elektricitäts-Gesellschaften, ihre Entwicklung und Unternehmertätigkeit. Dresden, 1904.

Friedmann, Georges. Der Mensch in der mechanisierten Produktion. Cologne, 1952.

Fürst, Arthur. Emil Rathenau. Der Mann und sein Werk. Berlin, 1915.

Fürst, Arthur. Das elektrische Licht. Von den Anfängen bis zur Gegenwart. Nebst einer Geschichte der Beleuchtung. Munich, 1926.

Fürstenberg, Hans (ed.). Carl Fürstenberg. Die Lebensgeschichte eines deutschen Bankiers. 1870–1914. Berlin, 1931.

Gedenkblatt zum 20. Juni 1915. Verein der Beamten der AEG und BEW. e.V. Berlin, 1915.

Gerhardt, Paul. "Die AEG." Westermanns Monatshefte 74, no. 147 (September 1929–February 1930), pp. 493–500.

(Geschäftsberichte DEG). Erster Geschäftsbericht der Deutschen Edison Gesellschaft für angewandte Elektricität betreffend das Geschäftsjahr 1883 (Berlin, 1884) and following reports.

(Geschäftsberichte AEG). Sechster Geschäftsbericht der Allgemeinen Elektricitäts-Gesellschaft betreffend das Geschäftsjahr vom 1. Januar 1887 bis 30. Juni 1888 (Berlin, 1888) and following reports.

Goldschmidt, Alfons. "Emil Rathenau." März 5, no. 3 (1911), pp. 239–241.

Haas, Robert. "Emil Rathenau. Zur 90. Wiederkehr seines Geburtstages." Spannung—Die AEG Umschau 2, no. 3 (December 1928), pp. 70–73; 2, no. 4 (January 1929), pp. 108–110.

Hasse, Hermann. Die AEG und ihre wirtschaftliche Bedeutung. Heidelberg, 1902.

Harden, Maximilian. "Emil Rathenau." Die Zukunft 91 (1915), p. 397.

Heinig, Kurt. "Der Weg der Elektrotrusts." Die neue Zeit. Wochenschrift der Deutschen Sozialdemokratie 30, no. 2 (1912), pp. 474–485.

Heintzenberg, Friedrich (ed.). Aus einem reichen Leben. Werner Siemens in Briefen an seine Familie und an Freunde. Stuttgart, 1953.

Herzberg, A., and D. Meyer (eds.). Ingenieurwerke in und bei Berlin. Festschrift zum 50jährigen Bestehen des Vereins Deutscher Ingenieure. Berlin, 1906.

Heyck, P. "Wesen und Wirtschaftlichkeit neuerer elektrischer Starklichtquellen." Zeitschrift des Vereins Deutscher Ingenieure 53, no. 32 (1909), pp. 1261–1268.

Hughes, Thomas P. Thomas Edison: Professional Inventor. London, 1976.

Jaeger, Hans. "Unternehmer und Politik im Wilhelminischen Deutschland." Tradition. Zeitschrift für Firmengeschichte und Unternehmer Biographie 6 (1968), pp. 1–21.

Jones, Francis Arthur. Thomas Alva Edison: Sixty Years of an Inventor's Life. London, 1907.

Kaelble, Hartmut. Berliner Unternehmer während der frühen Industrialisierung. Herkunft, sozialer Status und politischer Einfluss. Berlin and New York, 1972.

Kaelble, Hartmut. "Sozialer Aufstieg in Deutschland 1850–1914." Vierteljahrsschrift für Sozial und Wirtschaftsgeschichte 60 (1973), pp. 41–71.

Kampffmeyer, Hans. Die Entwicklung eines modernen Industrieortes und die Lehren, die sich daraus für die Ansiedlungs-Politik ergeben. Karlsruhe, 1910.

Kemmen, Gustav. *Die Berliner Elektricitätswerke bis Ende 1896. Geplant und Erbaut von der Allgemeinen Elektricitäts-Gesellschaft, Berlin.* Munich, 1897.

Klingenberg, Georg. *Elektrische Grosswirtschaft unter staatlicher Mitwirkung.* Berlin, 1916.

Kocka, Jürgen. *Unternehmensverwaltung und Angestelltenschaft am Beispiel Siemens 1847–1914. Zum Verhältnis von Kapitalismus und Bürokratie in der deutschen Industrialisierung.* Stuttgart, 1969.

Kocka, Jürgen. *Unternehmer in der deutschen Industrialisierung,* Göttingen, 1975.

Kreidt, Hermann. Die baulichen Anlagen der Berliner Industrie. Ph.D diss., Technische Universität Berlin, 1967.

Kreller, Emil. "Die Entwicklung der deutschen elektrotechnischen Industrie und ihre Aussichten auf dem Weltmarkt." *Staats- und socialwissenschaftliche Forschungen* 22, no. 3 (1903).

Kuczynski, Jürgen. *Die Bewegung der deutschen Wirtschaft von 1800 bis 1946,* second edition. Meisenheim/Glan, 1948.

Landon. "A.E.G." *Die Zukunft* 16, no. 35 (30 May 1908), pp. 337–340.

Landau, J. "An der Wiege der AEG." *Spannung—Die AEG Umschau* 3 (1929).

Lasche, Oskar. *Elektrischer Einzelbetrieb in den Maschinenbauwerkstätten der A.E.G* Berlin, 1899.

Laube, R. "Die Architektur von Elektrizitätswerken." *AEG-Mitteilungen* 13, no. 8 (August 1917).

Lenin, V. I. *Imperialism, the Highest Stage of Capitalism.* (Moscow, 1947).

Lindner, Theodor. "Vom ersten Berliner Kraftwerk zum Grosskraftwerk Golpa." *AEG-Mitteilungen* 18, no. 4 (October 1922).

Majerczik, W. "Elektrizitätswerke vom AEG-Typ." *AEG-Zeitung* 16, no. 9 (March 1914).

Martin, Rudolf. *Deutsche Machthaber.* Berlin and Leipzig, 1910.

Matschoss, Conrad. "Die geschichtliche Entwicklung der Allgemeinen Elektricitäts-Gesellschaft in den ersten 25 Jahren ihres Bestehens." *Jahrbuch des Vereins Deutscher Ingenieure* 1 (1909), pp. 53–72.

Matschoss, Conrad, E. Schultz, and A. Th. Gross. *50 Jahre Berliner Elektrizitätswerke. 1884–1934.* Berlin, 1934.

Miller, Oskar von. "Erinnerungen an die internationale Elektrizitäts-Ausstellung im Glaspalast zu München im Jahre 1882." *Deutsches Museum, Abhandlungen und Berichte* 4, no. 6 (1932).

Monasch, Berthold, and Leopold Bloch. Die gegenwärtigen elektrischen Lichtquellen (AEG lecture). *Technische Mitteilungen aus der AEG-Zeitung* 8 (February 1908); also in *Interne AEG-Zeitung* 10, no. 2 (1907–08).

Monasch, Berthold, and Leopold Bloch. "Fortschritte der Bogenlampentechnik." *Elektrotechnische Zeitschrift* 15–16 (1909), pp. 1–17.

Multhaupt, O. *Die moderne Elektrizität. Lehrbuch über die Anwendung der Elektrizität für Gewerbetreibende und Interessenten.* Berlin, 1901.

NAG. *Neue Automobil Gesellschaft m.b.h. NAG. 1901–1911.* Berlin-Oberschöneweide. 1911.

NAG. *25 Jahre NAG. 1901–1926.* Berlin, 1926.

Pinner, Felix. *Emil Rathenau und das elektrische Zeitalter.* Leipzig, 1918.

Pinner, Felix. "Emil Rathenau. Der Kaufmann und das Leben." *Beiblatt der Zeitschrift für Handelswissenschaft und Handelspraxis,* 1913.

Pogge von Strandmann, Hartmut (ed.). *Walther Rathenau. Tagebuch 1907–1922.* Düsseldorf, 1967.

Rathenau, Emil. *Aufgaben der Elektrizitäts-Industrie.* Berlin, 1910.

Rathenau, Walther. "Emil Rathenau." Memorial address at burial of Emil Rathenau, 23 June 1915. *Die Zukunft* 23, no. 40 (3 July 1915), pp. 23–30; also in *Gedenkblatt zum 20. Juni 1915* (Berlin, 1915).

Riedler, Alois. *Emil Rathenau und das Werden der Grosswirtschaft.* Berlin, 1916.

Roso, R. "Ein Elektrizitätswerk." *Deutsche Bauhütte* 14, no. 19 (1910).

Schiff, Emil. *Allgemeine Elektrizitäts-Gesellschaft und Berliner Elektrizitätswerke.* Berlin, 1915.

Schiff, Emil. *Sollen die Berliner Elektrizitätswerke verstadtlicht werden? Ein Gutachten von Emil Schiff.* Berlin, 1914.

Schulin, Ernst. "Die Rathenaus. Zwei Generationen jüdischen Anteils an der industriellen Entwicklung Deutschlands." In *Juden in Wilhelminischen Deutschland 1890–1914,* Schriftenreihe wissenschaftliche Abhandlungen des Leo Baeck Instituts, no. 33. Tübingen, 1976.

Siegel, G. "Das Elektrizitätswerk-Fürstenwalde." *AEG-Zeitung* 12, no. 9 (March 1910).

Sothen, Hans von. Die Wirtschaftspolitik der AEG. Ph.D diss., University of Freiburg, 1915.

Ufermann, Paul, and Carl Hüglin. *Die AEG, eine Darstellung des Konzerns der Allgemeinen Elektrizitäts-Gesellschaft.* Berlin, 1912.

Wenzel, Georg. *Deutsche Wirtschaftsführer. Lebensgänge deutscher Wirtschafts Persönlichkeiten.* Hamburg, 1929.

Wilhelm, Karl. *Die AEG.* Berlin, 1931.

Additional Credits for Illustrations in Catalog

AEG: A3, A6, A8, A13, A16, A21, A24, A25, A43–A57, A59–A74, A77–A96, A101–A103, A106–A137, A140, A143–A153, A163, A164, A183, P14, P35, P38, P41, P42, P44, P45, P47, P49, P74, P77, P79, P81, P82, P86–P89, P91, P93–P95, P97, P98, P107–P109, P117–P132, P134–P136, G73, G75, G76, G79, G80

Kaiser Wilhelm Museum, Krefeld: G29

Karl Ernst Osthaus Museum, Hagen: G41, G77, P3, P5, P6, P43, P46, P48, P78

Kunsthistorisches Institut der Freien Universität Berlin: A14, A15, A17, A19, A33–A35, A38–A42, A98–A100, A165–A170

Kraftwerk Union AG, Werk Berlin: A23

Foto Marburg: G23–G25

Fritz Neumeyer: A184, A185, A189, A190, A192, A197, A201, A204, A206, A212

Pfalzgalerie Kaiserslautern (Hans Günther Hausen): P37, G20, G32–G36, G54

Rat für Formgebung, Darmstadt: P116, P138, P139

Henning Rogge: A1, A18, A26–A32, A36, A37, A104, A105, A198–A200, A202, A203, A205, A207–A209, P1, P4, P8, P9, P15–P33, P39, P75, P76, P80, P90, P92, P96, P99, P106, P110, P111, P133, P137, P140, P141, G1–G19, G31, G37–G40, G42–G48, G50, G51, G53, G55–G58, G60–G69, G71, G74, G78, G81, G83, G84, G86

F. Stoedtner: A2, A7, A20, A22, A75, A97, A138, A141, A142, A175, A178, A180, A181, A187, A188, A191, A193–A196, P2, P7, P36, P112–P115, G49, G52, G59

Index